CONSIDERATIONS

UPON THE

NATURE AND TENDENCY

OF

FREE INSTITUTIONS.

BY FREDERICK GRIMKE.

SECOND EDITION CORRECTED AND ENLARGED.

NEW-YORK: DERBY & JACKSON.
CINCINNATI:
H. W. DERBY & CO.
1856.

CINCINNATI:
WRIGHTSON & CO. PRINT.
167 Walnut St.

PREFACE TO THE SECOND EDITION.

My design in writing the present work, has not been to produce a formal treatise, in which the parts are made to hang together by certain prescribed rules of art, but to unfold a system of thought, which will exercise the mind, and not the critical skill, of the reader. The two are distinct, and often irreconcilable. The reader, quick in apprehension, will have no difficulty in seizing the governing principle which pervades the whole work, and in marking the many important results to which it has conducted me. Another object which I have had in view, an indirect one to be sure, has been to *endeavor* to correct, as far as it is in the power of a single individual to do, the vitiated taste for reading which prevails in our country. Great numbers read from ennui, not from a genuine desire for knowledge. The consequence is that the works selected are either of a superficial, or of an exciting character. But nothing contributes more to enfeeble the understanding, and even to pervert the moral faculties. The mischief extends itself to the few who are possessed with a noble ambition. There is no tribunal to which they can address themselves. Their efforts are chilled by the mental dyspepsia which prevails around them, when they stand in need of being powerfully braced by a healthful and invigorating influence.

By laying open a field of thought which is peculiarly American (although allied with all other knowledge), and which has, in an eminent degree, both a literary and a philosophical interest, I flatter myself that I may contribute, however little, towards giving a more fortunate direction to the general mind. They who have studied the history of Europe during the middle ages, must have been struck with one remarkable fact, that there was no beginning even toward the formation of a literature, science and philosophy, strictly modern, until ancient literature, &c., had ceased to be studied, and that there was no other way, by which it was possible to create it. We call the period, which succeeded the disappearance of ancient, and laid the foundation of modern literature and philosophy, the dark ages, because the fermentation which the human mind underwent in this transition period, did produce a temporary mental eclipse. The instruction, afforded by this remarkable case, is not that we should fall back into a state resembling the dark ages, but that we should search in the rich resources of our own history, our form of society, our civil and political institutions, for the materials on which to construct an American literature. Until we do, our authors will have none of the originality and raciness, which give dignity and interest to mental speculations, and our population will continue to read only to assuage the pain of ennui.

Very material additions have been made to the present edition—a chapter on the great question of "the right of secession in a confederate government," another on the still more important question, "the ultimate destiny of free insistutions." New matter has also been incorporated into the former chapters—ten or twelve pages in Chap. vii. Book I., and the same number in Chap. vi. Book II., and Chap. iv. Book IV.; about eight in Chap. vi. Book I., and Chap. i. Book IV. In Chap. i. Book II. and Chap. vi. Book IV., four pages, and in several other chapters from a third of a page to three pages. The introductory chapter on our modern civilization has also been added to the present volume, and the numerous typographical errors in the former edition have also been endeavored to be corrected.

TABLE OF CONTENTS.

BOOK I.

BOOK II.

BOOK III.

BOOK IV.

NATURE AND TENDENCY

OF

FREE INSTITUTIONS.

BOOK I.

CHAPTER I.

INTRODUCTORY.

THE existence of free institutions presupposes the existence of a highly civilized society. An examination, therefore, of their genius and tendency, will very naturally be preceded by an examination of the origin and nature of civilization.

Civilization, then, is that state in which the higher part of our nature is made to predominate over the lower, and the qualities which fit men for society, obtain an ascendency over their selfish, and anti-social propensities. But as much the greater part of the human race have always been found at one period in an uncivilized condition, the question what has induced a change from one state to the other, is not one merely of curious inquiry, but of the highest philosophical interest.

History presents us with the earliest traces of civilization in those regions where the densest population existed. This is a striking fact; and perhaps it may afford a clue to the solution of the difficulty. A population which is only tolerably full, is inconsistent with the hunter state. One which is still more dense, is inconsistent with the pastoral state. Any causes therefore which give a decided spring to the population, are calculated to draw men from a savage into a civilized condition. When they have multiplied up to a certain point, the cultivation of the soil, which was before only occasional, and in particular spots, becomes, from the necessity of the case general. It is sure also to be continued from choice, in consequence of the variety of desires it satisfies, and the command it gives over both the moral and physical world.

But the difficulty still meets us, what in the first instance occasioned the increase of the population: for the hunter state will carry the population to a certain pitch, and the pastoral state will extend it still further. But although we speak of a hunter, and a pastoral state, these must not be considered as indicating what are the exclusive, but what are the predominant occupations of the population. A tribe of shepherds, and even of hunters, is always addicted to some species of agriculture, as an agricultural people are always addicted to the raising of flocks.

Civilization, then, would most probably commence in a region which combined the advantages of a genial climate, and a fertile soil. These assist in giving a predilection for the cultivation of the soil, and in gradually superceding both the hunter, and pastoral states. The multiplication of the population to a certain point, is the necessary condition of the progress of civilization, and how to obtain that condition is the precise inquiry we are engaged in.

When the climate is favorable, and the land rich, men will be attracted to agriculture as naturally as to any other pursuit. The relaxing influence of the climate will indispose to much activity, while the rudest cultivation, the mere scratching of the earth, will supply its fruits in tolerable abundance. But the diversity of productions among an agricultural people, lays the foundation for a more extensive barter than can exist in the hunter, or pastoral state. One neighborhood will exchange its products with another; and by degrees, a communication will be opened between the more distant parts of the community. The rude elements of trade will be introduced, and ultimately a regular commerce will be commenced. Some parts of the country will be more easily approached by water, than by land. Sometimes the rivers, at others the coasts adjacent to the sea, will afford the easiest channels. When society has advanced so far, the population cease any longer to be impelled by mere instincts. The circle of their desires will be enlarged, and the range of observation and experience proportionally extended. The occupations of society then become more complex, and more diversified. Men begin to reflect, to look more into the future, and to conform their actions to something like rule and system. Enterprise, though exceedingly limited, will be one feature of their character. The coasts of neighboring countries will be visited for traffic, as their own coasts had been explored before. And from that time we may date the rise of a regular commerce.

Even before this period, the inhabitants will be brought into such intimate communication, that the irsocial qualities will be distinctly developed, and those of an opposite character kept more in the back ground. In addition to the inanimate objects with which they will have to deal, their own minds will become the subject of observation. Each individual in order to regulate his own actions, will be compelled to make observation of the actions of others: and the range of observation widening with every increase of the population, the understandings of every one will be sharpened, and improved, whether they will or no. Industry and enterprise will not be the only traits in the character of the population. There will be symptoms of intelligence visible everywhere. And this will give a fresh spring to activity in every department of life.

The point of time when the minds of men begin to be the subject of observation, is the most important period in the history of civilization. The foundation is then laid for reflection in its most extensive signification. And it is for this reason, that I have laid so much stress on the cultivation of the soil, and the consequent increase of the population, as the last is the necessary condition of the growth of civilization. For then, not only are the desires of men multiplied, and the means of gratifying them augmented; but the beings whose minds act upon and stimulate each other, are also multiplied.

The notion of property in land is never fairly grasped, until agriculture has made considerable progress. Among a tribe of shepherds, this notion is very indistinct, among one of hunters, it is still more faint. It is only fully developed, when agriculture becomes the predominant pursuit. The foundation of the right is laid at the first dawn of civilization, but at that period it is not distinctly recognized, simply because the occupations of the inhabitants imply a use in common, and are incompatible with a division of the soil

When the land is cultivated, each individual tills the spot on which the accident of birth has placed him. The dominion over the land was once, what the dominion over the ocean always is. The one was once in common, the other continues to be so. As there is no superior right of one individual over another, to navigate the ocean, there was no superior right of one over another to cultivate the land. And yet precisely because there is no superior right, each individual is at liberty to make use of both. But the traversing the ocean by one vessel in a particular path, is inconsistent with its being traversed by another vessel in exactly the same path at the same time. The use of a particular path on the ocean becomes for the time being, exclusive. But more than this momentary use is necessary in the case of the soil; and precisely because, as in the former instance, there is no superior right of one over another, to the use, and this demands occupation, and occupation, protection; the right of private property in the land comes to be as legitimately established, as the right to a private use of the ocean.

As soon as the notion of property has sprung up, laws are necessary to enforce it. A system of legislation will be necessary, which however rude and imperfect in the beginning, will give shape, and consistency to the social organization, and push onward the march of general improvement.

But although civilization will originate among a people who have a genial climate, and a fertile soil, it may be transported to other regions, and give rise to even a higher condition of society. For as it is not in consequence of any original difference in the faculties of men of different countries, at least where there is no difference of race, but only from a difference in the circumstances in which they are placed, that some civilize themselves, while others continue in their primitive state, there can be no obstacle to the introduction of the arts, and refinement of the most cultivated people to every region where a foothold can be gained. This is a fine provision in the constitution of human nature. But for it, there is no reason to believe that northern and central Europe would have emerged from their barbarous condition. Britain, France, and Germany, were inhabited by barbarians, until Roman civilization was introduced. These countries are now the seats of a civilization more complete and refined, than existed among the people who first conveyed thither, the first rudiments of laws and manners. The conquest of the Romans first, and the dissolution of the empire afterwards, produced a mixture of the people of all parts of the continent, and caused the laws, and manners, the arts and sciences, of the people of Italy to penetrate into every quarter. No other, or further account need, or can be given of the matter. But for Roman civilization, London, Paris, Berlin, as well as St. Petersburgh, Copenhagen, and Stockholm, would at the present day be villages of straggling huts. There is not the least reason to suppose, that those spots would be inhabited by a race so far advanced in the scale of civilization as the present population.

No people, so far as our information extends, has been known to civilize itself. The civilization of ancient, as well as of modern Europe, was of foreign growth. Nevertheless, as civilization must have commenced somewhere, in order to be carried abroad, it is plain, that some one people, who were originally placed in singularly propitious circumstances, did originally succeed in civilizing itself. The earliest records of history place the first civilization on the eastern coasts of the Mediterranean, whence it has spread all over Europe.

The English, and Americans, are accustomed to talk of their Anglo-Saxon descent. This savors much of affectation, if it does not denote a defect of information. For if Roman civilization had not been planted in the island of Great Britain, before the Saxon invasion, the English and their descendants would have been very little lifted above the condition of the Saxons who inhabited the shores between Holland and Denmark. There was no European people at that day more thoroughly barbarous. This is more particularly true of the Angles, the chief tribe of the Saxons, and from whom the island derives its name of England. The lawless and piratical life they led, was absolutely inconsistent with the manners and habits which are so carelessly attributed to them. There was no way of even beginning the work of civilization, but by breaking them up, as a tribe, and planting them among a people who had already made considerable advances. The English, and Americans, have no more reason to be proud of their Anglo-Saxon descent, than the people of southern Europe have to be proud of their Vandal or Gothic descent. In every instance where barbarous tribes have invaded countries in which Roman civilization existed, they adopted, and grew into the institutions and customs of the more cultivated people, and built the fabric of society on that foundation. The mixture of the two people had precisely the same effect, only on a much larger scale, as the mixture, and intermarriage of the various classes in modern society. The stock of Patrician blood would run out, the upper ranks would become enervated, if they were not constantly recruited from the Plebeian orders. Nothing is more common than to mistake a mere coincidence for an antecedence and consequence—that is, for cause and effect. Thus, although circumstances peculiar to Great Britain (its being an island for instance) have secured to the people a better social organization than in any other European country, its great advances have been ascribed to a cause purely accidental, merely because it is more open to common apprehension. There can be no doubt, if the Franks or Burgundians, instead of the Saxons, had invaded the country, the march of civilization would have been the same.

The difference between the people of New England and of the Southern States of America, has been supposed to arise from the fact that the former were descendants of the Saxons, the last of the Normans. This is another instance of confounding a coincidence with cause and effect. The cavaliers (who we will suppose were descendants of the Normans) first planted Virginia, but the great bulk of the emigration afterwards were of the same class as that to New England. The difference between the two people is attributable solely to outward circumstances. The climate of the South was more soft, the land richer, the institution of slavery was better adapted to the country, and these are abundantly sufficient to account for the difference of manners (for that is the only difference) between the two people.

We should know absolutely nothing of the Saxons for three hundred years after the invasion, if it were not for Bede's history, and Bede himself was not born until A. D. 673. When there is so great a blank, and a blank only attempted to be filled up by the most superstitious of writers, it is easy to talk of Anglo-Saxon civilization without fear of contradiction.

It is now two centuries and a quarter since the English people emigrated to North America. During that period, their descendants have peopled it in every direction, and have covered it with the triumphs of art and science, so that if by possibility the country should be subjugated, there is no reason to believe that the laws, manners and institutions would be extirpated. On the contrary, they would form the basis of any future superstructure which might be raised, even if the invaders were as completely barbarized as the Saxons of the fifth century.

The Romans were in possession of the island of Great Britain for four centuries. We should make a great mistake if we supposed that it was only the Roman armies which occupied it. Roman citizens, of every class and occupation, emigrated there, as the English did to America. If we did not know this to be the fact, it would be a most improbable supposition that Roman civilization did not exercise a decisive and permanent influence upon the whole frame of Saxon society. Cities were founded even in the sequestered districts of Wales, in which the municipal government of the mother country was established, and the wealth and luxury displayed by the inhabitants, was evidence of a total transformation of the original society. From A. D. 80 to the fifth century, architecture and all the arts flourished, and beautiful buildings, after the Italian model, were erected in various parts of the Island. Every Roman colony and free city was a mimic representation of the city of Rome, encompassed with walls, adorned with temples, palaces, acqueducts, and other buildings, both for use and ornament; so that when the Emperor Constantine rebuilt the city of Autun, in Gaul, in 296, he was chiefly furnished with workmen from Brtiain. Schools were established in various parts of the country, in which youth were taught the Latin language, and other departments of knowledge.* The Theodosian code abounds in edicts relating to these schools. Savigny, in his great work, (Histoire du droit Romain), shows that not less than thirty-three towns lying between Winchester and Inverness were endowed with regular forms of municipal government; and the choice of the Magistrates was intrusted to the citizens themselves.

When the invasion of the Barbarians took place, the same consequences followed as in central and southern Europe. A long period of anarchy ensued. Society was in a state of fermentation until the process of mixing and amalgamating the two races was complete; but there never was a time, even during the darkness of the seventh, tenth and eleventh centuries, when Roman civilization did not exert a predominant influence throughout Britain, Gaul, Spain and

*Henry's History of Great Britian, vol. 2, page 92, 120. Allowance must be made for the coloring of the historian, but the facts are substantially correct.

Italy. The work of Savigne is devoted to establish the perpetuity of the Roman law, to show that there never was a period when it ceased to be the chief element in the jurisprudence of the European States.*

The diffusion of the Latin language over the west of Europe is an incontestible proof of the thorough root which Roman civilization had taken. It was the spoken language on the continent, in Gaul, Spain, Belgium, &c. Mr. Gibbon, (v. 1, p. 60), says that it was the spoken language in Britain also. Mr. Hallam, (Mid. Ages, v. 4, p. 159), thinks otherwise, and that Latin was never spoken as generally as in Gaul and Spain; and this is undoubtebly correct. But that it was the spoken language of the Roman and Roman-Anglo population, and that this population in the third and fourth centuries, was very considerable, will admit of no doubt. The Gælic was spoken by the Britons, as in the Welsh and German settlements of the United States, these people speak their own language, although the English is the prevailing language of the country. The Latin is the root of a great part of the English language. If the Saxon is the basis of the words used in common life, the Latin is the foundation of the intellectual part of the language, nor could it be otherwise. An uncivilized tribe cannot have the same range of ideas as a cultivated people; and not having the ideas, it is impossible for them to invent the corresponding words. The same fondness for uttering novel propositions which makes the English boast of their Saxon descent, has led them to

*When Julian, (afterwards Emperor), commanded in Gaul, the scanty harvest of the year 359 was supplied from the plenty of the adjacent Island. Six hundred large boats made several voyages to the coast of Britain, and distributed their rich cargoes of wheat among the towns and fortresses on the Rhine. [Gibbon, ch. 19.] Julian himself, (says Mr. Gibbon), gives a very particular account of the transaction; and if we compute the 600 ships at only seventy tons each, they were capable of exporting 120,000 quarters; and the country which could bear so large an exportation, must already have attained an improved state of agriculture." Same chapter, note 87.

In chapter 2, Gibbon, remarking upon the condition of the Island, long before the Saxon conquest, says: "The spirit of improvement had passed the Alps, and was felt even in the woods of Britain, which were gradually cleared to open a free space for convenient and elegant habitations. York was the seat of government; London was already enriched by commerce, and Bath was celebrated for the salutary effect of its medicinal waters."

boast of the Saxon origin of their language. Epicures whose taste is palled by living on a healthy diet, acquire a relish for the most repulsive food ; and the most refined and cultivated minds, satiated with the perfection to which their language has been brought by the transfusion of the Latin, take delight in descanting on the homely terms of Saxon origin. It carries them back to what they are pleased to consider an arcadian age, but which only exists in their own imaginations. Roman civilization, the traces of which, however obscured by time, are stamped upon every feature of the existing society, has given them a vantage ground to stand upon, and enable them to talk of the wonders which Saxon institutions achieved. If the question as to the structure of the English language involved a mere critical inquiry, it would be unimportant; but it necessarily assumes a character of profound philosophical interest, as it is connected with the whole problem of European civilization, and with the still deeper problem, what nation, if any, that has risen up in the world, has ever been known to civilize itself ?

It is supposed that the bulk of the Roman population was expelled from the Island after the invasion of A. D. 406 ; that the Roman legion had been removed some time before, in order to protect the empire in another quarter, is certain. It is highly probable, also, that numbers of Roman citizens among the employées and civil officers of the government also withdrew ; but that the entire Roman population and the population of mixed blood, which had been growing up during a much longer period than has elapsed since the settlement of the United States, also withdrew, is absolutely incredible. For what was the Roman population at the commencement of the fifth century? It was composed of persons who were Britons by birth, although descended from Roman ancestors; and this population which had been growing up for twenty generations, had become fastened to the soil, by habit and interest, as well as by early associations. If a thousand years hence, there shall be no authentic history of the dismemberment of Spain from her American Colonies, no one would place any confidence in the random conjectures that the Creoles had in a body abandoned Mexico, Peru and Chili. The belief would be, as is the fact, that they nearly all remained in the country of their birth.

The Saxon conquest was not the work of a day. It proceeded more slowly than conquests usually do. The armies which entered the country at considerable intervals, were too small to exterminate the inhabitants, even if they had desired to do so, although in the end they were sufficient to overcome the military force which they encountered. Nor could there be any motives to induce the Roman British population to retire, when all other parts of the empire were suffering from the overwhelming inroads of still more formidable Barbarians.

Historians speak of the expulsion of the Moors from Spain. With as much reason might a historian living three centuries hence speak of the entire emigration from Ireland to America of the Gælic race. The Moorish kingdoms of Spain were very gradually destroyed; the last, that of Granada, not until the close of the fifteenth century. But the Moors had been settled in Spain nearly eight centuries; and even if we possessed no positive information to contradict the general notion which is afloat, the fact that the national character to this day is strongly tinged with Moorish features, would be sufficient to prove that Mahommedan institutions had exerted a decisive influence upon Spanish society. No country, we may be well assured, has ever been emptied of its inhabitants to anything like the extent to which the careless and sweeping statements of some historians would seem to imply. The rich may remove, but the bulk of the population must stay behind.

With a much more formidable force than the Saxons conveyed to Britain, William the Conquerer was unable to extirpate the Saxon population. As soon as an invading army has succeeded in overawing the people, it has no interest in pushing its conquest farther. On the contrary, it is greatly to its advantage that they should remain. The Huguenots, notwithstanding the revocation of the edict of Nantz, always composed a numerous and compact body in France; and yet total expulsion was more practicable in that instance than in any other.

The history of Great Britain, for more than three centuries after the Saxon invasion, I have already remarked, is almost a blank. But we know that when this piratical horde planted itself in the island, they found regular government established, and all the arts of civilized life in considerable progress; and there is no way of accounting for even the slow advances which they made in civilization, but by supposing that a large proportion of the civilized people, and not merely the works of arts were permitted to remain. Knowledge is power, even in the hands of the subjugated; and the compiler of the

Saxon code was as ambitious as the compilers of the Burgundian and Visigoth codes, of copying after Roman institutions.

There can be no doubt, that the mixture of different peoples of the same race has contributed to the progress of European civilization, and has caused English society to attain its present high state of perfection. But I see no reason why it should not have made these advances, if the island had been invaded by any other German tribe. After making allowance for the powerful influence of Christianity, the civilization of modern Europe s chiefly ascribable to the fact that Roman civilization was engrafted on a northern stock. It was indifferent whether this stock should be a Saxon one or not. If the Franks had possessed themselves of Britain, and the Saxons of Gaul, the structure of society in the two countries would have been the same as it is now. Two things were necessary, that the barbarous tribes should be placed in contact with a civilized people, that they should live among them, and learn from them, otherwise, there would have been no beginning for the new race; and secondly, that Roman civilization should be so modified as to adapt itself to this mixed people. The sufferings, the distress, and anguish of mind which the people endured, threatened for a time to disorganize all European society. But these causes were never sufficient to tear up by the roots Roman civilization. On the contrary, the multiplied adversities to which men in all the relations of life were exposed, developed reflection and individual energy, and constituted a training and discipline for the new society, which rose up from the ruins of the old. In the seventh and eighth centuries, learning had made greater progress in England than anywhere else. On the Continent, profane literature had entirely disappeared. In England the schools were flourishing, and Greek and Roman literature were sought after with unusual ardor, as the history of Alcuin, the intellectual representative of the eighth century, completely attests.

Do physical causes exercise an important influence upon the human character? This has been a much debated question. But it is not difficult of solution. That difference of race produces a difference of character among nations, can admit of no doubt. But difference of race proceeds from an original difference of structure, or organization, and is entitled to infinitely more attention than food, air, and climate. The difference between the Chinese and the people of Europe is so marked, that it is impossible to mistake it. The Chinese attained to their present state of civilization when the people of Great Britain, France and Germany were in a savage condition. Education is universally diffused in China, and men of letters have a distinction which they possess in no other part of the world. But their education is confined within the narrowest limits imaginable, and their literature is mawkish and trifling in the extreme, without depth, or originality. They are the most lettered, and the most ignorant among civilized people. The Tartar conquest operated no change in society ; for the Tartars adopted the institutions and manners of the conquered people, as the Franks, Goths and Saxons adopted those which they found planted in Gaul, Spain and Britain.

In Africa, civilization never even begun to dawn, except on the Mediterranean coast, which was peopled by a race totally different from the Ethiopian. The brain is the organ of the mind, and any sensible difference in its structure must exercise a corresponding influence upon the character. There is a great difference in this respect, between individuals of one and the same nation. If we were to single out all the weakest minded persons in Europe and America, and plant them somewhere as a nation, they would probably be little inferior to the Chinese or Hindoos. We could not well compare them with the Ethiopians, because they would at least have the gloss of civilization, while the last are still addicted to the most savage habits. But it is still a problem whether this physical cause proceeding from race, and the original structure of the brain may not be countervailed by moral causes. The physical organization undergoes great changes in a highly civilized society. The moral causes which then exert an influence act upon the mind; and yet they act less directly than where the discipline is of a purely mental character. If we could transfer half a million of Chinese or Hindoos to Great Britain or the United States, place them socially, as well as politically, on the same footing with the people of those countries, but prevent intermarriages, except with the people of their own race, we might be able, after the lapse of a great many generations, to determine whether the structure of the brain, and not merely the external manners, is capable of alteration and improvement. No experiment of this kind has ever been made, nor probably ever will. It will then be forever a problem. For, although as I have remarked, moral causes would seem to be better fitted to act upon that part of our structure which is immediately connected with the mind, than upon that which is only so remotely ; yet it must be remembered that the mind, and consequently, its physical organ, have a power of resistance, as well as a principle of ductility, and this power might be absolutely fatal to any fundamental change in the intellectual faculties.

The consideration of physical causes has been generally confined to the influence of food, climate, and air. Climate, undoubtedly, exerts a powerful influence upon the character. The inhabitants of the frozen and torrid zones are distinguished from each other, by the most decisive traits; nor could any human device bring about a resemblance between them. In the first, the extreme rigor of the climate causes the whole of life to be spent in efforts to battle against the elements. The beings who are condemned to this dreary abode, are occupied with no other care, than that of sustaining animal life. Their faculties are dwarfed, and mutilated, and their feelings benumbed by the terrible agents which act perpetually upon them. In the torrid zone, the character is powerfully affected, but not in the same way, nor to the same extent. The extreme heat of the climate produces a lassitude, which is unfavorable to any vigorous or sustained exertion. In the first case, the mind suffers from being overtasked in ministering to the bodily wants. In the second, it suffers through defect of capacity for exertion. But the inhabitants of the torrid zone are capable of rising much higher, both intellectually and morally, than the inhabitants of the frozen. The climate does not act upon them with such unmitigated severity, as upon the inhabitants of the extreme North. Instead of a scanty subsistence, they have an abundance of food. Their numbers consequently increase greatly, society is fairly established among them, and the intercourse which takes place, makes great amends for the want of other motives to mental exertion.

In the temperate zone, the differences of climate are not such as to prevent all the people who inhabit it, from attaining a very high, though perhaps not an uniform civilization. Where physical causes are not absolutely overbearing in their operation, as in the polar regions, and near the equator, they are capable of being overpowered by moral causes, and bringing all the people subjected to them, to a near resemblance to each other. The difference between the people of southern and central Europe is not so great, that it might not be overcome by the operation of the same moral causes, acting upon both. The difference between the Italians and the English, is not so great as between the Italians and the people of Ancient Rome.

In the United States, the difference between the people of the North and South is not so great, as it is between the people of France, who inhabit different provinces in the same latitude.

The influence which moral causes exert, will be best appreciated by singling out those classes in different countries, which are most completely subjected to them. If the intellectual men, in different parts of the temperate zone, have in the chief lineaments of character, a strong resemblance to one another, it must be attributed to the influence which moral causes have in moulding the mind and disposition. The eminent men from the south of France in the Chamber of Deputies, do not differ materially from the eminent members of the British Parliament, who are natives of Scotland. Guizot, and Berryer, are not more distinguishable from Brougham, and Macauley, than they are from each other. There is greater difference of character between Mackintosh and Grattan, than between Burke and De Tocqueville. Education, absorbing occupations, pursuits, which demand judgment and reflection, overcome the difference of climate, where this is not extreme, and assimilate men wonderfully to each other. What is true in the higher walks of life, is true in the lower; and if the institutions, both public and private, are the same, the different classes in both will nearly resemble each other. The French are no longer the fickle and vivacious people they were before the year 1789. They begin to feel that they have some stake in the hedge, some interest in public affairs, and this has produced a marked seriousness of character. Thus, if difference of climate which is so well calculated to produce a difference of temperament, can make two nations appear to be of different races, a train of moral causes acting upon both, may make them resemble each other. The eminent statesmen of England and the United States, are very much the same sort of persons; but there is a very great difference between all of them, and Richelieu, or Mazarine, or Wolsey, and Strafford.

I have observed, that the bringing men into close communication with each other, and establishing some sort of society in the first instance, was probably the principal means of civilizing them. This influence is two-fold. It acts upon the manners by imposing a restraint on the excessive indulgence of the selfish, and antisocial propensities; it acts upon the mind, by presenting it with abundant materials for reflection. For the study in one form or other, of the minds and character of others, makes up the greatest, and the most valuable part of human knowledge. But free institutions lead to an association of people of all classes. The civilization, therefore, is destined to be more thorough, and uniform, than in any other species of government. In most countries, civilization can hardly be said to be an attribute of all classes. The various orders are separated as widely as if they were inhabitants of different ages, and countries. This condition of society could not exist in the United States, nor would it have existed in other countries, if the civil and political institutions had originally been so modelled, as to bring people of all ranks into a free and constant intercourse. No nation has ever been known to civilize itself; and the only way of civilizing the uncivilized orders of the same country, is to bring them under the direct influence of those which are civilized. The thorough civilization of the people of the United States, (when compared with that of other countries,) is more than any other circumstance destined to render their institutions lasting, and thus to falsify the maxim of Montesquieu, that a nation after it has attained a certain height, is compelled by some invincible law of its being to decline.

Although a southern temperament may make men fickle, passionate, and fond of pleasure, it also induces a contemplative turn of mind. This is a marked trait in the character of a southern people. Free institutions turn this quality to account, and prevent the contemplative disposition from wasting itself, as among the oriental nations, in vague, and unprofitable reveries. A vast field for active exertion is opened; and this mixture of the practical, and speculative, contributes to the formation of a very high order of mind. A most acute observer, De Tocqueville, has perhaps exaggerated, when he declares that the men of the Southern States of America, "are both more brilliant, and more profound, than those of the North." We shall not err, however, if we say that they have both these qualities in as great perfection.

In every country, which has run a career of long, and uninterrupted prosperity, there is a tendency to what may be termed excessive civilization. Extremes frequently meet, and excessive civilization carries men back to the indulgence of the same propensities which characterized them in savage life. The same vices, only under different forms, invade every rank, and the community would be in danger of universal dissolution, unless some terrible calamity occurred to give a rousing shake to society. But if there is a country, in which no wall of partition exists between the higher and lower orders, this catastrophe may be prevented, without breaking up the frame-work of society. The upper ranks will be constantly recruited from that part of the population, which being inured to industry, possesses greater simplicity of habits. The great disparity which exists in the condition of different classes, may seem unnatural; but it answers among many other wise ends, this important purpose; it prevents luxury, and effeminacy from taking complete possession of the ruling orders, and the whole community from running rapidly to decay.

The influence which food and air exercise, is very small. In the frozen zone, the first acts powerfully, but it is only as connected with the climate. The meagre, and scanty subsistence which the inhabitants obtain from the forests and rivers, does there stunt the growth both of body and mind. But in the temperate zone, the food although very different, in different regions, is on that very account better adapted to the various physical organizations. The inhabitants of a southern climate, have larger and more powerful muscles than those of a northern; which would seem to show that a moderate diet is not unfavorable to the complete development of the animal structure. No people in the temperate zone has been known to abstain from the use of stimulating drugs, such as tobacco, spirituous liquors, tea and coffee. If any such had ever been known, it would probably be found that the strength and health of both body and mind, was greatly improved, and that the human frame attained a perfection which it had not any where else. But no experiment having ever been made, we are deprived of the only certain means of verifying the conjecture.

The present has been termed the age of physical civilization; and it is even supposed that literature and philosophy, have already begun to decline. This, like many other general propositions has at least the merit of containing something striking. Its fault consists in presenting an imperfect, and incomplete view of the matter. There never was a period, when men were so much addicted to those pursuits, which minister to the comforts and enjoyments of life. There never was one when these were so widely diffused. The display of human activity in this direction, having been so little formerly, and so immense now, the intellectual exertion which is actually made, is thrown into the back ground, and to an inattentive observer the unprecedented progress which one pursuit has made, seems to imply the decay of all others. I doubt whether there ever was a time of greater intellectual exertion in France, Great Britain, and Germany, than during the present century. There is a fault common to the great majority of minds, even those of a high order. They can see nothing excellent, nothing eminently fine in anything which belongs to their own time. It is not merely that the living envy the living, not the dead. It is because the best minds are slow in analyzing, and appreciating what has not been analyzed before their time. I have known very excellent minds, affect great admiration for what are sometimes termed "the wells undefiled of English literature," and yet great part of the works so characterized, are heavy and dull in the extreme. A tinge of melancholy frequently pervades the finest minds in a civilized country. They are saddened by the present, not by the past; and they endeavor to escape from every thing around them, by studies which most effectually deaden and extinguish the sentiment of the present. This is a topic which is too large for me to dilate upon now. The reader must be satisfied with the few hints I have thrown out. These will exercise his mind more than if I were to explain the merits of the great number of brilliant, profound, and original writers, who have adorned the present century. Physical civilization lies at the foundation of all higher civilization. It constitutes the rudiments of moral, and intellectual cultivation. An age distinguished for it, denotes two things; first, that civilization is more thoroughly diffused than at any former period, and secondly, that preparation is making for the growth of a more various, profound, and original literature, than before existed.

The general taste for physical civilization at the present day, is an indication of a very important revolution in the structure of society. If we confine our views to its influence upon the social, and political organization, we cannot place too high an estimate upon it. Whatever contributes to raise the general standard of comfort, contributes to the development of the popular mind, and creates an improved taste and capacity for free institutions. And accordingly, the two countries, (Great Britain and the United States,) in which physical civilization has attained the greatest perfection, are the two in which civil and political freedom have made the greatest progress. Free institutions are endowed with a faculty of self preservation which is possessed by no other form of government. The reason of this is, that physical civilization diffuses property, knowledge, and power; and by so doing, conduces to the equal distribution of the physical, and moral strength of the community.

So far from believing that physical civilization is inconsistent with intellectual cultivation, I am convinced that the more the former is spread, the higher is the point to which the last will be carried. We must, at any rate, admit that physical civilization has something to do with the formation of the intellectual men who have adorned society. We cannot conceive of such minds as Locke, and Burke, Montesquieu and Cuvier, growing up in a society where they at least were not surrounded with the comforts of life. Health is a corporeal advantage; yet some degree of it is indispensable to the prosecution of any intellectual enterprise. And as a wise man will not wantonly neglect his health, he will not willingly forego any other outward advantage which conspires to the same end. Physical civilization supplies the materials on which intellectual men act. If we figure to ourselves two countries, one of which is covered with log huts, interspersed among palaces, the other filled with populous and well built cities, the truth of the remark will be obvious. In one the matter for reflection and study will be inexhaustible; in the other it will be sterile and unprofitable. All speculations in philosophy and literature may be said to be experiments upon the human mind. But it is impossible to make such experiments where the race of mankind is lifted very little above the condition of the brutes.

The more widely physical civilization is diffused, the greater will be the chance that superior minds will emerge from obscurity. When the progress of industry and the arts is so slow that a small proportion of the population is placed in easy circumstances, a great number of such minds may be said to perish annually, like seed sown upon a sandy soil. If on the other hand, the comforts of life are extended to the bulk of the population, the greater will be the number of the educated, not merely of the educated at schools and colleges, but of those who have encountered the severe intellectual discipline which follows. The number of those who will be thinkers and actors of the age will be greatly increased. Physical civilization may postpone the period of intellectual cultivation; but the longer it is postponed, the more certain it is of giving birth to the highest exertions in every department of philosophy and literature. Even excessive civilization is not without some advantages. The mind becomes wearied with the eternal round of heartless enjoyment, and is thrust upon its own resources for occupation. The apparent dearth of intellectual effort in the United States is remarkable. Never in any country has there been so much intellect in activity; in hardly any one has so little distinction been attained in the higher walks of learning. The reasons are obvious: 1st the wide spread political institutions, together with the learned professions absorb nearly all the talent of the country; 2p, this greatly retards the growth of intellectual men as a body. But until they become such, they feel as if they were placed in a false position to society, when in truth, it is society which is placed in a false position to them. When the minds devoted to speculation become numerous, the common sympathy, which will animate them will be a bond of unspeakable strength, and there will then, probably, be no country which will exceed the United States in every department of philosophy, science and literature. And there can be no well ordered commonwealth unless there is a full development of the intellectual as well as the active faculties. The first balances it and gives it a right direction, the second keeps it in motion. All the mechanical contrivances for balancing government are falling from our hands, and can only be superseded by the engine of knowledge. Take away all the intellectual men who have figured in public life, and in the learned professions, together with the influence which they have exerted upon other parts of society, and the United States would be a desert. But as the population becomes dense the demand for intellectual qualities will become more pressing, and cannot be satisfied by the amount which is expended in public life and the professions. And this demand is in due time answered. For in the natural course of things, political life and the professions become crowded to excess, and the various departments of knowledge begin to be filled up.

CHAPTER II.

GENERAL VIEWS AND DIFFICULTIES OF THE SCIENCE OF GOVERNMENT.

Amidst the general progress which the human mind has made during the last two hundred years, there is one science which has remained nearly stationary; and that is the philosophy of government.* It is true that all our knowledge is deduced from facts; and, it is equally true, that it is not in our power to create any one of those facts. The principles which go to make up what we denominate a science, are nothing more than the philosophy of facts; and until the facts are given, we cannot find the principles. But, it is remarkable that, during the period I have referred to, a wider range of facts has been laid open to human observation and scrutiny, than in any period of similar duration in the history of our race. For if we commence with the year 1642, in the midst of the great struggle between liberty and power in Great Britain, and come down to the present day, we shall find that nearly all the great revolutions in human affairs, which have sensibly affected the social organization, the structure of government, and the functions of rulers, are crowded into that compass. The inquiry, therefore, is not only the most natural in the world, but it forces itself irresistibly upon us, why, in the midst of so great and so general

* The intelligent reader is no doubt familiar with the distinction between art and science. The first is the result of our experience, however limited that may be. The second is the repository of those great principles which are deduced from all experience. The first therefore necessarily precedes the last. It contains the rule in the concrete, while the last contains it in the abstract, or in a philosophical form. In Quintilian's time, it was a question, whether oratory was a science, or an art. At the present day, I presume, no one will deny that government is both an art and a science.

a movement of the human mind, the science of government has seemed to stand still. It can never be necessary to know all possibly existing facts; otherwise no part of knowledge would ever be brought to completeness.

Several causes may be assigned for the slow progress of the science. The first consists in its intrinsic difficulties. There is no branch of knowledge which to so great an extent demands the application of abstract truth to particular facts; none in which the facts are so diversified, and so difficult to reduce to general rules. The very circumstance, therefore, that the two last centuries have been so prolific of materials, that they have afforded such an immense accumulation of facts, creates an impediment. Without these we cannot proceed a step, and yet with them the greatest powers of analysis are baffled in the endeavor to trace out those principles which shall everywhere be regarded as forming the great elements of the science. I can easily imagine that very many of the most thoughtful minds, both in Europe and America, have occupied a whole lifetime in surveying, with intense interest and an eagle eye, the changes which society and government have undergone in the last sixty or seventy years, and yet have recoiled from the attempt to reduce into a system such a vast mass of experience.

The second reason which I would assign is, that government is the science not only of what is, and what ought to be, but in addition to these, of what may be made to be also. It thus unites in itself the difficulties of all other sciences, and conducts to inquiries more complicated than any one of them singly. We can create no new facts, but we may vary indefinitely the combinations of those which are already known. If it is a painful effort, therefore, to apply abstract truths to particular facts, the difficulty is very much increased when we desire to make an entirely new disposition of those facts; when, for instance, we wish to alter existing institutions, and to give a new form to the whole, or to some part of the government.

Another impediment to the advancement of the science has arisen from the extreme backwardness which both writers, and statesmen have constantly discovered in speaking out all that they know and believe. It is supposed that there are a great many secrets in government which will not bear to be divulged to the generality of mankind. We have read of the secret and the open doctrine of the ancient philosophers. Some things they revealed to the multitude, while others were hidden from all but a select few. The same custom existed among some of the ancient fathers;* although it has been endeavored to be explained and palliated by eminent ecclesiastical writers. But the practice was by no means confined to the ancients. It has existed from all time, and has prevailed extensively, though not avowedly, among the philosophers and politicians of modern times. It is now beginning to fall into disrepute, since what are termed the multitude are increasing so fast in knowledge and information, that it is no longer an easy matter to keep any secrets, and since, on that very account, the disclosure can be productive of no detriment. For although the first effect, of finding out many things which were before hidden, is to make us fear nothing, not even the most violent changes; yet the ultimate effect is to make us fear many things, and to show us precipices and hindrances at every step which we take.

The last cause which I shall mention as retarding the progress of the science is, that in many instances the minds which are particularly fitted to extend its bounds are withdrawn from speculation into the field of active life. Profound thought, the ability to take the philosophical view, which belongs to things the most common and familiar, joined to a keen insight into men's character and dispositions, are necessary to penetrate into the principles of the science. But he who possesses these qualities is very apt to be won over to one or other of the great parties which share the mastery of the country. The field of speculation, the field of imagination, and the field of action, divide between themselves the empire of man's exertions. No one has been able to compass one of these in a lifetime; while the sense of enjoyment which is derived from mixing in active life is so much greater than is afforded by abstract speculation, that few minds have sufficient fortitude to forego the first for the sake of the more brilliant and durable fame which attends the last.

Writers on political philosophy have for the most part employed themselves in studying what is termed the mechanism of government,

* "*Some* of the Fathers held that wholly without breach of duty, it is allowed to the teachers, and heads of the Christian church, to employ artifices, to intermingle truth with falsehood." Riboff. Programme of the Doctrine and Discipline of the Fathers.

rather than in unfolding the structure of society. This is often the cause of great infirmity in the most ingenious speculations; since without pursuing the last course, we can neither thoroughly decipher existing institutions, nor see our way clearly in binding together the general principles which are fairly deducible from them. All governments are to a great degree dependent upon the manners, habits, and dispositions of the people among whom they subsist. This connection is closer and more striking where the institutions are democratic; and as the American constitutions are the only example of the thorough establishment of such institutions, it is no wonder the error, I have referred to, has prevailed so extensively in the old world. It is both our privilege and our misfortune, that our knowledge is so completely bounded by our experience: our privilege, because we are withheld from a multitude of visionary, and fruitless expedients to better our condition, and our misfortune. because we are sometimes inclosed in such a narrow circle of experience, as to remove us from the contemplation of a world of new facts which are transpiring beyond us.

The reason then why it is of so much importance to examine and understand the structure of society, and not merely the machinery of government, is because at the present day, more than at any former period, the political institutions are molded by the manners. It is true, every form of government may strictly be said to depend upon the constitution of society—upon the social organization in which it has taken root. But this dependence is of a totally different character in different countries. In some, the manners exert a positive influence; while in others, they have properly a negative influence only. In a commonwealth, where the standard of popular intelligence is high, and no impediment exists to the exercise of that popular authority which rightfully springs from such a state, the people may truly be said to create and to uphold the government. On the contrary, where the population is sunk in ignorance and apathy, government assumes the character of a self-existing institution, for there is no power beyond to direct and control it. In one instance, the will of society impresses itself as an active power upon the institutions, both ordaining and controlling them: in the other, for defect of will, the government is simply permitted to be what chance, or circumstances, originally made it. The political institutions of Russia, and the United States, equally depend upon the social organization; but in the former the influence is negative, in the latter it is direct and positive. In the former, the people, by their inaction, contribute to rear the fabric of despotism; in the last, they have created free institutions: It follows, that in proportion as the influence is of a positive character, will the institutions incline to the form of free government: for there may be every degree of this influence, stamping the greatest variety upon different schemes of government. Thus the English people are distinguished for the enjoyment of a greater degree of liberty than the French; and the last have made such noble advances in the same career during the last twenty years, as to place their government entirely in advance of the Spanish or Portuguese. Sometimes a positive influence is exerted upon one part of the government; one department undergoes a fundamental change, while others remain untouched. In other instances, no great alteration is made; the theory of the government continues as before; but such is the stringency and force of that invisible agent which we term public opinion, that the conduct and behavior of all public men, the tone and temper of the public administration, are materially improved.

The legislature is that department which is apt to be first molded by the direct intervention of the popular will. It becomes a representative body, long before it occurs to any one that it is possible to render the executive and judiciary elective also. The legislature seems to touch more extensively, if not more immediately, upon the interests of society than any other department; and it is the first, therefore, to which development is given. The judiciary would appear to have quite as intimate a connection with the business, the daily transactions of the people, as the legislature; but as its functions are supposed to consist simply in making application of a set of ready made rules, and therefore to be inconsistent with the attainment of any substantive power, it does not engage public attention so early, nor attract so general an interest, as it is entitled to do.

One great end which legislators in constructing government have proposed to accomplish, is so to adjust the parts of which it is composed, that they may act as checks upon one another. This scheme has given rise to the theory of checks and balances. But hardly any one has adverted to a balance of a very different kind, without which the structure of the government must forever be faulty, and its practical working inconsistent with its theory. I allude to that great balance which, in a society rightly constituted, is maintained between the government and the power out of the government. It is owing to the great alterations which the social and political organization has undergone in very modern times, that this new fact in the history of political philosophy has escaped attention ; at any rate, that a precise and definite place has not been assigned to it by those who have treated of government. The elevation of the lower orders, the formation of a great middle class, a thing but of yesterday, the creation of a genuine public opinion, have wrought changes in the composition of government corresponding with those in the structure of society. Because the legislative, executive and judicial departments comprehend that share of authority which is organized, and which assumes a visible and determinate form, it has sometimes been supposed that they contain the sum total of the political power of the community; but it is a matter for curious inquiry, to say the least, whether the outward force which sometimes resides in society, no matter whether we arbitrarily range it under the head of liberties and franchises, has not risen to the rank of a substantive power; whether, in short, it has not become a new wheel in the machinery of the government. Those departments do indeed exercise the administrative authority of the state; and if they were left to themselves, and permitted to use power without a constant and active control on the part of the people, they would constitute the government, in the largest signification of the word. The extent to which that control exists is the single circumstance which at first determines the form of any particular government, and afterwards gives a direction to all its movements. If it is extremely feeble, the government will be a monarchy or oligarchy, in the most unrestricted sense; if it is moderate in its operation, the mixed form of limited monarchy, or a tempered aristocracy, will grow up; and if very strong, it will give rise to free institutions, or a representative republic. If it could be conceived to be all powerful, it would not introduce the licentiousness of an unbridled democracy, but would rather supersede the necessity of all government. Wherever democracy in its extreme form exists, the control of society at large is very small, instead of being very great; and therefore it is that such a government never has more than a temporary existence; it soon degenerates into an absolute government.

As the power I have spoken of as residing out of the government, and in the society, represents for the most part a moral force, it may be supposed that I have assigned it too important a place in regarding it as a new wheel in the political machinery. But they who undertake to expound the ordinary theory of checks and balances, do not rely so much on the physical force which is exercised by the departments of government separately, as upon a set of moral causes which are recognized as belonging to human nature, and which, as they are known to operate upon men as individuals, are with equal certainty expected to act upon them when they are made public rulers. And with the same propriety, in order to form a just notion of that species of balance I have referred to, as existing between the government and the power out of the government, it is not necessary to consider the people as constantly invested with an armed force. The general tendency, at the present day, is to substitute moral power in the place of physical force; not because it is more convenient, but because it is more efficacious. The profound tranquility which has been enjoyed by the American government—a tranquility so remarkable as to constitute a new fact in the history of society—will easily lead us to comprehend how a check exercised upon so large a scale may be of so great importance; how it is that an invisible, but ever active power, which the term public opinion is of too narrow a meaning to give a competent idea of, may be sufficient to determine the form of the government, and after it is created, to superintend all its movements. The tendency of which I have spoken, may, at some future day, be carried so far as to render it doubtful which is the government proper, the official agents who administer the public affairs, or the more complex machinery which presides over them, and retains each department in its proper sphere.

Writers have divided governments into various classes. The most usual division is into monarchy, aristocracy and democracy. This classification has been adopted, not merely in consequence of the different manner in which those governments are put together; but proceeding upon a more comprehensive view, and considering each of them as founded in certain general and fundamental principles of human nature, those writers have treated the classification as a philosophical one of the highest importance. It is sometimes difficult to distinguish between an historical fact and a philosophical truth. That governments have existed under every variety of form, is an undoubted fact; and that their existence may be accounted for from well known causes, is equally certain. But what would be thought of the ethical philosopher, who ranged the virtues and vices under the same head, because they all have their root in certain principles of human nature. The error in both instances is precisely the same. There can be but one legitimate form of government, although there may be ever so many varieties, which force or accident has given birth to.

If I ventured to make a classification, it would be into the natural and artificial forms, considering a representative republic as the only example of the first, and every other species as coming under the second division. By arranging a truth in the same list with a number of errors, it loses the distinct importance which belongs to it, and ceases to be regarded as a truth. The aim of the writer is necessarily imperfect and unsatisfactory. Even admitting that it were absolutely impracticable to introduce free institutions into every country, that does not prevent their being considered as the only legitimate form of government, no more than the impossibility, if it exists, of engrafting the arts and refinement, which are found among the English and American people, upon the wandering tribes of Africa or America, forbids us from treating civilization and savagism, not merely as different, but as two opposite states. The great end to be attained by holding up some principles and some institutions as just and true, and others as the reverse, is to quicken and animate both individuals and states in their efforts to abjure the former, and to cultivate the last. The ancestors of the English and American people roamed like savages through the forests of Britain and Germany, and lived for centuries after under a stern and cruel despotism. The people, whom Cæsar and Tacitus describe as clad in skins, and sacrificing human victims, seemed to have no fairer chance of being raised to the arts and civilization, which their descendants have attained, than the great majority of rude tribes now in existence. By regarding and habitually treating some actions and some institutions as right, and others as wrong, we make a considerable step towards rendering the former attainable, since it is of the very essence of right, that it is something which can be reduced to practice. The distinction then is no longer between the possible and the impossible, but between things practicable and things which are only difficult to be attained.

Government when not founded upon the will of the people is necessarily an imperfect institution, because, failing in the commencement to represent their interests, it is almost sure eventually to be placed in direct opposition to them. Power, where it is condensed in a comparatively small class of the community, is obliged in self-defense to strengthen, in all possible ways, the influence and authority of that class ; and, to the same extent, to detract from the importance of all other orders of men. It is not a reasonable answer to this, to be told that abundant causes for the existence of such a mode of government may be found in the actual constitution of society in some countries, since there is no form of vice, however gross and detestable, which may not be accounted for and justified in the same way. We recognize the correctness of the historical deduction, but reject the general principle which is sought to be derived from it.

The political institutions of a country may be viewed as fulfilling two distinct ends: the one to administer all public business, the other to bind society together, in other words, to uphold civilization. But distinct as these two offices are, that constitution of government which is best fitted to promote the one, is also best calculated to advance the other. The wants and weakness of individuals give rise to the institution of government, and government, in turn, becomes the instrument of furthering the general improvement of society. The mere material interests which the public agents are appointed to superintend, the protection of property, the collection and disbursement of taxes, the guarding against foreign invasion, are not so absolutely connected with the moral and intellectual condition of the people, but what we may suppose the former to be competently managed, without any remarkable improvement in the latter. But it is certain, that the right constitution of government, joined to an upright and enlightened administration of what we denominate public affairs, does contribute wonderfully to impart freedom, activity, and intelligence to the general mind ; and it is still more true, that the diffusion of intelligence, the spread of the arts and sciences, and the growth of a vigorous morality, do produce a marked influence upon the working of the political machine. The wider the basis on which government is made to stand—that is, the more thoroughly it represents the interests of all orders of men—the firmer the purpose, and the more unremitting the efforts, of individuals in improving their condition. The most effectual way then of raising the intellectual condition of the people is to connect their interests so closely with their improvement, that these may be mutually dependent on each other; to throw knowledge in the way of every one, that it may become of daily use, and indispensable application in both public and private affairs; so that men in pursuit of their daily avocations, and government in the discharge of its official duties, may be compelled to run the same career of improvement. In this way, the maintenance of civilization, and the more direct aim which the institutions of government contemplate, are both answered at the same time.

CHAPTER III.

THE FOUNDATION OF GOVERNMENT, AND RIGHT OF THE MAJORITY TO RULE.

The foundation of government is laid in the nature of man; and this fact, simple as it is, explains how civil institutions came to have a beginning; and why it is that they have rightful authority to command. It is sometimes supposed that the most natural view would be to consider individuals as possessing, originally, the right of self-government. But that cannot be natural which contradicts the constitution of human nature. The mistake arises from overlooking, or confounding, the double nature of man. He has attributes which are peculiar to him as an individual: on the other hand he has innumerable relations to the beings who surround him. If we could suppose the former to swallow up his whole being, then it would be correct to say, not only that self-government was originally the rule, but we should be driven to the conclusion that it is now the rule, and must be so in all time to come. But as this is not the case, we are relieved from stating an unsound proposition, and from following it up by the most mischievous consequences. In truth the difficulty does not so much consist in conceiving how a collective body of men should be subjected to the government of society, as in imagining how such a body, constituting in its natural signification a society, should know no other rule than the government of individuals. To say that many thousands, or many millions, of men inhabit together the same region, is to imply that they have a multitude of relations to each other, and a system of interests which are common to all. No man can practice a duty, or exercise a right, without touching more or less upon the corresponding duties and rights of other men.

But as this view admits that man has a double nature, it may be inquired, what higher and stronger reason there is why those attributes which make him the being of society should have the precedence; why, in fine, they should be entitled to rule over the individual, rather than that the individual should be permitted to have control over society. And laying aside the impracticability and self contradiction involved in this notion, the answer is plain, that in society the whole of our nature may be completely unfolded; while out of it hardly any part is even tolerably developed. The scheme of self government, as it erects the will of the individual into the supreme arbiter of his actions, necessarily implies the violation, by each, of the rights of all; and would thus mutilate and destroy even the character of the individual, if it did not produce the utter extermination of the race.

It is no wonder, therefore, that men in all ages have instinctively taken shelter under some sort of political institutions. The imperfection of these institutions is a natural consequence of the very imperfect nature of man. This does not show that the scheme is wrong, but rather that its excellence is such that it cannot be carried thoroughly into practice. Imperfect as all human contrivances necessarily are, civil government has been found necessary to the supply of our wants, the protection of our rights, and to the lifting of our condition much above that of the brutes.

Several theories have been proposed to account for the first formation of government. Some writers consider it as a divine institution; while others suppose that it originated in compact. This compact, however, has been described very differently. Mr. Locke treating it as an agreement between the people and their rulers; while Hobbes and Rousseau suppose the agreement was simply among the people themselves.

There is this very important distinction between the exact and the moral sciences, that, in the former, a proposition is either altogether true, or false; while in the last, there may be, and very frequently is, a mixture of both truth and error. This renders it exceedingly difficult to deal with moral propositions. Truth and error may be combined in every proportion; and it is only where the balance inclines greatly to the one side or the other, that we can be sure we are right in adopting a given view. But there is this great compensation resulting from this defect, and the total dissimilarity between these two departments of knowledge, that, in politics, when we embrace an error, we very often embrace a considerable portion of truth along with it. Thus, in those matters which vitally affect the interests and happiness of mankind, the understanding is hardly ever condemned to the dominion of absolute and unqualified error. If one side of a proposition were altogether true, and the other altogether false, the adoption of the latter would give rise to something more than a theoretical error: it would produce consequences fatal to the peace and well being of society. The advantage which flows from this complete dissimilarity between two leading departments of our knowledge is not seen in those abstract propositions which, whatever way they may be decided, affect practice very little. But it is strikingly displayed in that vast multitude of questions which are of daily occurrence, in administering the complicated concerns of an established and regular community. That is to say, the advantage arising from the principle increases in exact proportion to its application to the actual affairs of men.

The two theories which I have referred to are an illustration of these views. The first, although exceedingly far fetched, has this much of verisimilitude, that the divine law constitutes the highest standard of right of which we can have any conception, and communities as well as individuals, in all their schemes of action, are bound to be guided by it. But if we were to interrogate a philosopher or mechanician as to the cause of the movements of some complicated machine, and they were to refer it to the divine agency, we should derive no satisfaction from the explanation. In one sense the solution would be correct, since the Supreme Being is the author of everything. But no addition would be made to our knowledge. So with regard to government; what we want to know, and what we are immediately concerned in knowing, is the process, the human instrumentality, which has given rise to the institution. If we were satisfied with the sweeping answer, curiosity and inquiry into the operation of those secondary laws which determine the form of particular governments would be damped, and we should make very little effort to improve an institution which was placed so entirely beyond our reach. Accordingly a doctrine which has the appearance of introducing the highest and justest rules into the conduct of political societies, is the one which has been attended with the most mischievous consequences. The advocates of the "jure divino right" have, at the same time, been the most idolatrous worshippers of the absolute power of governments; while the plain and homely understandings who have rejected it, have set themselves vigorously to work to extend the blessings of rational freedom, and to build up fortresses against the encroachments of power.

The other theory, which places the foundation of government in compact, especially the view taken by Hobbes and Rousseau, approaches the truth much nearer. It is not absolutely incorrect even as an historical fact. Compact is the only legitimate basis upon which government can stand. And if any one will turn his attention to the formation of the American constitutions, he will find that the idea is carried into actual practice. With an example so complete and decisive, it would be a very lame answer to say, with an eminent writer, that if the American procedure was not followed at the first dawn of society, where government, like the infant in the cradle, was the creature of circumstances, therefore it is not entitled to notice. No machine, no production of art, or science, which was the fruit of man's exertions, at the present day, or a thousand years ago, could have any claim to originality, if this view were correct. All must be referred to an infantile society, simply because the men who have since lived, descended directly from that society.

There are two principles which preside over, and give a direction to, the actions of men: reflection, and spontaneous feeling. And there is this fine provision in our nature, that where the attainment of an important end is desirable, which cannot be completely compassed without the aid of reflection, and yet the reflection is wanting, still there is a corresponding appetite, or sentiment, which enables us to feel our way. This, in a society which has made any considerable advance, is denominated common sense. In a rude one, it is called sagacity, or instinct. Thus, in those communities which existed at a period anterior to written history, although we cannot conceive anything like a formal agreement to have been entered into, we can very readily suppose, indeed we are compelled to suppose, that the minds of all the adult males, however untutored, spontaneously, and without any set purpose, conspired to that end. That those communities were societies, that is, collections of men in the aggregate, is abundantly sufficient to authorize the supposition. Certain it is, that in the rudest community, at the present day, that of the North American Indian, I discern far more evidences of the prevalence of a common will, as actuating the tribe, than of the independent and uncontrolled will of the individual.

We talk of tacit or implied agreements, even in jurisprudence, and give the same force and authority to them which we do to express ones. And with great reason. Our notions of right and wrong, of just and unjust, are not determined by our positive agreements; but the reverse. So much so, that the same force is sometimes given to that which ought to be, as if it were actually declared to be. For the same reason, although we might not be able to find any trace in a primitive community of an express compact, we should discover far more evidences of that form of society which results from one, than we should of the self government of individuals. In other words, the causes which lead men to society, and suggest the formation of political communities, for the management of the common interests are of such controlling efficacy, that they act independently of any formal agreement. And if the contrivances of government are very imperfect at first, the same imperfection belongs to the whole sphere of individual action. Although in the most perfect form of society, that of a representative republic, men possess far more personal freedom than they do as members of a rude tribe, yet it would be very incorrect to say, that they did not enjoy individual liberty in this last state.

Moreover, although societies of men may originally have been gathered by accident, and civil institutions planted fortuitously, the difficulty of conceiving such a thing as a social compact becomes less with every advance of civilization and knowledge. No one supposes that the authority of government, even in Great Britain and France, stands upon the same uncertain foundation as in the reigns of Henry VII. and Louis XI. The idea that some sort of agreement lies at the foundation of government is so inseparable from the human mind, so constantly present in every form of society that it survives all the mutations which human affairs undergo; and at length causes this compact to be reduced to practice in all its details. Thus at the present moment a convention is assembled in the most populous and powerful of the American States,* for the purpose of forming a new constitution; and that convention was elected by the votes of all the adult males in the State.

*New York.

Even in some of the European States, there is a settled conviction at the present day, not only among the reflecting, but with the great bulk of the population, that the promotion of the general weal is the only legitimate end of government. Obstacles may have to be encountered in realizing the idea; but the idea is predominant. I can easily imagine that all the adults of a society may assemble for the purpose of forming a constitution, and yet this constitution be very imperfect. Still it would be literally true, that the form of government was the creature of compact. The imperfection might be the result of some defects inherent in human nature, or of circumstances which were uncontrollable.

That all governments stand at least upon the footing of an implied contract, is of the greatest importance in politics. For then every advance in knowledge adds strength to the notion, and ultimately converts the implied into a solemn and formal agreement. And as our inquiries in political philosophy are not bounded by the actual, but are chiefly concerned with what ought to be and what may be made to be the theory of the social compact should ever be held up as constituting the firmest and the most rational foundation of civil institutions, and as that scheme which all people and lawgivers should make continual efforts to approach, even if it should not always be attained.

Great difficulty is sometimes expressed with regard to the rule of the majority; a rule which evidently lies at the foundation of free government. The difficulty is in truth no greater in the case of communities than of individuals, each of whom has conflicting and contradictory interests, opinions, and feelings, and yet knows that it is necessary to pursue some determinate plan, not merely to act successfully, but in order to act at all. And if one could conceive all the people of a State as composing parts of one mighty individual, this great being would be as much agitated and embarrassed by discordant views, as political communities are. He would be obliged to be governed by the majority of reasons in favor of or against a proposed line of conduct. Difficulties of this kind afford matter for curious and subtile speculation, but they rarely disturb the judgment or interfere much with practice. To say that the rule of the majority is a rule of sheer necessity, and must prevail on that account would be an imperfect explanation. But, if we say, that it resembles those great general laws, which bind together both the physical and the moral world, which are only rendered necessary because they produce beneficial results, we then shed light upon the reason as well as upon the mode of its operation.

If, in laying the foundation of government, our design is to consult the common interests of the whole population, there is no alternative but the rule of the majority. If when the vote is taken, either among the citizens at large, or in the legislative body which represents them, the will of the greater number did not prevail, the minority would be at liberty to act without rule, not merely as regarded themselves, but in regard to the majority also, and in this way we should fall into the solecism of self-government, where several distinct wills have power, not only to govern themselves in relation to their individual interests, but also to infringe in innumerable ways upon the general interests of the society. Even if we suppose that the majority should retire and form a separate government, a new minority would immediately appear, and this would be the case on every subdivision of the population, however minute it might be. The process, if continued, and it must be, once it is commenced, will unfold the preposterous and mischievous effects which would flow from departing from the simple and intelligible rule I have referred to. When the population, by repeated subdivisions, was morceled into the smallest fractions which would admit of a majority and minority, there would, in a country of twenty-one millions of people, be no less than seven millions of distinct governments. And, to be consistent, the division must be pursued still further, for in each of those seven millions of liliputian bodies politic, there is one individual to disagree to everything. The effect would be to create ten millions and a half of such governments; or, as it would be absurd when these assemblies were each reduced to two persons, not to accord to them equal authority, there would ultimately be precisely the same number of governments as individuals, that is, twenty-one millions. It is needless to add, that before the process had been repeated four or five times, society would be delivered over to wild uproar and confusion.

The rule of the majority does not disappoint the design of government, which is to represent the interests of the whole community, and not merely those of a part. On the contrary, it is the only principle which is calculated to secure the happiness and prosperity of the whole. The various opinions and views which are current in society, evidently do not exist for the purpose of being carried literally into practice. Their great use consists in this, that they rouse inquiry, sharpen discussion, lead to extended and thorough examination; and thus, by eliciting the truth in the only way in which it can be elicited, produce the greatest attainable advantage to the whole community. Men's opinions and feelings may be the most diverse imaginable, but their interests cannot be so. The giving free scope to the first, and then subjecting them to the will of the majority, is the only way to give consistency to the last, and of reducing to a system the complicated concerns of society. The keen and searching inquisition which, in a democratic republic, is made into all the schemes of public policy, constitutes a species of experiment upon their value and practicability, without which no permanent benefit could be secured to the whole, or to any part of society. Without this process, men would become mere automata in the pursuit of ends, to which instinct, not an enlightened reason, prompted them. So that the existence of a majority and minority, and yet the supremacy of the former, instead of marring the great design of civil institutions, contributes directly to advance it.

It may be laid down as a proposition, admitting of few exceptions, that whenever a majority is competent to take care of its own interests, it will also be competent to take care of those of the minority. This results from two circumstances; first, that all the prominent and substantial interests of the lesser will be included in those of the larger body; and, secondly, that parties in a republic, the only form of government in which the terms majority and minority are legitimate expressions, do not occupy the fixed position which they have in monarchy and aristocracy; on the contrary, the individuals composing them are constantly shifting places, some passing from the major into the minor, and others sliding from the minor into the major party.

The constant tendency in a republic is to the formation of a middle class, as the predominant body in the community. The consequence is, that so numerous a party as a majority cannot exist without being principally composed of that class. If the minority should be exclusively formed from it, a circumstance which cannot occur, the majority will at least draw the greatest proportion of its members from it. Now a middle class may be said fairly to represent the interests which are common to the whole society. The very rich and the very poor may be sure that their extravagant and unreasonable desires will not be consulted; but they may be equally certain that all their just claims will be regarded, and that, notwithstanding the occasional gusts which blow over society, their solid interests will be as carefully and effectually watched as, humanly speaking, can be the case. It can hardly be otherwise, as this great middle class was originally formed, and is constantly recruited, from the ranks of those who commenced life with little or no property, and as the ambition of every one is to move forward and to rise as fast as possible into the class of the rich. Moreover the laws which protect property in a democratic community are necessarily common to all who have property—to the man worth a million, as well as to one who possesses only two thousand dollars.

It is then correct to say, that in a country where free institutions exist, all the great interests of the minority will be inclosed in those of the majority, that the public men who conduct the one party will, in no important respect, be different from those who conduct the other, and that the great variety of opinions which divide the community will not in the long run, and in the general upshot of human affairs, affect fundamentally or even sensibly the well being of the state.

There is no other alternative than a government based upon the will of the majority, or some one of the artificial forms of government; and hereditary monarchy and aristocracy do not properly represent either a majority or minority. I speak now of pure monarchy and aristocracy. For by a partial combination of free institutions with the hereditary principle, the will of the minority may be introduced into some part of the government, but never that of the majority. The term minority is merely a comparative one. It is so intrinsically, and not merely verbally. A party in the minority is said to exist in reference to another party in the majority, because its opinions are formed in contradiction to those of the last. The minority may be said to spring from the majority. If in pure monarchies, as Russia and Spain, or in pure aristocracies, such as Venice and Genoa once were, there is no way of giving expression to the opinions, and collecting the will of the majority, there cannot, properly speaking, be a minority. Limited or constitutional monarchies, as Great Britain and France, make some approach to the formation of these parties, because a distinct element has found its way into the composition of the government. But monarchy and aristocracy, in their naked forms, are a species of self-existing government; although the notion of a social compact is never lost from the population, no more than the notions of right and wrong, the just and the unjust, are ever obliterated from the minds of the rudest people; yet these governments are upheld, for the most part, by superstition and fear, and have power to perpetuate themselves, without making any direct and declared appeal to any part of society.

But it is a very important step towards the formation of regular government when the institutions, or any part of them, come to be founded even upon the will of a definite minority. The end at which government should aim begins then to be seen in a clearer light. The mind is gradually weaned from the notion of the "jure divino" right of rulers. As a considerable part of the population participates directly or indirectly in the administration of the government, the exercise of political privileges by this part constitutes a school of instruction; which spreads its influence over the whole community; so that if we compare the England and Scotland of the present day, with what they were in the reign of Elizabeth, when, as has been finely said, the intelligent were "like gaudy flowers upon a putrid marsh," we shall find that the well informed are now as one hundred to one at the former period.

The moment that a considerable body of the people begin to exercise a visible authority in the state, the way is prepared for the ultimate rule of the majority. Men then begin, for the first time, to analyze their ideas on political subjects. As public men are now restrained by a force residing out of the government; as the party which wields the popular branch of the legislature, although it is a minority out of doors, is yet obliged to defer to the opinions of every part of the community, intelligent men, indeed persons of very ordinary sagacity, naturally interrogate themselves, why an artificial distinction, such as the possession of landed property alone, should be permitted to stamp the character of citizenship upon the population; why, in fine, a straight line should be drawn through society, placing beyond the pale of the political franchises great numbers of men of substantial condition, and every way qualified to bear a part in the administration of public affairs.

We may then make a more particular division of governments than that contained in the first chapter. We may divide them into three classes: 1st. One of self-existing governments, as absolute monarchy and aristocracy. 2d. Governments which rest upon the will of a definite minority of the population, of which limited or constitutional monarchies are an example; and 3d. Governments which represent the will of the majority, of which the democratic republic is the only example. The two first are mere subdivisions of the more general classification into the artificial forms of government. Nor is the classification a refined one. On the contrary it is entitled to the strictest attention. For the period when government succeeds in founding itself upon the will of the clear minority marks a most important era in the history of society. It denotes that a majority of the population, although politically passive, are yet intellectually active, and there is yet this further consequence flowing from it, that if the minority contain a large proportion of the substantial people, their interests, opinions and feelings will more and more resemble those which are common to the great bulk of the community. So that if government is not administered in the best possible manner, it will be infinitely better administered than in pure monarchy or aristocracy. I observe that in Great Britain and France every year adds to the force of public opinion; that the governing power no longer supposes that it is absolved from paying attention to the sentiments and wishes of even the most inconsiderable class; but that, on the contrary, it makes great efforts to accommodate the legislation to the interests of every part of the community. One of the most remarkable circumstances attending the rule of the majority is, that it is no sooner invested with power, than it sets about imposing limitations to the exercise of its own authority. This is an invariable consequence wherever a real majority, as in the United States, and not merely a constructive majority, as in France during the revolution, have the supremacy; and it is evident that it affords the most unequivocal test imaginable of the right and the fitness of the majority to rule. There is nothing surprising in this disposition on the part of the popular power. The same fact is observable in the conduct of individuals. There are few persons, given to the slightest reflection, who do not, on entering upon life, form for themselves a set of rules intended to act as restraints upon their own conduct, and to produce order and arrangement in the management of their private affairs. The merchant, the shopkeeper, the mechanic, all act in this way, and with fully as much judgment and discretion as men of the highest education. That these same persons, when collected into a body, should be suddenly bereft of a faculty of so much advantage in the pursuit of all their interests, would be difficult to explain upon any principles which belong to human nature. Self-interest, which prompts to its exercise in the first instance, will elicit it in the other also. The change which society undergoes when it has passed from a rude to a highly civilized state, does not imply that self-interest is extinguished, but that it has become more enlightened, takes in a great number of objects of gratification, and thus tends constantly to bring about an agreement between the general interests and the interests of individuals.

It would doubtless be a great improvement upon all ordinary systems of government, and would conduce materially to a just and regular administration of public affairs, if we could introduce among communities some principle which resembled the faculty of reflection in individuals. We should then succeed in imposing a control upon the passions, and remove the greatest obstacle in the way of free government. But whenever we have advanced to that point where the majority possess the supremacy, and yet consent to impose limitations upon their own authority, we may be sure that we have succeeded, to a very great extent, in introducing that principle into the institutions. These limitations, or checks, may be divided into three classes: 1st. Where a restraint is imposed upon both the majority and minority. 2d. Where peculiar advantages are accorded to the minority; and 3d. Where the authority of the community is so distributed as to give rise to a compound system of majorities and minorities.

A written constitution is an example of the first class. It is an instrument which undertakes to form, upon reflection, a body of fundamental rules for the government of the community, which shall be a convenient shelter against the temporary gusts of party feeling. Precautions are thus taken, on laying the foundation of the system, for securing the interests of every order of men, without reference to the fact whether they shall afterwards fall into the party of the majority, or of the minority. Every article of such an instrument is an authoritative declaration in behalf of general liberty. Opinions may vary, circumstances may change, rendering it desirable for the moment to depart from some of these fundamental rules; but this great covenant stares them in the face, and, although it is plain, that it is physically possible to overleap the bounds which it has set, yet such is the power which the rule of right exercises upon the minds of men, when it is recognized as a general principle of action, that there is hardly any faction but what recoils from the attempt, or if it is ventured upon, is compelled to retrace its steps. And what is very remarkable, the difficulty increases in proportion as the electoral franchise is enlarged, and the number of active citizens augmented; which is the reverse of what would at first be supposed to be the case. It is more difficult to maintain a good understanding among the members of a party which is very numerous, than of one which is small. Admitting that a majority of the majority should be bent upon infringing some parts of the constitution, in order to attain a desired end, there are always a numerous body of individuals, of calm judgment and solid reflection, who, although every way disposed to make sacrifices for the sake of keeping the party together, will never consent to sacrifice to a party what belongs to their country. These individuals stand aloof, or go over to the minority, which, becoming the majority, gains the ascendancy, and restores the balance of the constitution.

During the last twenty-five years, we have witnessed repeated attempts, by the legislatures of several of the American States, to violate their respective constitutions, and sometimes even that of the federal government. In every instance the attempt has been abortive. So many of the people have abandoned the party in power, that it became utterly powerless in the accomplishment of its plans, and, after a time, the whole community returned with renewed satisfaction to the wise and salutary maxims which had been handed down to them by their fathers.

The constitution of Ohio was framed in 1802, when the population was a handful. It has now become a populous and powerful community; so that it has outgrown its constitution, as the man outgrows the clothes which he wore when a boy. Great inconvenience has been experienced in consequence of some of the provisions of that constitution ; yet the people have submitted patiently to them, because, although a majority has constantly during the last twenty years been in favor of an alteration, yet the time has not arrived when the constitutional majority of two-thirds could be obtained.

An example of the second class of checks, is when the minority have a proportional representation in the legislative body. The constitution of the executive and judiciary is such as to preclude the adoption of this plan, but the legislature is composed of so many members as very readily to admit of it. As representation takes the place of an actual deliberation by the people in person, when all parties would have an opportunity to be heard, there is every reason why the same right should be recognized in elective government. But it is obvious the moment the door is opened to a representation of the minority in the legislative hall, that a most important restraint is imposed upon the majority. Some persons cannot conceive the existence of a check, unless it has a coercive force. But it is often of more efficacy, in consequence of being deprived of this quality. The minority, in its present position, are placed more upon their good behavior, exercise their wits more in finding out solid and substantial reasons for the opposition which they make; and from the single circumstance that they do not aspire to command, but only to persuade, are enabled to exercise very great influence at those critical periods when extreme measures are about to be pursued, and when the minds of men have become greatly exasperated. A seat in the legislature is the most commanding position which can be occupied in the government. There is no calculating to what extent public abuses are prevented, and the laws modified by the agency of a minority, although it may be impossible to lay one's finger upon the precise period when either was done. The instances are nevertheless without number.

The division of the legislature into two chambers, is another instance of checks. Where two chambers exist, and the members hold their seats for different terms, the more popular branch may alone represent the opinions of a majority of the people at any given period, while the more permanent one will reflect opinions which once had the ascendancy, but which are perhaps passing away. Whether the arrangement is an advantageous one—whether it is wise to permit this conflict of living with dead opinions, is a problem not easy of solution. Nor is it necessary in this place to enter into an examination of it. But, if the system is of doubtful utility, it more strikingly displays the disposition of the majority, on laying the foundation of government, to concede great and decisive advantages to the minority. All the American States, except Vermont,* have adopted the plan. At an early period the people of Pennsylvania established only one chamber, but very soon after added another.

In those countries where one chamber is composed of an hereditary aristocracy, as in Great Britain, or of an aristocracy for life, as in France, Holland, and Belgium, the institution is of an entirely different character. The creation of an upper house is not an advantage conceded to the minority of the society; but is a personal privilege conferred upon a very small body. No matter what opinions either the majority or minority may have, there stands this immovable bulwark, until the period has arrived when public sentiment has acquired so much power, as to control the conduct of the highest authority in the state.

In the federal government of the United States, the advantage afforded to the minority is permanent. And this has arisen from the fact that the Union was formed by a convention of the states, and not by the people of America, as constituting one aggregate community. The relative extent and population of these states are very different. But as they all held an independent rank prior to the formation of the constitution, it was impossible to do otherwise than to give all an equal representation in at least one branch of the legislature. This renders the structure of the government more complicated than that of the states. Neither a majority nor a minority of the general population are represented in the senate. The majority of the votes belong to a minority of the local population. But in that great confederacy of nations, over which international law now presides with nearly as much force as municipal law does over single states, large and small communities stand precisely upon the same footing, and are entitled to equal consideration. Moreover the difficulty is almost entirely obviated in America by the uncommonly skillful construction of the two systems of government. The federal and state interests are completely separated from each other, by which the most important part of the business of government is left to the exclusive management of the states. The veto of the executive may also operate sometimes as a check in favor of a minority. This power may be exercised in favor of a majority in

* In Vermont a second chamber has recently been created.

the nation, against a majority in the legislature; or in favor of a minority in the nation against a majority in the legislature; or, lastly, in favor, of a minority in the Legislature against a majority in the same body; without the means of knowing, at the precise time it is interposed, what is the actual state of public opinion among the people. Its operation is very different at different times, but the immediate effect is always to defeat the will of a majority in the Legislature. The institution presents a problem of as difficult solution as the one just referred to. The difficulty consists in balancing the probabilities for a long series of years, in favor of the rectitude of the opinions of the executive, against the corresponding probabilities in favor of a majority of the legislature.

The third class of checks, depending upon a more general distribution of the power of the community, is where a system of primary and secondary governments is established: one intended to preside over those interests which are common to all the parts; the other to administer those which are exclusively local. The perfect form of confederate government affords a full illustration of the plan, although it is by no means necessary that the community should be a confederacy, in order to give rise to it. Every state of great extent would find it its interest to create a set of local jurisdictions to manage the local interests, which are necessarily beyond the reach of the central government. The scheme does not belong exclusively to a confederacy of states. But its utility is first suggested by the practice under that form of government. The local jurisdictions of departments and "arrondissements" in France, and the separate legislatures of Sweden and Norway, are examples, though imperfect ones, of the plan. The United States is the only country in which it has been carried to its full extent. And as the restriction upon the electoral franchise is so very slight, it is easy to determine which party does in fact constitute the majority of the people. The creation of a national and state government has produced a double system of majorities and minorities. For instance, the minority in the National Legislature may be a majority in several of the state Legislatures, and vice versa. The interests to be administered are not the same in the two. They are therefore kept distinct. Under one homogeneous government, the party in the majority might rule over both.

But in the United States the scheme is not confined to the federal government, but is pursued in the separate governments of the states, each of which has created a system of local jurisdictions within itself, to manage the local interests. The county, and township jurisdictions, each with its board of officers attached, are examples.

It is unnecessary to refer to any further instances of the various checks and limitations which the majority constantly impose upon the exercise of their own authority. What has been said, contributes abundantly to fortify the position, that wherever a majority is capable of taking care of its own interests, it will for that very reason be capable of presiding over the interests of the minority. In the new states which are constantly springing into existence in America, and whose constitutions are based upon the principle of universal suffrage, we find that every precaution is taken in the outset, to impose limitations upon the power of the majority, wherever these are believed to be subservient to the general weal.

CHAPTER IV.

CHARACTER AND OPERATION OF ELECTIVE GOVERNMENTS.

If the extreme rigor of the rule, that the majority is entitled to govern, is thus tempered in practice, by the intervention of so many and such powerful restraints, imposed by the majority, it may be affirmed that the country which denotes such a condition of society, or anything which makes a near approach to it, is ripe for the establishment of free institutions. The right of the majority to govern, depends simply upon its capacity for self government.

But the inquisitive observer, fearful of the fate of free institutions in proportion to the interest he takes in them, may inquire whether the unbounded freedom of thought and action, which they engender, is not absolutely incompatible with the firm authority which government should possess; and whether they must not eventually perish, from the unceasing action of the very element in which they are destined to live. But it is that very freedom of thought and action, unbounded as it may be supposed to be, which gives being to public opinion; and without the influence of public opinion, society would be a mere waste. Although Europeans look with so much distrust upon the American commonwealth; yet it is remarkable that everything which is valuable in their own societies, has been brought about by the communication of a greater degree of liberty to the people. So far from weakening the bond which holds society together, the effect has been to render it stronger. In Great Britain, and France, in Prussia, and Belgium, it is in exact proportion to the power which public opinion has acquired, that the administration of government has become mild and enlightened, and that a character of firmness and durability has been imparted to the institutions. It was at one time believed that public tranquility could not be even tolerably preserved, without the constant presence of a military force. The people were terrified into submission to the government, rather than won over to obedience to the laws.

It may be laid down as a maxim in politics, that the employment of physical force is rendered necessary, by the absence, or deficiency, of moral force. If there is a happy distribution of the last through society, there will be less occasion to resort to the former. If, on the other hand, the distribution is very unequal, the discontent will be great because the amount of liberty is small, and hence as a natural consequence, inordinate authority will be condensed in the hands of the government. Now, it is public opinion, above all other agents, which contributes to produce a just equalization of the moral power of the community; and it is the freedom of thought and action which gives birth to public opinion. It was on the first dawn of a public opinion in England, or rather I should say in Europe, that Pym, and Selden, Coke, and Hampden, were roused to make such bold and intrepid exertions in behalf of popular freedom. Man feels strong when he is conscious that he is surrounded by a power, which represents not his feelings merely, but the feelings of mankind. Abundant compensation is thus made for that state of feebleness and isolation in which individuals, who cherish noble ideas, would otherwise find themselves placed in the midst of society.

It is not surprising that the freedom of the press has met with so much resistance in monarchial and aristocratical governments. The tribunal of public opinion, when fairly erected, is so formidable an adversary to the exercise of every species of arbitrary authority, that it invariably succeeds first in subduing the tone and temper of the public administration, and ultimately the form of the political institutions. Chateaubriand declared to the ministers of Louis Philippe, "on the day you decree the liberty of the press, you die." And if this audacious speech was not verified, it is plainly because the elements of public opinion are now everywhere visible throughout France.

In a country where a fixed aristocracy exists, some men are necessarily endowed with a much larger share of influence than others. A body of nobility and gentry have sometimes possessed more weight than all the rest of the community. This unequal distribution of power is a great hindrance to the formation of a public opinion which shall rule over all; but it is highly favorable to the creation of a particular or sectarian opinion within the class itself. When, however, the dispersion of knowledge and property has elevated that multitude of men who occupied the inferior ranks of society, public opinion rises up, and threatens to beat down the narrow and exclusive opinions which before existed. The array of physical force, which was before necessary, sometimes to quell insubordination among the masses, sometimes to curb the turbulence of the nobles, and at others to restrain the usurpations of the prince, gradually disappears. All orders of men begin to find their true relative position in society, and public order and tranquility are preserved with remarkable regularity. From whence it is very easy to understand why it is, that a just distribution of the moral power of the community, supercedes, to so great an extent, the use of mere physical force. The old ranks may continue to stand, but they will stand like broken and defaced columns amid the new structure which is reared around them.

One striking property of free institutions is, that they present fewer subjects of contention between the government and the people, than any other scheme of civil polity. I have already pointed to two characteristic features of a democratic republic: a written constitution, and the establishment of local jurisdictions, contrivances of great wisdom and utility. For by the first, the principal controversies which have shaken other communities are struck out of being; and by the last, a very large proportion of what may be described as the secondary interests of society are withdrawn from the arena of national contention, and are deposited with domestic governments, by which they will be managed in the most skillful and unobtrusive manner possible. Under such a system men are able to find very few subjects to quarrel about; and even if government has less ability to resist encroachments, there is also infinitely less temptation and opportunity to assail its rightful authority.

Not only however are the most dangerous controversies diminished; those which remain assume an entirely different character. They are unfit to be decided by force. The prerogatives of an hereditary monarch are so incapable of exact limitation, that he may often attempt to push them to the uttermost; or the strictly egitimate exercise of them may be productive of infinite mischief to society. The single power of declaring war may occasion the imposition of taxes insupportably burthensome to the community. The legislature may be a close body, in no way entitled to the appellation of representative of the people, and much more disposed to favor the projects of the prince, than to consult the solid welfare of the state. The questions which grow out of such a condition of things immediately suggest the idea of an appeal to force. But whether the legislature shall make internal improvements, charter banks, or encourage manufactures, however interesting and exciting they may be, are still questions which belong to a totally different sphere. They could not ever grow up in any other society than one which had been trained to the arts of peace, and where men had been habitually given to reflection. Such questions recommend themselves to the understanding alone, and it will be an exceedingly rare occurrence if one drop of blood is ever shed in deciding them.

This explains why it is that in modern societies men are so much addicted to reflection. It is not because they are by nature superior to the men of former times. It is simply in consequence of the independent condition to which they have risen. The cares and anxieties of life are multipled even more than its enjoyments. A vastly greater proportion of the people than at any former period are engaged in industrial pursuits. These demand the constant exercise of judgment, prudence and discretion, and being accustomed to calculate the consequences of their actions on a small scale, they are enabled to transfer the same habit to a larger theater of action, and thus to render the exercise of their political principles not merely harmless, but essentially beneficial to the community. At one time no one could practice a trade in a city unless he belonged to the guild: and hardly any one out of the ranks of the nobility and clergy was the proprietor of land. There was no school for reflection among the people, because there was no opportunity for its application, either in the walks of private or public life. It follows that in a democratic republic, where there is a more equal distribution of property, and where industry, whether in town or country, is unfettered, the mass of the population must be more distinguished for reflection than anywhere else. Thus, in that form of government where this invaluable quality is most in demand it is freely supplied, and where it is least wanted it is sparingly produced.

If it were possible so to construct government as invariably to connect the interests of individuals with those of the public, we should form a system which would bid fair to endure forever. I speak now of the interests of individuals, as seen and understood by themselves; for the real interests of private persons never can be inconsistent with the general weal. Now although it is impossible to realize this idea, in consequence of the great diversity in the faculties and propensities of different men, and the different manner in which these are combined in individuals; yet experience demonstrates that it is easy to carry it a great deal further than was once believed practicable. Philosophers who have sketched ideal plans of a republic, have failed, not so much because they have placed too high an estimate on human nature, as because they have not allowed room for the operation of some very homely qualities, out of which spring what we term patriotism and public spirit. If what makes the artificial forms of government so dear to the select few who participate in their administration, is that their whole interests are wrapped up in the preservation of them, there seems to be no reason why we may not imitate the scheme on a still larger scale, and cause the great body of the people to be deeply interested in upholding free institutions. There is no necessity for imagining the existence of any higher qualities than before, in order to produce this effect. For admitting that we cannot render the motives of human conduct more general in the one case than in the other, yet by giving to them an infinitely wider scope in the last instance, we found ourselves upon the same principle of interest, and thus communicate both more freedom, and more prosperity, to a greater number of people. If the superstition inspired by the artificial form of government is a prodigious support to their authority, there is a very similar but a still stronger feeling at work among the people who live under free government. They are alive to every attempt to impair it, not merely because they believe their institutions to be the best, but because they are the workmanship of their own hands.

In whatever light we may cast the subject, it seems evident that representative government is the only one which is fitted to fulfill all the great ends for which society was established. Not only is the general condition of the population greatly elevated, so as to render the care of its interests the chief aim of government, but a multitude of persons are actually employed in the public administration. Public magistrates of various kinds, periodically rising from the people and returning to the people, are dispersed over the whole country. The sentinels of liberty are so thickly planted as to keep perpetual watch, and the complicated and wide spread machinery of the government, makes it an affair of great difficulty to break it up, or to take it to pieces. In the artificial governments, the handful of men who rule over public affairs are staked to the preservation of power; in a republic, the great body of the people are heartily interested in the maintenance of freedom.

In the event of any great convulsion, occasioned by foreign war, or intestine commotion, the advantage is greatly on the side of popular government. Free institutions so thoroughly penetrate with their influence every part of the community, that although it may be possible to shake the government, the question will still arise, can you shake the society. In war, there is a distinction between conquering the government, and conquering the people; and a similar distinction is applicable in this instance. In a monarchy, or aristocracy, the overthrow of the government by foreign or civil war has sometimes nearly obliterated the traces of civilization. In a republic, where the great body of the people are fairly brought within the pale of civilization, such a disaster can never occur. Such a people feel deeper concern for their institutions, than the people of other countries, and yet they are not so completely dependent upon every vicissitude which may befall the government.

There is another advantage which free institutions possess. They lay the foundation for a great body of experience. It is of the highest importance that societies, as well as individuals, should be placed in a situation which enables them to make actual experiment of the utility of those diversified laws which the wants of the community render necessary. In hereditary government, the machinery is so delicate, that this can seldom be hazarded without endangering the whole fabric. I do not now speak of that bastard sort of experiment—the fruit of vain and fanciful theories—but of that which founds itself upon an intimate acqaintance with everything which appertains to the substantial interests of the community. As experience in its most comprehensive signification, including observation, is the foundation of our knowledge; as all science, in short, is nothing but the condensation of human experience, there seems every reason why we should be able to avail ourselves of it, in what concerns the positive interests of society, as well as in what relates to matters of more curious inquiry. The most gifted understanding, when relying upon its own resources merely, will forever be too imperfect to grasp all the conditions which affect the determination of any given enactment. As the whole groundwork of the institution is different in a republic, from what it is in any other form of government, the quantity of experience which is supplied is correspondingly large. For we then have a people in the genuine acceptation of the term. The laws, and the whole course of the public administration, take an entirely new direction. War, negotiation, and finance no longer absorb the whole attention of statesmen. Public affairs have then a different meaning affixed to them. The legislature embraces a vast scope of practical interests which, being more level to the capacities of all, call into requisition a great amount of popular talent; and as they who make the laws are the very persons who will derive advantage, or suffer inconvenience, from them, a most instructive school of experience is established, in which all are compelled to learn something.

I observe that more laws have been passed by the British Parliament in the last forty years, than in the three preceding centuries; that is, the laws have multiplied in proportion as the real business transactions of society have increased; and these have increased because so large an amount of the population have been raised to a higher condition than formerly. A similar change is very perceptible in France. But on the whole, I should say, that the democratic element, although it appears in bolder relief in France than in Great Britain, was not making so great and so sure advances in the former as in the latter country.

One of the most remarkable features of American society, is the facility with which changes are made in the fundamental laws, wherever experience has shown that there is an infirmity in some part of the system. A convention in any one of the American states, assembled for the purpose of making alterations in its constitution, creates no noise, or confusion. All the deliberations are conducted to a close with the same regularity as the proceedings of an ordinary legislative body. At an early period there was a remarkable sensitiveness on this subject. Constitutions, it was said by those who had not entirely escaped from the European forms of thought, were sacred things; and once ordained should never again be touched.

As if every institution did not acquire sacredness by being perfected and better adapted to its original design.

A great revolution was effected in the structure of society, when the inferior classes lost their dependence upon the higher; when the relations of patron, and client, of lord, and vassal, ceased. A new relation immediately sprung up. Instead of the dependence being all on one side, the two orders became mutually dependent on each other. Society began to assume the character of a great partnership among the members, instead of that of a series of ascending links in a chain, one end of which was fastened to the throne. From that period, the people have been constantly gaining in intelligence and power: so that it is doubtful whether, in more than one European state, if the laws of primogeniture and entail had been abolished a century ago, society would not be completely prepared for the introduction of the elective principles into every department of the government. There is every reason to believe that those laws will sooner or later give way. The force of habit among a whole people is as strong as it is in individuals. It frequently survives the existence of the causes which originally induced it, but it cannot survive them forever, when there are so many counter agents unceasingly in operation.

Two apparently opposite effects are produced by that alteration in the structure of society which I have described. Governments are rendered stronger, and yet, both the absolute and the relative power of the people is augmented. As it becomes more and more necessary to take counsel of public opinion, with regard to every important measure, it might be supposed that government had lost strength. But inasmuch as a man, mutilated in one part, is not able to exert so much general power as a man who is perfect in all his members, so a government which relies upon the entire strength of society, must necessarily be more efficient, in proportion as that strength is developed. In all the European governments, in which a legislative body exists, however inadequately it may represent popular opinion, there is notwithstanding an increasing anxiety to consult popular interests. Any important change in language, denotes a corresponding change in the ideas of the age. And the comparative disuse, in some parts of Europe, of the term subjects, and the substitution of the term citizens, or people, is an unequivocal indication that new things have come to pass. Mr. Fox was the first statesman who accustomed the English ear to this mode of speech. He knew well, that the way to fasten an impression upon the mind, was to give it a palpable form—to incorporate it into the dialect of the country. The crowned heads of Europe do not venture to sport with the lives and property of the people as formerly, simply because the people have acquired a weight in the political system which enables them to exercise a powerful, though it may be an indirect, control over all public affairs.

There are two properties inseparable from every well constituted government: the one a capacity to receive impressions from public opinion, the other a power of reacting upon society. There is no contradiction between the two things. On the contrary, the last is the natural consequence of the first. The use of public opinion is to inspire government with confidence, fortitude, and resolution, whenever public affairs are well conducted; and to impress it with shame, distrust, and fear, whenever the contrary is the case. Two forces act in different directions, and yet both tend to the same result: the causing public men to exercise a more legitimate, and therefore a more effective, influence than they could otherwise do. The more government reposes upon public opinion, the more susceptible it is of being acted upon; and yet, the greater is the facility it acquires of acting upon the community in difficult emergencies. I do not now suppose the case of general resistance to its authority; for the structure of representative government is such as to render it a guarantee against such a contingency. But I speak of those partial insurrections against the laws, originating in local discontents, and to which the best regulated society will be occasionally subject. European writers on public law, with nearly one accord, admit the right of resistance on the part of the people, whenever government has clearly and flagrantly transcended its authority; and very properly so, for where the institutions contain no provision for displacing men who have bid defiance to all law, and who have evinced a settled determination to render the public interests subordinate to their schemes of self aggrandizement, there is no other alternative but that of resistance. It constitutes an excepted case; but a case consecrated by necessity, by right, by the eternal laws of God and man. The deposition of Napoleon, and Charles X. in France; of Charles I. and James II. in England, stand upon this clear and undisputed principle. That of Louis XVI may admit of some hesitation, and yet it is exceedingly doubtful whether the scheme of constitutional or limited monarchy could have been achieved without it.

But in elective government, the case cannot occur. The powers of all public functionaries are not only very limited, but they are themselves quietly removed before they have had an opportunity to commit any great mischief. And I cannot help thinking, that the reason why America has been less subject to even partial insurrections than any other country, is owing to this circumstance. The power which is reposed with the government is conferred by all the parts equally ; and the notion that the will of the majority is entitled to command, is so indelibly impressed upon both people and rulers, that wherever a conflict occurs between the laws which that majority have ordained, and any particular section of the population, a degree of confidence, energy and alacrity is infused into all public men, which enables them to triumph speedily over all opposition, and that without depending to any degree upon the instrumentality of a standing army.

A democratic republic will then possess the two properties I have mentioned, in greater perfection than any other form of government. It will possess a capacity of receiving impressions from without, because it is the creature of the public will ; it will have the power of reacting upon society, not only because it will be powerfully supported by public opinion, but because the disturbances which will occur can never in the nature of things be more than local. Twenty times more blood was shed in Paris, on the memorable three days which closed the reign of Charles X. than in all the insurrections which have occurred in the United States since the foundation of the government.

It is the time now to direct the attention of the reader to a very material distinction, already hinted at, between a representative republic and the artificial forms of government. In the first the political authority of the community is divided into three classes ; the powers which are exercised by the government, those exercised by the people, and those reserved to the people. In pure monarchy, and aristocracy, there is but one class. The whole power is centered in the government. In the United States, it is common to make two classes only ; the second is left out. All the active power of the community is supposed to be conferred upon the government ;

and all its latent power to be lodged with the people; liable to be roused to activity whenever a convention is assembled for the purpose of forming a new constitution. But this is a very imperfect view of the structure of the American government. The powers actually exercised by the people are numerous, and of great importance. I have no reference now to the distribution of authority between the federal and state governments. That does in reality give rise to a fourth class, which it is not now necessary to notice.

First, if we could consider the various persons who are chosen to perform the duties of the great number of offices which exist in representative government, as naked instruments, mere conduit pipes, to convey the opinions, and to give an audible expression to the interests, of the people, the truth of the observation would be clear. The conduct of the representative would then be invariably determined by the will of his constituents. It might even be doubtful, whether the latter did not exercise all political power not reserved. If, on the other hand, there is a considerable approach to that scheme, or arrangement, the truth of the proposition will be still more manifest. The active power of the community will be partitioned between the government and the people. The arm is the mere servant of the will. If an individual had no immediate power in moving it, but was able to exercise an intermediate control, which might be relied upon as certain, in the great majority of instances, it would still be correct to say, that he exercised an important agency in determining its movements.

The physician who is employed to cure disease, or the lawyer who is engaged to prosecute a suit, are the agents in either case of those who apply to them. Yet the connection is not as strict, as between the elector and the representative; because in the case of the physician and lawyer, the skill demanded of them depends upon a body of scientific knowledge, an acquaintance with which is impossible for those who have not made it a special study. More strictly is he denominated an agent, who is selected to transact the private business of an individual. And although this trust will require judgment, sagacity, and industry; that is, the exercise of qualities which belong properly to the agent, yet his conduct, so far as concerns the substantial interests of the principal, will, in ninety-nine cases out of a hundred, be determined by the last.

There is this difference, however, between the two cases; that where one man employs another to transact his private affairs, there is a singleness, an unity of purpose, which it is easy to impress upon the agent, but which cannot be exactly imitated, where, instead of one agent, there are hundreds, and instead of one principal, there are thousands. The distinction is one of great consequence, and yet it does not detract from the truth of the observation, that the active political power which exists in a republic, is partitioned between the public officers and their constituents. But the distinction points to a very important end which representative government is adapted to accomplish.

For, as in order to execute the joint will of a very numerous society, it is indispensable that agents should be employed; these agents, whose number is very small when compared with the whole population, act as convenient instruments for separating the more prominent interests of society, from those which are of less moment. Their commanding position naturally leads them, amid the great variety of discordant opinions which are afloat, even in a small section of the country, to distinguish between those which are of vital and general importance, and those which are the offspring of temporary prejudices and local feelings. In this way, the multifarious business of an extensive community is brought under some systematic rules, and a character of oneness, and uniformity is impressed upon the movements of the government.

But there are instances in which the relation of principal and agent exists in its utmost strictness. The opinions and views which the representative is appointed to carry out, are not all of the same kind. Some are very complex: that is, they require a great many acts to be done, and a variety of unforeseen circumstances to be taken into account; and there are others, pointing to a single end, which cannot be mistaken. In the last the will of the constituent may be impressed upon the deputy, as completely as the stamp impresses its image upon wax.

The election of president of the United States is a remarkable example of this. On that occasion, a greater number of electors than ever was known in christendom are assembled, and although an intermediate body is chosen by them, for the purpose of making the election, yet those secondary electors invariably vote for the person who has been designated for the office by the primary electors. The result is reduced to absolute certainty, before the colleges of electors meet. Thus in a case where the electors are most numerous, and where it was supposed impossible to produce anything like harmony of opinion, the agreement is most complete. And what is of still more importance, where the public officer is elected to preside over the whole population, and to embrace the greatest diversity of views, a character of unity is most effectually impressed upon him. As the extent of country, and the great number of the electors, remove him to a great distance from the people, and tend to weaken his responsibility, it is of great consequence to exhibit before his eyes an example of the facility with which public sentiment can be united to all leading public measures, and of the equal facility with which he can either be made, or unmade.

In order to determine, with something like exactness, the closeness of the relation which exists between the representative and the constituent, where the duties to be performed involve a multitude of acts, the most satisfactory method would be to ascertain what proportion of the laws enacted have afterwards been repealed ; distinguishing between those cases where the repeal has taken place, in consequence of the representatives having gone counter to the will of their constituents, from those where it has been brought about by a change of opinion on the part of the people themselves. And I apprehend that cases falling under the first class would be found to be exceedingly rare. A repeal effected by a change in public sentiment is obviously an example of the strictness of the relation.

It is common to talk of the powers of government, and the liberties of the people. But this is rather in analogy with the structure of the European communities, than in accordance with the genius of free institutions. The people of the United States do enjoy a very large share of liberty; but its character is such, as necessarily to endow them with a large amount of active power. Their power constitutes the guarantee of their liberties. When we consider that, until very recently, all Scotland contained no greater number of electors than an ordinary county in America ; that the members of parliament from the cities were deputed by self constituted bodies, composed each of thirteen persons ; that a majority of the members of parliament are now elected by a minority of the whole number of electors ; that the throne, the aristocracy, and the ecclesiastical establishments exist, without any direct dependence upon the public will; that the right to bear arms, and the right of association are exceedingly restricted, we may form some idea of the importance of the distinction between popular power, and popular liberty.

It is remarkable that the three great maxims on which republican government reposes, were recognized, and formally promulgated, by the Italian states of the middle ages:

1st. That all authority exercised over the people originates with the people.

2d. That all public trusts should return periodically into the hands of the people.

3d. That all public functionaries are responsible to the people for their fidelity in office.

And yet it would be a great mistake to suppose that the people of these states, from the highest to the lowest, had any more idea of free institutions, than the philosophers of their day had of the theory of the terrestrial motions. We might with as much propriety rob Hervey of the credit of discovering the circulation of the blood, and attribute it to physicians in the time of Cicero. For when we inquire who the people (the inseparable condition of the three maxims) were, we find that they were a mere handful of the population. In the Florentine state, the best modeled of those republics, with a population of more than a million, the electors never amounted to more than twenty-four hundred; sometimes to a much less number. And the cruelties practiced by those invested with authority, were not excelled in any of the monarchial governments of even that day.

The artificial forms of government, by the oppression, and inequalities of one sort or other, to which they give rise, lacerate the mind, sour the temper, and goad to revenge. There is no escape from the ills they inflict. They are of yesterday, to day, and forever. Free institutions introduce heart burnings enough into society. But these only constitute a state of discipline, by which men are rendered more wise, more prudent, and more just, than they would otherwise be. A vast field is left open to individual liberty, so that the mind, instead of being deprived of its elasticity, and vigor, is incessantly braced to fresh exertions, in order to turn all the difficulties of life to the best account.

CHAPTER V.

THE PRINCIPLE OF EQUALITY—TO WHAT EXTENT CAN IT BE CARRIED.

It was a great imperfection attending society before the invention of printing, that there was no means by which human experience could be made thoroughly available at a subsequent period, or in remote countries. It is not only important that knowledge should be diffused among the men of the present day; it is also important that their successes and miscarriages should be recorded and appreciated by those who come after them, and by those who are separated from each other by the greatest distances. Printing has remedied this imperfection. It not only extends information; it extends the bounds of human experience; since this is very properly understood to include not merely what is personal to the individual, but whatever can be distinctly realized as matter of fact. Mere speculation does not move the great mass of mankind; but example, sympathy, imitation, all have a wonderful influence in molding their dispositions and conduct. Those who live apart from each other are now initiated into the form of society, the habits of thinking, and acting, and the actual working of the institutions which prevail among each. They are enabled to distinguish what is practicable, from what is proposed as a merely plausible theory; and, as very nearly the same feelings beat in the bosom of all men, every important amelioration of the condition of our race in one country, is regarded as a body of experience, which may be made more or less available in all others.

This enlargement of the bounds of human experience, so as to take in what is transacted in distant countries, as well as what is acted on the spot, is exemplified in the case of America. The political institutions of the United States may be described as the greatest experiment which has ever been made upon human nature. Their influence upon the European mind has already been immense. It is natural, therefore, that they should afford matter for deep contemplation, and that they should excite intense interest wherever they are known.

No one has even the right to indulge in fanciful and visionary speculations as to the form into which the institutions of society may be cast. But where our researches are pursued with care ; where they are bounded and limited on all sides by a long and instructive experience, they may be rendered highly instrumental in shedding light upon the two great problems in politics : what aught, and what may be made to be. It is not necessary that intelligence should be diffused in exactly equal proportions, among all the individuals composing a community, in order to found free institutions. It is true, knowledge is power, in politics as well as in private life, and may be made the instrument of detriment as well as of benefit. And if the interests of the great bulk of the population are delivered over to the less numerous body, who consist of the enlightened, it may seem difficult to escape from the conclusion, that a species of moral servitude must be established, let us adopt what form of government we please. Why it is not necessary, therefore, that all the members who compose a democratic community should be raised equally high in the scale of intelligence, and what is the extent to which intelligence should and may be actually pushed, are necessarily inquiries of great interest and importance.

In a commonwealth where the structure of society is such as to give rise to an uniformity of interests among the population, or to any thing approaching to it, it will, to a great extent, supersede the necessity of an equal distribution of knowledge. There may be the greatest diversity of knowledge amid the greatest sameness of interests, and without occasioning the least interruption to it. Knowledge is the instrument by which the interests of men are managed ; but it is not itself, at least in its highest degree, one of those interests. And if in a state where the elective principle prevails, this settled uniformity of interests is the result of causes which are inherent in the framework of society, public men will be disabled from interfering with the interests of others, without dealing wantonly with their own. The same laws which govern the ruled, govern also the rulers. The ability to act is restrained and limited by the principle of self interest. And the administration of public affairs is obliged to take a direction conformable to the public welfare, because the general welfare and private interests meet and terminate at the same point.

But this approach to an identity of interests among the whole community, does diffuse knowledge to precisely the extent which is wanted: 1st. Because it renders the intercourse of all classes more thorough and easy. 2d. Because it presupposes a tolerably equal distribution of property, and the diffusion of knowledge is inseparable from that of property. Not that the elevated attainments of the intellectual class will become the common property of the whole people, for that can never be; but that species of knowledge which has to do with the material interests of this world, will insinuate itself into the minds of all. Our acquaintance with any subject is in proportion to the concentration of the attention upon it; and the great bulk of the population, by having their attention constantly fixed upon that sphere of ideas which encloses all their substantial interests, may be trained to a degree of knowledge which will be more effectual for the purposes of society than the greatest learning, and the profoundest attainments. What is lost in variety and comprehensiveness, will be more than made up by the practical and serviceable character of the knowledge actually acquired.

If in France, before the revolution, four-fifths of the landed property of the kingdom was engrossed by the nobility and clergy; and if in the United States there is no such artificial monopoly, but the division of the soil has followed the natural direction which private enterprise and industry gave to it; the great difference in the structure of society in the two countries is sufficiently explained. All the moral causes, which in the last country now contribute to perpetuate the existing state of society, may be fairly deduced from this simple arrangement in the beginning. The principle of equality has thus found a natural support in America. It has not been the creature of the laws. These assist in upholding it, by giving it a visible activity in public life; but both it and the laws are the offspring of circumstances, which no legislature could have had power to alter.

Two inquiries of exceeding interest now present themselves: 1st. To what extent is political equality dependent upon the natural or civil equality of men; and to what extent can the last be pushed. 2d. If political equality is itself the result of causes which are peculiar to America, and these causes should cease to act, or act with less force at a future period; may not the political institutions, and the form of government, undergo in the progress of time an entire revolution. Each of the propositions: the laws secure political equality, and the laws have sprung from a given state of society, are clear enough. But it is important that our speculations should be built upon something more than a barren generality; that, so addressing ourselves to the reason of mankind, we may employ our own reason in throwing out hints for their meditation.

The distribution of property, in any community, will depend in some degree upon the amount of the population. In a state which is densely peopled, there will probably be a very large class of rich, and a still more numerous class of poor. Not that this proportion may not exist, where the population is thin. For it was undoubtedly the same, or even greater in the European states, five hundred years ago, than it is at present, although the population has more than trebled in that time. But in the one case, there is at least a physical possibility of rectifying the proportion, which does not exist in the other. Where there are large tracts of uncultivated land, human ingenuity, and industry, with a very slight assistance from the laws, may succeed in placing private fortune more upon a level. But where the soil has been appropriated for centuries, the inequality which shows itself, after a long period of commercial and agricultural activity, must be ascribed in part to that very ingenuity and industry, and in great part also, to the political institutions themselves.

But within certain limits, an increase of population may be highly favorable to the distribution of property. Capital and labor are augmented by it; and the supply of both affords the means of breaking up large estates into smaller parcels. It is only when the population becomes very dense, that on the one hand capital accumulates to such a degree as to create a large class of rich; and that on the other, labor becomes superabundant, which gives rise to a still larger class of poor.

There are several causes waich tend to counteract the increase of population, when it has reached a certain degree of density. The mortality becomes greater, the births fewer, and the average age of marriage higher. But these changes do not all of them take place, with anything like the regularity which might be expected. For instance, it appears to be certain that the mortality in Great Britain is much less than it has been at any preceding period: that it is less than it was when the population was only one half what it is now. Lord Brougham computes it at 1:58; Mr. Malthus at 1:51; while the census of 1839, taken since, and the only accurate register which has ever been made, finds it to be 1:45. The two first would have been an enormously low proportion. The last is low, and indicates a less mortality than in any country which ever existed, and containing an equally dense population. Although the population has increased greatly within the last fifty years, yet the general standard of comfort throughout the island has improved in a still higher proportion. And although it cannot be true, as has been conjecturally estimated, that the average age of death, or the expectation of life at birth, has mounted up from sixteen to thirty-three years, it is plain that it must be greatly higher than it was sixty or seventy years ago.

But increase the population a few millions more, and the mortality would then tell in a greatly increased ratio. Whatever may be the increase, however, and in spite of all the influences which have hitherto been brought to bear upon society, there is a tendency in every civilized community, to such an augmentation of the population as is inconsistent with anything like an equal distribution of property. Even the equal partibility of inheritances only partially corrects the evil. Primogeniture was unknown in the Grecian or Roman commonwealths. In France, it never prevailed universally. And in Spain, equal partibility was always the rule, and primogeniture the exception. Yet in all these states, there existed extreme inequality in private fortunes. The laws, the character of the government, may do much toward either promoting, or preventing, the disparity of estates. And it is one reason why free institutions are preferable to any other that they contribute to produce this last effect. But the inquiry of greatest moment is, whether there are any laws of our nature which, independently of the political institutions, or with every assistance which they may legitimately afford, can have power to establish, and maintain anything approaching to an equality of private fortunes. It seems natural to suppose, that when we are in possession of an advantage up to a certain degree, that it may be pushed on to a still higher degree; and so on indefinitely; and that cannot be an impossible state of society, which only consists in the addition to actually existing facts—of facts of the same kind. And this would undoubtedly be a correct mode of reasoning, if the new facts to be added did not depend upon the voluntary action of a vast multitude of persons, among whom there exists the greatest diversity of dispositions.

In tracing the generality of individuals through life, and observing how they conduct themselves, and the vehement struggle to acquire property, it is remarkable how little difference we can discover between the capacities of those who succeed, and of those who fail. Some move forward with amazing velocity, to the end they have in view, and heap riches upon riches ; some lag behind, and are only able, through the whole of life, to obtain a comfortable subsistence ; while others continue in a state of painful destitution, from the beginning to the end of their career. And yet but for the result, which, to ordinary observation, seems to set the stamp of superiority upon some, we should not be able, in the majority of instances, to perceive any adequate reason for so striking a difference. So far as the faculties of those individuals, either natural or acquired, are concerned, there seems to be no very material difference. But that there must be some difference, in that undefinable quality which we term the disposition, is clear : otherwise the consequences would not follow. We know too little of the individual man, to be able to handle, with anything like accuracy and discrimination, the secret springs which actuate human conduct. A fine writer has remarked of the character of the emperor Napoleon, that it has presented a problem to be studied. But in truth, the character of almost all the individuals we meet with, however obscure they may be, and however limited their faculties, presents very nearly the same problem. Whoever was able to unravel the mind of the least of these, would be able to decipher that of Napoleon at a glance.

Some men are roused and quickened by adversity ; while the faculties of others are clouded, and overwhelmed by it. Some are strengthened by prosperity ; others are blinded, and led astray by it. And as there is an endless variety in the working of these causes, arising from inconceivably small differences of temperament, and the perpetual interference of what is termed accident, their successes and miscarriages, will be marked by innumerable shades of difference, too secret, and too fine, for our analysis. It seems certain, however, that until we can master man's nature, it will be impossible to impress anything like an exact similarity of character upon individuals. And he who cannot take to pieces his own mind, must necessarily fall infinitely short of that task. The division of labor, which is introduced so extensively into every department of industry, is both a consequence and a cause of the inequality in the fortunes and condition of individuals. But if that were banished from society, not the ten-thousandth part of the comforts and enjoyments of life would exist for any one. To say that every one should be his own builder, manufacturer and cultivator; to declare that each one should be tailor, shoemaker, cook, would be very nearly the same as saying, that there should be no houses, no decent and comfortable clothing, and a very scanty supply of food. There would be nothing to set in motion that immense mass of industry which now affords employment and subsistence to the multitudes of men. The population would be gradually drawn within the narrow limits of a savage tribe; the most opulent and flourishing community would be carried back to the primitive state of barbarism. The annihilation of industry as a system, would involve the annihilation of all moral and intellectual culture.

At the same time, it is evident that the division of labor, which bestows such countless advantages upon society, cannot exist without giving rise to very great inequality among individuals. It is only necessary to consider any of the most inconsiderable of the objects of mechanical skill, to be assured of this fact. The workman who is employed in the manufacture of knives, or pins, is condemned to an occupation which, turn the subject in whatever light we may, cannot possibly improve his fortune, or elevate his faculties, so as to place him on a level with the master manufacturer. Nor would it remedy the difficulty, to divide the profits of the last equally among all the workmen. For even admitting that he would feel the same powerful stimulus as before, in the prosecution of his business, now that the disposition of his own property was violently interfered with; and that the workmen would submit to the same patient and indefatigable industry, without which the plan must fail; this distribution would only tantalize, without satisfying, the desires of any one. What would be a splendid income for one man, would, when divided among hundreds, be no sensible addition to their enjoyments. There must be some wise purpose intended in this constitution of society. It may be, that in a civilized community, this variety in the pursuits of individuals is absolutely necessary to maintain the mind in a sound and healthful condition; or it may be, that employment and occupation, without regard to the variety of pursuits to which they lead, are indispensable to balance the mind, and to restrain the animal propensities within due bounds. For without the division of labor, there would not only be little or no variety, but the occupations would nearly all cease to exist. At the same time, it is clear, that while some are engaged in the higher and more important part of the work, others must be engaged in the inferior, and subordinate branches. So that to maintain civilization at all, there must be inequality in the fortunes and condition, of individuals. There is no escape from our human condition, whatever may be the shape into which the elements of society are thrown.

If we suppose that the distribution of the incomes of capitalists, would place so large a number of the operatives in an improved condition, as to withdraw them from work, the supply of labor would be diminished, wages would rise, there would be more leisure, greater opportunities. But the high wages would, in a single generation, lead to an increase of the population, to a supply of the demand, and to a renewal of the old state of things.

The distribution of property by law, even if it placed every one in comfortable circumstance, would paralyze the springs of industry. It would diminish the vigor and activity of those who had acquired much, and increase the sloth and inertness of those who had acquired nothing. This equal division of fortunes would apparently tend to an equality of enjoyments; while an equality of industry and exertions, which is of far more consequence, would be overlooked. If all were placed in prosperous circumstances for one year, the next would witness the decline of great numbers; and in a few more, there would be the same inequality as before. We would absurdly introduce equality, for the purpose of bringing out inequality.

It would seem that not only our own infirmities, but that the infirmities of those around us, are absolutely necessary to goad any one to exertion. They who propose the plan of distribution, or, which is the same thing, to make the people work in common like so many galley slaves, forget that the true way of strengthening the public virtues, is to nourish the private affections, and that to turn all our efforts exclusively in one direction, would be to eradicate some of the best qualities of human nature. That is the best, because it is the natural, arrangement of society, which gives full play to the faculties of all orders of men. If it is beyond our power to control the private affections—if we cannot make men love other men's children as they do their own—it must be equally impossible to control the exertions which are the fruit of these affections. The instinct which leads men to become the center of a family, is as much a part of his constitution as that which leads him to society. To give an undue preponderance to one of these, would not be the application of a new regimen to his conduct; it would be a vain attempt to alter the laws which govern his nature. All the private affections, in reality, conspire to the general weal. They introduce into the moral world the great principle of the division of labor. More industry and sagacity are exerted—a greater amount of both public and private virtue is developed, than under any other government. To dislocate, therefore, any of the important springs of human conduct —to declare that one should have the mastery—would establish a state of society in which we should avail ourselves of only half the man.

If we could realize the views of Mr. Malthus, and introduce into a population which was threatening to become crowded the general prevalence of the check to early marriages, it would be followed by some very salutary consequences. But to carry it as far as is desirable, and so as to make it tell with a decisive and permanent influence upon society, might be attended with very many disadvantages. The idea is, that it would be an effectual way of elevating the condition of the masses, because it would keep down the numbers, and render the circumstances of the actual population more easy. Let us suppose then that the check had begun to operate in England about seventy years ago. Wages might now be so high as to cause every department of industry to languish. English manufacturers would have been undersold in every foreign market. Other nations would have been in a condition to supply the English people with every species of manufacture, and every article of food. But the last would be deprived of the means of purchasing from other nations, and the consequence is, that England may have been one of the poorest instead of the richest country in Europe. The more thin population which would now exist, would be in infinitely worse circumstances than at present. In Norway, the check to early marriages exists in greater force than anywhere else, and it is a poor country, and an abject population.

I know nothing which would confer more salutary and lasting benefits upon society, than to raise the general standard of comfort of the population; provided, it be done without producing effects which would counteract its operation. But to raise the standard of comfort in any European community as high as every lover of humanity would desire, would be the same as to raise wages so high as to enable every one to maintain his family in comfort, and to give them an education. And the consequences would be the same as before. The country would be undersold in every article of production; every branch of industry would decline, until a foreign population poured in, to receive lower wages, when the standard of comfort would be again reduced. The plan would undoubtedly succeed if we could introduce it alike into all countries. But if it has entirely failed in any one, except to be taken notice of by way of comparison with the condition of some others, it would require the will of Omnipotence to accomplish it.

All human exertions to better the social organization must necessarily be bounded within certain limits. Something must be taken for granted, as the elements of all our reasoning in politics as well as in other sciences. We cannot be permitted to construct ideas, which a fertile imagination has suggested, and which only approach toward being verified in part, because they cannot be verified universally.

Let us suppose that all those who have succeeded in life, and who are placed in good circumstances, were to go among the poor and ignorant, open up all the secrets of their hearts, recount the whole train of circumstances which contributed to elevate their condition, I can conceive of nothing which, for the time being, would so much expand the bosoms of those who believed, either rightly or erroneously, that fortune had frowned upon them. But, first: the thing cannot be done. Such a fearless and unreserved revelation of one's whole thoughts and actions can proceed from none but angels. Second: the exposition of so great an amount of infirmities, as the revelation would disclose, and as would be shown to attend frequently the most enviable condition, would cause the vicious and the ignorant to hug vice and ignorance still closer. The gerater part would become more bold and confident than ever, since there was no such broad mark of distinction, as had been imagined, between the highest and lowest condition. And one great check to irregularities of conduct would be removed. The counselors and the counseled in such an enterprise are equally covered with all sorts of infirmities. And the true way to get rid of these is to proceed upon the belief that they do not exist, or, at any rate, that they are only adventitious. In this way every one will be nerved to a greater amount of exertion than would otherwise be the case. If those who are placed in what is termed low life could penetrate the gaudy exterior of high life, they would find as little enjoyment as in their own humble sphere. Wealth creates full as many disquietudes as it heals. Fortunately they are unable to lift the veil ; for then, perhaps, all human exertions would speedily come to an end.

It may then be inquired why do legislators constantly inculcate the maxim that all men are equal. And the answer is plain : First. Because to teach and to act upon it is the only way of attaining equality, to the extent to which it is actually attained. Second. Because it is not in the power of government to make anything like an accurate discrimination between the inequalities of different men, and the attempt to do so would be to encroach upon those points in which there is no inequality. Third. Because the principle of equality may very well be recognized as the rule among men as citizens —as members of a political community, although as individuals there may be great and numerous inequalities between them. The utmost which the citizen can demand is that no law shall be passed to obstruct his rise, and to impede his progress through life. He has then an even chance with all his fellows. If he does not become their equal his case is beyond the reach of society, and to complain would be to quarrel with his own nature.

It cannot be concealed that a difficulty now presents itself which is entitled to particular attention. Here are two sets of ideas which do not quadrate with each other : equality proclaimed by the laws, and inequality in fact. And as, notwithstanding the artificial distinctions which we may make between the individual and the citizen, the former may be disposed to carry all his prejudices, narrow views, and selfish interests, into the arena of politics, it might be supposed that a scene of discord would be introduced, which, after lasting for a given period, must terminate in the ascendency of one or other of these rival principles. Hence the misgivings of many persons, otherwise possessing good sense and reflection in an eminent degree. If they do not believe, they at any rate doubt whether the undisguised recognition of the principle of equality in America is not destined to take entire posession of society, and ultimately to level the whole fabric of its institutions. The masses are put in possession of the same privileges as the educated and the wealthy ; and, in the event of a struggle between the two orders, will not numbers be sure to gain the advantage.

But the principle of equality is itself the parent of another principle, which sets bounds to it, and limits its operation in practice. The same laws which declare that all men are equal, give unbounded scope to the enterprise and industry of all. Neither family, nor rank, nor education confer any peculiar advantages in running the career which is now opened. In many respects they even throw obstacles in the way. Men without education, with ordinary faculties, and who commenced life with little or nothing, are continually emerging from obscurity, and displacing those who have acquired fortunes by inheritance. They constitute emphatically the class of rich in the United States. It is the principle of equality there which introduces all the inequality which is established in that country. The effects are visible to every one, and are understood and appeciated by the most ignorant men. Every one is a witness to the miracles which industry and common sagacity produce. No one distrusts himself; no one can perceive those minute shades of character and disposition, which determine the destiny of some individuals, making some rich, and leaving others poor. All place an equal reliance upon their own efforts to carve out their fortunes, until at length the period of life begins to shorten ; when cool reflection and judgment take the place of the passions ; and whether they have succeeded or failed, a new feeling comes over every one—a disposition to submit quietly to what is the inevitable, because it is the natural progress of things.

Thus as it is impossible among millions to say who, in running the career of wisdom, influence, or wealth, will attain the goal. Government very rightly establishes the broad and indiscriminate rule of equality, and the very means which it makes use of to effect this object, obliterates all artificial distinction, and yet brings out in bolder relief all the natural inequalities of men. And as a large proportion of the envious are constantly rising into the ranks of the envied; a powerful check is imposed upon the revolutionary tendencies of the former. They cannot reach, nor after reaching, will they be able to enjoy, that which is the constant aim of all their efforts, without lending an earnest and vigorous support to the laws under which they live. And in this way, free institutions are saved from shipwreck, by the thorough and undiguised adoption of a principle which seemed calculated to produce precisely opposite effects. It affords a remarkable example of the intimate union between two things apparently contradictory; and to what an extent the system of compensations exists in a country of free institutions, by means of which the defects of one part are cured by some effectual contrivance in another. Hence the surprise which has been constantly expressed by Europeans, from the day the corner stone of the American government was laid, down to the present, that although a degree of liberty has been communicated to the people, utterly unknown at any preceding period, society exhibits more evidences of happiness and prosperity than are visible anywhere else; that for so large an empire, wonderful tranquility prevails; and that the political institutions, instead of losing strength, are in reality increasing in solidity and firmness. There does exist in that community, as much as in any other, a powerful control upon the unruly elements of society. But this is not the result of an artificial system; the control is wider in its operation than anywhere else; and it is, for that reason, more effectual than in any other government.

They who entertain fears that the enjoyment of so much liberty in the United States will exert any other than a favorable influence upon the social organization, and the political institutions, should recollect that equality may be a regulative principle of the highest importance, without ever being pushed to any thing like the furthest extent. The laws may presuppose the possibility of pushing it so far, just as the precepts of morality suppose, that they may be carried in great perfection into the practice of an individual. The advantage of having some great principle constantly in view, is that it will then be sure of having some influence upon some individuals, and a very great influence upon all others. Human nature modifies, and sets bounds to all laws; but in order to render the principle of equality efficacious as a regulative principle, it is necessary to admit the abstract rule in all its universality. The more widely the rules of morality are circulated, and the more earnestly they are insisted upon, the greater will be the number of those whose conduct will be formed by them: and the more thoroughly the maxim of equality is taught, the more numerous will be the persons who will strive to make themselves equal to the wisest, and best. More vigor, enterprise, and intelligence, will be imparted to every one; and the moral force communicated to society will contribute to rectify the very disorders which are supposed to be inseparable from the recognition of the principle.

Although then the struggle for equality never can produce equality in fact, yet there is an immensely wide scope within which it may operate. If the wealthy, and those who found themselves upon the advantages of family, and rank, feel themselves incommoded by this eternal jostling—this continued struggle of inferior classes to rise to their level—I can easily conceive that the inconvenience may be productive of very great advantage.

If the difference between the higher and lower classes, in point of morals and intelligence, is not so great as is supposed; if the former wear, for the most part, an outside show; the struggle for equality, by unveiling them, by exposing their false pretensions, will apply a sort of coercive influence to compel them to act up to the duties of their station. They will at first endeavor to rid themselves of the inconvenience, by descending to the level of the lowest—by imitating their manners, and truckling to their prejudices. The effect will not be lasting; the plan cannot be carried out. And, after vain efforts to reconcile qualities the most incompatible, they will be driven to the necessity of cultivating habits which, as they most become, so they are universally expected from them. If adversity contributes to elevate the human character, and if the struggle for equality is to be regarded as a species of adversity which is constantly present with us, it cannot fail to exercise a salutary influence. The diffusion of property and education are not sufficient to produce the degree of reflection which is requisite to maintain free institutions. The acquisition of property, notwithstanding its manifold benefits, has a tendency to undo all that education has done. The affluent become too contented, too self-complacent, to be either virtuous or wise. The ever enduring struggle for equality is the only agent which, united with property and education, will conduce to the right ordering of society.

CHAPTER VI.

THE ELECTORAL FRANCHISE.

THERE are two plans upon which we may proceed in forming a constitution of government. By one, the political power is vested in a select number, composing what is termed the aristocracy of wealth and talent. And to accomplish this the electoral franchise, and the eligibility to office, are both restricted. The advantages of the plan are supposed to consist in the greater stability of the public administration, and the superior energy which the government will possess, in suppressing every species of insubordination. The second plan opens the door wide to the electoral privilege, and the admission to office. Doubtless the great problem in political science is to procure the greatest amount of liberty, consistent with the greatest degree of public tranquility. And as we are compelled to take for granted, that a large portion of the vice and licentiousness which have characterized the people of former times will always be found in society, it may be argued that the first plan is the safest and most judicious; but the republics which flourished in Italy, in the thirteenth and fourteenth centuries, were modeled upon this plan, and yet were a prey to the most atrocious violence and tyranny. For after this disposition is made of the political power, the question still occurs: in what way shall the governors themselves be governed? A large share of authority is conferred upon the government, for the purpose of preserving order, and yet this authority is without any effectual control. Opening the door wide to every species of political privilege, is the most certain means of increasing the natural aristocracy, and of combining vigor in the government with popular freedom. For it is remarkable that although in the Italian republics, the public officers were generally elected for very limited terms, for six, and sometimes for so short a time as two months, it imposed no check upon the exercise of the most arbitrary authority. The moral sense—the perception of the plain distinction between right and wrong, was wanting in the whole community. There was ample power and opportunity to render the principle of responsibility a powerful restraint upon the conduct of public men; but there was no adequate appreciation of that conduct; no more meaning was attached to the words just and unjust, than belonged to them in the monarchical governments of western and northern Europe;—a striking example of the important agency which the political institutions have in forming the manners and habits of different nations. In all those communities, the select few who were chosen to conduct the public administration were thoroughly trained to the requisite skill and intelligence: in the Italian republics to a much greater extent than in Great Britain and France, because at that day, the electoral franchise was much less restricted in the former. If, then, we extend political privileges of every kind still further, and convert the great body of the people into citizens, the conclusion is fair that the same skill and intelligence will be diffused among the whole population. Now, it is these very qualities which develop that moral sense—that quick perception of what is right or wrong in the conduct of public men—which I have noticed as being so deficient in the Italian communities. The men who held important posts in Genoa, Venice, and Florence, were sufficiently instructed, in consequence of their situation, in everything which affected their own interests. But those interests were, by set design, placed in contradiction with those of the mass of the people. Impart to the latter the same privileges, and the contradiction will disappear. For inasmuch as these will feel an equally strong interest in the protection of their own rights, and will possess the moral power to enforce them, public men will be compelled to conform their conduct more and more to this altered state of public sentiment. The standard of right and wrong will of necessity, and not from choice, have a just and definite meaning. No education can instill the moral sense in any individual. But a certain train of circumstances, and the discipline to which these subject the actions of men, are indispensable in order to develop it and keep it in constant activity.

In the history of society we may remark three distinct grades of liberty, which have existed in different governments. The first is where freedom is confined to the governors. This is the case in pure monarchy and aristocracy. Although the governments of Russia and Denmark are in no sense free, yet the Danish and Russian nobility, at any rate, enjoy as much political liberty as the American people. But the Danish and Russian people enjoy none. The second is where the people are divided into active and passive citizens; the former possessing political liberty, while the latter live securely in the enjoyment of civil liberty only. The British government is the fairest example of this class which has ever existed. The third is where all the people are full and complete citizens, possessing both civil and political privileges. This can only be the case in a country where free institutions are established.

It is not difficult to account for this great diversity in the structure of different governments. Society everywhere appears to have been at a very early period divided into distinct classes. This institution was, by no means, peculiar to Egypt and Hindostan. But the superstitious observances which were ingrafted upon it in those countries, and the immobile character of the population which prolonged its duration, have rendered it more striking than any where else.

The separation of the people into different orders lay at the foundation of the Grecian and Roman commonwealths. It may be distinctly traced in the history of all the modern European States; and vestiges more or less plain are discernible in the most of them down to the present day. The division of the population into nobility, clergy, burgesses, and peasantry, constituted at one time the settled classification of society in England and Scotland. Some of the ancient charters and statutes even went as far as the Roman laws, in forbidding inter-marriages among some of the classes. Guardians were prohibited from "disparaging their wards by wedlock with persons of an inferior condition." An inferior caste was recognized, into which the military tenants could not marry without degradation. It is not necessary to account for this from the fact that, long after the Saxon conquest, the Roman law composed the groundwork of the jurisprudence. The operation of the same general laws, which gave rise every where else to the existence of fixed classes, produced the same effect in England. No doubt now remains but what the institution originally grew out of conquest—probably out of successive conquests. The conquerers composed the superior, the conquered the inferior ranks. In the course of time the different races in England and Scotland were melted into one. And the progress of civilization in the other European States has, in a great measure, obliterated this as well as every other remnant of an antiquated society.

It is not the least remarkable of the circumstances attending the first settlement of the United States, that the native population were so thin and so immensely inferior to the emigrants, that it disappeared as fast as these advanced. If the country had been as fully peopled as Mexico, great difficulties would have presented themselves in the formation of that system of uniform institutions which now exist. The Indian race would have been disfranchised, precisely as are the Africans in both the northern and southern states. They would have composed as distinct a caste as these last do. The distinction would have been nearly the same as prevails in Hindostan.

The most obvious idea which we can form o f government is that it is an institution intended for tbe common benefit of the whole people. Nor is there any difficulty in realizing this idea, where the population does not consist of different races. Mere varieties of the same race oppose no obstacle, as has been proved in America, where one uniform system of laws causes these varieties to disappear in two or three generations. But where the community is artificially distributed into classes which possess unequal privileges, the term government loses its just signification. One part of the population is then forcibly elevated, and another depressed; and civil society becomes an institution, exclusively appropriated to the advantage of the former. The great body of the people live under, but not in it.

The disposition which governments shall make of the electoral franchise is destined to exercise a more important influence upon human affairs, than any other political regulation of which I am aware. And the reason is obvious. There is none which is calculated to produce so deep an impression upon the structure of society, and at the same time to affect so fundamentally the form of the government. The tendency everywhere at the present day, is to extend the privilege. For every enlargement of it increases the demand, by raising up a greater number of people who are fitted to exercise it. The improvement of the political institutions, and the improvement of the population, go hand in hand.

Why are the people in mass admitted to the electoral franchise in the United States, is a problem which has constantly exercised my mind. Wherever I cast my eyes, I seemed to see evidence of its being a solecism in politics. If I walked the streets of city or town, for one tolerably informed individual, I met with twenty who were the reverse. If I traveled on the highway, the same fact was exhibited even more glaringly. The great majority of persons I met, appeared to know nothing beyond the narrow circle of their daily occupations.

But there is another fact equally striking, which presented itself to my mind, although the number of the intelligent was in so small a proportion to the ignorant, the number of bad, or improvident laws, compared with those which were wise and salutary, was in an inverse ratio. They were even greatly less than one in twenty. I observed that the greatest stability reigned in those matters which concerned the general welfare. I witnessed a great deal of party strife; but in taking an account of the legislation for any series of years, I could not discover that there had been any material departure from one uniform system which had prevailed from the beginning. The constitutions of the different states did not appear to be the work of ignorant men; the whole code of civil and criminal law was modeled with as much judgment and ability as if none but the well informed had been the electors.

There are two forces necessary to conduct the affairs of society 1st. A certain amount of intelligence. 2d. A certain amount of integrity, or honesty of purpose. Now, admitting that so far as intelligence is concerned, it would be expedient to entrust the whole administration of the government to that very small class who possess intelligence; yet as the possession of office is corrupting in a high degree, the experiment must necessarily be a failure: that is, the affairs of government would be so conducted as to subserve the interests of those who enjoyed a monopoly of power, and not the interests of the whole community. Some plan must then be fallen upon, even though it should be in many respects imperfect, in order to rectify this great defect in the composition of society. We cannot find the requisite qualities of intelligence and honesty of purpose always united in the same individuals; but if we can find the intelligence in one class, and the honesty of purpose, though without the intelligence, in another, we may combine the two together, making one people of them, and thus answer the conditions of the problem we are in search of. It will be no answer to say that this will be done imperfectly. This is admitted; for every instrument of government must partake of the defect of the materials from which it is made. But it will be correct to say, that the plan will be more efficacious than any other which can be devised. It may be objected that honesty of purpose is no more characteristic of the masses than it is of the intelligent, that it is even less so, a certain amount of intelligence being necessary to make up the character of integrity in its genuine signification; that the common people are as much addicted to the practice of over-reaching each other in their dealings as any other class. This will also be admitted. But the material inquiry is, whether they are, or in the nature of things can be, so much so in what concerns public affairs. A small number of men to whom the electoral franchise, and eligibility to office, were confined, might very easily live upon the people. The taxes extracted from them, would be sufficient to gratify the most extravagant desires, and the most insatiable avarice. But it is impossible for the people to live upon the people. The taxes imposed are only sufficient to pay the small number who conduct the machinery of government, and the amount necessary for this must be derived from their labor. So far as regards the expenditure of public money, the common people may be considered as possessing honesty of purpose in a political sense, in a high degree. They are deeply interested in preventing the public revenue from being squandered. This integrity of conduct may be a negative quality, but it is not the less efficacious on that account. In politics, positive and negative qualities sometimes count for the same. It is the matter of fact we have to deal with; and it is clear that the interest of the people is identical with that of the public, for they are the public. But the interest of the office holders may be directly opposed to that of the public. It is self-interest which renders the former honest in political matters, and it is the same quality which, under the guise of a half courtly, half sanctimonious exterior, helps to make the latter corrupt.

It is in this way that we may account for what would otherwise appear to be an anomaly in the institutions of the United States: the permitting all classes to exercise the electoral franchise. It would seem at first view that we should, have regard not merely to the number, but to the intensity of the wills intended to be represented. And this is true, provided this intensity of will, or superior intelligence, was free from the vice of selfishness, and manifested itself in a due comprehension of the public interests, and are inflexible in pursuing them. But as we cannot find the two elements combined in one class, we are driven to the expedient of admitting all classes to participation in the electoral franchise. The power of control which is thus possessed by the governed over the governing, is indispensable in order to obtain all the ends of good government.

The system contains within itself a self corrective principle. The longer the people are habituated to the exercise of the franchise, the more completely will they grow into it. In France, when the revolution broke out, no class possessed the right of voting for any purpose. None had any voice in constituting any one of the departments of government. The consequence was, that the men of letters, the merchants, monied men, and principal tradesmen, were the instigators, and chief actors in that revolution. Had they been accustomed for a very long period to the exercise of the privilege, the government would have undergone a gradual reformation. In the three first volumes of Mr. Bancroft's history, the first rudiments of American institutions, are set forth with great judgment, and perspicuity. The historian deduces from the events he relates, the important fact, that whenever the people were left to themselves, and were rid of the rule of royal or proprietary government, their affairs were conducted with the greatest judgment and address. If any one should say, "admit the great body of the people to the elective franchise, but exclude the lowest class;" the answer is, that in a community where there has been a pretty equal distribution of property from the beginning, the mischiefs arising from the possession of political rights by even the lowest class, will be altogether less, than in a country where everything has commenced wrong, and where the laws are studiously intent on condensing property in the hands of a few. The lowest class will not be of sufficient magnitude in the former, to make any sensible impression upon the result of the vote. The United States are the first country which has made the experiment upon a large scale, and it is of infinite moment to pursue it until its practicability is fairly tested. The lowest class have a stake in the commonwealth as well as any other class; they are the most defenceless portion of the population; and the sense of independence which the enjoyment of political rights inspires, in innumerable instances acts as a stimulus to the acquisition of property. If the experiment fails, if the intervention of the lowest class in the elections, exercises too disturbing an influence upon the motions of the government, the expedient which has been adopted in the government of cities, and towns may be easily resorted to. The difficulty would be exceedingly great, impossible I may say, of effecting a change now. The lowest class are for the most part laborers, but their wages are such as to enable them to live in great comfort; they are closely connected with the great class which stands above them; and the sympathy which exists between the two, would not permit the enactment of any law which should exclude the former from their present position. But if a host of proletarians should rise up, whose voice in the government was detrimental to the public interests, unfriendly to the maintenance of that order, regularity, and justice, which makes up the true idea of a commonwealth, the feeling of sympathy would be lost, and as there would be no motive for continuing a rule after the reason for it had ceased, the great body of the commonwealth, who will forever be the majority, would unite in imposing some restriction on the electoral franchise.

One very important consequence follows from these views; that it will be necessary to enlarge the rule of eligibility to office in the same proportion as that for the electoral franchise. If one is without restriction, the other should be so also. The ground upon which the argument in the first part proceeds, is that it is impossible to find in one class all the qualities which are requisite to good government. But if we can find them separately existing in two classes, we may by combining them into one class for political purposes, attain the desired end. Although honesty in political matters may simply consist in an instinctive resistance of the general interest to the private interest of a few, yet if in practice the consequences are the same, as if it proceeded from natural integrity of character, the legislator will have attained all he has any right to expect. The public interest is promoted by honest views. If honesty of purpose is the moving spring, the end is attained in its greatest perfection. If on the other hand, an interest in the general weal is the moving spring, the same political end is attained. As a substitute for a property qualification for office, some have proposed to place the age of the candidate high, to require that they should be forty or forty-five before admission even to the legislative body. This is evidently impracticable, unless we raise the requisite age of the voters also. It is they who determine the rule of eligibility to office, and it is very improbable that they would deprive themselves of the privilege. But there are very wise reasons why this restriction should not be imposed. It would lower instead of elevating the capacity of candidates for office. At present, electors are the persons elected, and these again fall into the body of electors. If the legislature then, is a school of discipline for those who compose it, it is equally so for the electors. In this way a most advantageous influence is exercised upon the whole mass of the population. The consciousness that they are electors, and that they may be elected to a place of trust, sharpens the minds of individuals, and even amidst the confusion of party politics, rears up a much greater number of sagacious, and well informed persons, than might at first be supposed. If during the last seventy years, all the citizens under forty had been debarred from the elective franchise, or entering the legislative assemblies in America, there would have been less instead of more order in the conduct of public affairs ; for the great mass of the population would have possessed less intelligence, sagacity and prudence. Bacon has said that there is "but one mode of predicting political events, and that is by ascertaining the predominant opinions of the average of men who are under thirty." We are enabled to do this in a clear, determinate, and legal way, by endowing them with political privileges. It is for this reason, that even in the constitutional monarchies of England and France, the age of the electors and members of the legislature is placed so low. Some of the states which compose the Swiss confederacy, have erred on the other side. The age in some is so low as eighteen, and in others sixteen. The legislative assembly is the place where opinions are discussed, and where alone materials can be collected for predicting, as well as for providing for the future. It is very important that the opinions of the young should mingle with those of mature age. If inconvenience is experienced from the ardent character of the one, fully as much would be suffered from the narrow and obstinate prejudices of the other. The political prosperity of the United States, the stability in the midst of progress, which the institutions exhibit, are attributable to the young, and the old being admitted to the public councils. This has not given a predominance to the opinions of either. It has simply operated a fusion of the opinions of the two, and has placed at the command of society, all the genius, and activity of the one, together with all the wisdom, and ability of the other.

M. Chabrol, in his "Recherches Statistiques," calculates that nineteen-twentieths of the people of France are dependent on their labor, or personal exertions of some kind, for their subsistence; in other words, that not more than one twentieth are in a condition to live upon their income merely. Tucker, in his work on the census of the United States, has made the same calculation for the people of that country. The knowledge of this fact, M. Sismondi considers indispensable, in order to make a wise and safe distribution of the political power. If nineteen-twentieths of the population are condemned to employments which do not permit the free and vigorous exercise of their understandings, is it not absurd, asks M. Sismondi, to endow all the people equally with the electoral franchise; in other words, to give nineteen times more power to the ignorant, than to those who are capable of understanding the interests of the country. But we should commit a great mistake if we supposed that the calculation of M. Chabrol had the same meaning in all countries. Although in every country the number of those devoted to physical labor is nineteen to one, it will not follow that the condition of the class is the same in all. For instance, the majority of proprietors in the United States possess from eighty to two hundred acres of land; in France, from six to ten; in Great Britain, from fifteen to twenty-five; nevertheless, the American proprietor is as dependent for his maintenance upon the cultivation of his farm, as the French or English proprietor. But the maintenance of the former comprehends much more than that of the two last. In Great Britain, the rural population composes one-third, in the United States it is three-fourths of the population. These circumstances place a wide distinction between the population of the United States and that of Great Britain or France. The proportion of the rural population is as great in France as in the United States, but their condition is infinitely lower. Although nineteen-twentieths of the American people are dependent upon their labor, yet if more than one-half of this number are placed in an easy condition, and have a revenue greatly superior to the same class in other countries, their labor will not be anything like so intense and humiliating. The condition of the majority of French proprietors is little better than of the English operatives: neither earn more than enough to satisfy the lowest animal wants. American proprietors, on the contrary, live in comfort, and a fair opportunity is afforded for the development of their understandings. For even where the education is of a limited character, the feeling of independence gives a spring to the intellectual faculties. The difference between the American and European laborer is as great as between the American and European proprietor. The American laborer earns from three pecks to a bushel of wheat daily; the average wages of even the English laborer during the last five centuries have been a little more than one peck.

M. Sismondi insists [Etudes sur les Seiences Sociales, v. 1, p. 54,] that the most fortunate result which can be expected from an election by universal suffrage, is that the choice will be a mean between all the differences, so that if there are nineteen ignorant electors for one well informed, the legislative body will be nineteen-twentieths nearer the ignorance of the one than the intelligence of the other. This, however, is contradicted by universal experience. The opinion of Brougham is more correct, when he declares that, "if universal suffrage were now established in Great Britain, not one peasant would be elected to Parliament." Moral inability produces nearly the same results as physical inability. Those who are without knowledge, without ability, or aptitude for public affairs, feel themselves instinctively and irresistibly impelled to lean upon those who have these qualities in some respectable degree. There never has been a legislative assembly chosen by the people which did not contain men of high character and superior endowments. In France, after the revolution of 1848, such men as De Tocqueville, Berryer, Thiers, Barrot, Dupin, Arago, &c., were immediately elected to the legislative body. The same result has invariably taken place in the United States. Why this should be the case—why some men of superior merit are returned together with a greater number of inferior capacities, and why the first will be able to exert a decisive influence in the assembly, affords matter for curious inquiry: 1st. There is in all men a natural and instinctive respect for superior knowledge. It is not the result of reflection, and therefore cannot be got rid of any more than our other instincts. 2d. The sharp edge of envy is taken off by the knowledge which the people have that the successful candidates owe their election to them. 3d. Every one in the affairs of private life calls upon others to do what he cannot do, or do so skillfully himself: upon the lawyer, in a legal controversy; upon the physician, in sickness. 4th. These causes are greatly strengthened by a circumstance peculiar to political men. The public display which they make, the topics they debate, strike powerfully upon the imagination of the common people. They are not merely instructed; they are amused, and their feelings roused, by the animating spectacle which public affairs present. But there is nothing to produce animation when the public arena is occupied by dull, ignorant men, any more than there is at the theatre where the actors have none of the inspiration of genius. Through these various instrumentalities, some men of ruling intellect are sure to be elected to an assembly which has to do with great affairs; and such men, for even stronger reasons than have influenced the electors, will exert a commanding influence upon the other members. Superior minds, in whatever sphere they move, give unity to the thoughts and actions of other men. Profound writers, the pulpit, the bar, the seminaries of learning, all contribute to this great end. If we survey the condition of a savage or half-civilized community, we find this principle of unity entirely wanting: every thing which relates to the social, moral and political regime, is at loose ends. If we examine the condition of a civilized country, but in which internal commotions have for a time broken in upon the regular order of society, we find the same fact exemplified in a remarkable manner. If we look into the condition of the same country, when enjoying tranquility, we find a state of things entirely the reverse. Every thing is in its place; the thoughts and actions of men are controlled by a principle of unity, and that principle of unity is contained in the moral and intellectual machinery which is in operation. The institution of government contributes greatly to this end; it binds up the scattered, incoherent thoughts and interests of men, and makes them all tend to some common end. The use of representative government, as contra-distinguished from pure democracy, is not to reflect the vague and loose opinions of the millions of men who live under it, but to sift those opinions, to draw out what is valuable, and thus to give fixedness, consistency and unity to the thoughts of men, as well as to the plans of government. This want is infinitely more pressing in a country of great extent, than in one of narrow dimensions. But even the small republics of Greece were obliged to invent some plan in order to get rid of the disorder which would have arisen from an assemblage of the people in person; such as vesting the senatorial body with the initiative, confiding the reduction of the laws to special committees, or bureaus, and the appointment of a certain number of public orators. All these were representative bodies, and helped to make compensation for the inherent defects of the system. Without some such expedients, the legislative assembly would have been converted into a bedlam. A government which is representative throughout, attains these ends in much higher perfection. It is not necessary, nor even desirable, that a country should employ all its eminent men in political affairs. There are other and higher occupations for the ruling minds who belong to it; higher, because the eminent political men of every country are themselves formed, directly or indirectly, by the great thinkers and writers in every department of knowledge. America so far presents the singular spectacle of a country whose eminent men have been formed by the great minds of other countries. It is fortunate, therefore, that she at least does not convert all her gifted citizens into public men. Provision will thus be made for building up a profound literature at home, and preventing us looking abroad in order to obtain the great rudiments of knowledge. We shall then cease to be an eleemosynary people, in what relates to intellectual cultivation.

The notion of a property qualification, as necessary to entitle to a vote, seems to be derived from feudal institutions. A very few instances of the same kind are to be found in antiquity. The feudal law so completely united every species of political right with dominion in the soil, that even after a regular representative assembly grew up, the right of suffrage, as well as the capacity to hold office, was made to depend upon the fact whether the persons were landed proprietors, or not. In Great Britain, a qualification of this kind is still necessary: a freehold in county, and a leasehold in borough elections. In Scotland, until recently, none but tenants in capite, that is, persons who held immediately of the crown (whether really or constructively, was immaterial) had a right to vote in county elections. For the most extraordinary part of the system was, that it was by a fiction only they were so denominated. It was not necessary that they should have any interest whatever in the soil.

They possessed the franchise on account of what, in technical language, is termed superiority. They were originally tenents in capite; but it was in the power of any one to sever his superiority from his land; selling the last, and yet retaining the former: the purchaser consequently acquiring the right to a vote. This was a strange anomaly at any time; but that such a law should be found standing in the midst of the light of the nineteenth century, and in the most enligtened country of Europe, is difficult to explain by any sensible mode of reasoning. It shows that the artificial governments alone are able to reconcile the most heterogeneous and contradictory things—can insist that the public safety demands that property and power should forever go together; and then throw away the principle as unmeaning and valueless, and confer power upon those who have no property. The consequence of this state of things was, the electorial franchise was much more restricted, and the system of representation altogether more irregular, than in either England or Ireland.

In France, since the creation of a house of deputies, a different plan has been adopted. The right to a vote depends upon the payment of a certain amount of taxes, varying at different periods, from forty to sixty dollars for each individual. This presupposes the possession of property, but then it may be indifferently, either real or personal. The tax must be a direct one, but even if there is any real distinction between what are termed direct and what are termed indirect taxes, the former are deemed equally applicable to both kinds of property. In America, a property qualification was once necessary in all the state governments; and in the federal government, the right to a vote for members of the house of representatives was the same as it was in each state, for the most numerous branch of the state legislature. The laws, however, have undergone a total alteration in almost all the states. Universal suffrage is now the rule, a property qualification the exception; and the elections to the federal legislature are obliged to conform themselves to the changes made in the respective states.

The origin of a custom is never sufficient to determine its utility, nor to give us its true meaning at a subsequent time. Such changes take place in the frame of society, in modern communities, that an institution which was well enough adapted to a very imperfect civilization, may lose its signification and become highly injurious at a more advanced period. It is true, it sometimes happens that an institution which was fitted to answer one purpose, may, when that has ceased to exist, be found to answer some other end in a still higher degree. And, therefore, it cannot be stated as an universal proposition, that if the original design has failed, the institution should therefore be abolished. But it is still more necessary to guard against the opposite error, and never to take for granted that the antiquity of an institution is what entitles it to the respect of mankind. The prejudice is sometime of advantage, by correcting the precipitancy of innovation. But in the greater number of instances, it only darkens and confuses the understanding, and contributes to retain society in a stationary condition.

A property qualification has been defended in modern times, on two grounds: First, That property is the chief thing which the laws have to deal with, and therefore it is fit that the privilege should be worn by those who represent the most important interests of society. Second, That as a general rule, the possession of property affords a surer test of a capacity for the judicious exercise of the electorial franchise, than any other which can be devised.

To disseminate property is to disseminate power; and on the other hand, the diffusion of liberty gives rise to the diffusion of both property and power. And as the true plan of balancing power is to prevent its concentration in the hands of a few—to distribute it as widely as possible; so the only mode by which we can contrive to govern the governors, is to open the way to all classes of men for the acquisition of property. And the most effectual way of doing this, is to extend the electorial franchise as widely as practicable. Neither the abolition of primogeniture, nor any other enactment of the civil code, has in the United States assisted so much in effecting a distribution of property, as have the political institutions. So that even admitting, as a general rule, that it is fit power and property should go together: it cannot be wise to adopt a system, the direct effect of which is to prevent the growth and dissemination of property. Formerly, landed property constituted the principal capital of society. But the case is now very much altered. Industry, sagacity, and enterprise, though they can neither be seen or touched, compose, at the present day, the chief elements of wealth. No man, however affluent, can now tell with any degree of certainty how long his estate will continue to be enjoyed by his descendants;

such is the rapidity with which the inert habits of those who are born rich permit property to crumble, and such the corresponding activity with which those who are born poor acquire the ability to appropriate that property to themselves.

Why it is, that the communication of political privileges to a people imparts so much vigor and activity to their whole character, is not difficult to account for. It removes a feeling of degradation, the invariable effect of which is to benumb and stupify the mind, if it does not produce worse consequences. It is true, one can hardly say, that the peasantry of Russia, or Austria realize this feeling ; since having been habituated, from time immemorial, to a state of complete subjection, they can hardly form an idea of the value of the privilege. But in all the constitutional monarchies of Europe, where the electorial franchise is already extended to a part of the population, those who are excluded from its exercise are able to make a comparison of their situation with that of others ; and a sense of their own inferiority is forced upon them.

The great advantage arising from the free communication of the privilege consists, then, in its giving men new faculties, and not merely new rights. It enables them for the first time to realize a sense of degradation, which they were before too much debased to feel. It places the great body of the population in the only condition in which it is possible to place them ; where their understandings will be opened, their views enlarged, and their feeling elevated. Nothing can be conceived more dreary, and monotonous, than the time which is passed in the drudgery of supplying our animal wants, if there is nothing besides to give variety and interest to life. The beings who are condemned to this species of subterranean existence, are never able to acquire the proper character of men.

Medical writers have observed that nothing contributes so much to produce mental aberration as the habit acquired by some individuals, of brooding over one train of ideas. The mind which is exercised in this way, is deprived of its healthful action ; the balance between its different faculties is lost, and its strength gradually undermined. It is only in extreme cases that this takes place. But there is a condition of mind very similar to this, which may be termed fatuity — an intellectual torpor, which, in some countries, takes possession of whole classes ; produced by the addiction to an exceedingly narrow round of pursuits, and which prevents the natural play of the mental powers and affections. Long habit familiarizes the observer to this melancholy spectacle; but it is not the less an example of mental aberration, though in a much less degree than the state before described. Whoever has closely watched the countenances and behavior of the peasantry of most European countries, when they arrive in the United States, must have been struck with this characteristic mark. There is an obtuseness of intellect, a withered and sunken aspect, a bent and difficult gait, which contrast strongly with the alert step and animated countenances of American agriculturists.

There are two modes of rectifying this unfortunate condition of society—education and the influence of free institutions. Education alone is not sufficient. The mind may take in the mere rudiments of knowledge, and yet its faculties never be developed. The institutions under which we live, the social organization which encompasses us, are what give vitality and meaning to much the greater part of the knowledge which the bulk of mankind ever acquire. Liberty both imparts elasticity to the mind, and supplies the materials on which it is chiefly exercised. For the general communication of an important political privilege breaks down the wall of partition between the different classes. Men of low degree are brought into association with those who possess superior advantages. The former are taught to have more self-respect, more confidence in themselves; and the wide range of general information which is now placed within their reach, inspires the greatest inquisitiveness imaginable in regard to the conduct of public affairs, in which they have now become actors themselves. All this, so far from withdrawing attention from their private pursuits, adds fresh vigor to their exertions, simply because it supplies such a fund of variety to life. And thus this unexpected consequence follows, that in a country where no property qualification is attached to the enjoyment of political privileges, the number of people who possess property is the greatest. And wherever the qualification is highest, the less is the number of those who have property;—a remarkable instance of the false train of reasoning to which the mind is frequently conducted, by an obstinate adherence to what is called the ancient and established order of society.

There is an old maxim that the political institutions can never be made to rise higher than the manners. And a more pernicious one has never been incorporated into the book of politics. There is no difference in this respect between political and any other institutions. And if the maxim had ever been carried to anything like its full extent, society would never have made a single step in improvement. For what are religion, education, and the body of conventional rules which preside over a community, but so many institutions, which, finding men ignorant and weak, lift them up, and make them better and wiser. The true maxim is that the political institutions do exercise a most important influence upon the manners, and that every improvement of the former contributes to raise society to a higher level. And I am persuaded if some of the European governments I could name were resolved, manfully, but circumspectly, to rid themselves of the prejudice, that what has been must continue to be, and if they would impart a large share of liberty to the people, that it would redound to the strength and prosperity of both government and people.

There are several considerations, in addition to those already suggested, which go very far to show that a law which attaches a property qualification to the right of suffrage is unwise and without utility.

First. Public opinion is becoming more and more the great moving force of all governments. It is then of the utmost importance to inquire what part of the population it is which contributes to the formation of this public opinion. Is it certain that it is only the class of proprietors? Very far from it; there are great multitudes of people in Great Britain and France who are totally disfranchised, and whose opinions and interests are of so much consequence as to render their influence, even when deprived of suffrage, of infinite importance, whether for good or for evil. And this constitutes the test of the expediency of a property qualification. If whole classes who are disqualified have sufficient weight in society to bear a part in the formation of public opinion, it decides the question in favor of a liberal rule of suffrage. If those who have faculties to think, and an abundant curiosity with regard to all public affairs, are excluded from the privilege, they will succeed in spite of every effort the legislator may make in giving a direction to public opinion.

I venture to say, that all the great measures of reform which have been set on foot during the last twenty years in Great Britain, have been brought about in great part, through the influence of that numerous body of active and intelligent citizens, who are shut out from a direct participation in political power. But ciritical emergencies occur in all governments; when the passions of different orders of men are violently inflamed; and when what was before an invisible influence, will come to wear a more palpable form. The whole class of disfranchised, composed in part of sagacious and otherwise well disposed people, will then resemble a foreign force, rather than a body of orderly citizens, and may imagine, that in self-defense it is necessary to batter down existing institutions.

The British, and still more the French government, is placed in this position. Two hundred thousand electors in the last, where the adult male population is five or six millions, is too great a disproportion; and it is not surprising that the fear of a disputed succession, or some other speck discerned upon the political horizon, should produce so much apprehension among those who take the lead in public affairs. In Great Britain the reform bill extended the privilege considerably; but one thirty-fifth part of the population is much too small a proportion in a country where the standard of popular intelligence has been so much elevated during the last half century. I am not acquainted with all the views of the English chartists; but so formidable a body of men could hardly have been banded together in that great community, unless the electoral franchise was needlessly withheld from a very substantial part of the citizens, and unless those who were so earnest in endeavoring to effect a reform, had been animated by the characteristic good sense of the Anglo-Norman race. There is no necessity for acquiescing in the extreme views of Mr. Bentham, or Major Cartwright: a wide field for profitable legislation is opened, whether we adopt or discard them. The chartists have assuredly paved the way for further concessions at some future day. The present law of parliamentary reform was talked about by the party in power, and the party in opposition, by Pitt and by Fox, as far back as 1786, and was achieved nearly half a century after.

Second. A government which confines the electoral franchise within very narrow limits, fails to avail itself of the strength and faculties of the whole of its people. It is like the strong man cutting off his right arm with his left. In the United States, the enjoyment of the privilege by the great body of the people gives rise to order and tranquility, instead of tumult and insurrection. For an unmistakable test is thus afforded, that all public measures follow the course which the majority have decreed. And there is nothing which is so much calculated to subdue the will, and to produce an irresistible obedience to the laws, as the knowledge that they are imposed by an authority which has the only legitimate title to command. This alone is an immense advantage to society: so that even admitting that public affairs are not, in every particular instance, conducted with as much judgment, and discretion, as we could desire; yet if, on the average, they are characterized by more prudence, and good sense, a greater deference to the public weal than is discoverable in other governments, we may even afford to prize the flaw in the system, for the sake of its general utility. Montesquieu said, if the press were established in Constantinople, it would diffuse light even in that region. And it has actually done so; and I observe that every enlargement of the electoral franchise in Great Britain has had no other effect than to produce a greater degree of public tranquility. Invariably the introduction of free institutions, if it does not find a people already prepared for self-government, will in no long time render them so.

The general communication of the electoral privilege banishes the distinction of patricians and plebeians—a distinction which is quick in making its appearance, whenever it has any root in the laws. All the parts of society are thus combined into one firm and compact whole, and the strength and prosperity of the entire nation are proportionally augmented. On the other hand, where the right is very much restricted, two forces in the state are placed in opposition to each other: the legal and natural majority; the one conscious of the right, the other of power. The country is then sure to be torn by intestine divisions—divisions not created by a difference of opinion as to the ordinary measures of administration, which may follow one direction or another, without much affecting the public welfare; but divisions which are of fundamental import, as pertaining to the rights of the people, and the prerogatives of the government. It is not surprising, therefore, that even the extreme into which the people of the United States have run, of introducing universal suffrage, or nearly so, so far from destroying the public happiness, as was predicted, has been chiefly instrumental in promoting it. The natural and the legal majority being rendered identical, the surface of society is frequently ruffled, but the existence of the institution, is no longer jeopardized.

Third. It is a striking characteristic of human nature, that whatever is rendered common and familiar, loses on that very account its power over the imagination. Our feelings may be ever so much interested in the pursuit of an object, yet no sooner is it fairly attained than the charm of novelty begins to subside. The mind which was before tossed by contrary hopes and fears, recovers its composure, and a state approaching even to indifference sometimes succeeds to one of excitement. This is as true in the world of politics as in any other human concern. The same hopes and affections are set in motion in both, and they are liable therefore to be raised and depressed by the same causes. A privilege which, before it was granted was viewed as a mark of distinction, is deprived of a good deal of its attraction, when it is shared by millions.

The European governments discover the greatest alarm, and the most unreasonable timidity, whenever the subject of popular rights is touched. But we are not authorized to believe that there is so much danger to the political institutions from that quarter, when there is the fact staring us in the face, and which no one can gainsay, that those governments which have extended the sphere of popular rights the farthest, are the best administered, and are at the same time favored with the greatest degree of public tranquility. I would say to all those governments, if you are afraid of the temper and disposition of a people which is fast growing into manhood—if you feel alarmed at the intelligence and consequent weight which the people are everywhere acquiring, make haste to avert the mischiefs which are brooding over society, by imparting to them as large an amount of freedom as is practicable. Make what is now a privilege and distinction, the common property of a great number; it will then become cheap, common, and familiar. A state of popular excitement will not be perpetually kept up, and society will in no long time accommodate itself to the change. There is no difference, by nature, between Americans and the people of other countries; for the former were themselves Europeans originally. Their institutions have made them what they now are.

The electoral franchise has effected this important revolution in human affairs. Public measures are no longer decided upon the field of battle; hostile armies are now converted into political parties;

and military captains into civil leaders. Changes in the public administration, which years of civil war were unable to accomplish, are now brought about, silently, and imperceptibly, by the agency of the ballot box. If few are aware of the value of the mighty change which has taken place, or even of its existence, it is in consequence of causes to which I have already referred. Men cease to be moved by what has become the settled order of society.

But there is another benefit, which the general possession of the privilege will confer. A people who enjoy a long period of uninterrupted prosperity, are apt to become slothful and effeminate. The exercise of political privileges, by opening an arena for the operation of parties on the largest possible scale, keeps the minds of men in constant activity, and wards off the approach of that listlessness and decay, which have hitherto been the bane of society, when it has attained a very high civilization.

There is this advantage from founding government upon the will of the majority; that if alterations are afterwards found expedient, they will all originate with the same power. It is possible, that at some distant period, the public weal in the United States may require some modification of the right of suffrage. The true maxim in a republic is, that every right should be placed in subordination to the general welfare. If then the right is ever restricted, the change will be attended by this important advantage. It will be brought about with the consent of a majority of the people. This differs the institution fundamentally from what it is anywhere else.

It is not the mere abstract limitation of the right which is to be complained of. For none but males are now admitted; and as to them the age of twenty-one is arbitrarily fixed upon as the commencement of the right. It is the restriction of the privilege by a section of the community (as in the European governments,) which constitutes the chief ground of objection. It is remarkable, that the Americans have constantly adhered to the principle, that some other qualification than mere citizenship, or residence, is necessary in municipal elections. A property qualification of some kind, is uniformly imposed in this instance. This is not only the case in the large cities; it is the general rule in all the smaller towns which are scattered over the country. If, therefore, it shall ever be deemed wise to impose a limitation upon the right of voting at the general elections, the transition will not be a violent one. It will simply be the application of a principle in one form, to which, in another, the public is already habituated. Doubtless the qualification exacted at all charter elections interferes as much with the abstract principle of equal rights, as would a similar restriction imposed upon the general voter. Yet there is, at present, a very general conviction of the propriety of the rule in the former case.

As to the mode of collecting the suffrages of the people, whether it should be "viva voce," or by ballot, I do not believe that the question is of so much importance as is generally supposed. In the early history of most communities, the former was probably the practise. But this was owing to the inability to write, rather than to the simplicity of the manners. It is rarely a secret how any one votes, when the election is by ballot. Free institutions throw open the windows of society so wide as to unveil all political transactions. In the United States, the vote of every elector in a county has been sometimes calculated with absolute precision before hand. Cicero laments the disuse of the "viva voce" vote in his time. But in a period of deep gloom and adversity, such as existed when he wrote, the mind which is laboring under its depressing influence will lay hold of any circumstance, to give color to its apprehensions. The ballot does not render the vote of any one a secret; while at the same time, it has this eminent advantage, that an election becomes less noisy and tumultuous in consequence. It is made to resemble the quiet and orderly transaction of private business.

When the electors are very numerous, it is fortunately impracticable to organize them on the plan adopted in France. There the electors form themselves into what are denominated colleges, into which no one not privileged to vote is admitted. The elections are thus freed from violence, but they are shrouded in darkness, and are therefore subjected to the most sinister influence. Until 1830, the presidents of these colleges were nominated by the king — a circumstance which was understood to give them a decided advantage, if they were themselves candidates: so sadly does a monarchical government disfigure free institutions, whenever it attempts to imitate them.

The intermediate vote has been a favorite with some very able writers. Mr. Hume proposes it in his plan of a republic. The experiment has been made in France, on a more extended scale than was ever attempted in any other country. At one time, two intermediate bodies were interposed between the primary electors and the candidates : so that three successive elections, by as many different bodies, each diminishing in number, were necessary to the election of the legislative body. The whole plan, however, was abandoned in 1817. In the United States, a scheme in some respects similar, has been adopted in the election of the president, and senators ; and in most of the state governments, in the election of judges, and a few of the administrative officers. But in France, not only were members of the legislature elected by the intermediate vote, but what was infinitely worse, the electoral colleges who chose them were constituted for life. The small number of persons composing them, together with the permanent tenure of their office, rendered these colleges mere aristocratic bodies.

The election laws of France were at one time disfigured by another deformity. All those who paid a certain amount of taxes, seven hundred francs I think, were entitled to vote twice. In Great Britain the double, and even the triple vote is allowed ; but it stands on a slightly different footing. In France, the same elector might vote twice for a member of the chamber of deputies. In Great Britain, the same elector cannot vote twice in the same county ; but he may vote in different counties, if he has land of sufficient value in each. He may vote twice, and even oftner, for different members of the house of commons. All such schemes are entirely inconsistent with the genuine spirit of free institutions: and only serve to stave off, or to hasten the day, which sooner or later will come, when a more just system will be established. Indeed, in France the plan has already been established. In Great Britain it stands, notwithstanding the reform act of 1832.

It is a most valuable provision in the American laws, that the elections are held in the townships, or parishes. This contributes mightily to break the force of party spirit. The plan has been recently imitated in Great Britain. Formerly, the elections were held at but one place in each county. It is now held at several places. A similar arrangement has also been adopted in France. Instead of the elections being held by departments, they are held in the smaller subdivision of "arrondissements." The British and French plans are still imperfect. The American is thorough, and goes directly to its object. In Europe, the plan is to diminish the number of electors, instead of multiplying the places of election.

There is another difference between the British, and French, and the American elections. In Great Britain the polls were kept open for an indefinite period. In the celebrated Westminster election, when Mr. Fox lost his seat, they were open for six weeks; and were then closed only because the session of parliament commenced. The period is now restricted to one day in cities and boroughs, and to two in counties. In France, an election continues six days. In America, the polls are generally closed in one day, and nothing is more remarkable than the universal calm which immediately succeeds. The elections in America may be said to exhibit the extraordinary spectacle of prodigious excitement, in the midst of the profoundest tranquility.

CHAPTER VII.

THE ELECTION OF THE PUBLIC OFFICERS.

There is one property peculiar to representative governments, which I do not remember to have seen noticed. It doubles the responsibility of the public agents. The persons who are elected to office feel a general responsibility in common with their constituents; because the interests of both are substantially the same, and they feel an additional responsibility, in consequence of the station which they are selected to fill. An association of individuals, acting in common for their mutual advantage, are compelled to listen to some other motives than self interest; otherwise it would not be true that they acted in common. But the moment it is decided that all public measures shall be managed by deputies, instead of by the people in person, a new and very important element is introduced into the government. The incentives to good conduct on the part of the representative are increased. The very self interest, which before stood in the way of each one acting effectually for the public good, is made to operate advantageously upon the officer. He is no longer confounded with the crowd. He stands out to public view as one selected to discharge important duties. His constituents expect something more from him, than they do from themselves; and his conduct is obliged to be more prudent and circumspect than it would otherwise be.

The corrupting influence of office has often been taken notice of. But it may be made to have a directly opposite effect. I have in repeated instances known individuals to make use of untiring efforts to obtain some public trust, the duties of which consisted in the most laborious drudgery—in the performance of a mere round of clerical duties; and I have observed them closely, after their object was attained. To see the singleness of purpose, and the indefatigable industry, which they applied to their new occupation, one would suppose that they had made discovery of some inexhaustible source of enjoyment, which was unknown to any one else. Before they were chosen, their conduct seemed to be without any definite aim. It was a bundle of expedients; not a system of action. They were not only not distinguished for intelligence, industry, or sobriety of demeanor; but seemed to be absolutely deficient in all. As soon as the public confidence was held out to them, all these qualities were suddenly waked up, and they were transformed into active and valuable citizens. In most countries, the greater part of these individuals would have been cut off from all opportunity of obtaining office. They would have occupied the place of passive citizens merely; and not even have been admitted to the exercise of the electoral franchise. Thus, the extreme liberty which representative government imparts to the population, carries along with it its own corrective. Of all governments it is the one which creates, if I may use the expression, the greatest amount of business transactions; and it is, therefore, the one which demands the greatest amount of business talent, and industry.

It is very true that the separate interest which a public officer feels in the emolument and influence which office bestows, may be so much enhanced, as entirely to outweigh the interest which he has in the public welfare. The way to cure this defect is to distribute power as widely as possible; to assign moderate salaries to every place, and to limit the duration of office. The distribution of power, by calling into requisition the abilities of a large proportion of the population, prevents any one from acquiring undue influence: and by joining effective labor to almost every public employment, identifies the interests of the public with those of the officer.

The ancients never made a full discovery of the principle of representation; and, accordingly, their application of it was very feeble. The Roman commonwealth had recourse to another principle in the constitution of its legislative assemblies. Men were arranged into distinct orders; and the votes were taken by classes, instead of "per capita."

Thus where a modern republic is chiefly intent on melting down the inequalities of different parts of the society, by establishing the principle of representation, an ancient republic endeavored to perpetuate them by giving them full play. There is hardly an instance in antiquity, of a legislative body which was elected. The senate of Athens may be an exception, though that is a question which is involved in great obscurity. In the Roman commonwealth, the comitia of the centuries, and of the tribes, constituted, at successive periods, the real legislature. The senate was regarded in the light of an executive magistracy, and the members who composed it, although they were elected by the people, during the latter half of the republic, were not elected to the senate. They had previously been chosen to some other office, and by virtue of this choice became senators for life.

The elective principle, however, was thoroughly practiced upon in framing the executive department. In the modern European states, the rule is reversed. The legislature, or one chamber, is elected, while the executive is an hereditary magistrate, and the judicial and all the subordinate administrative officers are appointed by him. The United States is the only country where the principle of representation has been introduced into every department of the government.

To procure an upright and enlightened appointing power is the chief desideratum in the formation of a commonwealth. It is the final aim of all government; and all other devices are but means to the attainment of it. In Great Britain, this power is nominally a prerogative of the crown; in practice, it is exercised by the minister, or some other public officer. Thus all the puisne judges are appointed by the chancellor; and it has been observed by an eminent English writer, that the fitness of the persons thus selected, is "not only unquestioned, but unquestionable." It was a maxim of the French economists, that a legal despotism, if it were practicable, would be the best form of government. That is, the uncontrolled authority of one man, of the greatest wisdom and virtue, would conduce better than all other political contrivances, to the attainment of public felicity. But if we were able to find one such man in society, we should, for the same reason, be able to find a great many others. The diversities of human character, great as they are, cannot, in the nature of things, be pushed to such an extreme as to present us with one individual, rising supremely in virtue and intelligence, above all others. We might, therefore, with much more reason, desire that a great number of the citizens possessed these endowments; for although the wish would be as unavailing in the one case as in the other, the object of both is equally possible, while the last would indicate a more exact and comprehensive notion of the ends of civil government.

One reason why the selections by the English Chancellor are so good, is because that officer is not lifted so high as to be insensible to the influence of public opinion, and yet is so independent as to be able to resist the aberrations to which public opinion is occasionally liable. In a republic it is impossible to make such a disposition of the appointing power. The arrangement is an artificial and accidental one, and cannot be introduced in such a government without subverting its foundation. It is not merely because the character of the chancellor depends upon that of the Prince, and that of the Prince upon chance; nor that the existence of such an officer would be a solecism in a republic: it would frustrate one of the great ends in the formation of a commonwealth, which is to identify the administration of government with the interests of the people, and so to discipline them by an actual experience of this connection, that the appointing power may be freed, not for a season, but forever, from the caprice of an individual. It is not uncommon in a monarchy to find the civil rights of the citizens well guarded, although the political abuses are both flagrant and numerous. An assiduous care for some of our interests frequently withdraws the mind from hardships and grievances of greater magnitude.

How to constitute the appointing power is then a question of the deepest interest in representative government. There are two ends which we desire to attain: one, to make government an institution for the common weal; the other, to render public opinion as nearly conformable as possible with the public reason; that is, to reflect what we may suppose to be the most enlightened views with regard to the common interests. These two ends are not easily reconciled; for government cannot be made an institution for the common benefit, unless the people participate in it. Their exclusion, and the confinement of the political power to a comparatively small number, will be followed, in the first instance, by a careless regard to their interests, and will lead by successive steps to a fixed design to build up an authority so independent as to be inaccessible to attack, or observation. On the other hand, if public opinion, which sets government in motion, is not a reasonable and well informed one, the interests of the community may be sacrificed, whatever may be the share which the people may have in the direction of public affairs. These are the difficulties of the problem. We want government to be instituted and administered, by the majority; and yet we want public opinion, which reflects the sentiments of that majority, to be both vigilant and enlightened. If we say that the people are unfit to exercise the appointing power directly, and confide it to the executive, or the executive and senate, or the legislative body, the dangers will be only apparently lessened; for all these magistrates are themselves elected by the people, and will partake more or less of the same character.

Is there then any impossibility in the nature of things, any impossibility under all circumstances and conditions of society, in causing public opinion and the public reason, to be in conformity with each other. 1st. There is a very perceptible tendency towards something of this sort, even in communities which are not the best regulated. This arises from a principle of human nature, and is not at all dependant upon the mechanism of government. The most uncultivated men form to themselves a standard of excellence which they cling to until that period of life when the passions are silenced, and their conduct and actions become less dangerous to society. It is for this reason, that society everywhere exhibits a principle of progress, and never of retrogradation. 2d. This feeling is so spontaneous, and so little under the command of the will, that it disposes the bulk of the population to look up to, and to defer to the opinions of the superior classes. The ideal which is floating in the minds of find a visible representative in some other part of society. The the uncultivated, although not realized in themselves, is able to operation of these principles, as they lie at the foundation of all human improvement, lie also at the foundation of all the institutions of government. Let any one try, if he can, to worship ignorance and depravity: he will find it is impossible, even if he is himself ignorant and depraved. Let any one in the most obscure walks of life inquire what has induced him, by daily toil and labor, to better his physical condition: he will find that there has been a constant, though vague desire, to get beyond the narrow circle in which his physical wants are enclosed; hence the strong desire, the homely pride of the uncultivated, to lift their offspring, by education, above their own level. 3d. Without pretending to assert that there is no condition of society in which the two difficulties I have mentioned cannot be reconciled, we may at least affirm, that if there is a country in which knowledge and property are widely dispersed, in which consequently private and public interests are nearly identified, and the selfish affections do not swallow up the man, the problem can hardly be considered as insoluble. For, conditions of society which differ from each other, cannot afford the same results; if they did, they would not be different, but similar states of society. Spain and Portugal, Naples and Russia, exhibit a social organization entirely variant from that of the United States or Great Britain. It is only by ruminating on the things in which they agree, and leaving out those in which they differ, that the judgment is confused. The institutions of the two last countries are obliged to be different, in character, from those of the first, by a principle no stronger than that which links the effect to its cause.

In what way is public opinion formed? The groundwork is to be found in the principle I have already noticed: the standard of action which every one, high and low, forms to himself, and which always rises higher than his own conduct. Hence it is not true, that none but the enlightened contribute to the formation of public opinion. The uneducated have a share in it, for all the fundamental notions of morality are as strongly impressed upon them as upon the superior classes; and the hereditary monarch is visibly influenced, though never directly governed, by the opinions which pervade his peasantry. But public opinion, when it comes to be applied to the affairs of an extensive, wealthy and densely peopled community, becomes a very complicated organ; for although it reposes upon a few simple principles, these become greatly diversified in a highly civilized state. In such a state, public opinion may be defined to be the judgment which is formed concerning the rights, duties, and interests of the population in relation to the government, of the government to the population, and of the citizens to one another. If there is great diversity in the condition of the various classes, those rights, duties and interests will be seen under very different aspects, and there cannot, properly speaking, be any such thing as a public opinion. The term public reason will be employed to denote that there is another tribunal of still higher authority, although it may reflect the sentiments of a comparatively small part of the population. If, on the other hand, knowledge and property are pretty equally distributed, public opinion will not diverge materially from what is denominated the public reason. The diffusion of property alone may have this effect. For what is the consequence of a diffusion of property? It is to produce habits of business, industry, judgment and reflection in the management of property; and the very means by which private comfort is attained, contribute to discipline the understandings of the great majority of the population.

Notwithstanding these views, the subject still seems to be full of difficulty. The beings we meet on the highway, the operatives, common laborers, and menial servants, seem to be incapacitated by nature, or by circumstances as strong as nature, from forming any the most general notions of the end of government, even so far as their own interests are concerned. But these beings have, since the foundation of the American commonwealth, actually taken part in the election of the executive, and of both branches of the legislatures. The American legislatures are all elected by universal suffrage, or by a rule nearly equivalent to it. On entering these assemblies, an unpracticed eye will be startled with the boorishness and apparent ignorance of many of the members; a calm observer will see nothing inconsistent with a skillful and orderly management of the public business, and a well informed one will recollect that the composition of these bodies is infinitely better than was that of the provincial estates, or even of the states general of France, and and better than that of the English Parliament before the commencement of the eighteenth century. That there are great differences in the capacities of the members who compose the American legislatures, is certain. How, then, is business conducted with regularity? How are laws passed to meet the complicated exigencies of such wealthy and populous communities? That they are so framed, is matter of notoriety. For if we examine the codes of those states, whether criminal, civil, or political, we will find that they make a more wise, exact and judicious provision for the wants of all classes, than is to be found anywhere else. If these codes were imitations of those of older nations, the difficulty would not be removed; for great skill would be requisite in making the proper selection. But when it is considered that there are great departures from any existing code, and that these are every year becoming wider, that experience is the foundation on which these laws are built, the difficulty is increased. He who can collect experience into a body, and decipher its true meaning, is the wisest man. If we admit, then, that a considerable proportion of those who compose these legislatures, are incompetent to frame the laws, would it be an extraordinary circumstance that the smaller number who are able should execute the task. Does any one at all acquainted with human nature expect to find a legislative body, however constituted, materially varying from this description. It is the character of both the English Chambers, the Lords, and Commons ; that is, it is the character of those very bodies, which might seem worthy of imitation, if the elective principle which prevails in a republic was abandoned, not one fourth of the English Peers, or Commons, is able to grapple with the perplexing questions of foreign or internal policy which are submitted to them.

It appears, then, that there is a principle of human nature, by which, when a number of persons are assembled to transact any important business, the task will be voluntarily yielded to those who have most skill and ability ; although it will by no means follow, that the presence of those who are deficient in these qualities can be dispensed with.

The application of these views to the electors—the class who choose the public officers, is obvious. The same result will take place as in a legislative body. Those who are incapable of forming a clear estimate of the part they are called upon to perform, will be counselled and controlled by those of more intelligence, although it must not be inferred that the privilege should be confined to the last. Parents advise and guide their children, but the conduct of the parent, as well as of the child, is better on that very account. It is true, the electors are not collected into one body, like a legislative assembly, and cannot act so directly upon one another. But they are parcelled into families, neighborhoods, and townships, and this presents the same, or even a more advantageous mode of communication. Admitting, then, that among the common people the proportion of those who are capable of voting understandingly is only one to ten, that one will exert a marked influence. And how is it with the superior ranks : the proportion is not greater ; for if an humble condition of life rears rough and ignorant men, wealth rears feeble and effeminate ones. Thus the majority in each class is powerfully acted upon by a small number. That the superior knowledge of the few will sometimes be turned to sinister purposes is certain ; but this is a vice common to both classes, and does not interfere with the views I have taken.

If the structure of society is such as to permit the establishment of representative government, no reason absolutely satisfactory can be assigned, why some public officers should be elected by direct suffrage, while others are chosen by a close body. If the principle of responsibility is the hinge on which republican government turns, it does not appear clear why a thorough application should be made of it in some instances, and an imperfect one in others. If the judges should be elected by a pre-existing body, it would not seem improper that the executive aud legislative should be elected in the same way.

It is curious to trace the changes which have taken place in the appointing power in the United States. At first it was conferred upon the governor alone, as it is at the present day in Delaware. The next step was to vest it in the governor and council; and a third was to entrust it to the governor and senate. The taking the power from the governor was the commencement of a very important revolution. It broke the connection between him and the various civil officers of the state. It discarded the idea that the appointing power was an attribute of the executive magistrate. The transition was gradual: a council was created, who divided the power with the executive. As the council was created for this express purpose, it may be said to have produced a new organization of the executive authority, and not merely a new disposition of the appointing power. The effect was to create a plural executive. In process of time, the power underwent a further change: it was distributed among a greater number; and this was important, as it gradually paved the way for more decisive changes, which the structure of society rendered necessary. The next step accordingly was to confer the power upon the governor and senate. This was a more decisive change; for it divided the power between the governor and one branch of the legislature. It repudiated the maxim, that the power was an attribute of the executive, whether the the executive is a singular or a plural body. The reason of the change is to be found in the fact, that in America, after the revolution, written constitutions were adopted. Writing teaches men to analyze their ideas, and causes their speculative opinions to correspond more exactly with the results of experience. By no device, could the authority of the governor of a state whose institutions were democratic, be made to resemble that of an hereditary magistrate. The legislature, became at once the most important, and imposing of the three departments. The power of appointment, was not in the first instance, devolved upon the whole body, but only upon one branch. The successive steps, were not a departure from this design, but in furtherance of it, and prepared the way for its final accomplishment. But who can teach us, how to create a governor and senate, which shall be a thoroughly upright, and impartial appointing power. Whether composed of illiterate, or educated men, it would be subject to the vice of intrigue. The only approach to such an institution, would be a body so permanent, and composed of members so affluent, as to render them inaccessible to the solicitations of unworthy candidates. But it would be only an approach, for no sooner was the system set in motion, than the body would degenerate into an aristocratic cabal ; an interest separate from that of the community would grow up, and offices would be disposed of by a system of favoritism. Representatives will act more circumspect than their constituents, only when the trust confided to them, does not present a powerful conflict between private and public interest. Do what we will, we cannot raise men so high by wealth, or station, as to render them wise, and virtuous ; but we may easily render them the reverse.

The third step which was taken, was to devolve the power upon the entire legislature. This completed the design, which we may suppose to have been originally contemplated, which was to despoil the executive, not in part, but in whole of the attribute. The various civil magistrates then ceased to be his agents, and hence forward, held by a tenure as independent as his own. But the system, although relieved of one inconsistency, fell into another equally glaring. If the appointing power is not an appropriate part of the executive authority, it is as little so of the legislative. By wresting the power from the governor, and lodging it successively with bodies more and more numerous, the selections were apparently at least of a more popular character, and an approach was made to that plan, to which everything was irresistibly tending, to wit : a direct appointment by the people.

The chief objection to all the plans which preceded, is that they deprive us of the most effectual means of training the popular mind to self government. Experience, personal experience of the importance of correct appointments, of the connection between them and the public weal, is indispensable to fulfil not in theory merely, but in practice, the design of representative government. We desire to have a disinterested, and upright impartial appointing power. To procure that, is to procure everything. And we immediately set about devising a scheme for excluding the bulk of the population; in other words, we exclude those for whom government is made. In some conditions of society, this may be necessary; in others, the gradual transition from an appointment by a close body to a larger number, may facilitate the final transference of the power to the people themselves. But it is supposed, that it is impossible to get beyond one or two stages in this transition. The impossibility arises from perseverance in the plan of close appointment. By adhering to it inflexibly, we decree that it cannot be otherwise; we deprive ourselves of the only means of getting out of it. All knowledge is gained by experience: even that of a strictly speculative character, is confusedly apprehended, unless we apply our own faculties to the subjects we undertake to deal with. In the affairs of government, the proposition is true without any limitation. If the citizens have not a direct voice in the appointment of the public agents, they form a very inadequate notion of the purpose which those agents are intended to answer. They hear that certain functionaries are necessary, in order to administer public affairs; and they believe it, only because they are told so. They conceive government to be a species of self moving machine; and although they are told that it is established to preside over their interests, they apprehend this only in a vague and general way. Appointments are made, but as they are not made by themselves, they conceive that they have only an accidental connection with their interests, and that they have no control over that connection. Thus admitting that popular appointments are practicable, they cannot be made so, unless the power is brought into exercise. The danger of acting precipitately is not so great as is imagined. In a state habituated to free institutions, it is very slight. It might be otherwise in one which did not possess this advantage. In the former, experience would afford the rule; in the last, the rule would be the subject of conjecture. An enlightened ruler of one of the German principalities, visited the United States about 1825, and was so struck with the reasonableness and good sense of confidence to the people, the choice of those who make the laws, that he introduced an elective assembly into his dominions. His people protested, that they were incompetent to the task. He persevered, however, well understanding no doubt, that the difficulties and exigencies of human life, are the true school of human conduct. In the United States, where a great fund of experience has been acquired, I would, if necessary, force the appointment of the judges upon the people. I may have misgivings, but they are no greater than I have for the result of any human contrivance, which has not been tested by actual experiment.

It appears that in the United States, the plan of electing the judges by a close body, was retained long after it had been abandoned in the election of the executive and administrative officers. There must be a reason for this. Jurists are accustomed to distinguish between the question of fact and the question of right. An understanding of the first may shed light upon the last. In the American provinces, there was no order of nobility, with which to compose a senate; there were no materials for creating an hereditary executive. The country, therefore, very naturally slid, after no long time, into a popular election of both. But the judges had always held for life; and this circumstance withdrew them from the operation of the rule. The tenure for life had never been combined with a popular choice. The notion of responsibility is so closely connected with that of popular election, that the moment the last is introduced, it is united with a tenure for a term of years. The irregularity in the system, continued in consequence of the extreme difficulty of overcoming the prejudice, that the tenure of the judges must be for life. The governors had been generally appointed by the king; but there was now no king, and the senate had never been an hereditary body. Both chambers of the legislature, therefore, were elected by the people. The governor was, with some exceptions, elected in the same manner; not universally, because a vague notion still lingered in some of the states, that a distinction must be made between his election and that of the legislative body.

His appointment had originally been different, and this circumstance contributed to keep alive the distinction. At present there is but one state in which he is chosen by the legislature.

I have alluded to the remark of a very eminent statesman, (Lord Brougham) that the appointments to the bench in England, were unexceptionable. But the same statesman, in his celebrated speech on the reformation of the law, declares that "it is notorious, whenever a question comes before the tribunals, upon a prosecution for libel, or any other political matter, the counsel at their meeting take for granted, that they can tell pretty accurately the leaning of the the court, and predict exactly which way the consultation of the judges will terminate." I doubt whether a like character can be given of the administration of justice, in the higher tribunals of the United States, in those whose jurisdiction resembles that of the kings bench and common pleas. And I am persuaded that where this habitual bias exists, it must more or less, affect the decision of those civil controversies, in which the parties are of different political opinions. The same very able statesman speaks of "the incompetent judges," and "the slovenly administration of justice," as these are spoken of in the United States, in reference to some of the judges of the subordinate courts. In England, until 1809, no judge could hold court in the county in which he resided. In the United States, where no such prohibition ever existed, the judges often voluntarily decline sitting in their own county, lest an unfavorable influence might be exercised upon them. The "black book" confirms the observations of Lord Brougham. It informs us, that a tory ministry never selects a judge from the whig party, nor a whig ministry one from the tory party. This, the author remarks, "tends to lower the character of the judges in public estimation, by clearly evincing that politics, as well as legal fitness, have a share in ministerial promotion. It also instils into the minds of expectant judges, and of men already on the bench, a party feeling, fatal to strict justice, on political questions." An election for a limited time, diminishes the temptation to run into the excesses of party. The prize is not of sufficient magnitude to overcome the natural sentiments of justice, which, in order to have full play, only require that there should be no powerful provocative to depart from them. The judge elected for a term of years, balances in his mind the uncertain advantage of retaining his place, against the permanent advantage of maintaining his character. It does not follow, that he will be re-elected, even if his party should continue in power. The principle of rotation in office, never fails to exercise great influence in a democratic community, and it reduces the tenure of office to a mere contingency. If the public officers were appointed for life, the prejudices which they originally contracted, would cling to them without any countervailing motives to moderate them. Thus an election by the people, a tenure for a term of years, and rotation in office, which might be supposed to push the democratic principle to its furthest extreme, are the most efficacious means for restraining its disorders, and for giving to public opinion a more just, active, and pervading influence. The legal ability which fits a man for the bench, is very capable of being estimated by the generality of mankind. The capacity of the physician is much more a secret, and yet no one, in any condition of life, is at a loss to employ one eminent in that profession. Many may be unable to pay the best. But who the best are is a matter of notoriety in every town or neighborhood in which they reside. And for more obvious reasons, this is the case of the lawyer.

As the connection between the interests of the great bulk of the population, and the behaviour of all public officers, is very close, it would be a grand desideratum to establish a thorough intercourse between candidates and constituents. Men of elevated character, now recoil from any thing which might seem to have the appearance of soliciting for office. But I observe in some parts of the country, a corresponding disposition on the part of the people, an aversion to be caressed, and tampered with by the demagogue. "I do not know (said a mechanic in one of our southern cities) what these candidates proposed to themselves, in paying such assiduous court to us the people. It will not deter us from exercising our judgment, but it may deprive them of our vote." I predict that the reaction of public men on the one hand, and of popular sentiment on the other, will give rise to a more healthful public opinion than formerly existed, and that the intercourse of the two classes will be of a more rational character. This would complete the security for the preservation of free institutions.

We may refer to an example, which has only a partial application to the United States, but which is not the less instructive on that account. The remarkable solidity of the Venetian government, enduring as it did for a thousand years, is attributable to a circumstance which was peculiar to it among the other Italian states. The Venetian nobles engrossed the whole power, but they had no possessions on the mainland, no castles and strong fortresses in the country. They were shut up in a city built upon islands, in close contact, therefore, and under the constant observation of the other classes. They were unable to keep on foot large armies, to wreak their vengeance on each other, or to battle with the plebeians, as the nobles of Milan, Genoa, and Florence, were accustomed to do. The disadvantage of their position, led them to cultivate the good will of the plebeians, who were accordingly governed with more equity and moderation than in any other Italian state. Very similar causes, although operating on a vast and comprehensive scale, give stability to the American republics. There is no political aristocracy, no baronies, no military retainers; the civil aristocracy are mixed indiscriminately, or, to repeat the expression, are shut up with the other classes, and are both constrained, and disposed to consult their interests.

A property qualification for office has been retained in some of the American states, even where it has been abolished in regard to the electors. In the Athenian constitution, this species of qualification was at one period dispensed with, except where the office involved a pecuniary responsibility. In the United States, the rule is reversed. Property qualification is in some states required, to entitle to a seat in the legislative body, when it is not demanded of the administrative officers. But in the place of that qualification, another requisite, much more effectual, is substituted. The officer must give security for his fidelity in office. This reconciles the claims of the rich and the poor, and at the same time attracts to the public service the talents and industry of all orders of men.

In England, knights of the shire originally represented the counties, in the house of commons. They were the lesser barons—in other words, an inferior order of nobility. And although this chamber is no longer modeled upon that plan, a property qualification is still required of candidates. But, by the act of 1838, this may be either of personal or real property.

It is a great objection to a high property qualification, that it confines the competition for office to the rich exclusively. The rich only can afford to practice bribery; and hence the English elections have been corrupt to a degree utterly unknown in the United States. Thus, this remarkable consequence, and one not at all calculated upon, has taken place, that in those countries where the eligibility to office, as well as the electoral franchise, have been most restricted, the greatest corruption and licentiousness have prevailed; and where both have been thrown open to nearly the whole population, the elections are the most orderly, and the most free from sinister influence. The rich will forever put forth the lower qualities of human nature, unless they are controlled by those who are placed in circumstances of less temptation. A rich man going to attend an election where none but rich men can elect, or be elected, is like the twenty thousand nobles who used to march upon Warsaw to choose a chief magistrate. The extreme variety which characterizes the pursuits of the Americans, the diffusion of education, the unobstructed intercourse of all classes, and above all, the operation of the institutions themselves, disperse knowledge in every direction, and render the property qualification useless.

The duration of the term of office is a matter of still graver consideration. It is indispensable to the faithful administration of the government, that responsibility should be a vital and active principle, not a mere form. And the only way to accomplish this is by guarding against a too permanent tenure of office. Those are the wisest institutions which render it the interest of the officer to consult the public good. A system which succeeds in reconciling these two apparently contradictory things, is well calculated to beget habits of rectitude and good conduct, which a mere conviction of the propriety of such habits would be insufficient to instill. And it then becomes as difficult to lay down these habits as it was originally to take them up. Doubtless there is an intrinsic connection between morality and self interest. All the seeming exceptions to this rule arise either from some disturbing influence to the conduct of the individual who is called upon to act, and to which he is not a party, or else they arise from self interest not being properly understood. That scheme of government, therefore, which endeavors as well as it can to combine duty with interest, conforms best to the original design of our nature, and tends greatly to the preservation of public morality.

It may be supposed, if the duration of office is short, that it will lead to instability in the public councils. But there is such a thing as too great stability, as well as too great instability, in government. This may seem to be a paradox, and therefore requires explanation. A government, in order to pursue any plan of public policy with constancy and vigor, must be invested with power. But power is of two kinds, personal and political, and the last may be raised to so high a degree as to be transformed into the former—

to become, in other words, a mere personal authority in the chief of the state. Nevertheless all public measures will be characterized by the greatest stability and uniformity. There is more simplicity in the management of public affairs, fewer cross purposes to overcome, where government is at liberty to consult its own separate interests, than where it is employed in administering the vast and complicated interests of a free and intelligent people. In one sense the governments of Russia, Prussia, and Austria, possess this property of stability in a pre-eminent degree. The monarchs of these countries wield an independent authority. No obstacle stands in the way of their designs so long as they keep within tolerably reasonable bounds. There is a singleness of plan, an unity of purpose, belonging to such governments, which cannot in the nature of things be possessed by one into which the popular element is infused. Thus in Great Britain, where the political power of the community is shared to a considerable extent by representatives of the people, public measures vary more than they do in the governments of eastern Europe. And yet, in another and still higher sense of the word, the government of Great Britain does undoubtedly possess more stability than any European government of ancient or modern times. The stability of power and the stability of the government are, therefore, by no means the same thing. The changes of administration, and the changes of public men, in Great Britain and the United States, are more frequent than any where else, and yet the institutions possess greater stability than do those of any other country; and they possess it in consequence of and not in spite of these changes.

The enjoyment of an independent authority, by public rulers, has been the principle incentive to all the criminal enterprizes which have ever afflicted society. From time immemorial, power has been firmly secured in the kings and nobility, who have ruled the European states; and the consequence is, that from the Christian era, down to the peace of 1815, Europe was the theater of the most atrocious and sanguinary wars. Since this last period, the popular power, the real effective public opinion in Great Britain, has at least doubled. The public weal has therefore greater firmness and consistency, notwithstanding the changes of administration have been more frequent than before. If the President of the United States, and the members of the senate, were hereditary officers, and the house of representatives elected for a long term, it is more than probable that America would have embarked in frequent wars, when experience has demonstrated that the prosperity of the country demands that peace should be its permanent policy. And the vigor with which warlike enterprizes would have been prosecuted, would have impressed upon the government precisely that character of stability which is so much admired by unthinking individuals. A system which was even productive of considerable instability in the ordinary measures of government, would be greatly preferable to this. It would protect the state from infinitely worse mischiefs. The Americans, like most people who enjoy an uncommon share of prosperity, frequently complain of the fluctuation in the public measures. They complain, because they are not able to grasp all the minor as well as the more important advantages of fortune.

The compensation afforded to the public officers should be sufficient to insure competent ability, and should not go beyond this. High salaries create a separate interest in the office, independent of the interests of the people. On the other hand, low salaries render officers careless in the discharge of their duties, and the people, themselves, become gradually reconciled to a feeble and bungling administration of the laws, when they know that the reproach lies at their own door. The legislator therefore must bave sufficient judgment to strike a mean between the two things. Moderate salaries are one means of enforcing responsibility. And as this is the hinge on which free institutions turn, it is fit that we should avail ourselves of every device which is calculated to give strength to it. Moreover, moderate salaries enlist in the service of the state the abilities of persons in the middle walks of like. As the rich can best afford to dispense with a high reward, it might be supposed that this plan would cause them to be the principal candidates for office. But such is not the case. Moderate salaries chill and enfeeble their ambition; they do not gratify the ardent and impatient desires of the rich. But they contribute to raise solid usefulness from obscurity, and the officer who obtains an important post, finds himself disabled in every effort he makes to leap beyond the bounds of his legitimate authority. In the United States far the greater part of all public employments are filled by men in moderate circumstances.

The number, as well as the nature, of the public offices in a republic, will depend upon the fact, whether it constitutes one aggregate community, or has the form of a confederate government. I say the form, because in every extensive and populous state, it would be of the highest advantage to imitate the plan of domestic or local jurisdictions, even though the government is not composed of states which were originally distinct and independent.

A territorial division of the state, of some sort, is an arrangement known to every civilized nation. Even the most centralized government cannot dispense with it, since it is the only way by which the public authority can be present everywhere at the same time. The principle on which the division was originally founded was very different from what it is now. Most of the European states were at one time divided into feudal baronies. These inferior governments have long since disappeared. They are now merged into consolidated governments. But other divisions have been substituted in their place, whether known as departments, circles, or shires. These districts sometimes occupy the same ground which was once marked out as the domain of a feudal sovereignty. Accident has determined their extent, but not their use. When the authority of the central government was feeble, these inferior jurisdictions usurped nearly all power. Now that that authority is strong, they serve to convey it through all parts of the country.

But the principle on which this division depends is very different in different countries, even at the present day. In some the power which is set in motion in these smaller compartments flows from the central government as its source. In others the central authority is itself the creature of the lesser governments, and these continue, after the establishment of the former, to exercise a larger share of the power which originally belonged to them. The United States afford the most perfect example of this plan. Accidental circumstances gave rise to it. The states were independent sovereignties when the federal constitution was formed; so that this precise arrangement cannot be adopted where all the parts of society are melted into one homogeneous community. But there is no more interesting problem in government than to determine how far it is practicable to introduce the principle of the plan into all communities, no matter whether they have the confederate form or not. Not merely because this arrangement leads to a more convenient and efficient administration of public affairs, but because it is doubtful whether the maintenance of free institutions in any state of considerable extent does not absolutely depend upon it. The establishment of local jurisdictions gives a new direction to the whole course of legislation. Civil government is only a generalization of the principles on which the affairs of society are conducted. But generalization may be pushed to such an extent as to make us lose sight of very important interests which, although they are themselves capable of generalization, are yet incapable of being ranged under the same class. By effecting a separation of those interests which are common to the whole society, from those which are local or sectional, these last are brought distinctly into view—they are forced upon the public attention.

In most countries legislators have occupied themselves exclusively with those large and ponderous questions which further the aggrandizement of the nation rather than its solid prosperity. Even the emperor Charlemagne was impressed with this fact, and gave vent to the frank declaration that it was impossible for one central government to superintend the affairs of an extensive community. Princes are forward enough to tell the truth when they are not placed in a situation which obliges them to act upon it. But what was true during so early a period as the ninth century, when society was everywhere in a rude condition, must be still more true in the nineteenth century. For the affairs of every civilized state have become so complicated, and so minute, that they cannot be administered with the requisite skill and ability by a central legislature merely. Convenience alone would suggest the propriety of a territorial division, and the creation of domestic jurisdictions, if not as extensive as those of Scotland and Ireland before their union with England, yet much more so than the departments of France.

But what at first may be a rule of convenience leads directly to consequences of still greater importance. It lays the foundation of the great principle of the distribution of power, and reconciles two apparently opposite qualities—popular freedom, with vigor and efficiency in the government. No matter how popular the mode of electing the public officers is, yet if in the United States there were no domestic jurisdictions to preside over the local interests, the government would be republican in form only.

I know nothing which is more calculated to arrest the attention of the philosophical inquirer, as well as of the lover of freedom, than the new character which has been impressed upon the business of legislation in the United States. The state governments are confined exclusively to the care of the local interests; and this complete sequestration of those interests, from everything which appertains to the national administration, causes them to be more thoroughly studied and appreciated than could otherwise possibly be the case. There is no security that legislation will be for the people, unless it is by and through the people. Nor any security that it will be by and through the people, unless the subjects of legislation are brought so near as to be matter of immediate interest and constant observation.

The legislatures of the American states have applied themselves more diligently and effectively to the care of the substantial interests of the people, than it has been in the power of a single legislature in any other country to do. If there is ground of complaint, it is in consequence of the excess of legislation. But it is impossible to have enough of any good thing, without having a superfluity. Experience, which becomes a great instructor, wherever the system of representation is thoroughly introduced, will assuredly correct this defect.

We will suppose that, on an average, one month will be sufficient for the legislative sessions of the states; and that five months will be consumed by the national legislature. Thirty-four months then are required, in order to legislative advantageously for the national and domestic interests; a period nearly three times the length of the year. In Great Britain, with a population considerably larger than that of the United States, parliament sits on an average only six months. If we make a further allowance for the unnecessary consumption of time by the American legislature, and for the fact, that the United States is in a state of greater progress than any other country, it is still evident that the time employed by the British legislature is altogether too short to permit of an effective administration of the public interests in the sense in which the term is now understood. If the country were more extensive, and the population greater, six months would still seem sufficient. Necessity would compress the immense mass of public business into that short space; and the public mind would become habituated to it as the natural and reasonable period. The defect arises from having a single legislature to preside over the interests of twenty-seven millions of people. Nor will the defect ever be apparent, so long as the system continues to exist. The human mind possesses a wonderful ductility in accommodating itself to any set of habits which have been fastened upon it. Thirty years ago the American people were thoroughly persuaded that they got along well enough without canals, and without the employment of steam, by land or water. And it was with the greatest reluctance that they embarked in the plan of internal improvements. The first project of a canal, on an extensive scale, was literally carried through the legislature by storm, amid the most virulent and formidable opposition. And it is not improbable, if the position in which the American states were placed after the revolution had not given rise to the confederate form of government, that the public would have been completely reconciled to the establishment of a single legislature, where thirty now exist.

There is nothing peculiar to America rendering so much more time necessary to the successful administration of the public business than in any other highly civilized community, unless it is the single circumstance of its free institutions. For although society is in a state of progression, yet it is so only in consequence of these institutions. There is no country which contains more wealth, a more thorough civilization, and more general intelligence. It is then in the condition of one of the oldest, instead of one of the newest, nations on the earth. And it may be said, with great truth, that there is more room for progress and improvement in every state of continental Europe, if there were only the ability and opportunity to set in motion. In Russia and Denmark, the legislative body is nothing more than a council nominated by the king. No doubt these councils seem to transact all the requisite business, and the machinery of government goes on regularly from year to year, without any great feeling of inconvenience. Nevertheless the disproportion, in point of efficiency, between those mock legislative bodies and the British parliament, is nearly as great as between the last and the combined legislatures of the United States.

There may be an inconsistency in erecting a government for one aggregate community, and then morseling the public authority by distributing it among a number of lesser governments. There is no inconsistency, however, if the plan is the result of the natural economy of society. The principle on which it is founded may be discerned everywhere, even in those governments where it is intended that th national power should be the most firmly consolidated. The departments of France, the corporate cities of Great Britain, are in reality lesser governments, inclosed within a supreme government. And the only question is, whether the principle may not be advantageously pursued much further, wherever constitutional goverment exists, without reference to the fact, whether the state is one, or is composed of distinct members.

A people who constitute an undivided community, would possess this advantage over the plan adopted in the United States : that the creation of domestic jurisdictions, being the act of the whole, instead of the parts, there would be less danger that they would exercise a disturbing influence upon the central authority. One is so much accustomed to consider the American government as a system "sui generis," as deriving its meaning and utility from the originally independent existence of the parts, that it is supposed no system bearing an analogy to it is practicable in any other community. The mind is so habituated to consider cause and effect in the precise order in which they first presented themselves, that it becomes difficult to break through the association, and to make application of our experience, where the principle is the same, and the collateral circumstances only are different.

It is plain enough, that the independent character of the states could not be preserved, if they had not power to superintend the domestic interests. But these interests do not acquire the character of domestic ones, in consequence of the federal form of the government. The same reasons for regarding them in that light would have existed, if no such government had been created. In other words, if the American commonwealth had originally constituted one homogeneous community, the central authority would have been entirely inadequate to the management of them, unless powers not exactly the same, but resembling those which now exist, were distributed among a set of local jurisdictions. The effect of he progress of civilization is not to diminish, but to increase immeasurably, the whole business of society ; and unless this is skillfully and judiciously divided among a class of lesser governments, the institutions, however carefully modelled at first, must ultimately sink beneath the immense power condensed in a single government. The example then which America holds out is chiefly valuable, not because it proves the utility of the confederate form of government;

but because it teaches us, that in order to maintain free institutions in their true spirit, it is necessary to make an extensive distribution of the powers of society ; and that without any regard to the circumstances which give rise to the formation of the government. It presents a great problem in political philosophy, and not merely an incidental question in the history of one particular set of institutions.

Even in the consolidated government of France, long after the extinction of its feudal sovereignties, as late indeed as the reign of Louis XV, a plan, in many respects resembling the American, once prevailed. The provincial legislatures, or particular estates, as they were called, to distinguish them from the general estates, or national congress, possessed very considerable local powers. Independently of the inferior civilization of France when compared with that of the United States, at the period when this system existed, and which necessarily prevented it from working any thing like as well, there were several vices attendant upon it. It is only necessary to refer to two : 1st. The very imperfect responsibility of the deputies to those provincial legislatures to their constituents. 2d. The power which they acquired, after the abolition of the states general, if, indeed they did not exercise it before, of granting supplies for the whole kingdom, and not merely such as were necessary to defray the expenses of the provincial governments.

The same plan of local governments existed in the ten Flemish provinces, when they were a part of the Austrian empire ; and it is even more firmly established in both the Dutch and Belgian monarchies, notwithstanding the limited territory of each of them. That the system in these two last instances does not perform its movements with any thing like the same precision as in the United States, is not the fault of the system, but arises from a defective basis of representation, and from the imperfect responsibility of the provincial officers to the local population.

There is no foundation for the opinion that the existence of these domestic jurisdictions weakens the force of the central authority. On the contrary, this last is less embarrassed in the administration of the national interests. That the formation of a system of lesser governments constitutes a deduction from the whole mass of powers, which would otherwise be deposited with the central government, is evident. For that is precisely the purpose for which they are created. But as the sphere within which the former move is distinctly defined, and the duties allotted to it are more simple than before, it is enabled to act with more promptitude and energy. Like the man who is intent on accomplishing some important design, and whose attention is distracted by a variety of other pursuits, by ridding himself of all care for the last, he can prosecute the former without interruption.

A central government, armed with extensive powers, stands much more in need of checks, than of provocatives, to the exercise of its authority. And if the establishment of local jurisdictions gives greater force to public opinion, and raises up obstacles to the exertion of too much power, it is not the less valuable on that account. I have heard many persons express admiration of the wonderful energy with which the British government prosecuted the wars which grew out of the French revolution. But if the expense had been defrayed by taxes, and loans not resorted to, the people would have seen that their substantial interests were placed in direct opposition to the enterprises of the government. It was only because this fact was hidden from their view, that those wars were sustained with such amazing enthusiasm. The just fear of unpopularity would have prevented public men from embarking in such an unnecessary contest. And although this fear would have been regarded by some persons of very high notions as crippling the power of the government, yet it would only have crippled it in order to make the people strong. The same obstacle has constantly existed to the prosecution of similar enterprises by the American government, and the simple effect has been to accelerate the national power and prosperity to a degree absolutely unprecedented. And yet in a necessary war, there is no government which would be supported with so much enthutiasm, and would put forth so much power, as that of the United States. But more than ninety-nine out of a hundred of the wars which have ever taken place, have been unjust and unprofitable wars. And if the machinery of a system of local governments contributes indirectly to diffuse the popular will through every part of the country, and disarms the central government of the power to do mischief, it is not the less deserving of our admiration on that account.

But there is another view of the great advantages of that system, which is not apt to be thought of: the maintenance of the public authority at home—the inculcating a general obedience to the laws, is the principal object—the final aim indeed—of civil government. If that is attained, everything else will go right. But the system of local governments contributes directly to the promotion of this end. It brings the authority of the laws nearer to every one. The government which undertakes to preserve order is not removed to a great distance—is not regarded with an unfriendly eye—as if it were constantly intermeddling with the interests of a people with whom it had no direct sympathy. On the contrary, each individual feels as if he were surrounded by an authority, in the creation of which he himself bore a part, and which yet, some how or other, is more vigilent, and active, and imperative, than any other.

Thus, as the family and the school train men in order to turn them out in the world afterward, so the domestic governments create a species of moral discipline on a still more extended scale. They educate their own people to obedience to the laws, and then deliver them over to the national government. The authority of the last, instead of being weakened, is redoubled by this preparatory discipline.

Another advantage of the plan of local governments is, that it prevents geographical parties from exerting an inordinate influence in the national councils. These parties will inevitably make their appearance in every country of considerable extent. It is not desirable to extinguish them, but only to place them at a distance, where their reasonings will be heard, and their passions not felt. By creating local jurisdictions, geographical parties are enclosed within geographical limits, and are not brought into eternal collision at the heart of the government. Although such parties are actually found on the floor of the American congress, yet if the state governments did not exist, they would have displayed a front infinitely more formidable; and would have either jeopardized the integrity of the union, or the existence of free institutions. At present a vast amount of legislative power is withdrawn from the national assembly, and circumscribed within bounds so clearly defined, as to be not only harmless, but to produce a skillful, and orderly administration of the public interests. Although Great Britain is of very small extent when compared with the United States, yet if, when the Scotch union took place, a compact had not been formed, securing to Scotland its ecclesiastical and civil institutions forever, geographical parties would instantly have appeared, and would have had an influence fatal to the public prosperity. Although the separate legislature of Scotland was abolished, the effect of the union was to declare all its former acts to be permanent; and thus to compel all future legislation to take a direction comformable to them. It was the next thing to perpetuating the existence of the Scotch parliament. For want of this wise precaution, when the union with Ireland* took place, a formidable geographical party has been kept alive in that island, to the great annoyance of the peace of both conntries; and producing heart burnings which never can be cured, until England consents, or is compelled, to be just to Ireland.

What amount of power should be deposited with the local jurisdictions, where the confederate form of government is not established, is a question as novel as it is interesting. Doubtless, it would be necessary to adopt some medium between the comprehensive legislation of the American states, and the meager authority which is exercised by the French departments. The American states are complete governments within themselves, having unlimited power of taxation, except as to imposts on commerce, with an authority equally extensive over the whole field of civil and criminal jurisprudence. Education, private and public corporations, internal improvements, all lie within the scope of their jurisdiction. They have a written constitution, a regular legislative assembly, an executive magistrate, and a corps of administrative officers, together with a judicial system unsurpassed by that of any other country. No one would desire to make any alteration in this admirable plan of government, for it has not only contributed to a most wise administration of public affairs: it has done more, it has hastened the march of civilization. If it were impossible, in the case of a consolidated republic, to obtain the medium I have suggested, it would be better to adopt this system. But that there is such a medium is clear from the examples I have referred to, of the particular es-

---

*The articles of union between England and Ireland did, *in terms*, guarantee to the last her laws. But there were in truth no Irish laws to guarantee. As early as the reign of Henry VII, all the statutes made in England were declared of force in Ireland, and from that period to 1782, no subsequent law could even be proposed to the Irish parliament, without the consent of the English privy council. This last disability was removed only eighteen years before the union.

tates of France, and the provincial legislatures in the Belgian and Dutch governments; examples which, however imperfect, are nevertheless highly instructive, inasmuch as they present the existence of the system in monarchical governments, to which they are much less adapted than to countries where free institutions prevail. It is clear, also, from the various plans which were proposed in the convention which framed the American constitution; some of which seem to have proceeded upon the idea, that the United States composed one aggregate community, and were modeled upon the hypothesis.

A certain number of deputies then will be sent to the national, and to each of the local, legislatures. As regards the first, shall the whole country constitute one electoral district, or shall each of the local divisions compose one, the people voting by general ticket; or shall these divisions be subdivided into districts, each containing the population which entitles it to one member. The first plan may be dismissed as absurd. It has never been thought of, even in those European monarchies where the principle of representation has been introduced. The electors would be completely confounded in looking over a vast extent of country, for several hundred individuals, whom each was to vote for, and no choice could be understandingly made. The central government, or its managers, would choose for them.

But even if a selection in the genuine sense could be made, there would be no representation of the minority. The party in the majority would wield the power of the commonwealth without control, without the corrective influence, which an antagonist party is so well calculated to exert. The minority might approach to within one or two hundred of the majority, among two or three millions of votes, yet the last would elect every member. Even in the consolidated governments of Great Britain and France, therefore, the country is divided into electoral districts, which is a plain acknowledgment that, even where there are no local governments, there should be local representatives. The justice and utility of recognizing in some mode or other the local interests, is forced upon society, even where the form of government seems to forbid the idea. The arrangement which nature makes of human affairs sometimes rides over all the laws which are intended to counteract it.

With regard to the two other modes of election, by general ticket in each of the great local divisions, or by electoral districts carved out of those divisions, the reasoning which has already been employed, is equally applicable to show that the latter is greatly to be preferred, whether the elections are to the national, or the local, legislatures.

In England, as before remarked, knights of the shire were originally the representatives from the counties. The shires were local divisions of the kingdom, and the knights of each shire deputed one of their own number to parliament. The continuance of these parliamentary districts has survived the artificial state of society from which it sprung, and contributes in an eminent degree to the freedom and independence of the legislative body. It is this mode of election which has given rise to the question so often agitated: is the member elected the representative of the whole state, or of the district which chooses him;—which is in some respects similar to another question which might be put: whether man is an individual or a member of society. The answer would be nearly the same in the two cases. Man is both an individal and a citizen; and the deputy is a representative of his district, and at the same time of his whole country. And as that system of private conduct which most effectually consults the welfare of the individual, conduces most to the prosperity of the community, so that system of public conduct which most truly advances the interests of one part of the country, is certain to redound to the advantage of the whole. But inasmuch as men do not always see things as they really are, as ignorance, prejudice, and egotism lead them so much astray in whatever regards the public interests, the system of domestic government is contrived in order to prevent the interference of sectional with the national interests. And thus the question, is the deputy the representative of his district, or of the country, is of infinitely rarer occurrence in the United States, than it would be if the population composed one aggregate community. Election by districts mitigates the rigor of the rule, that the majority are entitled to govern. It draws the bond of responsibility closer, and it breaks the force of party spirit. Tne first has been sufficiently explained.

Where local legislatures are created, the effect is that the national interests are not represented in them, nor are the local interets represented in the national assembly. This is the general tendency of he plan; though as the boundary between the two jurisdicdictions cannot be drawn with exact precision, exceptions will necessarily occur. The responsibility of the deputy to the local legislature will be stronger, because, if his constituents are local, so also are the interests which he represents. The responsibility of the deputy who is sent to the national legislature will be more complete: because, although his constituents are local, the interests which he represents are exclusively national. Where this distribution of the powers of government is established, this further effect takes place. As the responsibility of a legislative body is in an inverse ratio to the number of its members, after a certain point is reached; so also the responsibility of the members is greater, where those to whom they are immediately accountable do not compose a great multitude. The representative of a district is constantly exposed to the gaze of his constituents. He might hide himself among two or three millions of people. He cannot do so among fifty or an hundred thousand.

Whatever contributes to afford a clear insight into public affairs, and enables everything to be seen in its true light, abates the violence of party spirit. Whatever shrouds them in mystery, and causes them to be seen confusedly, gives force to party spirit. The representative is the instrument of communication between his constituents and the world of politics; and whatever causes his conduct to be distinctly surveyed, causes the system of public measures to be more easily grasped, and more generally understood.

CHAPTER VIII.

PARTIES—THE OFFICE THEY FULFIL IN A REPUBLIC.

Many persons of great intelligence, and who are inclined to look with a favorable eye upon the progress which society is everywhere making, when they behold the scene of strife and contention which parties in a republic give rise to, recoil from it with dismay, and are instantly disposed to take refuge in what they denominate strong government. Nevertheless, it is most certain, that the distinguishing excellence of free institutions consists in their giving birth to popular parties, and that the annoyance and inconvenience which these occasion to individuals, both in public and private life, are productive of incalculable advantage. It is a great mistake, with our knowledge of the constitution of human nature, to suppose that society would be better ordered if its surface were a perfect calm.

The democratic principle has come into the world not to bring peace, but a sword; or rather to bring peace by a sword. One may easily conceive of an individual, that his various faculties may be so evenly balanced as to give rise to the justest and the most consistent scheme of conduct. And one may liken the state to some huge individual, and say that the rival views and opinions of different parties conspire to the same end; that when these are free to give utterance to their sentiments, a similar equipose takes place among all parts of society, and that something like a regular system takes place in the conduct of public affairs.

The human mind, with all its capabilities of thought and action, is wonderfully disposed to listlessness; so that it requires the most powerful incentives in order to rouse its dormant energies. And the condition of the great majority of mankind is such, that none but those sensible interests which touch them on every side can be relied upon as the instrument of moving them. By giving a full play, and a favorable direction to these, we succeed in imparting activity to the disposition. And this being attained, a great amount of thought and reflection is sure to be developed among the great bulk of the population. Party spirit at bottom is but the conflict of different opinions, to each of which some portion of truth almost invariably adheres : and what has ever been the effect of this mutual action of mind upon mind, but to sharpen men's wits, to extend the circle of their knowledge, and to raise the general mind above its former level. Therefore it is, that an era of party spirit, whether religious, philosophical, or political, has always been one of intellectual advancement. A powerful understanding may be sufficiently stimulated by the study and investigation of abstract truth : but the diffusion of knowledge in the concrete, seems to be indispensably necessary to produce this effect among the great majority of mankind.

The existence of parties in a republic, even noisy and clamorous parties, is not therefore a circumstance which should be regarded as inimical to the peace and welfare of the state. It should rather be received as a special and extraordinary provision, for furthering the interests and advancing the intelligence of the most numerous class of society. By creating an arena on which all men may be active and useful, we are certain of attracting an incalculably greater number to the pursuit of industry and knowledge than would be possible under any other state of things. The growth of popular parties constantly keeps pace with the diffusion of industry and property. The diffusion of industry and property, by exercising the mind intently upon small things at first, exercises it earnestly and seriously upon important ones in the end.

The true theory of popular parties then consists in multiplying the employments of private individuals,—in increasing the active industry of the whole community. The regular deportment and habits of reflection which these produce counteract the vicious tendencies of the system, and operate as a safeguard against the extreme excesses and the violent revolutions which occur in other countries. As the interests of private persons under this system become more and more identified with those of the state, each one has a desire and a motive for understanding and taking part in public affairs. The question in human affairs is never whether any particular arrangement shuts out all mischief and inconvenience, but only whether it excludes the greatest practicable amount; and not of one kind merely, but of all kinds. Thus, although, in a democratic republic, a vastly greater number of people take part in politics than under any other form of government, the minds of a vastly greater number are exercised by some healthful and useful occupation, which not only inspires sagacity and energy, but communicates a character of seriousness and reflection to the whole population. The weak side of human nature is thus constantly propped up and strengthened. The bickerings and animosities of parties are not extinguished; but there is, notwithstanding, a greater degree of public tranquility than would otherwise exist.

Popular parties are not only the natural result of elective government, but what is of much more consequence, they are absolutely necessary to uphold and preserve it. It is too common to regard certain arrangements of society as a sort of necessary evils; and thus very imperfectly to comprehend their true design, and the important agency which they have in securing the public welfare.

As the political institutions in a republic are of a totally different character from what they are in monarchical or aristocratical government, there is a corresponding difference in the machinery which sets each of them respectively in motion. In the artificial forms of government, a system of checks and balances is devised, to secure the influence of the public authority, and to maintain each department in its proper place; but such an expedient would be futile and powerless where government means vastly more than the rule of the persons who fill the various public offices. In a republic a substantive part of the political authority is designedly communicated to the whole population. We want something more, therefore, than a scheme of checks and balances within the government. As the forces which are set in motion, are so much more extensive, we must contrive some machinery equally extensive, for the purpose of controlling them. And thus popular parties very naturally, not to say necessarily, take the place of that curious system of checks and balances which are well enough adapted to a close aristocracy, or pure monaichy, but which play only a subordinate part in representative government.

In a despotism parties have no existence. Factions there may be, but not parties. In all the other artificial forms of government, the constitution of parties is more or less imperfect, because they are overborne by an extraneous influence which disables them from faithfully representing opinions. In a democratic republic, the people themselves compose all the existing parties. Hence opinions are not only submitted to examination, but they are submitted to the examination of those who are immediately affected by them. But the greater the number of persons, who are consulted with regard to any measure, which has an important bearing upon their interests, the greater is the probability that it will be adjusted with a view to their common welfare. The process may be tedious and circuitous, but this is an advantage, since it will cause a greater amount of reflection to be employed. Moreover, when opinions have to pass through a great number of minds, before they are reduced to practice, society does not experience a violent shock, as it does upon their sudden and unpremeditated adoption. Factions stir the passions of men, but parties introduce the conflict of opinions.

It would appear, then, that the wider the arena on which parties move, the more numerous the persons who compose them, the less dangerous are they to the state; which is the reverse of the conclusion to which the great majority of men are inclined to lean.

The absence of parties in a country of free institutions, would imply the existence of unanimity on all occasions. But in the imperfect condition of man, unanimity would not be desirable. As in the individual, one faculty is set over against another, in order to elicit the greatest amount of judgment, wisdom, and experiecence; so the mutual encounter of rival opinions, in different sections of society, constitutes a discipline of the same character, on a much larger scale. Unanimity, which has the appearance of being the only rightful rule, would, if it were conceivable, render society absolutely stationary. Man is not born with knowledge; and all the useful or noble qualities which he ever exerts are the offspring of variety, not of uniformity. Constituted as human nature is, there would be no virtue without some conflict of interests, and no wisdom without some conflict of opinions.

And this supposes a very important fact in the history of society; that although the majority rule, the minority, by virtue of the naked power which belongs to opinions, are able to exert an indirect, and yet very decisive, influence upon the course of public affairs. This influence is so great, that no one who has been accustomed to examine the workings of society in different countries can fail to have been struck with the repeated instances in which the opinions of a minority have triumphed over those of the majority, so as ultimately to become the settled and established opinions, and to transform the minority into the majority. And this, notwithstanding the civil institutions may not have been very favorable to the rise and growth of parties.

Among the important changes in the scheme of public policy which have taken place in Great Britain in very recent times, may be enumerated the abolition of the slave trade, the amelioration of the criminal code, the introduction of more liberal principles into commerce, the reformation of the civil jurisprudence, catholic emancipation, and parliamentary reform. In each of these instances the new opinion commenced with an exceedingly small party, and encountered in its progress the most solidly established authority. If the triumph has not been complete, it is certain to become so, in consequence of the strong ground which these very efforts have enabled popular parties to stand upon. So far from a minority not exercising a very marked influence upon the conduct of public affairs, the instances will be found to be exceedingly rare in any country where opinions are able to make themselves felt, in which a minority have not succeeded, if the cause it espoused, entitled it to be victorious. This fact would seem to show that so far as effective and permanent influence is concerned, it is of little consequence whether an enlightened scheme of policy is first suggested by the minority, or the majority. The fact that it is enlightened, gives it a claim to success, and that success is almost infallible.

Among the important movements which have taken place in American society may be noticed the revolution, the establishment of the federal constitution, and the ascendancy which the republican party attained in 1801. Each of these revolutions commenced with an inconsiderable band, which ultimately won its way to public confidence, and totally reversed the position of parties. The declaration of independence was only carried by one vote. The freedom of the colonies might have been rightfully asserted half a century prior to 1776. But although the struggle of opinions may be more protracted than that of armies, it always terminates in more decisive results. As to the second of those revolutions—the establishment of the confederate form of government, it was at one time deemed absolutely impracticable. Governor Pownall, in his work on the administration of the colonies, written about the time of the celebrated convention at Albany, declared that they had no one principle of association among them, and that their manner of settlement, diversity of characters, conflicting interests, and mutual rivalship, forbid all idea of an union. And Dr. Franklin, who was one of the commissioners to that convention, declared that an union of the colonies was absolutely impracticable—or at least, without being forced by the most grievous oppression and tyranny. The acutest observers, and the most experienced statesmen, underrated the force with which opinions are armed, when they are pursued with a steady and unfaltering resolution.

The third revolution was the natural consequence of the others. The two first acted upon the political institutions, and remodeled the government. The last acted upon the manners, and brought the laws, and the structure of society, into harmony and agreement with each other.

I will mention but two instances in the history of the state governments, in which the opinions of a party greatly in the minority have finally prevailed, and obtained an almost unlimited ascendancy. These are the amelioration of the criminal code, and the establishment of a system of internal improvements. Each of these enlightened schemes originated with a very small party—the one in Pennsylvania, and the other in New York. And they have not only conquered all opposition in those states, but have extended their influence over the whole union.

The struggle of new with old opinions will be more tedious in an old than in a new country. The abolition of the laws of primogeniture, and the simplification of the code of civil jurisprudence, did not occupy much time in the United States. In Great Britain, it is only within a few years that the second has been even partially accomplished. The first may not be effected in half a century or more.

Thus, whenever the general state of public opinion is least prepared for an important change in the existing institutions: that is, whenever agitation, discussion, and the encounter of rival opinions, is most necessary, and will be productive of most advantage—by developing a great amount of observation and experience—the struggle of new opinions is the longest protracted; and wherever these qualities already exist in great perfection, the contest is short, and soon brought to a close.

As soon as the period arrived when Congress had authority to abolish the slave trade, it was abolished. The debate on the subject is not one of the memorable debates in the American legislature. But it is one of the most memorable which has taken place in the British parliament, during the last half century.

It is curious to notice the manner in which parties deal with each other, and to watch the process by which opinions are communicated from one to the other. For parties would be without meaning and without utility, if they were eternally to battle with each other with no other result than the alternate loss and acquisition of power. The desire to obtain the ascendancy may be the moving spring which actuates each; but fortunately this spring cannot be set in motion in a country of free institutions, without rousing a prodigious amount of reflection among a very large portion of the population. Doubtless the true use of parties is very far from being to administer provocatives to demagogues to gratify their private ambition. Their selfish views may be necessary in order to animate them in the pursuit of certain opinions. But the moment these opinions are promulgated, they are subjected to a searching examination in all parts of society, because they are felt to have a practical bearing upon the substantial interests of all. The true office of parties then is to elicit and make manifest the amount of truth which belongs to the tenets of each; so that the great body of the people, who belong to no party save the party of their country, may be both easily and understandingly guided in the path they pursue.

In the progress of the struggle which takes place between parties, they will often be very equally balanced, and each will, for a time, alternately acquire the ascendancy. The first time that the party which before had been habitually in the minority, attains a decided preponderance, is felt as a presage of permanent success. The new opinions are then deemed to be practicable. Old associations are broken, and a new impulse is given to the new party. The party which had been accustomed to carry everything, falls back into the minority; and this example of the instability of power sets every one a thinking, and even amid the strife of politics, produces more prudence and moderation. The party in the minority, and now discarded from power, is at first disposed to cling to its most extreme opinions. Its pride has been wounded, and its ambition disappointed. It has no idea of turning to any sets of opinions upon compulsion. But a popular party contains a vast number of individuals whose temperaments, modes of thinking, and opportunities of information, are often exceedingly different, and whom it is impossible to fashion as you would a close body into one unalterable form. Reflection, sooner or later, takes the place of passion. And as the attachment of individuals to their own independent opinions is often much stronger than to the opinions of a party, every assurance is afforded that the new and enlightened opinions which have been introduced into the public administration, will not only be the rule for the party in power, but that they will spread their influence more or less over the men of all parties. Every one soon sees that there is really no such thing as compulsion in representative government; and that if a system of policy has fairly won over a majority of the suffrages of twenty millions of people, a very considerable portion of truth, to say the least, must belong to that system. They recollect that as no one man can represent the whole of humanity, so no one party can represent the whole truth in politics. Thus the minds of many, who were most obstinately set in the opposite direction, are gradually opened to the reception of new opinions. They begin to declare, for the first time, that some very important changes were necessary to secure the well being of the state. Great numbers openly go over to the opposite party; some from settled conviction, others from a sort of instinctive feeling that all was not right before. This gives additional strength to the majority, which, when it does not advance merely novel opinions, but appeals to truth and to the judgment of mankind, is sure to retain the supremacy for a considerable period. Everything then becomes fixed and settled.

But this very fixation of everything, so delightful to those who have been tormented by anxiety, and tossed by contrary hopes and fears, is not to last forever. This state of repose is often as fatal to the maintenance of free institutions, as the ill-regulated ambition of parties. Prosperity corrupts parties, as well as individuals. The long enjoyment of power persuades those who have possessed it, that it can never be wrested from them. Abuses, though not perhaps of the same kind, break out again. These abuses gain strength gradually. They are fortified by the prejudices which the prescription of time creates, as well as by the self-interest and cupidity of the leaders of party. Any attempt to root them up, is regarded as before as an attempt to change fundamental usages, and to tamper with the vital interests of the community. Then commences a new struggle, very much resembling the former; the same circle of opinions will be described as in the former revolution. Everything will again be set right, without shielding one drop of blood, without the employment of any other instrumentality than the simple dropping of the ballot. But it may happen that the new opinions which now spring up, will not be entitled to as entire confidence as in the former revolution. In the progress of the controversy, each party will cause some portion of its own opinions to be adopted. The issue will not be so decisive. A new party, or probably an old party, with views greatly modified, will succeed to power, and will preside for another term of years. It is in this way that all parties find themselves, somehow or other, represented in the state —some virtually, others potentially ; and although the government is frequently exposed to the most formidable power by which it can be assailed, that power is exercised so steadily, and yet so silently, as to overturn nothing, and yet to revolutionize everything.

There is another very curious inquiry connected with this subject; one which unfolds a very instructive chapter in the history of human nature. I believe it will be found, on a close observation, that parties in a republic, in great numbers of instances, originate in, and are nourished by, secret rivalships in private life; and that although questions of state policy serve to designate them, and to give them an outward form, those questions are, in great part, laid hold of in order to give force and effect to feelings of a very different kind. If the history of every hamlet and neighborhood in the United States were written, this fact would be found verified with wonderful exactness. But it is not necessary that we should be acquainted with the chronicles of all. It is enough to seize the events which pass under our own observation. What takes place in a few, will differ in no material respect from what transpires in all.

This is a view of the subject which is not only exceedingly curious, as affording an insight into the workings of human nature, but is highly instructive, as it sheds great light upon the formation and composition of parties. It is generally supposed, that individuals connect themselves with parties upon political grounds; that is, that they are influenced by a persuasion of the propriety, or impropriety of certain public measures. This is a great error. Numbers enter into these associations, from motives which are of a purely personal or private character. And this is true equally of the common people, and of the higher classes. In speaking of motives of a personal character, however, I do not at all refer to the preference which is felt for a particular leader; for this is generally of a negative character. It may help to decide the turn which parties sometimes take, but falls entirely short of the view to which I wish to direct the attention of the reader. To a very great extent, parties are formed and changed in consequence of the position in private life which individuals occupy. Any one who has lived in any town in the United States long enough to make an accurate observation of the structure of society, and the dispositions of the people who inhabit it, must have noticed that there is a constant tendency towards what may be called the supremacy, or precedence, of certain individuals or families. These will, perhaps, be composed of the old residents, of the merchants, of professional men, etc. As adherents of these, will always be found a number of the inferior classes, so that it cannot be termed a merely aristocratical party. Two circumstances, however, in the progress of time, contribute to weaken, or entirely to break up this association: 1st. Where any body of men, no matter how wide or how narrow the sphere of their influence may be, has maintained a certain degree of precedence for a considerable time, those who compose it become confident in themselves and annoy others, by making show of their influence. 2d. In the great majority of towns under twenty thousand, there will be a lack of talent in this body, owing either to the circumstance, that the long enjoyment of a fixed position in society diminishes the motives to exertion, or that there is not now enough for the strenuous action of mind upon mind. Either of these causes, and, of course, both combined, lead very naturally to the crumbling of the party, and to the formation of new opinions, and a new party. I visited several parts of the United States during the administration of James Munroe. Parties could not be said to be extinct, but they were feeble and inactive. In every town and village, and I may add neighborhood, a predominant and complacent nfluence was exercised by certain families, or individuals, on the principle I have suggested. I visited, or obtained accurate information, of most of these some years afterwards, when parties were distinctly formed. These parties were termed political, and, in outward appearance, had no other character. But political disputes only gave occasion to them, and afforded a plausible ground for open hostility, when, in truth, the actuating motives were of a strictly personal character, and it was the individuals who were arrayed against one another. Everywhere it was the new men against the old; very often the talented and the ambitious against the supine and unintelligent. In many instances, it was the reverse; it was the radical, the ignorant, the persons jealous of any influence which overshadowed them, no matter how rightful that influence was, who battled against superior talents, and long continued influence. In many instances, whole counties and districts of country, were revolutionized, the new men succeeding to the old. In others, the new men did not succeed in obtaining the mastery; but they notwithstanding wrought a great change in the habits and mode of thinking, of other people; for even ineffectual opposition may have a very advantageous influence. It wakes up those against whom it is directed; it leads them to soften, or correct their defects; otherwise they cannot maintain the victory they have won. In hardly any instance were political questions the springs which brought about these changes. One body of men simply felt uneasy in the subordinate position which it seemed to occupy. In general conversation and in public meetings, questions of public policy were seized as the ruling motives; in private conversation it was otherwise. There, people freely declared that political questions were of very inferior moment, compared with the annoyance which was daily experienced in private life, from the complacent rule of a clique, which could show no intrinsic title to respect.

It is of great importance that these views should be thoroughly studied by every one. Public controversies are not everything, even in politics. Every community requires, if I may so express myself, to be occasionally ventilated; and this can only be done by operating upon the secret and more delicate springs which work the machinery of society. We thus gain a clearer insight into the origin, character, and fluctuation of parties. It is as necessary to study the physiology of society, in order to understand the workings of government, as it is to study the physiology of man, in order to penetrate the character of the individual. The changes I have referred to are periodical. They take place about every generation. The reason is obvious: a period of twenty or thirty years is necessary to confirm the authority of any body of men, and until it is confirmed, it is not very troublesome to any one. Those who are growing into manhood then unite with the discontented among the older men. If this view does not present a very flattering picture of human nature, it at least shows, that through the instrumentality of some very harmless agents, important changes in the structure of society, are brought about silently and peacefully. A democratic community will not therefore be so liable to those terrible shocks, which, in other countries, are necessary to sweep away public abuses.

If we suppose that there are two or three men in a neighborhood who possess considerable influence, whether arising from family connections, wealth, or any other of the advantages of fortune, this at once lays the foundation for rivalship in its most secret forms. Envyings and heart-burnings insensibly grow up. This is a fact we are bound to know, only to draw instruction from it. This rivalship gradually extends to the connections of each, to their friends, and acquaintances—to all those who may be disposed to take refuge under the influence of one, rather than of the others— until at length the whole neighborhood is involved in their disputes. One perhaps acquires a decided ascendancy ; and in a few years this disproportioned influence incommodes great numbers of people in all the walks of private life. Many immediately declare, that they can see no reason why so much importance should be ascribed to any one who does not possess either eminent virtue or ability ; and they set themselves to work more vigorously than ever, in order to abate so great a nuisance. At the same time political questions are discussed, and agitated everywhere, and regular parties in the state are organizing. Each of these neighborhood clans connects itself with one or other of those parties, as the chance of success in their private views may dictate. The democratic party is understood to be the one which is most favorable to the equal rights of the citizens ; and all the opponents of this mimic aristocracy in a country neighborhood ally themselves with that party.

The influential man does not always put himself forward as a can didate for office. He feels that this would be to create envy among his own dependants—that it would be a dangerous test of his capacity and wisdom. But he brings some one forward who leans upon him, and who, if not the most capable, will be the most available man. And party politics now having two faces, the most available will generally be the most incompetent man. This mixture of private views with the political questions of the day, will sometimes render the machinery of parties very complicated and difficult to understand. And it will cause oscillations among parties when they were least expected. But we will suppose that the democratic party prevails. The influence which was before so serious an annoyance, and the subject of so much complaint in private, is then greatly diminished. Some one whose connection with the wealthy will be less obvious, and whose reliance upon the masses will be closer, is elected. He also may be nicknamed an available man—that is, a man whose face is smoothed—or a practical man, which means a man with a single idea. At any rate the personal weight and importance which political promotion gives him, and the bright prospects which every one beholds opening in his path, concur to clothe him with a very enviable share of influence. Or, if he also has been merely put forward to further the private schemes of others, the same effect is produced. A new influence is raised up in the neighborhood to act as a counterpoise to that which before prevailed. But in a few years, the same annoyance is felt in consequence of the ascendancy of this new party. Men begin then to exercise a bolder spirit of inquiry than they were willing to trust themselves with before. They see no reason why wealth, or any other fortuitous advantage, should give claim to precedence in society. The new favorite perhaps owed his elevation to personal motives and private views. But he is perhaps not fully sensible of this ; or, at any rate, it does not readily occur to him, that after being elected to a public station, of considerable responsibility, he has any other vocation than to attend to the public business. He separates the end from the means, and congratulates himself with the reflection that now a public trust is confided to him, he will be at liberty to act with a single eye to the people's interests.

After an interval more or less long, during which there will be great fermentation in the ranks of both parties, some new man will be selected, who will reflect the feelings, as well as the political opinions, of those who elect him. His success is almost certain; for the private aims and secret prejudices which were originally set in motion, have been continually gaining strength. And in order that the successful candidate may now well understand the line of conduct which he is expected to pursue, what were before regarded as motives, which might well enough influence without determining public conduct, are erected into opinions, on which full as much stress is laid as on any of the questions of public policy. This gives a deeper movement to the workings of parties. All sorts of opinions are now hazarded; men approach inquiries, which before were only touched lightly, and by stealth. The fault with the public man now is, that he runs into the opposite extreme. He takes his constituents literally at their word, and acts out his part even to exaggeration. He is intent only on gratifying his spleen: he indulges in personal invectives, in gross and indecent assaults. He has brought himself to believe that the public business is not merely of secondary importance, but that it is of hardly any importance whatever. He administers provocatives enough to the bad passions, but neglects and mismanages public business. The consequent derangement of political affairs is now more or less felt by the people in their private interests. Moreover, they are mortified in finding that some portion of the disgrace which their favorite has incurred attaches to themselves. Numbers then confer together, but in such a way as to avoid if possible the notice of the opposite party. They consult in private, how it may be possible, with the least noise and inconvenience, to remove the present incumbent, and to elect some one of prudence and discretion, even though his talents should be as moderate. A majority, perhaps, are candidly of this opinion; but a considerable number still cling to their personal views, as being the true index of public opinion; and without the aid of this body, it will be impossible to effect anything. Without their votes, the majority will fall back into the minority. All the private consultations are then hushed up, and the differences, which produced them, are forgotten for a time. The party displays a bold and decided front at the polls, and re-elects the former man. But the blow, which is to crush him, is already struck. His enemies are gathering strength. They even feel envious of him, that he is in a condition to display so much more energy than themselves. The minority of the party feel that it would be absurd that the majority should constantly yield to them. Besides, the new fashion of thinking begins to infect themselves. They regard their favorite with coldness, simply because so many people are disposed to discard him. They even permit him to feel this, in order that he may so act toward them, as really to deserve their cold treatment.

During all this time, and while these changes succeed each other, with more or less rapidity, the utmost inquisitiveness is excited among all orders of men. The connection which has taken place between politics and private manners, brings the former more completely within the reach of every one. It seemed impossible before to gain admission to state secrets, so as to have any notion of the complex machinery by which government is worked, simply because there was so little to stir the feelings, and through that medium to rouse the understanding.

This difficulty is in a great measure removed; and in spite of the eternal wrangling of parties, or rather in consequence of it, a greater amount of knowledge, a keener sagacity, and juster views, are created than would otherwise exist. Those who had formerly been invested with influence, and who imagined they were the hinges on which society turned, look on with amazement, to find public affairs conducted as well as when they took the lead. They observe that an entire revolution has taken place in the disposition and management of society. They ascribe this to envy, and doubtless envy had a great part in bringing it about. But, in human affairs, the inquiry is not always what is the cause of any particular change, so much as what is the character of the change itself. It is a great compensation for the existence of bad passions and propensities, when we cannot be without them, that they may ultimately be subservient toward rendering human nature better than it was before.

Through the instrumentality of the cause at which I have merely glanced, in order to set the reader a thinking, knowledge has been diffused, and power and influence, in both public and private life, have been more evenly balanced in every township and county of an extensive country. These views contribute to expain a remarkable fact in the history of parties in America. Taking any considerable series of years, it is surprising to find how often parties have been very equally balanced. The see-saw politics of some of the states seems even to be a reproach to them. But beneath this outside appearance there is always something to ponder upon. For if, on whichever side the scale of power inclines, the equilibrium of influence in every village and neighborhood is disturbed, the only way to restore it is by throwing more weight into the opposite scale, and thus the oscillations of parties may be almost as frequent as the annual elections. As soon as one party obtains a decided predominance, new rivalships grow up. A multitude of passions and desires (independent of the political controversies of the day,) are set in motion, for the purpose of displacing it, or diminishing its authority.

Hence another apparently singular phenomenon, that individuals of the most opposite political predilections, and of the greatest difference in point of character and mind, are habitually ranged in the same party. It would be deplorable if it were not so. And although one party is sometimes foolish enough to arrogate to itself all the virtue and talents in the community, yet there is, in truth, a very equal distribution among the men of all parties.

Another and equally curious fact may be noticed, that parties often seem to exhibit a mere struggle between the ins and outs. But if the power which is brought to bear upon political affairs is adjusted and regulated by the power and influence which are distributed in private life, and if this affects human happiness more than all other causes put together, the struggle may conduct to very important ends. I have already said that in a republic, parties take the place of the old system of balances and checks. The latter balance the government only, the former balance society itself.

Frequent changes of the public officers are a consequence of these vicissitudes among parties. But it is of the greatest importance, in a country where the electoral franchise is extensively enjoyed, that as large a number of the citizens as practicable should be initiated into the mode of conducting public affairs, and there is no way by which this can be so well effected as by a rotation in office ; and the direction, which party disputes take, affords the opportunity of doing it. If it were not for this, public employments would be continued in the same individuals for life, and after their death would be perpetuated in their families. But public office, of even an inferior grade, is a species of discipline of no unimportant character. It extends the views of men, trains them to the performance of justice, and makes them act for others as well as for themselves. It thus binds together the parts of society by the firmest of all bonds, and makes it tend constantly to a state of order and tranquility, in the midst of the greatest apparent disorder. If men were less quarrelsome; if an easy good nature was all that moved them, they would not be inclined to change their public officers as often as the interests of society demand. The detriment, which would follow, would be much greater than any which their quarrels produce.

It has been supposed, that where these changes are frequent, the persons elected must, for the most part, be inexperienced and incompetent. The fear lest this should be the case is wisely implanted in our nature. It holds us back when we are about to run into an extreme. The feeling is as much a part of our constitution as any of its other tendencies, and must be strictly taken into account in every calculation which we make as to the general working of the system. But public office itself creates, to a great extent, the very ability which is required for the performance of its duties. And it is not at all uncommon, when individuals have been snatched up from the walks of private life to fill responsible stations, to find that the affairs of society are conducted pretty much upon the same principles, and with as much skill and intelligence as before. Habits of order and method are soon imparted to the incumbent, and they constitute the moving spring of all effective exertion, either mental or physical.

In a republic, the rise and fall of parties are not merely revolutions in public life, they are revolutions in private life also. They displace some men from office, but they alter the relative position of a much greater number in private life. Political controversies afford an opportunity for parties to develop themselves : and these controversies do very often present a legitimate field for discussion. But they do not contain everything ; they do not express the whole meaning of parties. A given scheme of public policy may affect very remotely the substantial interests of the population ; but the jostling of men in private life is a perpetual source of uneasiness and discontent, and they seek to relieve themselves by an alliance with party, because, as individuals, they are powerless, while party associations are strong.

The views and actions of men may be the most narrow and selfish imaginable, and yet, they may terminate in consequences of the most beneficial character. The prominent men of each party exert themselves to carry extreme measures ; a great multitude of private individuals intend to acquire some advantage unseen, but not unfelt, over their neighbors. The fall of a party at such a time, like a sudden stroke of adversity, quells the pride of the politician, and inculcates prudence, caution, and forbearance, in private behavior.

The reason why the workings of party are so much more ramified and extensive in a republic, than in any other form of government, is easily explained. In monarchy and aristocracy, the bulk of the people are spectators, not actors; and the operation of parties is necessarily confined within a narrow circle. But free institutions presuppose that the mass of the people are active, not passive citizens, and parties not only regulate the conduct of the handful of men, who preside over public affairs; they regulate also the conduct of the millions, who, although out of the government, yet constitute the springs which set the government in motion. If this were not the case, if there were no regulative principle to shake society, as well as to act upon the government, there would be no way of maintaining free institutions. Men who hold office may be punished for misconduct; but how is it possible by legal enactments to punish whole parties? When, however, a party is tumbled from power, the individuals composing it, lose caste—lose some portion of that consideration, which before attached to them. If this produces more boldness and recklessness in some, it promotes more reflection and prudence in others.

CHAPTER IX.

A REPUBLIC IS ESSENTIALLY A GOVERNMENT OF RESTRAINT.

No one who is an attentive observer of human nature, can fail to be struck with the amazing influence which the opinion of a multitude of men exercises over the mind. We can stand up and confront a single individual even though we are far from being right, but we recoil with a sort of dread from any opposition to the opinion of a great number. Many causes concur to produce this effect :

First. If the individual feels awed by the presence, it is because he is conscious that they are rendered strong, by being in a body. This must necessarily be the case. Men are physically stronger, when they act together, and they are morally stronger when they sympathize together. The phenomenon then is easily explained. The principle even shows why the individual is awed, where he is in the right, and the multitude clearly in the wrong. That multitude, so far as physical injury is concerned, is as strong as before; so far as moral injury is concerned, it is not near so strong ; but it is much stronger than the individual. Their sympathy with one another is still a weapon of offence, against those who do not share in that sympathy. The individual then feels his weakness, because the sentiment of sympathy being a principle of his own nature, he is left without support, when he is entitled to the strongest. The first feel their strength as before, simply because sympathy is a principle of moral, as an actual union is of physical strength. The principle manifests itself in another shape. When an individual is conceived to represent a multitude, no matter whether it is an enlightened or an unenlightened multitude, his presence to a certain extent, conveys an impression of their presence, and produces a similar effect.

The institution of patron, and client which prevailed in Rome, for so long a time, is an illustration of the same principle. Individuals surrounded themselves with retainers, not merely to add to their physical power, but to increase their moral influence. The same custom was introduced into the Republics of Florence, and Genoa, in the middle ages, and gave an artificial weight and importance to those who adopted it. Even in England, traces of the same custom are closely discernible as late as the beginning of the sixteenth century. The practice of having a numerous body of retainers, and giving them badges, or liveries, was not put an end to, until 1509, in the reign of Henry the seventh. Even where no such custom exists, we can still perceive indications of a disposition moving in the same direction. Everywhere we see men allying themselves with other men, not merely openly as with parties, but tacitly with other individuals, in order to inspire themselves with confidence, and to give countenance to their behavior. In a democratic community, where individuals fear each other so much, the custom is difficult to be established, but the weapon of ridicule is wielded by cliques and coteries, as the most convenient mode of attack.

Second. The notion of right and wrong is implanted in all men That we should feel distress and anxiety when we do wrong, requires no explanation ; for this is running counter, if not to our propensities and passions, yet, at any rate, to the governing principle of our conduct. To say that we feel an immoral action to be wrong, whatever may be the allurements with which it is accompanied, is the same as to say that the sense of right is felt to be the authoritative principle, and that any departure from it fills us with uneasiness and apprehension.

But, in the second place, the training and formation of the human character are conducted in youth, when the mind is feeble and without much observation and experience. We, therefore, emerge into a world where a system of opinions and conduct is already established, and it does not seem unnatural but rather a necessary consequence of the process by which human conduct is shaped, that we should defer greatly to the standard of opinion which is erected, and our deportment (not so far as regards the fundamentals of morality, but) as regards those actions to which are affixed the appellations fit and unfit, proper and improper, reasonable and unreasonable, should be compressed into a conformity with it, and that any revolt against it should be followed with a sense of dread and uneasiness. And this more especially as so large a proportion of this class of actions affect other men, and carry along with them, not merely the force of opinion, but that of authority.

If it should be said, that the presence of such a force, constantly acting upon the faculties of men, and holding them in check, must frequently have a disturbing influence upon their actions, this will be admitted; but there is, on the whole, much greater security for the preservation of a tolerably right standard, than if every one felt himself independent of the opinions of all. This singleness in the character of the rule gives unity to those numberless actions which are isolated, and prevents their being drawn too exclusively in the direction of self-interest.

Each individual is apt to view himself from a point different from that where he is viewed by others. His horizon is more limited than theirs, not because he has fewer or feebler faculties, or because he has less correct notions of right, but because, in the case of the individual, these notions are liable to be obscured by feelings and interests which, although they may be common to all, are obliged to be kept under and restrained, when they come to think and act in a body. There is a high probability, therefore, that the opinion of an individual as to his own conduct is biassed, and an equal probability that the sentiment of the body is impartial. The mere apprehension that this may be the case hangs like a perpetual weight upon each one, and renders him, to say the least, more thoughtful and circumspect than he would otherwise be. He is thus better enabled, in those instances where he is in the right, and they in the wrong, to appeal from their judgment to the judgment of mankind.

That class of actions which are generally denominated selfish, carry for the most part their own antidote along with them. That they are selfish constitutes the great protection of the community against their inroads. For it will be easily seen that if there were the same sympathy with others in the gratification by them of their lower propensities, as there is in their noble and disinterested actions, the former would gain the mastery, and society be converted into a bedlam. However men may act therefore in particular instances, both the secret and the declared opinion of every one is obliged to be on the side of right. And this opinion is even fortified by self-interest, when self interest comes to be viewed from the proper point. For although the private interest of the individual may sometimes seem to coincide with the commission of wrong, when it is abstracted from all regard to his relations with others ; yet it can never do so when these relations are taken into the account. Now, our relations with others, if they do not create, at least modify, that whole circle of interests which we denominate private. I do not now speak of those actions which spring from the lower propensities, but of those which are employed by every one in the improvement of his outward condition. The pursuit of an absolutely separate interest by some would consequently break in upon the private interests of all others ; while, at the same time it is equally clear that a regard for the rights of all others is the only guarantee that our own will be preserved. Here, then, also, what is termed the general opinion is obliged to take a direction favorable to the common weal, and unfavorable to the selfish views of individuals. In this way the opinion of all is brought to bear upon each ; and hence it is that in a democratic republic, where the government appears to be wanting in authority, and individuals to possess unbounded freedom, what is termed public opinion is armed with so much power, inspires so general a respect for the laws, and so much terror on the infraction of them. In what is termed strong government society is divided into fixed classes, one of which sits in judgment upon all the others. But it is far less probable, that the opinion of a class should represent the opinion of mankind, than that the combined sentiment of a whole community should do so. The laws having consecrated that class as a separate interest, have to that extent confounded the opinion of right with that of interest.

It would appear, then, that liberty is essentially a principle of restraint. It is true, if others are free while I am not, the principle operates unequally—the restraint is on one side. But if I am admitted to the enjoyment of the same privilege, my actions will impose a check upon the conduct of others, and their actions will impose a corresponding check upon me : and the influence of the principle will be more or less felt throughout the whole of society. The exercise of unrestricted freedom by all, when all are free, is a self contradiction. It supposes a power in each to invade the rights of all others, in which case liberty would fall to the ground and no one be free. The possession of the privilege then by all, limits its exercise in practice, and men are restrained and controlled, precisely because they are free. My liberty of action is an habitual restraint upon the conduct of others, when they attempt to invade my rights, and their liberty is in similar circumstances a restraint upon me. It would not therefore be strong enough to say that where free institutions are thoroughly diffused, it is the evident interest of every one to impose a restraint upon his actions. It would be still more correct to say, that the constitution of society renders it necessary that he should do so.

The walks of private life furnish us with a fine illustration of this important principle. The youth looks forward to the time when he will arrive at manhood, with feelings of delight and exultation. His imagination paints it as the introduction to a state of unalloyed enjoyment. But he has no sooner entered upon the world, than he finds himself hampered and controlled on every side by a multitude of other beings who have acquired the same freedom as himself. The restraint whieh he met with under the parental roof was nothing when compared with the iron weight which now presses upon him ; and although no one can claim to be his master, so that physically his actions may be freer than ever, yet he finds, what before he very imperfectly understood, that the moral force which men exercise upon each other in society, is the sharpest and most powerful of all kinds of restraint,

Now, free institutions produce an effect of precisely the same character, and on a much larger scale. They advance the whole population to the condition of political manhood. If they do not confer anything like the enjoyment which was anticipated, they give rise to what is still more valuable : they multiply the cares and interests of life, and teach to the great majority of men habits of prudence, of reflection, and of self command. That they do not produce this effect in all instances, and in very few to the extent which is desirable, is no answer to the view here taken ; nor does it afford any good reason why we should never speak above our breath, when we are discoursing of the benefits of liberty. That there is a marked tendency to the production of the effect I have noticed, is an importane fact, since it shows that if liberty is power, it is also a a principle of restraint. And if a general acquaintance with the manner in which the principle operates, will contribute to strengthen this tendency, we have abundant reasons for speaking out all that we know.

When I make reference to the mighty influence which the opinion of a multitude of men exercises over the human mind, I do not shut my eyes to the fact, that the principle may operate sometimes, nay, that it does very frequently operate, so as to have a sinister and very pernicious influence, by giving an undue authority to associations and particular sections of society. I am aware that in this way a party, nay, even a cliquė, whether in public or private life, may acquire such dominion for a time, as to incommode and afflict great numbers of other men. Parties collect the opinions of a multitude into one focus, and make them appear like the judgment of an invisible being. They have been able therefore sometimes to oppress the most upright individuals, and even to countenance acts of insurrection against the public authority. No one has ever mastered a general principle, until he is cognizant of all the leading exceptions to it. The argument in favor of free institutions, therefore, never proceeds upon the ground that they are exempt from imperfection ; but that they are more so than any other form in which government has been cast, as much so as we dare expect from any scheme which human ingenuity may invent.

That invisible power which we term public opinion only tends to be right, in proportion as it resembles itself to the opinion of mankind. And I cannot help thinking, that this effect will take place in proportion to the number of men who are in the possession of liberty, and who on that very account, are driven to habits of thought and reflection. The parties and cliques which spring up in a republic, however noisome and hurtful they may be in some respects, may contribute to further this important end. For :

First. They either presuppose, or they excite to, an abundance of curiosity, observation and inquiry. Instead of one or two great eminences, and all the rest of society a dead level, we have a great many eminences, helping about as well as human imperfections will permit to lift the great body of the population to a higher condition.

Second. These parties, associations, and cliques, become so numerous in a republic, that they thwart, counteract, and control one another. Their frequent discussions and wrangling lead directly to the detection of each other's impostures, and serve to correct the aberrations into which the different sections of society are perpetually falling. By modifying, and limiting each other's views and opinions, public opinion is brought more and more into an accordance with the voice of mankind. It is an immense boon to society when, if any thing is transacted in society which is prejudicial to its interests, it shall at any rate not be done in a corner: that all who act for the public, or upon the public, in order to acquire any influence, are compelled to act openly. The so doing is the recognition of the existence of a tribunal of opinion above themselves, which sooner or later rejects all their false and pernicious opinions. Perhaps the majority of persons of intelligence and observation—all who have carefully pondered upon the experience which they have had of human nature, and from it deduced general results—instead of being perplexed by the exceptions, are sufficiently convinced of the wholesome influence which free institutions exercise. The only question with them may be, whether it is ever expedient to speak out so loud as to be overheard by the masses.

It is not necessary to scan American institutions with a very critical eye, to perceive that notwithstanding the great amount of liberty which is set afloat, and the inflammable character which this liberty sometime possesses, that there is some how or other a sort of self-regulative principle residing in the society, which tends to keep everything in its proper place: that this principle can no where else be so distinctly traced, and that it is entirely different from the formal authority which the government wields. And as there is no reason for supposing that there is anything very mysterious about the matter, when all the machinery of society is openly exposed to our observation, the fact, however novel, must admit of explanation, and what explanation so natural as is to be found in the restraint which the very enjoyment of liberty causes every individual, and each member of society, to impose upon one another. It is the partial distribution of the privilege, not the communication of it to all classes, which has occasioned so much disorder and insubordination in society. Rights and duties are reciprocal. My rights in relation to others are the foundation of their duties towards me, and their rights give rise to a set of corresponding obligations on my part. Hence we may say, in a general way, that the equal communication of liberty, by enlarging the circle of duties in the same proportion as it widens the sphere of rights, tends constantly toward the introduction of a principle of restraint, which reaches more or less every part of society. Not that the American people are naturally better than the people of other countries, but that the political and social organization renders it the interest of a greater number to respect and obey the laws, and that this feeling of interest operates in such a way as to have not merely a persuasive but a coercive influence. Not that there are not many evils incident to American society, but that there are fewer than in other governments, especially when we take into account those secret and uncomplained-of grievances, which are smothered by the hand of power, or which are made to appear insignificant amid the dazzling glare of the throne and aristocracy. Lord Coke has said of the court of star chamber, that "the right institution, and orders thereof, being observed, it doth keep all England in quiet." And if such extravagant and unfounded notions could be entertained at that period, we may be permitted at the present day, to search through society for some more homely, and yet more active and diffusive, principle of order.

There are two opposite plans of introducing order and good government into society. The one consists in arming the civil magistrate with a very large share of authority, and thus making every one feel as if an enemy were at his door. The other, not unmindful of the importance of clothing the public functionaries with ample power, is yet chiefly intent on enlarging the sphere of popular rights. It expects to fortify the authority of government in this very way. The first is the plan of almost all the European governments: the second is that of tne American republic. By pursuing the last, we add an additional force to society—we cause the people to control each other, as well as to be controlled by the authority of the laws. The working of the same principle may be observed in one or two of the European communities; but it manifests itself in exact proportion to the degree in which popular liberty has grown up

It is not placing an undue estimate upon free institutions, therefore, to say that in a republic, the distribution of justice, and general administration of the laws, will be attended with more weight and authority, than in either monarchical or aristocratical government. The fact is of the greatest consequence, since it enables us to draw so near the solution of the very difficult problem, how to reconcile popular liberty with political power. The experiment was deemed perilous in the extreme, until the firm establishment and thorough working of American institutions, when what was once a brilliant theory began to wear the character of a regular and well-compacted system. Sir James Mackintosh was perhaps the first English statesman who clearly descried a principle of order in this new community. The living under such institutions for a considerable period, might beget habits of acting which would insure their perpetuity, was very nearly the remark of that enlightened man. Many intelligent Europeans still hesitate. The difficulty of the experiment may be at an end in America: but they feel unable to calculate the exact amount of influence which American institutions may exert upon their own. They therefore prefer to exercise the obvious duty of patriotism, rather than to seem precipitate in espousing the most salutary principles. There is nothing so difficult and irksome as the taking up a line of conduct, however wise and reasonable it may be, provided it is something entirely foreign to our former habits. Its claim to respect only increases the awe which its novelty is calculated to inspire; but the plan once entered upon, it is amazing how fast the difficulties vanish, and how easily the new habit sits upon us. What is true of an individual, is, for obvious reasons, still more true with regard to a community.

If in Great Britain and France, there exists at the present day more public order, as well as a firmer and more regular administration of the laws, than at any antecedent period, I do not know to what cause we must ascribe it, unless it is to the infusion of a greater amount of popular freedom into the institutions of the two countries. Invariably, a wise and liberal communication of liberty has the effect of appeasing, instead of inflaming, the passions. But more than this, where the population only feels the pressure of their government, they are apt to herd together like miserable sheep; they are unconscious of any other danger than that which stares them in the face, and take little or no account of each other's actions, although these exercise so wide and so constant an influence upon the public weal. I think if any one will follow carefully and minutely the workings of American society, he will find that the people are fully as much occupied in keeping each other in order, as they are in checking the authority of their governments. It is only by doing the first, that they succeed in doing the last.

In a democratic republic, public opinion is a thing of more comprehensive import than it is anywhere else; and it is made to bear more extensively upon delinquents, public or private. In the artificial forms of government, the force of society is weilded by the few. It is an iron armor worn by a class set apart. The consequence is, that although the great bulk of society stand in awe of it, they also most cordially detest it, since whatever we fear, we also hate, and whatever we both hate and fear, we endeavor to beat down, openly if we can, furtively if we must. But in a country of free institutions, I discern a marked difference in the feeling of all classes, where crime has been committed, or insurrection set on foot. The guilty persons, as soon as they have time to reflect, are conscious that they are under the ban of public opinion. They wisper to themselves, "it is not a privileged class who seek to trample upon us; it is our fellow citizens whom we have arrayed against us; the judgment of mankind will condemn us." Such very nearly was the exclamation of one of the actors in an American mob. This species of awe has a wonderful effect in crumbling to pieces the stoutest league which was ever formed. The insurgents soon feel themselves to be powerless, their weapons drop from their hands, they fall off one by one, and seek to hide themselves from public view. The general truth of these remarks is abundantly confirmed, not only by the few instances of civil commotion which have occurred in the United States, but by the remarkable facility with which they have been suppressed.

This subject is obviously one of great and of increasing interest, and very naturally suggests many other very important views. In the first place, in must be admitted that hardly any instance of insubordination to the laws occurs in the United States, but what we hear complaint of the indecision and backwardness of the public magistrates, at the commencement of the affair. Whenever any circumstance is observable in the political history of this country, which is different from what takes place elsewhere, there is, to say the least, a high probability that there is some adequate reason for it, and that it is not necessary to suppose, because the precise mode of executing the laws which is practiced in other governments is not adopted there, that therefore the American police is very defective, or that it is infected with the same spirit of licentiousness which is displayed in other parts of society. The complaints which are uttered, the uneasiness which takes possession of all classes, lest the laws should not be executed, are themselves unequivocal symptoms of the soundness of public sentiment, and of the operation of that moral force which is of so much consequence in guarding the peace of society. In the second place, this apparent laxity in enforcing the laws, is in great part attributable to the few public disturbances which take place, and to the fact, that they are invariably of a local character. The American police, if I may use the expression, have not got their hand in—they have seldom had the opportunity to become initiated into the practice of using brute force. An insurrection does not, as in other countries, threaten to sap the foundations of the government, and to carry desolation into the heart of society. The Americans can afford, therefore, to proceed with a little more caution and deliberation than other governments. It is the strong, not the weak, who are most sparing of their strength.

Third. This caution is the result of another circumstance which is equally calculated to engage our attention. It springs from a conviction which, whether openly expressed or not, is constantly felt, that one side is not necessarily altogether in the right, and the other altogether in the wrong. The Americans have got to acting upon this principle as one of some appreciable value, and do not permit it to remain as a barren and unfruitful maxim in the code of ethics. It pervades both public and private society, in all their ramifications, and yet the supremacy of the laws is firmly upheld.

Fourth. This wise prudence, this apparent slowness to act, causes less mischief to be done, and restores order more speedily and effectually, than if a detachment from a standing army were commanded instantly to shoot down the rioters. The shocking enormities of the French revolution were not put an end to until the middle class took matters into its own hands, and by intervening between the two extreme parties, was enabled to exert both more prudence and more resolution. The great difference between the two countries is, that in America the population is almost entirely composed of this middle class. That is done constantly and silently, and by way of prevention, which in France could only be effected after the two parties had shed torrents of blood.

A habitual desire to avoid, if practicable, all extreme measures, is eminently favorable toward rousing reflection, and inspires all who would make opposition to the laws with a sense of insecurity and distrust in themselves. They see that the moral and physical force of society are against them, and they very soon learn that the forbearance which springs from humanity is invariably coupled with bravery, and that it is the invariable precursor of the most resolute and determined behavior. The government, which is strong enough to use forbearance in every act of authority, is sure to gather all the strength which the occasion demands. No band of men, however imposing it may be, can maintain a conflict of any duration with the public authority, unless it can go beyond itself, and derive support from public opinion.

Various conjectures have been hazarded, in order to account for the remarkable order and tranquillity which have existed in the United States. The most plausible are those which ascribe it to the exemption of the country from foreign war, and to the incessant occupation which the several departments of industry afford to the population. But in truth, these are only auxiliary circumstances, very well fitted to give full play to the operation of some other principle, but insufficient of themselves to account for the phenomenon. Very opposite effects have frequently taken place. A season of peace has sometimes been highly favorable to the growth of internal dissensions and conspiracies of every kind. In the Italian republics of the thirteenth and fourteenth centuries, the period of their greatest prosperity, the suspension of foreign war was invariably the signal for reviving the most implacable disputes within. The various branches of industry offered an inexhaustible fund of occupation to the people ; for Italy was then the greatest agricultural country in Europe ; and was also the principal seat of commerce and manufactures. But in examining the constitutions of those states, we find that no higher political privileges were accorded to the people, than are possessed in most of the monarchical governments now existing, and not near so high as are enjoyed by the English commonalty.

The Italian nobles looked upon government as an institution made for their benefit, and spent the lives and property of the citizens to gratify their personal ambition. The liberty which they possessed was not met by a corresponding liberty in other parts of society. The people were held in restraint, but there was no principle of restraint to operate upon the superior classes. Too little freedom in one quarter leads directly to too much power in another, and the very natural consequence is, an eternal conflict between the different orders of society. The foreign wars which have scourged the European states, have been the effect rather than the cause of the discontents and unequal condition of the population.

The wisest plan then, perhaps the only practicable one in the end, for all countries, is that pursued in America : to communicate equal rights to the people—to throw them indiscriminately together, instead of dividing them into fixed orders. They are then compelled to associate freely, and this ultimately ripens into a confirmed habit. Individuals and classes then act as a perpetual restraint upon each other. They are brought to an easy understanding of all these difficulties and interests which, under a different constitution of society lead to interminable feuds. Doubtless people incommode each other very much in a country of free institutions, but this is the secret of the good effect which takes place. They are made to act as watches upon each other, to consult each other's temper and disposition, to balance the great advantage of acting from reflection. They become keenly alive to each other's faults, simply because they have so deep a stake in each other's conduct. A new force is applied to society, which acts in detail, and not merely in the gross, and which, by regulating the conduct of individuals in the first instance, succeeds ultimately in regulating that of the masses. The machinery may be very imperfect after all, but it is the best which is placed in our power. Free institutions are the only instrument on a large scale for elevating the general condition of the people, because they are the only species of government which is capable of being converted into an instrument of moral and not merely of political discipline, for all classes.

As the preservation of order, the maintenance of the laws, the causing one part of society to be just to all others, are the great end of civil institutions, it is plain that unless the republican form contains some active principle of restraint, which shall take the place of the consolidated authority exercised by other governments, it will be no better than monarchy or aristocracy.

The tendency to reflection has been noticed as one of the striking characteristics of modern societies. Everything seems to depend upon the cultivation of this quality. Reflection is what distinguishes the civilized man from the savage ; and it is reflection which makes some men lovers of order, while others are vicious, and disorderly. In the midst of civilization, we are always surrounded by some remains of barbarous life. The great desideratum in politics is, how and to what extent we can get rid of them. Now the principle of equality is eminently calculated to teach habits of reflection. First, it makes men depend very much upon themselves, taxes their own resources, and obliges them to make exertions which they would otherwise never put forth. Second, it brings them more into contact with each other, and thus multiplies their mutual relations: since all our efforts to better our own condition have an immediate reference to others; and whatever multiplies the relations of man to man, enlarges the whole field of observation, and gives more both to think and to act upon. It may be that at some future day, it will not be necessary for some men to be vicious, in order to compel others to be virtuous. The principle of equality may cause jostling enough among men to keep them in order, without that wild license which not only makes them touch at every point, but causes them to trample on each other.

I cannot help thinking, that they who suppose when the population of America has grown to its full complement it will be exceedingly difficult to uphold free institutions, have magnified the danger arising from that source, or rather, that they have mistaken the influence which that circumstance will exert upon the destiny of the country. The denser the population becomes, the more will the people be brought into close proximity with each other, and the more rigorous will be the control which they will mutually exercise. This may be regarded as a law of society which, unless it is countervailed by other circumstances, is certain and invariable in its operation. It is a wise provision, and one productive of the most salutary consequences; the check increases in intensity, in proportion to the need which we have for it. More tranquility prevails among the European communities, than when their population was one-third or one-fourth of what it is now. To refer to the general progress of civilization would be reasoning in a circle, for the progress of civilization is itself in great part attributable to the increase of the population. The vast empire of China, where civilization has been stationary as far back as history goes, seems to show that the density of the population is not merely not adverse to the maintenance of tranquility, but that it is highly favorable to it. The form of civilization is greatly below what exists in Europe and the United States, but it is superior to that which exists in the South American states.

I know few things better calculated powerfully to arrest our attention, than the fact that, during two years (I think 1835 and 1836), there was not a single execution in London. London is itself an immense community; and that amid such discordant elements, such an eternal jangling of interests, such a craving of all sorts of wants and desires, so much order and tranquility should be maintained, is to say the least, a striking fact in the history of society. Nor is this state of things an accidental one. The diminution of crime, for a series of years before, had been very regular. The convictions for murder, and for assaults with intent to murder, were, for a period of ten years, commencing with 1816, no more in London than they were in New Orleans during the same time. The population of the one was not more than thirty-five thousand, of the other a million and a half. In the United States, it is in the thinly settled states of the west and southwest that outrages are most frequently committed, and the authority of the laws set at defiance. Those states, without doubt, contain an exceedingly sound population; but great numbers of the profligate emigrate to them, because they know they will be less exposed to the surveillance and control of others, than they would be amid the fuller population of the older states. If it should be said that this state of things is owing to a defective administration of the laws, it may be answered that this defect would be cured by a more numerous population. Public opinion is the most effectual auxiliary in the execution of the laws; but public opinion is necessarily feeble where the settlements are, to a considerable extent, composed of wandering adventurers. Those states are rapidly passing through the same purifying process which all the others have gone through. They will ultimately contain as sound, because they will contain as dense, a population as other parts of the union.

The reason then, why the control which the parts of society exert upon each other is more stringent and more active as the population increases, is obvious. Individuals, and collections of individuals, are placed more completely within reach of each other, and have a more immediate interest in each other's conduct. No one can then exercise his faculties, or perform any action however insignificant, without affecting many others. Each individual acts as a sentinel upon his neighbor, and thus, through the co-operation of all, the private interest of each is rendered as consistent as possible with the interest of all.

There are then two sorts of control existing in society; the one a control on the part of the government, thr other of the people upon each other. The last is a most important element in the social organization at the present day.

Free institutions give force to both species of control. The principle of equality which pervades them brings individuals into closer juxtaposition; and the check which these habitually exert upon one another's behavior not only familiarizes them to the authority of the government, but greatly interests them in upholding it, since the laws are only intended to accomplish what the great majority of private persons are aiming at, but which they are too feeble to effect.

BOOK II.

CHAPTER I.

WRITTEN CONSTITUTIONS.

The formation of a written constitution is one of the most decisive steps which has been made toward the establishment of free institutions. It implies the exercise of reflection in its highest degree, an ability to frame the most comprehensive rules, and to make application of them to the actual affairs of men. Most governments are easily enough initiated into the art of governing the people; but a written constitution is a scheme, by which the governors themselves are proposed to be governed. The commencement of this very important movement is of recent date. We cannot carry it further back than the era of the American revolution. For although a few examples have been handed down to us from antiquity, and one or two attempts of the same kind are recorded in European history, prior to 1776, the differences are so numerous, and so fundamental, that we are not entitled to range them in the same class with the American constitutions. It sometimes happens, that a mere difference in degree between two things is so wide as to place an absolute distinction between them, and to render them opposite, instead of resemblances of one another. The constitutions of antiquity confounded what we would characterize as political ordinances with the acts of ordinary legislation. This was the case in the code of the Roman decemvirs, and it was equally so in the systems introduced by the Athenian and Spartan lawgivers. One design of a written constitution, is to define the boundary between political and civil laws. For as it is not intended that the two should have an equally authoritative character, it is not intended that they should have an equally durable form. This incongruous mixture of two things so different was therefore an infirmity. It showed that the mind had not yet got so far, as to be able to analyze its ideas in matters of government; no matter whether this analysis is the product of great learning, or whether it is the result of a long course of experience. Not to estimate the difference between two things, is not to understand the nature of one of them at least; and so to make one, or both, occupy an unfit place in the system which we construct.

This subject has given occasion to very important discussions in France, since the establishment of constitutional monarchy; and it has sometimes required the efforts of the most enlightened French statesmen, to prevent the error I have alluded to from being committed in "the charte." Once settle the relative powers of the different departments of governments, and the office of the legislative body will be plain enough. Its power will be better guarded, and yet will be more full, and ample, than it would otherwise be. The varied exigencies of society, the unforseen changes which take place in human affairs, the slow accumulation of that wisdom which flows from experience, all demand, that once the orbit within which the legislature is to move is marked out, a large and liberal discretion should be given to it in the enactment of laws.

But that which places the greatest imaginable difference between the constitutions of antiquity and those of the United States, is that the former were in no sense the offspring of the popular will; while on the contrary, the latter have emanated directly from the people. The same may be said of those European states which now have written constitutions. Those constitutions have been the gift of some self-constituted lawgiver, or have been imposed by bodies of men who very imperfectly represented the supreme authority of the state.

The constitutions of antiquity showed clearly enough, that there were among the citizens some individuals of contemplative and cultivated minds. But they indicated nothing further. They afforded no evidence that those great truths, which lie at the foundation of all just and legitimate government, were seized and appreciated by the people at large; or rather they afford incontestible proof to the contrary. A conjectural plan of government is as easily drawn up as any other composition; which is one reason, perhaps, why many otherwise enlightened understandings affect to treat all such works very lightly. A constitution which deals in certain pre-conceived general principles, and seeks to mold the affairs of men into a conformity with them, is very different from a system of government which undertakes to arrive at the knowledge of fundamental maxims, by availing itself of a vast fund of experience and observation existing among the people themselves. The American constitutions were for this reason a really difficult and arduous achievement. The difficulty did not consist in the degree, but in the extent, of intellect necessary for the occasion. A plan of government in which the popular will has had a direct agency, presupposes a very wide diffusion of intelligence, and this at once stamps upon the undertaking both a practical and a comprehensive character. Lord Somers and his colleagues, who took the lead in the revolution of 1689; Benjamin Constant and Lafayette, who took the lead in the kindred revolution of 1830, were the real thinkers and actors on those occasions. But Hamilton and Madison, equally great names, who took the lead in the formation of the American constitution, were but spokesmen of the popular will. Hence the profound and impressive debates which took place at that time in popular assemblies; and hence the necessity which was felt of laying before the public a full exposition of the proposed plan of government. The letters of Publius are, in this respect, perfectly unique. No similar production is recorded in the history of ancient or modern civilization.

Some of the remarks I have made are applicable with still more force to the attempts which have been made, by individuals of ingenious and powerful understandings, to frame schemes of government for a whole people. We might as well tear out of the volumes of Plato, Harrington, or Mr. Hume, the plans of a republic which they conceived, and ordain them as constitutions, as to call Mr. Locke's and the Abbe Sieye's efforts by that name.

Nor is there any reason for surprise, that the popular mind, and not merely the popular will, should have so direct an agency in the formation of a constitution of government, as is manifestly the case in America. If the mere addition which a life of the closest study and thegreatest learning, makes to the mind of the highest capacities, is not so great as the knowledge which is possessed by the man of the most untutored understanding, a fact of which there can be no doubt, there is nothing unnatural in the supposition that the plainest men, when they are placed in a situation favorable to the acquisition and realization of a large amount of political experience, should not only be equal to such an undertaking, but that without their co-operation no such undertaking can be understandingly executed.

Some persons, eminent for their intelligence, have occasionally hazarded the assertion, that there is no force in constitutions on paper, and that we should be as well without them. Admitting that it is fair thus to withdraw the mind from the all-important consideration, that a constitution which is the work of the popular mind, marks an entirely new era in the history of society; no opinion can well be conceived, which is more completely behind the age in which we live.

The reasoning which has been relied upon to sustain this strange assertion, would be equally conclusive to prove that there is no force in written laws. And yet it is plain that without written laws, society would be a scene of discord and confusion. The occasional violation of a constitution would not even help to prove the assertion. The laws are repeatedly violated, and yet no one lays his head upon his pillow without feeling a wonderful sense of security under their protection. Even the English "magna charta," an instrument far less comprehensive in its scope, and possessing therefore much fewer guaranties, than an American constitution, was repeatedly violated, but it constituted a landmark amid all the troubles of the day, and the English monarchs were compelled to ratify and reratify it, until it acquired a weight and authority which no one was strong enough to throw off.

The precise and definite form which writing gives to our ideas, renders it an indispensable auxiliary in reducing those ideas to practice, and in spreading their influence over an extensive country. If instances are to be found where communities have been governed with considerable wisdom, without written constitutions, this is either because there has been some approach to one, some resemblance to an instrument, which, however imperfect, has acquired the sanction of successive generations of men, or such communities have lived in close fellowship, have been bound in an intimate alliance with others, which had written constitutions, and were moreover obliged by the league of which they were members, to owe allegiance to a federal constitution. The first is the case of England, the second that of Connecticut and Rhode Island. But all three of these examples prove that there is great force in written constitutions.

A written constitution is a repository of tried and experienced truths, with an authoritative sanction accompanying it, capable of being appealed to in all times of party conflict, when the minds of men are tormented by the danger of civil commotion, and when every means which is calculated to fix reflection, and to steady the public mind, is of so much importance to the peace of society.

In every department of life, it has been found that the collection of human experience and wisdom into some visible organ capable of making a sensible and durable impression on the mind, was the only way to give a fixed and permanent direction to the actions of men. It cannot be otherwise then with civil government, where the body of rules which are adopted has this additional advantage, that it is the result of a deliberate compact between the members of the community. It would be much more reasonable to assert, that there was no utility in a system of religious doctrines, or a system of education, in a code of jurisprudence, or in the rules which are adopted for the army and navy, than to affirm that there is no force in a body of fundamental ordinances for the government of the state.

We may pronounce of a country, in which a written constitution has been framed by delegates chosen by the people, that it is from that very circumstance placed entirely beyond the reach of monarchical or aristocratical institutions. A change in the structure of society, so thorough and so decisive, is absolutely incompatible with the existence of either of those forms of government. But this change may take place, although the great body of the people are not advanced to the highest pitch of intelligence, or to anything like an equal degree of intelligence. The system of common schools has existed in New England for more than two hundred years; and yet great inequalities still exist, and will forever exist, in the capacities of the men who inhabit it. But as there is a certain limit, beyond which knowledge must not advance, in order to insure the existence of any one of the artificial forms of government; so there is also a limit beyond which knowledge need not advance, in order to insure the establishment of free institutions.

Those rules which govern the interests of large collections of men, are never so recondite as those which are obtained by the study of the individual alone. And if we examine the history of any of the great revolutions which have changed the condition and destiny of the human race, it will be found that the leading ideas—those which presided over the whole movement—were the simplest imaginable. Let us take, for an example, the Protestant reformation. The principles with which the great reformer set out, and which were his constant weapon from the commencement to the close of the controversy, were so plain, so homely, so easy to be understood and handled by the unlettered man, that men of refined learning were puzzled to find out, how it was possible to create so great and so general a movement through the instrumentality of such trifling propositions. The public debates which took place throughout Germany seemed to turn upon mere truisms and puerilities. And yet these apparent puerilities could not be battered down by the greatest amount of learning which was brought to bear upon them.

It is the same with all the important and salutary revolutions which take place in civil society. The governing ideas are few and easily comprehended, because they contain general truths ; and the truths are general because they have reference to the interests of large collections of men. A highly intelligent man, who had been a member of the American legislature, remarked to me, that "he must give up all his notions as to the incompetency of farmers to legislate for the community. They have both more sagacity and more information than I had at all calculated upon."

The establishment of constitutional government in the United States has given a decided impulse to the public mind in Europe. Ten or twelve of the European states have adopted written constitutions. But none of them rest upon the same firm foundation as in America. A written constitution, emanating from the popular will, while the government was monarchical or aristocratical in character, would be a solecism in politics. Neither of those govrnments could possibly survive the establishment of such an instrument. If not immediately annihilated, they must speedily fall to decay. Men, whatever their physical strength may be, must at least have a fit atmosphere to breathe in. So that we must either say that the diffusion of knowledge is incompatible with the solid interests of mankind, or that monarchy and aristocracy are incompatible with the existence of constitutional government in its legitimate sense. There cannot be two inconsistent rules, at one and the same time, for the government of a community; the one founded upon the general interests, the other upon some particular interests only. One or the other must give way; and it is easy to see which will ultimately have the advantage, amid the general spread of knowledge which we witness in the nineteenth century. Where resides the moral power of the community, there also will be found to reside its physical power. The maxim, that power is constantly sliding from the many to the few, is false in a republic. The tendency is directly the reverse. The maxim is true only where the political institutions are unfavorable to the development and spread of knowledge, and where every contrivance has been employed to render the affairs of government complicated and mysterious in the extreme, and so to impress the popular mind with a conviction, not only that it has no right, but that it has no sort of ability, to bear any part in them.

But however imperfect the European constitutions may be, they are a great step toward the establishment of regular government. No event which has occurred in that quarter of the globe affords more signal evidence of the general advance of society. A written constitution never adds to, but always subtracts from, the power which previously existed. It is not only an open recognition of certain general principles favorable to liberty, but it is obliged to make a definite application of these principles. What was obtained when the community was struggling for freedom, can with difficulty be recalled when it has arrived at greater maturity. For a written constitution, together with the body of new laws which it gives occasion to, acts directly upon the manners, diffuses more inquisitiveness and information, and inspires all classes with a greater degree of self-confidence. The ability to guard the institutions is derived from the influence which the institutions have themselves created. There may be still more progress, but there will rarely ever be a retrograde movement.

The French "charte" is the most remarkable of the European constitutions. It was wrested from the king. And this indicates, at least, that knowledge and liberty have acquired sufficient strength to make a vigorous protest against the unlimited authority of kings. The leading men in the kingdom were obliged to fall in with this movement, in order to sustain their own influence, but they have contributed, however unwillingly, to strengthen the popular will. The "tiers etat," a name which one startled the ear, has become a body of acknowledged importance in the state.

The European governments had all grown by piecemeal. The fragments of which they consisted were put together as force or accident determined. Not representing the public will, the people were at a loss to discover the title which their rulers arrogated to themselves. There was no way of solving the difficulty but by having recourse to an authority from above. Hence the doctrine of the "jure divino" right of kings to rule. The minds of men were then filled with all sorts of superstition, and the prince, whose privileges flow from so exalted a source, seems alone entitled to place a construction upon them. Elizabeth told the English commons that they must not dare to meddle with state affairs ; and Charles XII, of Sweden, told the senate that he would send his boot to govern them. Constitutional government has effected the same revolution in politics, which the progress of physical science has produced in religion. Both have banished superstition ; the one from the domain of government, the other from that of religion. The human mind can no more get back to the notion of the divine right of kings, than it can get back to fetichism and idolatry.

A popular constitution is necessarily a restraint upon the majority so that that form of government which it has been supposed would be most exposed to the inroads of licentiousness, is the one which is most strongly secured against them. For as a written constitution is obliged to contain an exact distribution of the powers of the various departments, the persons who fill those places cannot separate themselves from the rule which created them, and say, because they are temporarily and for certain purposes the majority, that therefore they are the majority for all purposes and for all time to come. Do as we will, the moment we establish a popular constitution, we are compelled to afford a substantial security to the minority against the majority. It could not be a popular constitution, unless it contained provisions for securing the rights of all classes, without reference to the fact whether either shall afterward fall into the party of the majority, or into that of the minority. And although it is plain that it is physically possible to overleap the bounds set up by the constitution, yet so firm is the hold which this solemn covenant has upon the minds of every one, that the most ambitious and unprincipled men recoil from the attempt.

When this has become the settled habit of thinking among the people, their feelings and imagination come in aid of their convictions of right. The constitution becomes a memorable record; and the fancy clothes it with additional solemnity. If the altar and the throne become objects of veneration in monarchical government, the altar and the constitution become objects of equal veneration in a republic. In those rare instances, when attempts have been made by the state legislatures in America to violate their constitutions, there has been a redeeming virtue among the people, which has either compelled the majority to retrace their steps, or, by converting the minority into the majority, has brought the constitution back to its pristine spirit.

If there were no such instrument, parties would do very much what the exigencies of the moment dictated. For how would it be possible to argue upon the constitutionality of any measure, when there was no constitution in existence. The alarm may be given of a contemplated violation of some fundamental right; but how can the people be made to understand this. A written constitution affords the only plain test. Some of its provisions may be the subject of dispute, but in the great majority of instances, it will be a clear and most important guide in judging the actions of all the public functionaries.

The express, and the implied powers in a written constitution, are sometimes identical. This is a distinction which deserves great consideration, for from it very important consequences follow. The express powers are identical with the implied, whenever the former would be unmeaning and inoperative, unless laws were subsequently passed to carry them into effect. Without the aid of these laws, which are referred to the head of implied powers, the express powers would be a nullity. This is evident from the 8th section of the 1st article of the constitution of the United States. All the powers therein delegated to the legislature, are express powers, and yet not one can be exercised without passing laws. It is different with regard to the powers which are conferred upon the executive. These, for the most part, may be executed without the intervention of any laws. This is evident from the 2d and 3d sections of the 2d article. Some, perhaps all, the powers there enumerated, may be modified by the legislature. For instance, the power of removal from office may be forbidden under certain conditions; but they are all substantially exercisable, without any acts of legislation. This is the these powers also may be modified by the legislature, while the most important part of them execute themselves, and render it unnecessary to resort to any implied powers. This important difference between the legislative, and the other two departments, contributes greatly to enlarge the powers of the former, as the field within which the implied powers may be exercised is never precisely determined. On the other hand, there is this compensation for reducing to the case, also, with the powers conferred upon the judiciary. Some of character of implied powers, all those which are wielded by the legislature, that those which are possessed by the executive and judiciary, being complete without the intervention of any laws, these two departments are protected against the assaults of the legislature. If, then, it were possible to reduce to the character of express powers, all those which are conferred upon the legislative, in analogy with those conferred upon the executive and judiciary, a very important step would be made towards improving the whole structure of government. That this may be effected to a great extent, cannot be doubted. A very important movement has been lately made in this direction by some of the American states. It is no objection that it will render constitutions a little more voluminous. A constitution is faulty, when, by going into detail, its provisions are ambiguous. But when the opposite effect, that of greater clearness and precision, is attained, the objection loses its force. If in the federal government, the powers which appertain to the legislature are all of the character of implied powers, this is true, in a still higher sense, in the constitutions of the states. The former does contain an enumeration of the powers which are proper to be exercised by the legislature, although none can be exercised without the aid of the implied powers. But the state constitutions generally, do not even contain this enumeration. They simply create the legislative power, and then leave it free to act as the public exigencies and its own discretion may dictate. The reason of the distinction is obvious. The federal constitution is one of strictly limited powers; limited not merely in respect to the constitution making power, but as regards the state governments. It was necessary, therefore, to make a specification in gross of its powers, in order to separate them from those of the states. But there are powerful reasons, as I shall presently show, why a state constitution should be as well guarded in this particular, as the constitution of the Union.

One use of the veto of the executive is to protect him against the usurpations of the legislature, but another and still higher use is to protect the community against those usurpations. One reason why the executive, although a single individual, may succeed in the exercise of this power, is that he is armed with an extensive patronage. This clothes him with great authority, and enables him, when he acts with fidelity, to rally the sound part of the community. One reason why the veto is generally dropped in the state constitutions, is that it is impossible, even if it were consistent with the genius of free institutions, to create an executive with very extensive patronage: another is, that the states are not so extensive as to foster powerful local interests. Thus, the necessity of the veto is accompanied with a corresponding necessity of strengthening the magistrate who exercises it; and on the other hand, in proportion to its inutility, is the difficulty of rendering it authoritative.

It may be supposed that in an extensive country like the United States, executive patronage would be so great as to enable the chief magistrate to exercise the veto improperly. Doubtless, this will sometimes be the case. In every human institution we always make allowance for occasional aberrations, as we do in the most perfect machinery. But there is an antidote to the evil. Where universal suffrage is established, the amount of patronage, though great as regards the executive, is very small when compared with the number of the electors.

In a limited monarchy, the absolute veto is conferred upon the king, in order to protect him against the usurpations of the legislature, which represents the sovereignty: in other words, he is himself made a branch of the legislative power; for to give him the absolute veto, is to confer upon him legislative power. In a republic, the written constitution guards him against those encroachments, for his powers are clearly defined. But if the powers of the legislature are all of the nature of implied powers, which cannot be defined, it may be necessary to invest him with the qualified veto, the danger of usurpation not being as where there is no enumeration of either the express or implied powers. This would seem to afford an argument for giving the veto to the governor of a state; for as I have observed, the list of implied powers in a state government is vastly more extensive than in the federal, and the danger of encroachments on the community is as great, although there may be little danger of invading the prerogatives of the governor. There are, however, two ways of protecting society against the usurpations of the legislature. One in the manner I have just indicated, the other by circumscribing the authority of the legislature, that is, by inserting limitations in the state constitutions, on the exercise of every power which is intended to be withheld from the legislature, and express grants of every one which is intended to be exercised. There is a marked tendency in this direction in the state constitutions which have lately been framed. The prohibition of contracting a public debt, unless authorized by vote of the people, first inserted in the constitutions of Rhode Island and Iowa, and since in those, of New York and Ohio; the provision that special charters shall not be granted; that the legislature shall not authorize the suspension of specie payments; that the stockholders in a corporation shall be individually responsible, contained in the 8th article of the constitution of New York, and the whole of the 14th section of the 7th article of the same constitution, are remarkable examples. Of the same character are the 4th, 5th, 15th and 16th sections of the 3d article, and the 4th and 11th sections of the 6th article, and most of the provisions in the bill of rights, or 51st article. Indeed, it is remarkable that until recently the restrictions upon the legislative power, for the most part, have been carefully placed in the bill of rights. The great importance of controlling the department by express limitations, did not command public attention. Notwithstanding, however, that the constitution of New York has so far exceeded any other in the precision and comprehensiveness of its restrictions upon the legislature, the veto of the governor is retained. It will probably be retained until experiment has ascertained all the cases in which exact limitations may be imposed. When these are exhausted—when all the implied powers are converted into express powers, it may be dropped.

It would seem then, that the veto is only conferred upon the executive, in consequence of the imperfect character of the limitations imposed upon the leglslature. If society can be protected against the predominance of local interests, against the improper exercise of implied powers by express limitations, these will be much more efficacious than the veto. Even in the federal government, what an amount of mischief may have been averted, if precise provisions in relation to a bank, to the tariff, to internal improvements, &c., had been inserted. Nothing but experience could disclose where the weak points of the system lay. But the difficulty of availing ourselves of this experience in the federal government, is infinitely greater than in those of the states. It is exceedingly difficult to obtain amendments in the former. The veto will therefore be retained there, after it ceases to be employed in the latter.

An immense advantage will arise from this scheme of strict limitations, independently of its dispensing with the veto. It will, to a great extent, close the door upon party dissensions. If any one reflects upon the various questions which have agitated the people of the states, and kindled so fierce a spirit of party, he will find that they are nearly all attributable to the defect of the state or of the federal constitutions, in defining the attributes of the legislature. If a state constitution merely creates this department, and is almost entirely silent as to its powers, the door is immediately opened to the most unbounded discussion, as to the propriety of various acts of legislation. If the federal constitution does contain an enumeration of its powers, and this is wanting in the requisite precision, an endless controversy is kept up, not merely as to the expediency, but as to the constitutionality of various laws. A few words in the one case, a few lines in the other, would have prevented the mischief.

It would appear then, that so far from its being true, that constitutions are sacred, and should never be touched; that they partake of the character of all human institutions, and should be open to amendment. It is not in the power of the finest genius to draw up a constitution which shall be perfect at the time; much less, which shall be so in all time to come. Time and experience are indispensable to develop the true character of the powers which are marked out, and to reveal the secret flaws which have prevented the exact working of the system. England was convulsed with civil wars, or ruled with a rod of iron, until the revolution of 1788, when some precise limitations were imposed upon the power of government. And yet these limitations do not contain as much as is contained in the bill of rights of some of the American states. So far is it from being true, that written constitutions are of no avail, that the British constitution derives all its efficacy, all its healthful activity, from those written provisions which were made about the time of the revolution. It may be said, that that nation is not yet prepared for an entirely written constitution. But given the fact, that a nation is thus prepared, and then, the more exact and the more comprehensive are its provisions in relation to the legislative power, the more securely will the bulwarks of liberty be guarded.

A constitution is open to alteration by the same power which enacted it. The sovereign authority residing in the people is necessarily inalienable. It cannot be extinguished, because there is no human power superior to itself to have that effect. To assert that a constitution is of so sacred a character, that it can never again be touched, would be to return to the European notions of government. A constitution, however, may provide in what way alterations shall be made ; so as to get rid on the one hand of the difficulty which would arise from one generation attempting to bind all others ; and at the same time, to secure that the future generation which does make alterations shall be the people themselves, and not their rulers.

All the American constitutions contain provisions of this kind. But as it rarely happens that a constitution will require to be entirely remodeled, a way is provided by which particular amendments may be made, without the necessity of assembling a convention. In some states the proposed change must be deliberated upon, and agreed to by two-thirds of two successive legislatures, in others it is after a vote of two-thirds of two successive legislatures, submitted to the people at their annual elections. In Pennsylvania a majority of two successive legislatures is sufficient for this purpose. All these plans are substantially alike. By the first, it is the legislature which makes the alteration. But the members have been chosen by the people, with a direct view to the question of change or no change. In Ohio, Vermont, and New Hampshire, alterations can only be made by a convention, which in the former must be authorized by a vote of two-thirds of the legislature, in the second by a vote of two-thirds of a council of censors. But this vote cannot be taken oftener than once in seven years. And in New Hampshire the votes of the people are taken every seven years, by the selectmen, and assessors, as to the expediency of calling a convention.

The design of all these plans is to secure that alterations shall be made in so solemn and deliberate a manner, that there shall be no question but what they have emanated from the people.

In France it is a settled maxim that "the charte" can never be altered: that there is no power whatever competent to touch it. This seems to savor strongly of the school of Sir Robert Filmer. But in reality, it is a disguised departure from the doctrines of that school. "The charte" has shaken the power of the king and nobility. The danger of alteration, therefore, arises from that quarter. The notion of its inviolability is a check upon them; but it is not a check when popular sentiment calls loudly for some additional safeguard to liberty. Thus, the charte was remodeled in 1830, when provisions of vital importance to Frenchmen were inserted.

In great Britain the maxim is that parliament is the sovereign power. But I imagine that no parliament would dare to meddle with any of those fundamental enactments which secure English liberty. In 1689 it was deemed fit that "the convention," which seated William on the throne, and passed the celebrated "act of settlement," should be composed of the members who had sat in the two preceding parliaments.

Government, like every other human interest, is the subject of experience, and therefore capable of improvement. We are bound, therefore, in devising a system of civil policy, to avail ourselves of the same helps and resources which give strength and security to every other institution.

Society is not resolved into its original elements, by the call of a convention to alter the constitution. There is no instant of time, in the transition from the old to the new state of things, when there is not a subsisting government. Until a new constitution is ordained, the citizens are bound by the old. But a strange imagination exists among some persons, that whatever the people have power to do, they have also the right to do. It is not that such persons are at all friendly to the exercise of licentious power; but they can see no way of separating right and power, where there is no positive or organized authority, to limit and control the last. First, then, a distinction must be made between the power of voting and the power of executing. A convention might declare all existing marriages null, bastardise the children, confiscate the property of every one at death, authorize theft and murder, etc.; but it is plain, that it would not have power to carry these ordinances into effect. This distinction between the power of declaring and the power of executing, has been repeatedly illustrated in the history of all the European governments, even those which have possessed the most solidly established authority. The English parliament, armed with all the powers of a convention, was not able, in the reign of Mary, to exterminate the Protestants : it was not able in the succeeding reign, to abolish either the Catholic or Puritan religion. The French monarchs, prior and subsequent to the time of Henry the great, although they employed every instrument, both physical and moral, were unable to exterminate the Huguenots. That sect survived every effort to subdue them, and are now a powerful and influential body in the kingdom. No monarch ever possessed more absolute authority than Charles V., and Philip II. of Spain ; yet they were unable to execute their edicts among the people of the low countries. This people annulled their edicts, and became sovereign themselves.

Second. A constitutional convention has not the right to do everything which it has the power to do. Individuals every day have the opportunity to kill others, but they have not the right to do so. That an individual may be punished, and that a nation, or the majority, is dispunishable, makes no difference ; for it will be conceded, that if there were no means of punishing an individual, as there frequently are not, his guilt would be precisely the same, and his right without the shadow of foundation. There is no possible way, therefore, by which we can make right and power convertible terms. It is in vain to say, that these are extreme cases, and therefore prove nothing ; for they do, indeed, prove everything which is proper to be proved. They destroy the notion of universality, as a part of the rule ; and they, therefore, destroy the rule itself. They may also prove, that the same principles which falsify the rule in some particulars, operate throughout the whole system of legislation, and may be calculated upon with precision. But it may be said, that there are many questions, about which there is no such general opinion of right and justice, as to render the enactments of a convention at all uniform ; that this opens the door to a certain latitude of judgment, and that within this debatable field, it is free to declare what is right, and has power to enforce its decrees. This is admitted : there must be many questions, about which a difference of opinion will prevail, among persons of equal integrity and capacity. It is, however, a great boon gained to society, when all those questions, which are not debatable *in foro conscientiæ*, are withdrawn from the field of controversy. This happens more certainly in a society democratically constituted, than in any other. It is a fine observation of Mr. Hume, that events which depend upon the will of a great number, may be calculated upon with much more certainty than those which depend upon the will of a single individual, or of a small number of persons. Events which are dependent upon a great number, are governed by general laws, laws which are common to the species : those which depend upon one, or a small number, are subjected to the caprice, or momentary disposition of the individual. The reason, then, why the advantage I have indicated appertains to a society democratically constituted, is that the will of a great number, and upon that great number public events then depend, is consulted. No one has ever heard of a provision inserted in any American constitution or law, which did violence to any of the fundamental rules of morality. Individuals may be guilty of a violation of them constantly ; and, therefore, while we place no confidence in any calculation we may make as to what they will do, we may rely with great certainty upon a calculation, as to the conduct of a very large body of men. But when I speak of a society which is democratically constituted, I do not intend merely a society which has democratic institutions ; it may have them to-day, and lose them to-morrow. I intend a society in which not only the political, but the social organization is so advanced, as to render free institutions the natural expression of the national will. In such a community, the greater the number whose opinions are taken, the greater the probability that those opinions will be reduced to unity ; in other words, that the incoherent views which are entertained by some, will be swallowed up in the opinions of a great number. For to say that they are incoherent, is to say that they do not reflect the opinions which are common to the whole.

CHAPTER II.

THAT IN A REPUBLIC, THE GOVERNORS AND THE GOVERNED ARE IDENTICAL, AND DIFFERENT.

SOME persons find exceeding difficulty in comprehending how the people who govern should be one and the same with the people who are governed. The simplest and the most general notion which we ever form of government, is that it is an institution established to preside over society, to maintain the supremacy of the laws, and to resist all efforts from without, to shake and undermine its influence To accomplish this, it would seem to be necessary that government should possess an independent authority; that it should be armed with a power which could not be wrested from it, at the very time when it was most important to employ it. Self government, or a democratic republic, which presupposes that the governors and the governed are one and the same, appears then to be a solecism in politics. It seems to contain an inherent principle of decay, and on that account to be the least eligible form of government which can be adopted. The notions which we frame to ourselves on all subjects, but especially on politics, are so much determined by the forms of thought which have previously existed, that it is always a work of difficulty to break up old associations, and to persuade the mind, that any remarkable change in the institutions of society can be easily accomplished, much less, that it would be both safe and advantageous.

The actual operation of popular government relieves us from the difficulty which has been suggested. For there, parties in the majority and minority immediately rise up. And as the former is entitled by right and by necessity to the supremacy, an example is afforded at the outset, of a presiding power in the state which is distinct from that of the whole of society. Thus, if a small number of persons, when compared with the entire population, are disposed to be vicious, and to violate the private rights of any individual, inasmuch as the administration of the laws is deposited with a much larger number, a check upon the conduct of the former is created, which operates with certainty, in ninety-nine cases in a hundred. And if we suppose, that a still greater proportion—a proportion which constituted nearly or even quite a majority—were so inclined; still, if the distribution of property is such, that the major part of the citizens have some allotment, some stake in the hedge: their interests will outweigh the propensity to commit mischief; and the sense of interest, combining with the operation of the laws, after civil government is fairly established, redoubles its authority, and in the course of no very long time, beguiles the understandings of all men—the educated, and the illiterate, the honest, andthe depraved—into the belief that there is indeed an inherent power residing in the government, which can in no way be confounded with the local and discordant opinions which prevail without.

Nor, even if the unanimous consent of the people were admitted to be necessary to the first institution of government, would there be any great difficulty in obtaining it. Even the most abandoned men shrink from a public exposure of their hearts. Nor are crimes ever committed from habitual disposition, but from sudden impulse, or powerful temptation, which cannot well exist at the time when a popular convention is deliberating upon the form of government which shall be established. Nor, if it were otherwise, would it alter the case, since the worst men are as deeply interested in the maintenance of the general body of laws, as are the best. They would not be able to commit any crime, unless their own lives were protected up to a certain point. Their persons would not be safe, as soon as they discovered a disposition to commit violence upon others. This is the reason why what is vulgarly termed "lynch law," is so abhorrent to offenders, as well as to all lovers of law and order. Once established as a rule, and the mere suspicion that a crime was committed, or about to be committed, would lead to summary punishment; while the penalty inflicted, might be out of all proportion to the character of the offense. "Give me a fair trial," said a miserable creature, whom I once knew summarily dealt with. "If I have broken the laws, I am entitled to justice."

Instances have come under my observation, where individuals who freely voted for the establishment of a constitution, afterwards rendered themselves amenable to the laws, which were passed in conformity with that constitution. And I recollect two instances of individuals, members of a legislative body, who assisted in the enactment of laws, which punished forgery and perjury with great severity, and each of whom was afterwards the victim of one of those laws. Few men assist in passing sentence upon themselves. But all men are, some how or other, irresistibly impelled to create the tribunal which is destined to punish them, if they are guilty.

So far, we have considered government chiefly in its simplest form: tbe government of the people in person. But it is not practicable to conduct the affairs of a large state in this way. Almost all the ancient commonwealths were of small size. The Grecian states were none of them larger than an American county. Attica, the most famous, was of no greater extent than Ross county, in Ohio. Indeed, city and state were synonymous terms with the Grecian lawyers. By the government of a state, they intended the government of a city. Even in the Roman commonwealth, the governing power was for a long time, in theory, and almost always in practice, confined to the walls of the city.

But when the elective principle is introduced, the machinery of the government becomes more complicated. Those administrative officers, who were before appointed by the people, are invested with additional authority. And the legislative body becomes at once the most important and the most imposing of all the institutions of government.

There is no good reoson why a popular constitution should not be established in a simple democracy, as well as in a representative government. In both, the minority require to be protected against the majority. But the idea of a written constitution does not readily suggest itself, unless the state is sufficiently large to occasion the introduction of the elective principle into general practice. The fundamental ordinances of the ancient lawgivers were of a totally different character, not merely in their origin, but in their purport, from the American constitution. They were like the ordinary acts of legislation, which are intended to restrain the people;

whereas, one great design of a constitution is to restrain the government.

The adoption of snch an instrument, then, may appear to be a source of weakness, but in reality it is a source of great strength to the government. The individual whose conduct is marked by most propriety, no matter whether from internal or external motives, acquires most power in the circle within which he moves. And a representative government, which moves within the ample but well defined jurisdiction marked out for it, acquires unspeakable influence from that circumstance. And although the original intention, in framing a written constitution, was to supply the grand defect which existed in all preceding governments, to-wit, the absence of a control upon the governors, yet it operates with equal efficacy in restraining the rest of society. The existence of such an instrument, then, is another addition to the apparatus of the government, giving it an air of greater solemnity, investing its proceedings with a more regular and decisive authority, and thus contributing practically to separate, in the minds of every one, two ideas which are at bottom the same; to-wit, the idea of the people as governors, and of the people who are governed.

Various reasons have been assigned for the division of the legislature into two branches. The plan appears to have been unknown among the republics of antiquity. Where two chambers did exist, one possessed powers of a different character from those of the other, and therefore the co-operation of the two was not necessary; or else, one acted as a deliberative body merely, with at the utmost the power of initiating measures, while the others possessed the legislative power proper. Feudal institutions, which gave rise to a baronial nobility, seated by the side of growing and powerful cities, introduced the scheme as it exists in modern states. The population of the towns was of too much importance to be overlooked, while at the same time, the barons were too haughty and jealous to permit the representatives of those towns to have seats among themselves. The legislative body therefore became separated into two bodies, occupying at first the same hall, but afterward sitting in two, when the practice of public debate took the place of the private conferences, and rendered it impossible to conduct the proceedings at different ends of even a large apartment. And, although the reason for this arrangement has ceased to exist, the institution is still preserved. Perhaps we may be able to assign to it an office distinct from that which has been ascribed to it, and say that, although it has the appearance of being more out of place in a democratic republic, where the subordination of ranks does not exist, than in any other form of government; yet, inasmuch as two chambers render the machinery of legislation more complex than one alone, and communicate to the government a more imposing character than it would otherwise wear, this division of the legislative body may assist, although indirectly, in upholding the public authority, and in maintaining order and tranquility throughout the state. It is no objection to an institution that it exercises an influence over the imaginations of men, provided this influence does not interfere with the useful and legitimate purposes which were designed to be answered, but on the contrary, contributes to carry them out more fully.

A regular system of jurisprudence would appear to be as essential to a people living under the simplest form of popular government, as for any other community. The eternal principles of justice are not of man's creation; and they have on that account an authority which no man is at liberty to deny or disparage. A code of jurisprudence is nothing more than an exposition of those principles, so far as they apply to the affairs of society. But the existence of such an instrument is hardly known until after the state has passed from the simplest form of democratic rule, and has assumed the character of a representative government. The people, when sitting in judgment personally, cannot with any convenience make application of those principles of law requiring, as they do, the most concentrated attention, and the exercise of an undisturbed judgment. Indeed, such principles have the appearance of being out of place, where the form of government presupposes that there is no superior authority behind the judicial magistrates. We hear of the Roman or civil law. But no one has ever heard of Grecian law. The organization of the Grecian tribunal was exceedingly unfavorable to the growth of a regular system of civil jurisprudence. The principal court was composed of six or eight thousand people; and the decisions of such a tribunal must necessarily be vague and conjectural. Nor did Roman law make any progress until the judicial power passed from the popular assemblies of the comitia, and became exclusively vested in the representative magistrates termed prætors. It is not until the reign of Adrian, in the commencement of the second century, that jurisprudence began to wear the character of a regular system, such as it is known at the present day. The division of labor was then consummated. The judicial power was lodged with certain magistrates, set apart for that purpose, who were obliged to act upon some fixed, general rules. And the collection of those rules into a body constitutes in great part the foundation of the civil law. In the time of the emperors the prætors were not an elective magistracy: but the special character of the duties they were assigned to perform, after a beginning had been made, was far more favorable to the growth of a regular system than the tumultuous meetings of the comitia. In addition to which an absolute government in a highly civilized country, is very willing to purchase an unlimited political authority, by establishing exact rules of justice in what concerns the civil relations of men. If it were not for some principle of virtual representation at least, neither law nor civilization would ever make any progress.

But what the appointing power effects is accomplished still more fully by the elective power. In no country in the world has jurisprudence acquired a more regular and systematic character, than in the United States. The perfection which it has attained constitutes its only objection. All the leading principles on which it reposes have been so thoroughly ramified, and rendered so flexible with the professional man,, in their application to new cases, that the science no longer presents the same attraction as formerly, to minds of a highly intellectual cast. We may say of the law what has been said of mathematics, that it has become an exhausted science. But this regular growth of a body of laws, with appropriate tribunals and magistrates to administer it, the natural result of the introduction of representative government, has a wonderful effect in giving to the institutions an appearance of complexity, and in surrounding them with an air of authority, which only contributes to carry out the design for which they were originally created. These institutions are the workmanship of the people. And yet between the people and the government is interposed a vast and complicated machinery, difficult to break through, and which inculcates and enforces among the whole population, the notions of right, of obligation, of justice, more effectually than the decrees of the most absolute government could do.

The extent of country over which the government presides, assists in keeping up the delusion, in persuading people, that there is an authority residing in the government totally independent of the popular will: if that can be called a delusion, which has its origin in the most settled principles of human nature, and which only contributes to highten the reverence for the laws, and to maintain order and tranquility throughout the land.

Even where the territory is only of tolerable extent, government is called upon to act, through the medium of a host of functionaries, in a great number of particular instances. And, this acting in detail repeatedly, and on such an infinity of occasions, without any perceptible interference from without, separates the notion of governmental authority from that of the popular will, augments the authority of the former, and enables it to exercise an easy empire over the minds of men. And yet it possesses this influence, only in consequence of being founded upon the popular will, and on the condition of making itself eminently useful to society.

When men are called upon to act openly in face of the world, their actions are naturally more guarded and circumspect, than where they are free from so wholesome a control. This is the case even though the sense of right should be supposed to be no stronger than on other occasions. For when they come to deliberate in public, each one finds that the interests of others have an intimate relation with his own; and that, do as he will, their opinions will entitle themselves to equal consideration with his. This is the case in the simplest form of democratic government, where all the citizens meet together to consult upon public affairs. But the effect is increased where the elective form of government is established. In the first instance, the whole population constitute the public. The actors and the spectators, the delinquents and the judges, are indiscriminately mixed. The restraint therefore is not complete. Hence the tumultuous assemblies in the Grecian republics. In the second case, the legislature, executive, and judges, together with the whole body of administrative officers, constitute at any one time only a fraction of the population. The government and the public are separated from each other, in order that the last may bear with greater weight, and a more defined authority, upon the first. The keenness of the observers is hightened, and the conduct of the actors is more circumspect. Those who are invested with public trusts of any kind, find that they are no longer able to bury their motives and disguise their actions amid a vast and heterogeneous assembly. The circumstances in which they are placed rouse a feeling of responsibility to other men ; and this in its turn, awakens reflection, and a sense of justice. But, the circumstances in which men are placed, constitute a very large part of their education through life. And this sense of justice, and this habit of reflection, although originally induced by external causes, may in progress of time become very important springs of action. If all those public functionaries were accustomed to act as simple members of an immense assembly, called together on the spur of the occasion, they would be carried away by every temporary delusion ; and their actions would seem in their own eyes worthy of condemnation, only when it was too late to correct them.

This is the reason why what we term public opinion acquires so much force, and wears so imposing an authority, in representative government. That portion of the population which gives being to it, is far more numerous, the public much more extensive, than in any other form of government; while at the same time, the public officers of every grade stand apart and distinct from that public, and are therefore subjected to a constant and active supervision from without; and, if the separation of the two has the effect of hightening the sense of responsibility, and increasing the capacity for reflection in the former, it has the same influence upon the people. These are also placed in new circumstances, which are eminently calculated to promote thought and inquiry. And although the persons who fill the three great departments of the government, and all the administrative officers, are but the agents of the people ; yet this people now view the conduct of the former from a point different from that at which they view their own. They expect and demand better things than they would from themselves. And the constant working of this principle, in spite of all the tendencies to licentiousness of opinion, ultimately communicates, to both the public and the government, more calmness and moderation, and a disposition to view things not merely as they are, but as they should be. It frequently happens, that on the proposal of an important public measure, popular feeling seems to run in one direction, while the representatives of the people are disposed to take a different course. The discussion which takes place in the legislative body gives rise to discussion out of doors. The people and their representatives have time to compare notes ; and instead of a high state of feeling and exasperation, a greater degree of reflection is produced. So that when the final vote has been taken in the legislative body, it has received the most cordial approbation from the men of all parties. The settlement of the Oregon controversy is an instance of this. It is a memorable proof, that the question of peace and war is coming to be viewed in a manner totally different from what it was formerly : and that the American people and government are deeply impressed with the notion, that to preserve peace is to maintain civilization. The institutions of government in a republic have some other office to perform, besides that of giving occasion to the exercise of political power. They beget habits of reflection, and disseminate a spirit of inquiry throughout the land. Nor are those protracted debates which take place in the legislature, and which are so much the subject of criticism abroad, without their use. They allow time for public opinion to ripen, and bring the people and their representatives into harmony with each other. Half a century ago, the treaty negotiated by Mr. Jay, although it was exceedingly advantageous to the United States, created a degree of agitation which shook the confederacy to its very center. The institutions were then young ; the people had not grown into the new circumstances in which they were placed. Time, and the consequent increase of population, which it was predicted would develop in ten-fold strength, the mischiefs then experienced, has had a contrary effect. A dispute which, in 1795, may have kindled a bloody and unprofitable war was, in 1846, easily adjusted upon the same principles on which sagacious men of business act, in settling their private controversies.

In a democratic republic of considerable extent, the electors are so numerous that each feels himself like a drop in the ocean. So that the more the number of active citizens is increased, the greater is the power of the state, and yet in the same proportion is the importance of each individual diminished. The governors and the governed are in reality one and the same; but so exceedingly small is the share of influence which falls to each person, that everything seems to go on without any co-operation on his part. The movements of the political machine seem to be directed by an unseen hand, and to be conducted with as much regularity and precision as in the most consolidated governments. The difference between the two cases is, that in the former it is a mere illusion, while in the last it is all reality. But the illusion which is practiced upon the imagination, instead of detracting from the weight which the governed possess in the character of governors, adds greatly to it. Each one of the citizens is of importance; and yet if it were possible for him to realize this—to believe that he was of so much consequence, that his participation in the government was necessary to the general weal—public affairs would meet with constant hindrances, instead of proceeding with order and regularity. It is because each one does act, and yet so acts that his voice appears to be drowned in that of the public, that so much alertness and energy are combined with so much prudence and circumspection in the management of public affairs, and that one of the most difficult problems in government—that of conciliating the rights of each with the interests of all—approaches as near solution as, humanly speaking, is possible. It is in those countries where the electors are few, that the government feels most apprehensive, and is in danger of the most frequent revolutions. So that so far is the notion, that the governors and the governed may be one and the same, from being a paradox in politics, the more completely we succeed in practice in carrying it out, the more secure is the government, and the more prosperous and powerful are the people.

The same sense of feebleness and insignificance which each citizen feels as an elector, is more or less experienced by him when he desires to be a candidate for office. Although the elective form of government has the effect of multiplying the public employments, yet these are after all so few, when compared with the great number of persons who are eligible to them, that not one in a thousand dares flatter himself that he will be the successful candidate, or if he is, that he will be able to retain his place beyond the short period for which he is at first elected. This has one good effect. In spite of many untoward influences, acting in an oppose direction, it lessens the self importance of individuals, and puts every one on his good behavior.

Thus, in a republic, men demand that the utmost equality should prevail. They establish free institutions, and thus open the way to all the offices and emoluments in the state. But they have no sooner done so, than they find themselves crowded and incommoded in every effort to acquire the object of their ambition. If they lived under a monarchical or aristocratical government, they would have been obliged to contend with those who had the advantages of rank or fortune on their side. Those advantages are now annulled, but the number of those who are eligible to offices is multiplied more than a hundred fold, and the obstacles in the way of acquiring them, although of a very different kind, are yet fully as great as in any other form of government. But those institutions which have raised up so many barriers to the ambition of all popular candidates, and contracted their hopes and expectations within the narrowest possible dimensions, are the workmanship of the people themselves. They have neither the right, therefore, nor any the least disposition to quarrel with its operation. This is one reason why in the United States the profoundest tranquillity prevails after the elections. Up to the time when they are held all is excitement and agitation. But they are no sooner closed than the whole population seeks repose. The same institutions which extend liberty to all, establish the empire of public opinion, which, representing the sentiments and interests of all classes, presses with an irresistible weight upon the whole community, giving security to the government, and contentment to the people. All is brought about by the votes of a majority of the citizens, and to this majority all parties are habituated, by a sense of interest as well as from the necessity of the case, to pay unlimited deference.

Thus, although the electoral franchise is extended to the utmost, so that the government is literally wielded by the people, yet between the people and the organized authority of the state there is interposed a machinery which, as it is viewed by each individual, has an air of sanctity and importance which gives addititional force to the public will. It is illusion. The institutions are the direct and legitimate offspring of the popular vote. Each citizen contributes to the formation of public opinion; but once it is formed it represents a whole, and presses with an undivided weight upon each. So each individual of the majority contributes to make up the million and a half of votes which decide the election of the American president. But that majority is then viewed in the aggregate, and so acquires an easy empire over the imaginations of all.

But this is not all. As it is only a small number of the people who can fill the public offices at any one time, as it is a still smaller number who can ever succeed to the highest, the government and the people seem to be still more separated from one another. All the public officers are mere agents of the people. But they are as one to thousands. They are set apart for the performance of special duties, and are all clothed with a greater or less degree of authority. Although chosen for short periods, and constantly watched by the searching eye of public opinion, yet the separation is made, and this is sufficient to impress upon the laws an air of authority which commands respect from the whole population. Moreover there is no time when the public offices are vacant. The persons who conduct public affairs are continually shifting, and yet the government seems to be immortal. There is nothing more worthy of admiration than those numberless contrivances which exist in a society by which a system of compensations is established, and the irregularities of one part are corrected by an unforeseen influence in another. The process is noticeable in the individual man, and is equally observable in that collection of men which we denominate a community.

I do not see why so great difficulty should be felt in conceiving that the people who govern and the people who are governed may be one and the same, when the principal design of civil government is to bring out and to represent those qualities which are common to all. The individual may crave many gratifications, and pursue a great number of ends which appertain to his private interests. These may not interfere with the public weal; they may even contribute directly to promote it. But wherever there is a conflict, inasmuch as all have a right, if one has, to run athwart the public interest, while at the same time the attempt by all to exercise the right would annul it for each, it becomes a matter of necessity, and does not altogether depend upon reflection, that all learn to distinguish more or less carefully between those interests which are peculiar to each and those which are common to all.

But although it is not left to reflection to make the distinction in the first instance, yet, as reflection is powerfully awakened by enlarging the sphere of popular rights, it has a great deal to do with the matter afterward. In the great majority of mankind the formation of habits of reflection must necessarily depend upon the exercise which their minds receive from the daily occupations which engage them. The contrivance of means toward the attainment of the ends they are in pursuit of, the balancing of advantages against disadvantages, and the anxieties of all kinds which are consequent upon this employment of their faculties, makes them reflective in spite of themselves. It has been observed that the Americans are the most serious people in the world. And the remark is undoubtedly just. They are not the gravest, but they are the most serious, people. For there is a very wide difference between gravity and seriousness. The former may be the result of vanity, or dullness, or a frigid temperament. The last always implies thoughtfulness. It is a fine remark of Schiller, that the serene and the placid are the attributes of works of art, but that the serious belongs to human life.

But in a democratic republic, the field of human life is more thoroughly laid open than it is anywhere else. All the ordinary motives to reflection are increased, because the objects, about which reflection is employed, are multiplied. Individuals are thrown more upon their own resources. Each has more to do, more to quicken his exertion, more to kindle hope, and yet to sadden with disappointment. When we look over the vast agricultural population of the United States, and observe that it is almost entirely composed of proprietors, the reason why there is so much activity and yet so much reflection, so much stir and yet such perfect tranquillity, is apparent. Proprietors are charged with the entire management of a business which, in other countries, is divided between two or three classes. They are rendered thoughtful and circumspect, because they have so much to engross their attention and to tax their exertions. If the slaves of the south did not belong to a race decidedly inferior to that of the white man, it would be the highest wisdom to manumit them. The abolition of slavery would have the same effect as the abolition of the laws of primogeniture. It would melt down large properties into farms of a reasonable size. The number of proprietors would be greatly increased, and so would the number of those who would be trained to habits of independent exertion. The agricultural population of the United States are the conservators of the peace, and the great balance wheel of the constitution.

In a country where free institutions exist, not only is the sphere of individual exertion enlarged, the amount of business transacted by private individuals increased, but the interests which are common to all are also increased. If the effect were only to animate the cupidity of individuals, to sharpen the appetite for self gratification, and thus to nourish an universal egotism, it would run counter to all the ends for which civil government is established. But we cannot well enhance the importance of any one's private business, without placing him more in connection with others, compelling him to co-operate in their exertions, and causing them in their turn to be instrumental in his. If, in America, the rural population is for the most part composed of proprietors, and in the towns, the trades are thrown open to all, and not confined to colleges of artizans, there must be a constant tendency toward the creation of a system of common interests, since a great majority of the people have so deep a stake in the protection of property, and in the maintenance of those laws which guarantee personal liberty. Governmental regulation, of one kind or another, becomes more and more necessary. And this necessity is realized by a very great number of people. So that although men escape from the restraint which the artificial forms of government impose; they find themselves, when living under free institutions, surrounded by all sorts of restraints. The great difference between the two cases is, that in the last, the restraint is imposed for the common benefit of all, and with the free consent of all.

But this does not prevent the operation of that illusion to which I have constantly referred. Government has a vast and complicated business to transact, ever increasing with the increase of the population, so that the management of public affairs, in the single state of New York, is far more intricate and weighty than it was in the great empire of Charlemagne. The intervention of the governors stands out in bold relief, as something distinct from, and totally independent of, society. The people of that state created their government, and lend it a free and unanimous support. And yet, there is hardly one of them, perhaps, on hearing pronounced the words "people of the state of New York" in a simple indictment, but what feels as if an immense but undefinable authority was impending over him.

The property which elective government possesses beyond any other, of representing those interests which are common to the whole population, has this further effect: it tends to correct the idiosyncrasy of individuals. So that, contrary to all expectation, there is more sameness, more uniformity of character, among the American people than among any other. In other countries the inequality of rank, the inequality in the distribution of property, together with innumerable influences springing from these, produce the greatest diversity of character. The Americans enjoy more freedom than any other people; but if the structure of society is such that all are obliged to conform to some common standard, this freedom will simply terminate in rendering the manners and modes of thinking of all more alike.

Foreigners, in noticing the commanding authority which the will of the majority impresses upon American society, object to it, and even liken it to the awe which is inspired by monarchical government. But the two things are of an entirely different character. That majority after all reflects pretty much the substantial interests and the leading opinions of all. It could not be a majority of the people, if it did not produce this effect. Parties may afford to magnify their respective differences, if the only effect is to set in a more striking light the numerous points of agreement which exist among them. Moreover, if the superstitious submission, which prevails in a monarchy, contributes to fortify monarchical institutions, the authority, which public sentiment exercises in a republic, has a mighty efficacy in giving force and durability to free institutions. It is very true, that if in the United States any one is so wicked, or so unwise, as to entertain views favorable to the establishment of monarchical or aristocratical government, he dare not give utterance to them. But it is very certain that this species of despotism which is exercised over the minds of men, by causing public sentiment to run in one channel, places the institutions and the manners in harmony with each other, and gives strength and consistency to the first.

Thus, under whatever aspect we may view representative government, the same idea presents itself of an invisible authority residing in the state; which only represents the will of the people; and yet, in the imaginations of all, the high and the low, the rich and the poor, is clothed in a form, which exacts as unlimited obedience to the laws as any other government. Perhaps this phenomenon is only a manifestation of that tendency which the human mind constantly discovers, of figuring to itself some ideal standard of law and justice, which, although it may never be attained, yet acts as a powerful regulative principle in controlling the actions of man. This ideal cannot be found in the partial and half formed opinions of individuals. It is therefore endeavored to be obtained from that character of unity, which the collective authority of all, stamps upon society. We may occasionally notice something of the kind, even in the artificial forms of government, where the prince has pushed his authority to such an excess as to rouse a general popular sentiment for the time being. During the celebrated three days in Paris, a rumor was given out, by the the leaders of the popular party, that a provisional government was formed. Sentinels were stationed before one of the hotels, where La Fayette, General Gerard, and the Duke de Choiseul met; and when any one came to the door, these sentinels would say, the government is in session. This idea of a government, the historian says, gave ten-fold force and energy to the popular cause, and decided the revolution in its favor. But in the democratic republic of the United States, this notion of government, this abstract representation of law and justice, has a legitimate foundation. It, therefore, takes firmer hold of the imaginations of men, and prevents the occurrence of those dreadful commotions which have convulsed France and other countries. It not only prevents any rival notion from springing up; it prevents any rival institution from planting itself in the country.

There is an institution in America which is something new in the history of the civilized world, and which proves with what facility the notion of the governors and the governed being one and the same, may be carried into practice. The religious establishments are all supported by the voluntary contributions of the respective congregations. It was a prevailing idea at one time, even in the United States, that if the state did not take religion under its own care, the religious sentiment would fall to decay. Entirely the reverse has been found to be the case. There is no country in the world where the attention to religion is so marked and so universal as in the United States. The sum which is voluntarily contributed is greater than is collected in any European government, except Great Britain; and the amount which is paid to those who perform the actual duties is larger than in any other, without any exception whatever. So far from infidelity overspreading the land, and every one doing what seems right in his own eyes, the restraint, which religion exercises, is more manifest than anywhere else. Society is singularly exempt from the scornful hate and the pestilential breath of the infidel.

In this instance the governors and the governed are the same; the institution is on an exceedingly large scale, for it embraces a great majority of the population. And the interests, with which it has to do, are of unspeakable magnitude, as they involve all our hopes hereafter, and constitute the chief ties by which society is held together. For religion lies at the foundation of all our notions of law, and justice. Nor is there the least reason to believe that free institutions can be permanently upheld, among any but a religious people.

It is curious to note the working of this principle, that the governed may govern themselves, in some of its minute ramifications. There was a custom in Connecticut at one time (probably still existing), which permitted juries in all cases to retire to consider of their verdicts, unattended by any officer charged to keep them together. When the judge of the federal court first visited the state for the purpose of holding a term, he was startled at this custom, and was so convinced that the laws could not be impartially administered under it, that he expressed a determination to banish it from the tribunal over which he presided. But a previous residence in the state would have satisfied him, that the verdicts of juries in no part of the world were more free from suspicion—more unexceptionable in every respect—than in Connecticut. Too active an inquisition into the actions of men, frequently puts them upon doing the very things which were intended to be prevented.

There is a controversy depending in England at the present day, between the bench and bar on one side, and the press on the other. The press undertakes to report the proceedings of the courts in important public trials, while they are in progress; and the bench and bar deny the right to do so, maintaining that such a practice is calculated to forestall the public mind, and to influence the verdicts of juries. This controversy commenced, or at any rate assumed a threatening aspect, in the time of Lord Ellenborough. That eminent judge, anxious, no doubt, to hold the scales of justice with an even hand, gave it to be understood, that unless the practice was desisted from, the most severe and exemplary measures would be adopted. This was repeatedly proclaimed during the trial of some very important criminal cases : but I believe without effect. Now I do not pretend to say which side is in the right, relatively to an English population : but I do not believe that any harm has resulted in the United States, from the freest publication of similar trials, during their progress through the courts. As all trials are public, in America as well as in England, whatever is transacted within the walls of the court house is immediately spread abroad by the multitude of listeners who are present. And as, from imperfect apprehension, want of tact, or a variety of other causes, representations widely differing from each other will be made of the proceedings, the publication by a journal, which employs a reporter, for the purpose of taking down the evidence, so far from prejudicing the public mind, and turning the course of justice aside, may contribute to correct all the erroneous notions which are afloat. It may be laid down as an invariable maxim, that the good use of an institution will be in proportion to its constant and familiar use.

It is at a comparatively recent period that the comparison of hand-writing has been submitted to the jury. The old rule, which deferred the examination to the court exclusively, has been changed, and the reason assigned for the change is that the persons who composed the jury formerly could not write. As this is no longer the case, the court now derives great assistance from the judgment which is exercised by the jury on this difficult matter. Juries are able to govern themselves, although they are no longer subjected to the rigid control of the court

The freedom which females enjoy, is another remarkable trait in American society. In Roman Catholic countries, indeed in Protestant European communities, nothing of the kind is observed. It may have been supposed, proceeding lamely from a knowledge of what had been, to the conclusion what would be, that so much liberty would give rise to great licentiousness. The reverse is the case. In no country is the purity of the female character better preserved. In order to give to the laws of morality a controlling influence upon our actions, it seems indispensably necessary that we should share to some degree, even in youth, in the responsibility which attaches to those actions. And this can only be accomplished by a delicate mingling of the two things, freedom and restraint.

The liberty of the press is another example. It was once predicted that a press without a licenser would produce infinite licentiousness in conduct and opinions, and that the authority of the government, if not violently overturned, would be secretly undermined by the incessant action of so powerful an agent. All such conjectures have been entirely falsified. In no country is the press so powerful for good, in none is it so powerless for evil, as in the United States. If it were strictly guarded, and only circulated opinions by stealth, the appetite for change would be constantly whetted. The most startling doctrines would gain credence, simply because they were forbidden. By abolishing the office of licenser, the monopoly of the press is broken down. Opinions are harmless, because being free they mutually correct each other. Great multitudes of persons pride themselves upon holding opinions the most adverse to the public safety, when it is a privilege to promulgate them, whether that privilege is conferred by the laws, or is only obtained by stealth. Take away the privilege, and the appetite for all sorts of dangerous novelties gradually wears itself out; for what is novel to-day, becomes threadbare to-morrow, and juster and more sensible views, on all subjects, will be more likely to make their way among the whole population, because the disturbing influence of the passions will be less, instead of greater.

If any one supposes that it has been any part of my design to inculcate the notion, that free institutions are a panacea for all the evils which are incident to society, he will be greatly mistaken. No one can be more pressed down with a conviction of the vices and infirmities which cling to human nature, whatever may be the form in which the institutions are cast. All I have aimed at, is to show that the democratic form of government is free from the objections which have been made to it; that, without pretending to anything like perfection, it is, on the whole, the best form of civil polity which can be devised; the one which is best fitted to bring out the greatest amount of good qualities, both in the individual and the citizen.

I have, therefore, endeavored to show that representation, which in the beginning is an institution by the people, comes, in process of time, and through the instrumentality of causes which are immutable in their operation, to be an institution over as well as by the people. That it is the people who give being to this whole system, and that thus the governors and the governed may be identical and yet different.

CHAPTER III.

SOVEREIGNTY OF THE PEOPLE—IMPORT OF THE PHRASE.

It is certain that free institutions do not render men so perfect but what they may commit great mistakes in the exercise of the privileges which are committed to them. It is equally true that in that form of government men are often led away by the grossest delusions, and are persuaded even to travel beyond the bounds which the great law of morality has prescribed. The term "sovereignty of the people" is one of those which has been subjected to a most fatal misconstruction. Because, in a republic, the political authority of the state has been removed from the insecure foundation on which it formerly rested; because the will of the people has been substituted in the place of hereditary rule; it is sometimes supposed that this new power possessed unlimited attributes, and that it was free to make any disposition which it pleased of the rights of any part of the community. The "juro divino" right has been repudiated, and yet another maxim has risen up in its place equally terrible to humanity, and destructive of the very interests which free institutions are designed to protect. There is no power on earth, the people no more than the prince, which can be conceived to be absolved from the eternal principles of justice. To assert the contrary would be to deny the existence of some of the most fundamental laws of our being—of those laws which stamp upon all human actions a character of right or wrong. Such laws are not mere arbitrary rules, without any dependence upon some governing principle, and free at any time to be taken up or laid down. They are a part of our original constitution, as much so as any of our intellectual faculties or appetites, but with a far higher authority. There is a rule then which is superior to what is sometimes called the will of the people, and which obliges them to the observance of rectitude, with as high, although with no higher, authority than it binds the consciences of private individuals.

Right and physical power are not correlative terms. Right and moral power would be more nearly so. It is supposed, however, that there is a wide distinction between the conduct of individuals and of a whole nation; that inasmuch as the former may be restrained by positive laws, they have neither the power nor the right to commit injustice: that on the other hand, as there is no power actively to control the will of the people, they have from the necessity of the case both the power and the right to do as they please. But, some things are here too hastily taken for granted. There is, properly speaking, no way of preventing the actions of individuals, any more than of a whole people. Actions may be punished after they are committed, but the most absolute monarch is obliged to permit his subjects to be free until they have acted. A physical necessity compels him to do so. All the people cannot be goalers of all the people. If, then, because the state is at liberty to do as it pleases, it has the right also; for the same reason, private persons have the right to commit murder, or any other heinous offence. If it should be said, that as the latter may be punished afterward, this at any rate places an entire distinction between the two cases, the truth of the proposition might be admitted. But it would nevertheless be a surrender of the whole ground of argument, by making the distinction an incidental, instead of an intrinsic and necessary, one.

But even here, there is an important step in the reasoning, which is taken too hastily. Nations may be, and frequently (perhaps I should say, universally) are, punished for their misdeeds. Sometimes they are punished by other nations. At others they are cruelly scourged by intestine divisions. France, in the reign of Louis XVI, was visited by the heaviest misfortunes; and these misfortunes may be traced directly to the corruption, which had spread like a leprosy over those classes of society which had the management of public affairs. These misfortunes first fell upon the royal family, the nobility, and the clergy; because the abuses committed in those quarters stood out in bold relief, and shocked the common sense of mankind. The people, whom the general progress of knowledge had silently lifted into some importance, began to feel their own strength. But they put forth this strength by committing all sorts of enormities. And they, in their turn, were visited by the most frightful calamities: 1st, by foreign wars, occasioned by the excesses of the revolution; 2d, by furious parties in the bosom of France, which, after revenging themselves upon each other, delivered over that fine country to the wildest uproar and confusion; until at length these parties were themselves extirpated by a military despot. And this new power, having fulfilled the end for which it was appointed by Providence, was suddenly overthrown; leaving behind a warning to all nations, that neither kings nor people can commit crimes with impunity. Charles I, of England, and his infatuated mimisters, were punished by the people; the people were then punished for the violence of which they were guilty, by the re-establishment of the royal power in the full plenitude of its authority. James II persuaded himself that this counter revolution had lasted long enough to show that the prerogatives of the crown were consolidated for all time to come, and he acted upon this belief. He and his adherents were driven into exile; and it was not until all orders of men abjured the maxim, that might gives right, that any approach was made toward the establishment of regulated freedom.

Illustrations might be drawn from the history of the United States, though in that country they are not exhibited on anything like so large a scale, because the American people have never imagined that they possess the omnipotent authority attributed to them by slavish demagogues. There is a watchfulness and circumspection now visible in the conduct of nations, the result of the growing reflection of the age, which holds them back when they are about to leap to fast, and so prevents the occurrence of a world of mischief. But whenever the legislatures of the American states, acting upon the assumed will of the people, have betrayed the trust confided to them, and passed laws which infringed the great rules of justice, misfortunes of one kind or another have been the invariable consequence. I believe, if any one were to set himself upon making a searching and critical examination into a subject, which at first sight seems to be confused and mystified by the great variety of agencies which are simultaneously at work in society, it would be found that nations are even more certainly punisned for their misdeeds than individuals.

But it may be said, in reply to these views, which if true are of so great importance, that when calamities are the consequence of the unlawful acts of governments, or people, great numbers of innocent persons are involved in the suffering which overtakes the guilty. But,

First, This is no answer to the argument, which is, that the guilty are sure to be punished, sooner or later.

Second, The same circumstance occurs in the punishment of private individuals. We cannot put to death or imprison any man, without afflicting more or less numbers of persons who are dependent upon, or in some way connected with, him. We cannot do so without frequently casting a blight over the reputation and happiness of family and friends. This is an invariable dispensation of Providence. And it is doubtless so ordered, because in every such instance, some shadow of blame or reproach, although not immediately visible to the public eye, does in reality fall upon persons who are not openly guilty, or not guilty of the same identical fault.

The maxim, "the king can do no wrong," has been ingrafted into the monarchical constitutions of Europe, because it has been supposed that such governments were founded upon opinion. In other words, as the authority of the prince is a fiction, it is necessary to prop and support it by a fiction. Wherein, then, will a nation be the gainer by the establishment of a democratic form of government, if it shall be declared that the people can do no wrong. It will be to maintain that their authority is a fiction, and that it can only be upheld by a fiction. Human affairs will be a prey to as much disorder as ever. For as the people can never, in any country of even tolerable extent, personally take part in the public administration, society will be ruled by factions. And the maxim, that right and power are convertible terms, will be made to defeat itself in practice, by substituting, in the place of the will of the people, the will of a mere fraction of the state. I believe, that the greater the amount of power which is communicated to a whole nation, or to speak with more precision, the greater the proportion of the population by whom political power is exercised, the greater will be the probability that the laws will be just and wise, and that their administration will be impartial; and "vice versa," the fewer the number of citizens who possess political rights, the less the probability that the course of legislation will be characterized by an observance of the great principles of justice.

When the whole authority which appertains to government is concentered directly or indirectly in the people, as in the American commonwealth, the national power is the strongest; for then, not only is the will which moves the strongest, but the instruments by which it moves are most readily subservient to a common end. Such a community, if it chooses to put forth its strength, is equal to almost any achievement. If it never does exert its power to anything like the extent of which it is capable, it is in consequence of the self-limiting tendency which great popular power invariably has. For, consider for whom, and upon whom, this power is to be exercised. It is not enough to consider by whom it is exerted, without taking into account the manner in which it is obliged to operate, as we would do in the case of any other government, whose character we were desirous of sifting.

Now in a democratic republic the laws are made by the people, and for the people, and they act directly upon the people. And when this is the case, it becomes (not impossible to be sure, but) exceedingly difficult, to consult the interests of the few, to the prejudice of the many. The theory of such a government is, that the common interests of the whole community shall be consulted. But what does this phrase, common interests of the whole community, mean. It signifies, undoubtedly, that the rights of all the citizens shall be equally guarded and respected. It is where the privileges of A or B are violated for the benefit of C or D, that we say injustice is done to individuals. It is when the interests of one body of men are trampled upon for the advantage of another body, that injustice upon a still larger scale is committed. So that if the government is so constructed, as not merely to give the ability, but to render it the interest of the law-giving power to protect the rights of all, the probability is greatly increased, that the rule of right will be the standard, that the laws will be in accordance with the eternal principles of justice. Not because men, living under such a government, are naturally more disposed to the observance of rectitude than any other men; but simply, because there is no way by which any considerable number of people can obtain justice for themselves, but by consenting that justice shall be administered to others also. It is a circumstance of great importance, however, that although there may be no original difference between men in this respect, and that human nature is strictly the same everywhere—the same in Massachusetts and Ohio, as in Italy, or Turkey—yet that the habit of living under such institutions for any considerable period, and the consequent experience of the unspeakable benefits which in the long run accrue to every one, contribute powerfully to fortify men in the pursuit of the rule of right, to incline them spontaneously, and not merely upon compulsion, to act correctly; and thus to raise the general standard of the manners, as well as that of the laws. And although minds which are disposed to look upon the dark side of everything, or minds which are fretful and discontented, because they cannot jump immediately to the fulfillment of all their desires, or realize some preconceived theory of their own, may make all sorts of objections to such a constitution of government; yet it is not the least of the excellences of such a system, that it possesses the two-fold property of allowing the fullest latitude to the expression of private discontent; and yet of controlling it in such a manner that it shall do no harm to any part of the machine.

Thus, the more thorough the establishment of free institutions, the greater is the chance for the maintenance of just laws and the preservation of public tranquility; for the interests of each become more nearly identical with the interests of all, and the rights of each are only a reflection of the rights of all. But we must distinguish between a people who have a democratic character and democratic institutions, and a people who have democratic opinions only. The last may rush headlong into all sorts of excesses, and with difficulty escape the yoke of the most galling tyranny. The first is protected from such calamities, because it is the capacity for freedom, and not the possession of it, which is able to effect an advantageous distribution of the political power of the community. The one was the condition of France during the revolution, the other is that of the United States.

I have spoken of a democratic republic as the form of government in which the greatest amount of power resides. And persons who are captivated by appearances may suppose that this is a mistaken view. It may be argued, that the United States have never put forth anything like the amount of power which has been wielded by Great Britain, or France. But the possession and command of power are not the same with the actual exercise of it. I suppose, that if we could imagine the American republic to be animated and borne along by some one predominant idea, as was the case with

France, and England, in the gigantic wars of the French revolution, more strength, more resources, and a greater degree of enthusiasm would be called into requisition, than was the case in either of those instances. My argument has been purposely directed to show that where the greatest amount of power resides in the nation, it will necessarily be attended with a self-limiting tendency ; that the incapacity, or rather the want of inclination, to exert itself will continue no longer than is proper ; that if the solid interests of the state demand military effort, it will be made ; and that if this species of exertion does not become the habitual practice of the nation, it is because the greater the power, the more it is drawn into a direction favorable to the development of the interior interests of the state, and unfavorable to the concentration of power in the government alone. In other words, if we would carry national power in its genuine sense to the highest possible pitch, we must make every man a citizen ; but by so doing we render the wanton and useless expenditure of this power inconsistent with the common welfare, and therefore inconsistent with the maintenance of just and equal laws. If we were to suppose the United States attacked by a confederacy of all the potentates of Europe, for the express purpose of extirpating free institutions (an event, the opportunity for doing which has now passed over), I imagine that the amount of both moral and physical power, which would be put forth by the nation, would exceed anything of the kind of which history gives an account.

In the case of Great Britain and France ; if the people possessed a higher degree of power, that is, if the national strength were intrinsically greater, less outward display would be made of it ; the resources of those states would not be wasted in the maintenance of vast military and naval establishments ; the productive labor of those communities would have taken a direction less fitted to captivate the imagination, but infinitely better calculated to promote their solid prosperity. When we speak of one nation as very powerful, in contrast with some others, we ordinarily, but inconsistently enough, mean that the structure of society is such, as to enable a ruling caste to command the lives and fortunes of the major part of the population ; that is, we view what is in reality a capital defect in the institutions, as a system of strength ; we put a part in place of the whole, and because this disposition of the national strength is so imposing in appearance, and bears with such an enormous weight upon the mass of the population, we conclude that the nation is more powerful. Doubtless, if we were to imagine the vast resources of the United States placed under the command of a military despot, and the minds of men to be moved by an irresistible impulse, the national grandeur, as it is falsely termed, might be carried to the highest conceivable point. But the effective strength of the country would decline, and the moral energy which now animates the people would be speedily extinguished. As such a scheme of government would commence in injustice, it could only maintain itself by all sorts of injustice, and the laws would cease to be guided by the great rule of right, because the nation had become weaker instead of stronger. The formation of written constitutions, by the people themselves, is an incontestible proof that they believe there is such a rule ; that it is superior to the mere commands of men ; and that it has authority to govern in all public affairs, as well as in the private relations of society. Constitutions, which are originally designed to be a restraint upon the government, operate necessarily in a popular commonwealth as a restraint upon the people also. An individual who voluntarily places himself in a situation which disables him from doing wrong, gives proof of his superiority. He only who is strong enough to be wise can afford to be just. And the same is true of a whole nation.

There is this difference between a convention exercising the supreme power of the people, and an ordinary legislative body : the former enter upon the trust committed to them with a conviction that they are dealing with fundamental principles. The questions, what is right, what should be declared as rules, not temporarily, but for all time to come, are less embarrassed by the fleeting opinions of the day. And the ordinances which are framed have something of the absolute character of abstract truths. Hence no people would insert in their constitution any provision which was manifestly immoral or unjst though the same could not be said of a legislative assembly. All the things which it may or may not do, cannot be written down in the constitution. And so a field of limited extent is still left open to exercise the judgment and discretion of the legislature.

But may not this body transgress the bounds which have been marked out by the constitution, and pass laws which, to use a a term which is strictly an American one, are unconstitutional ? May it not do so, in compliance with the will of its constituents,

14

the people? And it is very certain that all this may be done. But in the United States the instances are exceedingly rare where it has actually been done. In almost every case, where an alledged violation has occurred, it has afforded subject matter for fair argument and debate on both sides, or the legislative act complained of was passed improvidently, and was subsequently repealed. The states of New Hampshire, New York, Maryland, Ohio, Kentucky, Illinois, &c., passed laws which were adjudged by the supreme court of the union to be unconstitutional, and those states immediately retraced their steps, although in one instance that tribunal went the length of decreeing that a prospective law impaired the obligation of contracts, and to the extreme length of declaring that, although such laws were not within the scope of state jurisdiction, it was competent to the federal legislature to pass them; and yet I confess it is exceedingly difficult for me to conceive how it can be competent to any legislative body to violate a fundamental rule of morality.

The admission of Texas might seem to be an exception to these remarks. It is certain that it was viewed by one party as an express violation of the federal constitution. But as that instrument does not contain an enumeration of the cases in which the treaty-making power may be exercised, the question is necessarily attended with great difficulties. Certainly it behooves a free people to guard against a too great extension, as well as a too narrow limitation, of the power. The authority by one government to accept an offer from another government, of a transfer of itself, so as to be incorporated with the former, appears at first blush to be too great an one to be confided to one department of the legislature. And as the most natural disposition which can be made of this right, is to deposit it with the entire legislature, we are free to do so, when the constitution is absolutely silent upon the subject. It will hardly be supposed that the English people are unreasonably latitudinarian in their notions of legislative power. The tendency is rather the reverse. The disposition is to guard scrupulously the prerogatives of the crown. The term treaty-making power has even a more indefinite meaning in that country than it has in the United States, and might seem therefore to swallow up every interest which concerned the foreign relations of the state, and which was not absolutely confided to the legislature. We might well suppose that the cession or exchange of European territory lay fairly within the scope of the treaty-making power. And yet it is the opinion of the greatest English statesmen, that no such cession or exchange could be made, unless it were concurred in by both houses of parliament.

There is no direct warrant for this interposition of the legislative authority. It can only be made out by admitting that the transfer of European territory, belonging to England, is theoretically within the treaty-making power ; and yet insisting that it is not within its spirit. Nor does it alter the aspect of the American question, that because the treaty-making power in Great Britain is vested in the king alone, it is therefore necessary to guard against its exercise, in so novel a case, by subjecting his action to the control of the entire legislature. The question still turns upon, what is the theory of the British constitution, and where is the authority for limiting the treaty-making power in one particular case. Nor does it affect the argument that British statesmen hold, that such a compact must at least originate with the king. The difficulty still recurs, by what authority is the treaty-making power curtailed in a government where it seems to be least ambiguous, and least open to construction. The difficulty is similar to another which occurs under the American constitution. The treaty-making power is conferred without limitation on the president and senate. Would a treaty, by which the United States were bound to lay a duty upon certain articles of export, be valid. The clause which forbids such an impost is contained in the article which limits the legislative power. There is no limitation whatever in the article which confers the treaty-making power. The settled construction, however, in America is, that a duty upon exports would be unauthorized in any shape whatever,—in other words that, in order to give effect to the spirit of the constitution, we must transfer a limitation from one part to another part to which it has properly no relation whatever. And if this construction is well-founded, there can be no doubt, but what the construction put upon the treaty-making power, in the admission of Texas, is also well-founded.

The "unions" of England and Scotland, and England and Ireland, were brought about by separate acts of the parliaments of the respective countries. The three governments acted upon the presumption that it was not enough to appoint commissioners to treat ; in other words, that the measure did not properly fall within the treaty-making power, and that therefore the legislative power must be appealed to. The unions, therefore, were decreed by separate acts of the English and Scotch, and the English and Irish parliaments, and the proceeding was by bill, as in all others acts of legislation.

There is a very interesting problem, which the power of altering constitutions presents in America. When the deputies of the people have assembled for this purpose, and have not been bound by any specific instructions, is society resolved into its original elements? can the mass of society be treated as mere "tabula rosa"? so that the whole body of laws and institutions can be, not only prospectively, but retroactively, annulled. If, for instance, numerous private associations have grown up under the protection of the former laws, can they be swept away without regard to the deep and permanent injury which would be done to great multitudes of private persons? This power has been contended for, in one state convention; but it was instantly rejected, although the population of that state was, at the time, perhaps the most democratic in the union;—a remarkable proof to what an extent the American people are impressed with the notion, that might does not give right, and how deeply all orders and parties, are convinced, that the great rules of morality and justice are not a gift by men, but a gift to men. It is admitted, that the authority of all public officers may be instantly abrogated by a constitutional convention; and the argument, that the analogy should be pursued through every species of private association, which the laws had created, would appear to have some color. Nevertheless, the distinction has been rigidly adhered to, and the contrary doctrine been proclaimed as both immoral, and anti-republican. If this were not the case, there would be nothing to prevent a convention from annulling all marriages; and so introducing a host of mischiefs, which no time could cure. I do not pretend to say, that instances may not occur, of associations which are semi-political and semi-civil in their character, and which may be abolished by an "ex post facto" constitutional ordinance. But there must be a great and overruling necessity to authorize it to be done. The mischief intended to be remedied must be so glaring as to shock the common sense of mankind.

What I have been most intent upon showing is, that the American people have been scrupulously jealous of their own power; that they have endeavored to guard against the idea that might gives right; and have thus given to the term "sovereignty of the people" an interpretation which it has received in no other commonwealth, either of ancient or modern times.

CHAPTER IV.

POLITICAL TOLERATION—IS IT PRACTICABLE?

Religious toleration has produced tranquility in the Christian world; and if toleration could also be introduced into the affairs of government, it could not fail to exercise a similar influence. But it does not very readily appear how this can be done. It is not necessary that religious sects should act; at least it is not necessary that they should act beyond the sphere of their own societies. All that is necessary, in order to render religious toleration complete, is to permit all denominations to enjoy freedom of thought, and to make such regulations within themselves as are conformable to their own creed and discipline. But the case is very different in the world of politics. It is made up of political parties, and of one or other of these parties is the governing power of the community composed. In other words, the government must be wielded by the majority; and this majority is not only obliged to act, but to act beyond itself; to make rules for others, as well as for itself; to preside, in short, over the interests of the whole community. There is then a wide distinction between religious and political parties, which seems to place insuperable difficulties in the way of introducing political toleration.

If it is possible, however, to contract the sphere within which parties, even the party in the majority, are permitted to act; if, without questioning the authority of this last to go beyond itself, and to make rules for others, the occasions on which it exercised this right were diminished both in number and importance, it is not impossible that we might succeed in introducing into political affairs, a spirit of toleration, which would exercise upon governments an influence very similar to that which religious toleration has exercised upon religious sects.

For that it is not at all necessary for a religious party so to act as to impress its authority upon others, is a maxim of very recent date, and is an effect of the very general progress which the human mind has made during the last hundred years. Religion at one time was regarded as one of the chief, if not the chief, political concerns of the state. Religious parties did constantly act, and act so effectually, as to affect the life, liberty, and property of the citizen. The system of intolerance seemed calculated to perpetuate itself; and so long as it lasted, the most enlightened understandings were borne down by the innumerable obstacles, which stood in the way of religious toleration.

It was easy to frame a plausible argument in defence of this state of things. It might be said that, from time immemorial, religious and political questions had been so mixed, that to attempt to separate them would be to do violence to both religious and political interests; would, at any rate, undermine the authority of government; if for no other reason, simply because the minds of men had constantly run in that channel; that when there was a multitude of sects in the state, their religious tenets would exercise a powerful influence upon their political opinions; that this would lay the foundation for intestine dissensions, which would rend the whole community; that the only cure was to give unity to religion, to establish it by law, and to exclude all dissenters from the privileges which were enjoyed by the favored sect; that in this way the unity of the government would be preserved, and its authority rendered inviolable. The inference then would be a necessary one, that government could no more avoid acting in religious matters, than it could avoid the duty of defending the state against foreign invasion. Arguments, in some respects similar, might now be employed to show the impropriety of political toleration.

The pope, at a very early day, became one of the most considerable potentates of Europe. Religious dogmas, of one kind or other, exercised complete dominion over the minds of men; and other princes, in order to maintain tranquility among their own subjects, and to preserve an equilibrium of power abroad, believed that it was necessary to add to their political, a very large share of ecclesiastical authority also. Through all the ramifications of society, in public as well as in private life, religious and political opinions were so interwoven that it seemed impossible to separate them. A war might be waged by the head of the church for the avowed purpose of imposing the most absurd and impious rites upon other nations, and if, as might naturally be expected, numerous adherents of these rites still lingered among those nations, their governments might persuade themselves that it was necessary to suppress freedom of religious opinion at home, in order to deal a successful blow upon the enemy abroad. This was the first occasion of religion becoming an engine of government in the modern European states, and of the universal introduction of religious intolerance. And as religion was thus erected into an affair of state, a further consequence took place, that ecclesiastics very generally became the statesmen of Europe.

The destruction of the papal power—the gradual decline of all the Italian commonwealths, which for centuries composed the most civilized part of the European continent—the employment of men in civil life, in all public affairs—and above all, the general progress of knowledge, industry, and freedom, have contributed to reverse the old order of things. A separation has actually been effected, between the political interests of the state and the religious doctrines which are taught.

The tendency of modern society, then, is to withdraw religion from the arena of politics, to put all sects in the possession of privileges which were formerly usurped by one, so that it shall no longer be necessary, nor even possible, for government to extend its legislation over some, in order to promote the agrandizement of others. The freedom of thought which has grown up everywhere, at the same time that it has disarmed the civil magistrate of a most dangerous authority, has created such a multitude of sects, that it would sometimes be impossible to bestow power upon one, without oppressing a very large majority of the population. It is not in consequence of any speculative notions, as to the justice and humanity of the principle of toleration, that it has gained ground so rapidly: the change has been brought about by a total alteration in the structure of society. The popular will, which reflects religious as well as political opinions, has gradually insinuated itself into the councils of all governments; until it has itself become a power of formidable import. It has attained this influence, either directly by virtue of the principle of representation, or indirectly through the instrumentality of public opinion. In the former case, the utmost freedom of opinion is obliged to be accorded to all religious sects.

There are two ways of imitating this system in the region of politics. One is, by extinguishing the cause of political disagreement; the other, by rendering it the settled interest of all political parties to tolerate each other's opinions respectively. The first plan would seem to be impracticable; but it is not so. Both plans are adopted in the United States, which being the only country where complete religious toleration has been established, it is natural, should also be the one in which the nearest approach has been made to the assertion of political toleration.

A written constitution, framed by representatives of the people, locks up, and forever withdraws from the field of party strife, almost all those questions which have been the fruitful source of discord among other communities. For almost all the civil commotions which have occurred in the Europen states, have been caused by a disagreement about questions which are no longer open to debate in America. The constitution, with the approbation of men of all parties, has placed them beyond the reach of the government. The authority appertaining to the political departments is also strictly limited ; and thus, a large class of powers which other governments have been in the habit of dealing with, without any control, cannot be exercised at all. In the same way as religion is withdrawn from the political world, and has given rise to religious toleration, the fundamentals of government are also withdrawn from all interference with by party; and all men agree to think and to act alike with regard to them.

As to those subjects which are left open to controversy, a great approach has been made, though in another way, toward the establishment of political toleration. In the first place, every one is free to think and to speak as he pleases; and in the second place, the minority, so far from being excluded from the government, are entitled to a representation in exact proportion to their numbers. This is of the greatest importance; because this body are thus placed in a situation where they may not only think and speak for all purposes, but where the exercise of so enviable a privilege may ultimately enable them to act for all purposes. It is very easy to construct a legislative body, so as to represent only one interest in the state.

It may be hereditary, or for life; in which case, it would wield an undivided influence, and there would be no effective and practical toleration for other classes; or the electoral franchise may depend upon so high a qualification, as to produce an effect similar in its operation. Very different, however, is the case in the United States. The legislative assemblies are composed of men of all parties; and although in politics, the governing authority cannot deliver itself from the necessity of acting, yet so much freedom is enjoyed by the members who compose those assemblies, that political questions borrow light from all parties. I believe if we were to take any considerable series of years, it would be found that the leading measures which have been adopted in the United States have been the fruit of the joint exertions of all parties; that they have been ultimately so arranged as to reflect in part the opinions of the majority, and in part those of the minority. And thus, the spectacle is no longer presented, of one fixed and immovable interest engrossing the whole power of the state.

The introduction of the principle of political equality is another step toward the establishment of the most complete toleration. Men are obliged to recognize the liberty of others, in order to maintain their own. The same revolution is effected in politics, as was formerly brought about in religion. The multiplication of sects was so great as to deprive any one of them of a predominant influence, and so excused government from investing it with exclusive privileges. This first suggested the notion, that toleration was not only just, but that it was eminently expedient. The great diversity of opinions, so far from being an obstacle in the way of religious toleration, was the means of establishing it. But the same causes which have multiplied religious, have also multipled political, opinions, so that there is no possible way by which one party can be free without permitting all to be free.

The confederate form of the American government adds additional force to the principle of political toleration. The country is divided into a number of separate, and to most purposes independent, governments. And it is a consequence of this arrangement, that all political opinions are not subjected to the control of a central legislature. The affairs of government are divided into two classes: one of which comprehends the federal interests, the other the domestic interests of the states. And this second class may again be divided into as many subordinate ones, as there are states composing the confederacy. If this system were not adopted, the local interests would be subjected to the jurisdiction of a single legislature, which could not adapt itself to the diversified wants of so extensive a country, and so the laws might follow one undistinguishing rule for communities whose pursuits were ever so different. But now, the governing party in the national councils may, or may not, be at any one time the goverining party in a majority of the states. The effect, in other words, is not merely to permit the people of each section of the country to exercise freedom of thought and speech, but to carry their opinions into practice—to frame their laws in conformity with their own wishes, instead of being governed by the general majority of the whole country. As all religious sects are tolerated, and placed in the possession of equal rights, because religion is divorced from government, so all local parties, however numerous, are tolerated, and have an equal share of power, because the administration of the state governments is wholly disconnected with that of the confederacy.

Political toleration, then, is not a solecism in politics: it is actually incorporated into American institutions, though, like all other great blessings, they who possess it are least sensible of its existence.

Political toleration is carried to a much greater extent in the United States, than is religious toleration in many of the most enlightened European governments. For let us consider what the term religious toleration imports, even in England. It does not mean that all sects are placed upon an equal footing. All sects are permitted to enjoy their religious opinions, and to adopt what forms of worship they please; but only on condition that they pay the tithe which is collected for the support of the established clergy. That is to say, all dissenters from the state religion are punished for the exercise of the rights of conscience. It is not necessary to recur to the fact, that certain oaths are still imposed upon all dissenting ministers, and that one class of dissenters is forbidden to hold some of the highest offices in the state. The assessment upon all denominations equally, for the support of an established hierarchy, makes a wide and important distinction between religious toleration in England and political toleration in the United States. And although all political parties in the latter are taxed for the support of government, as it is administered by the majority, yet there is, after all, a wonderful coincidence in the line of policy which is advocated by both parties. The points of agreement are a hundred-fold greater than those in which they differ. The latter acquire importance from standing out as exceptions to the general rule. They only contribute to keep up some animation in society, where otherwise all would be dull and monotonous. Besides, there is no party established by law. The laws which are passed by the majority are the supreme rule, but the majority to-day may be the minority to-morrow. But in England, a powerful religious party is established by law, nor is there any way of moderating its influence through the occasional ascendancy of other opinions. Its privileges are exclusive and permanent, and depend in no manner upon the exercise of the popular will. The injustice which is thus done, to a very large and enlightened portion of the English people, is plain enough. But it is still more glaring in the case of Ireland, where dissenters from the established church are an immense majority of the whole population.

CHAPTER V.

MONARCHICAL GOVERNMENT.

WHAT is the foundation of that illusion which has caused such multitudes of people in all ages to yield a willing and implicit obedience to the rule of a prince? A weak man, or woman, nay a child, once seated upon the throne, exercises a dominion over the imaginations of men which the longest time, the greatest reflection and experience, seem unable to conquer. This vast and disproportioned influence, of one individual above millions, seems an anomaly in the history of human nature. It cannot be ascribed to a persuasion among the community of the eminent advantages which spring from such a disposition of the political power. A considerable fraction of the community may have this persuasion in great strength; but to suppose that the community as a body reasoned in this way, that they proceeded upon any settled and deliberate view of the utility of the plan, would argue the existence of so high a degree of reflection as to give rise instantaneously to representative government. That fraction of the community who are so persuaded, are only so in consequence of their observing the operation of some other very different principles which rule over the mass of mankind. They notice the superstitious feeling which ignorance engenders; they then notice the idolatrous attachment of superstition to every species of authority, and still more to the gorgeous ensigns of authority. One may observe the workings of a similar principle in the government of private families. Children very generally believe their parents to be superior to other men and women. It is not until they become adults (and very often not then) that they are disabused of this prejudice. Some observation and experience are necessary to this end. But it is obvious how much this feeling contributes to the establishment of parental authority : it is equally obvious how much a similar and eqally mysterious principle contributes to the government of mankind.

The peasant who ascends a lofty mountain is instantly struck, no matter how untutored he may be, with the grandeur and sublimity of the scene before him. A vague notion of infinity is irresistibly thrust upon his mind, although he knows that the vast surface beneath him is composed of alternate patches of wood and cleared land, exactly like those in his own neighborhood. So when he confusedly calls to his recollection the vast population in which he lives, called a state, or community, he dwindles into insignificance in the comparison, although that vast body is only made up of men and women, like those in his neighborhood. In the first instance, a being beyond the world is suggested ; in the second, a being beyond himself, and yet not out of society. In both instances, the notion of unity seems necessary, in order to give support to his vague notion of immensity, and to make tolerably comprehensible what would otherwise be beyond the reach of his faculties. The conviction of the existence of a governor of the universe very naturally takes possession of him ; the notion of royalty, as the impersonation of the state, is thrust upon him with nearly equal force.

In a republic men all descend into the plain ; they are no longer overpowered by the indistinct notion of immensity. The understanding gains the ascendancy, and they are enabled to form more just notions on all subjects. Their religion, which was at first the creature of impulse, and therefore easily fabricated into some form of superstition, becomes both more rational and more devout. In like manner they are better able to survey calmly, and one by one, the men and things which make up the great community in which they live. The feeling does not leave them entirely ; but it now becomes subservient to very important ends, and is made to promote their own interests as men and citizens. Each individual has the sense of personal independence, not merely as applied to himself, but as applied to all other individuals, more and more impressed upon him, because the point from which he now views everything, is more favorable to cool analysis, and to setting everything in its proper light. But the reverberation of an authority from without still reaches him. He hears of millions of other people who are associated with him under the same government. Of these millions perhaps he never saw a thousand, perhaps not even an hundred. The existence of those beings, on that very account, makes a profounder impression upon his mind. On an analysis, perhaps it will be found that it is the notion of immensity which is gained by the view (the more indistinct the more imposing) of a vast population, which serves to cherish and to uphold the notion of royalty. The king is regarded as the special representative of that vast population. He becomes the state itself; so that if we can give to the terms "state," "people," sufficient unity, republican rule will exercise as potent an influence over the imaginations of man, as monarchical rule.

Doubtless, it would be as impossible to create the rule of an hereditary monarch in the United States, as it would be to carry physical science back to the condition in which it was before the time of Bacon; and for precisely the same reason. For want of a rational system of experiment and observation, phenomena the most simple, and the most easily explained now, were subjected to the most crude and fanciful speculations. Superstition reigned over physical, as it still does in many parts of the world, over political science. Actual experiment and observation have dissolved the superstition in the first instance; and it is possible that the sturdy good sense of the nineteenth century will go a great way toward undermining it in the last. The doctrine of occult causes was precisely akin to the political illusion of which I have spoken.

Where the people are immersed in ignorance, they feel themselves incapacitated to take any part, even the most indirect, in public affairs. This feeling cannot be shaken off; for knowledge is power, in every department of human life; and wherever there is great ignorance, the desire and the power to will effectually are both wanting. This state of things, for the time being at least, withdraws all political power from the masses, and reposes it in the hands of those who, either by rank or education, are lifted to a higher condition. Power is thus transferred easily, and without noise or violence, to a very small portion of society. But whenever a set of institutions come to represent the opinions and feelings peculiar to a class, those opinions and feelings will not be understood by those who are out of the class. The modes of thinking and acting among the former will begin to wear an air of mystery which time will only increase, until at length the whole machinery of what are termed great affairs, will be absolutely unfathomable by the multitude.

The great men will then begin to quarrel among themselves for the mastery. The most warlike, or the most crafty, will obtain it. In the event of a vacancy to the succession, he will possess himself of the crown. A new revolution will then take place. Before, the high places in the government, and the lustre which surrounded them, overpowered the imaginations of the people. They paid a sort of instinctive obedience to the prince; which is the same as to say, that a great power had risen up in support of the throne. Now, also, it is not against the assaults of the people that he stands in need of protection, for they are already overawed; it is against the assaults of the other great men. But the same sentiment of obedience, so undefined, and yet so enthusiastic, constitutes an impregnable barrier against those assaults also. The great men in the state soon discover, that although out of their own limited circle, nothing is understood concerning state affairs: yet that this very ignorance has given birth to a power which none but themselves have to fear. As soon as one of their number is made chief — as soon as he is fairly seated on the throne, the reverence of the multitude is directed toward him, and withdrawn from all others. The spell even begins to take possession of their own ranks. A sentiment of superstition in one part of society is converted into an universal conviction of right. The throne is fortified from within and without; it is equally guarded against the violence of the multitude, and the conspiracies of the nobles.

In the progress of time, it may be a very long period, the number of those who are placed in independent circumstances will be greatly augmented. Rich landed proprietors, great merchants, and opulent manufacturers spring up; and this will give birth to a new class, formed out of intermarriages between the families of the nobility and those of rich commoners, and which is denominated the gentry. Still later, education is extensively diffused; the press, although it should be under some restraint, spreads intelligence; a higher and wider civilization takes plaee. A popular branch is added to the legislature; or if one already exists, greater influence and authority are conferred upon it. A remarkable crisis now occurs. The lustre which surrounds the throne seems to be more dazzling than before. Notwithstanding the spread of intelligence, and the general elevation of the popular mind, its power appears to be firmer and more durable than ever. The class of the rich and influential have been swelled to a great magnitude, and this class, for the most part, lends its support to the throne rather than to the people.

Patronage, which supersedes the rough and irregular exercise of power, gives the monarch great influence among this class. Offices are multiplied in proportion as civilization advances. And in addition to all this, great numbers of people among the middle class, fearing more from the turbulence and licentiousness of popular freedom than from the exercise of the royal prerogatives in a limited monarchy, array themselves on the side of old institutions. A great party is for the first time formed, composed of persons whose opinions are founded upon the most mature and deliberate reflection. They would have more freedom imparted to the institutions of government, if they could only see their way clearly through the process which leads to it. They do not believe it can be done without endangering the whole system. Russia, and Austria, may be considered as illustrations of the first period; France, and Great Britain, of the second. Prussia must be regarded as trembling between the two.

The second period may be of indefinite duration. The country is then filled with wealth and intelligence; civil liberty seems to be secured to all conditions of men; a great middle class has been created, holding the balance of power in the state, and yet constantly inclined, whether from temperament, habits of reflection, or views of ambition, to throw the weight of its influence in favor of the superior classes. But, inasmuch as reflection has been roused, and a disposition to think and ponder upon the men and institutions which surround them has been developed in a great multitude of minds, it is plain that the artificial and unnatural principles on which government originally hinged, are beginning to be probed and comprehended, and that the great mysteries of government, in order to be unveiled, only wait for an opportunity favorable to calm and deliberate action. And when this is the case, as all knowledge is progressive, and even contagious, it will be difficult to predict with anything like certainty how long the institutions will be permitted to stand still, or how soon the hand of a thorough, and yet judicious and temperate, reform, may fall upon them.

When this interesting period has arrived, great numbers of men will unite, in order to obtain important changes in the government; associations will be formed with this avowed design, the majority of whose members will perhaps be composed of citizens who are politically disfranchised, and yet consisting of so large a portion of those who are not, as to give great weight and authority to the opinions of the whole body. A majority of that part of the middle class who do possess political privileges will be roused, and will recoil at every attempt of this new party, until at length the spirit of reflection, which has silently prepared the way to every species of salutary improvement, has effected a reconciliation between parties, when much will be conceded, and yet some substantial advantages will be obtained by the great movement party. This revolution will be repeated at successive intervals, until at length the entire body, of what may be justly termed the middle class, are admitted to the electoral franchise, and rendered eligible to office, when all further change will cease, not merely because none other will be wise, but because the moral force of society will be arrayed in defense of what has been gained, and in opposition to any further change. Before this revolution is accomplished, the notion, that the middle class comprehends none but persons who have an interest in landed estate, will naturally be discarded. The citizens who possess personal property will be placed upon an equally favorable footing; nay, the rule will perhaps be made still wider, and every one of good character, and who contributes to the support of government, will be admitted to the electoral franchise. For, so long as any one of those who go to make up the effective strength of the state is excluded, government not only commits great injustice to a numerous class of the people, but it deprives itself of a powerful support to the laws.

There is a fourth period which may occur; one deeply interesting to the cause of humanity, and to the final success of free institutions. The acquisition of so many blessings, the enjoyment of such delightful tranquility, both in public and private life, may lead to too much repose and inactivity. Sloth and voluptuousness may overspread the land, and the institutions may fall in the midst of the greatest prosperity. It is true society will be more completely protected against the disastsr, than at any preceding period. As the distribution of wealth will be more equal, the moral force of society will be better balanced, the means of recruiting the superior ranks from the classes below them will be more abundant than ever. Still all this may not be sufficient. It may be necessary for society to go backward, in order again to spring forward. For the dissolution of an old and worn-out society has sometimes the effect of breathing a new spirit into the whole population. All classes and conditions are then confounded together. The rich and the powerful are tumbled from their enviable position; they are brought down to the level of the obscure and humble, who now begin to run a new race for all the advantages of fortune. This is a provision inherent in the constitution of every community which has become effete with luxury and corruption. There may be no way of revivifying the elements of society, and of imparting fresh vigor to the population, but by passing them through the ordeal of a terrible adversity. But the experiment will be quite new, when any nation shall have traveled to the utmost limit of the third period. As the institutions will then have a sort of self-preserving faculty, and will contain powerful antidotes to the evils just indicated, we do not know whether any further revolution will be necessary. The high probability is that it will not; and this is the last term—the final consummation of our hopes.

CHAPTER VI.

NOTICE OF THE ENGLISH CONSTITUTION.

One of the most remarkable properties of the English government, is the faculty which it possesses of accommodating itself to alterations in the structure of society. The theory of the constitution is pretty much the same as it was in the reigns of the Tudors ; but its practical working is totally different. The social organization has undergone a great change during the last seventy years, and this has made a deep and lasting impression upon the political institutions. The king, the nobility, and the ecclesiastical hierarchy, occupy the same relative position to each other ; but they do not occupy the same position toward the people. This power of adapting itself to the altered condition of society, is one of the most valuable qualities which a government can possess. It is next in importance to positive changes in the composition of the government.

The revolution I have spoken of has been silent, but progressive. It has effected an entire change in the modes of thinking of all public men, and has wrought a corresponding change in the system by which public affairs are conducted. The prerogatives of the king and aristocracy are the same as formerly, but the people have been steadily advancing in strength and importance ; and how is it possible to employ power against the powerful ? As the general improvement of the population, and the consequent amelioration of the manners, has imparted a new character to the temper and dispositions of individuals ; so the inability under which public men find themselves, of exerting even an acknowledged authority, renders that authority in great part merely nominal ; and the administration of the government in practice no longer agrees with what the theory imports.

There are only two ways of effecting alterations in the political institutions. The one, is by sudden leaps; the other, by slow and insensible advances. The first is sometimes attended with so much violence and confusion, as to endanger the existence of the entire fabric. The second, although it avoids this evil, has, nevertheless, a tendency to postpone the most wise and salutary changes, to a period far beyond that when society is ripe for their introduction.

Montesquieu said, of the British government, that it was a republic in disguise; which shows what inadequate notions this eminent writer had formed of a republic. But it is not at all improbable, that it will become at some future day, not perhaps very distant, a republic in reality, and not one merely in disguise. When I perceive the great bulk of the people growing to the full stature of men; and when I observe that, in every contest between liberty and power, the advantages gained have been constantly on the side of the people, and never on that of the government; I see causes in operation which are not only sufficient to bring about this result, but which seem to lead straight forward to its accomplishment.

But how is it possible, without sudden leaps, to get beyond the point which has already been reached. How in other words, without creating an universal revolution, can the structure of the government be changed fundamentally. It is through the instrumentality of that invisible but powerful agent, which we term public opinion, that a spirit has been breathed into the institutions. But public opinion does not construct, it only influences and modifies. It may, step by step, and without noise and confusion, affect the working of the machine; but this is very different from taking the machine to pieces: very different from abolishing the royal power and the house of lords, and substituting in their place an elective chief magistrate and senate.

This is an obstacle, and a formidable one, in every attempt to alter the composition of an ancient government. Society, in Great Britain, is ripe for the introduction of free institutions, if there were no other system already in existence. The existence of that other system, with the vast patronage and influence appended to it, has a powerful tendency to counteract the force of public opinion, and renders it a work of infinite delicacy to make any radical alteration whatever.

But the process I have described may continue so long as to give rise to further changes of the same character; and, by molding the minds of men after a different fashion of thinking, may have power sufficient to overbear the influence of the throne and aristocracy. In this way, what would have been an abrupt and violent leap at an early period of society, may become an easy transition at a more advanced stage. Everything depends upon the shock which the mind receives. We do violence to the political institutions, only when we do violence to inveterate habits of thinking. But if old associations are broken in upon, there is no room for committing violence in any quarter. I think it cannot be doubted, that the footing on which the electoral franchise, parliamentary representation, religious toleration, and the freedom of the press, now stand in Great Britain, would, in the reign of Elizabeth, have been regarded as a much greater movement, than would at the present day the entire reconstruction of the executive magistracy, and the house of lords. Although the second appears to involve a more direct and positive interference with established institutions, it does not run counter to the genius and tendency of the age: it would therefore give much less shock to the understandings of men.

It is a remark of Mr. Hume, that there was, in his day, a constant tendency toward a diminution of the personal authority of the king. This fact has been still more observable since Mr. Hume wrote. And the reason why it is so is very obvious. The amount of real business which falls under the management of the executive, becomes so vast and multifarious with the advance of society, that no one man, much less a king, can attend to the one hundredth part of it. The consequence is, that the whole of this business has been gradually transferred to an executive board. So long as it was possible to conceal the cause of this change from general observation, the king continued to retain the dazzling influence which the vulgar apprehension ascribes to him. But now that this cause is apparent to every one, the royal and the executive authority have ceased to be even nominally the same. For not only is the king totally unable to discharge this huge mass of business; but ministers do not even hold their places at his will. The direction of public affairs was formerly a very simple concern. The gratification of the king's pleasures and ambition comprehended the whole. And although some share of business talent could not well be dispensed with, yet as public transactions consisted for the most part of war, negotiation and intrigue; the imaginations of the people very naturally figured the king as incomparably the most prominent actor upon the stage. But the case is very different now. Intellectual ability, extensive information, indefatigable industry, are all absolutely necessary to any tolerable success in the management of public affairs. The English statesman now a days has to deal chiefly with the interior interests of a densely peopled and highly civilized community. War, which formerly employed the whole attention of the state, is becoming a mere episode in its history. It is impossible for any monarch, however ignorant or bigoted he may be, to misunderstand the import and bearing of this great revolution in human affairs. With regard to the lords, I have in another chapter alluded to the process which seems destined to bring about the decay of their power and influence. Wealth constitutes the soul of an aristocracy. Other qualities may add lustre to the institution; but it is wealth, exclusive wealth, which gives it a firm hold, and a commanding authority, in society. But riches are now obtained by such a multitude of individuals, that they can no longer be the foundation of a privilege. What was once the chief element of an aristocracy, is now a great element of popular power. The same causes which conspired to create an hereditary order, are now at work to enfeeble it. The English nobility are no longer the haughty and powerful barons who formerly lorded it over the commons. They are simply among the most polished and affluent gentlemen of the kingdom: guarded for the present by a sort of conventional respect, but no longer wielding a formidable authority over the rest of the population.

The French have very recently made a fundamental alteration in the institution. The peerage is no longer hereditary. An event which seventy years ago would have startled the public mind throughout Europe, has been brought about with as much facility, and has created as little sensation, as an act of ordinary legislation. It is true, the English nobility are a much wealthier body than the French. But the English commons are wealthier than the French "tiers etat," in a still greater proportion. The materials for constructing an aristocracy are more near at hand in England than in France; but the uses of the institution would seem to be more apparent in the latter than in the former country.

An aristocracy is of two kinds. It may be so numerous, and

engross so large a share of the landed property of the country, as to form a component and very substantial part of the whole population. This was at one period the case in almost every European state. It has ceased to be so everywhere except in Russia and Poland ; or it may consist of so small a number, that the only way to compensate for its want of strength, and to preserve it as a distinct order in the state, will be to make the entire members a constituent part of one branch of the legislature. This is the case in Great Britain, except so far as regards Scotch and Irish peers, a certain number of whom are elected by their own order to seats in the house of lords. Scotch and Irish peers are not so numerous as to prevent their sitting in one chamber, along with the English peers ; but political considerations, growing out of the union of the three countries, have given rise to the present arrangement.

But where a nobility compose so very small a part of the population, and yet are endowed with such extensive political authority, the incongruity between the natural influence which belongs to them, as well-educated gentlemen, and the artificial privileges heaped upon them, must strike every one of the least reflection, no matter how familiarized he may have become with such a state of society. To remodel the institution, therefore, or to dispense with it altogether, would do no violence, would cause no disturbance to the public tranquillity. As the change would be strictly in accordance with the ideas of the age, and would but second a movement which is in full progress, so it would affect but a mere handful of men. And there are probably no persons in the British empire more observant of the course of events, more thoroughly convinced, that the day is approaching when it will be impossible to oppose their authority, even nominally, as a counterpoise to the commons, than the nobility themselves.

While the active political authority of the king and nobility has been gradually decreasing, that of the commons has been as constantly advancing. The same cause, the dispersion of knowledge and property, has produced these opposite effects. But as the people rise in the scale of intelligence (even though we confine the meaning of people, to that powerful body called the middle class), in proportion as they participate, although indirectly, in the affairs of government, they are brought to a clearer understanding of everything which appertains to the machinery of government ; and have a closer insight into the character and motives of all public men. Things which were before regarded as mysterious in the highest degree, and which were never approached without a feeling of awe, are now handled and touched, and become thoroughly familiar to common apprehension. Wealth originally gave privileges to a few hundreds; but it has now given intelligence to the million, and this enables the commoner to stand upon something like an equal footing with the nobleman. Men are never able to take exact guage of each other's dimensions, until they are made to stand side by side of one another; when those qualities, which were before so much magnified by the mist through which they were seen, assume their due proportions; and the individual man is valued more for what he possesses, and less for what he can make display of. The characters of public men appear grand and colossal, only in consequence of the illuminated ground on which they are exhibited.

There is one branch of the British legislature in which very great alterations may be made, conformable with the genius of the age, without immediately affecting the absolute theory of the government; although these alterations may ultimately disturb the whole balance of the constitution, and lead by an easy transition to fundamental changes in the structure of the government. The house of commons is elected by the people, but to what extent it shall be the genuine representative of the popular will, depends upon the high or low qualifications of the members, and the restrictions imposed upon the electoral franchise. If the qualifications in both instances were lowered, the power of the people would rise in proportion. Now there is an evident tendency in that direction at the present day. The reform bill, which is one of the most memorable acts of the British parliament, has gone a great way toward altering the relative influence of different parts of the government. But the achievement of one reformation renders the necessity of others more easily discernible, and very frequently paves the way for a change of the greatest magnitude, which had not before been dreamed of. The basis of representation, in all human probability, will continue to be enlarged, until the house of commons has acquired such a preponderant weight, as to make every one see the extreme incongruity of a legislative body, which fairly represents all the substantial interests of the state, standing in intimate connection with two institutions which have no immediate dependence upon the public will. It is true the concurrence of the house of commons will be necessary to any further reform of parliamentary representation. Indeed the laws, which are designed to effect that object, must be supposed to originate in the popular branch. And it may be said, that it will be the evident interest of the members to oppose every plan by which the field of competition for their own seats shall be widened, or by which the numbers of their constituents shall be so multiplied as to render them less easily manageable, by either intrigue or bribery. These considerations did not prevent the passage of the act of 1832. Public opinion, when it has acquired a certain amount of strength, acts upon the mind with as much force, and as absolute certainty, as the most powerful motives of self interest. The temper and dispositions of men become inflamed, as well as their understandings enlightened. The new fashion of thinking becomes contagious, and takes possession of society, without any one being aware whither it is carrying him. Indeed the causes which lead to any great changes in the structure of society, are never under the immediate control of men. They determine the will, instead of the will determining them,

It is through the operation of a great many causes the diffusion of knowledge and property, the growth of public opinion, the creation of a great middle class in society, and the giving to the representatives of the people a distinct voice and commanding influence in the legislature, that the public mind may be irresistibly conducted to a change in the fundamental laws, by which the officers of every department of the government will be rendered strictly responsible There is no good reason why the chief magistrate and the senate should continue to be hereditary, when the popular body has become so numerous and so powerful, as to swallow up the distinction ofi classes. The creation of a king and nobility may be said to have been originally owing to the inordinate influence which the imagination exercises over the minds of men, at an early stage of society. But reflection, the most striking characteristic of the present age, is a wonderful extinguisher of the imagination, in all affairs of real life.

It must be admitted that the principle of virtual representation, which is incorporated into British institutions, has been more successful than in any other government which has existed. But even if it were possible to perpetuate the system, it has many intrinsic defects. The great advantage of actual representation consists in its fixing the attention of all classes upon the conduct of public men. It thus initiates the people into an acquaintance with the practical working of the system, and founds their attachment to government upon their interests. Virtual representation is without these advantages. However powerful public opinion may be, and although it may prevent acts of injustice in the gross, yet it cannot reach them in detail. The system of public measures, and the conduct of public men, are made up of an infinite number of acts, each of which may be inconsiderable, and yet the aggregate of incalculable importance. When the rulers of the state are not subjected to a strict accountability, they become a law to themselves; they create a standard of opinion within their own circle, which necessarily weakens the force of that general opinion, whose office it is to watch over the actions of all the functionaries of government. It is true there is a species of adventitious authority attached to all human institutions which, after all, must come in for a very large share in the government of mankind. But the American experiment has demonstrated that free institutions possess this quality, to as great extent as either monarchy or aristocracy. The popular mind clothes all the symbols and insignia of a legitimate authority, with the same sort of veneration and respect which contribute to uphold the artificial forms of government.

There is one circumstance which might be supposed to stand in the way of all interference with the fundamental laws, and to prevent any alteration in the existing theory of the government. The middle class are, in effect, the governing class in Great Britain. By them everything must be done. And it may be insisted that, when this class reflect upon the perfect security which they now enjoy, they will be unwilling to exchange it for an untried state of being; that they will be more strongly impressed with the advantage which a system of institutions, in part artificial, has in producing domestic quiet, and inspiring an instinctive obedience to the laws. They may fear that all industrious occupations, which now confer comfort and independence upon them, may be interfered with, if they give countenance to any further changes, no matter how just, and how beneficial in many respects, those changes may be. In short they may be convinced, that if royalty and aristocracy are evils, they are at any rate necessary evils in the government of an ancient society.

There is, no doubt, force in these considerations: but they presuppose, and rightly too, a high degree of reflection among that class; and it is this reflection which, on the one hand, constitutes a guarantee against the mischiefs which are apprehended; and on the other, is a sure presage of very material changes in the structure of of the government. These changes will only be postponed to a period when they will cease to be regarded as a revolutionary movement, and will appear to be a natural transition of the institutions into a position already prepared for them. They will be preceded by a very important measure: one which will place all the members of the middle class upon the same footing, and give them all an equal voice in the government. For, although I have represented the middle class as holding the balance of power, yet it is not the entire body, but only a part, which possesses this influence. Not all the middle class are comprehended in the list of voters. The qualifications of electors might descend much lower, and take in a very numerous and substantial part of the population which is now left out. Moreover, the possession of personal, as well as real and leasehold property, might be made a qualification. When these two measures, so natural and so easy of adoption, are actually accomplished, the danger to society will no longer seem to consist in taking down a part of the government, in order to reconstruct it; but rather in permitting it to stand as it is, not representing the popular will, and yet, the popular will, possessing all power and authority.

As I have already remarked, there is no class of men who have a more distinct appreciation of the very general progress which knowledge, industry, and morals have made among the English people, than the nobility themselves; none which is more thoroughly sensible of the goal whither things are tending.

Mixed government, of which the English is the most complete model, proceeds upon the principle, that there are two permanent classes in society whose interests are opposed to each other: the higer and lower orders. It proposes, therefore, to secure a distinct representation to each, so that the two shall act concurrently, and yet each possess a veto upon the acts of the other. The legislature is divided into two chambers; one composed of an order of nobility, the other of deputies of the people. In addition to this, an hereditary monarch is placed at the head of the system. And it may be asked, where is the necessity of this arrangement, when the great bulk of the population are already represented. It is in consequence of the mixed character of the population. In a representative republic, the composition of society is exceedingly uniform: there is no order of nobility; a character of consistency and homogeneity is impressed upon it from the beginning. But in a state differently constituted, there must be some additional contrivance, in order to give this character of unity to the whole government. It is supposed that an hereditary monarch, holding his title independently of the two great classes, will answer this purpose. It may even be supposed that he will answer it better, in a highly advanced state of society, than in one which has made little progress in knowledge and refinement. In the former, both classes are powerful; in the latter, the nobility alone are so. In the first, he will be not merely disposed, but compelled, to act as arbiter between the two orders; in the last, he will endeavor either to render the nobility subservient to his designs, or, failing in this, he will be engaged in a perpetual conflict with them. In either event, the interests of society would be endangered. It is not surprising, therefore, that nations which have made great progress in cultivation, and among whom knowledge is widely diffused, should obstinately cling to the office of king, long after the state of society in which it originated has passed away.

There is an additional reason for the continuance of the institutions in an advanced state of society. The popular class itself becomes divided into two great classes, the middle and the plebeian class. Each of these grows in magnitude as the society advances; so much so, that the order of nobility loses its original character as a component part of the society, although it retains it place in the government. The great object now, is to bridle the unruly and licentious habits of the plebeian class, and the authority of a king, added to that of the nobility, is thought to be necessary for that purpose. If the power of the nobility had not declined, there would be no danger of their using the plebeian class, in order to curb the independence of the middle class. But the fact that they retain their place in the government, while their personal authority is diminished, enables them, in conjunction with the commons, to exercise just so much influence as is necessary to check the encroachments of the plebeian class. An invasion of the rights of the commons, now that these have become formidable from their wealth, would be an invasion of their own, unless they could make the whole body of plebeians instrumental in designs against the middle class. But this they are disabled from doing. And as the king was at first entrusted with the sword, in order to keep peace between the nobility and the people, he is now entrusted with it, in order to keep peace between the two orders into which the people itself is divided. The standing army of Great Britain is kept up solely for this purpose. It is part of the system of internal police, only designed for the whole kingdom as the constabulary force is designed for a town or county. There is this difference, however, between the old and new order of things. In the first, there was danger of encroachments of the nobility upon the people, and of the people upon the nobility. In the last, the danger apprehended is all on one side; it is of encroachments of the plebeians upon the middle class. May there not, then, be danger in the further progress of society, of an oppressive exercise of power as against the lower classes. If all other orders, king, nobility, and commons, are leagued together against them, may they not ultimately be driven to the wall, and one half of the population be subjugated by the other half. But in truth, the change is highly favorable to great moderation in all parts of the society. Instead of a powerful patrician class, and a handful of commoners, we have a handful of patricians, and a vast body of commoners. Power has been displaced from the position it formerly occupied. The influence of the middle class has been prodigiously augmented, and that of the nobles proportionally diminished Not only has power changed hands, but the new power which has risen up is of an entirely different character from that which it has superseded. The commons are too feeble, singly, to embark in any schemes detrimental to the public interests; they are too numerous to make it an object to do so. But their strength in the aggregate, enables them to exercise a decisive influence, and authority, over other parts of the society. The intervention of the nobility in the disputes between the commons and the proletarians, has ceased to be necessary. For, 1st, there is a stronger bond of connection between these two classes than between the nobility and the plebeians. 2d, the exercise of force in the name of the commons is productive of less exasperation than its exercise by the nobility. The great use of the commons at present, is to temper the power which the nobility might be disposed to exercise against the plebeian class. 3d, as the population has become more homogeneous, since the decay of the personal authority of the nobles, it is a system of general order which is now sought to be preserved; and that end is best attained where the authority which presides over the public welfare, represents the general will of the community, and not merely the particular interests of a class. When political power was very nearly divided between the nobility and the commons, it was necesrary, in addition to the means which each possessed for protecting its own interests, that a third power, an hereditary monarch, should be instituted to prevent any excess of power by either of the conflicting orders. And when the popular body became divided into two classes, the intervention of this third power was still deemed necessary, in order to compose their dissensions. But when in the further progress of society, the middle class entirely overshadows all others, and absorbs all influence, and all effective power, the personal authority of the monarch is also enfeebled. It is then that a government in which the commons are represented by an executive magistrate, and two chambers in the legislature, becomes abundantly strong to quell insurrection, and insubordination to the laws. The experiment of the American government is full of instruction on this subject. The utmost vigor and decision have been displayed by both the federal and state governments, in suppressing tumult and disorder. A government which knows that it represents the opinions and interests of the great body of the people, is necessarily a strong one, and goes straight forward to its end, without any of those misgivings which perplex the holders of a less legitimate authority.

Mixed government, then, may be described as the transition state from pure monarchy to representative government. We must not consider it as the form in which the institutions are destined to be permanently cast. The most eminent English statesmen of both parties are accustomed to pronounce it the best without any qualification. But there is a wonderful proclivity even among the most enlightened minds, to believe each step in the progress of society to be the best, and the final step. This law of our nature is not without its use. Each step may be one of indefinite duration. It is important, therefore, to render it popular, so that society may not go back, instead of moving forward. The force of public opinion is thus arrayed in favor of each successive advance; and when further change becomes desirable, society is prepared for it, by reason of the progress it has already made. And this leads to other and still more important views in relation to this matter. For a considerable period prior to each step in advance, there is a general fermentation among the minds of men. New opinions and doctrines are freely discussed, and resolutely proclaimed. A close observer of English society at the present day, one who has noticed the wide extent to which liberal opinions are circulated among all classes, will find more cogent reasons than those suggested by mere theoretical propriety, why the existing form of society is not destined to last forever. If popular intelligence and power continue to make much further progress, it will be impossible to preserve the *sentiment* of monarchy and aristocracy in its pristine force. It may be supposed that the commons will be disposed to uphold the existing frame of government from a conviction that it is the best on the whole: and undoubtedly in this event it will be maintained. But what shall we say, if among that very class, opinions of an opposite character are widely diffused. The commons may battle against the opinions of any other class, but they cannot make war upon their own. What is now the subject of frequent discussion will become matter for familiar every-day conversation. The principles which hold together the old fabric are already shaken, but the blows will be so constant, that it may ultimately be undermined. An illusion of the imagination cannot be kept alive by reasoning upon it, when the creature of the imagination becomes himself the reasoner. A close body, like the ancient priesthood of Egypt and Hindostan, might persuade others to accept their impostures, but they never accepted them themselves. And whenever any error or imposture is thoroughly penetrated by the popular mind, it is sure to be assailed on all sides, until it loses its force upon the imagination. When the secret can no longer be kept, because so many are let into it, there is an end of its influence upon society. A profound and original writer,* in exposing the unsoundness of what is termed "the development hypothesis," remarks, that it is impossible to travel by railroad, or steamboat, without hearing the freest discussion of this question. If a doctrine so abstruse, and so far removed from the ordinary pur-

* "Footsteps of the Creator"—By H. Miller.

suits, and speculations of men, has become the subject of bold and unreserved discussion, it is not surprising that political questions, which however abstract, are mingled with all the affairs of men, should be made the subject of general and familiar conversation.

In that form of society to which I have supposed the present current of events is tending, it will be unnecessary to disturb the question of universal suffrage. Every department of government in the United States was representative before universal suffrage was introduced. A moderate qualification for the exercise of the elective franchise would be consistent with the interests of that great body denominated the commons or middle class, but the artificial structures of king and nobility will be entirely inconsistent with those interests.

The system of patronage which has taken such deep root in the British government, depends for its existence upon the institutions of king and nobility. There is no subject which has more deeply engaged the attention of enlightened men in that country, ever since the memorable resolution introduced into the house of commons in the early part of this century, that the influence of the crown has increased, is increasing and ought to be diminished. It has exercised the minds of great numbers who had hitherto kept aloof from such speculations. The black book of England, a work of unimpeached authority, lets us into an acquaintance with the curious machinery by which this patronage is so wielded, as to enable a small number to domineer over the great body of the people. I shall notice a few instances only: 1st. Almost all offices in the West Indies, both civil and judicial, are discharged by deputy, the principal residing in England. 2d, Pluralities exist to an enormous extent, both in state and church. 3d. Nine hundred and fifty-six pensioners and placemen receive the immense sum of £2,788,907. 4. Sinecures exist for life, with reversions sometimes to persons in the cradle, to the amount of £1,500,0000. 5. Many offices even in Great Britain, are discharged by deputy. 6. From the returns of 1833, there were sixty members of the house of commons, holding offices and receiving emoluments from civil appointments, sinecures, etc., exclusive of eighty-three holding naval and military commissions. And there are so many as eighty-five members who enjoy church patronage. 7. The vast patronage of the church, of which the king is head, and to the principal offices in which he appoints. 8. The firm and irresponsible tenure of the whole body of civil officers. The power which this confers, the important agency it has in binding to the crown a vast organized corps, interested in holding all sorts of abuses, is equally evident.

The patronage of the American president is not only small in comparison with that of the British king, but is of a totally different character. Real duties are annexed to all the offices, which are dispensed by the former. If the president appoints with a view to his re-election, the influence emolument conferred on the persons appointed is inconsiderable. The tenure by which he holds his trust is short, so is that of his appointees. Both are placed on their good behavior from a consciousness of the insecurity of their places. But the king has an army of officers for life; for not one in twenty go out on a change of administration. The fluctuation of offices in America is a source of security to the institutions, independently of the good effect it has in introducing so large a part of the population to an acquaintance with public affairs. The displacement of a number of civil officers in the United States is simply an application of the principle of rotation, which takes place in the election of the president himself. The blind and arbitrary rule of the choice by lot, is superseded by one which is clear and intelligible. Removals may undoubtedly be made from improper motives; and I know nothing which would impart to political affairs so lofty a character, as that all the good which is done to society should be done from perfectly pure motives. If this cannot be accomplished, the next thing most desirable, is to make sure that the good should at any rate be performed. The great principle in the American government is, that power should never be conferred on the best man, which in the hands of the worst would be liable to abuse. Hence the rule which establishes a moderate tenure of office for the executive and members of the legislature; and the same rule runs through the appointment of all the subordinate administrative officers. If I were asked what is the secret spring which actuated the leaders of parties in the United States, in the selection of a president, I should say it was the desire to elect the man who was most approachable. Men of moderate talents are much more so than men of superior endowments. But from the choosing men of moderate talents, and of unexceptionable character, flow a great number of consequences which are of inestimable advantage. A patrician class is dispersed, as soon as it shows itself, while the power of the middle class is strengthened and consolidated. And with the frail materials we have with which to erect government of any kind, or under any circumstances, we can never do so well as by reposing the political power with that class chiefly.

English writers speak of the ease with which their government sustains an enormous patronage. But it would be more correct to speak of the ease with which a well organized system of patronage may be made to sustain government. For what is it we intend, when we speak of the ability of monarchical government to sustain patronage. It simply means, that the system of patronage is so firmly fenced in, so thoroughly supported by the rich and powerful, that it becomes a self-perpetuating institution, producing quiet, because it stifles, without removing discontent. The feature which is most calculated to produce alarm, is the very thing which hides the vices of the system from view.

The corrupting influence of patronage is less in a republic than in a monarchy. 1st. Because the power and emoluments bestowed are greatly inferior. 2d. Because they are so insecure. 3d. Because real duties, duties which demand unremitted attention and industry, are attached to all offices, 4th. The candidates are greatly more numerous in popular than in monarchical governments, so that the people exercise a perpetual check upon each other. 5th. The list of public offices is exceedingly diminutive when compared with the number of the electors. 6th. The multitude disappointed, and interested in voting against the chief magistrate, when he is a candidate a second time, is so much more formidable than that of the appointees. These circumstances render the mischiefs of patronage in a representative republic, much less than the theory of such a government would lead us to suppose. The executive dispenses offices to the people, and to the people he is indebted for his election. Yet this patronage is comparatively impotent in securing his re-election. The number dissatisfied, in conjunction with the still greater number who have no expcetation of obtaining office, is so immense that it is doubtful whether one chief magistrate in ten will be re-elected. The practice of electing for one term has grown up since executive patronage has been vastly enlarged. It may be supposed that the public interests will be damaged by not re-electing an officer who has already acquired a competent knowledge of public affairs. But in proportion as the institutions of a country are matured and perfected, less talent is requisite for conducting them. Public business becomes organized into a regular system, and little is left for the incumbent unless he has the temerity to depart from that system. To the stability of office is substituted the stability of a complicated system, easy to administer, and yet difficult to break in upon.

I have observed that the system of patronage in Great Britain contributes mightily to strengthen the power of the king and aristocracy. But there are some circumstances which, independently of the growing authority of the commonalty, have a contrary tendency, and not the less so that they are of a more hidden character, and act silently and imperceptibly upon the government. That the defects of a government should gradually lead to an alteration in its structure, will not appear suprising, but that its excellencies should have the same effect, is still more surprising, and would not be apt to strike the mind of any but a close observer. A very great change has taken place in European society in very modern times, in the habits and manners of what are called the superior classes. Formerly crimes, and every species of disorder, were committed by the men who belonged to those classes, fully as much as by those who filled the inferior ranks. In modern times, and more particularly in Great Britain, outrages against life and property are almost entirely confined to the lowest walks of life. This change in the manners, is one reason why society is so much more easily governed than formerly. Crimes are now strictly personal, and are no part of the habitual conduct of the governing class. This, to all appearance, confers a great advantage upon that class. It does so in reality, for a very considerable period. It evidently gives popularity to the government of that class, and wins over to it the obedience of all other orders. But it is also evident that the more the manners of the higher ranks are likened to those of the middle class, the greater is the authority and influence which the last acquire. The middle class in England and Scotland, are more distinguished for energy, sagacity, and information, than any other class during any period of European history. That the substantial excellencies of their character should be copied by those who wield so much political influence, is not so much a compliment (for with that we have nothing to do) as a recognition that that class have certain elements of public and private virtue, which, when they have full play, make up the whole of public and private prosperity. But if these are the qualities most essential both in public and private life, they are the very ones which are the best fitted to govern mankind. And as the commonalty are a numerous and powerful body, and the aristocracy a small one, it may happen that the whole effective authority of the state may slide, not from any set purpose or preconceived design, but insensibly and quietly, into the hands of the former; and then it must be admitted, it would not be a work of great difficulty so to change the institutions, as to make their outward form correspond with the genius which animated them. Perhaps it would be more correct to say, that it would not only not be difficult, but that it would be the end to which society would straightforward tend, as not only the most natural, but as affording, in the altered condition of the social organization, the most effectual means of giving strength and stability to the institutions.

There is another circumstance which is calculated to arrest our attention. A great change has taken place in the manners of European courts. The regime, the domestic police, if I may so express myself, of the princely mansion, is totally different from what it was formerly. Never were the manners so thoroughly dissolute, so corrupt, as in the time of Louis the Fifteenth of France, and Charles the Second of England. Nothing of the kind is witnessed at the present day. The French revolution of 1789 revolutionized the manners of the French court, and Napoleon was the first monarch who introduced something like decency and propriety in the princely household. The English revolution, a century earlier, effected the same thing in that country. The manners which formerly prevailed, and which were supposed to be peculiarly adapted to a court, would not be tolerated at the present day.

The cause of this great change is evidently to be found in the power which public opinion has acquired. The prince and the nobles, who were elevated so high, as to be exempt from its control, are now made directly responsible to it. But what has given being to this public opinion. Evidently the rise of that great class whom we denominate the commonalty, whose habits of life are for the most part alien to anything like unbridled licentiousness, and whose numbers add great weight and authority to the new law which is imposed upon society. Thus the prince, as well as the nobleman, finds himself involuntarily copying after the manners and habits of the middle class. The exterior may be more refined, but the ground work is the same. This singular and unexpected consequence, however, follows from this revolution in the manners. Kingly power, and grandeur strike the imagination with infinitely less force than formerly. The very fact, that the monarch was lifted so high, as to be absolved from all restraint, that he was not only not amenable to the laws, but not amenable to those conventional rules which preside over the manners of a civilized society, gave an imposing air to everything which pertained to his office. How this should happen, how he who was set so high, whose conduct should be so just, and his manners so unexceptionable, should be polluted with so many vices, seemed to be inexplicable; and the fact that it was inexplicable, imparted additional mystery to the royal authority. That so startling a contradiction should exist, and no one be able to answer why it was permitted, acted like a charm upon the imagination of the masses. Kingly power was not only a great office, but more than that, it was a great mystery. The heathen mythology exercised a sovereign mastery over the popular mind, although the gods were tainted with every species of vice. The human mind could probably give no other explanation of this anomaly, than that if they were not lifted so high as to be absolved from all the laws which govern mankind, they would partake of the character of men, and would cease to be gods.

Thus in proportion as princes mend their manners, and practise those virtues which give dignity to the individual, in whatever station he is placed, in the same proportion, do they contribute to break the spell which inspired unlimited obedience among all classes. If to come down to the level of those homely virtues, which adorn their subjects, has become the fashion of the day, a fashion not arbitrarily taken up, but imposed by the irresistible course of events, the notion may gradually insinuate itself into the minds of those subjects, that government is not a grand mystery, nor the prince an impersonation of the deity; that as it is now for the first time a received maxim in politics, that government should be administered for their advantage, that advantage would be most certainly attained by the appointment of responsible agents by themselves. Once a delusion of the imagination is broken up, men begin to reason; and although I do not undertake to predict what form the institutions will assume an hundred or even fifty years hence, yet there is nothing inconceivable, nothing unreasonable in the supposition, that within the shortest of those periods, a firm, wise, and vigorous representative government may be established in the British Isles.

There is, then, a very general conviction that the present state of things cannot last forever—that royalty and aristocracy cannot stand secure amid the light of the nineteenth century. When this is the case, the revolution is half accomplished. The middle class at a future day need not say to the king and his ministers, you may squander the wealth of the state, provided you will protect us against the assaults of the lower classes. For they will be able to protect themselves as effectively, and with infinitely less expense ; while at the same time, innumerable abuses and deformities in the system, which have no other use than to prop up an exceedingly artificial form of government, will be extirpated.

CHAPTER VII.

THE LEGISLATIVE POWER.

THE great defect of what is termed pure democracy, as distinguished from representative government, consists in this, that the former is without an established system of laws. The momentary and fluctuating will of the people constitutes the law on every occasion;—which is the reason why that form of government is the worst except despotism. Nor does there at first sight seem to be any reason why there should be any pre-established ordinances to bind the people, when they assist personally at every public deliberation. Their will constitutes the law, because there is no superior human power behind them to draw them back when error is about to be committed. For error, politically, is out of the question. Every such assembly is itself a convention of the people. Its last declaration, as it is the freshest expression of the public will, is also a full expression of the sovereign power of the state.

But there is no democratic republic which has existed, in which the inconveniences, not to say the manifold evils, which spring from such a scheme of government, have not been felt. There is not one which has not departed widely from the theory on which it professed to be founded. Solon drew up a body of laws for the Athenian state, and Lycurgus one for Sparta. But this departure from the naked theory of democratic government was not a step taken in favor of representative government. It was the introduction of a capital feature of monarchical government. It was a recognition in disguise of the one man power. Nor was the case very different with the Roman decemvirate. Commissioners sent abroad to make a selection from the laws of other countries, and exercising their own judgment as to what ordinances would be adapted to the Roman community, is very different from a convention assembled among the people for whom the new code is to be framed, drawing instruction from a deep and careful survey of the form of society which lay before them, and suiting the laws exclusively to their domestic interests.

Fortunately for most nations which have been inclined to establish popular government, the extent of territory has opposed an insurmountable obstacle to carrying out the naked theory of democratic government, while the extent and diverse character of the population have been equally fatal to the attainment of a predominant influence by one or two individuals. It becomes impossible for the people to assemble in mass, and still more so for them to perform the duties which appertain to an executive and judicial magistracy. This compels the adoption of the principle of representation in every one of the political departments. Representatives, when convened under this plan as a legislative body, pass laws from time to time, as the exigences of society require, until at length these laws become so numerous, and the chief part of them so adapted to the leading and permanent interests of the population, that they lose the character of mere temporary regulations, and are erected into a system of fixed rules for the government of the community. That is, they acquire a higher dignity and greater importance than they had before, notwithstanding they are not passed by the people, but by the people's deputies. The restrictions imposed upon the law-making power increase its solemnity, because they require a more exact and undivided attention to the duties which appertain to it, than would be possible in an assembly of millions or thousands, convened on one day, and dispersed the next. For in the first place, in a country of wide extent, and whose people are fitted for self-government, there will very naturally, if not necessarily, be a constitutional ordinance, prescribing the duties of the legislator and the limits of legislation. And in the second place, representatives, acting on behalf of others, in order to give any intelligible account to those who have deputed them, are obliged to proceed with considerable care in the preparation and consideration of bills. The laws are no longer carried by acclamation, but are conducted through a long and tedious process; and the language in which they are expressed is endeavored to be made precise and perspicuous, in order that the constituent may understand how the deputy has discharged his duty.

Thus representation, which was at first intended to cure one defect in democratic government, that is, to facilitate the transaction of public business, comes in process of time to cure all defects, by substituting, as nearly as humanly speaking can be done, a government of laws in the place of one of force. The people are the real lawgivers, the members of the legislative body their agents only; and yet, in consequence of the double machinery which is employed, the laws are made to reign supreme over the people themselves. For not only is the passage of all laws attended with certain solemnities, and published in a form which renders them accessible to every one; there is another circumstance which contributes to impress upon them the character of a system. The greater the number of persons for whom the laws are made, the greater must be the generality of the rules which they will contain. It is not difficult to legislate for a small number of individuals, or for a considerable number collected in a small space, by particular enactments. But there is no way of legislating for millions, inhabiting an extensive country, but by very general laws. We then make abstraction of everything peculiar to the individual, and take account only of those circumstances in which they all agree.

It is in proportion as the laws acquire this character of abstract general rules, that they are fitted to exercise authority over the minds of men; and that in proportion as the territory is enlarged, and the population multiplied, the restraint which is imposed upon society is augmented. To reconcile a high degree of freedom with a due authority on the part of government, is one problem which political philosophers have proposed to themselves. If we take refuge in monarchical or aristocratical government, we do indeed arm the public authority with a mighty power; but it is at the expense of popular liberty. If we have recourse to democratic government, we do not succeed in introducing a noble and generous freedom into the community, while at the same time we detract materially from the authority of the laws. Representative government, which is then the only alternative, is also the most natural direction which the institutions can take: the one which promises to answer all the desired ends, as well as we are permitted to expect.

Government, in order to fulfill the notion of a wise and useful institution, should aim to connect the private welfare of individuals with the public good of the state. To lose sight of the former—to suppose that the proper idea of government was that it had regard exclusively to public affairs, and took little account of men's private interests, would be to form a very inadequate conception of it. The political institutions are an accessary to a great end, rather than the end itself. To permit the various occupations of individuals to be conducted with freedom and security, is the final aim to which they should tend. But in the pure form of democratic government, the legislative, executive, and judicial powers would all be wielded by the same persons in mass; incumbering every one with such a multiplicity of public business, that their private affairs would go to ruin; and the people would cease to be men, in their efforts to become citizens; when the maxim should be, that in order to become citizens, it is first necessary to become men. And in such a constitution of society, the public interests also would fall to decay, as there would be wanting that concentrated attention which is indispensable to a skillful management of them. Representation, by applying the principle of the division of labor to the affairs of government, overcomes these difficulties. By collecting into a general system those rules which are intended to preside over the common interests, it gives additional authority to the laws; by abstaining from intermeddling too often and too minutely with the actions of individuals, it gives security and contentment to the people.

There is another view equally important. Men, even in the prosecution of their private business, have separate and selfish interests which they are ever intent upon gratifying. In a legislative assembly composed of a vast multitude, public and private interests would be confounded. The elective principle, without intending any such thing, effects a separation of the two. The number of private ends which are sought to be gratified, will be diminished as the assembly diminishes; not only because the number of individuals exposed to the temptation is reduced, but because the power of gratification is less. With no more wisdom, and fully as much selfishnes as the great majority of mankind, the members of this body are now placed in a situation where their attention will be more exclusively fastened upon the public interests, and one also which exposes their conduct more than ever to the scrutiny of other men.

The people say to their deputies, as we are physically precluded from looking after our private ends, we will, in revenge, observe your conduct more strictly, The deputies, on the other hand, although it may conflict with their private ends, are obliged to assume a character of earnestness and of devotion to the public business. They endeavor to place before themselves a standard of right by which to shape their conduct. A representative body, in other words, to make use of a homely phrase, operates as a strainer in separating the good from the bad qualities of individuals. It brings the public interests out in bolder relief, and weakens the cupidity of private persons.

An assembly so constituted is eminently favorable to reflection, not merely among its own members, but among the commnnity at large. The distribution of property and knowledge, in modern times, has created a wide basis for government to stand upon. But as it has multipled the number of persons who have an interest in public affairs, it has increased the intensity of party spirit. The legislative body has stated times for convening; it does not meet, like the popular assemblies of antiquity, on every gust of wind which may blow over the commonwealth. Between the first ebulliton of public feeling and the time appointed to deliberate, six months or more may elapse. This interval is eminently favorable to reflectian: not merely because it gives opportunity to so many minds to calculate the consequences of a proposed line of action, but because time itself has a sedative influence, and calms the most agitated passions. Or if we suppose that some event of very exciting character has occurred, when the legislature is on the eve of assembling, the set forms of proceeding to which such a body is addicted, and to which it becomes singularly attached, enable it easily to postpone the final determination for months, or even "to the first day of the succeeding session." The people willingly acquiesce in this delay on the part of their deputies, when they would not listen to it in a tumultuous assembly of themselves. The claim to the whole of Oregon would have been carried by acclamation in a popular meeting, when first proposed. But as the question had to be deliberated upon in a representative body, whose responsibility was increased, because they were acting for others, and not merely for themselves, it was held under consideration for three years. And the manner in which it was finally adjusted, although so different from what was at first expected, met with a more hearty and unanimous approval from the American people, than almost any other public measure which has been adopted.

Thus representative government is highly favorable to reflection, both in and out of the legislative body. It no longer speaks to itself alone, as was formerly the case. So far as regards the mere form of deliberating, the assembly sits within the four walls of the capitol. But for all important purposes, the whole state may be considered as an extension of those walls. If there is any species of information which is widely desseminated, it is that which relates to what is transacted in those walls. This is conveyed not once, and in one form only, but repeatedly, and in every variety of shape, so as to gratify the utmost inquisitiveness, and to rouse the attention of the most censorious observer of public affairs. It has been finely remarked, that one office which men of high intellectual endowments perform, is to act as instruments of communication between the intellectual world and society at large. And a representative body, with all its imperfections, performs a service of a very similar character.

There is no one circumstance in the history of modern communities, which more strikingly displays the great changes which have been wrought in the general structure of society, than the manner in which business is now conducted in a legislative body. There was a time, and that not very remote, when such an assembly did not pretend to deliberate upon, or in any sense of the word to conduct, the public business in person, but devolved the whole burden upon a handful of individuals. Thus the Scotch parliament, which was composed of the three estates of the clergy, nobility, and burgesses, never sat except on the day of meeting, and the day of adjournment. On the first, it made choice of a committee, styled, "lords of the articles," which was composed of three persons from each of the estates. And this committee drew up all the bills, and transacted the whole business. On the day appointed for the adjournment, these bills were submitted in mass to the parliament, and were all on that same day either approved or rejected. There was no free, open investigation, no debate, no account taken either one way or the other, of the serious consequences which might result from the proposed laws. Very similar was the mode of proceeding in the boasted Italian republics. The law was no sooner proposed, than the votes of the different orders were immediately taken. It is very easy to understand, what otherwise seems to be a riddle, how it came to pass that a legislative body, whether composed of one or more chambers, sat in one apartment. As there was no discussion, none of that bold and inquisitive spirit which now finds its way into such an assembly ; as, in short, everything was conducted in silence, the several estates or orders might very conveniently meet in the same hall. The mode of conducting the legislative proceedings in France was even worse than in Scotland or Italy. Madame de Sevigne, in her letters, has given a very animated description of the fashion of doing business. The canvassing the demands of the crown, the inquiry whether any and what taxes should be imposed, was not made in the legislative halls, but was carried on at the table of the nobleman who had been commissioned by the king to preside over the estates, or provincial legislatures ; and everything was carried by acclamation.

If there is any danger at the present day, it is of running into the opposite extreme. But it is better to err on that side. A superfluity of debate is infinitely better than none at all, or even than too little. It affords unequivocal evidence of two things : 1st, that the interests of the great body of the people have grown to be something ; and 2d, that the deputies of the people are compelled to set themselves earnestly to work, in order to acquire a competent knowledge of public affairs. In every deliberative assembly there are always a few individuals who stand out prominently above their fellows, and succeed in fixing public attention. But it would be a great mistake to suppose, that the speeches of other members, of inferior endowments, were unworthy of notice ; that they were to be regarded as empty and prosy harangues. It not unfrequently happens, that the reputation of a public speaker is not so much owing to his intellectual power, as to some external advantages. Some men succeed full as much in consequence of their physical, as of their mental, organization. And one is often perplexed, on reading the speeches of a leading member, to account for the fame he has acquired. The speeches of some other members are as full of good sense, and contain views as just and as comprehensive. Nevertheless, it is the fashion to regard these last as intruders into the debate, and as hampering the public business by their everlasting "longeurs."

It is the population residing beyond the walls of the state house who in our modern societies constitute the real and effective audience; and to them a sensible speech is always interesting, although the voice of the speaker may be unmusical, and his manner ever so ungainly. It was remarked of one of the most eminent statesmen America has produced,* that while he sat in the house of representatives, he gave marked attention to the speech of every member. There was hardly an instance, he observed, when he did not derive instruction, or when new views were not suggested to him, by the speeches of persons of even inconsiderable reputation. There was more wisdom in the observation, than would at first strike the mind. The habit contracted by this eminent statesman, gave him a thorough insight into the workings of other men's minds, and was one cause of the remarkable intellectual ability which he himself displayed. Doubtless there is a reasonable share of egotism to be found in every large assembly of men. But even egotism may sometimes become our instructor. For as it supposes a desire to obtain the public approbation, and as that approbation is very insecure, unless there is substantial merit, the representative, even in his efforts to attract the notice of his constituents, is obliged to make himself acquainted with the merits of the questions he undertakes to discuss. And as I have already observed, even if the speeches are unnecessarily prolix, there is an incidental advantage attending their delivery; they keep the public mind in abeyance, and contribute by their very defects to cool the feelings and mature the judgment. It might be supposed that the danger would be on the other side; that the country would be kept in a state of feverish excitement in consequence of the inflammatory harangues of demagogues. But the day of inflammatory harangues is gone by, when the competition for public speaking becomes so great as it necessarily is in a country of free institutions. Like everything with which we become abundantly familiar, those harangues pall upon the appetite, and make us ardently desire to hear something truly brilliant. In ninety-nine cases in a hundred, the inflammatory speaker succeeds in inflaming none but himself.

Shall the legislative power be divided? shall it consist of two or more branches? is one of those questions which the human mind

---

* William Lowndes.

hardly ventures to debate any longer. Public opinion everywhere, and in every form of government, except the absolute, has determined it in the affirmative. In the ancient commonwealths, in the limited monarchies of modern Europe, and in the United States, the division of the legislature has been regarded as an axiom in politics. An institution which is founded upon long-established custom, and which has apparently adapted itself to almost every form of society, has on that very account a strong claim to respect. This claim, however, must not be looked upon as absolutely decisive; for it is a fact of as ancient and as universal noteriety, as any other which falls under our observation, that the human mind is wonderfully disposed to accommodate itself to what it finds to be the established order of things. Here are two principles set over against each other; a consideration which should make us exceedingly careful, but which should by no means dissuade us from a critical examination of the subject.

The distribution of society into classes was, doubtless, the foundation of the division of the legislative body. Where this classification did not exist, or where the inferior classes occupied an exceedingly insignificant position in the state, the legislature was seldom a plural body. Thus, in the earlier stages of English history, the great council was composed of the wise men, or barons only; holding their seats, not by virtue of an express authority delegated to them, but by a tenure as firm, and as independent, as that of the king.

Society, in its rude beginnings is held together chiefly by the force of the imagination. Where there is an immense disparity in the condition of the upper and lower ranks, where the first possess nearly all the property, the superstitious reverence which this circumstance inspires, irresistibly invests them with the legislative authority. But in proportion as society advances, and a different distribution of property takes place, whether this is occasioned by the civil wars of the barons, which crumble their property, or by the growth of trade and industry, which raises up an entirely new class, this superstitious feeling loses its hold upon the mind. The appropriation of nearly all the property by the barons, conferred upon them an exorbitant authority in comparison with the great majority of the population, and the gradual division of this property, whether in fee, or in lease, afterward transfers some portion of that authority to other parts of society. A class below the nobility makes its appearance, first in the towns, and afterward in the country, and this class finally succeeds in obtaining a distinct and independent position in the community. While this new class is imperceptibly growing to manhood, the rivalry and disputes between the king and nobility reveal its importance, and enable it actively to assert a power which lay dormant before. The people have now got to be something, because their intervention in the controversies of the day may be turned to account by one or other of the parties. They now elect their own representatives, and this gives occasion to another chamber of the legislative body.

But on a further advance of society, the change becomes more marked and important. The barons dwindle into a mere handful. They cease to be even virtually the representatives of the community. Their weight in society is personal, rather than that of a class. If at an early period their number is small, this is compensated by their possessing the entire moral power of the state. At an intermediate stage their numbers and wealth are both diminished, but not so sensibly as to deprive them of their claim to constitute a separate branch of the legislature. At a still later period, their number is not only reduced, but their wealth becomes insignificant when compared with that of the aggregate of the population. The division of the legislative power then loses its original meaning: it no longer stands upon the same foundation as formerly. And it becomes not merely matter for curious, but for strictly legitimate inquiry, whether the plan shall be preserved. Society may have undergone great alterations, so that the causes which led to a particular political arrangement may have ceased to operate; and yet others may have sprung into existence, which equally demonstrate its utility. Perhaps the very prejudices which surround an ancient institution, may help us to ward off some other infirmity to which we will be exposed in constructing a new system.

In an old and established government there is this difficulty, the division of the legislature was not the result of any set design. Society fell into the arrangement at a period when circumstances controlled men instead of their controlling circumstances. The institution grows into an usage, which incorporates itself with the habits of thinking of every one. This gives it so firm a hold upon the imagination, that the legislator hardly feels as if he had power, much ess has he the inclination, to interfere with it. In a new society, and new government, the case is different. If there is no regular classification of society, no subordination of ranks, and the principle of representation is introduced, and yet the division of the legislature has been copied from older states, its entire want of adaptation either annuls its influence, or the influence which it has is of so vague and doubtful an appearance, as to withdraw public attention altogether from the consideration of it.

De Lalme is almost the only writer who has undertaken to examine this question. The reasoning is very ingenious. "Whatever bars," he says, "a single legislature may make to restrain itself, can never be relatively to itself, anything more than simple resolutions ; as those bars which it might erect to stop its own motions, must then be within it, and rest upon it, they can be no bars." This is undoubtedly true, if the members hold their seats by hereditary right, or where, being elected, the tenure is long, and the electoral franchise exceedingly restricted. But where the entire legislative body is chosen by popular suffrage, and for a limited period, a new principle rises up and takes the place of those bars, to wit, the responsibility of the members to their constituents. The condition which De Lalme was in search of, in order to restrain the legislature, is then found. The bars are truly without, and not within, the body. De Lalme, although investigating a general principle, confined his attention exclusively to British society, where, from time immemorial, the distinction of ranks existed : nor did he frame to himself any just conception of a commonwealth, where privileged orders had no place, and where the responsibility of the members shall be so direct and immediate, as to create an inevitable check upon their conduct.

From this view, it would seem to follow, that the question, shall the legislature be divided ? depends upon the mode of election, and the tenure of the members ; in other words, upon the provision which is made in the system for giving effect to the principle of responsibility, and not upon the nature of the power which is exercised. In most of the European states, the legislative body is composed of a class of nobles and of deputies chosen by the people and as these two orders are supposed to have contrary interests, each is protected against the encroachments of the other, by both possessing co-ordinate authority, and consequently the right to veto the acts of each other. No such reason exists in a democratic republic. Indeed, one great design of that form of government is to unite together, as far as is practicable, the different classes of which society is composed, instead of inventing devices for keeping them asunder. It is on that very account that the principle of representation is introduced into every department of the government. All the members of the legislative assembly are elected, and the reason is not very apparent why they should be distributed into two, any more than into three or four chambers. This incongruity between the institution and a democratic form cf society, may be productive of one or other of two results. It may give rise to much confusion and inconvenience in the working of the government, or its tendency to produce that effect, may be neutralized by the otherwise skillful structure of the body : the dead principle may be counterveiled by the living one with which it is incorporated. When the last is the case, the institution degenerates into a mere formal arrangement, which is preserved simply because it is found to be part of an old-established system. If no glaring inconvenience is perceived, people very easily persuade themselves that the institution is not only wise, but that it is an indispensable part of the machinery of free government.

Other reasons, however, than those I have referred to, may be assigned for this mode of organizing the legislative body. It may be argued that, it is calculated to introduce more reflection into the public deliberations than would be the case if the body were a single one. The United States is the only country which affords much light upon this part of the subject. So far as regards the state governments, and I purposely confine myself to them at present, it is by no means certain that experience justifies the conclusion. Perhaps, on a very close and attentive observation, it would be found that the division of the body has been productive of increased violence and exacerbation, although in ways which are at first calculated to elude observation ; or it may be, that a predominant idea having once taken possession of the mind, its influence is not easily weakened by all the observation which we have made.

In order to execute this plan of accompanying every legislative measure with a greater degree of reflection, it would seem to be necessary that the mode of electing the two chambers should be different, or that at least, the terms for which the members of the two are chosen should be of different duration. In both respects, there is little or no discrimination in much the greater part of the state governments. In Maryland the senate was formerly elected, like the president of the United States, by a college of electors. But this feature in the old coustitution has been superseded by the ordinary and more natural plan of direct choice. In Massachusetts, New Hampshire, North and South Carolina, a property qualification is necessary to entitle to a seat in either house. And the amount of property necessary for a senator is double that which is requisite for a representative. But, in the great majority of the states, no distinction exists. In Virginia a property qualification is indeed demanded of both senators and representatives, but the qualification is the same in both instances, and is none other than is required of the electors themselves.

As to the duration of the term ; in some states senators and representatives are elected for the same term. This is the case in Maine, Massachusetts, New Hampshire, Connecticut, Rhode Island, New Jersey, North Carolina, Georgia, and Tennessee. In Maryland senators are elected for six years. In Delaware, Mississippi, Arkansss, and Illinois, for four ; but in these states the sessions of the legislature being biennial, the four years is equivalent to two terms only. In Virginia, South Carolina, Kentucky, Lousiana, and Missouri, they are elected for four years, and the legislature meets annually. In Pennsylvania, Indiana, and Alabama, they are elected for three, and in New York, Michigan, and Ohio, for two. And in these six last states the legislature also sits annually. The only states in which representatives are chosen for two terms, are South Carolina, Lousiana, and Missouri.

All this shows an exceeding variety in the mode of composing the two chambers, or at least in the outward form which they are made to assume ; and indicates, moreover, that the notion of giving to senators a more independent tenure than to representatives, in order to create a balance between the two bodies, was often entirely lost sight of, and in no two instances thoroughly carried into practice. The division of the legislature was copied from older communities, in which a regular subordination of ranks existed. But in America, there was no similar classification of society, and the materials for constructing an upper house on the European model were entirely wanting.

In some of the states candidates for the senate must have attained a higher age than those for the house. But the distinction in this respect is so small as to create no material difference in the constitution of the two chambers. In no state does there appear to have been the least design to create a council of elders. But the scheme of a plural body having been adopted, it was necessary to give color to it, by creating a distinction, however unimportant it might be. Age undoubtedly, in the great majority of men, contributes to extend the circle of their ideas, and to mature the judgment. It would be difficult to fall upon any precise rule, applicable to all men, as there is not only a very great difference in the natural faculties of individuals, but a great difference also in the ripening of different minds, which possess equal power. Forty-five has been supposed to be the earliest period at which, in the average of men, the judgment is thoroughly matured, and the knowledge and experience which have been previously acquired, may be made available to the business of public life. But in no state, except Kentucky, is a higher age than thirty required, in order to entitle to a seat in the senate. In most of the states the candidate need not be more than twenty-five; and in Connecticut, New York, New Jersey, Rhode Island, and North Carolina, persons who have attained twenty-one years are eligible to either house. The provisions on this subject also show how very imperfectly the scheme of balancing one body against the other has been accomplished. In some respects the age of five and twenty is more unfavorable than twenty-one. The young man just arrived at majority is apt to be more diffident, to distrust his own powers more than he would if four or five years older. At five and twenty we feel more confidence, a greater degree of self assurance; even though there should be less ability to second our efforts. I am not sure, therefore, but what the constitutions of Rhode Island, New York, New Jersey, and North Carolina, have adopted the wisest plan. A man at twenty-one may be both more discreet, and better informed, than one at twenty-five. A man at twenty-five is sometimes superior in both respects to one at forty-five. Instead of establishing an unchangeable rule, the best plan is to defer the matter to the electors, and enable them to exercise their judgment in making the selection. Legislation in the United States is not, as in some other countries, an affair which is exclusively engrossed by the nobility and gentry. It is a matter in which the great bulk of the population have a deep stake; and in which consequently they are made to take an active part. Their observation and experience, although not affording an unerring guide, will ever prevent them from going very wrong.

There is another feature in which the upper and lower houses of the American legislatures differ. The last is invariably the most numerous body. But where the constitution of the two is in other respects substantially the same, this difference is little more than an arrangement of detail. One can easily conceive of an upper house composed of so few, and of a lower of so great, a number of members, as to create a complete antagonism between them. This was the case in the Athenian commonwealth, where the senate consisted of one or two hundred, and the popular assembly of eight thousand. It was so, also, in the Roman State, where the senate contained three hundred, and the comitia of the centuries, or tribes, twenty or thirty thousand. But the disparity in point of numbers, as well as in other respects, is so inconsiderable in the American states, that if there is any efficacy in an upper house, it is doubtful whether it is not attributable to the name, rather than the thing. We call it an upper house; figure it to ourselves as the most dignified body of the two; and thenceforward a firm conviction takes possession of the mind, that it must perform some office distinct from, and of superior utility to, that performed by the other house. In the English government, the house of peers is a less numerous body than the house of commons: the former consisting of four hundred and thirty-nine, and the last of six hundred and fifty-eight members. But the different operation of these two bodies, does not arise in the smallest degree from that circumstance. It is not the fewness of the number, but the fewness of the class, which renders the house of peers a totally different body from the house of commons. The former represents itself; the last represents millions. So that if the upper house were the most numerous body of the two, and yet the constitution of both was in other respects precisely the same as at present, the operation of the system would be the same.

Copying after English precedents, the American governments have sometimes sought to establish a difference in the functions, as well as in the composition, of the two chambers. Thus, in some of the states, money bills can only originate in the lower house. This is an arrangement which is obviously without meaning or utility in the local governments. It has accordingly been dropped in the constitutions of Connecticut, Rhode Island, New York, Ohio, Illinois, Michigan, and Arkansas. The members of both chambers are equally representatives of the people, and no very solid reason can be assigned, why any bill should not be permitted to originate in either. One thing is certain, that notwithstanding the efforts which have been made to create an artificial distinction between the two bodies, they remain essentially the same. This it is which constitutes a distinguishing feature of American institutions; that we may vary the paraphernalia of government as much as we please, but it still obstinately persists, in every one of its departments, to be a government based upon the popular will. In other countries, the different structure of these departments is occasioned by great diversities in the organization of society. The difficulty is how to retain these, and yet to obtain so much uniformity in the character of the population, as to dispense just and equal rules to all men. In America, this substantial requisite is already obtained, and American legislators can therefore afford to make experiments as to the mere outward form which their institutions shall wear. America may copy after Europe; but the great problem is, can Europe copy after America?

The materials then for constructing an upper house, such as they exist in Europe, are entirely wanting in America, and I have doubted (for it is perhaps impossible to pronounce an opinion absolutely decisive when the question is of taking down an old, not of erecting a new, institution) whether it was worth while to adhere to the principle of a division of the legislature in the state governments. The difference, however slight, in the tenure by which the members of the two chambers hold their seats, causes them sometimes to represent different parties; and this reflection of opposite opinions lays the foundation of a spirit of rivalry and animosity, which impedes the progress of business during a whole session. A single body having the public eye intently fixed upon it, and not distracted by the shuffling and the maneuvering of two chambers, would feel a more thorough, because a more undivided, responsibility to its constituents. The true office of a minority consists in its influencing, not governing. If the legislature consisted of a single chamber, the predominant party would abstain from those extreme measures which it is now driven to vindicate, in consequence of the equally extreme measures which are defended by the chamber of the minority.

Each dares the other to do as it says; each obstinately clings to its own opinions, because each knows that neither can possibly be carried, and in this way, both have in repeated instances endeavored to fly from the responsibility which they owed to society.

This is the reason why the veto of the governor, on bills passed by the legislature, has been abolished in nearly all the American states. That power was at one time supposed to answer the same purpose as the division of the legislature: to maintain a salutary check upon that assembly. But experience has demonstrated that it is as well, if not better, to place the legislative body in a situation where it will feel the undivided weight of the responsibility imposed upon it.

It sometimes happens, that although the duration of the term for which senators and representatives are chosen is the same, that the two chambers still reflect the opinions of different parties. This circumstance is ascribable to various causes. Sometimes it is in consequence of the mere difference of the number of members which compose the two chambers. The districts in which senators are elected will naturally be larger than for representatives. And although the qualifications of the electors may be the same in both, yet where parties in the state are pretty evenly balanced, a different territorial division will give rise to different results in the selection of the members. This was recently the case in Tennessee, where senators and representatives are elected for the same term. The melancholy spectacle was presented of one house obstinately refusing to go into an election, because, on joint ballot, the vote would be unfavorable to the predominant party in the house. It is a striking proof of the soundness of public opinion in America, that where a course of conduct of this character has been pursued, one so alien o the genius of free institutions, it has terminated in the overthrow of the refractory party. The ballot box at the succeeding election has converted the majority into the minority. But in none of the othe r nine states, where the term of senators and representatives is the same, do I recollect to have heard of such unjustifiable proceedings. This conduct, and other of a similar character, has been confined to those states where the duration of the term is different.

There is one of the American states in which, until recently, the legislature was composed of a single chamber. This is Vermont. And it is certain, that in no state has the course of legislation been more uniformly marked by good sense and propriety; in none has there been a more watchful attention to the interests of the people. At an early period, the legislature of Pennsylvania was also a single body. This arrangement was altered before there had been sufficient time to test the experiment. The brilliant repartee of Mr. Adams in answer to Dr. Franklin, who was in favor of a single chamber, captivated the minds of men, and was decisive of the question, at a period when the fashion of thinking in America was so much molded upon European institutions.

De Lolme attributes the wise and circumspect conduct of the English parliament to its division into two chambers. But the theory of the constitution was precisely the same in the times of the Tudors, and Stuarts, as when De Lolme wrote. At the latter period, England enjoyed a considerable share of internal tranquility, because the people, having risen in importance, had become a sort of make-weight in the government. During the two former periods, the government was little better than a despotism, and the laws were frequently the most iniquitous imaginable. So great a revolution, the theory of the constitution remaining the same, can only be accounted for, by supposing that some equally important change had taken place in the structure of society, and consequently, in the practical working of the government. And this change consists in nothing less than the gradual elevation of the popular body, and the creation of a well defined tribunal of public opinion which, impressing its authority powerfully upon the whole system, has maintained each department in its proper place. These are the bars which have been erected to fence off the encroachments of the legislative power. The condition which De Lolme demanded is obtained. The bars are not merely without the chambers; they are without the entire body; and are much more effectual than any curious adjustment of the interior mechanicism of the government.

I have, in a preceding chapter, alluded to the very important balance which is maintained between the government and the power out of the government; and the British constitution, at the time De Lolme wrote, and still more at the present day, affords an instructive example of it. Construct government as you will, if it is afterward left to itself, and permitted to command its own motions, the power it wields may be distorted to any purpose. But if there is a corresponding power—a presiding influence without — which subjects it unceasingly to the action of public opinion, even a faulty arrangement of the parts will be corrected. The English chambers no longer encroach as they formerly did on each other's rights, nor on the rights of the people; because the popular body has become the first estate in the realm, and holds in check, both the king and the nobility, as well as the commons. This is the simple explanation of the difficulty: and if one born under the Henrys could rise from his grave, he would be struck with amazement, at finding that British councils were conducted with so much more skill and wisdom than formerly; and that public men, in spite of the selfish interests which fill their bosoms, are placed under a restraint, from which the most powerful standing army could not deliver them.

In the times of the Tudors and Stuarts, not to go back to a still earlier period, the legislative power was divided as it now is. But under those princes, the country was either ruled by a stern and rigorous despotism, or it was a scene of incessant broils. At the present day, a species of virtual representation has been established in both houses of parliament, which, although it falls far short of an actual representation, has had power sufficient to work a most striking alteration in the conduct of public affairs.

De Lolme also attributes the remarkable solidity of the crown in Great Britain, in part, to the division of the legislature. But this is a circumstance which is not peculiar to that country. The same thing is observable of all the kingdoms and principalities of northern and central Europe, in some of which there is no proper legislative body; in some the legislative body consists of a single chamber, and in others of more than two chambers. The compact and vigorous authority of the royal power in Russia, Austria, Prussia, Sweden, and Denmark, is quite as remarkable as it is in Great Britain, and affords a strong contrast to the feeble condition of the crown in Spain and Portugal, in both of which there are two chambers modeled after the English system.

This singular stability of the royal power throughout the greater part of the kingdoms of Europe, a circumstance of apparently evil omen to the growth of popular power, but in reality favorable to it, is mainly ascribable to the fact that the most absolute monarchs are insensibly accommodating themselves to the new ideas of the age. They are more restrained, and are therefore permitted to be more secure. A king is compelled not so much to truck and huckster to the great men who surround the throne, as to cultivate the good will of the people. The close intercourse which now exists between all the European communities, has created a sort of informal league between them; and one member, although far behind some of the others in civilization, is powerfully acted upon by the institutions which exist in those others. Although the condition of society is such, that no powerful middle class exists, as in Great Britain, to control the government, yet public opinion in Great Britain, in France, Belgium, Holland, and throughout nearly all Germany, exercises a potent extra territorial influence, and is insensibly begetting habits of thinking and acting among princes, totally different from what they were accustomed to formerly. This influence has even penetrated the Turkish empire, and the sovereign is accordingly a wiser and more discreet ruler, than were most of the English Henrys. He has consented to do what they never dreamed of—to draw up an instrument imposing limitations upon his own authority, to appoint a commission to digest a code of jurisprudence, after the plan of the celebrated code civil of France, and to establish a system of public schools for the education of the people. The influence has obviously come from abroad; and without indulging in any idle notions concerning the progress of society, we may reasonably figure to ourselves a day when each of the European states will bear a resemblance to the various districts or provinces of one great commonwealth, and when the fashion of copying after those which have attained the highest civilization, will be even stronger and more general than it is at the present day. I know that when the most absolute sovereign of the north of Europe is concerting measures to introduce jury trial into his kingdom, that there is a power at work which belongs to the age, not to the individual.

I would not be understood as maintaining that there are not good reasons for the division of the legislature in the European states, nor that this arrangement may not have been productive of advantage. Given, a constitution of society in which a regular subordination of ranks exists, and is firmly upheld by the laws, and it may be wise for a time, the duration of which it is difficult to calculate, to place the privileged order in a separate chamber. But there are other causes which have contributed to the wisdom of English councils, and the general security of civil liberty, which are absolutely overwhelming in comparison of the division of the legislature. And perhaps the period is approaching, when it will be advantageous for both government and people, that some different disposition should be made of that department, so that even if the plan of dividing it is adhered to, it may at any rate be placed upon a wider foundation.

I have also, in treating of American institutions, confined myself to the domestic government of the states. And there does not appear to be any convincing reason why the division of the legislative power should be retained in them, other than that the institution has been incorporated in the general habits of thinking, and that an institution which is upheld by the imagination is sometimes as formidable and as difficult to be removed as any other.

But the national government presents an entirely different case. It is a federal, and not a consolidated, republic; and the most obvious way of executing this plan, and maintaining the separate existence of the states, was to establish two chambers of legislation; in one of which the people of the states should be treated as coequal sovereignties, and therefore entitled to the same number of representatives. An upper house was thus constructed, which instead of being composed of a body of nobles, consisted, like the lower house of representatives, of the people. But the apportionment of these representatives is different from what it is in the lower house.

This plan of constructing a senatorial body is entirely new. The chamber of nobles in the German diet bears no resemblance to it, as the members hold their seats "de jure," and not by election. The American system, in this respect, may be said to constitute the transition state, from the artificial structure of the upper house in all the European states, to the more simple and direct plan of founding it like the other house upon an equal representation of the people. The system may exert an unspeakable influence upon other communities, as it demonstrates the practicability of composing a senatorial body of other materials than an order of nobility, and shows that a house so composed may possess as great stability, and display as much wisdom and firmness, as any privileged body which has ever existed. The plan may suggest new views to the enlightened minds which help to control the destinies of other countries.

But I am treating of free institutions generally, and not merely of the particular form in which they have been cast in the American union. The separate and independent existence of the members of the American confederation, was an accidental circumstance. The republican form of government cannot be maintained, in a country of considerable extent, without the establishment of local or domestic jurisdictions; but it may well exist, although those jurisdictions should not possess the extensive powers which belong to them in the United States.

The question then presents itself directly—is there any solid reason for distributing the legislative power in a simple republic into two chambers? and I am of the opinion that there is, so far as regards the national assembly only. As, in such a form of government, the local jurisdictions would emanate from the aggregate authority of the state, instead of the central government emanating from them, the parts would neither be sovereign states, nor would they contain an unequal population. As a census is now taken in the United States, for the purpose of apportioning the representation in the lower house to the population; so in a simple republic, a census would have the double effect of varying the limits of the several compartments, and adjusting the representation equally among all. There would then be no reason for constructing an upper house upon the principle which governs the composition of the American senate. There would be no reason for so doing, even if the territorial divisions were ever so unequal; but as these divisions would not contain sovereign states, there would be no motive for making them unequal at the commencement, and of course none for permitting them to become so after the government had gone into operation. They would be created for the purpose of administering the local interests, pretty much on the same plan as these interests are administered by the state governments of America; because in an extensive country, a single legislature, whether its character be national or federal, cannot, either easily or advantageously, superintend the vast amount of business which properly falls under the cognizance of government. I have in another chapter declared, that it would be a mistake to suppose, because the republic was a simple, and not a confederate, one, that therefore domestic jurisdictions could be dispensed with. Their use would be the same as that of the local governments in America;

but the mode of constructing them would be different. In the United States, not only are the domestic legislatures a necessary part of the machinery of the government, but it would be impossible to get along without a great number of still lesser jurisdictions, subordinate to, and inclosed within the state governments, such as county and township jurisdictions. And the same would be the case in any other community, provided the form of government were republican.

We cannot expect that all the republics which may hereafter exist will be composed of independent states. Some may spring up in Europe out of the consolidated governments which now exist. At any rate the question cannot be avoided, shall the legislative power in a simple republic be divided?

I have said that I incline to the opinion that, so far as regards the national legislature alone, it should be. But my reasons are directly opposite to those which are assigned by De Lolme. He would divide the legislature in order to make one chamber control the other. This is the exterior bar to which he refers; not a bar exterior to the whole body, and residing in the society, but a bar exterior to each chamber, and therefore imposed by each upon the other. In a democratic republic this principle of control is superseded by another of far more efficacy, because of more comprehensive influence: the responsibility of the entire body to the people who elect it. The bars are then not merely exterior to each chamber, but they are exterior to the whole body, and act with a force which is in constant activity. The defect now is the reverse of that of which De Lolme complains. The bars are too strong, instead of too weak. The control is too stringent, instead of being too easy. In other words, as the legislators are the mere agents of the people, and elected for a short period, not merely will they be constantly subjected to the influence of public opinion in all their deliberations, which is a most happy circumstance; but there will be a constant tendency to the formation of a counterfeit public opinion also, which, in times of great party excitement, it may be difficult to distinguish from the other. This will unavoidably be the case in a country of wide extent. In order to condense public opinion, as it is termed, caucuses and cliques will be formed, and these may very imperfectly represent the opinions of the people. Public associations are the genuine offspring of free institutions; but it is not all associations which are entitled to this character. A knot of busy, active politicians will sometimes succeed in robbing other people of their opinions, instead of representing them. It becomes very important, therefore, to place the legislative body in a situation where it will be enabled to distinguish the real from the constructive majority, and to protect the community from the machinations of the last. By dividing the body the proceedings are attended with a greater number of forms, and with more solemnity. The discussions will be more thorough: the time consumed will be longer: add to which, dividing the body is like creating two bodies. The authority and influence attributed to it will be doubled, and all these circumstances will not only contribute to a clear perception of what is the genuine public sentiment, but will give to the body, or to one chamber at least, ability to resist the influence of the counterfeit representation without. It is, therefore, not with the view of detracting from the authority of the legislature, but of adding to it, and atoning for its weakness, that I would divide it. Doubtless it seems to be too strong, when it is carried away by the misguided passions of a part of the population, who cause their voices to be heard above those of a majority of the people. But this is a symptom of weakness, not of strength; since it exhibits the body as a prey to the artifices of those who are not its real constituents.

I have said that there are two essential properties of good government: first, a susceptibility of receiving an influence from without, of being acted upon by society; and second, a corresponding power of reacting upon that society. It is in order to conciliate these two opposite ends, that I would, in a country of wide extent, where it is difficult to collect and mature public opinion, divide the legislative body.

But it does not follow that it is necessary to pursue the same plan in constructing the legislative power of the domestic governments. The great principle of responsibility has superseded the check which one chamber formerly exerted upon the other. And that principle should never be modified, unless it is necessary in order to render the responsibility more strict. Money bills could only originate in the lower house, because the constituents of the lower house were the persons upon whom the weight of taxation fell most heavily. The possession of the privilege was an effectual check upon the proceedings of the upper house. But where both chambers are composed of representatives of the people, and the territory is of no greater extent than the American states, there does not appear to be any good reason for distributing the members into two chambers, unless it is that the plan is already identified with all the notions which have been formed of regular government; and that it is sometimes as difficult to root up an idea, as it is to build up an institution. Vermont had a single chamber until 1836; and the business of legislation was conducted with the greatest wisdom and prudence. The see-saw legislation, the refractory conduct pursued by the legislatures of other states, were unknown, because the simple character of the body took away the temptation and the ability so to act.

The allusion to the plan of local governments suggests another view of great importance. There is a division of the legislature, which proceeds upon a totally different plan from that contemplated by De Lolme, and Montesquieu, and which is much more efficacious than the old scheme. It consists in a division of the power, and not merely of the body. American institutions afford the only fair example of this plan. The legislative power, in this great commonwealth, is not devolved upon one body; it is divided between the national assembly and the thirty legislatures of the states. The powers which appertain to the domestic interests of the states are separated from those which relate to their exterior interests, and thus an arrangement, which was originally intended to answer one purpose, has the effect of answering another equally important. The care of the national interests is intrusted with the congress; that of the local interests with local assemblies; so that whatever might be the constitution of these thirty-one bodies, whether they were each composed of a single or a double chamber, the legislative power would be effectually divided. This arrangement is productive of far more important results than a mere division of the body. It is true, we may call it a division of the body. We may say that the whole legislative power of the union is confided to sixty-two chambers. But we should then lose sight of the principle on which the division is made, as well as of the manner in which it operates. It would be correct to say, that in Sweden, the legislative body was distributed between four chambers. But in America it is the power which is distributed. And although there are sixty-two chambers, yet these do not act co-ordinately, but each of the thirty-one legislative bodies exercises powers which are distinct, and independent of those of the others.

This disposition of the legislative power in America constitutes a deduction from the power which would otherwise be exercised by the national assembly. It erects still stronger and more numerous bars against the enterprizes of the legislature, and these bars are all without and not within the body. It does not merely balance power, it absolutely withholds it. If the whole mass of authority which is wielded by the national and state legislatures were delegated to one assembly, all the other bulwarks of freedom would be undermined. The political power of the community would be completely centralized. The minds of men would be distracted by the vast amount and the complex character of the business which would be transacted at a distance so far removed from their observation. Public affairs would become a great mystery, and whenever that is the case, government is in a fair way of acquiring inordinate power. But under the present admirable arrangement, public business, like all other knowledge, is classified and distributed, so as on the one hand to protect against usurpation, and on the other, to secure an orderly administration in every part of society.

A republic has been defined to be a government of laws: but as Rousseau has well remarked, a government may be one of laws, and yet be exceedingly imperfect in its construction. It must be one of equal laws, in order to fulfill the plan of republican government. Society has undoubtedly secured one great advantage, when public affairs are conducted upon some fixed and regular scheme, and where general rules are laid down for the government of individuals. This is better than to have everything dependent upon the arbitrary will and caprice of a handful of public rulers. Moreover, when this first step is taken, better things are in prospect, and only wait a favorable opportunity to be introduced. But there may be the most orderly arrangement in a system of government; and yet the system may act very unequally upon different parts of society. The laws may set out with taking it for granted, that there is a radical and permanent distinction between different classes of society; and when this is the case, the whole course of the subsequent legislation will be directed to uphold this distinction. In nearly all the European states, the executive is a hereditary magistrate, and the legislative body, or one chamber at least, is composed of the nobility. That this should be so, is in those communities regarded as among the most settled principles of wise government. If the laws did not originate the system, they everywhere confirm and support it. These communities may be said to be governments of laws. All public business is conducted with great precision and regularity. But this does not prevent the system from bearing with immense inequality upon different parts of society. The influence which such a scheme of government exerts, is not always direct: it may operate circuitously through many subordinate channels; but still affecting materially the manners, and consequently the character, of the legislation. Thus in Great Britain, where the nobility are a small fraction of the population, when compared with the middle class, parliament, in no act of ordinary legislation, ever avows the design of making a formal distinction between the two. But the influence and power of the former are upheld in a great variety of ways, by an overgrown church establishment, by the creation of monopolies, by the structure even of the house of commons, which admits persons principally who belong to the class of gentry, and who are therefore more or less connected with the aristocracy proper. All this inspires a general taste for aristocratic distinctions, long after the nobility have ceased to appropriate to themselves one half of the power and property of the community. The government of France is one of laws, but the house of deputies only possess one third of the legislative power, and represents only two hundred thousand persons, in a population of thirty-five millions.

There is another difficulty which meets us: although the laws do not accord any fixed immunities to one class, there will still exist great inequality in the conditions of the citizens. The same laws applied to all, will operate unequally upon some. A tax proportioned to the income of individuals, may reduce some to poverty, while it leaves others in affluence. The state invites all the citizens to enter the halls of legislation, or to fill other important posts. Accidental circumstances, natural infirmity of mind or body, or some other of the disadvantages of fortune, may prevent numbers from profiting of the invitation, while it will conduct others to wealth and distinction. We may alleviate if we cannot cure the defects of the first kind; we may take care that taxation shall never bear with inordinate weight upon the poor. But there is no way of rectifying the last species of imperfection, if an inequality which is stamped upon all created beings can be called an imperfection. But government has no right to exaggerate the inequalities which actually exist among men, and to create distinctions which would not otherwise take place. All men are not born equal, but all men are born with an equal title to become so; and government has no right to throw impediments in the way of making that title good. The high standard of popular intelligence in the United States is not owing to education alone. It is in great part ascribable to the absence of that mighty weight which presses upon the faculties of men in the middle walks of life, when they live in a state in which aristocratic distinctions lie at the foundation of the government.

The government of the United States comes as near the idea of a government of equal laws, as any we dare expect to see. The laws are made by the people, and they are consequently made for the people. There may be great difference in the legislation of two countries, although the laws are the same in both. For instance: laws which are designed to protect property, affect but a small proportion of the population where property is monopolized by a few, as is the case in Russia and Poland, and as was the case in France before the revolution, when nearly three-fourths of the land was appropriated by the clergy and nobility. Something of the same kind may be observed in countries much more enlightened than Russia or Poland. For instance: the law of perpetual entail exists in Scotland and Germany; so that in the former much more than one-third of the land is tied up for ever; the wholesome restraint which the English courts have imposed upon English estates being unknown. Scotland is under a government of laws, but those who are protected by the laws, are a privileged class.

This constitutes a leading distinction between the legislation of the United States and other countries. The Americans commenced where other communities will probably leave off. Property is more equally distributed than anywhere else. The laws, from the necessity of the case, are obliged to be more equal than anywhere else. But this lays the foundation for more important changes in their character. They will become more enlightened, less incumbered with subtle and unmeaning fictions, because they will acquire a greater degree of simplicity; and they will have this simplicity, because being enacted by the people, they will be more thoroughly adapted both to their wants and their comprehension.

Thus, although America derived the elements of its jurisprudence from England, material changes have been made, especially during the last thirty or forty years. And when, in 1828, the British parliament entered upon the great work of reforming the civil code, the laws of the American states furnished the pattern after which it was obliged to copy. In the laws of one or other of the American states, are to be found almost every material improvement which has been made, and a still greater number which may have been advantageously inserted in the new code.

The criminal codes of the American states are stamped with the same distinguishing features as the civil. The two go hand in hand, because the subject matter of both is closely connected. The temptations to violate the rights of property are increased, in proportion as property is confined to a few. And thus this new result will take place, that in a country where nearly every one is interested in the acquisition and secure possession of property, the laws will be more humane than in those where property is distributed to a few.

As to the mode of proposing the laws to the legislative body for its adoption, this has been very different in different countries, and in the same country, at different times. In the European states, formerly, the executive possessed the exclusive privilege of propounding what laws were proper to be enacted. The manner in which the initiatory step is now taken in some of those states, indicates a very great change in the relative authority of the two departments. The power of proposing the laws, when vested exclusively in the executive, gives him complete command over the motions of the legislature. This body was at one time regarded as a mere appendage to the executive. The last was in reality the supreme legislative tribunal. In course of time, this apparently slight change took place. The legislature addressed the king in the form of petition, as to what law they wished to be passed. This gave the former a more active part in their formation; but still fell very short of the appropriate office of a legislative assembly. The executive was still regarded as the ultimate arbiter of all public measures. In England, a further change took place. Bills were drawn up in general terms, and the judges performed the task of framing them into laws. But this was not done until the session of parliament was closed;—a strange practice, if we did not know that all human institutions, in their immature state, wear a strange and uncouth character. The judges at that period were dependent on the king, and the shape given to the laws was not always what was intended. This practice indicated very clearly, however, that something like system and regularity was beginning to be introduced into the transaction of business. It was the forerunner of still more salutary changes. Accordingly, in no very long time, parliament asserted the exclusive right of originating and framing the laws. The legislature then began to assume the character of an independent body. The prerogative of the king was transformed into a negative upon the laws, after they had passed through the two houses, instead of being exercised at the first stage of the proceedings.

A similar change has been brought about in the French government. The right of the king to propose the laws, which was retained in the "charte" of 1814, is abolished by that of 1830, and the power may be exercised indifferently by the king, the chamber of peers, or the chamber of deputies. But it is not so in the constitution of Holland, or Belgium, though in so many respects they are copied after the English model, and underwent a revolution in the same year that the new provision was inserted in the French constitution.

In the United States this power of initiating the laws could at no period be exercised by the executive: for the legislative power, both in the national and state governments, is vested solely in the general assembly of each. The privilege which is conferred upon the president and governors, of suggesting such changes as they may deem beneficial, is of a totally different character from the power of propounding the laws as it is understood in European language.

There are two customs which exist in the French and English governments, which may be regarded as relics of the ancient prerogatives of the executive. The one is the speech made from the throne, at the annual meeting of the legislature; the other consists in the right which ministers have to seats in that body, either "de jure," as ministers, as in France, or by virtue of an election, as in Great Britain. Wherever the executive is a hereditary magistrate, the last is an exceedingly advantageous arrangement, because it brings him within reach of the legislature, and subjects him to the immediate action of public opinion. The theory of the constitution places him beyond it; the practice draws him insensibly within the circle of its influence. But the speech which is made at the opening of the legislative body is a wise regulation, whether the executive is an hereditary, or an elective magistrate.

When we read the instructive and business-like communications of the president to congress, and of the governors to the state legislatures, the observation that they are the broken relics of a formidable prerogative of kingly power may appear to be new; yet such is undoubtedly the case. The American custom, however, is of unmixed benefit to the community. Some centuries hence, another Montesquieu, or Millar, will set about exploring American institutions, which will then acquire additional interest, from being covered with the rust of antiquity, and in poring over the history of the country, will fasten upon very many things as worthy of deep attention and study, which, in consequence of their familiarity, elude the observation of Americans at the present day. Existing institutions are often more difficult to decipher and thoroughly understand, than those of a remote age. They are mixed up with so much which is apparently familiar, and with so much which is really extraneous, that it demands a severe and comprehensive analysis, to disentangle the last, and to give to the former their just place. But when institutions grow old, things which were once familiar become striking facts, and whatever was extraneous has dropped off and fallen into oblivion; so that time operates the same analysis with regard to an ancient system of government, which it requires the utmost thought and reflection to effect in relation to an existing one.

The custom of sending to the legislature a communication, containing a clear account of the state of public affairs, not only maintains friendly relations between the two departments; it tests the capacity of the chief magistrate, and makes it his ambition to obtain exact information of everything which affects the condition and future prospects of the community over which he presides. The more the minds of public men are turned in this direction, the less the danger of their meditating schemes unfavorable to the general weal. And doubtless one reason why America has enjoyed such unexampled tranquillity, is that the administration of public affairs has assumed a thoroughly business-like character. Men of the finest understanding have been repeatedly governors of the states: Jefferson and M'Kean, Griswold and Clinton, M'Duffie and Everett, without mentioning many others who belong to the same class. If these men had been nurtured under a Spanish, or Portuguese government, or in an Italian republic, their minds would have been subjected to a discipline the most unfavorable imaginable, and their public conduct would have taken a totally different direction. When in reading American history, one comes across such a character as Aaron Burr, it seems as if we had encountered a being who properly belonged to another sphere. He also possessed faculties of a high order, but he stands alone in one respect: he appears never to have realized, what all other Americans find it impossible to forget, that he was born and educated in a country of free institutions. He seems to be a man of Venice, or Genoa, rather than one of New York.

The communities in which the executive messages are most full and comprehensive, are the very ones which possess most liberty, so much has the custom deviated from the institution out of which it sprung. In monarchical states, where we might expect the executive to dictate minutely what should be done, he says little or nothing. And in a republic, where from his authority being exceedingly limited, we might expect him to say very little, he traverses the whole field of inquiry, and appears to feel as deep an interest as if the state were his property, and the people his subjects. Nothing can be more jejune than a king's message, while few documents are more instructive and satisfactory, than the messages of the American president and governors. The king fears to show himself upon an arena where he would find so many private citizens his superiors. A few words are sometimes understood to be a sign of wisdom, and with kings it becomes an universal maxim that they are so.

The establishment of a written constitution necessarily introduces a great change in the character and functions of the legislative body. The effect is to create a division of the legislative power between the people and the ordinary legislative assembly: another contrivance much more efficacious than the distribution of the last into two chambers. The people exercise their share of authority when assembled in convention; they ordain fundamental rules for the government of all the departments; or when collected at the polls, they ratify or reject proposed alterations in the existing constitution. Sometimes a constitutional charter adds to the powers of the legislative body, but in a great majority of instances, it diminishes them. In the former case, it would perhaps be correct to say, that there was a displacement, or new arrangement, of the powers of the ordinary legislative body. Thus, in a republic, the authority to declare war is delegated to this assembly, but it has been taken from the executive. The same amount of legislative power as before may be delegated, but a very important part is wrested from one department, in order to be deposited with another.

But it is more important at present to notice those powers which are entirely withdrawn from the legislative assembly, and retained by the people. The freedom of religion and of the press, the organization of the political departments, trial by jury, the qualifications of electors, and of candidates for office, are a few of them. The legislature can no longer intermeddle with these matters, though the people in convention may make what disposition they please in regard to them. The noblest efforts have been made in France to introduce constitutional liberty. But the liberties of no people can rest upon a solid foundation, unless the constitution is the work of their own hands. The revolution of 1830, was occasioned by the daring interference of the king with the freedom of the press, and the law of elections: matters which should be carefully locked up by the constitution. The most exciting controverses, those which have caused nearly all the insurrections which have taken place, are precisely those which a popular constitution withdraws from the cognizance of a legislative assembly. A constitutional ordinance severs, if I may so say, the conventional from the legislative power. It marks out a limited field for the exercise of the last. The temptation and the ability to usurp power are not absolutely diminished, but they are greatly repressed.

There is another division of the laws, into those which relate to the manners, and those which have a direct reference to the rights of persons and property. In the first rudiments of society, a code of jurisprudence is very apt to touch extensively upon manners. The community then bears a strong resemblance to the family, and the government to the government of a family. The progress of society produces the same change in the laws, which a knowledge of the world produces in the character of individuals. It enlarges the field of observation and inquiry, and places in an insignificant light many actions to which the utmost importance was attached. All laws are the result of a process of generalization. But when the community has grown from a city, or an inconsiderable territory, to an extensive and populous state, it becomes impossible to regulate private manners minutely, and yet to preserve the system of generalization. The codes of some of the Germanic tribes, the Franks, and the Burgundians, interfered extensively with the manners. The blue laws of Connecticut are also a remarkable example of the same species of legislation, though it is a great mistake to suppose that laws of that character were confined to that province. Similar regulations, only not so numerous, nor carried to so great an extent, were adopted in others. They were not even confined to the northern provinces, but were in force in some of the southern also.

Sumptuary laws were very common among the ancient commonwealths. They even lay at the foundation of the government of Sparta. But Sparta was smaller than a moderate sized American county, and this system of legislation gradually gave way, after intercourse with the other Grecian states had produced a higher civilization, and given rise to more liberal modes of thinking.

The Oppian law enacted at Rome was one of the most remarkable of this class of laws. It imposed severe restrictions upon the dress of females, forbade ornamental apparel; and the legislature, which convened for the purpose of deliberating whether it should be continued in force, drew around the Roman forum a mob of women, as formidable as the band of men which in 1780, collected under the banner of Lord George Gordon, to intimidate the British parliament. The city of Rome, however, was the real Roman commonwealth: the Italian provinces occupied the place of dependences, rather than that of integral parts of one state.

But the list of such laws after all was not very extensive. It would have been an endless task to legislate for the manners and morals of the people. As positive regulations could not reach them, the matter was left to the discretion of the censor. But what the laws have not power to do, it is plain no individual will attempt, and this part of the duty of the censor was not very strictly performed.

It is sometimes difficult to draw a distinct line between the two classes of actions to which I have referred. Life, liberty, and property, are the subjects which the laws principally deal with. Yet in some highly civilized countries, duelling has not always been punished; the reason of which is, that the manners have been too strong for the laws. In some countries men fight in obedience to the manners; in others, they abstain from fighting, also in obedience to the manners. As the punishment of death has no terror for the man, who in order to escape death, seizes the last plank in a shipwreck from a weaker man, so it has no terror for the man who persuades himself that even an imaginary disgrace is more intolerable than death. But duelling is a relic of aristocratic institutions. It follows, therefore, that in proportion as the principle of equality gains ground, and becomes thoroughly incorporated with the fashion of thinking, the custom will disappear. The manners are then made to correct the manners. Equality has a wonderful influence in laughing out of countenance all fanciful notions. It is absurd to expose our own lives, when a grievous injury has been done to us. It is worse than absurd, when we have only been affronted. I observe that in the south-eastern states, where the principle of equality has gained ground so fast, and where in consequence the minds of men have been driven to reflection, the custom is falling into disrepute.

Some governments permit theatrical entertainments, while others prohibit them altogether. The legislature of Connecticut has resisted every effort to introduce them. Although these exhibitions, in some respects afford an innocent and even noble recreation, yet the sum of their influence is deemed as pernicious as any of those actions which immediately affect the persons or reputation of others. New Haven is as large as New York was in 1776, when the latter had a regular theatrical corps. But if it were as large as New York now is, or as large as Boston, it may be doubted whether the legislature would be enabled to persevere in its excellent intentions. The creation of domestic governments in the United States has this advantage: it enables particular sections of the country to adapt the laws to the manners, instead of being involved in the consequences of one general and sweeping system of legislation.

If the inquiry should still be pressed: why do legislators, for the most part, confine their attentions to those actions which immediately affect life, liberty, and property, and leave untouched a very large class of others, which have a very important, although it may be an indirect, bearing upon the public happiness? the following observations may be made, in addition to those which have been already suggested:

If there were no laws, actions which are now visited with a penalty would not go unpunished. The great benefit arising from a regular code of laws, and a corresponding system of procedure, consists in the restraint which these impose upon private revenge. For this would then pass all bounds, and punish too much. The influence of the laws is such, that it substitutes reflection in the place of passion. And with regard to those actions which affect others indirectly, but do not assume any tangible shape, although the laws do abstain from punishing them, yet they are most certainly punished. But inasmuch as the punishment is applied to a different class of actions, it assumes a different character. Acts of violence were before followed with violence; and vices in the manners are followed by a countervailing influence of the manners. Hatred, envy, and ingratitude, are exceedingly prejudical to public as well as to private happiness; and they are visited in private life with a penalty as certain as that which the law inflicts upon delinquencies of a graver kind. The state undertakes to punish these, because individuals would exceed all bounds, if punishment were left to them. And it abstains from noticing the former, because it could neither punish so generally, nor so judiciously, as when the punishment is left to the silent, but searching operation of opinion. Murder and robbery are very far from being driven from society by the severest laws, but they are rendered much less frequent than they would otherwise be. So, although the worst passions still infest society, yet without the punishment which now constantly attends them, the most civilized community would be turned into a pandemonium.

I cannot leave this subject without noticing a species of legislation which has lately made its appearance in some of the American states, and which has in a remarkable manner arrested public attention, both at home and abroad. I allude to the license laws; laws which are intended, if possible, to extirpate the use of intoxicating liquors. These seem to partake of the character of sumptuary regulations, and therefore to be an interference with subjects which are properly withdrawn from the care of the civil magistrate. But I hold that they constitute an exception to the rule.

It was not until public attention was particularly drawn to this matter, that any one was aware to how great an extent the commission of crimes was to be traced to the use of spiritous liquors. Still less did persons of even considerable reflection form any conception of the influence which the practice of moderate drinking, as it is termed, has in confusing the judgment, blunting the moral sense, and souring the temper. But it is evident, that a vast portion of misconduct, want of judgment, feeble, irresolute, and contradictory actions, which were supposed to be unacountable, and were not regarded as of great importance, are attributable to this cause, and have shed a most baneful influence upon society. This is a matter, therefore, which, even if it wholly concerned the manners, has an importance which belongs to no other of a similar class. And the efforts which have been made by the people of New England, Tennessee, and New York, are symptoms of an exceedingly sound state of public opinion. It is because the people have themselves taken this matter into consideration, that it possesses so much importance. In some countries, legislation by the people suggests the notion of licentiousness, of a predatory spirit. Here is a remarkable example, the most remarkable I am aware of, to the contrary. Without the co-operation of the people, it would be a herculean task to lift the popular mind; but with their co-operation everything good and useful may be accomplished. If the laws which have been passed in some of these states should remain unrepealed, they will be a lasting monument of the wisdom and virtue of the people. I am inclined to think that they will constitute the most memorable example of legislation of which we have any record, not so much in consequence of their widely salutary influence, as because they argue a degree of self denial and reflection which no one before supposed to belong to the masses. Let no European after this indulge in the fanciful notion, that the people are incapable of self government. As a single act, it is the most marked proof of a capacity for self government of which I have any knowledge.

Nor would it materially weaken the force of the reasoning, if these laws were repealed. That they have been proposed by the popular mind, that they have enlisted a powerful and numerous class in their favor, is decisive of the soundness of public opinion. If two millions and a half of people hold opinions which are eminently favorable to morality and good government, and three millions hold opposite ones, the influence of the first will be felt beyond all comparison, before that of the last. It would afford matter for curious and instructive inquiry, if we could ascertain the exact influence which government and the laws on the one hand, and the manners and habits of a people on the other, exercise respectively on society. The laws are the offspring of the manners, and yet when the former are fairly established, and have acquired authority from long usage, they exert a distinct and additional influence upon society.

1st. If there were no government and laws, there would be a voluntary association, or associations, similar to those voluntary conventions and societies which now spring up in the community, and which are employed in diffusing information relative to public affairs. But admitting that a large proportion of the population would be disposed to fall in with every measure which reason and good sense suggested, there would always be a number who would not be so disposed. Even if all assented at first, there would be numerous instances of disobedience, when those measures were to be carried into execution. The disturber of the public peace, the flagrant violater of private rights, would claim an exemption, on the ground that the resolves of the association were not laws, had no authoritative sanction, and the exercise of private judgment on the part of some would be as effectual in annulling, as the exercise of the same judgment on the part of others in maintaining them. So far, then, as one, and that a considerable portion of society was concerned, laws, that is, coercive enactments, would be indispensable to the peace of society.

But there are an infinity of other questions which would arise in every extensive community, besides those which bear directly upon the public tranquility. Dissent, with regard to these, would be very common, even among those who were agreed as to the necessity of fixed rules in respect to the last. There would then be no system of measures; everything would be thrown into confusion: the sense of a common interest, which might be sufficient to uphold the former, would operate in a contrary direction with regard to the latter. The total want of authority in carrying into effect the civil regulations of the association, would undermine its authority in executing the criminal resolves. Infractors of public and private rights, perceiving the confusion which existed in one part of society, would acquire boldness and activity in the perpetration of their deeds. The other part of society would lose confidence in their authority, simply because they were conscious of a disobedience on their own part, to measures, not of the same sort, but orginating in precisely the same species of authority. Civil government, then, has a two-fold influence, 1st, in controlling the population, and, 2d, in controlling those who undertake to govern. Society could not exist without coercive enactments to prevent crimes, and the authority which the laws acquire in restraining these, is very naturally transferred to all the political and civil regulations of the community, and thus carries one principle of obedience through all ranks of society. We see frequent opposition to every species of civil enactment, and very little to the laws which punish crimes. The first are intended to guard the rights of the highest, as well as the lowest, classes; the second are made especially to restrain the lowest. But the society is compelled to arm the first with the same authority as accompanies the last; otherwise the principle of obedience would be weakened at its source. The manners, the rules of conventional conduct, would be sufficient to prompt to the prohibition of very many acts, but they would be powerless in executing the wishes of the society, and equally powerless in commanding, or fobidding others to be done. Men are thus irresistibly led from society to government: the manners and the laws act reciprocally upon each other, and in the progress of time, the two are so intimately blended, that it is impossible to distinguish the exact influence which each exercises in molding the habits and conduct of individuals.

3d, It is in this way that the rule of the majority, a rule indispensable to the existence and well being of society, comes to be firmly established. The majority cannot win the minority to obedience to the laws, unless they also obey them. In numberless instances, individuals among the majority would desire to escape from the operation of the laws, but they cannot do so without breaking the bond which runs through the whole of society. They are compelled to adhere to the great principle of obedience, in order to maintain their own authority. They might command the physical force of society, but physical force is impotent when it is not accompanied with the opinion of right. This opinion, or sense of right, is like the self-possession and resolution of a small man, which make him an overmatch for a strong man who does not possess those qualities. Moreover, so many among the majority would be inclined to escape from the enactment of the laws, (the poor, for instance, from the payment of taxes), that the majority would dwindle into a minority: universal disobedience to a great part of the civil enactments, would take place, and the criminal laws, having no sanction, would also be trampled under foot. The manners and the laws again act mutually: the one upon the other; the maintenance of great principles is discovered to be identical with self-interest. The first as being better defined, and more easily appreciated, is laid hold of as of immutable obligation, and the sense of interest is ultimately swallowed up in the sense of justice. Every law carries with it a title to be obeyed, because one law contains as full an annunciation of a great principle, as all the laws combined, and to deny the authority of one, is to deny the authority of all. By multiplying the laws, we only multiply the application of a principle, but we cannot multiply a principle, for that is indivisible.

4th. The laws are a reflection of the manners. The manners give birth to the laws, but when the manners are incorporated in the laws, they acquire great additional authority. Legal enactments reduce to unity the great diversity of opinions which exist, and relieve the mind from the irksome task of perpetually inquiring into the reason of the laws. The value of the principle consists in this, that a great majority of the citizens are instinctively and habitually led to regard the law as the supreme rule of conduct. After a system of laws is established, the manners cannot be preserved, unless there is an adherence to the laws: the manners then become the powerful ally of the civil magistrate, and public order and tranquility are ensured.

5th. The wider the influence of the manners, the wider will be the influence of the laws: that is, the greater the number of people who will contribute to the formation of what we term public opinion, the stronger will be the authority of the government. Wherever, then, it is in our power to mould the institutions on the democratic model, the standard of both laws and manners will be elevated. In a democratic republic, the manners have necessarily a more extensive influence than in any other form of government. Public opinion, therefore, has a more direct influence upon the execution as well as upon the formation of the laws. In most countries, the laws are devised by the few. The opinions of the many and the few are thus placed in an antagonist relation to each other. In England, and Scotland, the manners have infinitely more influence in shaping the laws than in Spain and Portugal. English institutions contain a stronger infusion of republican notions, and the laws are infinitely better obeyed than in Spain and Portugal. In the United States, the spirit of obedience is still stronger, as is shown by the fact that no standing military force has ever been kept up. But, as a general rule, the laws are somewhat in advance of public opinion. The wider the sphere of their influence, therefore, the more powerfully will they act upon the manners, and the manners will be rendered more and more auxiliary to the execution of the laws.

6th. Constitutions and laws, then, are not mere parchment barriers. The instances in which they are violated, are to those in which they are obeyed, as one to ten thousand. But the reason why this is so deserves particular consideration. As a general rule, the constitution and laws are obeyed, because it is felt to be right that they should be. But this opinion of right derives great strength from the fact that each law, and each clause in a constitution, is the result of a mental analysis which has already been gone through with. He who can give us an analysis of his ideas, is listened to with more respect than he who can give us only his loose thoughts. But singular as it may appear, the great majority of mankind are even more affected with the result of an analysis, than with the analysis itself. It wears a more imposing character, 1st, because it presents them with the idea in a form too large for their apprehension. They are unable to comprehend the analysis, while at the same time they possess sufficient discernment to perceive that the end it leads to, is the result of a mental operation. 2d. A constitution and code of laws, are each a system of rules, and all men, the learned as well as the unlearned, are wonderfully affected with this notion of system. Each article in the one, and each enactment in the other, flows from some common principle; each part lends a sanction to every part, so that the sum total of authority which is possessed by the whole, is greater than that of the parts. The constitution and the laws are, for the most part, an impersonation of the manners, and yet they acquire an authority so totally distinct from the manners, that to speak of the two as identical, would appear to the common mind a violation of the rules of good sense.

7th. The co-operation of the laws and the manners is, then, evident. But there are a great number of instances in which the laws have a peculiar efficacy in giving a direction to the manners. It is sometimes even necessary to force a law, in order to bring about a given result. The first law which laid the foundation of the system of internal improvement in New York, the grand canal, was carried through the legislature by storm. The enactment of some laws is vehemently resisted for a long time, although the public opinion is in favor of them. The manifestation of public opinion is not clear and decisive, until they are actually passed: they then show a title to obedience, as well as to respect. The desired reform becomes more instead of less popular. It then represents a definite number of people who derive support from a mutual sympathy, and who, through the medium of the same principle of sympathy, gradually impart their opinions to a still wider number. If any of the American States succeed in abolishing the traffic in spirituous liquors, it will be on this principle. At first public opinion is only half muttered; its expression is only found in detached masses of men, although the aggregate of opinions of these masses would represent a decided majority. The law combines them, gives unity to the opinions of all, and the authoritative sanction thus afforded to them secures the triumph of the reform. As a first step toward bringing the Russians within the pale of civilized Europe, Peter I. made an ordinance prohibiting them from wearing their beards. In no very long time the disuse of the custom became not only popular but fashionable. There was great opposition in France, and many of the American States to the repeal of the law of primogeniture. In the last the law has so entirely molded the manners and set the fashion, that even desires which are unrestrained follow the rule of equal partibility. In France the same effect would follow, if the law had not controlled desires as well regulated the course of descent.

8th. The institutions of a country not only ought to be, but they necessarily are in advance of the popular intelligence. 1st. They must be so, because they are the work of the more intelligent class of community, even where intelligence is widely diffused. A constitution of government, a code of jurisprudence, institutions for the education of the people, etc., all demand information, together with powers of analysis and generalization, to which the common mind is incompetent. 2d. They ought to be lifted above the common run of opinions for the same reason. The intelligence displayed in those various institutions, taking advantage of the capacity for improvement among the common people, and presenting constantly to the view some permanent standard of action, pushes them forward, stimulates them to thought and reflection, and induces habits of conduct every way superior to what they would otherwise have attained.

The civil and political institutions, nevertheless, represent all classes. They represent the more enlightened, because they are the work of their hands; they represent all other classes, because they are designed to regulate their conduct toward each other and toward the government. They contain what they desire they should contain, although they are unable to give account to themselves of the manner in which the task has been performed. And if a fraction only of the three millions entertain different opinions, the majority agreeing with the two millions and a half, and only hesitating as to the expediency of positive legislation, we make sure of one of two things, that such laws will be passed at some future day, or the public opinion will be so searching and so powerful in its operation, that they will be unnecessary.

There are a multitude of subjects on which the legislative power may be exercised, which it would be unprofitable to recount in detail. Some of these will be more particularly noticed under distinct heads. The important modification which this department undergoes, in consequence of the existence of a written constitution, the abolition of a chamber of nobility, and the distribution of the power between a national and local legislatures, are things which it is of most consequence to keep in view. When the operation and influence of these are fairly grasped, it will be easy to understand the character and functions of the legislature in a country of free institutions, whether the form of government is that of a simple or a confederate, republic.

For instance: what a variety of subjects are withdrawn from the national legislature in America, in consequence of the existence of the state governments. This plan is attended with two important advantages. It alters the whole character of legislation. The domestic affairs of the population, which outweigh in number and importance all others, become the subject of chief importance, while at the same time more judgment and skill are devoted to those interests than could be the case, if they were all superintended by a central government. In the second place, the immense deduction which is made from the power of the national legislature, prevents its being brought in perpetual collision with popular rights. As the whole amount of public business, which is transacted in a country of free institutions, is incomparably greater than in any other, the danger of introducing a complete system of centralization would also be greater, if the legislative authority were not distributed among two classes of government.

At one time it was believed in America, that the power to make internal improvements, not merely military and post roads, but every other kind of roads and canals, might well be exercised by congress. The power was regarded as a sort of paternal authority which would be engaged in dispensing benefits to the whole population, and from which therefore no political evil need be apprehended. But reflecting and clear-sighted statesmen thought they could discern, behind this paternal authority, the germ of a power which, if it were permitted to take root and spread, would give rise to a system of centralization which would fritter away the authority of the states, and therefore be detrimental to popular freedom. They therefore opposed the exercise of the power, even where the state consented; and very consistently, for consent cannot give jurisdiction. A state cannot surrender a power to the federal government which the constitution has withheld. To do so would be to disarrange the whole system, and to alter the balance between the national and state governments. The school whence those opinions emanated was at one time derisively termed the Virginia school of politics; but with great injustice, for these opinions have been productive of unspeakable blessings to the American people. It should rather be denominated the American school of politics, as it is a genuine representation of the mode of thinking, which should be familiar to every one in a country of free institutions. All experience shows that there is more danger from a too lax, than from a too strict, construction of the constitution.

Every one may have read the interesting and graphic description of the solemn mission which was deputed by New York to Washington city, for the purpose of engaging the general government to embark in those public improvements which the state has itself executed in much less time, and with so much more skill and judgment, than if they had been left to a central government. The state distrusted its own ability to construct these works. This was one motive. Another probably was, that it would avoid the responsibility of laying the taxes necessary to defray the expense. But the mission to Washington met with an insurmountable obstacle. The federal government at that time was administered under the auspices of that Virginia school of politics to which I have referred: and for the first time in the history of nations, a government was found which openly avowed that it was unwilling to augment its own power. Fortunate result, in every aspect in which it can be viewed. The states have escaped a system of centralization, which would inevitably have impaired their just authority; and the great state, which first projected the plan of internal improvements on a broad scale, has succeeded beyond all expectation, in the execution of its gigantic works. The series of years of unparalleled activity in every department of industry which followed, has gradually enlisted every other state in the same scheme; and difficulties, which seemed too great for the resources of any single state, have been easily overcome by all.

This is one among many instances, of the advantages resulting from a division of the legislative power, between a national and local legislatures.

A striking example of the effect which a popular constitution has in altering the character of the legislation, is afforded by the disposition which has been made of the war-making power in the American government. It has been taken from the executive, and confided to the legislature alone. It is true that this arrangement may be adopted in a government where such a constitution is unknown. In Sweden, at one time, the states or diet had the exclusive power of declaring war. And at present they possess a veto upon the resolution of the king. But a popular constitution makes sure of abridging the power of the executive, and what is of still more consequence, it provides for the creation of a legislative body, which shall really, not nominally, represent the public will. The legislative power is the power to make laws, and the law which gives rise to a state of war is one of the most important which can be enacted. War was formerly made without any solemn declaration, and on this account, perhaps, the power was supposed to fall within the appropriate sphere of executive jurisdiction. Devolving the power upon representatives of the people is a step taken in favor of civilization, not merely in one nation, but among all nations. The power will be used with infinitely more caution. "War, says Mr. Burke, "never left a nation where it found it." It not only alters the relations between the belligerents; it produces the most serious changes in the internal condition of each. It annuls "ipso facto" some of the laws which were before of force; it renders necessary the passage of new ones, affecting immediately the pursuits of private individuals, and very frequently entails the heaviest calamities upon all classes of society. The law of war, therefore, has been attributed to the executive, in consequence of that confusion between the functions of the different departments which always takes place in the early history of governments, and which, once established, it is so difficult to remove.

It is true that in great Britain and France the supplies are voted by the legislature, and the bill must originate in the chamber in which the deputies of the people sit. But this sometimes is a very inadequate security against the prosecution of wars of ambition. The structure of the government must conspire with the social organization to throw discredit upon such wars, and to put them entirely out of fashion. If the manners exercise a powerful influence upon government, so also does government exert a like influence upon the manners. A hereditary monarch and an order of nobility, necessarily possess an amount of influence which cannot be measured by the mere formal authority with which they are invested. This influence too generally begets tastes and habits incompatible with the maintenance of peace, as the permanent policy of the country. These will extend more or less over every part of society, and give tone to the deliberations of the popular branch. Although, therefore, the two states I have named, as well as Belgium and Holland, are better protected than other European communities against unjust and impolitic wars, in consequence of the steady and vigorous growth of a middle class, the protection is very far from being complete. The crown and aristocracy still wield a disproportioned influence, and overshadow the deliberations of the more popular body, by contributing to prevent it from containing a genuine representation of that middle class. The only wise plan, therefore, is to confide the war-making power to the legislature, and to compose this body of representatives of the people. If this disposition of the power will not prevent republics from waging unjust wars, it will at any rate render such wars much less frequent.

In those governments where the popular representation is very slender, the right of petition is regarded by the people as one of the dearest they possess. In those where there is no popular branch of the legislature, it is the only means by which the people can cause themselves to be heard. In the democratic republic of the United States, this right has not the same use. The people have no need to petition a body which is created by themselves, and reflects their own opinions. Nevertheless, it is there considered more sacred, and is more extensively employed than in all other governments put together. And I am persuaded, that its importance is increased, instead of being diminished, in proportion as the institutions assume a popular character. In absolute monarchies, such as Turkey and Russia, the right is almost entirely confined to the redress of individual grievances. An obscure individual is permitted to carry his complaint to the foot of the throne, for this does not at all affect the solidly-established authority of the monarch. It only places that authority in bolder relief. But in a republic the right acquires a far more comprehensive character: it becomes an affair of large masses of men, who desire, in an authoritative but peaceable manner, to impress their opinions upon the governing authority. The opinions of an individual may sometimes be treated lightly; the opinions of whole classes are always entitled to notice. They are often indications of the propriety of some change in the legislation, for which the majority will not be prepared until public opinion has been thoroughly sounded; or they may denote some new movement in society which, whether for good or for evil, should have the fullest publicity, in order to be appreciated at its real worth. The great current of thought, which is constantly bearing the mind forward, is quickened, or interrupted, by a great number of lesser currents, whose depth and velocity must be measured, in order that we may determine our reckoning.

Petitions in the United States are of various kinds. Sometimes they contain the private claim of an individual upon the government. Sometimes they relate to the interests of agriculture, manufactures, and commerce. And in a few instances, they have been made to bear upon the political institutions themselves. The memorials accompanying the second class of petitions have often displayed consummate research and ability, and have shed a flood of light upon the subjects they have handled. It would be endless to refer to all the instances in which these compositions have sustained this high character. Two may be mentioned as samples : the memorial of the chamber of commerce of Baltimore, on "the rule of 1756," and the report accompanying the memorial of the merchants of Boston, in relation to the tariff; the first from the pen of William Pinckney, the second from that of Henry Lee. These papers are profound and elaborate disquisitions upon subjects which have greatly perplexed both American and European statesman.

As the legislature is immediately responsible to the people, it is of the utmost consequence that every channel of communication should be opened between the two. In this way, public opinion will exert a steady and salutary control upon public men ; and public men will endeavor to make themselves worthy of the trust confided to them, by the display of eminent ability, and the acquisition of information relative to the condition and interests of their state and country. In absolute government, the right of petition is an affair of individuals only ; in a democratic republic, it is one means by which the government and the people are more closely bound together, and the responsibility of the representatives rendered more strict. The views and opinions which prevail in different parts of an extensive community, are necessarily very various ; and the true way to reduce them to anything like uniformity, is to give free vent to the opinions of all. Notwithstanding the exceeding diversity in the modes of thinking of individuals, we may lay it down as a safe general maxim, that they are all in search of one thing, truth : and the mutual action of mind upon mind, although it at first increases the sharp points in each one's character, ultimately brings all to a better agreement. It is one distinguishing feature of American institutions, that the robust frame of the government permits it to wait the slow process through which opinions pass, without being at all incommoded ; whereas, most other governments too easily persuade themselves, that opinion is noxious because it is new, and strive therefore, by force, or by influence, to stifle it in its birth.

As to the stated meeting of the legislative body, I am of opinion that as a general rule it should be annual. In seven of the American states, the session is biennial ; but an annual meeting, accompanied with the limitation of the time during which it should sit, would be preferable. The indirect advantages which accrue from a political institution, are sometimes as important as the immediate end which is intended to be accomplished. Thus the appropriate office of a legislative assembly is to pass laws for the government of the community; but there are certain incidental benefits, growing out of the meeting of the body, which are of inestimable value. We stand in need of every help and device, by which to promote the intellectual communication of different parts of the country or state. As is the general standard of intelligence, so will be the character of the assembly which emanates from the people. To frame enlightened laws, experience, judgment, and information, are all necessary. It is the necessity of exercising the understanding about the material interests of this world, which raises men so much above the condition of the brutes. I would therefore employ every means in my power to advance the standard of popular intelligence. The capital where the legislature sits constitutes the center of information of the whole state. It may be a very imperfect contrivance, after all, for collecting the scattered rays of thought from abroad. The assembly may contain a great deal of ignorance, and a great deal of presumptuousness, but it very often contains a considerab.e amount of sterling ability and good sense. I think it will not be doubted, that if congress had been the sole legislative body in America, civilization, and intellectual improvement of every kind, would not have made anything like the progress which they have during the last sixty years; so true is it, that an institution, which was originally designed to perform one office, often succeeds in performing many others equally important.

The capital is the focus of general information. It is the place where the most important courts sit. Great numbers are attracted there from various motives. But I observe that the men who can impart knowledge, who can stir the faculties of other men, invariably command most attention in the private assemblages which take place there. Individuals of very superior minds, and who think they feel a sufficiently powerful stimulus from within to the attainment of mental distinction, may underrate the benefits which indirectly flow from the assembling of thirty legislative bodies. They are not aware of the influences which have given their own minds a firm ground to stand upon, and a wide field for observation and inquiry. They are still more insensible to the advantages which the general mind receives in this way. Yet, it is most certain, that the high standard of popular intelligence in the United States is in great part attributable to the annual meeting of the legislative assemblies.

In those states where the legislature sits biennially, there are doubtless some good reasons for the arrangement. The business to be transacted may be so small as not to require annual meetings, or the state may be burdened with debt, and may nobly resolve to adopt every practicable plan of retrenchment, rather than be unfaithful to its engagements.

As to the basis of representation, that is, the principle on which the legislative body should be elected, the rule in America differs greatly in different states. But notwithstanding this variety, it may be affirmed, that the United States have made a much nearer approach to a regular plan than is observable in any other country. In Great Britain, the apportionment of the representatives has always been arbitrary. It is less so now, than before the act of 1832. There are not so many flagrant discrepancies as formerly, not so many populous cities unrepresented, nor so great a number of unpeopled boroughs. But there are immense inequalities, notwithstanding. Not only is a majority of the house of commons elected by a part only of the substantial population, but it is elected by a minority of the legal electors. In France, the rule is attended with more regularity. The chamber of deputies is composed of four hundred and fifty-nine members, who are elected by so many electoral colleges. These colleges are nothing more than assemblages of the qualified electors, for the purpose of making the choice. They bear that name, instead of the simpler one of the polls, so well understood in England and the United States, because the election is not conducted in public, but has much the character of a secret meeting.

The number of "arrondissements" or territorial divisions next in size to those of the departments, is four hundred and fifty-nine, also. The colleges are composed of the voters in each of these, so that each "arrondissement" sends one member to the chamber of deputies. There is great inequality in the population of these territorial divisions. But notwithstanding this, there is less inequality in the apportionment of representatives than in Great Britain. The principal difference between the two countries, as regards the composition of the popular chamber, consists in this: in France, the basis of representation is less arbitrary; but in Great Britain, the number of persons who possess the electoral franchise is much greater in proportion to the whole population, than it is in France; so that the house of commons is a more popular body than the house of deputies. The population of Great Britain and Ireland is not as large as that of France by five or six millions; but the electors are four times more numerous in the former. In order to found a popular body, both principles should be combined. The apportionment of the representation should be as equal as is practicable, and there should be a liberal rule for the exercise of the right of suffrage.

Representation may be proportioned to the gross amount of the population, to the number of electors, to the number of taxable inhabitants, or the basis may be a compound one, of taxation and population; for these various rules have all been followed in the different American states. In addition to which there is a fifth plan, which has been adopted in the federal government and in a few of the southern states. The representation in Congress, and in the lower houses of Maryland, North Carolina, and Georgia, is determined by adding to the whole number of free persons, three-fifths of the slaves. In the composition of the federal senate, the rule, as I have already remarked, is necessarily different from all these. But so far as regards the state governments, the same reason does not exist for making the rule of apportionment different in the one house from what it is in the other. Yet there is considerable diversity in this respect. For instance: in Massachusetts, New Hampshire, and North Carolina, representation in the senate is based upon taxation; while in the lower house it is in the two former based upon the number of electors. In Rhode Island, South Carolina, and Georgia, senators are distributed by a fixed rule among different districts, without making allowance for a variation in the population or taxation; while in the second, representatives are according to a mixed ratio of taxation and population; and in the first, in proportion to the population, with this exception, however, that each town or city shall always be entitled to one member at least. In one respect, the rule in Connecticut and Virginia is different from what it is in the other states. The representation in both houses proceeds upon an arbitrary, or at least conjectural, rule. In the former, the senate is composed of twelve members, chosen by general district, and the number of representatives from each town is declared to be the same as it was prior to the formation of the constitution, with this exception, that a town afterward incorporated shall be entitled to one representative only. In Virginia, so many senators and representatives are distributed among different sections of the state, without any power in the legislature to alter the apportionment. In a majority of the states, the composition of the two houses is the same, being based in both either upon the gross amount of the population, or the number of the electors.

But notwithstanding the great variety of plans which are adopted in the several states, the basis of representation, either for the senate or the house, is in every one of them far more equitable than it is in any other country.

The plan which appears to be most conformable to the genius of free institutions, is to make population the basis of representation. 1st. The most populous will, as a general rule, be the most wealthy districts also. 2d. Where this is not the case, a representation of property interferes with the great principle of equality, as much as if we were to give to some men a quarter or half a vote, and to others a whole vote. If of two districts containing an equal population, one sends a single member, and the other, in consequence of its superior wealth, sends two members; the men of the last have what is equivalent to two votes, when compared with the first.

But the existence of slavery raises up a new rule in the southern states of America, and one which contributes greatly to complicate the question. The most wealthy will never be the most populous districts, where slaves are not counted as persons. If they are counted as property, there is nothing to correspond with them as persons. In other words, the very thing which is regarded as property is itself population. Shall these half persons, half things, form the basis of representation for freemen, although they have no representation themselves? It must be recollected, however, that this species of inequality will exist to some extent wherever the gross amount of the population affords the rule, whether that population is wholly free, or in part composed of freemen and in part of slaves. There is no way of avoiding it altogether, but by making the number of electors the basis of representation. There are only five states, however, in which this rule is adopted. But the number of electors and the number of the people are of course very different. The former are male adults only; the latter include both sexes and all ages. Is there, then, more injustice in a representation of slaves than in one of infants? It may be said, that whether we make the electors or the whole free population the basis, the distribution of representatives will be the same for all parts of the country; that is, that the electors are every where in the same proportion to the population. It is not the less true, however, that some persons are made the basis of representation, who are not themselves entitled to vote. Now the thing which forbids their voting, to wit: want of capacity, is the very thing which has induced all wise legislators to interdict the right to slaves. Moreover, the proportion of adult males to the whole population may not be the same in all the non-slaveholding states. This proportion is different in an old, from what it is in a new, country. And it is, for the same reason, different in one of the new and growing states of the American confederacy from what it is in older ones;—different in Indiana and Illinois from what it is in Massachusetts and Connecticut. And when we consider that it is not the whole number of slaves, but three-fifths, which ever enter as an element into the basis of representation, the rule adopted by the federal government and three of the states has neither the character of novelty, or of harshness. The same remarks may be made in reference to the plan of basing representation in one house upon taxation, to that of basing it generally upon the number of taxable inhabitants, and to that of assigning one senator to each town in the state. The first is the case in New Hampshire, the second in Pennsylvania, and the third in Rhode Island. Neither the amount of taxation, nor the number of taxable inhabitants, correspond with the number of the electors. Minors and females will frequently be subject to taxation. And the Rhode Island as well as the Virginia plan designedly rejects both the rules of population, and that of the number of electors.

But I am of the opinion, that the rule of federal numbers will ultimately be abolished in the three states I have named, although probably never in the federal government. I observe that in all the new states which have been formed to the south, the ratio of federal numbers has been rejected. This is the case even in Louisiana, the only state except one where the slaves outnumber the whites. As the old states have exercised a great and salutary influence upon the new, the new will probably, in their turn, exercise a like influence upon the old. Their experience will be a sort of double experience; that which their ancestors who emigrated from the older states handed down to them, and that which they themselves have acquired.

But there is a stronger reason. The tendency every where manifest, to incorporate thoroughly the principle of equality into the political institutions, will operate to produce this effect. The democratic principle will not lead to the emancipation of the blacks, for this would be to place the most democratic part of society in immediate association with them. But it will lead to the abolition of a representation of slaves, in the state governments, since that places different parts of the white popopulation on an unequal footing.

The English government, says De Lolme, will be no more when the representatives of the people begin to share in the executive authority. But when we consider how the executive authority in that government is constituted; that the king possesses numerous attributes which properly belong to the legislature, and that without any direct responsibility to the people; it would be much more correct to say, that the constitution will always be in jeopardy, unless the representatives of the people succeed in appropriating to themselves some of his vast prerogatives. The tendency of the legislature to become the predominant power in the state is visible in all the constitutional governments of the present day. But far from rousing apprehension, it is an unequivocal symptom of the progress of regular government. This tendency in Great Britain is more marked at the present time than when De Lolme wrote: it was much more so in his day than during the reign of the Stuarts, or during those of William, or Anne. The same changes have occurred in France. No monarch now dare go to the legislative hall to pronounce, as Louis XV did, the dissolution of the only body which served as a counterpoise to the throne. The whole kingdom quaked and was petrified by that memorable discourse, because the body to whom it was delivered had not been lifted up by the people, and was therefore unable to assert the rights of the people. The changes which have taken place, both in Great Britain and France, so far from endangering the executive authority, have given it strength; so far from filling those countries with confusion, have promoted public tranquility.

The preponderance of the legislative over the executive department, is the natural consequence of the system of representation. In a highly civilized community, in which the system is sure to make its appearance in one form or another, a larger amount of legitimate business falls to the legislature than to the executive; and that department which transacts the greatest amount of effective business for society, is sure to acquire the largest share of authority. We must quarrel with the principles of representation therefore, or admit that when the people have risen in importance, kings must part with very many of the prerogatives which have been attributed to them.

But if the legislature is destined to become the most influential body in the state, will not the balance of every constitution be overthrown? The balance of no constitution is upheld at all times by precisely the same means. On the contrary, an adjustment, which may have been skillful and judicious at one period, may afterward become very faulty, because illy adapted to the structure of society. If this has undergone material changes, it is most likely that the machinery by which we propose to maintain the constitutional balance will undergo a corresponding change. If at the present day the only way by which an equlibrium of authority in the British government is preserved, is by denying in practice powers which are theoretically ascribed to the king, it is plain that the day is not very distant when the theory of the constitution will be brought into a much nearer conformity with the practice. For the disguised and silent transference of power from the executive to the legislature is, in a highly advanced society, the certain forerunner of a formal and legalized appropriation of it by the latter.

In a representative government the legislature gains strength, while the powers of the executive either fall into disuse, or are distributed among a great number of administrative officers. But the responsibility of the legislature to the whole community is also increased. We cannot then adopt the opinion of De Lolme, but should rather insist upon it as an undeniable truth, that when all efforts to diminish the power of the king have become unavailing, the British constitution will be no more. Every scheme for widening the basis of representation, is a step in disguise toward lessening the regal authority. The reform act of 1832 strengthened the legislature, and saved the constitution ; and other reform acts will certainly be passed which will humble the powerful, but add strength and security to the government.

The preponderance of the legislative power, is the striking fact in the history of the American governments both national and state. No communities, to say the least, have been better governed. And it is but the other day, that one of the greatest English statesmen declared that "there was no reason why this system should not endure for ages." It is true, all human institutions are after all very imperfect. All fall infinitely short, not only of what is conceivable, but very far short of what is practicable. Let us cherish what we have, as the only means of extending the limits of the practicable. Some future generation may be able to do what now seems impossible: to resolve the great problem of the social, as the present have resolved that of the political, equality of men. All that is necessary to this end is to cause all men to obey the precepts of virtue, and to become educated. It is clear that there is no absolute impracticability in the first; and although the last, in the extended sense in which I use the term educated, is now totally inconsistent with the multiform, subordinate, and laborious employments of society, yet I am persuaded, that if the first is ever accomplished, the second will be made to follow, through instrumentalities of which we can only obtain an indistinct glance.

The opinion of Montesquieu is more plausible, because it is more vague and ambiguous, than that of De Lolme. The English constitution, says Montesquieu, will be no more, when the legislative becomes more corrupt than the executive. But to this term, corrupt, we are entitled to give a more extended meaning than is generally attributed to it. A legislative body is corrupt, when its members procure their seats by bribery and other sinister practices. This was the case when Montesquieu wrote, and it is to be feared that it is too much the case now. But a legislative body is still more corrupt, when exercising not merely the ordinary legislative power, but representing the sovereignty of the state, it permits, century after century, the grossest inequalities in the representation, without adopting some plan of remedying them. A legislative body is corrupt when, holding the relation of guardian to a sister island, it permits the most wanton oppression to be practised upon large bodies of men, because their religious creed was not the same as its own. All these things, and many more, were practiced, and undertaken to be be justified, when "the spirit of laws" was written. And yet the English constitution, as it then existed, was the beau ideal of government with Montesquieu. It is one advantage of free institutions, that they discountenance certain political vices, by putting them out of fashion. Time out of mind, there has been a constant tendency to exaggerate the vices of the weak, and to extenuate those of the powerful, because the powerful lead the fashion. And if the British parliament has relaxed its severities toward Ireland, has opened its doors to catholics, and placed the representation in other respects, on a more equitable footing, we must not conclude that it has become more corrupt; that it has usurped power, although these things do in reality increase the power of the legislature, and render it more than ever a counterpoise to the executive.

BOOK III.

CHAPTER I.

RELIGIOUS INSTITUTIONS.

THERE is an argument in favor of an established church, contained in Mr. Hume's History of England, which, on account of its extreme ingenuity, is entitled to great consideration. He admits that almost all the arts and sciences, which administer to the instruction of mankind, may be safely left to the voluntary efforts of those who undertake to teach them; but he contends that religious doctrines constitute an exception to the rule. This eminent writer supposes that the violent and immoderate zeal of different sects, each striving by every art and device to gain proselytes to its cause, will be productive of interminable contention, and that in this way the tranquillity and good order of the state will be deeply affected. He proposes, therefore, as the only cure for the evil, to give one sect the supremacy; in other words, to create an established church. But the mischief which Mr. Hume was desirous of curing, lies much deeper than in the mere number or the discordant opinions of different sects. It is to be traced solely to the mixture of politics and religion. It is the officious interference of the civil magistrate with religion, and the unbecoming interference of religious sects with state affairs, which whets the spirit of proselytism, and furnishes incentives additional to, and foreign to, those which the spirit of Christianity suggests to enslave the minds of men. By giving one sect a religious establishment religion is converted into an engine of government, and instead of curing we only give a different direction to the mischief. The zeal of religious parties is more inflamed by withholding from them privileges which are bestowed upon the established church, than would be the case if all were placed upon an equal footing. To be placed under the ban of public opinion, to be subjected to some disability or disadvantage which does not attach to other men, is a powerful and not always a commendable motive for making unusual exertions to diminish the influence of the last. There is no effectual plan, therefore, of doing justice to all sects and reconciling the great interests of religion with those of the community, but dissolving the connection between church and state, and so administering civil affairs that no sect, in the propagation of its doctrines, shall draw to itself any part of the authority which appertains to government.

Our speculations of any sort hardly ever rise much higher than the age in which we live. The use of all our knowledge is to be employed about the actual phenomena which are submitted to us; and it is the phenomena which surround us which rouse in us all our aptitude for thinking, and supply all the information which we are able to attain. Books give us the history of the past, while all philosophical speculation has reference to the present. But to be successful in our inquiries we must witness the development, up to a certain point, of the events which are submitted to us. In no other way can we make any sure calculation of the results. The superiority of some minds to others, often consists in the opportunity afforded to take advantage of the favorable point of view.

When Mr. Hume wrote, religious establishments had existed from time immemorial, and yet religious quarrels and religious conspiracies had constantly disturbed the peace of society. Neither the edict of Nantz, nor the English act of toleration, extinguished them. If he had lived at the present day, and witnessed the great advantages which have attended the abolition of a state religion in America, his views would have been more just, because more comprehensive, and he would have been led to a different conclusion. Warburton would not even then have been convinced.

The late Dr. Arnold, however, a most able and estimable man, in an appendix to his lectures on history, has insisted upon the right and the duty of the state to take the affairs of religion under its superintendence. His notions of the office and functions of the civil magistrate are such, that he would have government ordain the maxims of religion as laws, on the same principle that it makes any other enactments for the regulation of the citizens. If the public weal requires the imposition of taxes by a legislative body, for the same reason is it supposed that the public weal demands that the cardinal rules of religion should have the same authoritative sanction affixed to them.

These are the views of a man who hated every species of oppression, and who was sincerely and thoroughly devoted to the good of his fellow creatures. But although he can in no sense be said to have been wedded to a sacerdotal caste, yet it is evident that the institutions under which he lived exercised a powerful influence upon him, and communicated a tincture to all his opinions upon this subject. The plan of which he has given a sketch (for it is attended with such inherent difficulties that it will only admit of a sketch), is met by two arguments which it is difficult to answer, because they are both deduced from experience, and from experience on a very broad scale. And first, it is an undoubted fact, that there is as strong a sentiment of religion and morality pervading the American people, as exists among any other, and much stronger than among the great majority of nations who have had a state religion. In the second place, it will be admitted that if people would voluntarily consent to pay their taxes, or if they would faithfully comply with all their private contracts, and abstain from the commission of personal injuries, there would be no necessity for the intervention of government, by the appointment of tax gatherers, and the establishment of courts of justice. This is not the case however in matters of this kind; but it is so in all religious concerns. Men do actually discharge their religious duties, not as well as could be desired, but infinitely better than when the state interferes to exact the performance of them. The very reasons therefore which render it incumbent on the state to interpose for the protection of one set of interests lest they should fall to decay, prompt it to abstain from intermeddling with another set lest they also should fall to decay. It is immaterial whether we call one class secular, and the other religious, interests: we may call both secular, or both religious; but it will not follow that the actions which fall within these two classes should be subjected to the same discipline. The true theory then is, that inasmuch as religion creates a relation between God and man, the religious sentiment is necessarily disturbed by the intervention of the civil magistrate.

It is not necessary to notice the intrinsic difficulties which would attend the scheme of Dr. Arnold, if it were attempted to be put in practice. Shall the maxims of religion, which are proclaimed by the civil magistrate as laws, be subjected to the interpretation of catholics, or episcopalians, of presbyterians, or unitarians? Every attempt to prop up religion, by such a feeble instrumentality, would end in covering religion with dishonor.

There is another view which may be taken in reference to Mr. Hume's plan. The clergy of an established church, from their position in society, and their acquaintance with much of the literature and philosophy of the day, have much to do with the education of youths. Now, it is an undoubted fact, that the progress of religious inquiry is closely connected with that of philosophical inquiry; that freedom of thought in the one, contributes to enlightened views in the other; and that the true way to promote knowledge, is to extend the utmost latitude to all kindred pursuits. If it were only a question with regard to the progress of knowledge among the clergy themselves, this view would be of importance; but when it is recollected that they stand at the head of the schools of education, and thus assist in training to thought and speculation all the minds which are destined to figure in society in any way, the question becomes one of still greater magnitude. For although an ecclesiastical establishment, with freedom of worship to dissenters, is greatly preferable, to the supreme dominion of one sect; yet the evil is only mitigated, not cured, in that way. In place of the authority of the law giver, the influence of the law giver is substituted. And no one need be told, that the influence of government has a wonderful efficacy in repressing the efforts of the human mind, as well among those whom it takes under its patronage, as among those whom it discards from its countenance and favor.

The plan of curing the dissensions of religious sects, by giving monarchical rule to one of them, is a kin to the error which prevails in politics, that it is necessary to confer supreme authority on a prince, or body of nobles, in order to extinguish civil dissensions. Whereas, the true maxim is, that the peace of society is never in so much danger, as when authority of any sort is consolidated, and never so well guarded as when it is dispersed. Power may be condensed in ecclesiastical as well as in political institutions; and the scheme on which the American people have proceeded in religious affairs, is only an amplification of the great principle of the distribution of power. It is a mistake to suppose, that if some sects are disfranchised, they are therefore deprived of the ability to do mischief. On the contrary, their zeal and activity are increased, and their efforts are sure to take a direction prejudicial to the public tranquillity. We seek to shut them out from all interference with political questions by endowing one denomination with extraordinary privileges, and they are thereby more completely drawn within the vortex of politics. In other words, because religious parties are disconnected with the state, it does not therefore follow that they are disconnected with the political world. The sect between which and the state an alliance is formed, or which stands in the relation of dependent to the state, as its head, will naturally exercise its influence in favor of the government, and the dissenting sects will throw their influence in the opposite direction. These behold their own government as the author of the disabilities under which they labor, and only wait for a favorable opportunity to crush an authority so unnatural and so revolting to all persons of good sense. Ireland is an example on a great scale, and the American commonwealth, before the thorough dissolution of the connection between church and state, is an example on a small one. And even in England, from the commencement of the French revolution to the present day, political disputes have derived much of their acerbity from the same source. It is easy to see that all questions of parliamentary reform receive a complexion from the views and influence of the dissenting sects. It is equally easy to perceive, that many other projects, of a still more sweeping character, and which are only smothered, not destroyed, are engendered by the same cause.

It is now proved that the greatest interest which can occupy the mind of man—that which is fitted above all others to engage his attention from the age of puberty to the grave—may be entirely withdrawn from the care of the civil magistrate, and that both religious and secular interests will be thereby subserved. The plan of an established church was at one time adopted in all the American states, except Pennsylvania and Rhode Island. The nature of the establishment was, to be sure, not the same in all. In Massachusetts, Connecticut, New York, Maryland, Virginia, and South Carolina, the connection between church and state was as strict as in

Great Britain. In the others it existed in a modified form. In all of them this connection has been entirely dissolved; in the greater part, soon after the revolution. But it was not until the year 1816, that it was thoroughly put an end to in Connecticut; and not until the year 1833, that the finishing blow was given to it in Massachusetts.* Men of all denominations in every one of these states—those who were most opposed to the introduction of the new system—now acknowledge that it has been productive of great benefit to both church and state. There is more religious harmony, and consequently a greater degree of political tranquillity, because simply there is nothing to pamper the power of one sect, and to provoke the hostility of others. As the connection, wherever it exists is established by the laws, the sects who feel themselves aggrieved will take an active part in all political elections, for the purpose of delivering themselves from the burden of which they complain. Thus, in Connecticut, where the congregational sect was the favored one, all other denominations, episcopalians, baptists, methodists, and universalists, united themselves closely together in order to uproot the laws; and after years of struggle, which occasioned painful heartburnings in every part of society, they at last succeeded in gaining a majority in the legislature, and acquiring that Christian liberty to which all men are entitled. So in Virginia, after the revolution: all the dissenting sects combined to influence the elections, as it was only in that way that the episcopal, which was the established church, could be deprived of the authority and privileges which had been conferred upon it. The debate, which resulted in the dissolution of church and state, was one of the most stormy which has occurred in the Virginia legislature.

This great question, as to the political constitution of the church, agitated the German reformers at the commencement of the reformation. They were exceedingly anxious to get rid of the supremacy of princes in everything which related to the interests of religion. But they could conceive no way of doing this but by placing themselves under the dominion of an ecclesiastical hierarchy. Vain and fruitless expedient; for an ecclesiastical hierarchy will ever terminate in an alliance between church and state. It was reserved for the American states to solve this difficult problem. And

* Religion in America, by R. Baird, pp. 115, 116.

the religious institutions of this country may be said to be the last and most important effort which has been made in completing that great revolution which commenced in the sixteenth century.

I have alluded to the unfavorable influence which an ecclesiastical establishment has upon the progress of knowledge and the general freedom of thought. This influence is very striking in everything which concerns the political interests of the state. The ministers of an established church look with singular complacency upon the abuses which have crept into the state; since to question or discountenance them would be to impair materially the authority which assists in upholding themselves. Civil government is as much the creature of improvement as any other human interest; and whatever operates as a restraint upon inquiry, raises up obstacles to this end; the more formidable, as those who create them are insensible of their influence. The alliance between the government and a powerful and influential priesthood, enables secular princes to defy public opinion. The minds of men, pressed by the combined weight of superstition and authority, are slow to find out anything wrong in a system to which they and their ancestors have been habituated: and people soon persuade themselves that the king has the same right to govern the state which God has to govern the world.

Many causes may contribute to counteract this influence. No nation is permitted in the nineteenth century to sit securely locked up in its own institutions, without receiving numerous influences from abroad. The communication between the people of different countries is more constant now than it was between the people of the same country a century ago. In Great Britain it is in spite of, not in consequence of, the connection between church and state, that the general mind has been borne onward in the march of improvement. The existence of an established church has produced, what Mr. Hume was desirous of avoiding: it has multiplied the number of dissenters from the church of England; so that instead of being an inconsiderable body as formerly, they now stand, in England and Wales, in something like the proportion of six millions to nine millions. And it is not improbable that the growth of their numbers, joined to the superior energy which they possess, may at some not very distant day, bring about the same revolution, and by the same means, as was accomplished in Connecticut and Virginia.

The clergy of the established church in England were at the head of the party which first stimulated the American and then the French war. There was but one of the English prelates who voted against the first: the Bishop of Llandaff was the only one who declared himself in opposition to the second. The African slave trade—the barbarities of which are so shocking to every mind of humanity—was vindicated in parliament by nearly the whole body of prelates: so that Lord Eldon was heard to declare that a traffic, which he had learned to believe was the most infamous in which human beings could engage, could hardly be so inconsistent with the principles of Christianity.* It was the bench of bishops who opposed most vehemently the reform bill, an act demanded by every consideration of prudence, not to say of justice, and equity; and the only possible objection to which is, that it did not go far enough. If we inquire what body of men have been most lukewarm in the cause of popular instruction; who most hostile to the noble efforts of Romilly and Mackintosh, to ameliorate the provisions of the criminal code; the answer is the same: it was the clergy of the established church, who exerted themselves directly or indirectly to thwart these improvements.

It is clear, then, that the clergy of an established church, in consequence of their close connection with the crown, the elevated position which they occupy in the state, and their power of influencing the people, may become an engine in the hands of government, capable of being wielded as effectually as the army or navy.

That the principle of religion is absolutely necessary to hold together the elements of civil society, is a proposition which will be doubted by few. It is so, not merely as has been supposed, because it presides over a large class of actions of which the civil magistrate cannot take cognizance, but because it lies at the foundation of all our notions of right, and prevents, in innumerable instances, the commission of crimes which are punishable by the civil magistrate. Indeed it is doubtful, if human affairs were delivered over to the conduct of beings in whom the religious sentiment was not the master principle, whether the terms civil magistrate and laws would have any signification, and whether the universal licentiousness which would prevail, involving, as it must, both magistrate and citizen, would not disable any community from upholding institutions which were calculated to redress and punish crime.

* Black Book, pp. 6 and 7.

It may be supposed, that if the religious principle is of so great importance to the well being of society, that it should in some way or other enter as an element into the general legislation ; and admitting that an established church is as inconsistent with the spirit of christianity as it is with the genius of free institutions ; yet that there are a number of ways in which the laws might interfere, in order to secure the observance of religious duties. But it is not in the power of human legislation to reach all the actions of men, and although this might be thought to be a great defect in the constitution of human nature, yet in reality, it is a wise provision, calculated to strengthen the religious sentiment, and to cultivate a pure and genuine morality. For if the laws were to overshadow the whole circle of human actions, men would be converted into mere automata, religion into an empty ceremonial, and nothing being left to the natural impulse of the heart, the fountain from which the laws derive their chief strength would be dried up.

It is, to be sure, difficult to determine always what are the exact limits of legislation—to distinguish between those actions with which government should interfere, and those which it should let alone. But although the precise boundary between the two is invisible, yet in practice it is easy to find it. Something must go behind the laws, which cannot therefore be itself the subject of legislation.

A very eminent writer, and one of the greatest statesmen France has produced, Benjamin Constant, is opposed to an established church; but he believes it to be necessary that the clergy should be salaried by the government. This is one step in advance of the other European states, for it is not the clergy of one, but of all, denominations who are intended to be provided for. Great ideas seldom spring up in the mind more than half-formed. The understandings of the wisest men are in a state of continual pupilage. And here is one of the most powerful and enlightened advocates of civil and religious freedom, who desires in the mildest manner possible, to cement the religious interests of the people with their political institutions. He who is master of my income, possesses an influence over my actions, and if he is clothed with political power, he possesses something more than influence—he possesses authority. Benjamin Constant supposes, that the clergy will not be adequately rewarded, unless the state interposes to provide for them. And yet in America, where the voluntary principle is universally introduced, the ministers of religion are much more liberally paid than in France. The amount raised for this purpose in the United States, with a population of twenty millions, is nearly eleven millions of dollars. In France, the population of which is thirty-two or three millions, it is not much more than nine millions of dollars. The compensation which the American clergy receive is larger than is paid in any state of continental Europe. It is double what it is in Austria, or Russia, and quadruple what it is in Prussia.

The plan proposed by Benjamin Constant has been incorporated into the constitutional "charte" of 14th August, 1830. In some respects, it resembles the system which formerly prevailed in two of the New England states. Both plans may be characterized as a species of modified connection between church and state. In Massachusetts, the parish or township imposed the taxes necessary to the support of the clergy. In one respect, this is infinitely preferable to the French system; for in the first, the duty of defraying the expense was devolved upon the local jurisdiction where the church was situated; while in the last, being collected by the government, a system of universal centralization is established, both in church and state. But in another respect, the French system is most entitled to approbation; for it distributes the reward among all christian sects;—while in Massachusetts, it was reserved for ministers of the protestant faith exclusively. The Massachusetts scheme was a relic of those institutions which were planted during the early settlement of the colony when the presbyterian church was the established religion. The constitution of 1780 effected a great change in this respect. The funds collected, instead of being appropriated to the support of one denomination, were reserved for that sect to which the majority of voters in the township belonged. But the minority, however large, were thus compelled to support a clergyman of a different faith than their own; and were frequently deprived of the building which they had themselves erected. Like the English system the people were obliged to maintain a clergyman to whose creed they were conscientiously opposed. It was not until 1833 that this last remnant of superstition was obliterated, and the union of church and state finally terminated in America.

An established church is in no way subservient to the interests of religion, or the good government of the state. It does not allay the feuds between rival sects; it only inflames their zeal. It is surprising, when Mr. Hume had advanced so far as to admit of toleration to all dissenters, that the same process of reasoning had not conducted him to the end, and persuaded him that if such happy consequences were the fruit of removing some part of the unnatural restraint imposed by the civil magistrate, that still more salutary effects would follow from removing it altogether.

An ecclesiastical hierarchy does not contribute to the promotion of religion, among either people or clergy. Its tendency is directly the reverse. It lays the foundation for wide-spread irreligion and immorality. The cost of the church establishment in England is as great as in all the states of continental Europe put together. But a large proportion of the clergy have no more connection with their congregations, than if they resided in America. They receive the stipend, and employ deputies for a pitiful sum to perform the duty. Nor can it be otherwise, when the abominable system of pluralities prevails so extensively, and when the minister is entirely independent of his congregation for his salary, and may not even be the man of their choice. The church establishment costs about forty millions of dollars, and out of this enormous sum not half a million is paid to the four thousand two hundred and fifty-four curates, who are for the most part employed to do the real and effective duty. Not only have the congregation of the established church no voice in the choice of their minister; the right of presentation is as much the subject of traffic as the public stocks, or any other commodity in the market. The consequence is that immorality and licentiousness prevail to a fearful extent, among a large proportion of the English clergy. The mere ceremonial of religion is substituted in the place of religion itself; and may be said to constitute the system of modern indulgences, by which men purchase for themselves an exemption from reproach;—a system which does not differ essentially from that preached in the sixteenth century; but simply conformable to the fashion of this day, as the other was to the age of Leo the tenth: so that unless a second Luther appears, the day may not be distant when persons in whom the religious sentiment is not extinct, may set themselves about inquiring whether, in order to be religious, it may not be necessary to abstain from going to church. In the United States, although there is much connected with this matter which is calculated to make a thoughtful mind ponder, yet it cannot be doubted (since we have the testimony of impartial Europeans) that the observance of religious duties is more strict, and the conduct of the clergy more free from reproach, than in the great majority of the European states. Indeed it may be doubted whether, if there were no vicious clergymen, there would be any infidels.

The ecclesiastical establishments of Europe and the United States, then, present this difference: that in the former, the clergyman is independent of his congregation for his place and salary, while in the latter he is entirely dependent upon it for both. The American system is productive of one mischief. The minister is sometimes obliged to wink at many improprieties among his congregation, in order to retain his popularity. But there is no way of avoiding this, but by encountering still greater difficulties. Any scheme is preferable to one which would give us a fox-hunting, card-playing clergy, or a clergy which could afford to be slothful and idle because they were opulent. In the European system, corruption commences at the fountain head. Men cannot deliver themselves from it, if they were so disposed; and the new habits of thinking, which are inculcated by the example of those in high places, render them indifferent about doing so even if they were able.

In an American congregation, I can always discern some persons who are sincerely religious. But the minister is equally dependant upon all the members of his congregation: upon those who desire to see him true to the faith, as well as upon those who would have him countenance a lax and fashionable morality. Some compromise must take place between these two different classes. Those who are indifferent, do not wish to separate themselves from the rest of the congregation in order to choose a minister more to their taste. This is (most generally) the very last thing they would desire. Independently of the increased expense they would incur, and independently of the odium which would follow from an open rupture, there is that sense of justice among the great majority of mankind, that they respect virtue wherever it is to be found, and admire nothing so much as a fearless and unwavering performance of duty, even though it may interfere with their own practice. I observe, among an American congregation, a very general willingness, on the part of those who are indifferent to religion, to defer to the opinion, of those who are sincere. They distrust their own judgment and feel as if they had no right to command, where they had never learned to obey. The influence which is exercised in these ways is highly salutary. The clergyman feels that his moral power after all depends upon the religious part of his congregation; and those of his hearers who would have had things conducted after a different manner—who perhaps joined the congregation to promote their worldly interests—are at last persuaded, that if religion be true, religion must be preached. All parties are in this way made better than they would otherwise be. The sagacious clergyman, with his eye ever intent upon the action of so many apparently contradictory motives, and not wishing to dash the prospect of doing good, but rather to make everything turn up for the best, does not relax the strictness of his preaching, but dismisses that tone of authority which is so prevalent among the clergy of an established church. He uses the most straight-forward, and yet the most gentle means to accomplish his object. He renders the good, better; and wins over many who would be irritated, perhaps forever alienated, by a contrary course. So true is it, that a fashionable clergyman is not, therefore, a popular one, that I have known many instances in the United States, of pastors dismissed by their congregations for levity and unbecoming manners, and very few where they were dismissed in consequence of a fearless and upright discharge of thir duties.

In France, not only are the clergy dependent for their salary upon the government; they are dependent upon it for their places. The league between church and state is even closer than in Great Britain. In the last the minister collects his own tithes; in the first, government receives and disburses the taxes which are imposed for this purpose. The king of France nominates the archbishops, thirteen in number: he also nominates all the bishops. Both these orders of ecclesiastics receive canonical investiture from the pope, and make solemn oath to the king, as a condition precedent to entering upon the discharge of their functions. The bishops, on the other hand, nominate all the inferior clergy: but these nominations, with some exceptions, are submitted to the king, who may either reject or ratify them.

Another remarkable feature in this system consists in the control which the crown exercises over the clergy of the protestant church. This church is presided over by the ministers, by consistorial assemblies, and by synods. But the election of a pastor, although it is made by the consistory, must receive the approbation of the king in order to be valid; and although the synods may make regulations relative to church discipline and doctrine, yet their decisions are obliged to be submitted to the king for his approval. Nor have the synods liberty to assemble without the permission of the government. The state is not satisfied with being the head of one church; it is the head of all. It reigns supreme, not merely over the predominant sect, but over all sects. Like the Grecian and Roman commonwealths, it takes all denominations under its guardianship, and establishes all by law. Doubtless this state of things is greatly to be preferred to that which formerly existed, when this fine country was as much distracted by religious strife as it was by political dissensions. The step which has been taken toward the promotion of religious freedom is immense. And if government does interpose at all in ecclesiastical matters; it may be said with a good deal of justice, that inasmuch as the clergy of all denominations are provided for by law, all denominations should come under the supervision of the law.

But the introduction of the voluntary principle, which now prevails universally in America, is a prodigious step in advance of what any other government has attempted. It is a system "sui generis," and has grown up silently and steadily, without attracting much observation from abroad. Nevertheless, I regard this complete severance of church and state as the "chef d'œuvre" in ecclesiastical government, and as redounding more to the political tranquility of the state than any single civil regulation which has ever been made. The connection between all secular and religious interests is strengthened, just in proportion as the connection between government and church is weakened.

The rise of a sacerdotal caste in the United States seems to be forbidden by the great multiplication of sects. Religious and civil liberty are both protected by the same means. The unbounded freedom of thought which pervades every class of society creates the greatest diversity of opinions; and the influence which is possessed by any one sect is modified and controlled by the influence of all others. Each wants to be free; but none can succeed in obtaining freedom, unless all are permitted to enjoy it.

When one surveys the vast establishments of our bible, missionary, and other societies; when one considers the princely revenues which are received by some of the churches, in one instance, almost vieing with those of an eastern prince, the thought may very naturally cross the mind of one who is least disposed to take exception to anything, because it is not in conformity with his preconceived notions, whether all these things may not ultimately terminate in raising up an ecclesiastical hierarchy similar to what exists in most other countries. Religion was everywhere first preached in simplicity; but wealth and prosperity, in numerous instances, corrupted the clergy, who sought to conceal this deplorable change from the multitude, by assuming more pomp, arrogating more authority, and causing the unintelligibleness of their doctrines to keep even pace with the degeneracy of their manners. It is in this way that a sacerdotal caste, as distinguished from an independent religion, has been established in so many countries. Nor do I pretend to assert that there is any absolute certainty the United States will be saved from this destiny; nor that the approach to it may not even be more gradual and more concealed from public observation than it has been anywhere else. One way to guard against a public evil is to persuade every one that its existence is possible. The watchfulness and circumspection which are thus created, present innumerable obstacles in the way of those who might be disposed to abandon the simplicity of religious worship in order to build up a gorgeous fabric of superstition.

When we consider that not only are powerful religious associations constantly springing up in the United States, but that government and religious sects do not stand upon the same vantage ground, there might seem to be an additional reason for feeling alarm. The state is forbidden by all the American constitutions from intermeddling with religion; but the clergy are not forbidden to interfere with the affairs of state. They are not only at liberty to inculcate political docrines from the pulpit, but under the federal, and most of the state constitutions, they are eligible to seats in the legislative body, and may hold other important offices. An immunity, however, is not of equal advantage to all, unless all are equally able to turn it to account. The clergy and the laity may be placed on the same footing, so far as regards the mere possession of a privilege, but they may not be able to exercise it with the same facility. Now I observe among the people generally, a marked disapprobation of everything like political harrangues from the pulpit. I observe an equally general disinclination to elect ministers of the gospel to civil offices. The constitutional ordinance, which prohibits the government from interfering with religion, is founded upon the notion that religion is something beyond and above human legislation, and that to mix the two incongruously together would be to do violence to both. No class is more sensible of this than the clergy themselves. They feel that to mingle in the disputes of political parties, is to desert a strong for a weak position; that although an inflammatory harangue from the pulpit, or a seat in the legislature, may give them a temporary or local popularity, yet they lose in the same proportion, in point of weight and influence, as clergymen. The consequence is, that no class of men are so unambitious of political preferment, and (with very few exceptions) it is with exceeding caution and distrust, that they venture to touch upon the political questions which divide the community.

But it is the great multiplicity of sects in the United States which constitutes the chief security against the growth of an ecclesiastical hierarchy. The same causes which act upon political parties, act upon religious sects. Whenever one party in the state is disposed to carry thiugs with a high hand, and to arrogate to itself an exclusive authority, the alarm is instantly given, and hostile opinions grow up, which tend to counterbalance its authority. And as soon as one religious sect gives promise of becoming an aristocratic body, other denominations vie with each other in calling back the minds of men to the pure doctrines and manners which originally distinguished the christian community. It even happens sometimes that two or more sects are formed out of one. An incompatibility of views, arising out of causes similar to those I have mentioned, produces a schism in a whole denomination, and leads to a still greater multiplication of sects. We have seen a remarkable example of this in the United States within a few years. The three most numerous sects, the presbyterians, baptists and methodists, have been rent in twain, in consequence of dissensions among themselves. And although the interpretation given to some doctrines, or a desire to effect a change in some form or other of church government and discipline, have been put forward as the causes of these disagreements, I think I can discern behind them some other more powerfully operating motives. Thus to take a single example: although the new-school separated from the old-school presbyterians chiefly in consequence of objections to the doctrine of the necessity of the will, which the latter maintained, a doctrine which probably no argument will ever shake, yet it is possible for a religious sect to build up a well-compacted system of doctrines, and then, forgetting that this after all constitutes but the skeleton of religion, to fall down and worship it, instead of worshiping religion. I think I observed a strong desire on the part of those who seceded, to introduce more warmth into religious exercises, and a more practical manner of teaching and expounding the truths of christianity.

If I could fasten upon any causes which will arrest this multiplication of sects, I might then be able to discern the existence at some future day of a sacerdotal caste in America. Extreme indifference to religion, if it pervaded all classes, would undoubtedly have this effect. The institution would degenerate into a mere form, and then a pompous ceremonial. The priesthood would acquire power in proportion to the little interest which the general population felt in religion. And the manners of men would be molded into the form best calculated to fortify the worldly authority of the clergy. Where an universal indifference prevailed, there could be no incentive to diversity of opinion, and the distinction of sects would cease.

Will the same causes which threaten every where to demolish the idea of kingly rule, be equally fatal to the notion of a single ruler of the universe? Is the unity of the Governer of the universe so allied with that of a human governor, that if all traces of the last should be obliterated, religion would be in danger of being undermined? If it be true, that in other countries what are termed the enlightened classes are infidels at heart, and only profess religion because they believe it is a check upon the masses, what will be be the consequence when the thorough dissemination of instruction renders the great majority of the people well informed? I predict, that if ever the spread of equality is fatal to the notion of unity in religion, it will not give rise to a plurality of gods; it will sweep all religion from the face of the earth, and satan will be literally unchained, to turn earth into hell. I cannot but believe, that when the North American continent contains a population of one or two hundred millions, all speaking the same language and impelled by an irresistible curiosity to make inquiry into every thing; that when the sameness of manners and sameness of dialect have opened free access to every one's thoughts and schemes, it will exert an influence such as has never been witnessed upon the progress of knowledge, the social organization, and the religious institutions. But I am of opinion that the diffusion of equality will be fatal to the worldly authority of priests, and that the right modeling the authority of civil magistrates will add wonderfully to the reverence for God. I find that the greater the range of inquiry of a single mind, the more diverse the objects which it takes in the more certain it is of arriving at some general and presiding truths. There is nothing, therefore, in the diversified views of religious or political sects, which is hostile to the notion of a Supreme Governor of the universe.

It is true, until very modern times, the popular mind was unaccustomed to meddle with the subject of religion. Now, it approaches that as well as every other interest belonging to man, and grapples with religious creeds with the same freedom which it employs in attacking political opinions. The unlimited range of inquiry, subjects every institution to the most fearless and unscrupulous examination. Is there not danger, then, not that a passive indifference, but an universal unbelief, may seize upon the minds of men, and succeed in thoroughly rooting out the principle of religion?

There are some things which it is not in the power of man to accomplish, although these things have to do with his own interests exclusively. He cannot alter the structure of the human understanding, nor extirpate the affections of the heart. In every estimate or conjecture which we may form of the destiny of our race, we are safe in reposing upon these as undeniable truths. We can make no certain calculation in regard to individuals, so as to say what their conduct will be under particular circumstances; but with regard to the race of mankind, we may predict with absolute certainty. We are obliged to believe that the religious sentiment will never be extinguished upon the same, although not any higher, ground than that which convinces that insanity or idiocy will not be the lot of the human species, or that the private affections and desires, which have animated the heart since the first formation of man to the present time, will never be eradicated.

CHAPTER II.

INSTITUTIONS FOR THE EDUCATION OF THE PEOPLE.

THE great use of popular education, in a political view, consists in its incapacitating the people for any other than free institutions. Education tames ambitious men, and presents new motives and a new theater of action. It trains the people to a due sense of their weight in society, gives them new habits, new modes of thinking, and a different style of manners. In this way they not only acquire a decided taste for such institutions—they become morally unable to adopt any other. When the great bulk of the population is uneducated, a few men of ill-regulated ambition, banded together, may wield an irresistible influence in the community; but where popular instruction is widely disseminated, the additional power which is imparted to the mass acts as a perpetual counterpoise to this ambition. If the man who craves after public distinction is well informed, and expert in debate, so also will be the sons of the people. The former may set himself about studying the people, and may calculate upon success in proportion to his adroitness in moving their prejudices; but the latter acquire an equal facility in diving into the depths of all his motives. Those qualities which were dangerous when confined to a few, will be of unspeakable advantage when dispersed among a very numerous body. Education, then, is a constituent part of the plan of free institutions.

In some countries politicians who are bent upon their own aggrandizement, acquire an exaggerated notion of the importance of striking upon the imaginations of the people. But this is an instrument difficult to use where a system of popular instruction is introduced. Knowledge, information, habits of reflection, especially where these are employed about the daily business of life, act as a wonderful damper upon all flights of the imagination. Nothing is more amusing, and at the same time more instructive than to witness the awkward behavior of some men of untaught or unteachable minds, in a country where the people have acquired an elevated position. They want to imitate the great men of other countries, but for want of acquaintance with the temper of the times, every step they take places them in a false position, and reveals difficulties which they are unable to surmount. They become entangled in the web they had woven for others. If they move onward, they perhaps make themselves amenable to the laws ; if they falter and stumble, they are the subject of scorn ; if they make good their retreat, they are covered with ridicule. It is from constant experience of the unsuitableness of those arts of ambition which were formerly so successful, that the active spirits in a democratic community are gradually inured to new modes of thinking and acting. They acquire a clearer insight into the scope and aim of the institutions under which they live. They strive to render themselves eminently great by being eminently useful. And as this opens in the paths of eloquence, learning, and every species of intellectual effort, an almost boundless field of ambition, the altered temper which they acquire communicates an influence to others. The example once set, is soon erected into the fashion, is incorporated into the national manners, and becomes the standard of conduct for succeeding generations. So true it is, that the diffusion of education both elevates the people and tames the ambition of public men. No man in the United States dreams of running the career of Cromwell or Bonaparte. Intellectual distinction, capacity for business, large and generous views of patriotism, are the aim of every one, even in those countries where the noise of this revolution is just beginning to be heard. Such statesmen as Guizot, Brougham, and Lowndes, now rise up in society, and take the place of the Richelieus, and Straffords, of former days. The power which it is necessary to confer upon public men is not so great as it was, because the people are now able to do for themselves a great many things, which were once obliged to be devolved upon others ; and the authority which is exercised by government is wonderfully tempered in practice, in consequence of the course of discipline which the minds of all public men have to pass through.

This alteration in the structure of society, which is brought about solely by the elevation of the poular mind, is full of important consequences. As it sets bounds to the personal influence of ambitious men, it presents a natural obstacle to the introduction of monarchical or aristocratic institutions, and disposes all the artificial governments to imbibe some of the spirit and temper which belong to free institutions. In the early stages of society, the authority of a few men of commanding character may be highly salutary, although that authority may not be strictly bounded. But the employment of this instrument ceases with the advancement of society, at least, where that advancement is general and not confined to the superior classes. In other words, when popular instruction is diffused, the authority of government is abridged, because the people are then able to stand by themselves.

It is no inconsiderable argument in favor of a system of general education, that it tends greatly to preserve the identity of the language among all classes of the population, and consequently to maintain civilization. Where no such system exists, in a country of only tolerable extent, the people of different districts very soon fall into the use of different dialects, which by and by become distinct languages. The simplest elements of education, the knowledge how to read and write, uphold the standard of the language; and by so doing maintain the standard of the laws and manners. Newspapers which are the genuine fruit of education, exercise the same influence. The unexampled circulation which these journals have reached in the United States, is undoubtedly one reason why the uniformity of the written and spoken language is so well preserved. If then we do not confine our view to the present inhabited part of the United States; but consider that all North America is destined to be peopled from the Anglo-Norman stock, the benefits resulting from a thoroughly diffused education are incalculable. The present territory of the union will easily contain one hundred and fifty millions of people; and the use of a common tongue among this vast population will exert a mighty influence upon the progress of society. For as the difference of languages is one of the greatest obstacles to the diffusion of civilization, the doing away with this difference will cause a greater amount of civilization to bear upon the ruder and less-cultivated portion of this great commonwealth. And as the influence of America upon Europe will be prodigiously augmented, the nations of the old world will be brought more and more within the circle of American civilization. People who speak the same language, look upon each other in some sort as members of one family. Those who speak different languages are sometimes very little disposed to regard each other as fellow creatures. The easy communication and sympathy which the prevalence of one common dialect introduces, is singularly favorable to the spread of all sorts of improvement. The minds of Great Britain are now chiefly exerted for the people of Great Britain. Those of France and Germany for the people of those countries. But if all Europe spoke one common tongue, the intellect of any one country would be an addition to the stock of general intelligence. If the people of the American States had spoken different languages, there would perhaps have been no union: at any rate the advance of knowledge and civilization would have been materially retarded. The influence which has been exerted upon European society, in consequence of French, or English, the language of the two most enlightened nations of that continent, being spoken in all the great capitals, is very perceptible to any one whose attention has been drawn to the subject. More intelligence, and a greater amount of civilization, have been introduced into St. Petersburgh, and Hamburgh, Copenhagen, and Stockholm, Vienna and Berlin: and the effect has been felt, more or less, in the remotest provinces of those countries. But it would be very difficult to calculate the amazing influence which would have been exerted, if all Europe had spoken one language.

Before the American territory is peopled with one hundred and fifty millions, it will probably be divided into distinct confederacies; and the identity of the langurge will contribute powerfully to a good understanding among those separate communities. It is the maintenance of one civilization, not the maintenance of one union, which we are most deeply interested in. Identity of language, in some degree takes the place of an actual equality among men. The Scottish highlanders and lowlanders were, until a very recent period, like two distinct nations inclosed within the same nation. The spread of the English language among both has broken down the barriers which separated them as completely as if they had been distinct orders of men. The laws, the manners, and the intelligence of the more cultivated districts, were quickly diffused among all, when all were enabled to understand each other. Nothing contributes so much to the action of mind upon mind, as placing men on an equality; nothing so much to civilization, as this action of mind upon mind; and nothing so much to the maintenance of free institutions as the equal diffusion of civilization.

Leibnitz conceived the idea of an universal language; but he did not carry the thought further than to suggest the practicability of a language which should be common to the learned. He did not venture to propose to himself the idea of all the nations of a great continent containing one or two hundred millions of people, possessing a language which should be the familiar dialect of all classes.* Nevertheless, it would be an achievement of infinitely greater importance to the progress of the human understanding. Profound and inquisitive minds derive the materials upon which they work chiefly from the unlearned; and the unlearned derive their incitements to exertion from the learned. The observation and analysis of the minds of other men is the foundation of much the greatest part of human philosophy; and the broader the field of vision, the more exact and comprehensive will be the results. One of the principal impediments to the progress of knowledge consists in the extensive prevalence of what may be termed class opinions, in the different systems of thought. These opinions were originally taken up from a narrow view of human nature, and many of them are gradually discarded by the learned themselves; but a great number are still preserved, because they render philosophy a sealed book. If we compare a Chinese or Hindoo system of laws, or of ethical science with works of the same kind, which have come down to us from Greece and Rome; and if we run a comparison between these last and similar productions of English or American origin, we shall be made aware of the wholesome influence which has been exerted upon some of the most important human interests, by opening a wide field for observation and inquiry. The attrition of the popular mind does not merely render a system of philosophy or of laws more level to the common apprehension; it renders all human speculation more solid, coherent, and comprehensive.

Small and insignificant beginnings often give rise to important consequences, and influence the destiny of generations through the long-

*Leibnitz, in "Nouveaux Essais de l'entendement," B. IV., ch. VI., hints at the possibility of inventing an universal language. But in his letters to Mr. Oldenburgh, he contemplates only the construction of a philosophical language.

est lapse of time. The system of common school education, which originated in New England when the colony was a mere handful, has now spread over nearly all the American states ; and has contributed more than any other cause to preserve the identity of the language, to advance civilization, and to bind those republics together in a firm and beneficent union. When this system is introduced among a population of fifty or a hundred millions, it will present a spectacle from which the whole race of mankind will be able to derive instruction.

It has been supposed, that government has properly nothing to do with the education of the people ; that it is an affair which concerns the private citizen exclusively, and does not fall within the province of the legislator. But the maxim, "laissez nous faire," must not be be interpreted in such a way as to destroy its own value. The whole body of laws, the direct design of which is to promote the good government of the community, the civil, criminal and commercial codes, all interfere necessarily with the behavior of individuals ; yet, it is admitted, that they do not lie within the range of the maxim. I do not know that any precise line can be drawn between those actions which affect the public weal, and those which have a relation to private persons only. For as no system of legislation can avoid interfering to some extent with the conduct of individuals, so there is no scheme of private conduct but what may affect the whole community. It is not because there is any exact and definite distinction between the two classes of private and public actions, that government is bound to interfere in one instance, and yet to abstain in another. It depends upon who can most effectually and most advantageously, for both government and people, preside over the one and the other.

Governments, in many instances, originated colleges, and other institutions of learning and benevolence. Government first set on foot newspapers. By anticipating the existence of these important instruments of science and information, the time was hastened when the people appropriated them to their own use. There are some subjects which fall under the superintendence of government, in the early stages of society, which cease to belong to it when a people have risen up. And there are others, where the care exercised by government becomes more intense, in proportion as free institutions take root.

There is one sure test which may be applied to all such questions; one, however, which is not capable of being employed in any but a democratic republic. This test is afforded by the rule of the majority; not the majority of to-day, or to-morrow, but the majority of a considerable series of years. We may be quite sure that if the people themselves agree that government shall undertake the management of a particular interest, and adhere to this agreement after long experience of its effects, the arrangement is a wise and salutary one. It is possible for the majority temporarily to oppress the minority. But it is a much more difficult matter than is generally supposed, for it to persist in so doing. It is impossible in a country of free institutions, in a country where the electors number three millions, to present any such prominent distinctions in the circumstances of different classes, as to insure the rule of a fixed majority, if it is disposed premeditatedly, and of set purpose, to run counter to the substantial interests of the minority. Any such effort will forever terminate in converting the minority into the majority. It may frequently happen, that on the first proposition of a most wholesome and beneficial law, the minds of many men may be taken by surprise, and that it it will require a good degree of reflection on their part to be convinced of its propriety. That the majority have agreed to it; that is to say, that a body of individuals; no way distinguishable in their habits and condition of life from the great body of the minority, have given their consent to a particular enactment, is strong "prima facie" evidence of its reasonableness; and if this enactment remains in the statute book for a considerable period, it is almost conclusive evidence of its wisdom. I observe that at the present day, in New York, and in all of the New England states but one, there are laws prohibiting the sale of ardent spirits. One can hardly imagine a case where the interference of government with private conduct is more direct and imperative than it is here. But it is very difficult to conceive any case where private conduct is capable of exercising a deeper and more extensive influence upon the public weal. These laws have been too recently passed to enable us to say with certainty whether they will stand. I am disposed to think that ultimately they will prevail; that although there may be fluctuations of public opinion, leading to their alternate repeal and re-enactment, they will in the end conciliate the minds of the great bulk of the population, and bear down all opposition.

The difficulty, then, of distinguishing in theory between those things which the civil magistrate should take under his jurisdiction, and those which should be left to the discretion of private individuals, is resolved in practice by the simple rule of the majority. Where government is truly the representative of the people, we can afford to trust it with the doing of many things, which under other circumstances it would be desirable to place beyond its reach. Where it is a self-existing authority, it is too prone to intermeddle with private conduct, it seeks to thrust itself into every corner of society, because its own influence is increased in proportion as the people are rendered dependent. But this is a mistake which can rarely be committed in a republic, where those who are affected by the laws are themselves the authors of the laws.

It is remarkable that while Mr. Hume is in favor of a strict superintendence of religious interests by government, that he would leave every other department of instruction to the voluntary and unassisted efforts of individuals. In America the rule has been entirely reversed. There, the people claim the interposition of their state governments, in securing a system of popular instruction, while they deny the right or the utility of interfering in any degree with religion. And this system has been attended with incalculable advantages to both government and peeple. It is the existence of an established church, which in England has opposed so many obstacles to the introduction of a system of popular instruction. A fear has been constantly felt by episcopalians lest, in that course of training and discipline which the minds of youth undergo at school, opportunity might be taken to instil notions unfavorable to the doctrines of the church of England; while on the other hand dissenters of all denominations have taken a totally opposite view, and have concluded that there was even greater probability, that principles adverse to their own particular creeds might be insinuated into the minds of their children. A system of common school education established in England, and headed by an ecclesiastical hierarchy, might have so many bad features as to counterbalance the good, of which it would be otherwise productive; while the same system in America, originated by representatives of the people and superintended by them, would be fraught with unmixed advantage. A country in which free institutions are sought to be perpetuated, presents a strong case for the interposition of the government in every thing which concerns popular instruction. The system of common school education is applied to the formation of the mind, at a period of life when it is too feeble to originate any scheme of mental discipline for itself. And the great object is so to train the youth of the country, that when they come to be men, they may render themselves useful members of the great commonwealth in which they live. And it is a consideration of great importance, that where the population of a country is well instructed, the interference of the legislator is unnecessary in a multitude of instances where it would otherwise be demanded.

When education is widely diffused the whole population is introduced into active and useful life, at a much earlier period than could be the case, if the means of instruction were limited, and difficult to be obtained. This necessarily constitutes an immense accession to the strength and resources of the state. The great body of the people then become not merely the bone and sinews of the community, they become its soul, and its vivifying principle. Lord Bacon, like Cicero, complains that men who have obtained a tolerably advanced age, are frequently withdrawn from public usefulness, when their inflence and counsels, would be most profitable to the public. This great man would not have had so much reason to indulge in this lamentation if, instead of the brutish and ignorant population by which he was surrounded in the beginning of the seventeenth century, he had lived in the midst of an instructed people. In the United States, a very considerable part of the business of society falls under the management of young men. The liberal professions, the legislative assemblies, all the branches of trade, of manufactures, and the mechanic arts, derive immense accessions from their exertions. And it is perhaps one reason why all these pursuits have caught so liberal a spirit, and are freed from the cumbrous forms and antiquated usages which hang around them in other countries. The effect is similar to that which is produced by the substitution of free in the place of slave labor. General education imparts general freedom of thought. And this freedom of thought is the parent of vigorous exertion, of self reliance, of that thorough sense of responsibility, which causes every one to walk alertly and yet cautiously over the difficult paths of life.

Until recently, no one was eligible to the French house of deputies until he was forty. This fact sheds an abundance of light upon the social organization in France. The laws are a pretty sure index of the manners, and where we find the age of political majority raised so high, we may be very certain that the age of civil manhood is also high, and that both the minds and characters of individuals are slow in maturing. In some countries, the hour glass of life is more than half run out before the faculties of men can be made available and effective for any part of the business of society. At present, the age of admission into the house of deputies is thirty years, and contemporary with this alteration of the constitution, a great change took place in reference to popular education. Formerly, the government appropriated twenty-five thousand dollars for that purpose. At present, twenty-five millions are granted. More than forty-two thousand schools are maintained by the state, the departments, and the cantons: while at the same time, the private schools have also been augmented. For although the laws are an index of the manners, yet in a country where a system of artificial institutions has existed for a very long period, government may, nowithstanding, originate the most important improvements, and thus bring about a change of the manners themselves. The whole number of pupils at school in France is very nearly three millions, and the cost of primary instruction alone is estimated at two and a half millions of dollars.

In the United States, it is very common to see men, by the time they are thirty, already established in some useful and profitable employment. At that age we see them conducting with judgment and ability an extensive practice as lawyers, or physicians, or embarked in the most difficult branches of trade. It is evident that such a constitution of society must contribute materially to augment both the moral and physical resources of the community, and that it must be equally instrumental in giving strength and solidity to the political institutions.

Those persons who are prone to look upon the dark side of human nature, and to magnify the licentiousness of the present age, would derive great instruction from looking into the interior of society, as it was only one hundred and fifty years ago, and that among some of the most enlightened European states. The system of common, or parochial, schools was established in Scotland, in 1696. Fletcher, of Saltoun, the celebrated Scotch patriot, and a person eminently distinguished for soundness of judgment and purity of character, writing about this time, draws the following vivid picture of the general state of manners in that country: "There are at this day in Scotland (besides a great many poor families provided for by the church boxes, with others, who, by living on bad food, fall into various diseases), two hundred thousand people begging from door to door. These are not only no way advantageous, but a very grievous burden to so poor a country. And though the number of them be perhaps double to what it was formerly, by reason of the present great distress; yet in all times there have been about one hundred thousand of these vagabonds, who have lived without any regard or subjection to the laws of the land, or even to those of God, and nature: fathers incestuously accompanying with their own daughters, the son with the mother, and the brother with the sister. No magistrate could ever discover, or be informed, which way one in a hundred of those wretches died, or ever that they were baptized. Many murders have been discovered among them, and they are not only an unspeakable oppression to poor tenants (who, if they give not bread, or some kind of provision, to perhaps forty such villains in one day, are sure to be insulted by them), but they rob many poor people who live in houses distant from any neighborhood. In years of plenty, many thousands of them meet together in the mountains, where they feast and riot for many days, and at country weddings, markets, burials, and other like public occasions, they are to be seen, both men and women, perpetually drunk, cursing, blaspheming, and fighting together."

This state of abject poverty and wild disorder cannot be attributed to the density of the population. Scotland, at the close of the seventeenth century, contained hardly a million of inhabitants. By the census of 1841, it contained more than two millions and a half. But at the former period, the Scotch were destitute of education; destitute, therefore, of those moral capacities which could alone lay open to them the resources of nature. At present, they are among the best educated people in Europe; and the condition of the country is totally changed from what it was when Fletcher wrote. In the place of a lawless band of marauders, traversing the country and inflicting all sorts of injuries upon unoffending people, we have, from one end of the country to the other, a shrewd, active, and industrious population; the great bulk of whom possess a very reasonable share of the comforts of life, and live in a state of strict subordination to the laws. Doubtless, we may find very great defects in the social organization of any country; and the disposition to magnify these may even sometimes be a favorable symptom of the general soundness of society. It may indicate that a very high standard of excellence is constantly held up by every one, which, although it can never lead to the attainment of all which is conceivable, yet is the only means of reaching so much as is actually attainable. ,But to make any comparison between the moral and industrial state of Scotland, in the seventeenth century, and its condition since the system of parochial schools has been matured and borne its fruit, would be to forego the use of our faculties. We might as well institute a comparison between the annals of bedlam and those of New England or Ohio.

What will be the effect, ultimately, of placing men so much on an equality as the general diffusion of knowledge supposes, is an inquiry at once novel and interesting. The great qualities which we admire, in the eminent men who take a lead in public affairs, are in very great part formed by their power of acting upon other men. But this power depends for its exercise very much on the structure of society. A state which contains a handful of intelligent and sagacious individuals, all the rest of society being condemned to a state of intellectual inferiority, presents the most favorable opportunity for the development of those qualities. Men who are surrounded by the ignorant, feel a stimulus to exertion, in one walk of ambition at any rate, the force of which it is difficult to calculate. Under such circumstances, they are inspired with a wonderful degree of assurance, resolution, and self-command: mighty agents in counterfeiting as well as in making great qualities. But if we contrive to scatter knowledge, and so to multiply the number of independent thinkers among the people themselves, much of this artificial stimulus to an artificial greatness is taken away. It becomes then a much more difficult matter to manage men; less easy to control their wills, so as to render them subservient to the designs of ambitious leaders. In such a condition of society, the aspiring man sees a great number of sagacious individuals, not merely in the sphere in which he moves, but interposed between himself and the people, and in the ranks of the people themselves. His power is by little and little frittered away, until at last it becomes doubtful whether there will any longer be opportunity for the display of those qualities which have hitherto attracted so large a share of the public attention.

And admitting that this will be the consequence, it is clear that society will be infinitely the gainer; not merely because qualities which depend so much for their formation on the ignorance of other men, must necessarily contain a great deal that is factitious and superficial; but because the community as a body will be rendered wiser and stronger, and the political institutions be made firmer and more durable.

There is one inconvenience attending society when knowledge is widely circulated; and the principle of equality consequently gains strength—the feeling of envy is apt to pervade all classes of men. Every one seems to forget that although the dispersion of knowledge does in truth break down many of the distinctions which before existed between individuals, that it cannot destroy the natural inequality which the God of nature has stamped upon different minds. Every one, however, fancies that he is capable of every thing. All want to be great, and yet are too indolent to make themselves wise. And as chagrin and disappointment must follow the indulgence of such vain hopes and pretensions, men instantly fall into the deplorable vice of detracting from the merit of those who have run before them in the attainment of reputation. If they cannot reach the object of their ambition, the next most desirable thing is to prevent others from obtaining it. In a barbarous or half-civilized community men slay each other to make room for themselves. In a highly-civilized one, they rarely go further than to wish the death of each other.

But although this is to a considerable extent the character of every society where knowledge is diffused and people are placed pretty much on a footing of equality; yet it is attended with so many compensations, that a wise man is not at liberty to desire a change. We must avail ourselves of every spring of improvement which is planted in human nature. If we cannot rely solely upon the noble ambition of excellence for its own sake, we may very reasonably tolerate some other qualities of an inferior kind, provided they are productive of effects any way similar. Our nature is so admirably adjusted, that even our defects are often converted into instruments for our improvement. But there is this very important distinction to be made: that we intend our virtues shall redound to the good of society, whereas we intend no such thing with regard to our vices. These are made to produce results without our knowing it, through the interposition of an overruling providence. Root out envy from the human bosom, and we take away one of the strongest incentives to all sorts of exertion, from the lowest, the mere acquisition of wealth, to the highest, the perfectionment of our moral and intellectual nature.

In surveying the extensive provision which is made in America for the promotion of popular instruction, the inquiry may very naturally be made : what is to be the result of the plan if it is not turned to some account, reaching beyond the years of puberty ? The system of common school education gives the ability to read and write ; but the possession of this ability is one thing, and the application of it after leaving school is another and very different thing. In other words, even admitting that the whole youth of the country are taught those important arts, what will it profit them if, after the acquisition is made, it is not employed in getting knowledge. The ability to read and write is merely mechanical—it is only a means to the attainment of an end. If the means is possessed, and yet the end totally neglected, in what respect is society better off than when this mechanical art was entirely withheld from the general population.

I imagine, however, that when the matter is considered attentively, the deficiencies of society will be found to be much less than this view supposes, and I have purposely placed it in the strongest possible light. It is true, when we take a survey of some of the best educated communities, the United States and Holland for example, we are struck with the unintellectual character of the masses. But the fault is in ourselves : we compare the condition of these masses with that of the most cultivated class, instead of comparing it with the condition of those masses prior to the diffusion of education. In pursuing the first course, we are disappointed, perhaps even shocked ; in adopting the last, we will find that our most sanguine expectations are realized. Reading and reflection, unless carried beyond a certain point, cannot be productive of what we term striking results ; and yet when employed short of this point, they may have a decidedly intellectual influence. There is in reality much more read by the people than is generally supposed, only it is not visible to those who live in the full blaze of knowledge. The single fact, that a greater number of newspapers are circulated in the United States than in the whole of continental Europe, is pretty good evidence that the Americans turn the ability to read to some practical purpose. The reading of the daily journals is an occupation to which the most accomplished minds are addicted : for they contain, with all their demerits, a great part of the history of the times in which we live. They do not contain this information in the gross, as is the case in works professedly historical ; but they present the transactions and events of the day minutely, and in detail; and although the narrative is on this account less imposing, it is doubtful whether it is not more instructive. This species of reading, although it produces in some a disrelish for any other study, has a contrary effect with others. It whets the appetite for knowledge, opens up the connection between those things which are contained in the newspapers and the ten thousand other things which can only be alluded to by them. A great many persons among the mechanical, agricultural, and commercial classes, are thus beguiled into habits of reading, who would never otherwise have taken up a book. Newspapers first created a general taste for reading : and reading is of great assistance in grasping and analyzing the information which newspapers contain. The profitable use which may be made of these journals, is in exact proportion to the general stock of knowledge which individuals possess. Facts related by them, which a casual observer would pass over as signifying nothing, may with minds of reading and reflection possess a great deal of meaning, and conduct to very important conclusions.

The system of popular education has many negative advantages which are not inferior to the positive benefits which it bestows. The training of the hearts of youth is very properly confided to the domestic circle ; but intellectual occupation, the acquisition of the mere rudiments of learning, exercises a decidedly moral influence upon the character. If it only to some extent shuts out the temptation to vice, it prevents the lower appetites from gaining the mastery.

In Sismondi's History of the Italian Republics (iv. 193) we have some insight into the state of popular education in the republic of Florence, in the fourteenth century. The city then contained one hundred and fifty thousand inhabitants. In the territory beyond the city, there were about seven hundred thousand. From eight to ten thousand children learned to read, twelve hundred learned arithmetic, five or six hundred, logic, or grammar. In Scotland, at the present day, one eleventh of the whole population go to school. In New England and New York, this proportion is about one-fourth, or one-fifth, in other words, three-fourths of the children, between five and fifteen years of age, go to school. The proportion then in Florence, which was greatly advanced beyond any of the other Italian states, in this, as well as in every other respect, was surprisingly small. It was only about the eightieth part of the population. It is exceedingly small, even when compared with England, where one in nineteen, or with Ireland, where one in thirty-two of the whole population, are trained to the first rudiments of education.

The moral influence exerted upon society in these different communities, has been in about the same proportion as the diffusion of education. It was less in Florence than in Ireland, less in Ireland than in England, and in England less than in Scotland, New England, or New York. The register of crimes shows this fact very conclusively. The number of criminals in Ireland is about one in five hundred; in England, one in nine hundred and sixty; in Scotland, New England, and New York, out of the city, one in about five thousand. We have no materials from which to form any exact calculation as to Florence. But we do know that it contained an exceedingly disorderly population, and that it was a scene of the most sanguinary civil feuds, during the period to which I have referred. The riots of an American city are a mere episode in the history of the country; those of Florence were barbarous in the extreme, were fomented by the chief citizens, and were of so frequent occurrence as to constitute the principal part of its annals.

There is still a difficulty, however, connected with this subject, which demands attention. All the people cannot be expected to be educated. Even admitting, that with the munificent provision which is made for the establishment of schools in New England, New York, and Ohio, all the males receive the first rudiments of learning, it would be going too far to suppose that all will get much further than those rudiments, and become well informed. We will probably have in those sections, and ultimately throughout the whole country, a better instructed people than have ever existed. But very many will still remain wrapped up in ignorance. The number of the electors then will be much greater than that of the educated. Whereas, the theory of democratic institutions seems to require that all who exercise the right of suffrage, should be at least tolerably instructed. In other words, the administration of public affairs in America, both in the federal and state governments, gives rise to a multitude of questions of great magnitude and complexity, which cannot be understandingly apprehended without information and reflection. Nevertheless, the people are either directly or indirectly invested with the whole power of deciding upon these questions ; and yet, numbers are very ignorant in relation to them. How are we to reconcile this plain discrepancy, between the demand for knowledge on the one hand, and the lack of it on the other? The difficulty is startling at first view. It is one which has constantly exercised the minds of the most thoughtful and judicious men in the United States.

In the first place, then, it must be recollected that a like analogy runs through every department of human affairs ; that political knowledge is like every other kind of knowledge ; that it is subject to the same rules which apply to all other human interests ; and that if a slight observation does disclose the strangest incongruities, greater attention will reveal a system of compensations, by which the mischief is in a great degree neutralized. In the whole circle of human interests, there is hardly an instance where theory and practice are united to any great extent. It is one of the most striking and beneficent provisions in the constitution of our nature, that the combination of the two is not always necessary, in order to act efficiently and correctly : that on the contrary, our conduct may be determined with the utmost promptitude and regularity, without our being able to analyze our thoughts ; that is, without our comprehending the processs by which we are impelled to act. The commonest laborers will skilfully apply all the mechanical powers, without understanding their nature. Millions of men are engaged in the processes of manufactures, without any insight into the world of knowledge of chemistry and natural philosophy, which their occupations seem to imply. Many who successfully and skillfully pursue the professions of law and medicine, are unacquainted with the philosophy of those sciences. There are no subjects upon which a greater amount of thought and learning have been employed, than upon theology and ethics ; yet the religious and the moral are to be found among the unlearned as well as among the enlightened. The analogy may be traced through every interest appertaining to human life. Indeed, if the ability to act were dependent upon knowledge of the machinery by means of which we act, our condition would be more deplorable than that of the brutes.

It is worthy of observation, also, that on all the important questions which agitate a civilized community, a wide difference of opinion exists among the enlightened, as well as among the uninstructed. The utmost which we can reasonably demand is, that public affairs should be conducted by those whose vision is the keenest and most comprehensive, and whose intentions are the most upright.

But even such minds are constantly ranged upon different sides. Perhaps the difficulty is more apparent than real. It may be that it is the egotism and narrow views of politicians, which give an importance to questions to which they are not entitled, and that those who are uninstructed, by being less ambitious, and consequently more impartial, serve to moderate the ultra views of politicians of all parties. A great nation may do great injustice to itself, by imagining that its substantial interests are dependent upon the existence of a central bank, or the enactment of a high tariff. Public men feel as if they must have a wide field opened, on which to make a display of their abilities, and such questions present the opportunity, although the advancement of the country in riches and power would not be sensibly affected one way or the other, whether such schemes were adopted or discarded.

But although the difficulties which beset free institutions are great, it is plain that there is no way of elevating the great mass of the population but by disseminating the benefits of education. If the mischiefs complained of are not cured, they are at any rate greatly abridged. The question is not, whether the social organization, and the political institutions of a representative republic, are preferable to such a picture as our imaginations may draw; but whether they are not the best which we can reasonably hope to attain; whether they do not present a state of society infinitely better than that of Spain, Italy, or Russia; better even than that which exists in Great Britain, where the laws and the manners have a fairer aspect and a more wholesome influence than in any other European state, only because they approach nearer to the model which the American commonwealth has set up.

CHAPTER III.

MILITARY INSTITUTIONS.

THERE is no fact in the history of our race more striking than its addiction to military pursuits. From the earliest period, and in every form of society, whether barbarous or civilized, war has been one of the habitual occupations of mankind. It might almost be supposed that it answered some necessary want of our nature, and that the propensities which lead to it were as much entitled to be considered a part of the original constitution of man, as any of those which rule over his ordinary actions.

The least insight into human nature, apprises us of the great variety of faculties which are planted in our constitution. Qualities which tend to raise the species to a condition almost above humanity, are immediately associated with others which sink it to a level with the brutes. And it is plain that if the former were not capable of exerting a control over the last, the human mind would be a mere jumble of contradictory properties, each acting with the force of a separate instinct, and giving rise to actions the most incoherent and unmeaning imaginable.

It is true, war is sometimes productive of beneficial effects. In the absence of any more powerful stimulants, it scourges the lazy elements of society, brings to light some dormant spring of improvement, and gives a totally different direction to human affairs from what was intended. If our bad qualities are not controlled by ourselves, a higher power has ordained that they shall be instrumental of good in some other way. By rendering it necessary for individuals to act under circumstances of the greatest peril, and amid the most deplorable calamities which can fall upon society, war calls out some of the noblest qualities of our nature; inspiring some with a lofty patriotism and self denial, and training others to humility, resignation, and fortitude. If conquering Rome had not penetrated a great part of Europe, and if the hordes from the northern and central part of that continent had not in turn penetrated Italy, it may be doubted whether civilization would have made much progress, up to the present day, beyond the confines of the Italian peninsula. Christianity and Roman civilization lie at the foundation of our modern civilization; and I do not see how it would have been possible to diffuse one or the other, if there had not been that complete mingling of races consequent upon the Roman conquests, and the irruptions of the barbarians. I believe, that if it had not been for those events, the inhabitants of Britain, France, Germany, and Prussia, would have continued, down to the present time, the same wandering and barbarous tribes which they were in the times of Cæsar and Tacitus. That there was no spring of improvement within, is demonstrated by the fact that they had remained in a stationary condition for more than two thousand years. If then there had not been some powerful causes set in motion from without, there is every reason to believe, that those countries which have made such prodigious advances in knowledge, and in all the arts of life, would still be inhabited by an ignorant and barbarous race.

The subsequent wars which have prevailed among the European states, have probably contributed to produce an effect of a similar character. Doubtless the guilty individuals who fomented them were only animated by a desire to gratify their selfish ambition; and they have been subservient to ends which they neither desired or contemplated. I will only take as an example the wars which scourged Europe, from the commencement of the French revolution to the general peace in 1815. Assuredly no one can take a survey of European society before and since that period, without noticing the immense progress which has been made in knowledge, industry, and the arts, and the corresponding improvement which the social and political organization has undergone in that quarter of the globe.

The influence which these wars have exerted, is similar to the effect produced in the United States by breaking down the distinction of ranks. Civilization has circulated more freely in consequence of the last, and the wars of the French revolution, by contributing to break down the barriers which separated the European states from each other, have brought the inhabitants of all to a more intimate acquaintance and connection than existed before. The intercourse of all kinds which now takes place, political, commercial, and personal, between different communities, is greater than it once was between the people of the same country. Civilization is contagious; the manners of a cultivated people exercise an amazing influence upon others which are less advanced, and the European nations, which were once distinguished by the greatest inequalities in this respect, are gradually assuming the character of one great commonwealth of civilized states.

These views conduct to others equally important. Historical works which, for the most part, contain a narrative of foreign and intestine wars, would have been doubly instructive if their authors had constantly drawn the attention of their readers to the difference of races. I imagine it would be found that this difference lay at the bottom of nearly all those wars. China, whose population is greater than that of all Europe, has, with very inconsiderable exceptions, enjoyed profound tranquillity for more than two hundred years. During the same period, the European people of the same country, as well as of different countries, have been tearing each other to pieces. Let us take as an example a single historical work: Sismondi's History of the Italian Republics. What a flood of light would this profound and eloquent writer have shed upon the times of which he treats, if he had throughout the whole work directed the attention of his readers to the original diversity of races, and to the very slow process by which they were fused into each other. The mixture of Goths, Vandals, Lombards, Normans, and Saracens, with the Italian population, produced a total disorganization of society, and made men of the same district, and even living within the walls of the same city, implacable enemies. I have no reference now to the times immediately succeeding the invasion of those hordes; for then it is plain enough, without the historian pointing to it, that the incongruous assemblage of peoples of different civilization was a fruitful cause of disorders. I allude to periods much later, to the twelfth, thirteenth, and fourteenth centuries, when the descendants of all these various races inhabited Italy, and when, notwithstanding intermarriages between them, the original lineaments of character had not disappeared. The same view might be taken of the intestine troubles of Spain, France, and Great Britain. We know that it is not much more than one hundred and fifty years since the Saxon and Norman population, in this last country, could be considered as completely amalgamated; and that the amalgamation of the Gaelic population of the highlands of Scotland with that of the rest of the country, dates from a much more recent period.

This suggests anothor important view, which is, that in proportion as the various races have been melted into each other in the same country; in proportion as they have tended to form one homogeneous population, the character of war became gradually changed. The different people no longer inhabited the same country, but belonged to different countries. Hence in very modern times, instead of domestic wars we have had foreign wars. The extraordinary uniformity of character in the population of the United States, has undoubtedly been one great cause of the unprecedented tranquillity it has enjoyed at home. It is not merely that this sameness of character presents fewer points of actual difference, but it has led to a thorough intercourse between men of all classes, and between those inhabiting different parts of the country.

No nation is composed of a greater variety of races than the United States. But the English type is predominant above all others. The emigrants who flock thither are from the most civilized parts of Europe. Although for the most part they belong to the inferior classes of society, their minds are more ductile on that very account—more capable of receiving impressions from the manners and institutions which surround them. They behold a high standard of civilization existing in the country. Their natural instincts impel them to imitate it: since in no other way can they compete with the native inhabitants in the acquisition of comfort and independence. The older emigrants adhere to their own language. After a certain period of life, it is difficult and irksome in the extreme to learn a new language. But their descendents do not find the same difficulty. Their dispositions and organs are more pliable. The intercourse between all parts of the population is so great, that they insensibly acquire the language of the country, and learn to regard that of their ancestors as a foreign tongue, which is now both useless and unfashionable. This obstacle being surmounted, intermarriages take place. Their transactions of business lie with the natives, much more than with their own countrymen. American courts are opened to them, when they have any difficulties to adjust. They must converse with their lawyers in English, in order to make themselves understood. Their interests, no less than a desire so natural to the human heart, to imitate those who have wealth, power, and intelligence, conspire to weld them thoroughly to the institutions among which they live. So that in process of time the English type promises to be not merely the predominant but the universal one.

The distinction of race may be regarded in a two-fold aspect; as it arises from physical or moral causes. When we speak of difference of race, we generally have reference to some variety of conformation and habits which has been wrought by physical causes. But there may be a difference superinduced by moral causes. For instance, independently of the varieties which have been noticed by philosophical writers, the political institutions of different countries may differ so widely from each other in their structure and influence, as to render nations who have sprung from the same stock, as alien to each other as if they had emerged from totally distinct tribes. And so also, the institutions of the same country may act so unequally upon different parts of the population as to create great diversity of habits, manners, and modes of thinking; and so to estrange from each other men inhabiting the same country. It is in the power of governments then to create artificial races among their own population. Monarchical and aristocratical institutions, together with an imposing ecclesiastical hierarchy, may contribute to perpetuate distinctions long after the original lineaments of race have disappeared. So long as this is the case, the seeds of intestine war exist; and whatever foments intestine war, acts in one way or another as a provocative to foreign war. Soon after the breaking out of the French revolution, the party in the ascendency waged war against some of the European governments, in order to prevent their interference in re-establishing the odious privileges which divided one part of French society from another. And when strong government was established, war was still waged in order to keep down the insubordination of men of all parties at home.

There is one part of the policy of the American government which is entitled to great praise. I allude to the laws for the naturalization of foreigners. I will not stop to inquire into the propriety of a little shorter or a little longer residence, in order to entitle to citizenship. The main design of the plan, which is that of a speedy naturalization of foreigners, is marked by the soundest wisdom. These laws have been regarded as something entirely new in the history of governments. And it is true that they do differ materially from the laws which exist in the European states. But they are pretty much the same as those which prevailed prior to the establishment of American independence. Similar laws were passed by the mother country, for the purpose of encouraging emigration to a country which had a vast extent of fertile land, and too few inhabitants to cultivate it. America, although its population is now greater than that of many of the kingdoms of Europe, has still an abundance of unoccupied land. The same reasons, therefore, which lead to the original enactment of these laws would prompt to their continuance.

But without denying that these laws offer strong inducements to emigration, it is doubtful whether the emigration would not be nearly as great without them. The immediate temptation to the inhabitants of densely-peopled countries to emigrate, arises from the prospect of bettering their condition. The desire to become proprietors when before they were serfs, to acquire comfort and independence, and so to raise their offspring reputably, when otherwise they would have been sunk low in the scale of society; not to mention the absolute cravings of want among great numbers, which make them satisfied with merely wages sufficient to uphold life; all these motives conspire to bring great crowds of people to the new world. Although they might not be admitted to the possession of political privileges for fifteen or twenty years after their arrival, they would enjoy freedom of religion, and a larger share of civil liberty than falls to the lot of any European people.

But it is of infinite importance to assimilate as speedily as possible all parts of the American population: to melt down all the different races into one race; and thus to produce the greatest harmony and agreement between the manners and the political institutions. This is a more powerful and convincing reason for the enactment of the naturalization laws of the United States, than would be the mere desire to encourage emigration. Examine all history from the earliest records down to the present time, and it will be found that the presence of different tribes in the same country, and yet separated from each other by unequal privileges, and consequently by dissimilar habits, has been the most fruitful source of internal dissensions and civil disturbances. We know that the Roman patricians and plebeians were not originally different classes of the same people; but that they were in reality two different people: that they assumed the relation of different classes, only in consequence of the laws which kept them asunder after they were incorporated into one commonwealth: and that Rome enjoyed no tranquillity until the laws were repealed. When this was effected the two people were easily melted into one, and a character of unity and solidity was imparted to the political institutions. If you traverse Italy, or Germany, you will find vestages everywhere of the same policy which guided Rome in its infancy. A close examination would probably disclose many traces still unobliterated of similar laws growing out of similar circumstances, in almost all the large kingdoms of Europe. It was therefore a fine idea of the American government to begin at the beginning—to take speedy and effectual measures for fusing into one the diverse tribes of which its population would be composed. A monarchy, or aristocracy, may suppose that it is greatly for its interest to impose severe restrictions upon its foreign population, or even to make aliens of one part of its native population, as has been too often the case. But a republic is deeply concerned in smoothing as far as practicable all the inequalities and unevennesses which obstruct the intercourse of society; that so the political institutions may be adapted to the whole people, and the whole people be made heartily interested in upholding those institutions. In 1708, an act was passed by the English parliament for the naturalization of all protestant aliens. The *reasons* urged were, that it would encourage industry, improve trade and manufactures, and repair the waste of the population by war. But one of the *motives* was to counterbalance the power of the landed aristocracy. The objection was, that the new citizens would retain a fondness for their native country, and, in time of war, act as spies and enemies: that they would insinuate themselves into places of trust and profit, become members of parliament, and by frequent intermarriages, effect the extinction of the English race. The act was repealed 1711. In 1751, another bill was introduced, but failed. It was strenuously supported by Wm. Pitt, (Chatham), and other enlightened members, but fell through, in consequence of the same narrow and bigotted views which were urged in 1708.

Great numbers of people who now emigrate to America are catholics, and fears are entertained lest they should exercise an untoward influence upon the rest of the population. But these fears are without foundation. The institutions of the United States will protestantize the Roman catholic religion, for protestantism is a vigorous protest against both religious and political superstition, and whatever contributes to check the one, contributes equally to check the other. Maryland was settled by catholics, yet it is certain that the protestant population have exerted a much more powerful influence upon them than they have exerted upon the protestants. I can observe no difference in the manners and modes of thinking of the people of this state from what I observe in other states. So true it is, that in everything which addresses itself to the reason, the true policy of government consists in permitting the utmost latitude of thought, and the freest exercise of conscience. To pursue an opposite course, would be to fill a country with dissensions, perhaps civil war, which has hitherto enjoyed unparalleled tranquillity.

The risk which America has to encounter, in the absence of those causes which ordinarily produce heartburnings and jealousies in other communities, arises from the institution of slavery. There is no danger of any serious and lasting contest between the white and the black race. But it is possible, for the white man of the north to fight the white man of the south, through the black race. Such is the perversity of human nature, that it will sometimes create differences where nature has made resemblances, and a diseased imagination may convert the white man of the south into a being of different race, in order to enable him of the north to indulge in a misguided fanaticism.

But the security against this danger is after all very great. It consists in the substantial identity of the white population of the north and south, which, although a gust of feeling may occasionally obscure the horizon, will force itself upon the attention of every one, and cement the two sections of the country, until the natural period of their separation has arrived. A certain degree of zeal, of even enthusiasm, is always necessary to set the mind a-thinking, and to enable it to apprehend the bearings and consequences of any important measure. It must never be supposed, because passion and feeling mingle in public disputes, that they are going to run away with the understandings of people. That passion and feeling only act as a healthful stimulus to the faculties, and by producing greater intensity of thought, may ultimately conduct to conclusions very different, perhaps totally the reverse of those which were at first seized. There is a species of intelligence, which is bottomed upon good sense and a sound judgment, which is eminently unfavorable to an over indulgence in fanaticism. And there are no people who as a body are more distinguished for this same intelligence, than are the people of the north.

The reader may suppose that I have lost sight of the subject on which this chapter professes to treat. Such is not the case however. But it is my desire to present a different view from what is usually taken. In other words, it is no part of my design to describe either the military institutions of any particular country, or to make inquiry what system would most conduce to promote the power and aggrandizement of a nation. My object is the reverse: it is to examine very briefly, those causes which have hitherto given rise to foreign and civil wars, and more especially to consider the train of events, and that constitution of society, which at the present day give promise of checking the propensity to war. For although war may have its uses, yet these uses may in the progress of time be exhausted. Not that there is any probability that wars will absolutely cease to be waged by nations, but the tendency of public opinion everywhere is such as to discountenance the practice. Not only do the interests of communities impel them in an opposite direction, but what is of infinitely more consequence, the understanding, the conviction that such is the case, is continually gaining strength. Foreign wars, so far as they are occasioned by the unequal civilization of different states, may become less frequent, when civilization is more evenly diffused; not because the power of different nations will then be more equally balanced, for the reverse may be the case; but because a more equal civilization in all, produces a superior civilization in each, and a high state of civilization, such at any rate as exists in our modern world, is absolutely incompatible with the habitual pursuit of war. So also civil wars may become much less frequent, in consequence of the more thorough civilization which will exist among the population of the same state. For then the interests of different parts of the state will some how or other be found to be better adjusted to each other, and will more seldom be brought into violent conflict.

If hitherto, appeals to the humanity and good sense of nations have been insufficient to put an end to the atrocious practice of war, a train of causes may be set in operation by the Governor of the universe, which will accomplish the same end. The people of Europe may at least be made to see, and to feel, that their interests are identified with peace; and as the control of popular opinion upon the actions of the government is continually gaining ground, the same sense of interest which disinclines the people to war, may disable rulers from making it.

When these causes have been in operation for a considerable period, when the wisdom which is learned from experience has had time to produce some sensible alteration in the habits of thinking prevalent among men, the moral sense will be powerfully and effectually awakened. It is amazing with what facility the human mind will reconcile itself to customs the most abhorrent to reason, and the most revolting to humanity; and it is equally surprising how easily it may be weaned from them, when new circumstances have arisen to produce a clear judgment and a sound state of feeling. For in what respect does the killing in war—in war which is not absolutely in self defence—differ from private murder, except that in the former case a great multitude of people have leagued together to do the deed, and by so doing, have organized among themselves a species of public opinion, in order to drown remorse and to absolve from condemnation.

An almost total exemption from war is one of the memorable things in the history of the American republic. One war, of short duration, in a period of nearly seventy years, is a phenomenon without a parallel in the history of European society.* It is true, America is removed to a distance from the great theater of modern wars. But the vast countries of South America are near at hand, and present an arena for warfare much more tempting to that sort of cupidity, which formerly impelled both people and governments to fall upon the weak and defenseless, in order to aggrandize themselves. Rome, when it made war upon all the nations of Italy, was a more unequal match for them, than the United States would be against all South America. But Rome and the United States have been placed in very different periods of the world.

* The Mexican war has occurred since this was written.

But whatever may be the causes which have produced so marked and so general a disinclination to war among the American people, it was of the greatest importance that the experiment of peace, as a part of the permanent policy of a state, should be fairly made. The experiment has proved that an abstinence from military pursuits, is not only consistent with the highest civilization, the greatest national power, and the most enduring prosperity, but that it contributes directly and powerfully to the furtherance of these ends. It has proved that the passion for war bears no resemblance to any one of those natural instincts which are planted in the constitution of man for the purpose of stirring up and quickening his higher faculties, and that it may be easily counteracted by principles which possess much greater force.

The true secret of the steady adherence to a pacific policy on the part of America, is to be found in the inconsistency of any other policy with the maintenance of free institutions. The moment it was determined to establish a republican form of government, it became necessary to throw away military pursuits. For war is the most effectual instrument which can be employed to undermine public liberty.

But even though we should admit that the policy pursued by the United States is attributable to the peculiar position in which it was placed, the example may be of unspeakable importance in its influence upon other nations. An experiment made under one set of circumstances may suffice to show that it may be made under all circumstances. For the circumstances are a mere accident, while the experiment itself is conformable to the interests of every civilized nation on the globe.

A new state of things seems to be growing up in the European world; entirely variant from the old, and although it does not entitle us to predict the total destruction of this last, yet promises to make some approach to it, and distinctly indicates that the tendency to peace is one of the predominant characteristics of the present age.

First, then, I observe that since the peace of Paris, which closed the unexampled wars of the French revolution, princes have made efforts such as have never before been known to cultivate a good understanding among themselves. It is immaterial whether this combination has been formed for the purpose of checking the progress of the democratic principle, so visible every where. Princes very often intend to do one thing; and the course they are compelled to pursue insures the accomplishment of another and totally different thing. The fact that such a concert does exist is inconsistent with the continual wars which once prevailed in that part of the world. And if it is adhered to for another thirty years, by the principal European powers, it may eventuate in very important consequences. It has created a counter revolution to the French revolution: and this counter revolution only stands in need of time, in order to render it successful. For in the second place, the democratic principle instead of losing is constantly gaining ground. Crowned heads are afraid of their subjects, and combine in order to secure their own authority; and the steady growth of industry and popular intelligence, which is the consequence of this pacific policy, is all the time adding to the moral power of the people, and placing in their hands, instead of in those of their rulers, the means by which alone peace can ever become the permanent policy of Europe. For, in the third place, the prodigious impetus which has been given to every department of industry within the last thirty years, is directly calculated to render the middle class the predominant class in society. When it has fairly become so, the disinclination to war will be nearly as manifest as it is in the United States; not, perhaps, because the people of one period are intrinsically better than those of another, but because, in the vehement and obstinate pursuit of their own interests, they have become insensibly inured to habits of peace, and realize what the mass of an European population was not formerly in a situation to do, the importance of making peace the fundamental policy of the state.

When the embargo was laid by the American republic in 1806, it was for the first time authoritatively announced to the world that war is inconsistent with the prosperity of a free state. And when in 1833 the industrious classes in France protested against war with the United States, it was for the first time authoritatively announced by an European people, that it is inconsistent with the interests of even a monarchical state. Military pursuits then are irreconcilable with the highest degree of national prosperity. War contributes to alter the relative distribution of both property and power. It takes property from the industrious classes in order to bestow it upon a very different order of men: or what is worse, it causes the destruction of wealth without any retribution whatever. I know of but one instance which seems to form an exception to this view. During the wars which grew out of the French revolution, Great Britain did not appear to suffer materially. On the contrary, there were evident symptoms of a regular advance in wealth. Every department of industry was alive and active. The maritime ascendency of the nation enabled it to open new channels of commerce, and to protect its vessels in almost every quarter of the globe. This is the favorable view of the subject. But the true question is, what would have been the condition of the country, if the expenses of the war had been defrayed by taxes collected within the year? Instead of this being done, a debt has been created so overwhelming, that no one dare believe that it will ever be paid; and which, whether it be paid or not, will equally postpone the disasters of the war to a period far beyond its termination. For if, on the one hand, a national bankruptcy will dry up the income of great multitudes of people; on the other, the reimbursement of the debt will trench so largely upon capital, as to shake to its foundation the commercial prosperity of the country. When either of these events occur, we will be able to form an adequate idea of the influence of war in disturbing the natural distribution of property.

Similar views are applicable to the question of the distribution of power. Property and power are invariably connected. Whatever affects the disposition of the first, affects that of the last; whether as between different classes of the people, or as between the people and the government. War, more than all other circumstances put together, assists to condense power in the hands of a few. Its effect upon the distribution of power is more immediate and decisive, than it is upon property.

It is not difficult to follow the process by which this revolution is effected. Impending danger, at home or from abroad, may alarm the mass of peaceful citizens, but it inspires the ambitious with resolution and boldness. If the crisis is at all doubtful, if either civil or foreign war seems to be brooding, a vague sense of patriotism persuades people that it is right to confer ample power upon government to beat down the evil, and a large military force is raised. But the use of this instrument, where liberty is not most

23

solidly guarded, is apt to give an exorbitant authority to the government. The imaginations of the people are intoxicated by the pomp and circumstance which are introduced upon the theater of public affairs. They lend a disproportioned importance to those who are the principal actors, and are led, step by step, to intrust a larger and larger authority to public rulers. The army becomes an end instead of a means; war is provoked when peace might easily have been maintained. And whether in consequence of the altered modes of thinking which every one then adopts as to the general tendency of war, or through the instrumentality of the army itself, the way is prepared, if not for the conquest of the people, at any rate for greatly abridging their liberties.

It is not surprising, therefore, that the great mass of the American people should feel such an aversion to war. There is no instances to be found, where this sentiment has been any thing like so general or so strong. The nation no sooner goes to war, than it sets about framing expedients by which to obtain peace. It is not from fear of the enemy, for no country possesses both the "materiel" and "personnel" of war to a greater extent. But the nation fears itself, and would put away the temptation to acquire a dangerous greatness. Hitherto the disinclination to military pursuits has been so great among all parties, that it is not easy to form an estimate of the consequences, if there should be any thing like a general change in the tone of public sentiment. Military men have been bred in civil pursuits, or have lived during the greater part of their lives in a state of profound peace. Their character consequently partakes more of that of the citizen than of the soldier. If they are introduced into political life, they find themselves entangled in the complicated net work of our free institutions, and the last thing which a soldier president dreams of, is to employ the army for the purpose of perpetuating his power. But let public opinion run for any considerable period in an opposite direction, let military pursuits become more popular than trade, agriculture and manufactures, and I, for one, would desire to hide myself from contemplating the countless evils, which would be the consequence. For as no nation ever was endowed with such a capacity for doing good: none has ever been endowed with such a capacity for inflicting evil.

It is impossible to foretell with any accuracy, what will be the issue of those immsense political assemblages which are constantly held in evrey part of the United States. The effect may be to discipline two vast armies, which will ultimately take up arms and tear each other in pieces. The experience which we have had of domestic violence in some of our large cities, proves that it would not be an impossible thing to embroil parties to such a degree as to occasion the most disastrious civil wars. On the other hand, the people may become so familiarized to peaceful assemblages, and so habituated to reflect upon the wide-spread ruin which would be the consequence of a resort to arms, that the greatest political excitement may always terminate, as it has hitherto done, in merely affecting the ballot box. On the issue of this experiment are suspended the destinies of this great republic.

The disposition to reflection, is one of the remarkable characteristics of the men of the present day. Two circumstances have contributed to awaken it. 1st. The prodigious development of industry. Commerce, agriculture and manufactures are now conducted on so immense a scale, and interest so great a number of minds, that they have to a great extent superseded the practice of war. 2d. The men of the present day have more individuality, if I may so express myself, than at any former period. The first circumstance supplies materials on which reflection may exercise itself. The second develops the faculty itself. For by rendering individuals more dependant upon themselves and less dependant upon a class, they are thrown upon their own resources, and exercise more caution, prudence and judgment in their behavior. And when this habit has been established in private life, it is very naturally and even necessarily transferred to the scene of public affairs.

When I was a young man, I have heard older persons relate, that in their time it was expected that at all dinner parties the guests should not only be of good cheer, but that they should drink until they were merrily drunk. The custom had been of time immemorial, and not to conform to it, was considered as an indication of a poor spirited fellow. This practice is now unknown among any thing like good company. It is banished to the night cellars and other haunts of the dissipated. I also observed that a great many other changes had taken place in the manners; that for ten duels not more than one was fought now. I concluded that there must be some general cause for so great a change, and I traced it to the strong habit of reflection which had grown up. I found that the alteration in the manners showed itself in public life also; and I will only refer to one or two examples. At the time when the struggle between the Union and the nullification parties was at its hight, when the exacerbation of feelings was so intense, that the least circumstance, a look or a gesture might lead to a sanguinary conflict, the leaders of those parties entered into a formal agreement that not only should no wanton insult be offered by any individual of one party to any individual of the other, but that the most active and vigilant precaution should be taken to prevent any occurrence which might by possibility lead to it. During the extreme excitement of feeling which preceded the presidential elections in Tennessee, in 1844, a similar agreement was entered into by the two parties in Nashville.

Nothing is more common than to see politicians pursue a line of conduct which they intend shall advance their own influence and authority, and which, nevertheless, terminates in setting bounds to both. What the leaders of the parties often design to effect, by these political meetings, is to promote their own selfish aims: to obtain office immediately, or to prepare the way for their elevation at the first favorable moment. If endowed with ambition, resolution and self command, they may be disposed to wink at the most offensive conduct on the part of their adherents, in order to bring matters to extremities. By embroiling the two parties in a civil dissension, they would render themselves more necessary to their respective partizans. But the course which they are insensibly impelled to pursue, once they have fairly entered upon the career of public debate, is calculated to give an entirely new turn to affairs. Civil war rarely makes its way through the medium of public debate. Discussion and reasoning on such an extended scale presuppose a wide diffusion of information, and a very general disposition to reflection among the great mass of the people, both of which are greatly assisted by listening to these debates. The independent condition in which the bulk of the population are placed, their educated habits, and the strong masculine sense which the two conjoined produce, impart to them a strong appetite for public discussion. When the plan of holding these conventions was first introduced, the public mind seized upon it with avidity, as something which it had long been in search of. For nothing presents so imposing and animating a spectacle as do these assemblages, since they bring into play a living instead of a merely fictitious sympathy. The love of strong sensation is an universal trait in the human character; and it finds vent in this way. Hence political assemblages may be said to constitute the amusements of the American people. The crowds who attend them desire to hear public affairs talked over and reasoned about. And the leaders of parties are compelled to follow this bent of their disposition. However incompetent a great number of the speakers may be, their ambition is at any rate directed into a new channel. They strive to make display of their information, to show their acquaintance with the political history of the country, to grapple with the most difficult problems of legislation. Every step they take only raises up fresh obstacles in the way of civil war. An intellectual cast, in spite of themselves, is given to the whole machinery of parties; and instead of those dark conspiracies and acts of desperate violence which have been so common in other countries, the efforts of these politicians simply terminate in curbing their own ambition, and in making the people more deeply sensible than ever of the deplorable consequences of civil insubordination. The European kings raised the privileges of the towns, in order to use them in bridling the power of the nobility. The result was, that the towns succeeded in checking the power of both kings and nobility.

It is one great advantage of these meetings, that they bring the country and the town population into contact and association with each other. Political conventions, which were once held only in large cities, are now equally common in the agricultural districts. The meeting may take place in the county town: but vast numbers from the country flock to it. I have known twenty, thirty, fifty thousand people assembled on these occasions. Now the rural population are the natural balance of the city population. In other countries, in consequence of the want of combination among the former, and their destitution of the means of instruction, the inhabitants of the towns have had things all their own way. But in the United States, the means of instruction are imparted to all parts of the population; and political conventions afford the most favorable opportunity for concert and united efforts.

The military institutions of the United States stand upon a different footing from what they do in Europe. In the European states an army is kept up, ostensibly to provide against the contingency of foreign war, but with the further design of maintaining the authority of government at home. That which is the principal end among the nations of the old world, is not even a subordinate end in America. The government of the United States relies upon the people themselves for the preservation of order. And that this reliance has not been misplaced, an experience of nearly seventy years amply testifies.

This very remarkable difference between the military institutions of these nations is the natural and necessary consequence of the difference in their civil institutions. As in the United States the government is the workmanship of the people, by the people is it most naturally preserved : but as in the old world it is a sort of self-existing institution, it is driven to rely upon its own resources for the maintenance of its authority. The European princes complain that obedience to the laws cannot be insured, unless they are placed in possession of an imposing military force. And how can it be otherwise, when the laws are neither made by the people, nor for the people. In Italy and Spain, when a murder has been committed, persons who are spectators of the deed flee instantly, in order that their testimony, if possible, may not be used against the criminal. So detestable in their eyes is the whole apparatus of government, that they involuntarily shrink from lending assistance in the detection or condemnation of the criminal. And the same feeling seizes every one, on occasion of those civil disorders which are infractions of the law upon a much larger scale. The army is the king's, not the people's ; and let the king take care of himself, seems to be the language of the spectators.

In the United States an insurrection against the laws, in which a majority of the people should be embarked, is an event which cannot take place. In the European states, it has frequently occurred : and would happen still oftener, if the few did not grasp a weapon of powerful efficacy in repressing popular grievances. In the United States the militia, which is only a collection of the citizens, constitutes the reliance of government in suppressing disturbances, whenever the ordinary police is not sufficient for the purpose.

The difficulty of creating a militia in the European states, arises from the extreme repugnance of those governments to permit the people to have arms. The permission, wherever it exists, is regarded in the light of a privilege, and is accompanied with the most odious restrictions. The celebrated statute of William and Mary, generally known as the bill of rights, allows persons "to have arms for their defense, suitable to their condition and degree, and such as are allowed by law." The words which qualify the privilege are provokingly ambiguous ; and were doubtless intended to be so, in order to wait a more favorable opportunity for asserting the full authority of government. Accordingly, the statute of George III, c. 1. and 2, authorizes justices of the peace to seize arms, whenever they believe them to be in possession of persons for dangerous purposes.

Now one can conceive of a militia to whom arms were never intrusted, except when they were actually called into service, but it would be a militia without a soul. The single circumstance that the American government feels no jealousy whatever, as to the carying of arms by private individuals, sheds a flood of light upon both the civil and military institutions of the country. In truth, there is no such institution as a militia, in the proper signification of the term, in any European state. It is the offspring of free government, and can only exist in conjunction with it. In Great Britain, by an act passed in the reign of George II, a certain number of the inhabitants, selected by ballot, were to be organized as a militia for successive terms of three years. They were to be annually called out, trained, and disciplined for a certain number of days, and the officers to be appointed among the lords, lieutenants of counties, and the principal landholders. But this force was only intended as auxiliary to the regular army, and the whole scheme has been long since abandoned. The plan of training and disciplining the whole adult population, in peace, as well as in war, has never been entertained except in the United States. The national guard of France approaches the nearest to it. In theory, it is composed of the entire adult male population; but in practice it is otherwise. The disinclination of the great majority of the lower classes to leave the employments on which they depend for subsistence, has established a sort of dispensation for them from this service: so that the national guard rather resembles the uniform companies, than the ordinary militia of the United States. It is very much the same in Great Britain. The militia there simply means the yeomanry, a body of men organized in each county, but selected from among those who are known to be well affected to the government. The election of their own officers by the national guard has not grown out of the revolution. The practice was introduced by Louis XI.

As is often the case, where what was once a privilege has become the common property of all, the people in some of the American states appear to set very little value upon their character as soldiers. Public opinion appears to have undergone a very great change with regard to militia duty. In Massachusetts, Maine, and Vermont, compulsory drills became so unpopular, that they were at length abolished. In Massachusetts, the sum of fifty thousand dollars is annually appropriated to any number of the militia, not exceeding ten thousand, for voluntary duty a certain number of days in every year. In Maine, the militia system is retained by continued enrollment of all who would be bound at her call to come forth for the support of the laws, or the defense of the soil. In Vermont, the laws requiring militia drills have been repealed, and in their place has been substituted an enrollment similar to that for jury purposes, of all who under the old system would have been liable to militia service. The militia system is retained in these states as the only effective military force, but the frequent mustering deducted so much time from the civil pursuits of the people, that it has been dispensed with. They only who compose the substantial power of the commonwealth, can afford to abstain from making continual display of it.

CHAPTER IV.

INSTITUTION OF THE PRESS.

The press is a component part of the machinery of free government. There would be an inconsistency, then, in arguing whether it should be free. It is the organ of public opinion, and the great office which it performs is to effect a distribution of power throughout the community. It accomplishes this purpose by distributing knowledge, and diffusing a common sympathy among the great mass of the population. Knowledge of some sort or other all men must act upon in the ordinary affairs of life, in order to render their exertions fruitful of any result. Political society, which connects men together while living in the most distant parts of an extensive country, is in need of a still wider range of information. It would be correct, therefore, to say that the freedom of the press was to knowledge, what the abolition of primogeniture was to property: the one diffuses knowledge, as the other diffuses property.

If we inquire, why in most countries so much power is concentered in the hands of government? the answer is, plainly, that knowledge is condensed in the same proportion. If we could suppose it to be uniformly diffused, government would cease to be a power: it would become a mere agency. For although it would be necessary to confide exclusive trusts to the public magistrates, in order to conduct the joint interests of society, yet the extent and activity of public opinion would give control to the power out of the government. This is an extreme case; and an extreme case is the most proper to illustrate the intermediate degrees, where the shades of difference are so minute as to run into one another.

If, in a state where representative government was established, we should suppose the press to be suddenly annihilated, the political institutions would not long preserve their character. As there would be no superintending control any where, and no acquaintance with what was transacted in public life, the affairs of state would soon be involved in the deepest mystery. Knowledge would be confined to the men who were the chief actors upon the stage of public life, and the very necessary authority which had been conferred upon them, in order to further the public welfare, would be converted into a mere engine of power. Usurpation would be heaped upon usurpation. Society would at first be a scene of infinite confusion. During this period, there would be many violent struggles between liberty and power. But as a state of disorder can never be the permanent condition of any community, the contest would terminate in the consolidation of power. And this vantage ground once obtained, the population would easily be molded so as even to co-operate in carrying out the designs of the governing authority.

If the press were extinguished, the great principle on which representative government hinges, the responsibility of public agents to the people, would be lost from society; except in those few instances where the duties to be performed were confined within so narrow a circle as to render them the subject of as direct supervision as the affairs of private life. The parish and the township officer would continue to be watched and controlled, until the revolution I have described established a system of universal centralization, and wrested the power of electing even those officers from the people.

These views afford a sufficiently clear illustration of the truth of the observation, that the principal function which the press performs in a political view, is to equalize power throughout all parts of the community.

The power which opinions exert upon society, is in direct proportion to the intrinsic value they possess, and to the publicity which they acquire. Both these circumstances are affected by the condition of the press, which gives impulse to thought, and free circulation to opinions. The action of mind upon mind, sharpens the faculties and kindles enthusiasm: and the extent to which an opinion prevails, indicates the number of persons whom it interests, and the degree of concert which is established among them. A thought, wrapped up in the bosoms of a few individuals, can never acquire importance; but when it engages the sympathy of a great multitude, it becomes more than a thought: it is then a new power added to public opinion.

What we term public opinion, is not the opinion of any one set of men, or of any particular party, to the exclusion of all others. It is the combined result of a great number of differing opinions. Some portion of truth often adheres to views and speculations which are apparently the most unreasonable, and it is the true side which they present, that goes to swell and to make up the sum of public opinion. Not that this is always the case—not that it is the case in any particular instance—but the tendency is constantly in that direction.

Very important consequences follow from this in a political point of view. The mixture of so many opinions, causing light to be shed upon each, contributes to moderate the tone of party spirit. However irreconcilable the views of parties may appear to be, a free communication cannot be established between them without producing a visible influence of each upon all. The press, in its efforts to widen the breach, and to make one opinion predominant, is compelled to make all opinions known, and creates the very process by which all are sought to be rectified. The free exposition of the views of parties constitutes a sort of lesser experience, which supersedes the necessity of actual experiment as a means of testing the utility of each. The public administration is prevented from running rapidly from one extreme to another, and in spite of the machinations of all sorts of parties, the people are insensibly drawn to the defense and adoption of wiser and more wholesome measures. Political contentions, in a monarchy or aristocracy, are like those personal rencounters in which one party is beaten to the ground. But the war of opinions is not conducted after this manner, for there the weaker side often rises from the conflict with redoubled strength.

Opinions may be even absolutely absurd and preposterous, and yet may contain a sort of negative truth. A system of religious belief, founded upon the grossest superstition, may simply signify to the men of other sects, that their practices are totally at war with the pure doctrines which they profess to teach. So it is said that in some parts of the United States individuals are to be found who have a predilection for monarchical government. Such fanciful notions cannot put out the light of the nineteenth century; but they may read a very instructive lesson to the men of all parties. They may signify to many who espouse free institutions: "Your conduct is inconsistent with the noble sentiments you profess to admire. Your designs are the most selfish and unpatriotic imaginable; and you would leave no stone unturned in order to compass them. If this were not so, our opinions could not stand up for a moment. In America, at least, they would never have gained entrance into a single bosom." Thus the existence of error often leads to a clearer sight of the truth, and the wide dissemination which the press gives to opinions, increases the intensity of the light by which all parties are enabled to see their sentiments reflected.

The facility with which opinions are promulgated, might seem to be unfavorable to stability in the public councils. And if it were so, it would be preferable to the complete despotism of one opinion over all others. But all change, which is the result of liberal inquiry, invariably leads to stability, for this never consists in the inflexible pursuit of one line of policy, but in listening to suggestions from all quarters, and causing the public administration to rest upon the widest foundation possible. Certain it is, that although this may never be the design of those who stand at the head of public affairs; yet in a democratic republic, the existence of the press, some how or other, insures that it shall sooner or later be brought about.

In France during the reign of the Bourbons, and in England in that of the Tudors, one set of opinions ruled the state, and it was ruled with a rod of iron. In America, where one party has never been able to succeed to the extent of an extreme opinion, the public administration, although wearing occasionally the appearance of fickleness, has in the main preserved a character of remarkable consistency. It has been made firm only at the cost of being enlightened.

The press may then be regarded as an extension or amplification of the principles of representation. It reflects the opinions of all classes as completely as do the deputies of the people. The difference consists in this, that it has the ability to influence, without that of compelling. And there is this advantage attending it, that it is in constant activity before the public mind, and does not like the legislative body speak only periodically to the people. Checks in government, as I have before remarked, are of two kinds: positive and indirect. The European states afford instances enough of the first: the American republic exhibits a great example of the second. Public opinion is the great preventive check of civil society, and wherever it is firmly established, the necessity of a recourse to the system of positive checks is to the same extent diminished.

When Cecil, the celebrated minister of Elizabeth, established the first newspaper in England, he little thought that he was creating a powerful counterpoise to that throne of which he was an idolator. To disseminate information with regard to the movements of the Spanish armada, and thus to assist the country in making a vigorous and concerted resistance to a foreign enemy, was his design. The most exaggerated accounts were circulated with regard to the Spanish armament, terror was spread among the inhabitants, and Lord Burleigh, who had reflected maturely upon the moral influence which the press was calculated to exert, fell upon this expedient as a certain means of relieving the public mind from anxiety, and inspiring it with resolution. The journal which he called into being, diffused information far and wide, corrected the misrepresentations which were afloat, and produced union and combination among all parts of the population. But the plan has resulted in a vast and complicated system, by which the rights of the people are protected from invasion by their own government. A new engine was created, which has contributed materially to effect all the great changes which have since taken place in favor of civil liberty. In 1821, there were twenty-four millions of newspapers annually sold in Great Britain. In 1827, there were twenty-seven millions circulated in the United States.

The process by which this great revolution has been brought about is very obvious. The press has given a voice to an immensely numerous class of the population who before composed a mere lifeless and inert body, but who now contribute essentially to the formation of what we term public opinion. A single newspaper may be very barren and uninteresting ; but the sum of all the information which is in this way brought to bear upon the public mind is incalculable. What we stand in need of, is information, and not merely the result of information. The great mass of mankind acquire knowledge with surprising facility, when it is communicated in detail. Facts thus presented have a distinctness which gives them an easy admission to the mind, and the conclusions which are deduced, are both more comprehensive and more practical. The sagacious and inquisitive spirit of very obscure men in the inferior walks of life, frequently stirs the public mind on questions of the greatest interest to society. Such persons often suggest hints and anticipate improvements which men of cultivated understandings, and more intent upon past history than upon the character and genius of their own age, would not have had the boldness to adopt. Perhaps it would not be too much to affirm, that almost all the great revolutions in human affairs may be traced to this source. The wealthy and educated, having attained the goal of their ambition, have nothing further to desire. Their views and exertions are confined to their own order. If such is the case with the men who occupy a lower position in society; if they also are intent upon advancing their own interests; we at any rate make sure, when activity is imparted to them, that all orders of men in the state shall be taken care of. But to give activity to the great classes of society, is in effect to connect them together, to form substantially one class, and to create a system of opinions and interests which shall be common to the whole population. Accordingly in the United States, men of all conditions are found associated in endeavors to extend education, to promote public improvements of every kind, and above all to further the interests of religion and morality. The great advantage which the towns formerly possessed over the country, consisted in their superior intelligence, and greater ability to combine for any public purpose. But the dispersion of knowledge by means of the public journals, has placed the city and the rural population on nearly the same footing;—another example of the influence of the press in producing an equal distribution of both knowledge and power, throughout the community.

The freedom of religion, of suffrage, and of the press, which has been introduced into some countries, was brought about by the very reasonable complaints of men who occupied an inferior position in society. The learned and the educated consulted their books, interrogated history: they paused, they doubted, they refused, until at last public opinion grew to be too strong. Suddenly, a great change was effected in the political institutions, and as government was thenceforward made to stand upon a broader foundation than before, and to interest all classes in its preservation, those who had predicted that the most fatal consequences would follow from such innovations, were surprised to see their calculations falsified, and to find that every interest which pertained to society had acquired additional stability.

The political press in the United States has a different character from what it has any where else. As there are no privileged classes, it is emphatically the organ of popular opinion. Society is divided into parties, but they are all parties of the people. The moment the people drew to themselves the whole political power, public disputes began to wear a new aspect. They ceased to be the feuds of distinct orders of men, and became the quarrels of members of one of the same family. And it is needless to add, that this was not calculated to lessen the acrimony of political dissensions; on the contrary, it has greatly increased it. But there is this compensation for the mischief: that instead of the terrific assaults of two hostile combatants upon one another, the power of the press is broken up into small fragments, and we have only a war of skirmishes.

The journals of no country surpass those of the United States in ribaldry and abuse. But a great part of what we term public discontent, is in reality only private discontent in disguise. Our private troubles we do not care to divulge, because hardly any one can take an interest in them; they are deposited among the secrets of the human heart. But the burden is too great, and every one endeavors to find out some circuitous means of giving vent to them. As soon, therefore, as the exciting topics of political controversy begin to agitate the public, the fiery elements of the character are seen to burst forth. All those private discontents which originated in envy, personal animosity, neighborhood bickerings, the finding one's self placed in a false position to the rest of society, in fortune, reputation, or understanding, immediately disclose themselves, and give a bitterness and vulgarity to public disputes which do not properly belong to them. Men throw the mantle of politics over their faces, and fight each other in masks. The consequence of this state of things is, that private character and personal conduct of almost every kind, are the subject of attack, beyond any thing which is known elsewhere.

So long as legislators are reduced to the necessity of governing by general rules, society must in part be regulated by the rival passions and propensities of individuals. They who narrowly scan American society may believe that it is in danger of being universally overrun by backbiting; and what in its vulgar form is party politics, but backbiting reduced to system?

But this melancholy infirmity, like many other defects, is designed to have a salutary influence. In private life it assumes the character of a regulative principle, by which, in the absence of any better corrective, men succeed in keeping each other in order. Nor is its influence in public life less conspicuous ; for there also it contributes to put every one upon his good behavior. If the American journals were exclusively the organs of the refined and educated, their tone would undoubtedly be more elevated. But it must be recollected that the ground work of the human character is pretty much the same in all classes. People living in polished society have passions and propensities as well as the common people ; only in the former case they are not put forth with so much nakedness. It may then be inquired, whether it is not one capital object of all institutions, whether in private or public life, to draw a veil over the bad side of human nature, so as to hide from view the selfishness and deformities of the character. And the answer is plain : such is the object, wherever the concealment does not have the effect of protecting from censure and rebuke the vices which are in disguise.

As all the parties which exist in the American republic originate among the people, and are essentially popular parties, it follows that the press is a censorship over the people ; and yet a censorship created by the people. There would, consequently be no meaning in the office of a censor appointed by the government. That institution is superseded by the very nature of the American press. Where a censorship is established by the political authority of the state, it is applied to restrain one class of publications only. No one ever heard, in a monarchical or aristocratical government, of any attempt to forbid the circulation of writings which were calculated to increase the influence of the prince and nobility. The utmost indulgence is extended to them ; while a rigorous control is exercised over every appeal in behalf of popular rights Popular licentiousness is bridled ; but there is no restraint upon the licentiousness of men in power. There is but one way of remedying the defect, and that is by causing the press itself to perform the office of censor : in other words, to grant such absolute freedom to all the political journals, that each shall be active and interested in detecting the misrepresentations and impostures of the others. There is a real and formidable censorship of the press in America, but the institution is in and not out of the press. The consequence is, that the efforts of all parties are more vehement and untiring, and yet more harmless and pacific than in any other country.

I shall conclude this chapter with two reflections. The first is a very obvious one: it is that the existence of a free press is not alone sufficient to inspire a people with a just sense of liberty; and to cultivate in them those qualities which are necessary to the establishment and maintenance of free institutions. The press was free in Denmark, Sweden and Prussia, until very modern times. It is nearly so in China. But in all these countries the moral power to set in motion this vast engine is wanting. The Prussian and Danish youth may be as well educated as the American, but the Prussian citizen is not half so well educated as the American citizen.

The second reflection is, that the press must not be regarded merely as the representative of political opinions. The dissemination of information in the daily journals, in magazines, pamphlets and books, on a variety of subjects interesting to the popular mind, withdraws the attention of the people from a too intense devotion to party politics, and educates them to be both men and citizens.

CHAPTER V.

ARISTOCRATICAL INSTITUTIONS.

There is a fine observation of Adam Smith, in the "Theory of Moral Sentiments," relative to the formation of ranks. He remarks, that where there is no envy in the case, we sympathize more readily with the good than with the bad fortune of individuals; and as much envy cannot be supposed to exist among the great mass of common people, they feel a real delight in beholding the prosperity and luxury of the rich; and in this way the foundation of an aristocracy is laid. The observation is neither recondite nor farfetched; on the contrary, it is both solid and ingenious, and is founded in the deepest insight into human nature. The same idea seems to have struck Bonaparte when he was revolving the plan of establishing the "legion of honor." He was struck with the curiosity which the populace exhibited in surveying the rich uniforms and decorations of the dignitaries who surrounded him. There was always a crowd in the neighborhood of his residence to witness the show. "See," said he to those who objected to the unpopularity of the institution, "see these futile vanities which geniuses disdain. The populace is not of their opinion. It loves those many-colored cordons. The democrat philosophers may call it vanity, idolatry. But that idolatry and vanity are weaknesses common to the whole human race; and from both great virtues may be made to spring." In order to the existence of an aristocracy, it is not merely necessary that there should be great inequality in the distribution of wealth; it is necessary, also, that this condition of society should fall in with the prevailing tastes and prejudices of the people. A privileged class may be created by dint of force; but to maintain its existence for any considerable time, it must some how or other interweave itself with the affections and sentiments of the people.

But Adam Smith does not direct the attention of his readers to another fact of still greater importance, inasmuch as it prevents the rise of a privileged class, or prepares the way for its extirpation after it has been established. We may very easily suppose a state of society in which the common people, being lifted to a considerable share of independence, will feel more self-respect, and have less admiration for outward show and splendor; at any rate, in which the envy of which Adam Smith speaks will stifle that sentiment of admiration. About the time he wrote, commenced that extraordinary prosperity of the English nation which has continued with little interruption to the present day, and which has given a prodigious impulse to all sorts of industry: to commerce, manufactures and agriculture. But the effect has been to raise up from among the ranks of the people, once so poor and humiliated, a formidable class whose wealth eclipses that of the nobility. And a further consequence is, that the sympathy which was before felt in the fortunes and reputation of a privileged body is now engrossed by an exceedingly numerous class of the population. The envy of which Adam Smith speaks now begins to show itself. The people feel that they are able to rival the aristocracy in wealth and intelligence, and they envy the exclusive privileges which are accorded to that aristocracy. I think I can discern many symptoms of a loosening of the hold which the institution once had upon the popular mind. As the absence of envy among a thoughtless and ignorant people contributed to the formation of ranks, an opposite cause may tend gradually to undermine their influence. The institution has already ceased to be hereditary in France, and some other countries. The curious trait of character which Bonaparte observed in the French populace, has been wonderfully modified by some other circumstances.

In the United States there is no foundation upon which to build an aristocracy. Landed property is very equally distributed; and the laws prohibiting primogeniture and entails, prevent its accumulation beyond a very limited period. It is the greatest nation of proprietors which has ever existed. One may observe signs of the same love of splendor and outward show which are visible among the people; for, as the French ruler remarked, it is common to the whole race of mankind. Nevertheless, the feeling is different from what it is in other countries. Instead of making people contented with their own condition, and satisfied with beholding the splendor and outward show which others make, it renders every one uneasy and restless, and goads them to unceasing exertions to procure to themselves some of the advantages of fortune.

As it is the effect of free institutions to take power from the superior ranks, and to add power to the popular body, in the progress of time these two classes change places. The aristocracy is converted into the democracy, and the democracy into the aristocracy; for there where the political power resides, will reside also the aristocracy. What was once the governing power, becomes the subject body. Hence, in popular government, one may observe a general disposition, not only to pay court to the people, but to imitate their manners, and to fall down to the level of their understandings.

Declamatory talent takes the place of genuine eloquence, superficial views of profound thinking. It may also be said that the people set the fashion in every respect. And if it were not for a tendency in an opposite direction, if the people were not making constant efforts to elevate themselves, the condition of society would be melancholy in the extreme. For the true democratic principle does not consist in letting down the highest in the land to the level of the lowest, but in lifting the greatest possible number to the highest standard of independence and intelligence. Although those who endeavor to ingratiate themselves with the people are intent upon advancing their own interests, they some how or other succeed in giving an impulse to popular improvement. Foreigners suppose that the democratic institutions of America are calculated to degrade the character of all public men, and to lower the general tone of intellectual and moral excellence. But it is important to look to ultimate and permanent results, and not merely to immediate consequences. Candidates for office are doubtless, in numerous instances, led to the employment of arts, and the cultivation of qualities, which are unfavorable to the growth of a sturdy and manly virtue. But independently of the fact that these qualities would, under any other form of government, be found to exist, only under different forms, and with more mischievous tendencies, the great desideratum is obtained—that of bringing about an association among the different orders of men of which the state is composed. The superior man may for the time being be lowered, but the inferior man will be sure to be elevated. The opportunities which most of the candidates have enjoyed in some degree, their pursuits in after life, their addiction to politics, even if it be only the superficial part of the science, enable them to impart some things to the people which the people are very inquisitive to learn, and the knowledge of which would be otherwise withheld from them in consequence of their daily occupations. The general intercourse which is thus established gives the most ordinary mind some tolerable insight into public affairs, initiates the uninstructed into the conduct of public men, and the import of the public measures, so that the mind the most captious and the least disposed to estimate free government at its true value must see, upon reflection, that the advantages springing from this order of things greatly preponderate over the mischief which is incident to it. It is impossible to produce as general an intercourse among all classes as is desirable, without incurring the mischief. But the intercourse gives to the popular understanding a very important discipline. Curiosity is the first step in the acquisition of knowledge; rouse that among a whole people, and you possess yourself of the masterkey to their faculties. The common people even form exaggerated notions of the advantages of information, after listening to repeated conversations and discourses of public men. A strong and general taste for education is diffused among them; and in progress of time a new people grows up, which is able to detect the hollowness of those artifices which were before employed to gain its favor. The evil is corrected by that same instrumentality which it was supposed would augment and perpetuate it. Doubtless politicians are bent upon promoting their own interests in their efforts to win the good will of the people. But some how or other, public and private interests are inseparably connected. Providence has wisely ordered that there shall be no way by which men can substantially and permanently advance their own interests, without advancing that of others. The lawyer, the physician, the merchant, are all chiefly intent upon lifting themselves in the scale of society; but they cannot do so without scattering benefits around them, and lifting the condition of others as well as of themselves.

Wealth and refinement, when they are not confined to a separate order, are not necessarily unfavorable to a high standard of intelligence and morals; on the contrary, they may be made highly instrumental in the promotion of both. If this were not the case, the condition of a free people would be the most hopeless imaginable; for they are destined to make the most rapid advances in the acquisition of riches.

Let us walk through the apartments of the rich man, and survey the interior economy of his house. We can only obtain a lively and correct picture of society, by examining the minute and delicate springs which govern it. The first thing which strikes us is the number of persons who compose the household. Besides the family proper, the easy circumstances in which he is placed enable him to employ several persons to attend to the various offices of the house. There is at once the introduction of a principle of order and regularity. The larger the family, and the more numerous the occupations, the greater the necessity for rules by which to govern it. The very subordination in which the members of the household are placed, is favorable to a system of discipline in every part. The head of the family is constrained to exercise a certain degree of authority, and this authority is chiefly displayed in the maintenance of order and arrangement in each one's occupations. The education of his children, is one of the first things which engages the attention of a man placed in independent circumstances. If he has not been educated himself, his heart is the more set upon it on that very account. This contributes still further to introduce the elements of good morals into the bosom of the family. If there is refinement and luxury, and even ostentation, there are also some powerfully counteracting principles in operation. The authority of the head of the family cannot be maintained, the obedience of his children cannot be easily won, if he breaks through the rules of morality, and sets an example which is at war with all the precepts which he undertakes to inculcate. There cannot be one code of ethics for parents, and another for children. The consequence is, that children will impose a restraint upon parents, as well as parents upon children. And however ineffectual the former may sometimes be, yet in the great majority of instances, it will exercise a marked influence upon the interior economy of the household. Individuals make great efforts to acquire property, in order that they may live in what they term elegance; and they have no sooner succeeded in their desires, than they find themselves surrounded by beings whose appetite for novelty and splendor is even stronger than ther own. The only way to maintain a due authority in their families, without which everything would run to confusion, and there would be neither elegance nor enjoyment for any one, is to introduce a system of rules for the government of the family. And these rules, to have any effect, must some how or other connect themselves with the principles of morality. And when that is the case, the wealth which was amassed in order to enable its possessor to live independently and free from control, is the means of creating an active control in the bosom of private families. Manners, that is, good breeding and civility, are one of the attendants upon a well-ordered, domestic society, and this creates a new bond of connection, not only between the members of the family, but between them and the great society out of doors. And it is very easy to see, even from this rapid sketch, how the acquisition of wealth may contribute to elevate the general standard of morals and intelligence in the community.

But the man placed in independent circumstances, has a great variety of relations to society at large. He walks abroad, and he finds other men engaged in enterprises of private and public improvement. If he were a subject under a monarchical government, he would perhaps lend his fortune to aid in conducting a foreign war. If he belonged to the order of nobles, in an aristocracy, he would expend it in furthering his own aggrandizement, and that of his order. But he is simply the citizen of a republic in which different modes of thinking prevail, and he is absolutely unable to free himself from their control. His whole conduct, whether he will or not, is governed by laws as fixed and determinate as those which guide the actions of men in less-easy circumstances. He becomes the member of various societies for the promotion of knowledge, the diffusion of benevolence, the amelioration of the face of the country in which he lives. All this is calculated to give him great influence; but this influence is bounded by the very nature of the enterprises in which he embarks, for they contribute directly to the distribution of property and knowledge among other men. He can only attain weight and consequence in society, by efforts which tend to elevate the condition of those who are below him. So that in a country of free institutions, the acquisition of wealth by individuals may be decidedly favorable to the cultivation of both public and private virtue, at the same time that it can hardly fail to promote the intellectual improvement of the whole population.

The influence of property is necessarily modified by the structure of society, and the character of the institutions which prevail at different times. At an early stage of civilization, a military aristocracy makes its appearance. There is then little wealth, and that little is condensed in the hands of a few. To this succeeds a species of baronial aristocracy, in which there is more wealth, but the distribution is as unequal as before. And when free institutions are established, both these forms are superseded by the dispersion of knowledge and property. The title then ceases to be a distinction. It is shared by so many, that there is no possible way of causing wealth to enter as an element into the structure of the government, without at the same time giving supremacy to the popular authority. In the Italian republics of the middle ages, the term, nobleman, signified simply one who was the proprietor of land. In Florence alone, mercantile wealth was able at one time to dispute this title with the possessors of the soil.

In the United States, where the distribution of wealth is more complete than in any other country, one may remark a difference in the groundwork of society in different parts of the union. In New England, a species of ecclesiastical aristocracy, if I may so express myself, once prevailed. But the growth of commercial and manufacturing industry has modified that state of society, without at all impairing the force of the religious principle. The term, "merchant princes," is still more applicable to the merchants of Boston, than it was to those of Florence. In the south, a sort of baronial wealth exists; but two circumstances have concurred to prevent its assuming the character of a political aristocracy. The laws of primogeniture and entail have been swept away; so that a new distribution of property takes place at every successive generation. And although wealthy proprietors have a great number of dependents, or retainers, yet this class, possessing no political privileges themselves, are unable to confer any upon those who are masters of the soil. There is, in other words, this peculiarity attending the cultivation of the soil in the south, that tillage is performed by a class different from, and inferior to, the proprietors. Such an aristocracy, although it may confer personal independence, cannot create political authority. In the middle states, where there are no such distinctive traits in the composition of society, an aristocracy of parties may be said to predominate. Party spirit, accordingly rages with more violence in these states, than in any other part of the country.

But, notwithstanding these differences, there is an infinitely greater uniformity of character among the people of America, than is to be found any where else. As M. de Toqueville remarks, there is less difference between the people of Maine and Georgia, who live a thousand miles apart, than between the people of Picardy and Normandy, who are only separated by a bridge. So it is said that people inhabiting different districts in the kingdom of Naples are entirely strangers to each other. And when two gentlemen from the city of Naples lately visited the Abruzza, in quest of information as to the natural productions of the country, they found there many medicinal plants, growing in the greatest profusion, which the Neapolitans were regularly in the habit of importing from foreign countries.

The leading fact in the history of American civilization, undoubtedly consists in the very equal distribution of the landed property of the country. And this is owing to the circumstances in which the country was found when it was settled by Europeans. The population was so thin, and so entirely below the standard of European civilization, that it quickly disappeared, and left the whole field of enterprise open to the whites. This is a fact quite new in the history of society. Two effects immediately followed, each having an important bearing upon the character of these settlements. First, two distinct races, one the conquering, the other the conquered, were not placed side by side of each other to nourish interminable feuds, and to obstruct the quiet and regular growth of free institutions. Second, if the country in 1607 had contained as dense a population as Italy, at the foundation of the Roman commonwealth; if it had only contained as full a population as Spain, Gaul, or Great Britain, when they were subdued by the northern tribes, the territory in all human probability would have been found divided among numerous chiefs and petty nobles: and the colonists would most certainly have accommodated themselves to this condition of society. The new proprietors, instead of vacant land, would each have acquired cultivated estates, together with a retinue of serfs and vassals, from whom the most ample revenue might be drawn This would have been so gratifying to the adventurous spirits who emigrated, some of whom were connected with the best families in England, and their notions consequently tinged with the modes of thinking then prevalent, that the distribution of property would have become very unequal, and would have been perpetuated to this day. But as it was, the whole country was a wilderness ; the high and the low had to begin the world, by turning laborers themselves. There were no great estates cultivated and adorned, and ready to be taken possession of ; no body of retainers, who might help to form an European aristocracy. All men were compelled to begin at the beginning. Men were from the first trained in the school of adversity and hard labor. The land was obliged to be sold, and cultivated in small parcels, in order to give it any value. Its treasures were a thing in prospect only, depending upon what should be done hereafter, and not upon what had been done already. To rent it was almost impossible, since the product was not more than sufficient to reward the labor of the cultivator.

Two effects followed from this : the land was pretty equally divided, and the agricultural population, instead of being divided into the two classes of proprietors and renters, assumed almost universally the single character of proprietors. That this has contributed to give an entirely new direction to the political institutions and the whole social economy of the state, must be obvious to every one.

When the colonies were severed from the mother country, an immense body of vacant land was claimed by the respective states. This was ultimately ceded to the federal government ; and the system established by that government for the sale of this land, has insured a still more uniform distribution than existed before the revolution.

Similar causes influence the growth and municipal government of the American cities. Neither the aristocratic "regime" of the Roman "commune" which prevails in the south of Europe, nor the gothic system of tradesmen and artificers, which grew up in the middle ages, and still prevails in central Europe, could well be introduced. It was the country people who founded the villages, and continued to replenish them, until they became large cities. These, when collected on the present sites of New York, Philadelphia, Baltimore, etc., found themselves in a state of as complete dependence as the rural population. The foundation of equal privileges was laid, and took the place of that equal division of the soil which prevailed in the country. Nothing at all resembling the close corporations which have existed in Europe, even in Scotland, and Holland, has ever been known in America. That in Edinburg, a city containing one hundred and thirty thousand inhabitants, the city council should have been a self-existing body, perpetuating itself by filling up vacancies in its members, and that the member of parliament should be chosen, not by the men of Edinburgh, but by this same city council, is a monstrosity which could hardly gain belief, if we did not know as a historical fact, that such was the case up to the year 1832. M. Guizot, in his admirable work, "De la Civilization Francaise," (v. 5, ch. 18,) has drawn a comparison between the rise of the cities in the south of France, and of New York, Boston, *New Haven*, and Baltimore. If he had pointed out the striking contrast which exists in the municipal "regime" of these two very different species of "communes," he would have afforded most solid instruction to his European readers.

But whatever may have been the beginnings of society in America, if the country is destined to make prodigious advances in wealth, will not aristocracy ultimately show itself? will not society, even more than in other countries, contain a very large body of wealthy individuals, who will attract to themselves an unreasonable share of influence? And if we mean by an aristocracy, a class of rich individuals, such will undoubtedly be the case. But when we call them individuals, and say that they will be exceedingly numerous, we point to two circumstances which will limit their power and cast the institution, if institution it can be called, in a different form from what it has assumed anywhere else. There would be no meaning in democracy, if it did not open up all the avenues to distinction of every sort, and we may with much more reason hold up such a condition of society as exhibiting the "beau ideal" of the democratic form of polity.

For aristocracy may be divided into two totally distinct kinds; a civil and a political aristocracy. The first is the very natural consequence of the unobstructed progress of the population in wealth, refinement, and intelligence. The second is the workmanship of the laws, which, proceeding in a course directly opposite, undertake to mold society into a form most favorable to the condensation of power and property in the hands of a few, and by so doing, gives an artificial direction to the political authority of the state. In the United States a political aristocracy is unknown ; but as the country has advanced with unexampled rapidity in the acquisition of wealth, and the diffusion of knowledge, a civil aristocracy is everywhere apparent. If there are any causes which condemn one part of society to great inferiority to another part ; if slothfulness, want of a wholesome ambition, or vicious habits, make some men the natural enemies of this admirable state of things, Providence has very wisely ordered that an antidote commensurate with the evil should pervade the system : that the class to whom influence belongs, having themselves sprung from the people, should know how to temper moderation with firmness, and not be able to bear down upon any class with the weight of a titled aristocracy.

The civil aristocracy which I have described, may be said to consist of the learned professions, of capitalists, whether belonging to the landed, the commercial, or the manufacturing classes, and of all those associations whose efforts are directed to the furtherance of public or private prosperity.

The profession of the law differs from that of medicine in this particular. Lawyers are called upon to make display of their knowledge in public, and this circumstance invests them with a sort of public character. They wear more nearly the character of a corps, or class. Moreover, their pursuits have a close affinity with all political questions, which cannot be said to be the case with the members of any other learned profession. The professors of medicine, whose services are performed in private, and whose position in society is necessarily more isolated, endeavor to make compensation for these disadvantages, by establishing everywhere colleges and universities, dedicated to instruction in their particular science. The colleges which were at one time established in England, for teaching the civil law, and the inns of court in London, a rival institution for teaching the common law, have nearly fallen to decay. In the United States, medical colleges are very numerous, but no college of jurisprudence exists. And yet the science of law is divided into fully as many distinct branches as is that of medicine, to each of which a professor might be assigned, and thus give rise to the establishment of law as well as of medical colleges. Lawyers, however, seem to be satisfied with the share of public attention which the nature of their pursuits attracts to them.

Although the efforts of the clergy are all in public; yet each minister stands alone in the performance of his duties. And they seek to relieve themselves from this disadvantage in two ways: first, by establishing, like physicians, seminaries devoted to teaching their own system of doctrines; and secondly, by the institution of ecclesiastical assemblies of various grades, sometimes embracing the whole clergy of one denomination throughout the country, sometimes the clergy of one state, and sometimes of districts only, in the same state. The first, under the names of general conventions, assemblies, or conferences, transact the business common to all the members of a denomination throughout the country. The second and third classes attend to those matters which concern the churches of one state, or of one district. And all contribute to bind together the members in one league, and to give them a just weight and influence with the whole lay population.

The strength of the natural aristocracy of a country depends upon the worth and intelligence of the members who compose it. Neither wealth, nor any other adventitious advantage, are of any moment, unless they tend to the cultivation of these two master qualities. And it is because the acquisition of wealth in the United States does actually tend in this direction, that its influence is so beneficial. The civil aristocracy becomes so numerous and so powerful that it is impossible to found a legal or political aristocracy. But it has been supposed that the popular sentiment in America is unfriendly to intellectual distinction. And yet a very fair proportion of men of eminent endowments have been elevated to office. This envy of intellectual distinction which has been ascribed to the people, if it does exist, indicates at any rate that that species of distinction is appreciated and coveted by them. Men envy in others those qualities which confer respect; and in so doing give no slight evidence that they are themselves ambitious of the same distinction. It is the first step in the intellectual progress of a nation. When the population is an inert, ignorant mass, it has no envy, because it has no inward spring of improvement. Moreover this jealousy of talent, although it may for a time cast very eminent men into the shade, is sometimes attended with very great advantages to themselves. The revolution which brought Mr. Jefferson into office, found the great body of American lawyers enrolled in the ranks of the federal party. They were consequently very generally excluded from office. This withdrawal from the noisy field of party politics caused them to devote themselves more exclusively to their profession, and the consequence was, that the legal profession attained an unparalleled eminence during the twenty-five succeeding years. American jurisprudence was built up into a compact and regular science, and acquired such a commanding influence, that it became a sort of make weight in the constitution.

The revolution which lifted General Jackson to office, confounded all the former distinctions of party. Lawyers were therefore appointed to office, without regard to the particular party to which they had before belonged. The taste for public life, which has in consequence been imparted to them, has been in the same proportion injurious to the profession. The present race of lawyers are not equal to their predecessors. It must be admitted, however, that this state of things is not without its advantages also. As lawyers are now very generally introduced into public life, they are less exclusively addicted to the technical forms of their profession; and this contributes to enlarge and liberalize their understandings. The great work of forming jurisprudence into a regular and well-defined system having been accomplished, the community can afford to let them mingle freely in public transactions, in order that they may impart the influence of their own habits of business to other classes; and at the same time, bring back from those classes some portion of their varied and diversified views.

There are two ways by which mankind have hitherto been governed: the one by a fixed authority residing in a select class, the other by a sense of common interest among all the members of the society. In the first, the imagination may be said to be the ruling principle of government: in the second, we avail ourselves of the same simple machinery by which all other human interests are managed; good sense, a love of justice, the conviction that the interests of the individual are, after all, identified with the public welfare. The idea with European statesmen is, that a government fashioned after the first plan will possess a greater degree of impartiality—that it will be more completely freed from the influence of parties. But inasmuch as the structure of society in modern times is constantly tending to weaken the influence of the imagination upon all the business concerns of society, the time may very speedily come, when there will be no choice as to the form of government which shall be adopted.

Nor is it true, that a government which is absolved from a dependence upon parties, is more impartial on that account. Parties are simply the representatives of the various interests of the community, and these interests will never be able to attain an adequate influence, unless they can make themselves felt and heard. Doubtless monarchical and aristocratical governments may be very impartial in one respect. They may be so strong as to turn aside from the claims of all parties. But as no government which is not founded upon men's interests, can administer those interests with skill and success; so no government which is not animated by popular parties, can ever be made to understand those interests. It is only since the rise of parties in Great Britain and France, that public affairs have been conducted with anything like impartiality.

CHAPTER VI.

THE INSTITUTION OF SLAVERY.

THE institution of slavery has an entirely different character in the United States, from what it possessed in the ancient commonwealths. In these, the servile class occupied very nearly the same position as the inferior ranks in the modern European states. They might not only be freed, but they were afterward capable of rising into the ranks of genuine freemen. At Rome, after the second generation, their blood was considered sufficiently pure to gain them admission to the senate. As slaves were most generally brought from barbarous countries, the restraint imposed before the manumission was favorable to the acquisition of habits which would fit them to be freemen. But before manumission, they filled a number of civil occupations, which at the present day are assigned exclusively to freemen. Even the professions of physic and surgery, notwithstanding the doubts suggested by Dr. Mead, seem at one time to have devolved upon them. Thus the servile class of antiquity, may be regarded as a component part of the general population; connected with all other classes by numerous links, and recruiting the ranks of the last with citizens of hardy and industrious habits.

This great difference in the relative condition of freemen and slaves in modern and ancient times, arises from the fact, that in the last, the two classes were composed of one race; while in the United States, they belong to distinct races. This renders the whole question of slavery at the present day difficult in the extreme. The light of the nineteenth century very naturally stimulates the mind to inquiry, nay, imposes upon it the duty of making an examination. And yet, the problem presented for solution—"Is it practicable to do away with slavery ?"—is surrounded with difficulties so numerous, and of so grave a character, as almost to baffle the best-directed efforts we can make. For how shall we emancipate from civil disabilities two or three millions of people, without admitting them to the enjoyment of political privileges also ? And yet how can this be done without endangering the existence of the very institutions which are appealed to as the warrant for creating so great a revolution ? In some of the American states, the colored population might constitute a majority of the electors. Where this was the case, the plan would simply terminate in raising up a black republic. For although it should be possible to overcome the prejudice of caste among the whites, yet the still greater difficulty of overcoming it among an inferior and unenlightened order of men, remains to be disposed of. The probability is, that long before the colored population could become educated and informed, if such an event may be deemed possible, the whole management of public affairs would fall into their hands ; or, by a combination between them and the worst part of the white population, the political power would be divided between the two. The extraordinary spectacle would then be presented, of a highly enlightened people voluntarily exerting itself to turn the tide of civilization backward ;—for assuredly, if the scheme succeeded, society would return to the barbarous condition which it has cost the human race so many ages of toil and suffering to emerge from. In Hayti the whites are a mere handful, and create no jealousy. In the British West Indies, the property qualification which is imposed upon voters continues the black race in a state of political servitude; so that the experiment in neither has produced any result which can shed light upon the most difficult and perilous part of the undertaking. In the United States, universal suffrage, or very nearly so, is the rule. It would then be impossible to make a distinction between the two races, without running into direct contradiction with the principles with which we had set out. How could we refuse to impart the benefit of those institutions, whose existence is the very thing which has suggested the change. And yet on the other hand, how could we consent to commit violence upon those institutions, by placing them in the power of a race who have no comprehension of their uses.

The earnest and extended inquiry which this great question has given rise to, cannot fail to to be attended with advantage. If there is any plan by which the institution of slavery can be gotten rid of, that plan will be suggested through the instrumentality of discussion. If there is no practicable mode of abolishing it, the freest inquiry will have the effect of confirming the public mind in that conviction. In either case, the tranquillity and welfare of the state will be better secured, than where every thing is seen through the twilight medium of doubt and ignorance. The great advantage of discussion consists in this : that by engaging a number of minds in the investigation of a particular subject, that subject is no longer viewed from one position only. The point of observation is continually changed and the conflict of so many opinions, each of which contains some portion of truth, ultimately elicits the whole truth. Before the press had roused the human understanding to vigorous and earnest inquiry on all subjects, society was full of all sorts of exclusive opinions and exclusive institutions, each of which was pent up in a narrow circle, and defended from the approach of any improvement. That was formerly, and to a very great extent is still, the condition of much the greater part of the civilized world. Force, disguised under one form or other, was once the principal means resorted to, to set things to rights. But in America, the discovery has been made, that the agency which is most powerful and most comprehensive in its operation, consists in the moral force of public opinion, which acting incessantly and in every direction, silently introduces changes which would otherwise have disturbed the whole order of society.

When the same object is seen under different aspects by different minds, the most partial views are acquired in the first instance. Nevertheless each one, uninstructed in the process by which opinions are gradually matured, is vehement in the promulgation of his peculiar dogmas; not because they are true, but because they are his. This is the danger which society runs, in that intermediate period when opinions are yet in a state of fermentation, and before time and reflection have been afforded, to separate what is true from what is erroneous. This danger is diminished, instead of being increased, in proportion as the spirit of inquiry becomes more free and independent. For then, to say the least, the shades of opinion are so infinitely varied, that the advocates of one and the same plan are frequently obliged to pause, in order to come to an understanding and compromise among themselves. Half-formed and sectarian opinions are very apt to produce sinister feelings and designs. This diminishes their influence still more, and prevents their acquiring an exclusive authority in the community. In the nonslaveholding states of America, the population is universally opposed to slavery. Public opinion, however, is so justly tempered, that the party which desires to carry out the extreme measures of the abolitionists constitutes a small minority. But opinions which are even tinctured with sinister views, ought never to be disregarded on that account. Our enemies always tell us more truth than our friends; and they are, therefore, frequently the best counsellors we can have.

There is another danger to which society is exposed. In times when schemes of public improvement are agitated, the spirit of philanthropy is sure to be awakened. This is more particularly the case, where these schemes are intended to affect private manners. But a well-informed understanding is as essential to the execution of any scheme of philanthropy, as is a benevolent disposition. The two, put together, make up the only just and true idea of philanthropy. Not only a correct discrimination between the possible and the impossible, but a wise and cautious adaptation of means to ends, in every thing which is practicable, are necessary to insure success. Without an enlightened understanding, there is no governing principle to guide; and without benevolence, there is no motive power to give vigor and effect to our actions. Hence, when these two qualities, each exerting a prime agency in the constitution of man, are dissociated, or not properly balanced, all our efforts become abortive or mischievous. They become so, simply because we have not acted up to the genuine notion of philanthropy.

In a country where free institutions are established, and unlimited freedom of discussion exists, this danger is increased, since every one then persuades himself that he is in duty bound to give utterance to his opinions, and that if these opinions are only conceived in a spirit of benevolence, they must necessarily be entitled to command: thus reversing the whole order of our nature, and making the feelings an informing principle to the understanding, instead of the understanding acting as a regulative principle to the feelings.

On the other hand, this danger is greatly countervailed by the very causes which give occasion to it. An unbounded freedom of thought and inquiry being exercised by all, those who hold contrary opinions are equally earnest in the promulgation of them, And even if the views on either side are pushed to an extreme, as they probably will be, the incessant disputation which takes place gradually wears out and exhausts the feelings, and enables the understanding to take clearer and more comprehensive views of the whole field of inquiry.

There are three errors to which philanthropists (those of the unphilanthropic are without number) are chiefly exposed:

First. By fastening attention upon some one defect in the social organization, and giving it an undue importance, they weaken the sentiment of disapprobation with which other defects, equally glaring and mischievous, should be regarded. This forms no part of their design, but it is the inevitable consequence of the course they are driven to pursue. Great multitudes of persons, who are entirely free from the stain which is endeavored to be wiped out, but who are overrun by other vices or infirmities equally offensive to genuine morality, join the association of philanthropists. They do so because this presents one common ground, upon which people of the most contradictory opinions and habits in other matters may meet; and, because, by combining with the philanthropic, in a philanthropic design, they withdraw public attention from their own defects, nay, they even seem to make amends for them, and to purchase the privilege of persevering in them, by lending their efforts to a single undertaking, whose avowed object is to ameliorate the condition of mankind. Hence, the extraordinary spectacle which is frequently presented, that a party dedicated to a benevolent purpose is, notwithstanding, crowded by persons whose designs are the most sinister imaginable, and whose feelings are nothing but gall and bitterness.

Second. There is another mistake into which philanthropists are apt to fall. In every society which has attained a high civilization, there are always numbers of persons who, from a variety of causes too indefinite to be described, are discontented with the social organization amid which they reside. No matter whether this proceeds from temperament, or ill-fortune of one kind or another, from disappointed ambition in any favorite end, whether in the walks of public or private life, or from being placed in a false position to the rest of society, the fact is so, and it exercises a deep influence upon human actions. Such persons seek to administer opiates to their troubled feelings, by brooding over the infirmities and binding up the wounds of others. The sombre and melancholy interest which pervades all their actions, impresses them with a character of earnestness and sincerity which irresistibly commands respect. The opinions of this class of persons are never to be shunned; for as human nature is constituted it seems impossible to sympathize with the sufferings of others unless we have been made to suffer much ourselves. We should avail ourselves of the feeling, but join to it an enlightened understanding, that so we may be more intent on relieving the infirmities of others than of curing our own.

The present has been correctly termed the age of eclecticism in mental philosophy. It is so in every department of thought. The tendency, in every thing connected with the knowledge or the interests of man, is to draw light from every quarter; not to consider different opinions on the same subject, as forming distinct systems; but rather, as all conspiring to form one consistent and comprehensive scheme of thought.

Third. There is frequently among philanthropists a want of tact in distinguishing between the practicable and the impracticable. This causes the path they would follow to be strewed with numerous difficulties and temptations. I do not use the word "tact," in its vulgar signification, as importing mere adroitness, or empirical dexterity; but as simply denoting an ability to make application of our theories to the practical affairs of men. In this sense, it may be said to be the consummation of all our knowledge. But it implies a wide observation, and a profound acquaintance with the history and constitution of man. It is well when actions which abstractedly have a character of benevolence, have in practice an opposite tendency to describe them as they are; and it is equally proper, when words which exercise such dominion over one half of mankind have usurped a foreign or ambiguous meaning, that we should call them back to their appropriate signification.

The man of the highest faculties, and who devotes them exclusively to improve the condition of his species, on being placed in society, immediately finds himself pressed with this difficulty. On the one hand there is a rule of right which, in consequence of its being a rule, is in theory conceivable of universal application. On the other hand stands the fact, that in spite of all the efforts of the individuals who have preceded, him, a vast amount of poverty, suffering and vice exists every where. As the causes which produced this state of things were beyond his control, so no remedies which he will apply can have more than a partial application. Is he to stop short, to abate his exertions? Not at all. There is a wall of adamant somewhere, over which he cannot leap, and which yet he is unable to discern. He should, therefore, endeavor to make constant approaches to it, as if it were, no where; but at the same time. never to part with the conviction that it does actually exist. This will not diminish the force of his exertions, since within the bounds of the practicable there is more than enough to give employment to the most active benevolence. But it will render those exertions more enlightened, and therefore more efficacious. There is another thing which he may do, and one which is neglected above all others. He may in his own person afford an example, that the rule of right, not in one particular only, but in all, is carried to the furthest extent of which it is capable. It is because we fail to do this, that all our efforts to improve the manners of others fall entirely short of the mark. Nor can I conceive any thing better calculated to exercise a powerful influence upon the actions of other men, than a genuine example of purity of life, if it were to be found, even though it should never assume to intermeddle with the conduct of others.

These three circumstances contribute to corrupt the manners, by rendering some abuses more prominent than others, which are equally or more deserving of animadversion; and by investing the last, and the men who practice them, with an air of authority which no ways belong to them. 2d. The moral sense is perverted, by making our own uneasiness and discontent the prime mover of our actions. For then it only depends upon accidental circumstances, whether the individual shall plunge into dissipation, become the victim of misguided ambition, enlist in the ranks of the soldiery, and throw himself into an association, the novelty of whose enterprises will create strong sensation, and prevent the mind from preying upon itself. 3d. The judgment is obscured by a failure to know and to appreciate the very thing which a being of limited capacities is bound to be acquainted with; the extent to which he may carry his exertions, and consequently the means which should be employed for that purpose. So that they who undertake to instruct and improve mankind, and who suppose that the very nature of their vocation places them beyond the reach of public opinion, very frequently find that they are equally obnoxious to it, and that they themselves stand greatly in need of instruction and improvement.

The term slavery has sometimes an odious meaning attached to it; and yet it deserves very grave consideration, whether the distinction between what we call slavery and some other forms of servitude is not for the most part an artificial one. The former denotes in its highest degree the relation which exists between master and servant, or employer and employed. The immature faculties of children give rise to a similar relation. The disabilities of both a moral and physical character, under which menial servants and the great body of operatives in every civilized country labor, give rise to the same connection. What avails it to call these by the name of free, if the abject and straitened condition in which they are placed so benumbs their understanding as to give them little more latitude of action than the slave proper. In an investigation of so much importance, it is the thing, not the name, we are in search of. It is true, it would be infinitely desirable, to cure all these inequalities in a society where servitude does not ostensibly exist, as well as in one where it is openly recognized. But in order to do this, we must be able to regulate invariably the proportion between capital and labor, which would imply on the part of the legislator a complete control over the laws which govern the increase of population. Nor is it certain then that we should be able to succeed; since there are so many inequalities in the faculties, disposition, and temperament of individuals, as to give rise to every conceivable diversity of sagacity and exertion, from the feeblest up to the most strenuous and energetic.

It is vain to say, that what is termed the institution of slavery contradicts the whole order of Providence; for society every where exhibits the most enormous disparities in the condition of individuals. Nor is it possible to conquer these disparities unless we abjure civilization and return to a state of barbarism.

That one race of men should be inferior to another, is no more inconsistent with the wisdom of Providence, than that great multitudes of the same race should labor under the greatest inferiority and disadvantages, in comparison with their fellows. We know not why it is, that so many wear out life in anguish and sickness, nor why a still greater number are cut off in the blossom of youth.

We are only permitted to conjecture, that if it were not for these inequalities, the little virtue which has place in the world would cease to exist anywhere.

The institution of slavery, when it is imposed upon the African race, may simply import, that inasmuch as the period of infancy and youth is in their case protracted through the whole of life, it may be eminently advantageous to them, if a guardianship is created to watch over and take care of them. Amiable and excellent individuals have descanted upon the ill treatment and severity of masters. But no one has been bold enough to rise up and tell us all he knows. Domestic society in all its relations, if its secrets were not happily concealed from public observation, would as often exhibit mischiefs of the same character. Perhaps it may be asserted that every new country has to a great extent been peopled by young persons who at home were surrounded by influences of one kind or another with which they were not satisfied. There is always a limit at which the most downright and headlong philanthrophy is fain to halt, and that stopping place is the inmost chamber of domestic life; although there it is that the foundation of all the virtues and vices of our race is laid. It would not do to lift the veil here, else it might show us how little genuine virtue exists ; and thus cast a blight over the exertions of philanthropists, as well as take away from the authority with which they speak. It is painful to think, that a great part of mankind are driven to talk much of the defects of others, in order to convey an impression that they are free from any themselves.

It must never be forgotten, that no institution can stand up amid the light of the nineteenth century, without partaking greatly of its influence. As the species of servitude which formerly existed in all the European states has been wonderfully modified in some, by the surrounding institutions and the general amelioration of the manners, the system of slavery which prevails in the southern states of the American union has received a still more decided impression from the same quarter. In the Eastern division of Europe, where money rents are unknown, where even the metayer plan of cultivation had not been introduced, but the system of serf labor is almost exclusively established, the treatment which the laborers receive is not near so humane as that of the American slaves. In Austria, the "Urbarium of Maria Theresa" still continues to be the "magna charta" of the peasantry. Nevertheless the absolute authority which landed proprietors exercised over them has been very imperfectly removed. In 1791 the peasantry of Poland succeeded in obtaining a new charter of liberties. But it was only in name, and their condition has not materially improved. During the last half century, laws, customs, and manners have undergone a great change. But this change is nowhere so perceptible as in the United States. It is not surprising, therefore, that intelligent foreigners should have been so struck with the fact, that the condition of slaves in America is altogether more eligible than that of free laborers, even in the western division of Europe. It is impossible to communicate an impulse to the institutions of society in one part, without causing it to be felt in every part. And for a very obvious reason, that every species of moral influence acts upon an institution, not as a dry system, but goes to the bottom, and affects the manners and dispositions of the beings who set it in motion.

Thus the institution of slavery, growing up with the manners, and partaking of the spirit which animates free institutions, may be gradually so molded as to acquire a still more favorable character. It may become in effect a mere branch of the domestic economy of the household, differing from others in no one respect, except the nature of the occupations to which it is devoted. In the Roman commonwealth the treatment of slaves was cruel in the extreme. Branding, the torture, slitting the ears and noses, and crucifixion, were employed for the most trivial offences. It has been reserved for the people who first established free institutions, to introduce also the only humane system of slavery which has ever existed.

M. Sismondi, in his History of the Italian Republics (v. 7, p. 68, n.) remarks that it was not due to christianity to have abolished slavery. And he mentions several instances (v. 8, pp. 160, 226 and 157) where the captives taken in the wars of those republics were indiscriminately reduced to slavery. And this as late as the commencement of the sixteenth century. But in the last passage he qualifies the remark by saying: "That it is not to the Roman church that we should accord this high praise." For christianity is the parent of philanthropy, and the parent of those institutions which in America have abolished the barbarous system of slavery once in vogue, and reared up an institution differing from it to precisely the same degree, that the political institutions differ from those of the European commonwealths.

The influence of race is a subject which has recently engaged the attention of philosophical inquirers. It may be that the light which has been shed upon it is still too imperfect to enable us to solve all the difficulties which meet us. But it would be a great mistake to suppose that the inquiry is in no way connected with the question of slavery in the United States. On the contrary, it is the single circumstance which renders the inquiry difficult in the extreme, both as regards master and slave. Philanthropists, in treating the subject, desire to deal in the most abstract propositions imaginable; but it is of infinite importance to make application of these principles, in order to ascertain whether they are not limited, and qualified by an extensive range of experience and observation. It is certainly very remarkable, that Europe is the only one of the four continents which has been thoroughly civilized. And Europe is the only one which is exclusively inhabited by the Caucasian, or white race. It is equally remarkable, that throughout Africa no trace has ever been discovered of civilization, except where the white race has penetrated. The ancient commonwealths of Egypt, Cyrene, and Carthage, were not, as some people suppose, composed of Ethiopians. They were all three settlements from Arabia, Ionia, or Phenicia. The black race do not appear to have possessed even the faculty of imitating, so as to build up any institutions resembling those which were transported to their soil. This race still continues wrapped up in that immovable state of barbarism and inertia which existed four thousand years ago. Denmark, Germany, France, and England, were inhabited by barbarians only two thousand years since; and yet, through the instrumentality of causes which have acted upon Africa, as well as upon Europe, the latter has been reclaimed, and the fabric of civilization which it has built up exceeds in beauty and variety the model from which it was taken. According to all the laws which have hitherto governed the progress of civilization, Africa should have been civilized as early as Europe. We can give no further account why it has not been, than that there is an inherent and indelible distinction between the two races, which retains one closely within a certain limit, and permits the other to spring far beyond it. To deny the distinction is not a mark of philanthrophy, but rather a defiance of those laws which have been imposed by the Deity, and which are no more inconsistent with his benevolence, than innumerable physical and mental differences which exist among individuals of the same race.

The revolution in Hayti dates back half a century: a period of sufficient duration to ascertain something of the capabilities of the negro race. Two generations of freemen have come upon the stage in that time. But we can no where discern any distinct trace of European civilization. The inert and sluggish propensities of this people have already created habits which preclude all hope of any substantial advancement. If they had found the Island a wilderness, it would now be covered with wigwams. Instead of the strenuous industry which carries the white man forward in the march of improvement, and makes him clear up the forest with as much alacrity as if he were subduing an empire, the negro is satisfied if he can appropriate one or two acres of land. All he cares for, is to obtain just enough to satisfy the wants of animal life. He has the name of freeman only: for liberty is of no account, unless it absolves us from the yoke of our own propensities and vices, which are far more galling and degrading than any physical disabilities whatever.

I differ with those who suppose that the worst effects of emancipation will be disclosed immediately. On the contrary, I believe that they will be developed very gradually, and that the impediments to the introduction of order and industry among the blacks will become more instead of less formidable, with the progress of time. On the establishment of the new system, in the British West Indies, the novelty of the situation in which the blacks found themselves placed, infused for a time an unwonted ardor and alacrity into their exertions. But this soon died away. They have fallen back into their natural apathy. It is impossible to induce a race to make strenuous exertions to better their condition, when they are satisfied with a mere garden patch to sustain animal life. In the small islands of Barbadoes, and Antigua, where there is hardly a foot of uncultivated land, they have been obliged to labor. But in Jamaica, where a great proportion of the soil is still uncleared, and where consequently it has been an easy matter for the negroes to obtain one or two acres apiece, they manifest the same disposition as in Hayti, to squat themselves down, and to drag out a mere animal existence. It is no wonder, therefore, that the plan of importing laborers from abroad was at one time seriously agitated in Great Britain, nay, carried into effect; nor that after being abandoned it should again be revived at the present moment. The experiment so far has been anything but successful. It seems to be impossible to train this emasculated race to the hardy and vigorous industry of the white man. To have made slaves of them originally, was a deep injustice. To introduce them into the society of whites, and to leave them to contend with beings so greatly their superiors, is a still more flagrant injustice. Even if there were not an incontestible distinction between the two races, still if there is a total defect of sympathy, arising from causes which it is impossible to remove, all efforts to melt them into one people must fail. The statesman is bound to take notice of all those secondary principles which are planted in our nature, and which exercise so wide and permanent an influence upon human conduct. He must make allowance for them, as the mechanic does for the operation of friction. If he fixed his attention exclusively upon certain primary laws, which do indeed lie at the foundation of human society, but which are so greatly modified in their operation, he runs the risk of losing every advantage which may be derived from either the one or the other. No one supposes that the prejudices of kindred can be conquered, or if it were possible, that it would conduce to the welfare of society. They constitute an important part of our structure, and are no more to be disregarded than are those general principles which rule over extensive associations of men. Yet the affections of kindred confine our attention and views within a very narrow circle, and consequently modify all our conduct beyond that circle. The same analogy is visible throughout the whole economy of human nature. It is therefore the part of sound wisdom to gather up all these inequalities, and to assign to each its appropriate place.

The philanthropic association which planned the colony at Liberia were fully aware of the truth of these principles. They, therefore, made it a fundamental regulation that white people should not be permitted to settle there. One can easily conceive that immense advantage might be derived from the presence and influence of the white race. But this is only on the supposition that that influence would be of the most unexceptionable character. And as it is not allowable to make this supposition, wise and discerning men have determined to effect a complete separation of the two races. The settlement at Liberia is one of the most remarkable schemes in which human enterprise has engaged ; even in an age distinguished above all others for noble and generous undertakings. But the philanthropy which planned it was obliged to take into consideration the distinction of race, as constituting one of those secondary principles of our nature which influence human conduct in spite of all that we can do.

We may say that a difference of color, and of physical organization, are to be regarded as accidental circumstances only. But accidental circumstances exercise a very wide influence upon the actions of men. The particular period when we were born, the institutions under which we live, the country which bounds our views and engages our patriotism, were all of them accidental circumstances, originally. But as soon as they exist, they cease to be accidents, or subject to our will. We may have been born at another period of the world, or in another country ; have been nurtured under totally different institutions, when our habits, our character, and our whole scheme of thought would have taken a different direction. If in all those particulars, our lot has been most fortunate, let us use our privileges discreetly, and not trample under foot the blessings we enjoy, because we cannot mend the works of the Deity, according to our own crude conceptions.

As the distinction of color is not at all dependent upon climate, there is every reason to believe that a meaning was intended to be attached to it. Doubtless, it was intended to signify that there is a difference in the intellectual structure of the two races ; and that it is the part of true wisdom, therefore, to keep them apart. The physical make and constitution of individuals of the same race are frequently of so great consequence as to give a coloring to the whole of life, and to stamp an impression upon their conduct in spite of themselves.

There is one class of philanthropists, who would have us consider men as merely disembodied spirits, and as entirely freed from the incumbrance of matter ;—a generous error, if the narrow and one-sided views in which it originates did not lead to consequences of an entirely opposite tendency, and afford a striking example of the untiring operation of the lower part of our nature, upon those who fancy they are the most completely lifted above it. We are never more in danger of sensualizing our whole being, than when we believe we have attained the highest degree of illumination. The founder of the Moravian sect wished to introduce some of the obscene rites which are practiced in the Brahminical religion of Hindostan. The quakers of New England, at an early period, entered the places of public worship and danced stark naked. It is but the other day, that an association of perfectionists was announced in the city of New York, which proclaimed the right and the duty to practice promiscuous concubinage. It requires but one step of false and detestable reasoning, to stride over the gulf which separates virtue from vice. If we have attained perfection, there is no way of manifesting it so decisive, as to practice all the things which are denominated vices, in order to prove that we are incapable of contamination from them.

It has been predicted that when the population of the southern states of the American union has attained a certain degree of density, slavery will disappear. It is remarkable, however, that the existence of the institution has no where hitherto depended upon the greater or less compactness of the population. It existed in the holy land, in India, and in Italy, for centuries after the population had reached its maximum. And on the other hand it disappeared from the northern states of America, and from most of the European communities, while the population was very thin. In England, the final blow which was given to the institution may be said to have been in the reign of Charles II, when the population of the whole island was not greater than that of the two states of New York and Ohio, at the present time.

There is one circumstance, however, which at this period is calculated to have great influence upon the existence of the institution. The present is beyond all comparison the most commercial age which has been known. Nations do not live within themselves as formerly. Each is striving to produce as large an amount of surplus commodities as possible, in order to exchange them for the superfluity of other nations. And as there is no doubt but what the labor of the freeman is, as a general rule, more efficient than that of the slave, a nation which employs slave labor, will labor under great disadvantages when it goes into the market of the world, and finds that the price of every species of produce, which is not a monoply one, is regulated by the supply of those nations which obtain it at the least cost. The nation which employs the cheapest labor will command the market. It may be true, therefore, as applicable to the present state of the world, that when the population of the southern states of America has acquired a certain density, the labor of slaves will be less profitable than that of freemen. And when this is the case it would seem, still proceeding upon general principles, that the slaveholders will be the persons chiefly instrumental in effecting the abolition of the institution.

But lest we should proceed too fast, there are here a good many things which must be taken into consideration. When we talk of the density of the population in a region where slaves already constitute a great proportion of the laborers, we must mean a density occasioned by the multiplication of the whole people, and not merely of the freemen, Our calculations, therefore must be founded upon the supposition that the community will be able to avail itself of the labor of those who have been emancipated, to the same extent as before, and with the additional advantage of finding their exertions more strenuous and effective than ever. This at once lays open the source of all the difficulties which attend the abolition of slavery in the United States. For is it quite certain that the labor of the free black will be more, or even as productive as the black when a slave ? I imagine that the reverse is the case: and that although the labor of the white man, when free, is altogether more efficient than when he is a slave, precisely the contrary is the case with the negro. None of these difficulties attended the abolition of slavery in Europe. Freemen and slaves were of the same race: and the last, after they were emancipated, slid by an easy process into the position of the first. Maryland and Kentucky may abolish slavery, but the effect will be not so much to get rid of slavery as to get rid of the African race altogether. Persons born after a certain period will be declared free, and in the intermediate period, the slaves who might give birth to this race of freemen will be disposed of in the southern market. The number of slaves in New York, at the first census of the United States, was more than twenty-one thousand. The number of colored persons in the state should now be somewhere about eighty thousand, if the increase was only equal to that of the slaves: and this independently of the great number of colored freemen and fugitives from labor, who have gone from the southern states. The aggregate number of colored freemen should have been greatly above one hundred thousand. But the census of

1840 makes it fifty thousand and twenty-seven. Either a great part of the original stock of slaves have been sold, or the free institutions of the United States are singularly unfavorable to the growth and prosperity of this portion of the population.

The efforts which any class of men will put forth for the purpose of bettering their condition, will be in proportion to their own ideas of the standard of comfort, not to the notions which other people have formed of it. If the man is endowed with strong moral energy, his exertions will be vigorous. The circle of his hopes and desires will be enlarged. It requires but little food and raiment to satisfy our mere animal wants, and little toil, therefore, if these are all which bound our exertions. It is the disposition to go beyond this limit, the desire to acquire the faculty of enjoyment, and not merely some of the things which administer to enjoyment in its lowest form, that has given occasion to that immense mass of industry which is now wielded, and which has covered Europe and North America with thriving and powerful communities.

Now, if we suppose that the American negroes, on being emancipated, will fall into the inert and sluggish habits which characterize their race throughout Africa, in Jamaica, in Hayti; that they will be content with a few acres of ground, upon which to seat themselves, and to vegetate in a condition little above that of the brutes, we cannot make the same calculations as if the country were peopled by the white race alone. The population may be numerically dense, and yet in reality thin. And I do not see how it is possible to avoid making the supposition. All history bears witness to the existence in the Ethiopian of a character totally dissimilar to that of the white man. And the former, equally with the last, is thoroughly convinced of the fact. "Black man is nothing by the side of white man," was the exclamation, says Mr. Park, of the negroes, on witnessing some very indifferent exhibitions of skill at Pisania.

This then is the great difficulty which is to be encountered in the United States. There is no doubt, but what the labor of the white man, when free, is more productive than if he were a slave, and this whether the population is dense or thin. But the reverse is the case with the negro. His services, when placed under the controlling guidance of the white man, may be rendered very valuable, but when left to himself he invariably falls into habits totally incompatible with strenuous and vigorous exertion. I remember a few years ago remarking to an intelligent individual, who was active in promoting the formation of a Fourier association, that the great objection to the plan of a system of common labor and property was that it destroyed the incentives to exertion. His reply was a sensible one. He said he did not suppose it would answer as a general rule for society, but that from long observation he had become acquainted with a fact, perhaps new, but one of great interest and importance in the history of the individual: that there are always a number of persons scattered through the community, who, from causes difficult to discern or explain, felt themselves to be too feeble and inert to take the management of any business into their own hands, and more particularly their own business; that such persons would show themselves alert and active in attending to the affairs of others, but lost their self command, and labored under a confusion of judgment, as soon as they set about managing their own. He maintained that it was to relieve this class of persons from the weight which constantly hung over them, and which cast a blight over all their exertions, that such associations were formed: that they constituted the exception, not the rule for society. And is it at all incredible, or inconsistent with the benevolence of the Deity, that qualities which are inherent in numbers of individuals of our own race, should belong to an entire race. Are the members of Fourier associations withdrawn from the pale of humanity on that account? No more than is the African race.

There is nothing which the human mind so much delights in as to generalize its ideas. The faculty of doing so is the highest which belongs to man. To be able to deduce a great truth from a given number of facts, is alike flattering to human ambition, and serviceable to the cause of general knowledge. But at the same time that the legitimate exercise of this faculty is of great advantage, the unskillful and imperfect use of it is often of exceeding detriment both to morals and knowledge. To fasten upon a few isolated facts, or upon facts ever so numerous, and to bind them together in the same class with other facts to which they bear some resemblance, but from which they disagree substantially, is not in any degree to subserve the cause of knowledge; and if our efforts are designed to have an application to the practical affairs of men, they denote something worse than an error of judgment. They are noxious and mischievous in the extreme. But it is this extreme fondness for constructing general propositions, this worship of abstract ideas, if I may so express myself, which constitutes the besetting sin of very many of the associations which have sprung up recently. Because some people are exceedingly good and benevolent, perfectibility is possible. Because some men are not so active and energetic, when working alone as when united into an association, all men should be herded together in associations. Because the white and the black man have one generic name, from that name are deduced the most absolute and sweeping propositions.

But in the event of the whites multiplying to such an extent as to fill up all the occupations of society, to become the sole operatives and agricultural laborers every where, what will be the condition of the blacks? They would be gradually deprived of their little possessions, which would become more and more valuable with the increasing density of the population. The whites would have the means to purchase them, and the blacks would be unable to resist the temptation to sell. Or if we suppose that a considerable number continued in the employments in which they were engaged before their emancipation, what still are their prospects? The accounts which we have of the abject condition of the lower classes in Europe, are enough to sicken the heart, and almost to cause minds which are not powerfully fortified by reflection, to despair of the cause of humanity. A vigorous writer, in the Boston Quarterly Review for 1840, on surveying the deplorable condition to which the white laborer is doomed by the operation of the inexorable laws of population, concludes that it is idle to talk of the evils of slavery, when American slaves are placed in a far more eligible condition than any class of European laborers; that there are certain mischiefs in the social organization of every free community as now constituted, and that it is incumbent upon all enlightened men and lovers of humanity to probe the mischief to the root. And he proposes, that the property of all deceased persons should fall to the state to be distributed among the population. The views which this writer took of the condition of the lower classes was, for the most part, correct; but the remedy he proposes would be utterly powerless. If, however, there is among all intelligent observers, such an unanimous opinion as to the abject condition of the white laborer, when the population has attained a certain density, what must be the condition of the African, when he is placed in close and death-like encounter with beings so greatly his superior? If that period were suddenly to come upon us now, the most extraordinary revolution would take place in the opinions of philanthropists. They would take ground precisely opposite to that which they now occupy. They would cry out against the cruelty and injustice which would be done to the blacks by emancipating them; they would, if true to their principles, inculcate the duty of maintaining a guardianship, the yoke of which would then be so easy and so desirable to bear.

The probability is, that the same fate which has overtaken the Indian race would be that of the negroes. The process of extinction would be more gradual; but it would be sure. The Ethiopian disappeared before the march of civilization in Egypt, Cyrene, and Carthage. And the more thorough civilization of the United States would assuredly bring about the same result.

It is evident, then, that difficulties of the greatest magnitude surround this question. Now, there are few obstacles which a powerful and enlightened people cannot overcome, if it can be made to see them clearly. But long familiarity with the institution of slavery, is apt to beget partial and indistinct views among slaveholders, as well as among abolitionists. I do not suppose there is any danger that the blacks will ever gain the ascendency. They never succeeded in expelling the whites who founded so many commonwealths on the Barbary coast. On the contrary, they were themselves driven to the wall. And what has been the fortune of communities founded by an Asiatic race, will be the fortune of those which have been founded by the Anglo-Norman race in the United States. Insurrections would take place among the liberated blacks. And they would be quelled. But humanity recoils from contemplating the stern an inexorable justice, which would have to be dealt out in so terrible an emergency.

Two alternatives seem to present themselves: to transport the African race bodily to some other country, or to retain them in their present condition. The first would be literally a gigantic undertaking; or rather, we may regard it as an impracticable one. Independently of the violent shock given to every species of industry, by the sudden withdrawal of such a multitude of laborers, the expense would surpass the resources of the slave states, even if those resources were unaffected by the deduction of such an immense mass of labor from the soil. The mere cost of removal would completely exhaust them. To transport a number sufficient to keep down the annual increase, and to continue this plan until the country were emptied, would be beyond the ability of the southern states. The Moors of Spain, and the Huguenots of France, were expelled, not removed. And the expulsion in neither instance was anything like complete. The Moors and Huguenots had effects to take with them, to enable them to begin life again. The first had a kindred race on the neighboring shores of the Mediterranean, who were glad to receive them. The second were welcomed in every protestant community throughout the globe. The state incurred no expense. It lost a body of valuable citizens; but the laws of population soon filled up the void. These cases differ widely from the present. Not that the analogy fails in every particular, but that when we sum up the difficulties on both sides, they are incomparably greater in one case than in the other.

If then it is impossible to melt the two races into one; if to transport one of them is impracticable, and to emancipate it would be an act of injustice and inhumanity, there is but one alternative: to retain the institution of slavery. We are never masters of the circumstances under which we were born. We may desire a change in every one of them. But the wise and inscrutable decrees of Providence have ordered otherwise, and we can in no way fall in with its designs so completely, as by accommodating ourselves to difficulties which cannot be surmounted; in other words, by acting up to the rule of right, in every situation in which we may be placed, and this not merely where our duties are plain, but where they lead us over a dark and difficult way. To attempt to beat down an institution, because we were not consulted as to its establishment, is to arrogate an authority which does not belong to us. But we may convert that institution into an instrument of good. We may apply to it the same rules of justice and humanity which are applicable to every other part of the economy of society.

The men of the south find themselves born under an institution which they had no hand in creating—which their fathers did not assist in building up, but vehemently protested against when it was introduced by the mother country. Their course is plain. If it cannot be removed, to employ the same judgment and discretion in the management of it, as are due to every other institution which is placed beyond their control. The relation of parent and child is the most extensive and important which exists. The relation is different in degree, but not in kind, from that of master and slave. Parents, by harshness and severity, may, and probably in great numbers of instances actually do, cause the fairest and gentlest virtues to wither in the blossom, when, by tender and judicious treatment, they may have reared men and women, who would have been ornaments to society. And although all our exertions to produce a different conduct may be of no avail, although we may not even have the right to intermeddle with the private relations of others, yet the duty of parents to act otherwise, stands as firm and unalterable as ever, and this notwithstanding the innumerable crosses to which they are subject in the management of their household. Precisely the same is the case with the master. Great numbers of parents, in all parts of the world, are compelled to make use of the labor of their children, in tillage, in manufactures, in every species of employment. A very large proportion, in densely peopled countries, do actually task them to occupations, the recital of which makes us shudder. And if this be an evil inseparable from the density of the population, so that all efforts to extirpate it will be ineffectual, it affords another example of those uncontrollable circumstances under which we were involuntarily born; but one which far surpasses in magnitude the institution of slavery as it has hitherto existed in the United States.

CHAPTER VII.

THE JUDICIAL POWER.

Montesquieu has said, that the judiciary is the weakest of the three departments of the government. There are few general maxims which do not admit of some limitation—there is hardly one which does not demand this limitation in order to be true. The observation of Montesquieu is perfectly correct, in reference to some particular forms of government. In hereditary monarchy, where the executive is a self-existing authority, from which all appointments flow; in an aristocracy, where the legislative and executive authority is condensed in a body of nobles, the judicial power is necessarily feeble. But in a democratic republic, where the legislative and executive power is strictly bounded on all sides, the judicial may become a very imposing department. Its relative if not its absolute strength is then increased, for while the other two departments have been deprived of some of their most important attributes, the judicial power retains very nearly the same position and character which it before held. It even seems to possess a disproportionate share of importance, which is probably the reason why some of the state constitutions of America have substituted the tenure of a term of years, in the place of a tenure for life. By so doing, the great principle of responsibility is applied to all the departments indiscriminately. As the power of impeaching the chief magistrate, and of punishing in some way equally effectual the various administrative officers of the government, is not deemed a sufficient reason why they should hold their places for life, it has not been deemed sufficient with regard to the judges.

The judiciary does not deal so directly nor so frequently with political questions, as do the other departments. But it does sometimes deal with them, and that too definitively; in addition to which, it extends its authority over a vast multitude of private transactions, many of which receive a hue, more or less distinct, from the political disputes of the day. If then the judges are appointed for life, they may have the ability to act upon society, both inwardly and outwardly, to a greater degree than the other departments. For when we talk of political authority, we must distinguish between the abstract power which belongs to the body, and the active authority which may be wielded by the members. If, for instance, the deputies to the legislature are never the same for any two successive years, while the judges are elected for life; then, although the legislative authority of the state may be ever so great, yet still the power and influence of the judges may be greater than that of the deputies.

Courts of justice may well be described as an institution framed for the express purpose of putting an end to the practice of private war. The legislature is well fitted to make general rules for the government of the people, and the executive to keep watch over the public safety. But without the instrumentality of the judicial tribunals, which act in detail and not merely in the gross, society would be a prey to perpetual civil dissensions. Disputes between private individuals are occurrences of every day. The manifold relations which men have to each other in a thriving and cultivated society, multiply them greatly. These disputes have relation to the most valuable interests of society: life, liberty, and property. And to have devised a mode by which they may be quietly appeased, is one of the greatest achievements of modern civilization. In a state of imperfect civilization, the quarrels of individuals frequently assume a formidable shape, and become matters of the gravest public interest. The injured parties interest first their relatives and friends, then the neighborhood, and finally whole districts of country are involved in the ferment. A dispute respecting the boundary of lands, or a mere personal trespass, is kindled into a furious insurrection, which nothing but a military force can subdue. An institution, therefore, which goes to the bottom of the evil, and takes up each case as it arises, separately and in detail, and which is so constructed as to inspire a very general confidence in its impartiality and integrity, necessarily occupies a very important place in the complicated apparatus of government.

It is curious to mark the successive steps by which the practice of private war has been finally put down; how, from the most confused and discordant elements, a regular system for administering justice has sprung into existence. The trial by ordeal and judicial combat which make such a figure in the codes of the European states, at an early period, were the first rude attempts to mitigate the custom of private war. There may be said to be this natural foundation for the combat, that all ignorant people, when they are offended, immediately feel like fighting; and for the ordeal, that all superstitious people have faith in the determination by lot. But it would be a great mistake, as an admirable writer* has remarked, to suppose that these customs were calculated to fortify or to continue the practice of private war. On the contrary, they were designed to have an opposite effect. The legislator said to the injured party: if you insist upon revenging yourself, you shall at any rate do it according to certain forms, and in the presence of the public. The secret pursuit, the midnight murder of an enemy, were thenceforth put an end to. The pecuniary composition was a step still further in advance. Although at first it was at the election of the injured party whether he would accept it; in time it came to be absolutely binding upon him. And thus the practice of even regulated warfare was completely checked. When we read, in some of the most ancient European codes, of the trial by ordeal, of judicial combat, and of the "wehrgeld," we are apt to regard them as anomalies in the history of society, of which no just and satisfactory account can be given. They were undoubtedly relics of a custom still more barbarous; but the true view is to consider them as the first feeble efforts which were made to rid the community of the practice of private war. The duel was substituted in the place of private assasination; and in progress of time the relations of the murdered man were compelled to receive a pecuniary compensation, instead of revenging themselves by the murder of the criminal, or his family.

Although the pecuniary mulct excites surprise, when we read of it in the history of the middle ages, it has notwithstanding occupied a considerable place in the criminal codes of some of the most enlightened modern states. In that of Ohio, passed so late as 1809, it

* Guizot's "Civilization Francais," 1. p. 365.

makes a part of the punishment of every felony except four. There was this difficulty attending this system, under the Salic and Ripuarian laws, that the delinquent having no property might be unable to pay the fine. What then should be done? Montesquieu says, that he was placed out of the pale of the law, and the injured party was permitted to redress the wrong. But this was not the course resorted to by all the German nations. Some of them imposed outlawry, banishment, transportation, or slavery. The laws of Ohio avoided the awkward predicament of the Salic and Ripuarian codes, by combining the penalty of imprisonment with that of the fine; so that the maximum of the first would alone be sufficient, if the circumstances of the criminal made it necessary to abstain from the fine. The existence of the pecuniary composition in the American laws, and in the Saxon, Salic, and Ripuarian codes, marks two totally different states of society. In the last it denoted a feeble effort to get rid of the lawless violence which every where prevailed: but in the other it was a step from one regular mode of procedure to another still more regular, but more humane and judicious. In other words, it constituted the transition state from the system of capital punishments to the scheme of penitentiary discipline. There was another difference still more striking. The Germanic tribes held fast to the notion that a crime was an offense against an individual. They were not able to raise themselves to the higher conception, that it was an offense against society, much less that it was an infringement of the laws of God. Hence the fine was never so high but numbers to whom revenge was sweet could afford to pay it: hence also it was not paid to the state, but was given to the injured person, or in case of homicide, to the relations of the deceased.

The whole course of modern jurisprudence runs counter to such ideas. A crime is not merely regarded as an infringement of private rights but as a violation of the great rules of morality, so much so, that the private injury in the most flagrant cases is merged in the public offense. For it is the chief design of legislators, at the present day, to impress every one with so deep a sense of the heinousness of crime, that the guilty man shall both regard himself, and be regarded by the community as an outlaw from society. In this way the remorse of conscience is added to the physical punishment which is inflicted. For want of such just notions, society was formerly a prey to the wildest disorders. For as long as the license to commit crime could be purchased at a price, the power of conscience was necessarily very feeble. The license was regarded as a privilege, instead of as a badge of disgrace. The life and reputation of man seem to be cheap, until he is raised high in the scale of civilization. He becomes more accustomed to the degradation of his own existence, and views the existence of others as being equally degraded with his own.

I do not mean to give any opinion as to the propriety of compelling the criminal to make additional satisfaction to the injured person, or, in the case of felonious homicide, to his relations. But this should never be enjoined as the chief end of punishment. If the plan is adopted, it should never, in the graver offenses, be by way of fine. The delinquent should be condemned to hard labor in the penitentiary, and that labor be made available to the widow and children who had been deprived of their support. There are even then some difficulties in carrying out the plan in detail. The murdered man, for instance, was perhaps so worthless, that instead of sustaining, he was sustained by his family. At the same time, therefore, that the public punishment cannot be dispensed with, there is no room for compensation to private individuals. And although cases will occur, where the degree of private injury can be easily ascertained, there will be others where it will be exceedingly difficult to compute it in advance, since no one can determine how long the murdered man may have lived, and may have been able and willing to maintain his family. The laws in modern times never give the fine to an individual, except in those cases where there is the least propriety in so doing; that is to say to the base informer.

The judiciary is considered by Montesquieu, as a branch of the executive power. That there are resemblances between these two departments, is certain; and that the points of resemblance between the two are different at different stages of society, is also clear. But it is necessary to trace the gradual rise of both, in order to ascertain in what respects they differ, and in what they agree. A proposition may sometimes be true as an historical fact, and yet untrue as a principle. And the reverse may also be the case. In the former instance, the business of the political philosopher is to make use of the fact, only so far as it may be the means of eliciting the principle.

At an early period of society, the king, or chief of the nation, by whatever name he was known, dispensed justice in person. It would be correct to say, that the judiciary then formed a branch of the executive authority. But the great multitude of controversies, both civil and criminal, which grow up with the progress of civilization, put an end to this arrangement, and cause it to be superseded by another. The executive magistrate has neither the time, nor the ability, to attend to the ten-thousandth part of the controversies which are perpetually springing up in an industrious and densely populated country. He is obliged to employ a great number of subordinate agents: and this immediately introduces new combinations, and a new element of power, into the government.

What was orignally regarded as an arrangement of convenience, turns out to be an important step in the advancement of society. These deputies of the king render themselves so useful to the community, and acquire in consequence so large a share of influence, that they are no longer viewed as his dependents. The administration of the laws, by a class of men set apart for that purpose raises the whole body of judicial magistrates to an independent position in the state; and not only renders it unnecessary, but absolutely forbids that the executive magistrate should take part in judicial proceedings. James I. was the last British monarch who ventured to take a seat on the bench; and he was reminded by the judges that he had no business there—no right to give counsel and advice on the trial of any cause.

But as the judges still continue to be appointed by the king, and to hold their places at his pleasure, the next important step is to render them irremovable after they are commissioned. And this was not effected in Great Brtain until the act of settlement in 1689, nor even then completely until the first year of George III. In France, at one time, the tenure of the judges went beyond any thing known in England. The office was hereditary. It was the absolute property of the incumbent, capable of being disposed of by sale or devise. And we know that Montesquieu, the celebrated writer made sale of his when he retired into the country to write "The Spirit of Laws." At present the tenure is the same as it is in Great Britain.

These changes are afterward followed, though at very long intervals, by another of still greater importance. The executive not only ceases to be judge, but he loses the power of appointment. The same causes, the general spread of intelligence, and the complicated transactions of society, which gave the judges so independent a position in the community, act with even more force upon another department. The legislative body, the more immediate representatives of the people, attains an entirely new rank and importance; and the appointment of the judges is devolved upon it. And if, when these were nominated by the king, it was correct to say that the judiciary was a branch of the executive power, with equal reason may we assert, that it has now become a branch of the legislative department. But suppose that the chief magistrate, and the members of the legislative assembly, are themselves elected by the people for limited terms, we shall not be at liberty to make either the one assertion or the other. In the early stages of society, the king is literally the sovereign; and it is by virtue of this attribute that he then centers in himself the powers of both the other departments. He is not merely judge; he is supreme legislator also. In proportion as the state becomes strong, he becomes weak. He is deprived of his prerogatives, one by one, in order that they may be distributed by the real sovereign, the people; which now, for the first time, makes its appearance upon the stage. The government then assumes the character of a regular system. Three distinct departments are created by one common power; neither of which can lay claim to any part of the sovereignty of the state.

But there is one sense in which the judges may be said, in a very advanced state of society, to exercise a very important share of the executive authority. When the chief magistrate is elected for a short term, and none of the subordinate officers are chosen by himself, his power is so greatly abridged, that he is known by the name, rather than by the functions he exerts. The decisions which he makes are not one in a hundred to those which are made by the courts: and to these tribunals are attached officers, who carry into immediate execution the orders which they receive. This is the case in all the state constitutions of America, which afford the most perfect models of government that have ever been established. In Ohio, for instance, the judges are perpetually active; while the executive, having little or nothing to do, is almost inert. If the executive officers of the courts were only appointed by the courts, we might say that the judiciary had usurped nearly all the executive power of the state.

The independence of the judiciary has been considered as a fundamental principle in government. But by that term is understood, in Great Britain and France, and even in the United States, where European ideas sometimes contribute to modify the institutions, a tenure for life. And yet the same arguments which are employed to vindicate the propriety of this arrangement, may be used with nearly equal force to show that the executive and the legislative body should hold their places for life. In some respects there would be even greater propriety in establishing this rule in the latter than in the former case. For the chief magistrate and the popular deputies stand in the midst of the party conflicts of the day, and if we wish to protect them from the storms of political life, that so their judgments may not be swerved from the path of rectitude by the changeable currents of opinion, no way would seem so effectual as to withdraw them from this influence. There may be the most solid reasons why, in a monarchical government, the judges should be independent, in the English sense of the term ; and yet these reasons may be inapplicable in a republic, and not have sufficient force to lay the foundation of a general maxim. That only is entitled to the dignity and value of a maxim which, although it may not be applicable to all circumstances, and to every condition of society, is yet applicable to the most perfect disposition of the subject matter which we have to deal with.

In Great Britain and France the executive magistrate is a hereditary officer, and the appointment of the judges is vested in him. The only plan, therefore, of creating anything like an independence of him, is to make the tenure of their office permanent. The only alternative is between removability at the pleasure of the king, and a tenure for life. The last plan has been adopted, in order to produce an effect which, in a country of free institutions, is unnecessary and out of place. As the station which the king holds is so far removed from the wholesome influence of public opinion, the judges, if dependent upon him, might be subservient to his worst designs. The influence of the crown would be felt everywhere : in the walks of private life, as well as in political affairs. So great an authority centered in one person, might render him the preponderant power in the state. By breaking the link of connection from the moment the appointment is made, there may be good ground to expect that the judges will feel a due sense of responsibility to the community which they are appointed to serve.

For what we intend, or should wish to intend, when we reason in favor of the independence of the judges, is that they should be freed from the control of any individual; that they should not be subjected to any species of personal influence. But this by no means implies that they should be independent of the society or community whose interests they are designed to administer. The two things have been constantly confounded, although, in reality, they differ from each other in most respects. If in the United States the appointing power was a hereditary body, or one elected for life, the analogy would hold. It would then be necessary to render the judges independent of that power, in order to secure their dependence upon, and responsibility to, the people. But if the appointing power is itself chosen by the people, for a short term, a tenure for a limited period may not only be compatible with the independence of the judiciary, it may be the true way of reconciling that independence with a due sense of responsibility. If the term independence of the judiciary does necessarily mean an emancipation from the control which electoral government imposes, the people of America would be led to pull down the whole fabric of the institutions which they have constructed, in order to introduce so salutary a principle into all departments.

Notwithstanding the independence of the judiciary, as understood in Europe, is an anomaly in some of the American constitutions, there are some circumstances which have caused it to work well in practice.

First. The pursuits of a judge are of a highly intellectual character, and all intellectual pursuits exercise a favorable influence upon the character. They have a decidedly moral tendency. Although the investigation of legal questions may not contribute to open and invigorate the understanding so much as some other mental occupations, it assists powerfully in strengthening the moral qualities. The duties which the judge is called upon to discharge, consist in the application of the rules of morality to the affairs of real life, and are therefore calculated to impress his whole behavior with an air of seriousness and conscientiousness. To be called to act as umpire in the numerous and important controversies between individuals, to sit in judgment upon the life and reputation of a fellow being, to hold the scales of justice with a firm and unfaltering hand : these are duties of no common import, and except in natures very illy formed are every way fitted to purify and elevate the character. The judge, too, is removed from the scene of party conflicts, nor is it expected that he will mingle in all the gayety and frivolity of fashionable life. He is thus placed out of the way of temptation more than other men, and is insensibly beguiled into a train of conduct the most favorable for the practice of both public and private virtue.

Second. The system of judicial precedents acts, to a considerable extent, as a check upon the conduct of judges. As it is necessary that there should be rules to restrain private individuals, so it is also necessary that there should be a law to restrain the court, and precedents constitute that law. The respect for cases which have already been adjudged, although it should never be carried so far as to render them absolutely binding, prevents any marked or habitual derilection of duty. The profession are apt to be keenly attentive to both the motives and the reasons of the bench, when it undertakes to overthrow a decision which has grown to be a principle; and in this way a system of responsibility is created, which, in the case of all other public functionaries, can only be brought about by short terms of office.

These views are of considerable importance in surveying this interesting question in all its parts. But they rather show that there are some compensatory contrivances incident to the system, than that the system is as perfect as it may be made. The theory of compensations is sometimes of inestimable value. It is even our only resource, where the structure of society is of so fixed a character as to give us a very limited control over the political institutions. But if these contrivances will not always continue to act with effect; if they do not cure all the defects which it would be desirable to reach; above all, if the society in which we are placed presents entirely new materials, it may be the part of wisdom to endeavor to reconstruct, in part, a system which has grown up under other and very different circumstances. To permit it to stand forever in the same position, would be a confession that what we term compensations are something wich makes amends for our own want of foresight and ability rather than for any inevitable fault in the system itself.

Public opinion in America was at one time universally in favor of the independence of the judiciary. In some parts of the union, there are at present many individuals of the greatest intelligence who are firmly attached to the scheme. They believe that the most untoward influences may be brought to bear upon the administration of justice, unless this is inserted as a fundamental principle in the government. My own opinion is, that once a nation has entered upon the task of self government, it is bound to encounter all the perils which are incident to it; and that these perils, numerous as they are, are among the means provided for preserving the integrity of the system. A nation which has once fairly entered upon this arduous career, has overcome the principal difficulty; all other obstacles will be surmounted as the people grow into the system. Perhaps many of the mischiefs which now incommode society, are a consequence of the rubbing together of old and new ideas. But when the new ideas become a thing of familiar apprehension and of daily exercise, the minds of men will take a wider survey of the whole field of experiment, and acquire more confidence in the results which may be expected. And this increase of confidence will add strength to the institutions—will give them the very support which they stand in need of. Nothing throws so many obstacles in the way of self government, as a denial of the right and ability of the people to engage in it. If on the other hand these are frankly conceded, and all intelligent men lend their assistance in carrying out the plan, everything will go easy.

An election for a term of years may be necessary, to enable the mind of the judge to keep pace with the general progress of knowledge, and more especially to make him acquainted with the diversified working of the institutions under which he lives; in the administration of a part of which he is engaged, but all parts of which are thoroughly connected. A public officer may be wonderfully skilled in all the mysteries of his profession, and yet lag miserably behind the age in which he lives. It is a great mistake to suppose, that because the judges are called to expound the principles of an abstruse science, that they should be insensible to the general movement of the age and country in which they are born; that they should live in society, and come perpetually in contact with the practical concerns of men, and yet be unaffected by the influence of public opinion. There is a very wide difference between being drawn from the path of rectitude and duty, by every temporary gust of party spirit, and submitting the mind to the healthful influence of those opinions and feelings which grow up in the progress of every improving society. The first unhinges the mind; the last refreshes and invigorates it. There is no public magistrate whose mind will not be enlarged and liberalized, whose views will not be rendered both more wise and just, by catching something from the influence of that public opinion which constitutes, to so great an extent, the regulative principle of society. There is no art, or calling, or profession, which is not greatly modified in practice through the instrumentality of this influence. But when the judge is sure, provided he commits no technical violation of duty, that he will retain his station for life, he is very apt to regard himself as entirely absolved from this control. And although he may not outrage the law in a single instance, he may give evidence of the narrowest views and the most rooted bigotry, which, although unperceived by himself, will give a tinge to the whole administration of justice. There is always a vast amount of large and enlightened views, and these popular ones too, pervading every society in which free institutions are established, which do not deserve to be treated as mere algebraical quantities; for although they do not exactly constitute the principles of any particular science, they surround every science and profession which have to deal with the interests of men, and afford light and assistance at every step which we take.

But the chief argument in favor of a limited tenure of office, is derived from the peculiar character and functions of a court of justice: so different from what they appear to be in theory, and so different from what they are actually supposed to be from a cursory observation. Such a tribunal does in effect partake, to a great extent, of the character of a legislative body. The idea commonly entertained is, that it is simply invested with the power of expounding the laws, which have been ordained by another and a distinct department of government; and this office it does undoubtedly perform. But this power of expounding comprehends a great deal, and reaches much further than is generally imagined. It at once communicates to a court of justice, the double character of a legislative and judicial tribunal. This is inevitable, and arises from the inherent imperfection which attends all human institutions. It is not in the power of any collection of men, formed into a legislative assembly.

however fertile in resources their understandings may be, to invent a system of ready-made rules which shall embrace all, or anything like all, the cases which actually occur. The consequence is, that a judicial tribunal which has been created with the avowed design of applying the laws as they are made, finds itself engaged in an endless series of disquisitions and reasonings, in order to ascertain the precise rule which is applicable to any particular case. The innumerable contracts, voluntary dispositions, and delinquencies of individuals, are perpetually giving a new form to private controversies, and present new views and new questions to the examination of the court. However full and however minute the code of laws may be in its provisions, a vast field is still left open for the exercise of the reasoning powers, and the sound discrimination of the judges. The cases of the "first impression," as the lawyers term them, are as numerous now as when Marshall and Kent took their seats upon the bench. It is not a reproach to the legal profession, that this should be so ; it is merely a curious and interesting fact in the history of jurisprudence, that the exigencies of society, the ever varying forms into which the transactions of business are thrown, should ramify to such an endless extent the rules which regulate the conduct of individuals. Perhaps it is no more than happens to every other department of knowledge ; for every conquest which science makes, every fresh accession it receives, only presents a new vantage ground, whence the mind can see further and take in a wider scope than it did before. But in jurisprudence, the experiments which are made are infinitely more numerous than in any other science ; and this contributes to modify and to attenuate, to a wonderful extent, the rules which have been made and the principles which have already been adjudged. For every question which arises, every case which is tried, is a new experiment which lays the foundation for new views and new analyses, and which the finer and more subtle they are, the more they escape from the grasp of general principles, and the greater the discretion which is conferred upon the courts of justice.

It is sometimes supposed, that all the decisions which are now made, all the rules which are declared, are mere deductions from some general principles which had been previously settled. But how far back, and by whom, were these principles settled ? Not by the legislature. The greatest genius which had devoted itself exclusively to the task, would be incompetent to its performance.

Hence the laws are comparatively few, while the books of jurisprudence are immensely voluminous. The human mind is able to invent very little. Its true employment consists in the observation and analysis of phenomena, after they have been developed, and in then binding them together into classes. And as this process of development, in the case of jurisprudence, is constantly going on, after as well as before the legislature have passed the most comprehensive laws, the functions of the judge, do what we will, or turn the question in whatever aspect we please, are compelled to bear a very close analogy with those of the law-making power. If all the rules which are now declared by the courts are mere corollaries from the statute book, or from previous adjudications, the same may have been said one or two hundred years ago, and then what is the meaning of that vast accumulation of learning which then exercised, and still continues to exercise, human ingenuity? Admitting that there are some sciences, where a few elementary truths being given, the whole mass of subordinate principles may be readily evolved from them—a proposition which may require further investigation, before it is admitted—yet, this cannot be the case with jurisprudence, which does not deal with abstract propositions simply; but with a state of facts, where the question is perpetually recurring—what does human experience prove to be the wisest rule, which can be adopted? or what does it prove to be the wisest construction of a rule already in existence?

Profound writers, and among others Leibnitz, and Dugald Stewart, have supposed that jurisprudence might be reduced to a regular and exact science, in which all our conclusions may be deduced with absolute rigor, and with the force of demonstration from certain previously established principles.* But to the question, how

* In "Nouveaux Essais de l'entendement," b. iv. chap. vii, Leibnitz says that jurisprudence and medicine differ widely in this respect; that in the former, we can deduce all our conclusions from certain general principles; that we want few books therefore, but in medicine we cannot have too many. But medicine depends upon our physical structure, jurisprudence upon both our physical and moral structure. Medicine is adapted to the constitutions of individuals, jurisprudence to collective societies of men. The last, therefore, must be the most complicated; it must require as much experience and observation, and therefore as wide an induction of facts, and as full a collection of those phenomena which we call *cases*. And, therefore, it is, that law books have always, in the age of Tribonian as well as that of Kent, been more numerous than medical works.

numerous shall these principles be, the most acute understanding can give no satisfactory answer. In every department of moral science, in order to be able to range a case under any particular principle, we must first go through a process of analysis more or less tedious. The principle may be taken for granted, and yet its applicability be determinable only after much investigation. If it is not only applicable to the whole extent, but requires to be modified, a thing of common occurrence, the foundation is immediately laid for a host of other principles, equally authoritative, and each claiming to control all the cases which can be brought under it; until at length, the process of analysis being pushed still farther, these principles give way before others still more numerous, which assume to be the guide, because they are more exactly applicable to a given state of facts. So that, admitting the great value of what are termed general principles—and hardly any one will deny it—what a wide field is notwithstanding opened to human ingenuity in tracing out the fine analogies which may connect a given controversy with an elementary truth. How different may be the judgments of different minds equally astute and ingenious, when exercised upon precisely the same state of facts. The functions of the court will still be resembled to those of a legislative body. There will be ample room for the operation of sinister motives, which will both warp the judgment and blind the moral vision. And the position which I have endeavored to enforce, will be true: that if it is not wise to confer a permanent tenure of office upon the executive and legislative, it should not be conferred upon the judiciary; and the more so, because the legislative functions which the last perform is a fact entirely hidden from the great majority of the community.

It is remarkable that some very enlightened minds should be so wedded to the independence of the judiciary, when in the nature of things, men must sometimes be elevated to the bench who are deficient in both the moral and intellectual qualities which are requisite: and when the only remedy which can be applied consists in re-eligibility. I, for one, protest against the adoption of a principle, which would secure an incompetent or badly-disposed judge in the possession of his place, for thirty or forty years, because he committed no flagrant violation of duty. It is not always a reflection upon the wisdom of the appointing power, that an improper person has been elected.

Very excellent lawyers have sometimes made indifferent judges ; and lawyers not the most eminent, have sometimes become very distinguished judges. Nor are the moral qualities of the man always sufficiently developed, to assure us what his future conduct will be, if he is placed for life in a situation of even tolerable ease. The experiment however must be made; and our only alternative is to provide a plan by which an unworthy or ignorant judge may be removed, as well as a fit one be continued in office. And admitting that no scheme will be entirely successful in accomplishing either the one or the other, I do suppose, that none which can be invented will so well answer all the ends which we are in search of, as an election for a moderate term of years.

The purity of character and the eminent learning of the English judges have always been the subject of commendation, and certainly it does not become any one who is not furnished with the most exact information, to detract from this high praise. That the English judges, as a body, have been superior to those of the states of continental Europe, may be conceded ; but at the same time it is clear that there may be numberless improprieties and aberrations from the strict path of duty, which the exceedingly technical character of the English system of procedure would entirely conceal from the public eye. Moreover, the English bench is connected with the aristocracy. The two institutions are glued together. And whenever society is distributed into distinct classes, it is difficult for those who are out of a particular class to penetrate into its interior, so as to observe and understand everything which is transacted within it. It is only incidentally that we are able to catch anything which sheds light upon the manners of English judges.

The peculiar interest which attached to the life of Savage, caused his biography to be written by one of the most remarkable men of the day, who has related the very extraordinary behavior of the judge who sat upon the trial. An eminent Englishman, in his sketch of Lord Ellenborough, has detailed the high-handed course which that eminent judge pursued on the trial of some very important state cases.

In France, where the tenure of the judges is the same as in Great Britain, it has always been the custom for suitors to visit the judges. The practice, to say the least, does not look well. It may not be attended with any improper influence. But a violation of decorum is often a stepping stone to the commission of some graver fault. The system of bribery, once universally in vogue, may have been entirely abandoned, but an intelligent traveler who lately attended the trial of a case in a French court, tells us that he saw the judge who presided driving the splendid equipage in which a few days be fore the successful suitor traveled to the assizes.

Indeed if one were disposed to look to England, to furnish us with a body of experience, which would help to decide this interesting question, we might find arguments in favor of the absolute dependence of the judges, as decisive as those which are employed on the opposite side of the question. For the chancellor, the judges of the admirality, and of the ecclesiastical courts, are removable at any time, and yet these magistrates have been in every respect equal to their brethren of the common-law courts.

The judicial system of the American States, differs in many respects from that established in Great Britain. As civil government is not understood to exist for the purpose of creating a splendid and imposing pageant of authority, all the institutions are made to administer in the most easy, effectual, and unostentatious manner, to the practical wants of the community. To cause justice to be dispensed thoroughly, extensively, and with the least cost and parade, has been the governing idea in the organization of the courts. It is not enough to possess such tribunals unless they are completely within the reach of every one who has a complaint to make before them. England, and Wales, with a population of eighteen millions, have about twenty judges assigned to the superior courts. The United States, with a population a little larger, have more than two hundred.

I take no account in the enumeration of the county courts, courts of request, and other subordinate tribunals, which are established in the former country, since the business transacted by them all falls within the jurisdiction of justices of the peace in America, whose numbers amount to many thousands. I simply confine myself to those courts, which in the two countries exercise a corresponding jurisdiction. The disparity there is immense, and it is a fact full of interest, and instruction. No man who is not clad in an armor of gold can gain entrance into the English court of chancery : and no man can litigate effectually in the king's bench, or common pleas.

unless his circumstances are very independent. Very different is the state of things in the United States. Local courts, of a high as well as of an inferior jurisdiction, are established throughout the whole country; and amply compensate by their intrinsic utility for the want of pageantry and show. But this consequence follows, that however easy it may be to select twenty men with splendid salaries, to occupy very imposing stations in the government; it may be a matter of very considerable difficulty to induce two hundred to accept office, where the duties are unremitting and arduous, the salaries low, and where the occupation, although of an intellectual character, is yet seldom sufficiently so to fill the mind and to gratify a high ambition. The law being an exhausted science, so far as regards the leading principles, the business transacted by the courts becomes one chiefly of detail, not requiring faculties so high as formerly, but demanding more patience and assiduity, and a greater degree of tact in the performance of the duties. What is sought after in America, and what should be the object of pursuit in every other civilized state, is a judicial system which shall do the business, the whole business, and nothing but the business; and this in the most prompt and effectual manner practicable. And this end cannot be attained without the establishment of numerous courts of superior jurisdiction, and without therefore running the risk of sometimes procuring incompetent persons to act as judges. The average number of court days in all the six circuits in England (exclusive of London) is one hundred and thirty-five. The average number in each of the fifteen circuits in the single state of Ohio, whose population is not more than two millions, is one hundred and sixty-three. It is no wonder that want of time to try the case was assigned as one reason for proceeding by impeachment, rather than by indictment, against the late Lord Melville. That the risk incurred in selecting proper persons to set upon the bench in America has turned out to be much less than was calculated, may be matter of surprise: but that it will always exist to some extent, is a decisive reason why the judges should be chosen for a term of years. Even in England, we are assured upon very high authority, that not more than twenty lawyers can be found competent to fill the place of "puisne" judge. But if the courts were more numerous, and the demand for ability greater, there can be no doubt that the supply would keep pace with it; and that there would be no more difficulty in obtaining two hundred, than there is now of obtaining twenty judges.*

At the present day the tenure for life is abolished in nearly one half of the American states. The term of office varies considerably in different parts of the Union. In Pennsylvania it is fifteen years, while in Vermont it is only one year. In the greater number the period is seven years. So far as we may judge from the books of reports, I do not know that any courts have given evidence of more solid and extensive learning than those of New Jersey, where the duration of the office under both the late and present constitutions is eight years. And Indiana, where the system is the same, furnishes the example of a very young community immediately springing forward in this career of improvement. The decisions of her supreme court are also marked by uncommon ability and learning.

In Pennsylvania, the system has been recently adopted; but there is every reason to believe, that her courts will continue to maintain the high reputation which they have hither enjoyed. In Connecticut, it is quite remarkable that before the independent tenure was introduced, and when the elections were annual, the bench was eminently distinguished for the learning ability, and integrity of the members who composed it. I believe I do not exaggerate, when I say that five or six of the judges who sat in her superior court prior to the constitution of 1818, would have done honor to any of the courts of Westminster hall. By causing the administration of justice to penetrate every part of the community, the conduct of the judges, in America, is submitted to a more thorough observation and scrutiny, by the public at large, than in any other country. And as it is the people, and none but the people, who are interested in the upright and impartial administration of the laws, an unworthy man, who has fortuitously wriggled himself into office, will stand an uneven chance for re-election.

For what period shall the judges be elected? is a question to which different minds may give different answers. Nor is it very

* During the Cromwellian Revolution in England, the professors in the universities were removed, and dissenters appointed in their place. On the restoration of Charles II, the new incumbents were found to be so entirely competent to the discharge of their duties, that no thought was entertained of removing them. They all retained their places.

important what the precise period shall be. Once the system of responsibility is established, we have made sure of the ruling principle which is to guide in the constitution of the courts, and the greater or less exactness with which it is applied, is a matter of minor consideration. I should say that the term should not be less than five, nor more than ten years. One reason why the members of the legislative body are elected for so short a period as one or two years, is to introduce the great body of the citizens to an acquaintance with public affairs, and to cultivate in them an ability to take part in their management. Free institutions are a security for the preservation of liberty, only because they lay the foundation for that discipline of the character, which enables us to know and appreciate what liberty is. But the law is a science which no more than theology or medicine, can be made the study of the great bulk of the people. It is necessarily the exclusive pursuit of a small number, whose training and education, both before and after they are admitted to the bar, is obliged to take a direction which conspires to a single end. The legislature is a numerous body; the free and discursive character of the debate, and the large dimensions which very many questions assume, force upon the mind of almost every member some tolerable acquaintance with their purport and bearing. But a single controversy at the bar, in order to be grasped, may demand the most minute and painful attention of even the professors of the science: so much so, that it is not at all uncommon for a lawyer who has been present, but not engaged in a particular trial, to feel himself at a loss, if he undertakes to give a distinct account of the testimony, and of the precise legal questions which were mooted. It is not because the law is a cabalistical science, that it is full of perplexity; it is because it deals so much in detail, and because it is impossible to get rid of this detail, when we are obliged to apply our knowledge to the multifarious transactions of human life. The general principles by which the mercantile body conduct their affairs, are pretty much the same everywhere; yet how much caution, attention, and sagacity, are sometimes necessary in settling a long and intricate account, even where no difficult, legal question intervenes. I would, therefore, make the tenure of the judges long enough to induce lawyers of competent ability to abandon the profession in exchange for that office; while at the same time, I would not make it so long as to absolve the judges from a strict responsibility to the community. I would rather increase the salaries than part with the dependent tenure.

The manner in which the laws are administered, the exterior deportment of the bar and bench, are a matter of very great importance. The business habits which are acquired by an experience of some years, insure promptitude, skill and dispatch, in the decision of legal controversies. The trial of cases is conducted with ease, order, and regularity. The confidence of suitors is greatly and justly increased by this circumstance. Instead of altercations between the judge and the advocate which so much disturb the regular course of business, and detract from the weight of the court, every thing proceeds in an even and regular manner. Integrity of purpose is not of more consequence than ability; for without knowledge, there is no room for the exercise of integrity. A judge may intend very well in the general, and yet be unable to mean any thing distinct, when it becomes all important for him to act and to make his integrity apparent in the things which he does. The term of office, therefore, should be long enough to enable the public to make a fair trial of the ability and moral qualities of the incumbent; and not so long as to prevent a removal in a reasonable time, if he is deficient in either.

I have referred to the system of legal precedents, as constituting a salutary check upon the conduct of judges. It now becomes necessary to approach this subject more closely, and to explain distinctly the view I have taken, in order that we may be able to understand, in its full extent, what is the force and operation of precedents. But if any thing is said which goes to qualify the proposition I before laid down, the reader must not therefore run away with idea that there is contradiction. Political philosophy has to encounter the same difficulties which beset jurisprudence. Our principles have to be constantly modified, but they are not therefore to be dispensed with.

When one considers the vast amount of adjudged cases which are already reported in the United States alone, it is obvious that the utmost attention and patience may be necessary to decipher them, when they are appealed to as rules, or as mere guides in the determination of particular cases. They will be a very ineffectual check upon one who is unable to seize their import, and to appreciate them for exactly what they are worth. The principles of jurisprudence in almost every one of its departments have been so exceedingly ramified by the multitude of similar, or very nearly similar controversies, that the shades of difference between different precedents are often so minute, as to hold the judgment in suspense as to which should be relied upon. And yet they may conduct to totally different conclusions in a given case. The consequence is, that a very considerable proportion of the cases which are actually decided might be determined either way with a great show of reason, and with a like reliance upon precedents in either case. This observation will startle the general reader, but it will not fail to be comprehended by the learned and experienced jurist. Nor is it more remarkable than what is daily exhibited in all courts of justice, to wit, the appearance of lawyers of known integrity, on different sides of a case, each arguing with zeal and perfect conviction for the correctness of the views he advocates. Persons who are imperfectly informed, believe that this practice is totally inconsistent with the uprightness which should belong to the members of any profession. Others look upon it as something which can be explained in no way whatever. But in truth it is not imputable to dishonesty, nor is it incapable of reasonable explanation. It is a natural consequence of the nature of the science, which having to deal with an infinity of detail, necessarily runs out into an infinity of deductions and conclusions, which perpetually modify and cross each other. Independently of a number of cases which are settled out of court, by the advice of the profession, and of a number which might be equally settled in the same way, there are still a greater number where the principles appealed to on either side are very evenly balanced.

But this very important consequence follows: that in many cases where the distinctions are fine, and the authority of precedents is half obliterated, an ill-disposed judge may cast his piejudices into the scale in order to decide the controversy, without his motives being suspected by an one, or if suspected, without the possibility of being detected. The judge who has a competent share of the pride of human opinion; the lawyer who believes that jurisprudence is a science "par excellence," a science of strict and immutable rules, may demur to these views; but I am satisfied they will gain the assent of a majority of both the bench and the bar. And if they are well founded, they afford powerful reasons why th judicial tenure should not be for life. By submitting the conduct of the judge, during a limited period, to the observation of the public, in those instances where his motives and reasons will be apprehended, the probability is less that he will on any occasion, free himself from the restraint which a sense of duty should invariably impose upon him. The public feel as if they had no right to scan the conduct of a public magistrate who has a freehold right to his office. He is protected from all intrusion of this kind, except where he is guilty of some open delinquency. An election for a term of years removes this indisposition on the part of the public to observe the course which the administration of justice takes. The judge, sensible that his actions are the subject of attention, and not knowing to what extent this scrutiny may be pushed, becomes more circumspect in his conduct; and as it is difficult to impress two contradictory habits upon any one, whether public or private individual, his conduct will more readily conform to that one which is dictated equally by self interest, and by a regard to duty.

I have not yet adverted to another, and a deeply interesting question: whether the judges should be elected directly by the people, or by an intermediate authority. The last is the plan adopted in the great majority of the American states, as well as in the government of the union. But the intermediate body which appoints, is not the same in all these instances. In Maine, Massachusetts, and New Hampshire, the appointment is made by the governor and council. In eight states, as well as in the federal government, the executive and senate appoint. In rather more than one-half of the states, the election is made by the two branches of the legislature. Delaware stands alone in this respect, for the governor has the sole power of appointment.

The great object to be obtained in organizing the courts, is to select persons who are every way qualified to discharge the duties. But the qualities which are requisite in a judge, are different in many respects from what are demanded in any other public officer, and the selection is proportionally more difficult. It is not because the ability of the people to make a fair choice is distrusted, that this power has been delegated; it is because they are supposed not to have the opportunity of forming a correct judgment. The seat of government is the place where information from all parts of the state is collected, and where abundant materials exist for forming a proper estimate of the qualities of candidates. Members of the legislative body are properly elected in districts in which they reside; and these districts are of so convenient a size, that the qualifications of the candidates are under the immediate observation of the electors. With regard to the governor, whose duties in most of the states are few, it is not necessary that he should be versed in any particular science, though no species of learning or accomplishment is amiss in any public officer, but adds greatly to his reputation, and gives illustration to the state over which he presides. The case of the judges differs materially from both these classes of public officers. The learning and accomplishments which are demanded of them are of such a character, that the great body of the citizens are neither desirous nor have any interest in acquiring them. As an individual therefore of the soundest judgment and the fairest intentions, who has not within his reach the information upon which he desires to act, deputes another to act for him, so the American people, for similar reasons, have delegated to agents immediately responsible to them the difficult task of selecting fit persons to preside in the courts of justice. That an individual voluntarily avails himself of the intervention and services of another, is proof of his liberty, not of his constraint; and that a whole people should proceed upon the same obvious and rational views, may denote the exercise of the most enlightened freedom.

It must not be imagined, that in every instance where the public authority is delegated, the power of the people is therefore abridged. Rousseau was mistaken in supposing that, wherever the people act through the instrumentality of agents, they are free only during the moments of the election; that the choice being made, power has departed from them, not to be resumed until the return of another election. This may be true to a greater or less extent in the artificial forms of government, where so many of the magistrates not being elective, but holding by hereditary title, wield an authority which counterbalances that of the people, and so effectually controls public opinion. But in a democratic republic, it is precisely the reverse. As the principle of responsibility runs through all the institutions, no one can escape from it in order to shelter himself under an independent authority. It is true that, construct government as we will, there will always be a tendency, in some part or other, to elude the control of public opinion. But where the great body of the institutions is sound, the utmost degree of exactness and theoretical propriety may be a matter of indifference: like an individual possessing a fine constitution, and robust health, and who does not take every sort of precaution against changes of the weather; a people in the full possession of free institutions, need not guard themselves too tenderly against every possible contingency. The intervention of a jury in all common law trials, renders such extreme scrupulousness less necessary in the constitution of the judiciary, than in that of the other departments.

But a great revolution has just been effected in one of the American states. The new constitution of New York has ordained that the judges of all the courts shall be elected directly by the people. This I regard as one of the greatest experiments which has ever been made upon human nature. This single feature in that constitution, stamps the convention which framed it as the most important which has ever sat in America since the formation of the federal constitution. Nor can it be viewed as a hasty or visionary scheme, since the assembly which planned it was composed of an unusual number of able men; of men who united, in a high degree, all the qualities which are necessary to make up the character of wise and enlightened statesmen: experience, sagacity, and information, and a desire to innovate for the sole purpose of reforming. No public measure which has been adopted in America has so powerfully arrested my attention, or given me more painful anxiety. The conclusion to which I have come, forming my judgment from the general character of the population, is, that if the experiment does not succeed, the people will cheerfully retrace their steps. But I am strongly inclined to think that it will succeed. There is such a thing as making an institution succeed, however much it may appear to run counter to the received opinions of the day. This repugnance may be the only obstacle to success. If the people of New York persevere in the immense exertions which they have hitherto made, to educate themselves; and if, in consequence, a thorough conviction is imbibed, not merely as something gained from others, but as realized by themselves, that an upright and enlightened administration of justice is indispensable to the protection of their interests, I cannot doubt that the experiment will succeed. Mischiefs will exist, and precisely of the same kind as those which now trouble the community: the disposition to centralization; the effort on the part of political leaders to control public opinion; the substitution of a constructive majority, in place of the real majority. But with a state of society such as is fast growing up from the operation of causes which I have referred to, I can easily conceive that these evils may be warded off as effectually, and perhaps more so, than under the old system. So important a movement can only be regarded, at present, as an experiment; and it has been most justly remarked of the Americans, that they possess the faculty of making experiments in government, with less detriment to themselves than any other people.

But any one who was attentive to the circumstances under which the New York convention assembled, and who watched throughout the course of the proceedings, must be sensible that there is a soundness of public opinion in that state which will prevail upon the people to retract, if the experiment is not successful. It should be observed, however, that the same constitutional provision exists in the state of Mississippi, and has been in operation for more than ten years. Even this experiment is too recent to enable us to pronounce a decisive opinion upon. The scale upon which it is made being so much smaller than in the other case, the plan has attracted very little public attention. But if it does succeed in both these states—if it succeeds in New York alone—it will probably be adopted throughout the greater number of the American states. And I predict that it will then be the parent of more important changes, in both government and society, than have been brought about by any other single measure.

The theory of the judiciary cannot be well understood unless we take into consideration the uses of jury trial, an institution which exercises so wide and salutary an influence upon the administration of justice.

First. The juries act as a check upon the conduct of the judge. He discharges his most important functions not only in the presence of, but with the co-operation and assistance, of his fellow citizens. The jury are not chosen as in the Roman commonwealth, from a patrician body; they are taken indiscriminately from the great mass of the people. The responsibility is consequently increased; his deportment and actions are not merely observed by the spectator, they are narrowly watched by those who participate in the trial, and to whom is committed the ultimate determination of the issue. Benjamin Constant proposed that the juries should be selected from the class of electors: that is, from among those who pay a tax of from fifty to sixty dollars. And this is now the law. In Great Britain the qualifications of jurors are also very nearly the same as those of the electors. But the latter being much more numerous than the French electors, the jury is a more popular body. In America, the same reasons which led to the adoption of a liberal rule of suffrage, have also augmented the number of persons qualified to act as jurymen.

Second. The institution of the jury introduces the great bulk of the people to an acquaintance with the practical working of the laws, interests them in their faithful administration, and contributes to train them to an ability for self government. "He only," it has been said, "is fitted to command, who has learned to obey;" he only is fitted to take the lead, who has already passed through the subordinate ranks.

Third. The intervention of the jury helps to mitigate the extreme rigor of general rules, to give effect to the import of general maxims, and yet occasionally to make allowance for that infinite variety of shades in human transactions, of which the laws cannot take cognizance.

Fourth. Juries stand in the place of impartial spectators, and are therefore well calculated to act as umpire in settling controversies among their neighbors. This is an office which could not be so well performed by a pre-existing tribunal. As I have already observed, it is an inestimable advantage which we derive from a regular judicial establishment, that it extinguishes the motives for private war, the most deplorable of all the calamities which can visit society. This benefit, however, would not be so perfect, if it were not for the jury, whose composition is such as to inspire general confidence in the fairness of all law proceedings.

Fifth. The intervention of a jury gives publicity to trials. The disuse of the institution on the continent of Europe, consequent on the introduction of the Roman law, was the cause why the proceedings in a court of justice became secret. As long as the "prodes homines," the jury, were a necessary part of the machinery, judicial investigations were a matter of curiosity to the public. As soon as they were dispensed with, and the whole evidence was collected in the form of depositions, legal controversies gave rise merely to a discussion of technical points, and the public no longer felt an interest in them. The halls of justice were thenceforth abandoned to the judge and the advocate. What was once a custom soon became a law, and at the present day, trials are for the most part conducted in secret, throughout the greater part of continental Europe.

The non-introduction, or rather the partial introduction of the civil law into England, accounts for the preservation of jury trials there, and for the remarkable publicity which law proceedings have always had. The fifty-fifth section of the French constitution of 1830, declares that the trial of criminal causes shall be conducted in public, except in those instances where publicity would be injurious to decency and good morals; and the court is bound to announce that as a reason for sitting in private;—a very remarkable state of society, when it was reserved for a constitutional ordinance, to provide that the halls of justice should be thrown open to the inspection of the public. But jury trial was unknown in France until the revolution; it is no part now of the procedure in civil cases. Its introduction in criminal trials is the reason why they have been rendered public. Not only was the examination in secret, but there could be no cross-examination; for the only person entitled to ask questions was the judge. It is but recently that this unnatural custom has been put an end to, and that counsel on behalf of the prisoner have been permitted to assist in the examination. In Scotland, where the civil law has from time immemorial constituted the foundation of the jurisprudence, juries were unknown until 1815, in any but criminal cases. They were then for the first time introduced as an experiment into one of the civil courts of Edinburgh; and they are now a constituent part of the procedure in the court of sessions. The practice of conducting trials in public secures two distinct and very important ends. It operates as a safeguard against corruption, and it prevents the administration of justice from becoming odious to the people. In some parts of Europe, the criminal magistrates and officers are regarded with detestation and horror. They are looked upon as the instruments of an infernal tyranny; whom the innocent shun, and even shudder to approach. This is not the feeling in Great Britain or the United States. As the proceedings are conducted openly, the public may be said to take part in them. The fate of the criminal may be deplored; but every one feels that he is condemned rather by the public voice than by the sentence of the judge.

There is one respect in which the institution of jury trial has been disadvantageous. It has caused the rules of evidence to be more strict than they would have otherwise been. The manner in which this has been brought about is very easily explained. The composition of juries originally, and for centuries after the institution took its rise, was such as not to permit the committing to them any evidence, which might by possibility be misinterpreted, or misapplied. Certain rules were consequently adopted, which shut out every species of testimony which, in order to be rightly used, would demand a degree of caution and discrimination which could not be expected in the persons who made up the jury. The evidence excluded (and which was denominated incompetent) might shed abundant light upon all trials, if it were confided to persons of judgment and good sense. But the condition of European society was generally low; and juries necessarily partook of the same character. The consequence is that the rules of evidence have been gradually molded into a system so exceedingly artificial and complex, that in the endeavor to correct one mischief, another equally dangerous has been incurred. A great deal of truth has been shut out, in order to prevent some falsehood from gaining entrance. And this system, having once taken root, has been continued long after the state of things which occasioned it has passed away. The constitution of American society is such that juries are every way competent to the management of that testimony which is now declared inadmissible. By the Belgian code, lately promulgated, the only persons who are absolutely excluded from giving testimony, are the parties, relatives in the direct line, and husband and wife.

At an early period of society, the human mind does not dare to trust itself with any but the roughest and the most general rules. It feels an utter inability to enter into long inquiries: to compare and to balance a great many items of testimony, in order to elicit the truth from the whole, instead of from a part. For fear of doing wrong, it shuts itself up within a narrow circle; although the effect is to preclude a great deal of information and knowledge. But as society advances, the vision becomes more clear and distinct, and the rules which are framed for the conduct of every department of life are rendered more free and liberal.

The Livingston code of Louisiana, as originally drawn up, excluded none as witnesses, except attorneys and catholic confessors. Parties, however, were admitted with this limitation : their evidence could not be proffered by themselves ; but must be demanded by the opposite party, by the court, or by the jury. In England, and New York, efforts have recently been made to annul the distinction between competency and credibility : to permit parties and persons interested to testify in all cases, leaving their credit to be determined by the jury. And what sensible reason can be given, why parties should be permitted to testify in one form of proceeding, and not in another ? in chancery suit, and not on a common law trial ? When the grand jury ("jury d' accusation") was introduced in France, the experiment for many years was deemed absolutely hopeless. It was found impossible to make the members understand the distinction, between the finding of a true bill and a sentence of conviction. They supposed that the first involved the last, and often refused to find bills where there was the strongest "prima facie" evidence of guilt. No such misapprehension exists among the English or American grand juries. Still less would there be any misunderstanding with an English or American traverse jury, as to the relative weight of the testimony, some part of which was unexceptionable, and another open to examination ; for the daily transactions of life, their ordinary business avocations, thoroughly initiate them into this manner of viewing and employing testimony. I think there can be little doubt, that in no long time, a more liberal system will be established, and that every one will be convinced that it conduces to a much more enlightened and satisfactory administration of justice.

The admission of the testimony of all those persons who are at present excluded (and I know of no case which should form an exception) would diminish the number of suits, and in those which were tried, would cause the truth to be elicited more promptly and successfully. Greater solemnity would be imparted to all judicial proceedings, when the evidence of persons who knew all about the transactions was thoroughly sifted, instead of applying, as is now the case, to witnesses who know very imperfectly or only by piecemeal. If a defendant in a criminal prosecution were in all instances examined, real delinquents would feel more terror of the law, and innocent persons would have greater respect for it.

Whether the rule of unanimity, or that of a majority, should prevail in the finding of a verdict, is a question which has been much debated in France, since the introduction of jury trial in 1789. The rule of the majority has been constantly adopted there. By the law of 1789, this majority was fixed at 8 : 4. By that of 1791, at 9 : 3, and by that of 1835, at 7 : 5. And recently a proposition for another change has been discussed in the house of deputies, but I am not informed what the result has been. M. Isambert says, if the English rule of unanimity had been adopted in France, such men as Bailly, Lavoisier, and Malesherbes, would never have been condemned. The greater part of the judgments of the revolutionary tribunal were made by a fraction. M. Fermot has calculated, that where the majority is 7 : 5, the probability of error is as 1 : 4, indifferently in favor of and against the accused. Where it is 8 : 4, the chance of error is 1 : 8, and where unanimity is required, it is 1 : 8000. These are calculations which should make Englishmen and Americans prize the rule of unanimity even more than they have done. For although in the even tenor of ordinary times, there should be as little probability of error under the French as under the English and American rule, yet, when the elements of society are greatly disturbed, and the minds of men are heated by party spirit, the jury, and the unanimity of the jury are the shield of the innocent. Unanimity is attended with this advantage: it compels to more discussion and deliberation among the jury. The verdict which in practice is very generally the verdict of a majority, is the result of a more patient examination, and is therefore more likely to be unexceptionable. In Scotland, the rule of unanimity prevails in civil, and yet not in criminal cases: the reverse of what one would suppose should be the case. But the employment of the jury (composed of fifteen) in criminal trials, dates very far back, and was a distinguishing feature of Scotch institutions; whereas, the jury of twelve, in civil causes, was copied directly from England; the court in which the experiment was first made was presided over by an English barrister, and nothing seemed so natural as to establish the English rule of unanimity.

One of the greatest difficulties which attend the administration of the law, is the exceedingly technical character which the system has acquired. This is the chief of the popular objections which are ever made to it, and I am persuaded that it had great influence in carrying forward the plan of judicial reform in New York. The objection may be ill conceived, and yet the reform may prove to be salutary. For let us analyze our ideas. Does this character of technicality arise from the fact that the legal profession have been in the habit of following a principle, or has it arisen from an adherence to precedents. If the first is the case, the law differs in no respect from any other pursuit in which the exercise of mind is demanded, from the practice of medicine down to the most inconsiderable of the mechanic arts. One cannot conceive of administering justice in a civilized community, except upon some previously established rules. But this difficulty presents itself: that where a science deals so extensively, and yet so much in detail, with the practical interests of men, as is the case with the law, principles which were at first broad, and clearly distinguishable, become in the course of time exceedingly ramified, and our distinctions are then so fine, that it is almost impossible to found a conclusion simply upon a rule of abstract justice. When this is the case, a new course is adopted, as subsidiary to finding the principle. The question then raised is, what does human experience as tested by a great number of adjudications, prove to be the best mode of applying the law, in those countless instances where the rule of right in the abstract seems to be indifferent? As jurisprudence is eminently an experimental science, it is very important to ascertain to what extent a system of practice contributes to the public weal. Now, in innumerable instances, precedents are looked to, because the abstract principle is so shadowy that it cannot be explored, and yet it is of infinite consequence, if we can, to cling to some rule which has a near affinity to a principle, while at the same time, a number of years of experience may bring the matter to a test, and enable the legislator to ascertain whether any and what changes will be advantageous. The frequent revisions of the laws in the American states is one effort to attain this end. And there is a further plan which would recommend that it should be made the duty of the judges to make annual reports as to the working of specified parts of the system.

In administering this technical science then, the inquiry is, are we following a principle, or only a precedent? If the former, how do we obtain the principle? When it is asked, is it right to murder or steal? the answer is plain enough. If it is asked, ought B to pay A a sum of money he borrowed from him? the answer also is plain. But the instances are without number, where our principles become so dim that we are warned to pursue a new direction in order to find them. We are enabled to discover what is useful, by knowing what is right, and we are enabled to find out what is right, by understanding what is truly useful. The two are never disjoined.

But whatever may be the cause of the exceeding technicality of the law, whether it arises from the adoption of principles, or the adoption of precedents, or from both together, as is undoubtedly the case, there is no possible way of avoiding it; nor is there any one science, profession, or art, to which the same difficulty does not adhere. It is more apparent in the case of the law than in any other calling, because the science is applied in such infinite detail to the actions of men, and because this application is to so great an extent the subject of popular observation. That is to say, the very thing which stamps upon the law its character of excellence and utility, its application to the infinitely diversified affairs of society, is the foundation of the objection, and the open and public administration of it is what gives occasion to the complaint. If the law were applied as sparingly as it is in despotic countries, it would lose this character of complexity immediately. It is in proportion as civilization advances, and the institutions become free, that our knowledge becomes both more full and more minute, and that every profession or art which springs from knowledge becomes more difficult in the management. This is doubtless a wise dispensation of Providence: that in proportion as the temptation to abuse our power or our liberty increases, new bulwarks may be raised up to restrain our actions.

But in what I have now said, I do not mean to be understood that a great deal may not be done to free the law from the artificial character which it has acquired. On the contrary, I am persuaded that a field is here opened, in which wise and judicious minds may perform inestimable good for society. The abolition of the distinction between competency and credibility, would go a great way. And the abolition of the various forms of action at common law, and the substitution of one simple form, as in chancery proceedings— these two alone, would sweep away a multitude of refined and artificial rules which now incumber the practice. But what I do mean to say is (and I know the exceeding difficulty of propounding or conceiving two things which appear to conflict, although, in reality one only qualifies the other), that do as we will, make what disposition we please of jurisprudence, it is absolutely impossible, even if it were desirable, to free it from its character of technicality. This is a quality which will forever belong to it, so long as it has any pretension to the character of a science, and so long as it is understandingly and uprightly administered. If we suppose all our present legal institutions destroyed, the courts abolished, the books of law burned, society a mere "tabula rosa" to begin again, new tribunals established, with directions to have no reference to any existing elementary works or precedents, a system would nevertheless, in process of time, grow up, quite as technical as that which now exists. One single circumstance, and yet one which cannot be dispensed with, would insure this : to wit, the commanding that the decisions of all the higher tribunals shall be reduced to writing and published. English law never assumed a decidedly technical character, until this important safeguard was interposed between the courts and the public. And what, in the case supposed, will be the consequence of this admirable practice, independently of its operation as a check upon the courts ?—that the minds of the profession will immediately fall into a train of generalization. Certain fundamental principles will be grasped, a classification of them will be made, as applicable to different departments of the law, other principles subordinate to them will be seized, principles within principles, as in all other sciences ; and yet the last not evolved from the first, but only classed under them after the induction is made. The amount of business will increase, the pile of precedents will also increase, an abundance of elementary works will be written, embodying the decisions, and rendering the law more scientific in form, and yet more approachable and more intelligible to the profession. The same process will be gone through as heretofore. A fabric will be erected, vast, complicated, and full of labyrinths to the ignorant, and yet differing in no one respect from any other system ot knowledge, except in its more extensive application to the actual business of men.

For what are technical rules ? It is of the utmost importance to distinguish between what is artificial and what is technical. Every rule which is artificial is technical ; but very many are technical without being artificial. A technical rule, then, is nothing more than a general principle. When we begin with it, in the case of A or B, there is nothing intricate about it ; it is more like a simple statement of the circumstances of the case. But the case of A or B, soon comes to be the case of thousands, each varying in some particulars. Then, our difficulty commences. The mind is compelled to look further, to extend its principles more and more, and yet at the same time to be minute and ever on the watch in its examination. As the research will embrace objects entirely new, a new class of ideas will be formed, and new names will be given to them. Or, as is very commonly the case, old and well understood words will be used, and yet the connection in which they are found, although the most natural imaginable, will instantly give them a character of abstruseness. For instance, the words remainder and condition are ordinary English terms, familiarly used in common life. And yet what an infinite fund of learning is attached to them, of which there is no possible way to get rid, without encountering difficulties infinitely more formidable than those which are complained of. No man not a physician can understand the language of a physician. No man not a mathematician, or chemist, or political economist, can understand them. Nay, no man not a mechanician, a horticulturist, or agriculturist, can go but a very little way along with those who have devoted themselves to these pursuits, and have made them the subject of direct application to the affairs of life. The language of every one of these persons is highly technical; because having bent their minds upon one particular pursuit, they have obtained new ideas, have learned to classify them, and have given them appropriate names. How, then, should there be such exceeding difficulty in understanding why the law is, and forever must be, a technical science. No one can feel a greater interest than myself in seeing what is artificial in the law swept away; but no one is more sensible of our utter inability to give it any other character than that of a technical science.

The law applied to land titles in Virginia, and to the military districts in Ohio, is a remarkable example how vain all our efforts must be to communicate to any branch of jurisprudence a phraseology which shall be other than technical. This part of the law is almost exclusively the creation of the courts of Kentucky. It grew up when these courts were in their infancy, when there was no previously accumulated learning to help to give it a technical air, and in a state which was less disposed than any other to adopt any part of the refined system which prevailed in England, and other states. It is the only state, I believe, in which there existed a positive prohibition, not only to the reference to English reports as authority, but against reading them at all in court. The state of society was simple; the community was composed of farmers; the foundation of titles was different from what it was anywhere else; so that it could borrow no assistance from the real-property law of Great Britain. Everything was favorable to the building of a system which, if possible, should be free from technicality. But it was found absolutely impossible to effect this. The simplest elements of title, a warrant, an entry, and a survey, familiarly apprehended by all the settlers, and called by those names as soon as the process of legal investigation commenced, were recognized in every case, and yet in cases so endlessly diversified, that a system of classification and of rules became speedily necessary in order that a court of justice should not be converted into the bed of Procrustes. For technical rules are adopted, not to obstruct, but to further the regular and just administration of the laws. This system, so perfectly unique in its principles, and yet reduced to so much precision, is a monument of the wisdom and ability of the courts of Kentucky. It has now nearly performed its office, that of settling land titles, and will hereafter be regarded, by those who are fond of looking into the history of laws and institutions, as a remarkable instance of the fertility of the human mind, and of its capacity for framing general rules, even where the materials are the most scanty.

I can imagine one way in which the popular institutions of the United States may succeed in modifying, perhaps in entirely overthrowing, the vast system of technical jurisprudence which is now in use. The profession of the law may come to be regarded as an aristocratic institution. The path to it may be laid open, by admitting every one who pleases to practice, as is the case in some of the states with the medical profession. This by itself would effect very little; for so long as a learned and enlightened system was upheld by the courts, it must be appealed to by all practitioners; and the license to plead would be an empty privilege. The lawyer must still show his ability, in order to succeed. But in addition to this arrangement the judges may be selected, not from the class of jurists, but like members of the legislature, from the citizens indiscriminately. This last movement would at once sweep away all use of precedents; for it would be impossible to construct them. The law would cease to be a science, or a branch of knowledge. The administration of justice would be likened to that of a Mohammedan judge, who founds his judgments upon the circumstances of each particular case as it arises, who professes to be guided by the dictates of good sense merely; and whose appreciation therefore of the value of experience, as well as his notions of right and wrong, are the most crude imaginable.

But first, there is less probability that the profession in the United States, will be regarded as an aristocratic institution, than there is any other country. Lawyers do not compose a distinct corps. They are not collected in one great city, as is pretty much the case in England and Scotland. They are dispersed over the whole country; and are not distinguished by any privileges from the general mass of citizens. I shall take occasion, hereafter, to notice more particularly this very remarkable feature of American society.

Second, as regards the scientific character of the law, and the use of precedents; or what is the same thing, the appointment of persons to administer justice, who shall be capable of analyzing their ideas, of forming an intelligible exposition of their judgments; and then causing their opinions to be recorded, there is no way of dispensing with these things, unless we resolve to go back to a state of society different in so many respects from the high civilization which now exists. We desire to free the law from its technicality, and we remove all check upon the judge. We wish to make the principles of law familiar to all the citizens, and we adopt a procedure which forbids that there shall be any principles whatever. The Mohammedan judge does as he lists; he acknowledges the authority of no rule, nor the value of any experience. He is absolved from all regular control; and the public have no insight into the motives or reasons of his judgment. What we term precedents, are in reality a great volume of human experience; and it is upon the wisdom which is gained by experience that free institutions are built, and by which they must be preserved. Indeed the system of precedents is peculiarly adapted to a democratic commonwealth, which seeks to establish equality, and demands that the same rules, wherever applicable, shall be applied to all the citizens equally.

The absence of all reports of adjudged cases, was a great defect in Roman law. It led first to a nearly arbitrary exposition of the law by the Pretors. Second, to a recourse to the opinions of the lawyers, as to what the law was. The edicts of the Pretor are an example of the first. This officer, on entering upon his duties, (and the election was annual) published an edict, or little code, containing the rules by which he intended to be governed in the decision of cases. It was understood that he could not depart from the enactments of the twelve tables ; but the power of expounding the laws opens a wide field to construction, when it is not guarded by the force of precedents. The meaning of those laws was constantly tortured, and all sorts of subtleties invented, in order to introduce new rules of interpretation. The pretor could not depart from the provisions of his own edict : this was inviolable during the year he was in office. But this was no security for the permanence and stability of the law under succeeding pretors. And it was not until the time of Hadrian that a perpetual edict was established. When I say was established, I mean only to state the fact, aud not to engage the reader in the unprofitable controversy, whether this was the result of a positive decree of that emperor, or was brought about by the silent operation of other causes. The English common law was never rendered authoritative by an act of parliament. Hugo, in his history of the Roman law, declares that the annual edicts of the pretors, afforded the means of harmonizing the legislation with the spirit of the times. It was one step, but a most dangerous one in that direction. The spirit of the times could not be so fluctuating as to require a new edict every year ; and the Roman legislature was constantly in session. The reports of adjudged cases, which constitute the crowning glory of English and American jurisprudence, perform this office, without opening the door too wide to construction. The respect for adjudged cases becomes a habit : they are of general notoriety to the profession, because they are in print, and any eminent departure from them is viewed with extreme jealousy ; while on the other hand, as no judgment is absolutely binding, (except in a few specified cases) unless between parties and privies, no positive impediment is thrown in the way to prevent a re-consideration of the principle in future cases. The collection of the opinions of eminent civilians, was the next contrivance to help the defect, arising from the want of law reports ; but it was inadequate to this purpose. A compilation of this kind will cover an exceedingly small part of the ground, comprehended within the list of adjudged cases. The Pandects or Digest was a work of this character, but it afforded a very feeble light, in the administration of the laws, compared with the English and American reports, and the learned treatises which are founded upon them. The last not only announce a greater number of leading principles, but these are so ramified as to shed light upon a still greater number of subordinate ones.

BOOK IV.

CHAPTER I.

ON WHAT IN AMERICA IS SOMETIMES TERMED THE VETO POWER OF THE STATES.

It seems difficult, at first view, to assign any reason completely satisfactory, why the judiciary should be the final arbiter in determining upon the constitutionality of the laws. For if we say that the courts are the expounders of the constitution, it may be answered, that the enactment of a law, involving a constitutional objection, is itself an exposition of the constitution, and that if the judges by repeated adjudications decide one way, the legislature by repeated enactments, reaffirming its own construction, may decide another. The difficulty does not consist in attributing to the judges the right to decide, since whenever a constitutional question is involved, the court must give a construction ; it consists in making that tribunal paramount and supreme. It is perfectly correct to say, that the judiciary is invested with the power of applying the laws, but whether it has a right superior to the legislature in expounding them, does not appear so clearly. Nevertheless it is this very power of applying the laws, distinguishable as it is from that of expounding them, which has enabled the courts to assert and maintain the exclusive right of expounding them, and caused them to be regarded as the natural and ultimate arbiter in all such questions. The legislature declare the construction of the constitution ; the judges not only make declaration of their construction, but in addition to this, they carry that declaration into execution. For the various executive officers, marshals, sheriffs, etc., together with the "posse comitatus," are appended to the courts, not to thel egislature. Now it is plain, that that tribunal which is able to decide the law, and also to carry its judgment into immediate execution, must ultimately acquire the supremacy. When, therefore, the question is asked why is the judiciary the tribunal of dernier resort ? the obvious answer is, that its office as such is the natural and necessary consequence of the manner in which the government is constituted. The question confounds two entirely different things, the theoretical propriety of the arrangement with the plain matter of fact that it does exist. Even if we were to admit that the first is open to debate, upon the second the door to discussion is closed. The legislature in America bears to the courts the same resemblance which the present national government has to the old confederation. The present government acts upon persons, the latter acted for the most part upon states only. And the reason why this last did so act, was that (with a single exception) it was unprovided with courts to enforce the execution of its resolves. The national legislature now in existence, like the state legislatures, passes laws affecting the community at large, and the judiciary executes its decisions upon all the individuals in the land. The courts never arrogate to themselves the imposing authority of making general declarations. They act only in detail, and yet it is the exercise of this more humble duty which has rendered them the undisputed arbiters in construing the constitution. Humility and modesty in private life, often procure a high authority and reputation for those who practice them ; and it is fortunate when governments can avail themselves of the same salutary tendencies, in order to strengthen the authority of the laws, and to maintain order and tranquillity in the state.

Notwithstanding the right to which I have referred sometimes affords matter for disputation in America, (for although discussion is the proper office of the understanding, its place is often usurped by the feelings, yet nothing has struck foreigners with more admiration than the firm establishment, and general recognition of the principle in America. It is a necessary conseqence of the introduction of free institutions. For a constitutional chart is itself an act of legislation. It is the supreme law of the land. To determine therefore upon the constitutionality of a law, is not more improper, than the construction of any other enactment in which a question of constitutionality is not involved. It does not place the judge higher than the lawmaker; it only maintains the supremacy of the sovereign legislature, the people.

And if the original propriety of this arrangement should be questioned (its existence as a matter of fact being admitted), it may be answered, that all our knowledge is more distinctly apprehended when it is in the concrete, than when it is clothed with an abstract and general form. The legislature view the law in its general features. The courts deal with it in detail, and in its application to a particular case. It is not because the judges have mental powers superior to the legislature, that the duty of deciding is devolved upon them; it is because the form which the question assumes, distinct, and unembarrassed by any extraneous matter, facilitates the process of analysis, and it is by this process alone that we are able to give precision to our ideas, and certainty to our conclusions.

But this power of deciding constitutional questions has a much wider application than I have yet supposed. The state courts decide upon the validity of state laws in reference to their own constitutions. The courts of the union do the same in reference to the federal constitution. But the supreme court of the United States is also the tribunal of last resort, for determining the validity of state laws, whenever these conflict with the federal constitution. And this, also, is a consequence of the structure of the government. The introduction of the perfect form of confederate government, its substitution in the place of the imperfect form which formerly existed, has produced a corresponding change in the constitution of the courts, and given a new direction to the exercise of judicial power. As the laws of the union do not operate upon states, but upon individuals, the decisions of the courts do not act upon governments, but upon persons.

One of the most striking features in the American government, is the double system of representation which it contains. It is a great achievement to introduce the elective principle into all the departments of a consolidated government; to render the executive and judiciary, as well as the legislature, elective. But the American is not a consolidated, but a federal government. Separation has, therefore, been made between the general and local interests. Each have been deposited in distinct governments, and the principle of representation has been established in both. The states are not mere municipal corporations, deriving their existence and franchises from the central government. Their separate jurisdiction is secured by the same instrument which created the confederacy, and is therefore equally fortified against attack. It is the independent character of these two classes of government, which has caused some eminent minds in America to doubt whether the judicial power of the union extends to the determination of the validity of state laws, when they conflict with the federal constitution. It has been supposed that there could be no arbiter in the case; and that the states, nay, each of them separately, must necessarily possess a veto upon the decisions of the national tribunal.

Mr. Hume, in a short essay "on some remarkable customs," has stated as a singular fact, that the legislative authority in the Roman commonwealth resided in two distinct assemblies: the comitia of the centuries, and the comitia of the tribes, acting independently and not concurrently; each haviug a veto upon the acts of the other, and a right to carry any measure by its single authority. And this example has been relied upon, together with other views, by the able author of "New Views of the Constitution," in support of the veto power of the states. But the American government is a government "sui generis," and it is not safe to resort to other political systems for the purpose of finding analogies. Admitting the fact to be as stated by Mr. Hume, there are some very important differences between the Roman and the American plans. The two comitia were parts of one and the same government, and not institutions of two distinct governments. Conquering Rome annihilated all the confederacies which once existed in Italy, the Tuscan, Volscian, &c., and substituted in their place one homogeneous government. Second, the two legislatures were not distinct bodies in the same sense as the English houses of lords and commons are; but were composed of nearly the same persons: only in one, the vote was collected by classes, and in the other "per capita." Third, they did not always preside over the same interests. A similar organization of the legislative power has taken place in every country where civilization has made slow progress, and where the melting down the various classes of society into one body has been the work of time. In England, at one period, the nobility, burgesses, and clergy, taxed their own order separately. Those assemblies did not act concurrently, as is the practice now; each voted separately, and did not wait for the concurrence or disapproval of the others to its own bills.

But inasmuch as the two Roman comitia did frequently vote upon the same subject matter, upon the question of peace or war, for instance, there is a difficulty even greater than in the case just referred to. There is no part of history which is more obscure, than is the constitutional history of Rome. Things which were plain enough to contemporary writers, which involved no contradiction whatever and which are therefore not related with precision, but even with carelessness, are full of perplexity at the present day; nay, were so at the time Livy wrote. That two legislative assemblies should exist, each possessing an independent jurisdiction upon the same matter; and each therefore armed with authority to undo immediately whatever had been resolved by the other, involves so glaring an inconsistency, that we are compelled to believe that there must be something further in the case which, if it could be seized, would at once dispel the difficulty. Such a theory of government, if there were nothing further, would lead to absolute inaction. The vote of the last assembly ought to decide the matter; but there could be no last, if each was absolutely independent, and could incessantly revoke the bills passed by the other. On the other hand, if there was a stopping place, the vote in the last decided the matter, and gave to that body alone the supreme legislative authority.

We know that the plebian assembly were at first confined to legislate about matters which concerned their own order. Afterward they procured the privilege of deliberating, and deliberating only, on all matters which affected the general interests. If prior to 372, a proposition was discussed in both assemblies, and was carried by the vote of the centuries in contradiction to that of the tribes, it could hardly be said that those two bodies acted independently. For the proceedings in the first were only like the proceedings in one of those voluntary conventions which are so common in America. It might deliberate and resolve; but it had no power to carry any measure into effect. It had in other words no real power of legislation. This constitution of government is a very common thing even in modern societies. The French tribunate in the Abbe Sieyes constitution, and which existed for several years, was merely a deliberative body. So also the Danish, Prussian, and Russian councils deliberate, but do not enact. A still more remarkable example is afforded by the Germanic legislature. It is composed of three chambers, the princes, electors, and deputies of the towns. But the last, although it may discuss, is never admitted to vote. An example on a small scale is exhibited in the American congress, where the delegates from the teritrories enjoy the full privilege of debate, but have ho right to vote on any question.

In the course of time, the two Roman assemblies shifted their positions. The popular body which before met to deliberate only, acquired complete legislative authority: precisely as would be the case in the Germanic confederation, if free institutions were introduced, when the deputies of the people would exercise the entire legislative power, leaving it free to the other orders, to meet and deliberate if they chose. If this revolution were to take place, if the art of printing did not exist, or through some calamity or other, all public records and histories were lost, or mutilated, the same puzzle would exist as in the case of the Roman comitia, and from the same causes. Suppose that the same catastrophe should happen to American institutions, and that two or three thousaud years hence, some one were to read this passage in the very able speech of Mr. Calhoun on his resolutions: "the powers not delegated are reserved, against the judiciary as well as against the other departments." If no copy of the constitution could be found, nor any document which shed light upon the subject, he might suppose not only that the proposition was true, which it undoubtedly is, but that it proved the existence of a veto power on the part of the states, even as against the determination of the supreme court of the union. But with a copy of the constitution in his hand, he would find that that court was by irresistible implication clothed with the power of deciding upon the constitutionality of state laws; and that what he had taken to be the statement of a fact, was the statement of the view of an individual.

But the most remarkable circumstance is, that in the debates which recently took place, the existence of a veto power, on the part of the states, was taken for granted. Its advocates did not confine themselves to showing that there would have been propriety in so organizing the government. They asserted that its existence was an undoubted fact. And such is the exceeding fertility of the human mind, not merely in finding reasons for what it conceives ought to be, but in converting its conceptions into reality, that numbers of people in one part of the union, who had never dreamed of the existence of such a power, began to hesitate. It may be allowable to doubt, where one is obliged to search in the dark caverns of antiquity for materials to guide our judgments. But the institutions of the United States are open to the apprehension of every one. If what they ought to be admits of discussion, what they really are is matter of history.

The extreme novelty, not to say the alarming tendency, of such a power in a country where infinite pains have been taken to establish regular government, compelled those who advocated it* to assume that congress were bound to call a convention to amend the constitution, whenever a single state dissented to a law as unconstitutional. In this way the mischief of civil war, which would otherwise be inevitable, was sought to be avoided. But in order to attain this end, the assumption went still further. It was insisted, that when the convention assembled, the proposition should be, not to insert by way of amendment the limitation upon the power of the federal government which a single state had contended for, but to insert the power claimed and actually exercised by congress, with the consent of every state but one. Every one will perceive the immense difference which is made by only changing the form in which the question is put. In the one way, the constitution will be amended by a very small minority of the states; in the other, it can only be effected by a very large majority. Now admitting that congress may sometimes transcend its powers, and that this way of proceeding would arrest it; the inquiry properly is, not what would be the effect in one or two instances, but what would be the effect in all time to come, and in the numberless instances in which the states, encouraged to resistance, would succeed in paralyzing the operations of the government? Is there not, so far as we proceed upon any known principle of human nature, infinitely more security in the vote of a majority of congress and three-fourths of the states, than in a very small minority of both? We may admit that there are certain dormant powers residing in every community, and that the right to resist an intolerable tyranny is one of them; but this does not permit us openly to recognize the existence of a wild excess of power, and to insert it as a standing provision in the constitution of the government.

* "New Views of the Constitution," by John Taylor; and Calhoun's peech, 1832–3.

The mode of calling a convention to amend is one of the parts of the constitution which is least liable to misinterpretation. It can only be assembled with the consent of two-thirds of the states, or two-thirds of both houses of congress. The effect of the doctrine in question would be to give this power to a single state. Not that this view would be taken by its advocates, for our own arbitrary conceptions are able to give shape and form to almost anything. It would still be insisted that two-thirds of congress, or two-thirds of the state legislatures must concur in calling a convention. But if two-thirds or a majority in either case were convinced of the constitutionality of the law in existence, it is plain that a convention could only be assembled by the authority of the single dissenting state. For there is no way in which we can conceive of a legislative body acting, at any rate of its having a right to act, but by persuasion of the correctness and lawfulness of what it does. To assert that it is bound to call a convention, against its most settled convictions, is to assert that it is bound to call one upon compulsion. Nor can any human ingenuity make it otherwise.

It is an established maxim in American institutions, that the government can no more concede an ungranted privilege, than exercise an ungranted power. To concede a privilege is to communicate a power; and is guarded with the same caution as the usurpation of authority. If it had been intended that a convention should be assembled, not only when two-thirds of congress were convinced of the expediency of so doing, but upon the complaint of a single state, the constitution would have said so in plain words. There cannot be a shadow of doubt upon the subject. The two cases are totally distinguishable from each other. Each affords a specific occasion for acting: and to suppose that the one was intended to involve the other, would argue a confounding of two things, unnecessary, improbable in the extreme, and full of mischief. But to have inserted in plain language the provision contended for, would have been so startling, that every member of the convention would have recoiled from it. Strange as it may seem, therefore, there is no possible way of claiming the existence of any such power, except upon the ground that it has been absolutely omitted in the constitution. It is impossible to defend usurpation by law, but it is often possible to argue plausibly against law.

Not only has the constitution forbidden the exercise of the veto power, by refusing to grant it, and by prescribing a mode of amendment absolutely inconsistent with, and repugnant to its exercise; it has closed the door upon all controversy, by creating a tribunal which shall be the ultimate judge in all controversies between the state and the federal goverments. On the 13th June, 1787, in the convention which framed the constitution of the United States, it was moved by Mr. Randolph, and seconded by Mr. Madison, that the jurisdiction of the national judiciary shall extend to all questions which involve the national peace and harmony. The resolution was passed, and was embodied by the committee which had charge of it, in the precise and definite language in which the power is clothed in the third and sixth articles of the constitution as ratified. Now I do not pretend to say, that a doubt may not still be raised; for it is possible for an ingenious mind to doubt every thing. But when I observe that the constitution, and the laws made in pursuance of it, are declared the supreme law of the land, any thing in the constitutions and laws of the states to the contrary notwithstanding: and when I observe that the exclusive right to expound the law in these cases is conferred upon a federal tribunal, I am compelled to believe that there can be at least no solid foundation for doubt.

The celebrated author of the Virginia resolutions and report, admits that the supreme court of the Union is the tribunal of last resort, whenever the validity of a state law asserting the existence of an unconstitutional power in the states is called in question. The construction of that clause, which prohibits the states from issuing bills of credit, etc., he declares is referred to that tribunal. This is in effect a surrender of the whole ground of argument; for the prohibitions on the power of the states are as much a part of the constitutional compact, as are the limitations on the power of the federal government. And if it be true that, in all questions which relate to the boundary of power between the two governments, there is no common umpire, and neither has the right to decide, there is no reason for ascribing supreme authority to the court in the one case, which does not equally exist in the other.

There is an interesting problem in government, which may be thus stated: when is it that two political powers in the state being set up, one against the other, their mutual rivalry will lead to a just balance of authority, and conduce to a successful administration of public affairs? And the answer is, that this adjustment of the parts of government will be safe, whenever these two rival authorities are compelled to act concurrently, and when they are controlled by some common authority, which is superior to both. The various departments, the legislative, executive and judiciary, have rival interests; but they are amenable to one common power, and they co-operate in carrying out one plan of government. So on a smaller scale, the court and the jury are set up against each other, with power in each to overrule, "ad infinitum," the determination of the other. But they are bound by one common ligament to the people, and combine in administering the same laws. The Roman tribunate may be mentioned as an example of the same class. It was, like the senate and the "comitia," a constituent part of one and the same government.

In the artifical forms of government, only one of these conditions is complied with; the three departments conspire in the administration of the same system, but their responsibility to a common constituent is very imperfect. And the consequence is, that one usurps nearly all power, or an interminable conflict exists between them. In proportion as the popular power is raised, and pure monarchy is transformed into limited or constitutional monarchy, the responsibility becomes direct and positive, and the departments are more easily retained within their respective spheres. The walks of private life afford a similar analogy. How is it that so many thousand individuals, all armed with propensities and desires which constantly stimulate them to run counter to the general interests, are so restrained as to produce any thing like tolerable tranquillity in society. The tribunal of public opinion, which represents those interests, controls them all, and produces regularity of behavior in those numberless instances which the laws would never reach.

It would have been wonderful then if the American people, after establishing free institutions, had so far spoiled the original design as to create a counterbalancing force to the system, in the sectional and particular interests of one member of the confederacy. Circumstances may occur, which would render it meritorious in a state to remonstrate, and to take high ground, in order to induce a change in the public measures. But it must be a very extraordinary case—a case which must make the law for itself, which would justify civil war. There may be secrets in public as well as in private life, and a state which resists the laws of the union, may calculate on the length it may go, in order to procure a compromise, and may at bottom determine to go no further. But the statesman who should draw the sword, if compromise failed, would incur the transcendant ignominy, as well as merit, of going into battle without his shield. No man has a right to be brave at the expense of his patriotism.

In the Germanic confederation, there was a tribunal in some respects resembling the supreme court of the United States. The chamber of Wetzlar, or Westphalia, possessed exclusive jurisdiction in deciding upon disputes between members of the empire. But it had no power to execute its decisions. The laws operated not upon individuals, but upon states ; and a sentence of the supreme judicial tribunal had no higher effect. The consequence was that it became necessary to resort to force, and to this end the empire was divided into circles, the entire military force of which was at the disposal of the emperor, to enable him to execute the sentence of the court against a refractory member. Under the new constitution of 1815, a different organization took place. If the rights of one state are invaded by another state, the injured party must choose one of three members of the diet, selected by the defendant; or if the defendant neglect to select, the diet is bound to name them. And the court of final resort, in the state of the member thus chosen, decides the case. And if the party against whom the judgment is pronounced does not obey, a military force is resorted to, to coerce submission. There does not appear to have been any judicial tribunal, either under the old or the new constitution, for the purpose of settling disputes between the states and the confederacy. The diet, or national legislature, seems to have possessed this power. The American system stands alone amid the institutions of the world. And although it was a natural consequence of the adoption of the perfect form of confederation, yet as this species of government is a work of the greatest refinement, and the result of a very high state of civilization, the organization of the national judiciary may be pronounced one of the greatest achievements which political science has made.

There is a tribunal of another European state, which it is curious to notice, in consequence of its novel mode of procedure, although it is never called to decide upon the conflicting rights of different governments. The court of errors, or of cassation, in France, is the highest judicial tribunal in the kingdom. And the principle on which, until recently, it proceeded was this; if the judgment of an inferior court was reversed, the case was sent back to be tried again. If the court below persisted in its error, and the cause was again appealed, and the court above reaffirmed the judgment before pronounced, it was sent back a second time. But if the inferior court still persevered in its error, the decree of the court of cassation no longer afforded the governing rule. The legislature was then appealed to, to settle the law, by a declaratory act. But the absurdity of the scheme, the temptation which it held out to the local tribunals to resist the judgment of the highest court, and to unsettle all the principles of law, produced so much mischief, that in 1837, the English and American procedure was adopted; and the determination of the court of cassation is now final, and absolutely binding upon all other tribunals.

It is not uncommon to meet with this odd combination of liberty and power in monarchical government. The system of monarchical rule is itself a compensation of errors; where if the weight presses too much in one part, it is carelessly relaxed, or altogether removed in another part. The most remarkable example of this is contained in "magna charta," which authorizes the barons to pursue and to kill wherever found, the monarch who presumes to violate any of its provisions. It legalizes civil war all over the land; and England was accordingly a scene of confusion and violence for more than two centuries afterward. It is to the regulated liberty which free institutions introduce, that we must look for a salutary restraint upon the actions of men, and as the only means of giving supreme authority to the laws.

The reason why no tribunal, like the supreme court of the United States, is known in monarchical or aristocratical governments, is because too much instead of too little power is condensed in the political institutions. The king and nobility having acquired an extravagant share of authority, there is no way of subjecting their public acts to the scrutiny of a regular legal investigation. Questions cannot arise, because as there is no popular constitution, the right is all on one side. The establishment of such a system as the American, is a sure indication that the odious maxim of the sovereignty of the government is abjured, and that of society substituted in its place. Then for the first time questions arise between government and the members which compose it; for the same fundamental ordinance which is obligatory upon the one, is obligatory upon the other. The notion that public rights are unsuited to such a mode of proceeding, grows out of the idea that they are of too high a dignity to be submitted to the same examination as private rights. The notion, then, is anti-republican in the extreme. All public as well as private rights, are rights of the people, Formerly government was not amenable to any tribunal, while private citizens were. But as soon as the basis on which government rested was changed; the moment that its whole authority was referred to the consent of society, the rights of government and those of its members were placed upon the same footing. The constitution of the United States does not imitate "magna charta,"—the makeshift of a semibarbarous age—and authorize one member of the confederacy to place its veto upon the most solemn acts of the government. It does not, in order to settle a question of right, first unhinge the notions of justice, but fortifies the one by guarding and maintaining the other. It submits national and state controversies to the calm and patient investigation of a tribunal, which, as it represents both parties, is eminently adapted to compose the angry feelings of both.

There is infinite convenience in administering the government, where the public authority is made to act directly upon individuals. The laws are then executed with promptness and facility. But it is not for the sake of convenience merely, that the plan is adopted. There is another and a higher end which is designed to be effected; and that is to banish civil war, to preserve internal tranquillity, in short, to uphold civilization itself. The form which all questions take, their submission to a judicial instead of a political tribunal, is an immense advantage to the cause of free institutions. And admitting, what must be admitted, that every human tribunal, however skillfully contrived, must be subject to error; yet all who have had any experience of human affairs, will see the great importance of having some tribunal of dernier resort; some tribunal, in other words, which shall be able to speak with authority, after it has deliberately examined and decided.

There is a peculiarity in the form of confederate government established in America, which sheds great light upon this subject, and points to the supreme court of the union as the most fit tribunal to decide upon questions of controverted jurisdiction. The national government is not represented in the states, but is itself a mere representation from the states. Senators are elected by the local legislatures, the president and representatives are chosen by the people of the states, and not by the people as composing one aggregate community, and the judges are chosen by the two first, and from the districts in which they reside. But there is no similar representation of the national government to be found in the executive, legislature, or judiciary of the states. Now all confederacies are not constructed in this manner, nor was there any absolute necessity why the American should have been so. But a little reflection will show that it contributes materially to promote one very important object, and that is, the complete separation of the powers of the two classes of government, the national and the state.

Before the union of Scotland and Ireland with England, independently of the fact that there were no local executives like the governors of the American states, the two former countries being presided over by the king of England, this officer as representing the central government, appointed the members of two estates in the Scotch parliament, the nobility and bishops, and nominated a certain proportion of the lords of articles, by whom the real legislative business of Scotland was transacted. In Ireland, until within a few years before the union, no law could even be propounded to its parliament, until it had received the previous assent of the English parliament. The case in both instances was the reverse of what it is in the United States. The federal head was effectively represented in the local governments; while, on the other hand, those governments were not represented by the national executive, legislature, or judiciary. Or, to take another example: the provinces of Holland are a confederacy in a much more strict acceptation, than was the British government; for there is a more complete separation of the local from the general interests. Each province has its own legislative assembly, and one chamber of the states general, or federal legislature, is composed of representatives chosen in the provinces. But the provincial governments differ exceedingly from the state governments of America. They are intended to administer the local interests; and should, in order to carry out this design, represent exclusively the local population. But this is not the case.

Not only is the number of the members of the chamber of deputies, and of the electors who choose them, fixed by the federal executive, but he nominates the members who compose the upper house in every one of those provincial legislatures.

The American government would have resembled the Dutch, if the plan of a constitution presented to the convention by Mr. Hamilton had been adopted. The plan proposed that the governors of the states should be appointed by the federal government, and that they should have a negative upon the laws passed by the state legislatures. The federal government would then have been effectually represented in the state governments. The same object would have been accomplished in another form, if the plan advocated by Mr. Pinckney and Mr. Madison had been accepted. This proposed that the national legislature should have power to negative all laws of the state legislatures; not merely such laws as were repugnant to the federal constitution, but all laws which appeared improper. There would still have been this difference between the American, and the Dutch and former British confederacy: that in the former, the states are represented in every department of the national government, whereas in the second, they are very imperfectly represented, and in the last, they were not represented at all. There would have been much stronger reasons, therefore, in the first, than in the two last instances, for creating a supreme tribunal to decide upon the conflicting rights of the two classes of government, and vesting the appointment of its members in the federal head. Those plans, however, and others of a similar character, were avoided; and the constitution adopted is accordingly the only example of the perfect form of confederate government which has any where been known. It fulfills the three indispensable conditions of that species of government. First, there is a complete separation between the general and local interests. Second, the laws operate upon individuals, not upon governments; and third, the federal head is a mere representation of the states, but has no power to intermeddle in their domestic legislation. This mode of constructing the government, determined the character and jurisdiction of the tribunal of last resort. It was a judicial tribunal: 1st. Because the laws were designed to act upon persons. 2d. Because the process of analysis, by which the unconstitutional feature in a law is detected, is more completely reached in that form of proceeding. 3d. Because the constitution and character of such a tribunal necessarily shuts out the influence of party feelings, so fatal to the firm and just appreciation of wha is right. The members of this tribunal were appointed by the federal government, because that government is made up of a representation from the states, and is in no way represented in the state government. And if ingenious minds should still seek to raise objections, and insist that a jurisdiction of the kind conferred upon the supreme court savors too much of political power, it may be answered: 1st. That this constitutes one of its chief recommendations. 2d. That political power must necessarily be wielded by some one or more of the citizens, and that the members of the court are alike citizens with the members of any other department. 3d. That it is infinitely desirable to break up political power as much as possible, to distribute it among several tribunals, instead of condensing it in one.

We may illustrate the great advantage which is derived from giving to all the movements of the government, the greatest simplicity imaginable, by an institution which prevails in America, and which is now sought to be imitated in all the constitutional monarchies of Europe. The popular elections are not conducted in counties, much less in larger divisions of districts, but in the townships or parishes. Instead of assembling a vast multitude of people on one spot, to engage in broils and fights, this army of electors is cut up into minute parcels, each of which is separated from the other by miles. The force of party spirit is broken; and when the election is over, universal tranquillity is established. This is an emblem of American institutions in the general, which undertake to compass the most important end in the easiest manner possible. The organization and procedure of the supreme court of the union, is an application of the same principle to things apparently different, but which are in reality the same. We want an institution which shall have power to protect us against the rage of party spirit, in those cases where party spirit would be most fatal; an institution which shall be able to appease the sharpest discontents among the states by the employment of calm judgment and reflection. The reaching rights of this ponderous character, through the simple and unostentatious forms of the law, is, as I before said, the chief recommendation of the system. If it savors of political power, this power is at any rate morseled into small fragments, is only employed in detail, and on occasions where there is the least temptation to render it subservient to political ends. And although we may not be authorized to say that it is the best conceivable plan, we are well justified in declaring it the best practicable one.

The constitution of the United States is a compact. Every popular constitution is both a compact, and a delegation of power, whether the government be a consolidated, or a federal one. In the first, the compact is between the people, and the delegation of power is by them : in the second, the compact is between the members of the confederacy, and the delegation of power is by them only. And when the constitution is framed, the government created represents the joint authority of the states. This different mode of proceeding does not render the authority actually granted less binding in the one case, than in the other. It alters the structure and form of the government ; but the compact, or constitution, is equally obligatory in both. And as in an aggregate community, neither the citizens, nor even a majority of the people, can go beyond the compact, and interpose a veto upon the acts of the government ; so in the confederate government, neither a single state, nor a majority of the states, have any right to do the same thing. No one ever heard that when government was acting within the legitimate sphere of its jurisdiction, the jurisdiction itself should be questioned, because the measures pursued were not agreeable to every one. If there were no discontent in the state, government would be unnecessary. Civil institutions are appointed for the purpose of melting down the idiosyncrasies of different parts of society; and it is not merely from a noble self denial, but from a sense of evident interest, that men are ordinarily persuaded to lend their support in upholding the influence of these institutions.

The division of the territory of the United States into distinct states, was an accidental circumstance ; but the advantage which has sprung from it, is not accidental. If the people of America had composed one aggregate community, it would have been the hight of wisdom to imitate the present plan, to have created local governments, with complete jurisdiction over the local interests, and a central government to preside over the common interests. The scheme is in effect carried out to a considerable extent in the individual states. The counties and townships are lesser jurisdictions inclosed within a larger one, administering their domestic affairs skillfully and economically, because they are not mixed up and confounded with the general interests of the state. And if this form of civil polity was the result of a constitutional compact at the first foundation of the government, the counties and townships would possess complete sovereignty within their respective spheres, which could only be alienated, or altered, in the mode prescribed by the constitution. For the soveignty of the parts of which the community is composed, does not depend upon the time when they became sovereign; but upon the fact that they are so. Nor is it possible for ingenuity to frame further objections, and insist that the parts would in that case be the offspring of the central authority; whereas, in the confederate government, the central authority is itself but an emanation from the parts. For in both instances, the form of government is the offspring of the voluntary consent of the parts: only in the one, the parts are more numerous, as they are made up of individuals; in the other, they are composed of states, or separate collections of individuals.

Now if, in a state government thus constructed, the original compact should appoint a tribunal for the purpose of settling constitutional disputes between these two sets of government, no one of the parts could object to its jurisdiction and interpose its veto, because the law complained of did not equally benefit all the parts. Nor could it do so, even if the law declared to be valid, were in reality invalid; since in theory such a supposition would be itself unconstitutional, while in practice it would undermine all authority—that of the parts, as well as of the whole.

It is remarkable that those who advocate the veto power of the states, have taken for granted the existence of a power which is no where recognized in the constitution; and at the same time deny the jurisdiction of the supreme court, which is contained in language as unequivocal as could be desired; as unequivocal as that which confers jurisdiction on any other department; so much do times of high party excitement confound all our notions of justice, and make shipwreck of the most settled principles of government. As a large part of our opinions and beliefs are not absolutely determined by the objects with which they deal, but are modified by the structure of mind and the temperament of each individual, it is perhaps surprising that uniformity of opinion does exist to as great an extent as is actually the case. But in order to correct those aberrations in which we are so liable to fall, upon all political questions, it is of great importance to view them at a time when the judgment will be least liable to be perverted by any disturbing influence. The doctrine of the veto power of the states was for the first time proclaimed in the case of the commonwealth vs. Cobbett. At a time when party spirit ran high, C. J. McKean, ventured to express the opinion, that it was the duty of congress to call a convention, whenever a state protested against a law as unconstitutional. This singular opinion, was easily molded by the fertile genius of John Taylor into a regular system, and has been defended by other minds of equal vigor and fertility, as the panacea for all the irregularities in our system of federal government.

The United States is not the only country in which geographical features have made their appearance. The southern provinces of France have, for a long time, shown a disposition to counteract the legislation of the kingdom, because it was deemed too favorable to the northern provinces. At the very period (1833) when geographical parties in the United States, threatened the Union, two parties in France of the same character, and founded upon the same principles, were arrayed against one another. In 1834 was drawn up the celebrated manifest of the southern provinces, demanding that the kingdom should be intersected by a line east and west, separating the vine growing from the non vine growing provinces; and that south of this line the customs should be abolished. The then minister, M. Theirs, declared that "he had given great consideration to the subject, but in endeavoring to consult the interests of Bordeaux, I should do violence to those of Lyons. In attending to the complaints of Elbouf, I must sacrifice the interests of Havre." The vine growing constituted the predominant in the south, but it was not the predominant interest in the kingdom, nor the exclusive pursuit in the south. As the north was not an exclusively manufacturing, the south was not an exclusively agricultural region. The government of the minority then, would be subject to more abuse than that of the majority. But I return to a consideration of the veto power of the states.

If, in America, a single state, in consequence of its possessing this power can compel congress to assemble a convention, whenever it supposes a power not delegated is exercised, there must be a corresponding right on the other side, whenever a state assumes a power which is not reserved; otherwise the equilibrium of the system would be destroyed. On this subject, Taylor and Calhoun are silent. We will then suppose, that in this case, congress will be obliged to call a convention, as well to protect the rights of the other states as its own authority. The question in that convention will be, not whether the constitution shall be so amended as to delegate a given power, but whether it shall be so amended as to reserve it. The discontented state derives every advantage in the first instance, from the singular mode of propounding the question; but it loses this advantages in the second. The question is so framed, with the express intention of enabling a small minority of states to overrule a large majority. But this small minority, which in the first instance, determined the question adversely to the federal government, will now decide it adversely to the discontented state. But much the greater number of questions which have arisen between the two jurisdictions, have related to powers assumed by the states as reserved. The consequence is, that by this novel construction of the constitution, the rights of the states would be placed in jeopardy. As all the powers reserved are not enumerated, it would be peculiarly necessary to call a convention to determine whether the power exercised by the state was usurped or reserved. And the right of North Carolina, South Carolina, and Louisiana, to regulate the ingress of free people of color, would be decided against them. This would also be the case with regard to constitutional provision in Indiana, prohibiting the immigration of the same persons; for it is certain, that three-fourths of the states could not be found to declare that these powers were part of the reserved rights. The same disposition would have been made of the Dartmouth college case, the laws of Kentucky suspending the payment of debts, and those of Massachusetts, Rhode Island, and Maine, prohibiting the sale of spirituous liquors, for they might be supposed to interfere with the delegated power of congress to permit their importation. The two writers I have referred to, contend for a new and unheard of power, but do not seem to be aware that the rule which permits it, would operate in contrary directions; that if a state has a right to veto a law of the federal government, because it is not a delegated power, for the same reason will the federal government have a right to veto a law of a state because it does not fall within the reserved powers; and that the same consequences will follow the assembling of a convention, in which by the same mode of propounding the question, the right would be authoritatively and finally settled against the state.

It must not be supposed that no case can be conceived where a power is assumed to be reserved, which does not raise the question whether it is delegated. For 1st. A power prohibited to the states cannot have that effect. 2d. A power neither directly prohibited to the states, nor reserved, may be assumed before any law has been passed by Congress. 3d. If the delegated powers presuppose the existence of the reserved, the reserved equally supposed the existence of the delegated. Nor does the non enumeration of all the reserved render it necessary to propound the question always in the same form, for a considerable number are enumerated, and the enumeration of the delegated is ipso facto a designation of the reserved. It will be remarked that the question is between the authority of a single state, and the joint authority of the other states. If it were between the state and some depository of power created by itself alone, the presumption might be that an authority not delegated, had been exercised; for the two would stand in the relation of inferior and superior. But there is no such relation between a state and the Union. Each of the other states is the equal of the one which complains; and jointly they are its superior, because the constitution was the result of a joint act, and not the act of a single state. The presumption, therefore, is that the power is not reserved, and not that it is one not delegated.

The greater the number who concur in doing an act, the more of a popular character is stamped upon it; but that is on the supposition that it is actually done. The merely making provision, that several shall concur to render an act valid, is something very different from their actually concurring: for if they do not, the consequence is that the measure adopted, instead of enlisting a greater number than a majority, may enlist one that is much less. The rule that requires a number greater than a majority, is only adopted in order to preserve the old order of things. For this reason, it is very sparingly used, because all legislation supposes alteration. The moment it is employed to introduce a new state of things, it becomes mischievous. And that is the old state under which a government had hitherto been uniformly administered, and that the new, which would overturn the old. If the unconstitutional doctrine of calling a convention were put in practice, it would follow that whichever asserts a power inconsistent with the established order of things, is bound to show its validity. If a state attempts to impair the obligation of contracts, by violating the visitatorial power in a collegiate institution, (1,) or by enacting a law suspending the collection of debts, (2,) or by an insolvent law discharging the debt, (3,) or by imposing a tax on packages of goods imported, in the hands of the merchant, (4,) or by laws abolishing the duties, (5,) or by laws annulling the fugitive slave act, (6,) the question appropriately submitted to a convention would be, shall the right assumed be deemed a reserved one ? shall a declaratory amendment be passed to that effect ?

There is another view of great importance. I have considered the scheme as a two edged sword, as operating equally against the states and the federal government. But in truth, it would operate very frequently against the states, even where the convention was consequent upon the veto of a state, and the question was shall the power be delegated to the Union. Vermont and Massachusetts, have vetoed the fugitive slave law. If a convention were assembled for the prepesterous purpose of delegating the power to pass the law, it would be very difficult to obtain the votes of three-fourths of the states in the affirmative. If the same course had been pursued in 1836-7, when the act prohibiting the circulation of incendiary papers by the mail, was passed, a declaratory amendment delegating the power to pass the act could not have been procured. If one of the non slave-holding states had vetoed, as unconstitutional, the act admitting Missouri into the Union, the constitutional number of the states could not have been found to vote in the affirmative, shall the power be delegated to the national legislature. It will be observed, that the right asserted does not depend upon the fact whether the law may or may not be executed within the territory of the discontented state, nor upon its ability to oppose any actual resistance to its execution : it is sufficient that a state protests against any law, and congress is immediately obliged to assemble a convention. If, in 1802, any one of the states had protested against the constitutionality of forming new states, out of territory acquired since 1789, a convention would

1. New Hampshire. 2. Kentucky. 3. New York and Louisiana. 4. Maryland. 5. South Carolina. 6. Vermont.

not have delegated the power. Or, if the protest had been against the acquisition of territory by treaty, Louisiana may not have been purchased. Great Britain would have seized it during the war which was soon after rekindled between herself and France. It was to prevent this catastrophe that Napoleon consented to part with it. Even Mr. Jefferson declared he was not satisfied that the United States could accept the cession, unless the people inhabiting the territory voluntarily submitted to live under the American government. He saw no difficulty in the alienation, or division of the sovereignty by the people themselves; but he saw great difficulty in an alienation or division by the government which presided over them. But there is no intelligible way of dealing with a question of this sort, unless we suppose an anterior consent, tacit or implied, to the alienation, or the joint consent by the people of France and Louisiana to the same. Any other interpretation, would throw into confusion the boundaries of every state on the face of the globe.

It would appear, then, that the operation of the system under the present and only true construction of the constitution, is more favorable to that wise and just spirit of compromise which should forever preside over the counsels of a federal republic. Taylor and Calhoun suppose that the veto will always be interposed by a southern state, and that that state will always be triumphant. But the scheme would be equally fatal to the southern and northern states.

The two authors I have referred to, suppose that because the American states entered separately into the confederacy, and separately ratified the constitution, the government of the Union is the agent of the individual states. All constitutional government is strictly an agency; in a democratic aggregate community, it is the agent of individuals; in a confederacy, it is the agent of states. But although individuals form the first, they do so jointly, and, therefore, no one individual can unmake it; and for the same reason, although states formed the last, they did so jointly, and no one state has power to take it to pieces. It is immaterial, whether the joint power which created, and the government and constitution which were created, were all one act, or successive acts. The existence of the joint power is undeniable; otherwise we fall into the absurdity of supposing that one individual made the one, and one state the other form of government. It follows, therefore, that as the sovereignty in the former, resides in individuals jointly, in the last, it resides in states jointly. This separates the sovereignty in both instances from the agency, and renders it as easy to find it in one form of government, as in the other. The sovereignty resides in those who make the government; in aggregate community, in the people jointly, in a confederate government, in states jointly. In the former, the sovereignty is not lodged in individuals, because they voted per capita, nor in the second, does it reside in the states separately, because they also voted per capita. For all this was necessary to be done, in order to render the act in each instance a joint one. This gives rise to a division of sovereignty, though this sometimes creates confused notions, as it seems to import a division of the faculty of sovereignty at one and the same time, instead of a division between two distinct political beings. The first is impossible, the second is easily understood. The states jointly, not the government, are sovereign as regards the federal interests; the states singly, as regards their domestic interests. Nor is there any difficulty in conceiving how a state should be sovereign as to some things, and not sovereign as to others, the difficulty is the other way; in conceiving how a state should be solely sovereign over other states. If there is any act of sovereignty, it is in the creation of a government, or in the alteration of it after it is created. The joint power of the states, is as distinguishable from the government, as the joint authority of individuals in an aggregate community, is distinguishable from the government they create. No single state framed the constitution, nor has a single state power to alter it. It was framed by the states jointly, each voting separately, for there is no other device, by which a joint act can be made to originate, and the concurrence of three fourths, not the voice of one is necessary to alter it. It follows, therefore, that the sovereignty is partitioned between the states jointly, and the states individually. For as it would be contradictory to say that a joint association could act in the capacity of a single member, it is contradictory to say, that a single member can act in the capacity of a joint association. For the same reason, that the states jointly cannot alter the constitution of a state, no single state can alter the constitution of the Union. It is contended, that this renders the states sovereign as to the reserved, and not sovereign as to the delegated powers; and how should it be otherwise. The reserved powers are simply those powers which belong to each state separately. Over these it must be supreme, because they have never been alienated; over the last it cannot be, because they were created by the states jointly. The reserved powers are placed in the constitution, but it is for the express purpose of separating them from the body of federal powers. If the objection were, this makes the states separately, sovereign as to the reserved, and separately, not sovereign as to the delegated powers, its futility, and want of meaning would be apparent; but by making use simply of the word states, in both instances, an ambiguity is created, which gives rise to a confusion of ideas. If the objection were, this makes the states separately sovereign as to the reserved and jointly, not sovereign as to the delegated powers, its falsity would be immediately seen. By using the word states in both instances without qualification, that hazy state of mind is created, which is most favorable to the admission of every kind of error.

The argument in the "Discourse on the Constitution," is woven out of a sophism. The states are said to have formed the constitution separately; but with *concert* and *mutual understanding*. The infirmity of the argument would be flagrant, if something *resembling* a joint act were not alluded to. Hence, those words of half meaning are employed. The appropriate terms compact, or united wills, are not used; though so much stress is afterwards placed upon the first, in passages where it is not of more importance that they should be used. The reason is obvious; the frailness of the reasoning, would be instantly seen, if that precise, and unequivocal language were employed. States may with concert, and mutual understanding, agree to establish separate constitutions. Very different is the case, where a compact is entered into for the formation of a single constitution for the whole. In the last the constitution is by irresistible implication, the result of the joint will of the states thus united. The argument of Taylor, and Calhoun, is this: the states separately sent delegates to the convention; in the convention, the vote was taken by states, and each state separately ratified the constitution; therefore, the constitution was ordained by the states separately, as completely as were their domestic governments. The argument has an air of plausibility, especially when connected with the words, "with concert" and "mutual understanding;" for these by their ambiguous import, contribute to hide the sophism which lurks beneath. They are not inconsistent with the formation of either a federal, or a state government. But they do not explain with precision, the foundation on which a federal government rests. The states did separately send delegates to the convention, the vote in the convention was taken by states, and each state separately ratified the constitution, as each party to a treaty, separately ratifies it. It will not be denied, that a federal government may be established by the joint will, or authority of the members, and a little reflection is sufficient to convince us, that it is impossible it should be established in any other way. In subsequent parts of the "Discourse," "compact," and "contract" are frequently used. The reason is obvious; the author is there engaged in considering the violations of the constitution, and to represent that instrument as having been framed merely with concert, and mutual understanding, would be language too loose, and ambiguous, to answer the purpose there intended. That the vote in the convention was taken by states, and that the states severally ratified the constitution, does not prove that all was not done by the joint will of the states, for the joint will of separate states can only be ascertained in this way. It merely proves that the population was not an aggregate one, and that the government was not a consolidated republic.

To hear some persons talk of the federal government of America, one would suppose that it was a foreign government, seated in a remote country, presiding over the general interests of the states, and yet without any visible connection with or dependence on them. One would hardly recognize a government which derived its whole being from the states, and which was constantly recruited and supported by them.

There is one way in which I can conceive that an important revolution may be effected in the structure of the supreme court. The judges may be appointed for a term of years, and the marshals may be elected by the people of the respective states. The relation which the judges bear to the federal government will not be changed, the bond which now connects them will not be broken; but it will be materially weakened. The wisdom and authority of the judges will be in some degree eclipsed, not only in their own eyes, but in the eyes of all those who are called upon to assist in executing a judgment. I think I can already discern symptoms of a reluctance, in those state courts whose judges are elected for a term of years, to touch a constitutional question, if it can be avoided: a disposition which is in every way commendable, as it does not necessarily imply a shrinking from duty, but may produce much more caution than would otherwise be observed. There is an important rule on this subject, which is, that every law is "prima facie" to be deemed constitutional, and that the reasons to show the reverse must be very convincing. But the duty of judges in America is peculiar: they may have to decide upon two conflicting laws, or two conflicting constitutions, when the "prima facie" presumption cannot be presented with so much distinctness. The result, however, may be the same; more prudence and caution will be observed in weighing the arguments on both sides. The court will more readily retract an erroneous judgment, when it is less accessible to that pride of opinion which makes it desire on all occasions to give an example o consistency with itself, even at the expense of inconsistency with the rule of right.

CHAPTER II.

THE RIGHT OF SECESSION IN THE CONFEDERATE FORM OF GOVERNMENT.

This is an entirely new question in political philosophy. No confederate government has ever provided for the emergency. In America the constitution is equally silent upon the subject. It provides for amendments; but amendments imply the continued existence of a constitution, whereas secession is a partial dissolution of it. Nor do the 9th and 10th amendments affect the question; for these merely guarantee to the states, the exclusive control of their domestic interests, and presuppose the continued existence of the two governments, state and federal, instead of the extinguishment of one of them.

States, before they form a confederate government, are distinct and independent communities; and the question very naturally arises, whether the entering into a compact of this nature, necessarily forbids a withdrawal from it. The determination of this difficult and interesting question renders it necessary to examine the principles which lie at the foundation of the confederate form of government.

If the individuals composing an aggregate society, establish a consolidated government, whether that government is republican, aristocratical, or monarchical, a part of the society have not the right, they have not even the ability to secede. Such a government comprehends a defined and undivided territory, the territory inhabited by all the people within it; and there is a plain inconsistency in supposing that some of the people may be politically, out of the government, while territorially, they are within it. Territory, and government, where the community is homogeneous, are corresponding and convertible terms. If independent states enter into the same form of government, they will be subjected to the same disability. They will have created an aggregate society, and erased the existence of separate peoples. Although the former boundaries of their respective territories may be traced, their population is completely merged. In half a century, a new people have grown up, total strangers to the original lines of demarcation, and absolutely knowing but one country, and one government. Although the boundaries of the states, occupied by their ancestors, may be preserved in tradition, or record, the political geography of the country is altered, the moral boundaries of the population are obliterated, and secession would be a solecism.

These difficulties do not exist where independent communities enter into a confederacy. Each separate state is an aggregate community: its people therefore, cannot withdraw their allegiance from it in any other way than by removal. But if a state secedes, the people who inhabit it, are instantly placed, both politically and territorially, without the federal government. A confederate, as such, possesses no territory. In the case of secession, therefore, the laws would at one and the same time, cease to operate both territorially, and politically, over the state withdrawing. The great difference, then, between a consolidated and a federal government is, that in the first, there are no parts, or if originally there were, they are merged; in the second, the parts continue to have a distinct existence.

The soundness of a principle is said to consist in its operating both ways; and a mind fertile in resources, may inquire whether if a people composing one aggregate community, whose territory was either inconveniently large, or inconveniently situated, were to divide the state into two states, first receiving the vote of the new state in favor of this arrangement, and that this last proceeded to organize a separate government; it may be asked, whether it would be competent for the people inhabiting the old division, to annul the compact, and to reabsorb the new state into itself. The answer is, that it would not, the reason of which is, that in the case supposed, there is a double compact, giving birth to two distinct governments. The dismemberment of Massachusetts, by the erection of Maine, is an example. The consent of the people, as composing one entire community, was first obtained, and then the separate vote of the newly contemplated state. But in the formation of a federal government, by independent states, the vote of the states is alone taken; the vote of the people, as forming one aggregate community, is not and cannot be. In the first case, there is a double compact, in the second, a single one. The principle therefore would be misapplied. In order to render the analogy complete, the hypothesis should be, that the people composing one aggregate community, carved out of the territory distinct, local, or municipal governments, but without any regard to the consent of the local population, and consequently without forming any compact with it. In this case it would be competent for the former to annihilate those local jurisdictions. Their formation is only a mode of administering the government, not a contrivance for severing it. The erection of departments, provinces, or districts, is an example. They all stand upon the same footing. The greater or lesser extent of authority possessed by some of these domestic jurisdictions, makes no difference in principle between them. It is not the extent but the nature of the power, the source whence it is derived, which determines where there is a similitude or difference between them. And as it is competent for a state which is a member of the confederacy, to extinguish the municipal governments within its territory, it would be competent for a people composing one undivided empire to annihilate any of the local governments upon its surface. There is no necessity for the reservation of the right. It springs from the charter and constitution of the society. The same is true of a confederate government, formed by independent states. It is the creature of a single, not of a double compact; and each state for itself, and for itself only, may withdraw from the union. The right flows by irresistible implication, from the original structure of the society. But although a formal recognition of it is unnecessary, I am by no means satisfied that it would be unwise to insert it. For the minds of men are as much moved by magnitudes in the moral, as in the physical world. Whatever protects us from the delusions of the imagination, or from the effect of a train of inconsequential reasoning, in matters pertaining to political society, is as much to be valued as the deliverance from a present calamity.

I have spoken of a single, in contradistinction to a double compact. The distinction is of great importance. Some writers, in treating of the social compact, regard it as a contract between the government and the people, while others, with much more reason, consider it as a contract between the people themselves, for the establishment of a government. If both took place, it would be a double compact. So in the division, by an aggregate community of the territory, into local governments, the compact is single, and in the formation of a central government by independent states, the same is the case. The compact in the one, is between the individuals composing the society ; in the other, between the states. Where a people have established a single government, they may alter or abolish it, for that government is an agency. Where they have established local or municipal jurisdictions, they may annihilate them ; and where independent states have entered into a confederacy, any one of them may secede from it. The reason of the last will not be so readily apprehended : for it may be supposed, that, as in the first and second, a majority of the people would be necessary to exercise the powers described, in the third, a majority of the states would be necessary to annul the central government, as regards even a single member. But the two things are *diverso intuitu*. In the two first, the original organization of the government is effected by the majority : in the last, it is effectd by the separate vote of each state. The principle of the majority is entirely foreign to the constitution of a federal government. It only begins to play a part, after it is set in motion. It is an instrument in the administration of the government, not in laying its foundation. So that the analogy fails ; and we are brought to the same conclusion, that each state, each member of a confederacy, may for itself but for itself alone, abdicate, and silently withdraw from the confederacy.

First. It has been attempted to deduce the right of secession from the hypothesis, that the sovereignty is inalienable and indivisible. The argument may be thus stated: the sovereignty originally resided in the states ; it is incapable of alienation or division; therefore, the right of secession is a perpetually subsisting right. This opinion is, however, without foundation, and I have therefore called it an hypothesis. Those who maintain it, regard it as a settled and fundamental maxim of government. Even if it were so, it would not be applicable, for secession does not imply the exercise of sovereignty, but the reverse, as I shall presently show.

A striking thought sometimes crosses the mind with the rapidity of lightning; and its novelty and brilliance forbid a vigorous examination of it. But analysis is the only test of the validity of any opinion. Our knowledge is so multifarious, and lies in such confused heaps in the mind, that nothing is clear until it is reduced to its simple elements. When we assert that the sovereignty is inalienable, or indivisible, we in effect impose limitations upon the sovereignty, which is a contradiction; we annul the very principle upon which the proposition rests; we take from the sovereignty its most capital attribute in the very sentence which is intended to give it the most extensive signification. Once the notion of sovereignty is admitted, it follows, as an unavoidable consequence, that it has power to do, at least, what will contribute to the well being of the nation in whom it resides. Emergencies may occur which would render it highly desirable that one people should come under the government of another. If we say that the former is unable to do so—unable to merge its sovereignty in that of the latter—we in effect declare that it has not the capacity of self-preservation; that it is deprived of the choice of means for furthering so important an end, and yet sovereignty has no meaning, unless it supposes the power of making this choice. Scotland and Ireland merged their sovereignty in that of England by the acts of union, and it is certain, that if the United States had been a consolidated, instead of a federal, government, it would have been competent for the people of Texas to ask to be incorporated into it. It would have been so, if, instead of a republic, the United States had been an unlimited monarchy, like China or Russia. When, in the reign of Elizabeth, the people of Holland made overtures to the English nation to become united to it, as Wales is to England, it was an exercise of that very sovereignty which belongs to every independent people.

The dogma of sovereignty, if pursued in all its ramifications, and followed out in all the consequences to which it leads, is full of absurdity. The people of France have undoubtedly transferred all sovereignty over Louisiana to the United States; and although it may be said that this was a renunciation of sovereignty over a colony, and not over themselves; yet, first, the fact is certain (which is all I care for), that the sovereignty has been alienated; has been displaced from where it once resided, and that it cannot be recalled. Secondly, we can form no conception of sovereignty, unless it is attached to all the people living under the same government. The mere distance of the parts of an empire from each other, can make no difference in the principle, if there is any force in it. But to render the view still clearer, the French nation, instead of ceding Louisiana, may have ceded a part of European France. In this case, there would be absolutely no ground to stand upon in maintaining the dogma of the indivisibility of the sovereignty. Either the sovereignty did not reside in the French nation, or if it did, they would, by the cession, have alienated it in perpetuo. In the whole range of political philosophy, I know of no opinion which has been seen in so confused a manner, and which, perhaps, on that very account, has been seized with so much avidity. By the treaty of Vienna, Genoa was ceded to Sardinia, Finland to Russia, Norway to Sweden. In all those instances, the sovereignty over the people was irrevocably transferred to other nations. The sovereignty in neither Persia or Turkey resides in the people; but it would be absurd to say that the prince and sultan in whom it resides, are incompetent to alienate it, or that the progress of knowledge, and the advancement of popular power, may not gradually displace it from where it is now lodged, and deposit it with the people. Knowledge is power, especially in the political world. Where that resides, the sovereignty is to be found. Writers on political philosophy do not limit the maxim to one form of society, but extend it without distinction to all; and therein they have reason, and argue at least consequentially; for the power to alienate, must depend upon the faculty of sovereignty, not upon the body in whom it resides.

In a confederate government, the states composing it always reserve to themselves certain rights; and it may be supposed that in that case there can be no alienation of sovereignty. But in the English and Scotch union, where the merger was almost complete, Scotland reserved various rights to her people, the ecclesiastical establishment, the judicature, and private law, &c. And on the cession of the District of Columbia, a similiar course was pursued; but the sovereignty over the residue was forever alienated. It is incapable of being resumed, except with the consent of the United States. In the instances of Norway, Genoa and Finland, the sovereignty was transferred; in that of Scotland and the District of Columbia it is divided. If the United States had been a consolidated government, and without any representation of the people, the annexation of Texas would also have operated as a complete alienation of the sovereignty, if it were without any reservation, and with it, would have been a division. Some very excellent minds are ready to admit that there may be a division, while they are unprepared to admit that there can be an alienation. The keen mind of Rousseau saw clearly enough, that unless the indivisibility of the sovereignty was admitted, the dogma of inalienability must fall to the ground. He has, therefore, declared peremptorily, "that sovereignty is inalienable and indivisible." For it will be evident on reflection, that there is no difference in principle between the two. A division of the sovereignty is *pro tanto* an alienation.

On entering into political society, the individuals composing an aggregate community may make an entire surrender of their rights to the joint society created; or they may reserve to themselves a portion of those rights. The bill of rights of every state constitution in America is a reservation of this character; but this does not prevent the transfer of the sovereignty over the residue to the people of the state as composing one homogeneous community. The celebrated maxim, therefore, to which I have referred, is as untrue as it would be injurious. It is one of those generalities which are so fascinating to the mind, because they seem to condense a great deal of knowledge in a very small compass. It has no foundation in reason, because it assumes to set bounds to the sovereignty: it has none, in fact, because the course of human affairs has repeatedly contradicted it.

The author of "New Views of the Constitution" argues that there are only two ways in which it is conceivable, the sovereignty of the states forming a confederacy can be alienated: to the people in the aggregate, or to the government; and as there is no aggregate people in such a community, and as those who administer the government are only agents, he concludes that in the formation of the federal constitution of America, no alienation has been made. The objection is easily answered. There is a third mode which may be, and actually has been, adopted. The alienation was by the states separately, to the states jointly.

When individuals unite to form a government, each conveys to all. When states do the same, each also conveys to all. Not merely does the administration of the government appertain to this newly created power, but the government itself, the federal authority, resides in the states jointly. That the American states entered separately into the confederacy, and separately ratified it, does not contradict, but is in exact agreement with this view. For how can the concurrence of all be ascertained but by taking the vote of each separately, upon the question whether they do concur. No other device can be imagined by which this consent can be effected. The states are, by the supposition, separate, and independent communities, and we wish to ascertain whether they concur in lodging a vast mass of power in a joint association, and displacing it from the separate jurisdictions where it before existed. It is clear that every act done, up to the time when the new power is actually created, must be separate ; otherwise the states would be a joint association, before the compact creating them such would have been made. The consent of each is then necessary to create the joint society of states, and when this is effected, a large amount of power which before resided in the states separately, is made to reside in them jointly. Nor does it vary the matter whether the consent was given before or after the formation of the constitution. When several act together, the consent of each is necessary ; for how could it become the act of all, if it were not the act of each. A treaty which is separately ratified by two or more nations, is the joint act of both, precisely because it is the act of each. It would not be more effectually the act of both, if each had given full power to its ambassadors to make the treaty, consenting to be bound by their acts, and waiving all ratification. The separate consent of each would still be necessary to this agreement. But that the treaty would be the fruit of a joint, not of a single authority, is manifest ; for the consent of all the parties, not the will of one, would be necessary to unmake it. And yet the ratification by the American states, after the constitution was formed, is supposed by the ingenious author I have referred to, to prove that it was the act of each, and not the act of each and all, between which there is the the greatest imaginable difference. That it was not the act of a majority of the states, but of the states unanimously, does not prove that it was the act of each separately ; for the consent of each would be necessary to make the act of a majority binding.

In a consolidated republic, the united wills of individuals make the constitution, although the vote of each is taken ; and in a confederate republic, the joint will, not the will of any one member, makes the government, although the vote of each is also separately taken. In those private associations, which reflect the image of a large state, on a small scale, each member has entered separately ;

but its constitution is a joint act: every exercise of authority is from the necessity of the case, joint, and not several: all effective power over the subject matter within its jurisdiction, resides in the association, not in the government set up by it, nor in the agents appointed to administer it, but in the joint society to which the separate wills of individuals have given birth. In like manner, in a federal government, the sovereignty over the common interests is transferred by each, not to the government, but to the states jointly. No other supposition is admissible; nor does it require any metaphysical acumen to perceive that power may reside in states jointly, as well as in states separately. That the consent to make the transfer, and the transfer itself, are *uno flatu*, need not puzzle us, for such is the case in every species of political transaction.

Second. Secession is not the exercise of an act of sovereignty, but the reverse. Between it and the veto of a state, there is a clear and broad distinction. Secession is an unequivocal admission, that the sovereignty does not reside in the state seceding. An act of sovereignty removes officers, abolishes offices, alters constitutions, extinguishes the powers exercised by the government. In the case of secession, instead of the constitution and laws being removed out of the way of the discontented state, the state itself removes out of the way. This is a plain recognition, that it is not vested with sovereignty over the federal government, has no right to assume it, and that it is obliged to succumb to it. It is precisely like the emigration of individuals from a country whose government is a consolidated one, who become discontented with the condition in which they are placed, or with the institutions under which they live, and remove to another country. They are aware that, as individual members of society, they have no right to control the government. Instead of assuming to do so, they quietly withdraw from it. A confederate government, being the result of a joint compact between the members, and not the act of any one singly, the veto would be the usurpation of a power, which cannot belong to a single member. It would transform a joint into a single government. Secession admits the incompetency of the seceding state to do so, and instead of bending the government to its will, it is compelled to bend to the will of the government. Great mistakes have been committed from confounding secession with the veto. They are entirely different from each other, as the preceding observations sufficiently show.

There are different forms of confederate government ; and it may be supposed that the question whether the right of secession exists cannot be decided, without having regard to the precise form which is adopted. The Amphyctionic, Achæan, Italian, and German confederacies, were all different. The Achæan had this peculiarity, that the states composing it were obliged to adopt the same domestic institutions, as well as to submit to one uniform rule of federal legislation. The former and present confederations of the United States were also very different. There is one circumstance, however, in which they all agree, and that is in possessing a common federal jurisdiction, distinct from the jurisdiction which each state possesses within its own territory. They were all governments, although the amount of power which was wielded by the federal head varied in all. Thus the former and present confederacies of the United States were constitutions ; otherwise, they would not have been governments. We term both federal Unions, in order to distinguish them from the consolidated form of government. The principal feature in which they differed, was in the operation of the laws. In the first, these, as a general rule, acted upon the states, but not universally, for they were sometimes executed upon individuals. On the other hand, the laws, as a general rule, operate upon individuals, but not without exception. There are some instances in which they operate upon the states directly. There is one feature, however, in which these two governments resemble each other, and that is in the binding and obligatory force of all the federal laws upon all the people. The mode in which these laws are executed cannot vary the obligation to obey them. In both, congress was the source whence these laws emanated ; in some instances, executing them through the instrumentality of agents appointed by the central power. The disposition and arrangement of the federal authority presents a question of more or less convenience in the administration of the government, but does not affect the validity and supremacy of the laws.

When the federal government depends upon the states for the execution of the laws, and they are not executed, the delinquent member may be coerced into obedience by the whole force of the confederacy. But the coercion of a state implies the coercion of the

31

individuals composing it: and thus we are led to the same conclusion, that every form of confederacy is a constitution and government; that the laws are equally obligatory upon the citizens, and that the distinction between them consists in the more or less perfect machinery which is employed to enforce them. In all there is a division of the sovereignty, one portion being retained by the states separately, and the residue alienated, not to the central government, but to the states jointly. The distinction, then, so far as it affects the right of secession, is not between the more or less perfect form of federal government, but between a federal and consolidated government. This is the only test in our power, in order to determine when the right of secession exists.

Very imperfect notions were entertained, even under the former confederacy, of the structure and attributes of the state governments. In the debates of the convention, (Yates notes, p. 184,) Mr. Madison says, "the states at present are only great *corporations*, having the power of making *by-laws*." "The states *never* possesed the essential attributes of sovereignty. These were always vested in congress." He then compares the states to the counties of which they are composed, and argues, that as the counties are not sovereign, the states cannot be. If so fine a mind could err so greatly with regard to the appropriate authority of the states, it will not appear surprising that very inadequate notions are entertained at the present day. From one extreme, political writers have plunged into another.

A great principle can never depend for proof of its validity upon examples, since these may contradict some other principle of equally high authority. But where the example has been deduced from the principle, and could not have existed without it, it is of wonderful use in testing its value. It is then a direct corollary from the principle, and not merely a happy illustration of it. The confederation of 1778 was broken up by secession. The articles on which it was founded provided that no alteration should ever be made, unless with the unanimous consent of the states who were parties to it. The states were not unanimous in the change which substituted another ordinance, and converted the government into the present confederation. Rhode Island and North Carolina rejected the scheme, and may have remained out of the Union to the present day. Eleven states thus seceded from the old confederation. If it should be said that these states did not secede because the new government erected in place of the old, was itself a federal union; the answer is, that any change of the articles, much more the radical change which led to the formation of a new government, was absolutely prohibited unless the consent of each state was obtained. Indeed the futility of the objection will be manifest on a very little reflection. If two or more states were now to assemble in convention, or if all the states were so to assemble, and by a majority of votes should form a different federal government, it would be absurd to say they had not seceded, because the form of polity which they had established had one or more features in common with the former. But if, in order to test the bearing of the objection, we should admit it to be well-founded, the difficulty still exists. The states of North Carolina and Rhode Island then seceded. Their right to remain out of the new union, was never disputed; it was openly and unequivocally admitted. The congress under the new government never dreamed of coercing them into an adherence to it, but dealt with them as independent nations; and as I have before observed, they may have continued to this day separate and independent states.

There is another difficulty which presses upon us, and which creates more than a doubt whether the states composing a confederation are mere corporations, or municipal bodies, like the provinces and departments of a consolidated government. The states of Rhode Island, New York and Virginia, in ratifying the constitution, expressly reserved the right to secede. The first declared "that the powers of government may be reassumed by the people, whenever it shall become necessary to their happiness." The second made a declaration in precisely the same language. Rhode Island entered the union a considerable time after New York, and copied the language which had been used by the New York convention. The ratification of Virginia declared that "the powers granted under the constitution, being derived from the people of the United States, may be resumed by them, whenever the same shall be perverted to their injury or oppression." No language can be more precise and unequivocal. Each of these states declare that, although on entering into the confederacy a division of the sovereignty was made between the states jointly and the states separately, this partition was not inconsistent with a withdrawal from the Union, and that the right to secede was reserved to the states respectively. No tribunal is erected or contemplated, in order to determine the course of action of the states, when the crisis arrives. The question whether the trusts conferred upon the federal government have been perverted, or in the unqualified language of New York and Rhode Island, whether "the happiness of their people would be promoted" by a resumption of the powers granted, is not submitted to any tribunal under the federal government. The supreme court of the United States is never alluded to. Its interference is, by necessary implication, precluded. No such disposition could possibly be made of the matter. A judicial tribunal is unable to determine a question of expediency: it is only adopted to adjudicate cases where the naked question of right is presented. The constitution has skillfully guarded the peace of the confederacy, while the states remain in it, by referring the constitutionality of the laws to the supreme court. But what causes shall be of sufficient magnitude to induce a state to withdraw altogether from the operation of the constitution and laws, and by thus withdrawing, to avoid all conflict between state and federal jurisdiction, is, from the necessity of the case, submitted to the state itself. This is the undisguised avowal of the three states I have referred to; it is equally so of the whole Union, which accepted these declarations as conformable with the fundamental principles of a confederate government, and thereby ratified them. As one member of a federal union cannot possess any higher federal right than is enjoyed by all, the inference is direct, that even if the right of secession were not an inherent attribute of confederate states, it is at least reserved to every American state. The time has gone by when we can conceal the truth, from a persuasion that the knowledge of it may be abused. The discovery will assuredly be made, and if made in the midst of a settled and determined opposition to its promulgation, all the institutions of society, and not one merely, will be in jeopardy. The European doctrine is, that in matters of government, it is necessary that statesmen should have both a secret and a declared opinion. The maxim in America should be, that the justest use will, in the long run, be most likely to be made of every right, where it is clearly, frankly and unreservedly admitted.

The value and importance of the principle I have been endeavoring to unfold, will be appreciated, when it is recollected that in every community whose population comes to be spread over a wider and wider arena, a diversity of views, habits and customs will necessarily grow up, over which the laws can very imperfectly preside. Even Charlemagne, who wielded the power of one of the most consolidated governments which ever existed, was compelled to declare that "it was impossible for the central authority to watch over every interest with all the care which was desirable, or to retain every one in the path he should follow."

All writers on public law, agree that in the event of intolerable oppression, the people are justified in making resistance to the government. The terms in which this proposition is conceived are very remarkable. 1st. The cases which will authorize so violent a departure from the settled order of things, are not enumerated and defined. The principle is expressed in language the most general and ambiguous. 2d. The idea of a tribunal to sit in judgment upon the controversies which may lead to revolution, is not entertained, but is directly repudiated. 3d. The maxim is proclaimed in governments which are supposed to possess an absolute and self-existing authority. The principle is attended with dangers of the greatest magnitude, and yet we can discover no way of escaping from it. The great desideratum then, is to be able to contrive some expedient which will exempt us from this stern necessity, which will substitute peaceable in the place of violent revolution. The aggregate form of government does not admit of this remedy; the confederate does. Instead of forcible resistance to the federal head, instead of unlawful attempts to annul the laws of the Union, while the member is within it, that member is at liberty quietly to depart, while others retain their position in the confederacy. This is one of the most important attributes of a federal government. Secesion is the instrument happily substituted in the place of open hostility to the laws. So that in the confederate form of government, the law itself provides against those great emergencies which in other countries are said to make the laws for themselves.

The great risk which will be incurred by the seceding member, the disadvantageous position in which it will be placed, standing alone in the midst of a firm and compact league, will operate as a powerful check upon its conduct, and will prevent recourse to such an extreme measure, unless it can be justified before the bar of public opinion. At the same time, the open recognition of the right to secede, will render it disgraceful to embark in any scheme of concerted resistance to the laws while the state continues a member of the Union. The explicit recognition of the right wlll also operate as a salutary restraint upon the central government. If one or two states seceded, they would inevitably be the losers: it would be staking every thing upon the cast of a dye. But if several threatened to do the same, the confederacy would be in danger of being deprived of so much strength and importance, that every measure which prudence and calm judgment could suggest, would be adopted to avert so great a calamity. The public councils would be marked by more reflection, when a moral agency was substituted in the place of brute force. Rhode Island and North Carolina were resolute in their opposition to the present constitution, and for a time refused to enter into the Union. Congress pursued towards them the same course which it did towards the European states: it treated them as independent nations, and applied to them the laws relative to discriminating duties. This contributed greatly to change their resolution. They entered the confederacy, one of them two years after it was formed; and motives still more powerful, will deter either from now seceding. The right of secession, then, is a weapen of defence of great efficacy in the hands of the states, but it supposes one still more efficacious in the hands of the federal government. The advantages of union are so manifold, the position of a member, when isolated is so insignificant, and when united with others, so commanding, that nothing but the greatest injustice, or the most irreconcilable diversity of interests will occasion the exercise of the right. Instances of secession are accordingly very rare. Two of the states composing the Boetian confederacy seceded, and the dismemberment of the provinces of Holland and Belgium may perhaps be regarded as similiar. They were united in one confederacy in 1814, and were disunited in 1830, by the withdrawal of Holland. The rupture was occasioned in part by an irreconcilable difference in the religious creeds of the two peoples, and in part by the improper interference of the central government with the education of the people.

The principle of representation is one of the finest expedients which has been devised, for perfecting the machinery of government. In a country of great extent, it is ineffectual, unless it is combined with another principle of equal importance. This consists in dividing the territory, if it has not previously been divided into separate jurisdictions, and investing each with complete control over its domestic interests. If this is not done, the general and local interests will be confounded. The last can be but imperfectly represented or understood, and yet will be subjected to the same undistinguishing majority, which rules over the national interests. The principle of representation, would then fail to answer the end it was intended to reach. The United States, in consequence of the great extent of country, presented greater obstacles than any other country, to the solution of the difficulty; and it is the one in which the nearest approach has been made to that solution. But it by no means follows, that the confederate form of government may be carried to any extent, that there is no limit to the number of states which may be combined in one Union. It would be more correct to say, that there is a limit, although happily, it is difficult to define it. It is like a great many other interests appertaining to society, in which the rules are certain enough, and yet the precise circumstances under which they are applicable, are difficult to predict. The time will certainly come, when the same causes which led to the formation of the present Union, will lead to the formation of two or more Unions. The institution of government, as I remarked in a preceding chapter, is an experiment to classify, to reduce to unity, the diversified rights and interests, which spring up in society. But the generalization may be pushed so far as to tresspass upon the interests of the parts, in spite of the machinery of the local governments. The time, however, must not be anticipated. Union is itself one means of overcoming geographical differences, and harmonizing geographical parties. These parties were appealed to in the convention of 1787, and in the succeeding state conventions, as opposing insuperable difficulties to the formation of a federal constitution. In the period which has elapsed, no country has been so happy and prosperous, none so free from civil dissensions, none which has so well succeeded in reconciling a large amount of liberty, with the requisite energy in government.

CHAPTER III.

THE EXECUTIVE POWER.

It is more difficult to form a distinct idea of the executive than of any other department of the government. In some countries it comprehends nearly the whole authority of the state, not to be sure dispensing with laws, but usurping to itself the sole power of ordaining them. In absolute monarchies, the prince is legislator, judge and ministerial magistrate. The permanence of the executive is doubtless one reason why, in the majority of governments, it has been the most imposing authority. The minds of men are more strongly impressed with the notion of government, when its image is constantly before them, than by the occasional or periodical exercise of authority by a legislative body, the members of which are disbanded during a great part of the year. The political institutions of a state may be said to perform two distinct offices: First, to hold society together, to maintain civilization; and secondly, to administer the interests of that society. The last implies a mere agency, a delegation of power by the members to conduct the affairs of the community with judgment and discretion. Nor is the first at all inconsistent with the same notion of delegated authority; on the contrary, the various elements of which society is composed, its divers population, and different interests, are never so firmly cemented together, as where government represents the will of the people. But this is a character which it has seldom acquired. The institution of a prince, termed by way of eminence the executive magistrate, has been deemed necessary almost every where, to bind together the parts of society, and to give a character of unity to the authority of the state. It is this notion of unity perpetually revolvving in the mind, in matters of government as well as religion, which gives a shape to the political institutions, and enabled the prince to center in himself nearly all power. The gradual and unobstructed progress of society, wherever it takes place, at length sets bounds to this state of things. As civilization advances, public affairs become so unwieldly and complicated, that it is physically impossible for one mind to preside over them, much less to administer them in person. The prince communicates his authority to subordinate agents, in order to relieve himself from the burden, but by so doing he, step by step, diminishes his influence, loses his prerogatives, and prepares the way for more regular institutions. He appoints judges and administrative officers, to do thoroughly what he had been able very imperfectly to perform. A legislative body soon after makes its appearance, at first only representing constructively the society in which it is assembled. And as this body will necessarily have a close connection with all those affairs which are immediately superintended by the ministers of the crown, it ultimately acquires a considerable control upon the crown itself. It at first influences, but in the progress of time, it absolutely determines the appointment and removal of those ministers. The prince, in order to relieve himself from the cares of public business, and to have more time to devote to the gratification of his pleasures, or ambition, assists in raising up a host of officers in the state; by so doing he causes a larger proportion of the people to be trained to the understanding and management of public affairs, and without intending any such thing, creates a counterpoise to his own authority. Through the operation of the same causes, which speedily give birth to some species of legislative assembly, the judges no longer expound a code of laws enacted by the sole authority of the king. The legislature is at first permitted sparingly to interfere with such high matters, but in progress of time it is enabled to speak out audibly and intelligibly, and the judges are then freed from a servile dependence upon the executive magistrate. He retains the power of appointment, but as soon as it is made, a new relation is established between the judges and the community at large, and they are declared irremovable at his pleasure. Their responsibility becomes both more strict and more extensive, and the laws are consequently administered in a much more enlightened manner than before. The powers which are thus gradually wrested from the king are not extinguished, but they are deposited in other hands where they are even amplified and strengthened. The commonwealth gains in power much more than the monarch loses. In order that the increasing demand of the state for the services of its citizens may be fully answered, knowledge and education are sought after by every one. And thus at length, that invisible but powerful authority which we denominate public opinion, comes to preside over every movement of the government, and to fulfill more completely than ever the notion of unity, which continues to float in the mind, whatever may be the mutations which the political institutions undergo.

It is through a circuitous process, then, that a gradual separation of the executive from the legislative and judicial authority takes place, and that three distinct departments are created. But this separation is hardly ever complete. The same difficulty which we have to encounter in every other branch of knowledge, meets us with redoubled force in political philosophy. The principles are given, but the facts do not all agree, or the facts are given, but the principles which we look to do not exactly correspond. The limits however which are drawn around the human mind, even in matters of this kind, are never so absolutely fixed but what we may sometimes escape from the dilemma. It is often possible, by the application of principles which do not strictly correspond with the facts, to produce an alteration in the facts themselves, to give rise, in other words, to an altered condition of society, and then the disagreement will in great part disappear.

The thorough introduction of the elective principle into the government, effects a separation of the different departments from each other. This is a natural and a very important consequence of the establishment of representative government. Where public officers are chosen by the people, it is with a view to the performance of some prescribed duty, and the exercise of some precise and definite power. But as soon as a practical and determinate end is sought after, the functions of the different officers lose all the vagueness and ambiguity which before hung over them. The prince consulted materially the interests of society when he laid down some of his prerogatives, although it was only for the sake of his convenience. But the people go straight forward to the same end, as soon as they possess the electoral franchise in its full extent. A feeling of convenience also determines them to remold the institutions. But as this view to convenience has reference to the general good, to the practical affairs of society, the work is performed more completely by them.

As the prince is not elected but is a hereditary magistrate, the powers with which he is clothed have been determined by accident only. Hence his prerogatives are neither adjusted by any distinct rules, nor to the actual exigencies of society. His title commenced at some remote period, when society was full of noise and confufusion—when the human mind was not sufficiently instructed, nor the interests of the community sufficiently developed, to give any determinate character to his functions. At first, by dint of superstition, or force, afterward, by means of the vast influence which his strong position enables him to command, he succeeds in maintaining the most extravagant and contradictory powers, and this long after society is prepared for an entire change in the structure of his office.

When not merely the public officers who fill the various departments are elected, but in addition to this, the entire system of government is founded upon a written constitution, the opportunity and the power to effect a separation between these departments are both increased. The experience which has been previously acquired, the adaptation which each part of the government has obtained in practice, to one appropriate end and no other, are seized by those who assemble in the constitutional convention, and suggest certain fundamental rules, by which to give fixation and stability to the plan. A constitution is indeed only a generalization of the diversified rights, duties, and exigencies of men in society. And when the generalization is made upon reflection and deliberation—when it is brought to bear upon matters which have been the subject of actual experiment, it is necessarily more distinct as well as more comprehensive.

It has been proposed to elect the president of the United States by lot. This mode of choice is thought to be peculiarly adapted to a democratic republic, which presupposes that all the citizens stand upon an equality. This is to take a one-sided view of the matter, a course which is always attended with error. The great principle of equality demands that all the citizens should have free liberty of choice in selecting persons capable of managing their affairs. We attribute to them equal rights, and straight forward adopt an arrangement which overthrows the most important of those rights. We start with the principle of liberty, and then inconsistently introduce a principle which causes the actions of every one to be controlled by a rigid necessity. The principle of equality does not require that all the citizens should succeed in turn to the presidency, for that is an impossibility: but it does require that all should be equally eligible. Now the only way in which it is possible to reconcile this right with that of free choice, is by the establishment of the elective principle. If there were any inconsistency between the two, it is plain that the former should yield to the latter, as being of superior importance. But in truth, there is no inconsistency. The right to hold office would be a frivolous and unmeaning one, if it were not combined with the principle of election. That cannot be called a right, whose existence is absolutely dependent upon blind chance or an irreversible necessity. That only is a right in society which springs from the free consent of society. It is because the principle of election is calculated to carry to perfection all the other rights of mankind, that it is made the corner stone of a republic; and it is because the lot would confound and subvert those rights, that it should be rejected.

If in a community of twenty millions of people, the chief magistrate, legislature, and judges, were chosen by lot, it is evident that the selection would, in the greater number of instances, be very unfortunate. That it might be so, would be a sufficient objection; but that it would necessarily be so, is an insuperable one. Offices are created because they are indispensable to the management of the public interests, to the well being of society. But the office is an empty thing, a mere abstraction, unless it is filled by some one who is competent to discharge the duties; and integrity, ability, and experience, are all necessary to fulfill this design. A state, then, which is founded upon republican principles, which undertakes to procure the greatest happiness of the greatest number, is entitled to the services of those citizens who possess these qualities. That the elective principle will not invariably secure this advantage, is no objection to it; but that it does actually attain it, to a much greater extent than any other system which has been devised, is a conclusive reason why it should be adhered to.

In order to avoid the difficulties which attend the lot, it has been proposed to combine with it the principle of free choice, as in the case of the Venetian doge. Hillhouse's plan, the earliest which was presented to the American public, and the parent of all others, contemplated the election of president by lot from among the senators. A plan, presented twenty-five years later, proposed that he should be chosen in the same way from members of the house of representatives. This, to be sure, reversed the Venetian scheme in which the doge was elected by forty-one nobles, they themselves having been appointed by lot. The two plans, however, are substantially the same; in both, there is a combination of choice and chance. But there is no arrangement in which the lot enters as an element, which is not objectionable. The lot might fall upon some senator or representative who was eminently unfit for the station. The manner in which the fortunate individual succeeded to the chief magistracy, would be exposed to the same objection as exists to monarchical government. The prince reigns by accident, and the selection of the president would be determined by accident, also. The community would be unable to profit by the lessons of experience; it would not have the power on a succeeding occasion, to cure the error which had been committed. The lot might fall successively upon those who had not the requisite qualifications.

The objections to a free and untrammeled election, are the very argument I should employ in favor of it. They who propose the lot, have fastened their attention upon the prevailing spirit of party. It is to prevent the eternal din and confusion which it occasions, that they have presented this plan. Zealous and patriotic individuals they are, for they wish to attain all the good which is attainable; but they are not sufficiently apprised of the means through which alone this desirable object can be reached.

It may be very important that the president of the United States should be chosen by a party. Parties, whatever may be the exterior form which they wear, almost always contain the elements of great improvement. They are among the instruments which are appointed to push the race of mankind forward. The heated passions and fierce disputes through which they sometimes cause themselves to be heard, are the only means in a society not enlightened above what it falls to the lot of humanity to be, by which any signal change in the public policy of the state, or the condition of the people, can be attained. In elective government, public men may be said to be the representatives of the ideas of the age, as well as of the grosser interests with which they have to deal; and to give those ideas a visible form, is the most certain way of commanding public attention, and of stimulating inquiry.

It would be a noble undertaking, if it were practicable, to separate the mischievous qualities of parties from the good they contain; to suppress the one and retain the other. But that is impossible as men are now constituted. To endeavor to rid ourselves of the anxieties and sufferings of life, would be an attempt to free society from the most wholesome discipline to which it is at present subjected. No important end can be attained, perhaps none is worthy of being attained unless it is through some sort of difficulty and danger. These are not merely to be viewed as obstructions in the way, which it requires some strength to overcome, but as constant monitors to remind us of our own imperfections, while we are endeavoring to rectify those of others. The innumerable annoyances of which party spirit is the occasion, are planted in the walks of public life, in order to exercise a similar influence. That we complain of them, may be only a proof that they have the desired effect. That the lot would contribute to banish parties from the commonwealth, instead of being a recommendation, therefore, is a solid and conclusive objection to it.

Men undoubtedly take upon themselves a difficult task, and involve themselves in a great many troubles when they undertake to elect the highest officers in the state. But it is the only way by which the people can be trained and habituated to the practice of self government. If public affairs go wrong, they cannnot say it is government which has done the mischief, and we will revolt and overturn the existing authority; but they are brought, after a painful and instructive experience, to understand that they are themselves the direct authors of the public distress, and that they alone have the power to remedy it. Thus a great number of petty misfortunes have the effect of averting an enormous evil.

The popular election of the American President has not been productive of the mischiefs which were anticipated. Instead of wild disorder and misrule, it has been eminently favorable to public tranquillity. This is a necessary consequence of the elective principle as it is applied in the United States. By communicating the electoral franchise freely, and at the same time distributing into small fragments the bodies which exercise it, the ability to do mischief is very much abridged. The machinery which sets in motion the elections, is like the machinery of a federal government. It acts upon the whole mass; and yet through springs so numerous and so fine, as to combine all the strength of a consolidated government, with all the freedom of a popular one. The share of power which each individual exercises is so small that he is constantly reminded of his insignificance, and does not boast of his importance, while the principle of the majority is so imposing and authoritative in its influence, as to command instant and universal obedience to the laws. It may, indeed, be laid down as a maxim in politics, that the danger to the institutions is diminished, rather than increased, in proportion to the enlargement of the electoral franchise.

Representative government imposes a check upon the electors, as well as upon the elected. It is not apt to be viewed in this light. The accountability of the public officer to his constituents, was the thing to which public attention was directed, when free institutions were first established. That was a novelty before. No man, it is true, ever ventured to deny that he was under an obligation to consult the welfare of the people over whose interests he presided; but amid the contradictory elements of monarchical and aristocratical government, the principle could never be made to have a practical operation, much less to assume the supreme authority to which it is entitled. A responsibility, however, on the part of the public agents, cannot exist in full vigor, without creating a counter principle of equal strength and efficacy. The numerous magistrates who are created, the regular system of administration which grows up in spite of the popular character of the institutions, stamps upon the government a degree of authority which either wins or compels the obedience of all. Not only is the responsibility of the citizens to the public increased, but what is of more consequence, the responsibility of each to the whole society is hightened.

The public officer is made responsible to the people, for the very obvious reason, that their interests are involved in every act of his public life. A perception on their part of what is advantageous for the public weal, is necessary to place the officer in that relation. Unless this condition is admitted, the whole theory of representative government falls to the ground. Nor is it necessary to entertain any fanciful views with regard to popular intelligence, in order to suppose that this condition may be fulfilled. There is but one way in which that perception of what is useful and fit can be gained, but one way in which any sort of practical knowledge can be acquired ; and that is, by placing those for whom such knowledge is desirable, in a situation where they will be sure to realize the consequences which will follow from pursuing opposite courses. It is supposed that if the lot is established, we shall get rid of all the noise and confusion of elections, that everything will go on smoothly, that the officer will feel greater pride in the discharge of his duties, when he occupies an independent position, than when he was a candidate, and obliged before hand to shape his conduct so as to meet all sorts of contradictory opinions. But this extreme smoothness of public affairs I have constantly observed to be inconsistent with much progress in society, and to be invariably followed by commotions and disturbances afterward. These commotions are the compensations of a bad system of government, and have been the only means by which European society has been prevented from falling into the sluggish and inert condition of a Chinese population. Popular elections not only afford employment to the superabundant activity of the people, but they create innumerable checks upon the conduct of public men. They thus act by way of prevention, in warding off great mischiefs, instead of encountering them, after they have arrived, by calamities still more formidable. It is a great mistake to suppose that public men would possess more integrity, patriotism, or knowledge, if they were less interfered with. The mistake would be fully as great, if we were to suppose that the people would be more peaceable and orderly, or anything like as inquisitive and well informed on public matters, or indeed on any matters whatever, if the lot were substituted in the place of elections. I am so persuaded of the utility of the last, so well satisfied that the advantages which they procure could be obtained in no other way, and these advantages accrue not merely in spite of, but in consequence of the inconveniences which are complained of, that I would dispense with even more of the ease and comfort of individuals, if that were necessary, in order to retain them. I know no other plan by which it is possible to keep alive the intelligence of the great bulk of the adult population ; none by which it is possible to give activity to the popular mind, and at the same to exercise it upon subjects which shall have interest and importance enough to lift it above the narrow round of ordinary pursuits. I know of no other plan by which it is possible to maintain the integrity, industry, and activity of public men. An eminent physician has said that life and bodily health are forced states. And so are intellectual and moral health. Many hard and disagreeable things are necessary to preserve the former, and annoyances, privations, and inconveniences, of one kind or other, are equally necessary to preserve the latter. There is hardly any one but what would pass away life in a state of careless ease, if he were permitted. In youth we are constrained to do otherwise by the superintending hand which guides us, and in manhood we are driven to exertion, and to the pursuit of laudable ends, not less by the wants of life, than by the constant interference of others with every plan of conduct which we may pursue. The elective system only carries out this part of the economy of human nature; the difficulties and temptations with which it surrounds both the electors and the candidates, may force a state of moral and intellectual culture, but after it is obtained, it becomes the natural state. And everything then goes on more easily and quietly than it would in any other society. For I do not find that public affairs in the United States have been reduced to less system, that they have been conducted in a less orderly manner, or with a view to the attainment of objects of less magnitude and importance than in other countries. On the contrary, I believe that in consequence of the conflict of parties, the public will has been more steadily directed to the advancement of the public weal than in any other country. The disputes and contentions of parties have been favorable to that unity of purpose which is demanded in all human affairs. The more frequent and varied these disputes are, the more they help to strip both public men and public measures of whatever is adventitious about them. The former are observed more readily, and the analysis of the latter becomes easier.

It is not surprising that the popular election of chief magistrate in the United States has never led to any political disturbance. The elective principle cures the mischiefs which have been apprehended from the contests of parties. The lot would deprive us of the most valuable means for maintaining free institutions. It would annul the use of experience, or render its application impossible. It would cut asunder the bond which now connects the representative with his constituents; and would remove the check which the exercise of the elective franchise imposes upon the electors themselves. It would be better that the lot should be applied to the choice of any other officer than that of president, for in this, the election is on so large a scale, that it raises the minds of the people above the narrow and contracted views which they are sometimes prone to take of public affairs. It gives them large objects to look at, and thus refreshes their feelings, and expands their minds.

There is the greatest imaginable difference between the election of a king of Poland, and of the American president. It was precisely because there were no parties of the people in Poland, that that unhappy country was filled with confusion whenever the time of election came round. The body of nobles who were masters of the landed property, had thereby a mortgage upon the understandings of the people. Factions there were, but parties had no existence. It was not because the prize was so high ; it was because the election was managed by a close body, that Poland was a prey to every species of intrigue and violence. Parties are unfavorable to civil commotion, while factions engender and support them : one reason of which is, that parties in any country of tolerable extent are so large, that in order to enable them to act, they must be subdivided into still smaller parties—into bodies so numerous as to render intrigue or intimidation very difficult : whereas factions concentrate immense power in a small compass. The principle of the distribution of power, is applied in the one case, but not in the other. Thus in the United States, the people assemble at ten or fifteen thousand places to vote for a president ; and in Poland, the election was conducted by a ferocious band of nobles all armed and collected upon one spot. The experiment of electing the chief magistrate has succeeded in America, because it has operated in a manner different from what was expected. It has succeeded, because the election is in effect by the people, and not by the electoral colleges.

The unity of the executive power is regarded as a fundamental principle in political science. In this, there is a striking distinction between antiquity and our own times. It is remarkable that almost all the capital rules of government have undergone a revolution in modern times. In the ancient commonwealths, the principle of representation was applied to the executive, but not to the legislature. A hereditary nobility, which has made a figure in the modern

European states, was unknown to the ancient. And the constitution of the executive presents us with a third example of the great diversity between the old and new systems of government. A plural executive was considered, by the ancient lawgivers, as indispensable to the right ordering of a state. In the Spartan commonwealth, there were two kings, in the Athenian the archons, at Rome two consuls. The elevation of the great body of the people in modern times, has given birth to the principle of representation, as applied to the legislative body. A hereditary nobility is the offspring of feudal institutions, and to the decay of those institutions we may trace the unity of the executive power. The chieftain who centered in himself the greatest amount of authority, who was able to bridle the ferocity of the other barons, and to impose an iron arm upon their will, usurped the supremacy under the title of king.

De Lolme is the most vigorous defender of the unity of the executive, and his views are entitled to great attention. This indivisibility of the executive authority, he says, fulfills two very important and apparently opposite conditions. Power is more easily confined when it is one ; while at the same time, it is placed more completely above the reach of assault. But a train of reasoning which is suggested by the frame of the English constitution, may be very inapplicable to other forms of government ; still less may it be entitled to rank among the fundamental principles of the science. If our design be to establish regal government, if we determine to create an executive magistrate, with vast powers and prerogatives, it is certain that we will produce one effect. The prestige and luster which will surround the office, independently of the positive authority which is conferred upon it, will make a powerful impression upon the imaginations of the people. They will be awed to obedience, to a bad as well as to a good government. The throne will acquire great stability, conspiracies to overturn it will rarely be formed; although it may be free from the wholesome interference of public opinion, it will at any rate be placed above the assaults of ambitious men. But these are all consequences of the artificial character which is at the outset communicated to the executive : and unless its imposing prerogatives are an inseparable condition from its existence, we are not obliged to leap to the general conclusion, that therefore the executive should be one. For if, on the other hand, we intend to establish a republican form of government, the executive will be elective; the precise authority assigned to it will be settled by a constitutional ordinance, and not be left to stand upon the debatable ground of opinion. The office will be less dazzling, but it will on that very account be less open to attack. It will not affect the imaginations of men so strongly, but it will acquire a firmer hold upon their understandings. It will be protected by a real force, instead of by an invisible agency, and will secure the obedience of the people by the practical benefits it dispenses.

In these two examples, the structure of the government is totally different, and yet results in some respects similar may take place, but without any regard, so far as we can yet see, to the fact, whether in the last the executive is a single or a plural body.

The second position of De Lolme, that the executive power is more easily confined when it is one, is as a general proposition more questionable than the first. The condensation of power is the chief circumstance which renders it formidable and difficult to be restrained. And it is for this reason that free governments proceed upon the plan of distributing power, as the most certain means of controlling it. The splendid attributes which are ascribed to a hereditary prince, overpower the minds of the great majority of mankind; the people are incapacitated from making resistance to the most alarming exercise of authority, or from rectifying the most inveterate abuses; for a feeling of superstition has taken possession of them, and they feel as if they were ruled over by a force superior to society. And when to this is added the physical power which is placed at the command of this single individual, it is obvious that if he is restrained, it must be by some compensatory contrivance, totally independent of the unity of the executive, and indicating perhaps that there is a faulty rather than a wise constitution of that department. I speak now of the unity of the executive as understood by De Lolme, whose reasoning is founded upon the notion of a hereditary monarch, although his views are conceived with a design of laying the foundation of a general principle. So difficult is it for even the finest understanding to analyze its ideas, that the argument is a defense of the unity of the executive, as the only way of maintaining the hereditary principle, rather than a defense of the first, for the sake of establishing a principle of universal application.

The subordinate end is made to take the place of the superior one; a very common error when the mind has fastened upon one set of phenomena, and is determined to deduce all the principles of a science from them alone. It was after the usurpation of Octavius Cæsar, when the executive authority which was before divided came to be centered in the hands of a single individual, that it was found impossible to set bounds to it. The theory of nearly all the European governments, so far as regards the constitution of the executive, is the same now that it was centuries ago. And yet history shows that it was absolutely impossible to control it in England, in the times of the Stuarts, and in France under the reign of the Bourbon princes, not to go back to periods still more remote, when it swallowed up every other authority.

What has occasioned the remarkable change which has taken place in very modern times? Not the recognition and establishment of the maxim of De Lolme, for that was the corner stone of government when all Europe was filled with the most frightful tyranny. Causes of a very different character must have given rise to this revolution. It can only be ascribed to the growth of a new power in the state, to wit, that which is represented by the popular will. And that this new power will acquire still more influence, and ultimately succeed in modifying the whole constitution of the executive, is as certain as any event which is the subject of human speculation. It was formerly sufficient to study the mere mechanism of government in order to explain the phenomena of government, but it is now necessary to look a great deal further, and to take in the structure of society as a most important element in the character and working of the political institutions.

All the tendencies of society at the present day, all the new forces which are created within it, are unfavorable to the condensation of power in any department of the government. This was not the case until very modern times. When De Lolme wrote, the English house of commons was just beginning to acquire a due weight in the constitution: the people were making slow but steady advances in the acquisition of knowledge and property; public opinion, for the first time in the history of society, showed signs of becoming a power of commanding influence in the state. All these agencies have received a wonderful accession of strength during the last seventy years, and begin to press with an enormous weight upon the executive authority. In other words, the power out of the government more nearly balances the power within, and produces the two opposite effects of confining and yet giving stability to the regal authority. This is evidently attributable to the altered structure of society, and not to the unity of the executive.

There is this difference between a monarchy and a republic: that in the former, the government is more simple as a whole, and yet very complicated in its parts; while in the latter, it is exceedingly complicated as a whole, and yet very simple in the construction of its parts. In a republic, power is not condensed in any single institution as in a monarchy. It is divided among a great number of offices. When, for example, the chief magistrate is elected, his term of office short, his powers greatly abridged, the executive department will not be so complex and artificial a contrivance as it is in a hereditary government. It may even be a matter of very little importance whether it is composed of one or more members. Its original structure, in other and more important respects, is such as necesssarily to confine it within its appropriate sphere. And the same power which confines it also protects it.

In modeling the executive department in a republic, a double plan is pursued. Certain attributes which were before regarded as inseparable from it, are extinguished; the hereditary principle, the right to create peers, the absolute veto, the authority to dissolve the legislative body are all annihilated; they are deposited no where. The residue of the power is then divided between the officer who still maintains the title of executive, and other departments, or offices, some portion being extinguished as to him, but yet remaining in other parts of society.

But two plans may be pursued in distributing power. A certain amount of power may be conferred upon two or more individuals to be jointly exercised by them, or the power itself may be divided, that is, lodged in different institutions and not merely distributed among several persons, all holding the same office. Examples of the first were common in the ancient commonwealths. The executive authority was confided to two or more; but all composed one body. The French directory, and afterward the consulship, when composed of three members, and the governor and council in some of the American states, are instances of the same arrangement. The executive power is exercised by a plural body. The German, Swiss and American confederacies, are examples of the second plan. The executive authority is not divided among a number of persons all composing one body, or one department, but is distributed among a great number of institutions. In the German and Swiss confederacies this power, so far as regards one class of objects, the exterior relations of the members of the confederacy, is deposited with the general diet, which in both is a numerous body ; and as regards the local interests of each of the members, it is sometimes confined to a plural, and sometimes to a single executive. In the American government, the same power is apportioned between the president and the thirty states. For it is plain, that if the United States were a hereditary and consolidated monarchy, the entire authority which is possessed by the state executives would be wielded by a single individual. This might also be the case, if it were one aggregate community, and yet a republic. But it would fall very far short of the true notion of a republic, which absolutely requires not only that the public authority should be divided among several persons, but that it should be distributed among a number of sections or local departments. And although we way view the American confederacy as composed of several distinct governments, rather than as parts of one system of government, yet it is neither necessary nor advantageous to do so; not necessary, because the same or a similar scheme must have been adopted, if the country had not been accidentally divided into distinct colonial provinces: and not advantageous, because a scheme analogous to the present is indispensable to the maintenance of free institutions. By taking the view I have just adverted to, the mind fastens upon a circumstance entirely accidental, and loses sight of the principal point to be gained in constructing a democratic republic, whether it be composed of one homogeneous people, or of several distinct peoples: and that is, to subdivide the executive authority, to make such a disposition of it that it shall no longer be the inalienable attribute of one man, and thus to falsify the maxim of De Lolme.

Or in order to make the train of reasoning still clearer. We must not suppose that the principal design, in founding the American government, was to preserve the identity of the states, and to make a merit of necessity by assigning to them very extensive powers. The prime object was to establish a government thoroughly republican; and there was no way of effecting this, but by abridging the immense power which would otherwise have been exercised by the political departments: and no way of accomplishing this but by dividing power, not only among several persons, but among several bodies. The government may have been a confederacy of monarchies, as in the German league, or a confederacy of aristocracies. The principal design, then, would have been to unite the whole for the sake of defense, to consult the exterior rather than the interior interests of the parts. But the American system went a great way beyond this; and it became necessary to retain the state governments, in order to subtract power from the central government, and to render the creation of a republic even possible. And although the American government is generally viewed as a system in which the federal authority superintends the external and the states the internal interests; yet the true view is to consider it as a whole, in which the principal design was to consult and secure the interior prosperity and welfare of all the parts; and the division into local jurisdictions was an accessory, indispensable to carrying out this design.

Where the whole executive authority of the commonwealth is distributed among several distinct departments, or jurisdictions, three plans may be adopted. The whole, or the greater part of the administrative officers appertaining to each of those jurisdictions, may derive their appointment from one person, who will thus be constituted the chief magistrate in regard to one class of interests; or the power of nomination only may be conferred upon him, subject to the approval or rejection of one or both chambers of the legislative body: or their appointment may flow from an entirely distinct source; in which case they will all, from the highest to the lowest, be independent of each other, as well as of the head of the state. The first is the plan of monarchical government, whether absolute or limited. The second is the theory of the federal; and the third is that of the state governments of America. On either of these three plans, however, it is evident that the maxim, that the executive should be one, loses great part of its force. Thus, if the German confederation were presided over, as formerly, by the emperor, all federal appointments might flow from him, while all the administrative officers in each of the states would hold under some magistrate, or council, which was established in each; none of these magistrates, or councils, having any dependence upon the chief of the confederacy. The confederate form of government is then a device for breaking up the power of the different departments. It is not a mere arrangement of convenience. Convenience, or even necessity, may have determined it in the first instance; but the result is, that a much greater amount of liberty is introduced into the state. The character, and not merely the form of government, is altered.

But the state governments of the United States afford the most remarkable example of an entire departure from the maxim, that the executive should be one. In most of them, the governor has no participation whatever in the appointment of the other executive, or administrative officers. There is in truth no way of constructing free government, without doing violence to that maxim. Executive power, as it is understood by all writers on government, implies the appointment of the whole host of administrative officers by a chief magistrate. This is an authority too large, too vague, and too dangerous, to be confided to any one individual. We are compelled to divide and to subdivide the power, in order to uphold another principle of still greater value and importance, the responsibility of the public agents to the people. The European governments proceed upon the plan of conferring enormous power upon a single executive; and then the difficult problem is presented, how shall this unnatural authority be controlled? The American governments get rid of the difficulty, by getting rid of the problem. The executive power is distributed between the president and the thirty state governors: or it is in part devolved either upon the people themselves, or upon agents appointed by them. And this arrangement, while it causes all public business to be conducted with a greater degree of exactness and regularity, imposes numerous and powerful checks upon the exercise of the power. The plan which is the most natural, the one which falls in best with the convenience of society, will be sure to be the best constructed. The effect may be to spoil the beauty of a favorite theory, and to render what was once a cardinal principle of government, a mere formal arrangement, or a matter of detail. But it will not be the less valuable on that account.

In the federal government of America, it is only a small proportion of the public officers who are elected by the people. Not to mention officers in the army and navy, as well as foreign ambassadors, officers of the customs, heads of departments, the judges, the attorney general, and district attorneys, together with the marshals, are all appointed by the president and senate. The postmasters of higher grade are appointed in the same way ; those of an inferior grade are appointed by the postmaster general. The president and members of the house of representives only, are elected by the people, and the senate by the state legislatures. In a democratic republic, this at first appears to be a novel arrangement. But the confederate form of government naturally, if not necessarily, leads to a system of centralization within itself. And hence the importance of local jurisdictions becomes more manifest, in order to prevent the whole authority of the state from being swallowed up by a single government. To centralize the powers of the federal government seems to be the only way of preventing the two jurisdictions, the national and the domestic from being confounded and ultimately running into each other. The same reason does not exist in a consolidated government, for there all the public officers may be elected by the people. But what more particularly deserves attention in the structure of the American federal government, is, that those officers whose administration is central, the president and members of the legislative body, are chosen in local districts ; while those whose administration is local, are appointed by a central authority. It is not so in the state governments, where nearly all the administrative officers are elected by the people. For there is no danger, in the domestic governments, that any rivalship will grow up between their public officers and the state authority.

Thus the federal government still clings to the system of patronage, while almost all the state governments have, since 1789, gradually introduced the elective principle, in the appointment of civil functionaries. The consequence is that the relative position of the two governments toward each other is different, and the balance between the two materially altered. Federal politics now create the only existing parties of moment, and these parties not only rule in the national councils, but control the local parties within the states. And the only question is whether, by controlling their local politics, they will finally succeed in controlling their local interests also. There can be no objection to the natural influence of general politics within the states, for that contributes to fasten more closely the bond which connects the national with the local interests; but when to this natural influence is added the artificial strength derived from the patronage of the federal government, a doubt is suggested whether the state jurisdictions will retain the independent position which was originally assigned to them. It is this patronage which creates the system of centralization in the federal government, and which not only raises up two great parties, but subordinate to them, the local parties in the states.

In a democratic republic, then, there are two apparently opposite tendencies: the one to a distribution, the other to a centralization, of power. As soon as the elective principle is extensively introduced, it leads directly to the creation of local jurisdictions, as the only way of connecting firmly the constituent with the representative. The advantages which they procure are not thoroughly realized, until the population comprised within them have become habituated to the management of their own affairs. The experience then acquired inculcates all the skill and ability which are requisite. But as there will be a residuum of power left after the institution of these local authorities, to wit, that which represents the state as a collective whole, the notion of a central government forces itself upon the minds of the most democratic people. And the question then is, how to avail ourselves of the great benefit of such a government, without introducing a system of centralization also.

When the constitution of the United States was established, the state governments were all differently modeled from what they are now. The administrative officers in each were by no means so generally elected by the people as they are now. The constitution of New York, at that day, vested the power of appointment in a council; that of Pennsylvania conferred it absolutely upon the governor, whose authority in that respect closely resembled that of the British monarch. And the other state governments tended more or less to the same system. Important changes have been made since that period in many of these states, while in the new states which have since risen up, the elective principle greatly predominates. Thus, at the time the federal constitution was established, state patronage contributed to balance the patronage of the national government, that is, created state parties on a large scale, and armed them with great influence. Those parties then absorbed a corresponding share of public feeling, and served to break the impetuosity of the national parties. Perhaps if the system since introduced, had existed in 1789, it may, so far as regards some of the public officers, have been copied after in framing the federal constitution.

The executive power is commonly defined to be the authority to carry the laws into execution. But the constitution of nearly all the European governments shows the widest possible departure from this idea. The institution is made to correspond to the name, not the name to the institution. The power of declaring war, and of making treaties, which are devolved upon the prince, without the participation of any other department, signify a great deal more than the right to execute the laws. They amount to the declaration of a new law for the community, and appertain more properly to the legislative department. The creation of an order of nobility, or the adding to their number, has no shadow of connection with executive power. It is not merely the creation of a new and a fundamental law, but it influences the making of all laws which shall be subsequently passed. How these attributes, together with the vast patronage which the appointing power implies, came to be associated with the notion of executive power, may be gathered from the observations made in the commencement of this chapter. In a society which has not attained a high civilization, men are governed more through their imagination than their reason. That mysterious principle of our nature which, in some respects, is even stronger in the common race of mankind than it is among the educated, and which makes them figure to themselves a higher standard of excellence than can be found in real life, affords the explanation of this phenomenon. It is for this reason that regal power exists in the greatest vigor in the most imperfect form of society—in Russia, Turkey, and Persia, than in Great Britain, France and Belgium. When the masses are very ignorant, and a prey to all sorts of superstition, they are the most disposed to take refuge, from a sense of their own degradation, in the creation of an ideal phantom of sovereignty, which commands their obedience because it enchains their admiration. The throne, with its immense and imposing prerogatives, gives to this brilliant image a visible form and existence. It seems to the imaginations of the people, that the further the source of all political power was removed from themselves, the nearer was its approach to the supreme fountain of law and justice. And an institution which has once fairly acquired this preternatural authority, is in a condition to retain it, long after society is prepared for a thorough and permanent change. The executive power will still comprehend a great number of attributes which do not properly belong to it.

Even where the chief magistrate is deprived of the war and treaty-making powers, and the right to create one chamber of the legislative body, the interpretation put upon the executive power, that it is the authority to carrry the laws into execution, must be received with very great caution. It will have some semblance of truth, if we intend to describe the power as it exists in some particular countries, instead of defining it as it belongs to a regular and well constituted government. Nor will it ever be rigorously true, except in theory, for in practice the execution of the laws is reposed in a great multitude of officers, scattered over a wide extent of country, whose official transactions cannot be understood, much less superintended, by a single individual. The advance toward a state of general, and not merely of high civilization, the increase of the business transactions of society, necessarially sets bounds to the executive authority. The public interests become so diversified and complicated, as to require the laborious attention of many thousand officers where a handful was before sufficient. This produces two effects of great importance. It first separates the administrative officers from the chief magistrate; he continues to appoint them, and yet the duties performed by them are removed from his inspection. It then disconnects entirely their offices from his, and alters the theory as well as the practice of the government. It is needless to add, that this last change is never brought about except in a democratic republic. As the chief magistrate can neither execute the laws in person, nor see that they are executed by such a multitude of agents, the idea is sooner or later suggested, that the great majority of the administrative officers have in reality no connection with him. He is consequently deprived of the power of appointment, and the theory of the government is then made to correspond exactly with its practice. But this is the result of time, and is only brought about by great reflection, and by a minute as well as extensive experience of public affairs.

I observe, in the new constitution of New York, an arrangement which is not to be found in any other state constitution. The administrative department is separated from the executive proper, and is classed under two distinct heads: "administrative" and "local officers." An arrangement of the parts of a constitution may sometimes be a matter of detail; but in this instance it is the result of a strict logical analysis, and indicates that the true notion of executive power has been seized and thoroughly appreciated. The effect is to disconnect, more clearly than has ever been done before, the administrative officers from the chief magistrate; in other words, to produce a division of the executive power.

In some of the state constitutions, under the head of executive power, the language is, the "chief" executive power shall be vested in a governor. This is the case in the constitution of Mississippi, where all the other executive officers are, as in New York, made to derive their appointment directly from the people. The election of the principal of those officers, however, is prescribed in the article which defines the executive power. In New York, the word "chief" is omitted; but the distribution of power, which would seem to render the employment of it very natural, is actually made; and so the use or rejection of the word is even less than a matter of detail.

In some of the state constitutions, the appointment of some of the administrative officers is ranged under the head of executive power, while others are placed apart and under no distinct head whatever. This is the case in the constitution of Ohio. The office of secretary of state is created by the article which defines the executive power; while those of treasurer and auditor, are placed under no distinct head. On the other hand, in the constitution of Kentucky, the offices of secretary of state, of attorney general, district attorneys, and sheriffs, are ranged under the head of executive power; while the state treasurer and printer, are to be found in the article which confers judicial power. The two last officers, being elected by the legislature, would more naturally have been placed under the legislative department. This very confusion, however, which is to be found in many of the other state constitutions, is an unequivocal proof of an entire change in the structure of government in America. The convention of New York have adapted the arrangement and phraseology of the constitution to this change; and by so doing, have communicated to a very important principle of government a degree of clearness which it did not before possess.

At one time, the chief magistrate was regarded as very much the state itself. But when he came to be divested of prerogatives which have no shadow of connection with the executive power, he ceased to be viewed in that light. A great change took place in the ideas of men of all classes. The responsibility of the administrative officers, which was before referred to him as their chief, is now referred to the people. The term "subordinate," when applied to these officers, is then used to denote the relation which they hold to the community, not to indicate their dependence upon him. In other words, responsibility to the people is substituted in the place of acountability to one individual.

And yet the reasons for divesting the chief magistrate of the power of appointment, are not so strong in a republic as in a monarchy. Where he holds by a self-existing title, there would seem to be a greater necessity for rendering the appointment of the other executive officers independent of his control than where he is elected by the people, and his responsibility to them is immediate. But a dependence of the public officers upon the community, however consistent with the interests of society, would be totally incompatible with the genius of monarchy. It would cease to be monarchy from the moment the change was effected, and the prince himself would fall into a dependence upon the new appointing power, whether that was composed of agents of the people, or of the people themselves. The federal and a few of the state governments have endeavored to reconcile the two plans by pursuing a third, which combines some of the features of both. The power of appointment is wrested from the chief magistrate, but he retains the power of nomination. This is sometimes viewed in the light of an absolute power of appointment. And this is correct so far as regards the political party from which the nominee is selected, but no further. The control which the body to whom the nomination is made possess over the appointment, may not always be discerned; because in the great majority of cases it acts as a preventive check, deterring the officer from the nomination of persons whom he would otherwise select. But there are many instances in which its direct operation has been distinctly shown. Presidents have sometimes so conducted on these occasions, as to persuade the impartial among their own party that they did not so much "believe in the rule of the majority, as in the rule of him who had obtained the majority;" and the senate have been compelled to perform the austere but patriotic duty of rejecting persons who were eminently unfit for the station which they were named to fill.

There are many defects in this system, however, notwithstanding the control of the senate. The person nominated may, in common acceptation, be both capable and honest, so that he could not be rejected with any show of reason. And yet his dependence upon the president for renomination, or for a continuance in office for a single week, will be very apt to impel him to a course of conduct which will be completely subservient to the personal ambition of that officer. He may, perhaps it is not too strong to say, that he will, inevitably be nominated with a view to that result. This greatly mars the plan upon which the executive authority is constituted, which proceeds upon the idea that as the president is himself elected, he may be as much confided in, in making nominations, as in the performance of any other duty. The design in both instances is that he should act as the representative of the people. But there is this difference between the two cases, that in one the president simply influences the opinions of men, in the other he acts directly upon their will and determines their actions. The effect is in some degree to counterbalance his responsibility to the people. For if he can place in lucrative situations a multitude of persons who are bound to him by the powerful motives of interest, he is possessed of an authority entirely foreign to any which the elective principle contemplates. He is provided with an instrument of no mean force in promoting his re-election. The original design of the government so far fails, because one great defect of the monarchical regime is attached to it. The prince holds his station independently of the will of the people, and the president is armed with a power which may ensure his re-election in spite of well-founded objections to his administration. Thus the principle of representation is made to defeat itself. The political institutions are themselves converted into instruments for corrupting both public officers and people.

There are but two plans by which this defect can be cured. The one is, to cause all or the greater part of the administrative officers of the federal government to be elected by the people in the districts where their offices are located, precisely as in the state governments; the other is, to declare the president ineligible a second time. The first plan would carry the division of the executive further than it is now; the second, would render the president comparatively powerless in the dispensation of the patronage which is attributed to him.

It may be supposed that if the first plan were pursued, the effect would be to confound the authority of the two governments, to obliterate the boundary which now separates them; and to make the citizen forget that he was as much bound in allegiance to the national as to the state government. It is true that the president is himself elected by the people of the states, and not by the people of the United States; and so are members of the senate and house of representatives. And these elections not only take place in each state separately; but in the third instance they are conducted in local districts, and on the same plan that members of the state legislatures are chosen. The election of president has also been sometimes held in electoral districts. It is at any rate always conducted in minute subdivisions, smaller even than those of counties. But the chief magistrate of the union is stationed at the seat of government, where all his duties are centered. It is there only that we are familiar with him as one exercising political authority. Congress holds its sittings at the same place. It is to this spot that all its proceedings are referable. This contributes to keep these parts of the machinery of the national government in activity before the public eye, and to draw a broad line of discrimination between it and the state institutions. But if the whole corps of administrative officers were chosen in the same way, it might be to be feared that they would lose their separate identity, since their functions are necessarily performed in local districts within the states, and not at some central point. It may be apprehended, if this scheme were adopted, that the centripetal force of the federal government would be much weakened; that the love of union and the spirit of patriotism, which takes in the whole country, would be extinguished. The power of nomination may originally have been conferred upon the president, because it was supposed to be an attribute of the executive authority. That may not be its true character, and yet it may fulfill another purpose of still higher importance.

The power which the imagination exercises upon the opinions of men, is a thing not to be absolutely neglected; at any rate when it comes in aid of any of the legitimate objects of government. But it has never been found that the minute division of the state authority, the creation of county, township, and city jurisdictions, relaxes the bond which holds together the parts, and connects them with one presiding authority—that of the state. On the contrary, the bond is made firmer and stronger. The complete centralization of the appointing power does indeed affect the imaginations of men sensibly, because it sets in motion a power which is beyond themselves ; but the communication of the same power to the people gives it a more palpable connection with their interests, and in the end produces a more durable, if not a more vivid impression upon them. Instead of referring the authority of the state to one individual, it is made to represent the joint power of the whole society ; a thing equally mysterious and invisible in its operation, and yet constraining the actions of men with a force almost irresistible. The delinquent in America, whether his crime be of a political or a private character, as soon as the officer pronounces the words, "I arrest you by the authority of the state," delivers himself up. He quails before an authority which means so much, and which only speaks through an humble individual whom he has himself been instrumental in electing. More is gained than can ever be lost by founding government plainly and directly upon the interests of the people. The practical working of the system will gradually inculcate the requisite skill and experience ; and while the influence of the imagination will still count as something, powerful motives will be added to render the people prudent and circumspect in the selection of the public officers. I should not err if I were to say that it is to the over exercise of the imagination, that the greatest defects are to be traced, even in a country of free institutions. Like the children of the rich, who believe that they will be abundantly taken care of by others, the people, when the management of their interests is placed far from them, are disposed to concede everything to the showy authority which presides over public affairs. But when they are cast upon their own resources, and are compelled to grapple with business as a matter of serious concern, they are taught to be more cautious and wise in every step which they take. In America, the population increases so rapidly, generation crowds upon generation so fast, that society may be said to be still in a state of fermentation. It is (contrary to the opinions of European writers) when the population becomes dense, and society is thickly planted with the sentiments of public liberty, when long and inveterate habit has rendered republican rule both firm and durable, that a due estimate will be placed upon the political institutions.

We have no reason to believe that public officers in Great Britain are selected with more judgment than in the American states. To take one example—that of justices of the peace, who are so numerous that the aggregate amount of business transacted by them is of immense consequence to the community. These magistrates do not exercise in the first country the very important civil jurisdiction which they do in the last. But they possess some other powers of considerable magnitude, and their criminal jurisdiction wholly exceeds anything which is known in the United States. For they can sentence to almost unlimited imprisonment, and even to transportation for seven and fourteen years. In England they are appointed by the lords lieutenant of counties, a class of officers who are totally irresponsible. In the United States they are almost universally elected by the people of each county or township. These officers perform their homely but useful duties very much to the satisfaction of the public, although their jurisdiction in some of the states extends to one hundred dollars, and a very great amount of money consequently passes through their hands. But in the British kingdom, the malpractices of these magistrates, of one kind or another, have been so flagrant and notorious as to engage the attention of the leading men in parliament. Lord Brougham, when in the house of commons, dilated upon them with much severity, although there was every disposition on his part to soften the censure which they deserved.

I am aware, that although the president's patronage exercises a disturbing influence upon the domestic politics of the states, this is in some degree counteracted by another effect. By strengthening and consolidating two great national parties, the sectional jealousies, the narrow and contracted views which mere state politics would create, if not swallowed up, are at any rate mitigated and kept more out of view. The domestic jurisdictions are prevented from tearing each other to pieces, by placing them on an arena where one common sympathy, one mutual interest, may animate equally the citizen of Georgia, and the citizen of Ohio. These are effects of no light moment, and if they can be brought about in no other way, than by clothing the president with the vast patronage he now enjoys, it cannot be doubted that the evils incident to the system are amply compensated. But national parties must exist, and will ever have a commanding influence, since the questions with which they deal are so weighty, and of such general interest to the whole country.

I am persuaded that a genuine devotion to the national interests and a generous patriotism would not be lost to the community, even if a considerable portion of the administrative officers of the federal government were elected in the states. The two governments would be more identified in interest than before, and the execution of the laws by a federal officer, would be accompanied with the same authority which attends the execution of state laws. It is the operation of the laws upon individuals, which gives efficacy to the system of confederate government. The laws of the United States are in truth laws of the states, and admitting that there is never unanimity in their enactment, there is as seldom unanimity in the passage of state laws. And yet, there is rarely any resistance to the execution of a state law in those counties whose representatives have voted against it. The state is an aggregate of counties, as the nation is an aggregate of states. And although in the first, the parts are carved out of the whole, while in the last, the whole is formed out of the parts; yet the whole cling as tenaciously to the local divisions of counties and townships, as they do to the larger division into states. Hardly any of them would submit to the unbroken central authority of the state, more than it would to the authority of a consolidated national government. The existence of those minor jurisdictions accordingly is coeval with the foundation of the state governments. Logically, if not chronologically, it would be correct to consider the states as originally issuing from the settlement in townships and counties, rather than the reverse. This is so true, that if the states in which they have subsisted from time immemorial were to undertake to abolish them, public opinion would be as much shocked as if the national government were to invade the undoubted rights of the states. Those lesser jurisdictions then contribute to bind together the parts of which the states are composed. And the existence of the larger jurisdictions of the states, so far from weakening the authority of the central government, adds strength to it, on the same principle that the division of the judicial power between the judge and the jury, increases the effective authority of the former. The judge is relieved from the performance of duties which, although the least difficult in themselves, are the most apt to engender heart burnings in society. And the federal government is in like manner relieved from responsibility in so many matters which engage the attention and feelings of the people, that its authority has more freshness; and where it does act, it has the advantage of greater vigor and alacrity. I am not disposed therefore to think that the election of one class at least of the administrative officers of the federal government would subtract in any degree from its legitimate authority.

Cases may arise where there will be a collision between the authority of the state and federal governments. And to guard against the consequences flowing from this, there is one class of officers whose appointment might well remain as it is. The attorney general, district attorneys, and marshals, as well as the judges of the federal courts, might continue to hold under the president and senate. The share of patronage thus devolved upon the chief magistrate would not be great, and would do no harm even if it were unattended with one particular advantage. Perhaps it is not certain that the laws would not be as faithfully and energetically executed, if the district attorneys and marshals were elected by the states. Instances have already occurred, where these officers have resigned in consequence of some temporary obstruction to the discharge of their duties, and their unwillingness to make efforts to surmount the difficulty. For the officer is nothing unless he can clothe himself with the armor of public opinion. The instances of resistance to the execution of state laws, have certainly been more numerous than of resistance to the laws of the union. The executive officers of the former as well as of the last have notwithstanding invariably triumphed. But if there is any uncertainty whatever, that is a sufficient reason for retaining the appointment of those officers as it is now. An experiment with a more numerous class of public agents, will shed great light upon the practicability of extending it still further.

Postmasters are the most numerous class of civil officers appertaining to the federal authority. They outnumber all others put together. Their duties are essentially of a local character; that is, are confined to certain territorial divisions within the states. I see no good reason, therefore, why, if a convention were now called to frame a constitution of government, the appointment of these officers might not be devolved upon the people, precisely as is that of members of the house of representatives. The scheme seems to run counter to our notions of theoretical propriety; but that is the most which can be said of it. This notion of preserving a certain symmetrical arrangement, no doubt had great influence with the conventions which first organized the state governments. The power of appointment seemed at that day to be peculiarly an attribute of the executive; and almost all the states conferred the right of nomination, at least, upon the governor. A great change has been effected in almost all the old states; and in the new, hardly any trace of the system can be discerned. Yet the conduct of all public business is, to say the least, as orderly, upright, and intelligent, as it was under the old plan. There is no possible way of making free institutions succeed, but by training the popular mind to habits of self government; to make it feel and realize the consequences which ensue from any mistake in the management of public business. And even if we should admit that the frequent elections acted as a provocative to party spirit, this would be no argument against them. No great good ever was obtained, but by contending with great difficulties.

Experience, however, seems to prove that popular elections are highly favorable to public order. We may account for this unexpected fact, in a variety of ways. First, public jealousy is very much softened, when place and emolument are not confined to a close body but are laid open in reality, and not merely in name, to free competition. Second, there is a principle of human nature almost universal in its operation, that once the desires of the mind are fairly gratified, they lose their attraction and have no longer the same power to stir the passions. Third, the more equal distribution of power which popular elections necessarily introduce, gives rise to a more equal distribution of benefits, also. Men are no longer favored by classes or sections, for all classes and sections participate in the management of public business. Fourth, the popular mind becomes infinitely better educated, than under the old system. I am aware of the silly affectation of perpetually underrating the present, in comparison with the past, no matter at what period of time the present may be placed. But I believe I have not been an inattentive observer of the progress of society; at least I have endeavored to make it a chief object of my thoughts; and I think I can discern very visible marks of improvement, both moral and intellectual, in every part of America. The two countries which in very recent times have been most convulsed by party spirit, and which have been a prey to all sorts of crime and immorality, are Spain and Portugal. An election, which in America makes very little noise beyond the district or county, and which as soon as it is over leaves every thing behind tranquil, renders those countries scenes of perpetual strife and disorder.

In the event of a constitutional amendment which would refer the election of postmasters to local districts, there are several important checks upon their conduct which would be retained by the federal government. First, they would be commissioned by the president of the United States, on the same principle that state officers, who are chosen in territorial divisions of the states, are commissioned by the governors. Second, they would be governed by the federal laws, which would not only mark out the election districts, but which would prescribe all the duties to be performed. Third, they would be amenable to the federal courts. And fourth, their transactions would all be referable to the seat of government; so that in the event of any charge against them, they might be suspended by the president. A president would be apt to be very cautious in the exercise of this power of even temporary displacement, where the public officer did not hold directly under him. The present system holds out temptations which very few public magistrates can withstand. It invites the president to treat all the administrative officers like the men upon the chess board, and to use them for no other purpose but to play the old-fashioned game of politics. The plan proposed would contain abundant checks upon the conduct of those officers, while it would create a powerful and most salutary restraint upon the actions of the president.

I believe there are few presidents who would not greatly prefer to be relieved from the annoyance and heart burnings which these appointments create. As long as the authority exists, no one holding the station feels at liberty to turn away from the arbitrary exercise of it. The party, if not the public generally, expect that changes for political ends will be made. The constitution and laws have thrown out a challenge to that effect, which the chief magistrate dare not decline; although he would cheerfully part with the prerogative, in order to be delivered from the eternal clamor and the despotic dominion of cliques. At present he makes changes just as caprice dictates ; but he is first rendered a capricious being, by having so unnatural an authority cast upon him.

There is a difficulty with regard to the removal of public officers which has pressed upon the minds of thinking men. If an officer is elected by the people, and is guilty of gross misconduct, while at the same time the period for another election does not come around until a year or two afterward, in what way shall we deal with him? One way of curing the difficulty is, to make him give security for his good conduct. But this may not always be sufficient: he may commit more mischief than can be compensated by any bond which can be taken. The Italian republics of the middle ages endeavored to get rid of the difficulty, by electing their officers for exceedingly short terms; sometimes for six months, and sometimes for only one. It was believed at that day, that there was no possible way of reconciling the two principles, of responsibility and election, but by rendering the duration of the office so limited that the officer would hardly have time to commit any flagrant delinquency. They required no bond; and they not only never removed before the expiration of the term, but it was held to be a fundamental principle, that there could be no trial for misconduct until that term had elapsed. These difficulties are all easily avoided in the state governments of America. They are met in a very plain and effectual manner. In Ohio, county treasurers are removable by the county commissioners, without waiting for the tedious process of a trial and conviction. So also the governor of the state, upon being impeached, ceases for the time being to be governor; and in the meantime, the president of the senate supplies his place. In New York, the treasurer of the state, and other administrative officers, may be suspended by the governor, whenever there has been a violation of duty. These provisions, which seem never to have suggested themselves to the Italian politicians, are perfectly familiar to the Americans. The officer has been elected by the people. No magistrate, therefore, should have power to deprive him of his office. But there is every propriety in suspending him for the time being. If he is ultimately removed, it is only upon conviction by a tribunal of the people.

In the great majority of instances, the bond taken from the federal officers would be sufficient to insure the faithful performance of their duties, as is the case with the state officers. The same system throughout, which has been adopted in the state governments, might, with equal advantage, be introduced into the federal government. It would act as a check upon both the president and the administrative officers; while we should also get rid of the corrupting influence of executive patronage.

I place reliance upon the plan of distributing the power of appointment among the people, not merely because it best agrees with the genius of free institutions, but because I do not believe that the ineligibility of the president a second time will reach the mischiefs which it is so desirable to remedy. Where the desire of re-election cannot be gratified, a new passion will take its place. The chief magistrate will become deeply interested in the choice of his successor. The ambition of living even after we are dead, is one of the most powerful springs of human conduct, and unfolds itself in every variety of form in our progress through life. Before feudal institutions had firmly planted the hereditary principle in government, kings were as ambitious of being instrumental in the choice of their successors, as if it were a matter of personal interest to themselves. The Roman emperors, even when there was no question of kindred in the case, were as desirous of this reputation as they were of extending the limits of the empire. The American president will always be surrounded by powerful and aspiring men, who will seek to ingratiate themselves in his favor, and to some of whom he may be under inestimable obligations in prosecuting his plan of administration. He will strive to live in the person of his successor.

There is another consideration of great importance. As free institutions delight to lift up the man of the humblest pretensions to the most exalted station, they also teach the man who has attained the highest honors, that he does not tarnish the luster of his reputation by afterward accepting an inferior station. In two instances have ex-presidents consented to fill offices of inferior grade. It is the man who ennobles the office, and never the reverse. The precedent has only to be set when it will be generally followed; especially where the retiring president is in the vigor of life, and in the full possession of his faculties. The experience of one who has seen so much of public life in all its allurements and anxieties, may be full of instruction to those who are just entering on the stage of public life. This presents a powerful motive of interest, as well as of ambition, to engage the president in the choice of his successor. He may be the future ambassador of the nation, or he may aspire to any other office to which his extensive fame and abilities recommend him. He may have retired from the presidency, very creditably to himself, a poor man. Instead of a pension, which free governments never bestow, he will be ambitious of earning a reward, by being in some way useful to his country. But it will be impossible for him to lose sight of the influence which party connection will have in promoting his desires.

A political arrangement which is destined to further one chief end, generally succeeds in answering some other subordinate ones. The complete centralization of the power of appointment, gives unbounded sway to the government of the majority. But if this power is distributed among the districts where the officers are located, the extreme rigor of the rule that the majority is entitled to govern, is very much mitigated, without substantially impairing its force. The various administrative officers, also, will be chosen by those who have the best opportunity of judging of their capability. For, as I have before remarked, free institutions, if they do not find men absolutely fit for self-government, are some how or other, wonderfully adapted to make them so.

Doubts however, will still suggest themselves to even the most intelligent minds. It will be inquired, how it is possible to succeed in the government of a mighty population, if the chief offices in the state are not surrounded by something of the prestige of authority. If the hereditary principle is dispensed with, and the prerogatives of royal power are abolished, what plan can be fallen upon to atone for this diminution of the authority of government; unless it is by centering the whole power of appointment in the chief magistrate. In what way can we keep alive the notion of unity as an attribute of the government: a notion which has hitherto been of so much efficacy in the government of mankind. If we are bound to take notice of the good qualities of human nature, it may be said that we are equally bound to take notice of its bad qualities. And while all statesmen, from the earliest times, have been convinced that the chief desideratum of government was to place all sorts of checks upon popular feeling; shall the American government part with the only one which is left, and one which is merely indirect in its operation? Even if these objections have not been sufficiently considered in different parts of this work, I feel so firmly persuaded that the system of patronage cannot always maintain its ground, that I would even make a merit of necessity, and forestall the period when it will fall into disuse. There is a strong current of public opinion running against it. And I have constantly observed, that whenever there has been a very general and decided tendency to any great movement in society, it has been sure to be brought about; and what is of equal importance, it has been accompanied with safeguards and compensatory contrivances, which were entirely overlooked. There may be particular or local tendencies to change, and these never tell anything. But any event, the tendency to which is of so general and marked a character as to stamp an impression upon the age or country, is sure to take place and to succeed.

I observe that a very great change has taken place in the mode of procuring appointments. Formerly, one or two individuals in a state arrogated the right to dictate to the president the nominations he should make. It was one way of subserving their own private ends. Most generally, it was with a view to strengthen their political connections. But sometimes the motives which governed them were purely personal. I knew one instance where an individual of some influence, procured the appointment of a near relation of his enemy, in order to bind the former to his own interests, and to inflict a deadly blow upon the last. The appointment was absolutely unexceptionable: a better could not have been made. But the example was of pernicious influence.

Within fifteen or twenty years, a very great change has taken place in the management of this matter. A public man, no matter what his influence may be, feels constrained to defer considerably to the opinion of the people, among whom the appointee is to reside, and to discharge his duties. Recommendations are drawn up, and even if the persons designated are not altogether to his liking, he feels himself in duty bound to second them. This change in the mode of operation of the system is a sure indication that the sys tem itself is on the eve of being changed.

The system of patronage belongs properly to monarchical government. It is not adapted to the genius of a republic. Cecil was the first European minister who seems to have been aware of its importance as an engine of government. He announced it as a maxim in politics, that the nation must be governed through, not by, the parliament. James I, was the first king who acted upon this maxim, by seducing a parliamentary leader from the popular cause, and making him prime minister.

The rise of this system in monarchical government, is an infallible proof that a great change is taking place in the working of the institutions. It denotes that the government is passing, by insensible degrees, from absolute to limited monarchy. All absolute monarchs reign by dint of force or superstition. They may be obliged, as Mr. Hume remarks, to "truck and huckster" to some particular men; but the great bulk of the community are ruled by fear or superstition. If, in a society, thus organized, a train of causes can be set in motion which will rouse the popular mind to activity, and spread knowledge and industry throughout the land, a more direct communication will be opened between the people and the government. Public opinion will be something, as in after times it will grow to be everything. The prince will be obliged to throw away the coarse instruments of government which he had before employed. As men can no longer be driven by force, he will resort to the seductive influence of patronage. And this is undoubtedly a great improvement upon the old system, inasmuch as it supposes that men are endowed with free agency, that they must be governed by some sort of persuasion addressed to their understandings, even though it should be through their interests.

This mode of governing a community, may be denominated the transition state from absolute to limited monarchy. Its continuance may be of indefinite duration, as it possesses a faculty of self preservation greatly beyond the old system. It may last so long, but in a greatly mitigated form, as to render it, also, the transition state from limited monarchy to free institutions. It may raise up so large a body of educated people, and independent thinkers, as to create an effectual counterpoise to the throne and aristocracy. The American government commenced where all other governments had left off; and if here and there the federal government exhibits features of a monarchical character, it must be attributed to the absence of all experience in modeling a republican government upon so extensive a scale.

There is one circumstance, however, which has tended greatly to diminish the mischiefs of patronage in the United States. This is the immense disproportion between the number of offices and number of the electors. The influence which the system of patronage exerts, evidently depends upon the number of persons who can be gained over, and this depends upon the number of active citizens; not meaning thereby the number of adult males, but the number of those who are admitted to the enjoyment of political rights. We do not talk of patronage as applied to the brute, unformed mass of a Turkish or Russian population. They are easily governed, without the employment of this delicate but powerful instrument. The king of France appoints to one hundred and thirty-eight thousand offices, the aggregate salaries of which amount to forty thousand dollars. The president of the United States "nominates" to fifteen thousand, the salaries of which amount to five millions of dollars. There is not merely a great disparity between the number of lucrative places to be disposed of in the two countries, but what is of infinitely more importance, there is an immense disproportion between the number of offices and the number of citizens who can be influenced in this way. One hundred and thirty-eight thousand public officers, with two hundred thousand electors only, discloses a patronage literally gigantic, when it is contrasted with fifteen thousand officers, and three millions of electors. The reform act of Great Britain, which has increased the number of electors from three hundred and forty thousand to eight hundred and thirteen thousand, has in the same proportion diminished the power of the British monarch. The American president cannot nominate to office more than one in every two hundred of the electors. The king of France has the absolute disposal of so many places, that he can present more than every second man in the kingdom with one apiece. The effect of the one system is, to train a vast corps of civil officers in the service of the government; that of the other is, to create an independent body, and one vastly more numerous, out of the government. And this view alone is abundantly sufficient to show how greatly mistaken they are, who have run a parallel between the European monarchs, and the chief magistrate of America.

There is a circumstance of an entirely different character, which does increase the power of the American president, and one which is peculiar to representative government. The immense development of the democratic principle, a thing of yesterday, without entering as a distinct element in the composition of the government, cripples incalculably in practice the effective power of the French and English monarchs. The structure of society and the political institutions are not in complete harmony with each other. In the United States it is the reverse, and the predominance of the popular power may be said both to limit and to fortify the authority of the chief magistrate.

For the true notion of political power does not consist in contesting and running counter to the general interests; but rather in founding itself upon the general will, and so placing at the command of government a greater amount of both physical and moral energy, than it would otherwise be able to employ. But nothing contributes so much to give strength and influence to a public officer, as the confidence and support of a free people. It is more than equivalent to the obedience of a great army. Free institutions do not detract from the legitimate authority of any public magistrate; but they do give a new direction to ambition, and insensibly habituate the most aspiring genius, to fasten all hope of acquiring a brilliant and lasting reputation upon the ability to advance the solid prosperity of the state. And the untrammelled authority which may be exercised to carry out so noble a design, is as truly power as are the prerogatives of any potentate on earth. This new direction of power, is one of the most marked characteristics of the age. Even the emperor Napoleon, who lived amid elements little calculated to inspire such feelings, was obliged to take refuge in one monument which he had constructed for the public welfare. "I shall go down to posterity," he exclaimed, "with the code of laws in my hand." And although this code was in no sense the work of his hands, but was drawn from the profound writings of Pothier, and other eminent jurists, yet circumstances enabled him to call it into being; and one can easily pardon, nay greatly admire, the vanity which seeks in any degree to associate itself in part with those who have been the real benefactors of mankind. On a more recent occasion, an English king, William IV, placed himself at the head of the party which contended for parliamentary reform. Elizabeth countenanced the establishment of newspapers, but little thought that this was the first step toward raising up a new power in the state. And a subsequent monarch ratified "the mutiny bill," without exactly deciphering the consequences which would follow from it. But William IV, well understood the import of the bill which introduced parliamentary reform, and manfully leaped to the conclusion that although it circumscribed his authority, it added wonderfully to his influence. The institutions of a democratic republic help to render that the habitual temper of public men which in other countries is only an occasional burst of magnanimity.

I have noticed one change which very gradually takes place in monarchical government: the substitution of patronage as an instrument of power, in the place of superstition and fear. There is another, equally remarkable, and one which is every way calculated to arrest the attention of an inquisitive mind. The regal and the executive authority which are originally united in one person, in progress of time, come to be entirely separated from each other. They may both continue ostensibly to be exercised by the head of the state; but in practice, in the actual administration of public affairs, the tendency is to disconnect them entirely. This is an event which contributes to break the force of the royal authority, and to nullify the maxim, "the king can do no wrong," by introducing something like a regular responsibility into the management of the public business. It hastens the passage from absolute to limited or constitutional monarchy, and facilitates the ultimate transition to free institutions.

Two causes may be assigned for this important change. First, that diminution of the personal authority of the king, which invariably takes place in a community which has attained a high civilization. So many, and such powerful interests then spring up to obscure the luster of the throne, that the officer ceases to exercise the magical influence which he formerly had upon the minds of men. In the meantime, the power and importance of the other departments are as regularly advancing. They attract to themselves a large portion of the influence and respect which were before exclusively bestowed upon the monarch. The words of Louis XIV, "the state, why I am the state myself," come to be regarded as an empty ebullition of vanity rather than as a treasonable expression.

In the second place, the duties appertaining to the executive become, as before observed, so intricate, and demand the exercise of so much ability, industry, and information, as to be absolutely unmanageable by a single individual. A regular board of executive officers then takes the place of those pompous and luxurious functionaries who were the mere servants of the king. The members of this board will continue to be nominated by him ; but the business devolved upon them will be so complicated and difficult, as not even to be understood by the prince. This will give to the board a distinct character and importance, which, in process of time, will ripen into something more than a nominal independence of him. The importance of the principal is not always increased by the ability of the agents he employs. It is often the reverse. The relation which the executive officers ultimately bear to the community is so much more extensive than to the king, that they may even act as a counterpoise to his authority.

The seats which ministers have in the legislative body, contribute to consummate this great change in the constitution of the regal power. The arrangement was originally intended to give support to the throne. But in a highly civilized community, the legislature is sure to acquire the supremacy, and turns all the instruments of the crown to its own advantage. By placing the chief members of the ministerial board in the popular branch of the legislature (as is most usually the case), they are brought into immediate contact with the representatives of the people, are subjected to the direct control of public opinion, and are sure to be displaced, whenever the majority is decidedly against them. Thus, by a slow, but irresistible process, the executive is effectually separated from the royal power. The prince is a hereditary magistrate, the people have no voice in his appointment ; but to compensate for this unnatural arrangement, he loses the executive functions. The persons who exercise them are virtually appointed by the representatives of the people. It is not surprising that an English premier should prefer a seat in the house of commons to one in the lords ; for as nothing can deliver ministers from the omnipotent control which public opinion exerts, they are certain by acting in conjunction with it, to add to the weight of their authority.

By the act of settlement of twelve and thirteen of William III, it was declared that no person holding an office or place of trust should be eligible to parliament, This provision was afterward altered, so as to exclude persons holding pensions, and to vacate the seat of any member of the house of commons upon his appointment to office. He was, however, immediately re-eligible. Instead of being incapacitated from holding a seat, by a fixed constitutional provision, it was referred to the people themselves to determine whether, under the circumstances, he should again be elected. This change has been disapproved of by some eminent writers ; but it is plain that the ordinance, as it was originally penned, would have increased instead of diminished the power of the crown. The admission of members of the executive to the hall of legislation, has a decidedly democratic tendency. It brings them within speaking distance of the people, and when that is accomplished much of the mystery and state craft which would otherwise surround public affairs, is dissipated. It has had another very decided advantage. It has led to the practice of appointing ministers from among distinguished commoners, rather than from among the nobility. The king makes a merit of his dependent situation, by courting popular favor, and relying upon it as his chief support.

The compelling ministers, then, to appear in presence of the representatives of the people and to show their hands, is a contrivance for breaking the power of the crown. By bringing the conduct and views of the king himself under the notice of a legislative assembly, it makes him indirectly a representative of the people. If we could suppose the British monarch to be brought upon the floor of the house of commons, the effect would be instantaneous in diminishing the luster of the office. It would almost annihilate his personal authority, and in no very long period he would become an elective magistrate, like the president of the United States. By placing members of the executive board there, his authority is to a certain extent preserved ; but the executive and regal power are completely separated. Instead of the king governing the people through parliament as an instrument, parliament and the people control the king through the instrumentality of ministers.

Thus in proportion as government approaches to anything like perfection, there is a constant tendency to a division of the executive power. If there is no fundamental ordinance to bring about this result, the vast expansion which the whole framework of society acquires, the entire change which takes place in the social and political organization, become a law to the government; and even in a country where monarchical institutions have existed time out of mind, mold the authority of the chief magistrate into a new form.

The maxim that the executive should be one, is true only in despotic government.

In the United States the executive officers are not eligible to Congress, and the reason is apparent. There is no hereditary prince whose authority it is desirable to limit by breaking it in pieces. The people choose the chief magistrate, he holds his office for a short period, his salary is small, his powers few, and his responsibility to the people is immediate. It is unnecessary then to subject him, or the other members of the executive board, to the same species of control as in the British government. For the authority which they exercise is circumscribed by other and more effectual means. In a hereditary monarchy we are obliged to cut in two the office of chief magistrate, leaving the kingly authority to the monarch, and erecting ministers into an executive board; and in order to give them a substantive authority distinct from his, they are introduced upon the floor of the legislature. But there is no necessity for the last in a republic. A much more exact distribution of the executive power than this implies is made by the fundamental laws. If in the former government the personal influence of the king is diminished, this is the very object sought after by the institution. But in a republic, we do not attempt to detract from the influence of the president, since being permitted to deal with his office by fixed laws at the first organization of government, there is no occasion for any compensatory contrivances afterward.

In France, since the reconstruction of the government, the same plan is adopted as in Great Britain, and the same consequences have followed from it. Ministers are named by the king, but they must act in conformity with the will of the deputies. The system of public administration must have the sanction of public opinion, in order that they may be secure in their places. In the former country, however, they are by virtue of their office entitled to a seat in the legislative body, and are at liberty to pass from one chamber to the other, for the purpose of explaining their views. In both these respects they differ from the English ministers, who must be elected in order to have a seat, and can only appear in the chamber of which they are properly members. That part of the French plan which permits ministers to appear in either chamber is an improvement on the English. If ministers are selected from the peers, it makes sure of bringing them into immediate contact with the deputies of the people.

In Great Britain and France, ministers go out of office in obedience to the will of the legislature; in the United States, to that of the president. It may then be supposed, that the force of public opinion is stronger in France and Great Britain, than it is in the United States. The case is entirely the reverse, however. In the two first countries, ministers are appointed by the crown; they are brought into the legislature to weaken the authority of the king, who would otherwise be beyond the reach of public opinion, as he is already beyond the reach of the laws. But the president is himself the creature of public opinion; and the reason why his secretaries do not abdicate on a change of parties in the legislature, is because public opinion is strong, instead of being weak; so strong as to render their influence comparatively null, notwithstanding their continuance in office. But these two contrary practices are both indications of weakness in the executive power. Only in limited monarchy the king not merely submits to it, but is obliged to make confession of it. If his ministers were not entitled to seats in parliament, there would be no occasion to remove them.

This notion of a double character as belonging to the head of the state, this distinction between the functions of the governing and the executive power, was doubtless revolving in the mind of the celebrated Sieyes, when he drew up his plan of a constitution, in 1799. And it was a capital feature of that plan, to carry out the distinction more precisely and thoroughly than had ever been done before. The chief magistrate, with the title of grand elector, was to be maintained in princely splendor; he was charged with the appointment of all the administrative officers of the state, who were thenceforth declared irremovable by him. He was to be elected by a close body of two hundred members, denominated the constitutional jury. Although living in splendor, like a hereditary prince, and surrounded with all that luster which is calculated to captivate the imaginations of the people, he was not permitted to exercise himself any part of the executive authority. His authority was strictly confined to the appointment of the executive officers.

This was to resemble the system of government to those mechanical contrivances fashioned by the hand of man, which perform all their movements in exact compliance with the impulse originally given to them. But political institutions possess more or less a self-determining power, which perpetually interferes with any artificial rules which the lawgiver may prescribe. The great defect of this, as of most other theoretical plans of government, was that it proposed, by a set of curious and complicated contrivances, to check one part of the government by another, and this at a period when the power out of the government had grown to such magnitude and importance, as to demand the chief consideration. The mere internal mechanism of the government, was once everything; its relation to the social organization, almost nothing. Very different is the case now. A scheme of government, in order to have any chance of success, must connect itself, in some way or other, with the popular will. How much more simple, and how much more effectual for France, is the present arrangement; where a house of deputies is elected immediately by the people, and exercises a complete control upon the appointment of ministers. The effect is to establish practically and not merely theoretically, a division between the regal and the executive power. When the structure of government is rendered very artificial, it becomes, in the progress of time, unadapted to the condition of society. But if it only has the merit of simplicity, no matter how incomplete it may be, it acquires the faculty of accommodating itself to the progressive change without. As the popular strength and intelligence are developed, so will be the political institutions also. It may be no difficult matter to enlarge the electoral franchise gradually, so as to create a million of electors of the house of deputies. But how can such odd and grotesque contrivances as the mute legislative body, the grand elector, and the constitutional jury, be improved, unless it is by abolishing them? The most complex and artificial contrivance ever devised, was proposed by one of the profoundest minds France has produced, at a time when, above all others, society was least prepared to receive it.

The scheme of a double cabinet, which originated in the court of Frederick, prince of Wales, proceeded from an effort on the part of the heir apparent, to escape from the wholesome control of parliament. This control, in the reign of George II, was beginning to assume a regular form, and to be regarded as an important feature in the constitution. It was not unnatural, therefore, that the king should feel uneasy under a restraint, from which every other European monarch was free. Hence this attempt, to raise up one set of ministers among the court, to thwart and humble another set, who had come in through parliamentary influence. But it was in vain to resist the current of public opinion, which was silently effecting a separation between the regal and the executive power; and notwithstanding renewed efforts, in the early part of the reign of George III, to maintain the prerogatives of the crown unimpaired, and to render the whole ministerial board dependant upon it, the control of parliament, over the appointment of ministers, has been thoroughly established, and is at this day regarded as a fundamental principle of the constitution. No finer illustration can be found in all history, of the constant tendency of public opinion, in a limited monarchy, to bring about a separation of the kingly and executive power.

In Great Britain, the separation of the regal and executive office has only been brought about by the gradual rise of the commons. And the same will be the case in France. But the French "tiers etat" is not yet as powerful a body as the middle class in Great Britain, and therefore does not exert as sensible an influence upon the movement of the government. Abbe Sieyes's constitution, at the same time that it deprived the grand elector of the power of governing, annulled the authority of the second legislative chamber, by taking from it the right of debate, and by rendering the basis of representation exceeding narrow and confined. The grand elector was only placed in the system to keep alive a pageant, which might subdue men to obedience through the influence of the imagination; and yet he is robbed of all the attributes which are calculated to have that effect. But the governing idea of the plan is very visible: to cut in twain the executive power, and to bestow the largest share of authority upon those who have the management of the real business of society.

In the state governments of America the idea which was floating in the mind of the Abbe Sieyes, has been carried into practical operation. But all the other institutions are framed in harmony with this arrangement. The governors are elected, not to direct the movements of the government, but simply to keep watch, to see that all is right, and upon any critical conjuncture, to ring the alarm bell to the legislative assembly, which is dispersed during the greater part of the year. Government, in those communities, is so plainly founded upon the interests of men, that it has been found the easiest thing imaginable to dispense with all the trappings and insignia with which the chief magistrates of even the German states surround themselves. As the real and effective business of the state is transacted by the legislature and judiciary, there, accordingly has the active authority of the state been deposited. And as every agent upon whom power is conferred, may be tempted to abuse it, the basis of representation is rendered so wide as to create a strict responsibility to all orders of men, and not merely to one class. The chief magistrate is there placed like a sentinel, upon the highest position, to give warning of any approaching danger. There is no blind, mechanical contrivance, as in the constitution of 1799, by which each department is expected to act as a check upon the others; and without any presiding power without, to keep the whole in order. Free room is allowed for the development of public opinion; since it is upon public opinion after all, that all legitimate government must rest. Without public opinion, in other words, without the elevation of the great body of the people to a condition which will enable them to obtain some insight into the management of public business, responsibility would be a dead, instead of a living and active principle.

The American system has answered the desired purpose; and it may be termed the "beau ideal" in politics. It has demonstrated that all the great ends for which civil government is established, may be attained without the employment of those curious and artificial contrivances which render men unfit for self government, simply because they hide government from their observation. By rendering men free; by satisfying all their wants, so far as it is in the power of human institutions to do, it has removed out of the way the prime cause of all public discontent, and has thus guarded against the dangers to which both government and society are exposed.

Perhaps with the help of so instructive an experience, it may be found an easy matter to balance the government of the most extensive community upon the same plan. The fact that no commonwealth formed upon the same model had ever before existed, gave rise to the belief that none such could exist. The firm persuasion that a thing is impossible, often creates a real and invincible obstacle to its attainment. And as the imagination has a wonderful influence upon all our opinions, we get rid of its disturbing influence and of the notion of impossibility, where we have the example of thirty states (many of them singly more populous and powerful than Venice, Genoa, or Florence, in their palmiest days), in which the elective principle is thoroughly introduced, and where the political institutions possess both more consistency and firmness, than has been witnessed any where else.

The absolute veto is one of the attributes of the executive in monarchical government. The design in creating the office of king, we may suppose to have been to raise up some one who should occupy the place of mediator between the higher and the lower ranks. Hence the office is rendered hereditary, in order to clothe it with the greatest possible influence. Originally the king had no occasion to exercise the veto, because he had the initiative of all measures. But after the transition of the legislative assembly, from a mere council to the rank of an independent body, his situation became very different. The legislature was then able to run counter to his views, and he was consequently endowed with a corresponding power to ward off the attack, and to protect his own prerogative. But in the course of time, an entire change takes place in the nature of his office. The executive authority gradually falls into his hands. And this places him in a still more advantageous position for acting as a mediator between conflicting parties. For a hereditary monarch can hardly be said to belong to any of the parties in the state. This complete independence of all of them, exempts him from all interest in any question of party politics; and if his personal influence is undermined, in consequence of so many rival powers growing up around him, his ambition is less provoked to indulgence, and his prejudices have less room to show themselves. He therefore not only removes his ministers, but refrains from the exercise of the veto, in order that he may conform as much as possible with the views of the legislature. This is the last term, the final aim, to which the veto tends in the progress of monarchical government. It becomes, in other words, a dormant power in practice, as soon as the legislative and executive boards meet upon the same floor, and are obliged to co-operate in devising plans for the public welfare.

In the earlier stages of that form of government, the prerogative is employed to compose the dissensions of the patrician and plebeian classes, or as a defensive weapon against assaults upon the executive. But those two classes are at length succeeded by another, the great middle class, which itself conciliates the rival interests of the other two, by containing a tolerably faithful representation of the opinions of both. This class, then, occupies the place of umpire, which the king before held: and having drawn to itself, by its commanding influence in the legislature, a complete control over the executive board, it ceases to meddle with the prerogatives of the king.

In a republic, the chief magistrate is an elective officer. He is chosen by the party in the majority, because he belongs to it. He is, therefore, designed to be its representative, and is expected to speak its sentiments. For this reason, the exercise of the veto may be more frequent than in a monarchical government. And it is because the political institutions are more instead of less democratic, that this will be the case. The authority of the king is so independent of public opinion, he is so completely exempted from all party connection, that he will readily assent to any measures proposed by the legislative body, provided they do not trench upon his prerogatives. But the president is altogether the creature of public opinion. He has no prerogatives. His authority consists in exercising the power which the majority of society have conferred upon him. His ambition is to represent and to give effect to the will of that majority.

But here a difficulty occurs: the president is elected for four years, the popular branch of the legislature for two, while one-third of the senate retires every two years. The majority which elected the president, therefore, may not be the majority two years after he is chosen. The exercise of the veto, then, at that period, may seem to contradict the public will, while in reality, it may be in accordance with it. It presents a doubtful case; a case in which a wise magistrate may well pause to reflect, in order that he may be saved from the reproach of too hastily giving into every measure which a temporary majority may favor, and the still greater reproach of contradicting the settled and well understood opinion of a permanent majority of society. If he were a hereditary officer, and these doubts were very perplexing, the true way to sclve them would be to ratify the proposed law. He would then make sure of conforming himself in some degree to the public will, since one chamber of the legislature is elected, although the electoral franchise may be very restricted. The president, in aiming at the same result, that is, in seeking to find the real majority, may be driven to pursue an exactly opposite course. If the king should refuse to ratify a law, when his consent should have been given, the mischief is without remedy. For his veto is absolute. But if the president does the same, and thus contradicts the unmistakeable will of the public, the legislature may place their veto upon his, or if the majority is not sufficiently large to do this, he may be quietly displaced in a year or two after. It is very remarkable, that very few instances have occurred of the rejection of a law by the president, which has not met with subsequent approbation. That is, if we may judge from the succeeding election of president. But as the patronage which is at present attached to the office, gives him a great advantage in molding public opinion, we must beware of speaking too positively on the subject. We cannot be sure what would have been the result, if that patronage had not been created.

But it is obvious that the exercise of the veto must necessarily have a more democratic tendency in a republic, than it is possible for it to have in a monarchy. In a republic parties take the place which is occupied by classes in monarchical government. The advantage of this is, that as the great body of the citizens will be admitted to the enjoyment of the electoral franchise, no parties can well exist which are not of a popular character. The great object is to make even the suspensive veto represent the opinions of at least a large body of the community. In a monarchy it might represent the opinion of a single individual. The electoral franchise is usually so restricted, that there is no way of certainly ascertaining how large a portion of the community is enlisted for or against a particular measure. In France, whose population is thirty-four or five millions, two hundred thousand electors are a very feeble representative of the public will. Either the majority or the minority of the deputies chosen by them, are an equally feeble representation of the parties whose sentiments they undertake to speak. In elective government, properly so called, the basis of representation is so wide, that both the great parties which divide the country are essentially of a popular character. And thus where the veto is in accordance with the vote of the minority, it has the merit of founding itself upon the opinions of a very large section of society, an advantage which it can only accidentally possess in monarchical government. And it is for this reason that the veto is suspensive, not absolute in its operation. The design is to prevent the chief magistrate from contradicting the clear and unequivocal expression of the public will. Armed with the absolute veto, he might persist in its exercise, whatever was the strength of the majority against him; or what would be more common, he might refrain from exercising it when the public good very clearly demanded it. The suspensive veto enables him to make efforts to find out what the public will is. And if two-thirds of the legislature annul his veto, it becomes impossible for him to run counter to the declared opinions of a majority of the people. Do what he will, however, he must act in obedience to the wishes of a popular party, and that party, whether in the majority or minority, must compose a very considerable portion of the legislative assembly.

It has been proposed, as one means of insuring a system of enlightened legislation, that the consent of two-thirds or three-fourths of the legislature should be required to the enactment of all laws. Great inconvenience and mischief, however, would be the consequence of this. In the first place, a very large proportion of the laws are not of sufficient importance to require it. 2d. It might have the effect of delivering the legislative power permanently into the hands of the minority. Now it is never the design in representative government to make the government of the minority the rule, but only the exception to the rule, so that in a few isolated cases the majority in the country may be sought through the minority in the legislature. The invariable rule of two-thirds would be better adapted to monarchical than to republican government. In the last every law is an experiment submitted to the people, and it is often very desirable that this experiment should be gone through with, in order that the effects of any given measure may be distinctly understood, and that public opinion may be firmly united one way or the other. The temporary inconvenience is overbalanced by the benefit attending it.

To avoid the mischiefs arising from the invariable rule of two-thirds, it has been proposed to subject only those laws which affect interests of great magnitude to this ordeal. But it is impossible to discern beforehand what laws will possess this character. Many enactments derive great importance from the circumstances, or the particular crisis when they are made. The suspensive veto is intended to reconcile all these difficulties. It may be described as a power, or rather as a duty, which renders it incumbent on the chief magistrate to inform the legislative body when the measure about to be adopted is of so grave a character as to require a reconsideration, and to render it expedient that two-thirds of the members should concur in its enactment. If the clause in the constitution were couched in terms signifying this, the veto would not have been thought of, any more than one talks of the veto of the jnry upon the opinion of the court, or that of the court upon the jury, although the effect is the same, leading sometimes to a change of opinion on the part of the court, and sometimes to a change on the part of the jury. The president simply says to the two chambers: you are in the heat of the battle; you would not, therefore, trust yourselves with the power of deciding precipitately, when the emergency is such as to demand a reconsideration. I am, it is true, not entirely removed from the conflict. But the independent position, in many respects, which I hold, and my election by the people at large instead of by a district or single state, impels me, whether I will or no, to form a judgment which doubtless will sometimes be erroneous, but which may in the great majority of instances be conveniently relied upon. This is the reason why the constitution vests the whole legislative power in congress. The chief magistrate is not considered as a third estate. He is, therefore, not permitted, as in the European government, to have a part in the enactment of the laws. His office is simply to notify the legislature when a measure is of so great importance as to demand a reconsideration, and a vote of two-thirds.

There is another circumstance which differs the exercise of the veto power in the American government, very materially from what it is any where else. In Great Britain and France, the legislative power constitutes the sovereignty, and is competent to change the constitution. In the United States it is otherwise; the sovereignty resides in the people, and none but a convention of the people have authority to change the constitution. In the European states the king may prevent any fundamental alteration in the government, however wise and beneficial it may be. In the United States no constitutional change can be made by a mere law, and the president has no opportunity of defeating the public will in this important particular. The veto, even the suspensive veto, is unknown to a constitutional convention, because the forms under which it assembles, the rules which are necessary to be observed before it can be called together, presuppose that consideration and reconsideration, on the part of the community, which are indispensable in handling matters of so grave a character. It is easy to adopt the rule of two-thirds or three-fourths in this instance, when it would be impracticable or highly inconvenient to do so in the ordinary business of a legislative body. The king may persist in maintaining the vast prerogatives which were conferred upon him centuries ago, although material changes in the structure of society have occured to render them desirable. This power is absolutely denied to the president, If in monarchical government it is necessary to confer so great an authority upon the crown, in order to enable it to protect its prerogatives from the assaults of other branches of the legislature, no such reason exists in a republic, because the powers of the chief magistrate are placed beyond the reach of the legislative body.

There is another view which is entitled to great attention. Every law alters more or less, the existing state of things. It is intended to effect a change in some measure or measures, which were themselves brought about by the act of a majority. But it is quite otherwise in almost all other communities, where government is a self-existing institution, never representing the majority, often not even the minority of what may be termed the substantial population. So that in the United States, whether the veto be exercised or not, we know that the old state of things, if it is permitted to continue, or the new, if it actually takes place, have both been effected by a clear majority of the community. The great desideratum, in other words, is that the legislation of the country shall be based upon the will of the majority, and in the only instance where this rule is departed from, the laws in being still stand as the expression of a majority of but a few years antecedent, to which is added the vote of any number less than a mere majority of both chambers of the existing legislature. We make sure that the veto shall never represent the mere arbitrary will of a single individual; that the chief magistrate, whatever his personal wishes may be, cannot free himself of an alliance with public opinion.

In the compound republic of America, there may be a further use in vesting a qualified veto in the president. Notwithstanding the utmost care in separating the domestic police of the states from the national jurisdictions, they will sometimes conflict. Geographical parties will occasionally make their appearance, influencing the course of legislation, and demanding the interposition of an umpire, in order to compel them to be just to each other. Senators are elected by the states, and representatives by districts comprised within the states. But the president is elected by the united suffrages of the whole. Although, therefore, there might seem to be an incongruity in setting up the will of an individual to control that of the legislature, yet if the mode of election is such as to render that individual a more exact representative of the community as a whole, than the members of the legislature, the incongruity will immediately disappear.

The disparity between one man and the two or three hundred members who compose the legislative body, is the circumstance which strikes the mind with so much force, and makes it appear both unnatural and unjust to array the opinions of the first in opposition to those of the last. But this is a very imperfect way of making a comparison between the two things. When one considers the immense disproportion between the handful of representatives who make up the legislative assembly and the twenty millions who compose the community, the disparity in the first instance ceases to make any strong impression, not because it is not greater than in the second, but because the difference between one man and two or three hundred men is so little when both are compared with the whole population, that the disparity in the first instance is reduced to insignificance. And as no one considers the legislature a defective institution, because it contains an exceedingly small fraction of the community, for the same reason, no one can consistently maintain that the office of chief magistrate is absurdly contrived, because it sometimes interposes the opinions of a single individual to counteract the wishes of that small fraction.

The power which the English house of commons possess to grant or withhold the supplies, has been regarded as an important check upon the enterprises of the executive. But this check has no application in a republic; the constitution of the executive presents no occasion for its exercise. To declare war and to make treaties, are the exclusive prerogatives of the king in a monarchical government. In the United States, the war-making power belongs to the legislature, and the treaty-making power is under the control of the senate. A refusal on the part of the legislature to make the necessary appropriations, would interpose an obstacle to measures which had originated with itself, or to which one chamber was a party, instead of creating a restraint upon the executive power. The necessity of conferring the absolute veto upon the prince, has been argued from the nature of the office. It is necessary, it is said, to enable him to defend himself against the assaults of the legislature. He may refuse his signature to a law in the passage of which the legislature is deeply interested, in order to coerce it into some other measure, which will be favorable to the prosecution of his own plans. Such an adjustment of the powers of government is unnatural in the extreme. Representative government, therefore, proceeds upon totally different principles. It is not the executive, but the whole community, who are interested in the question of war. The power to declare it is therefore intrusted with the legislative body. Even in Great Britain, the check which has been so much relied upon, no longer possesses the same efficacy as formerly: for the commons have acquired so much importance as to make itself in practice a party to every declaration of war.

But there is this great defect in monarchical government, that not only is the direct authority of the king very considerable, but the fashion of thinking prevalent in a court has a wonderful influence in shaping public sentiment. A war, therefore, may have the approbation of a great majority in the legislature, although it is clearly repugnant to the interests of the people. The elevation of the middle class in Great Britain, has done much to rectify this unnatural state of things ; but it cannot accomplish everything, as long as there is a powerfully-disturbing force in some other part of society ; at any rate, not until that middle class is thoroughly and genuinely represented.

In the United States there has been a marked disposition of late years, to elevate men of moderate talents to the presidency. And this has been regarded as a circumstance of deep omen to the future, and as indicating a retrograde movement in society. But there is no reason why we should take this view of the matter. The election of such men, where there is no question of their integrity and patriotism, may not only be very consistent with the public welfare, but it may have a distinct and very important meaning which it is our duty to decipher. I have generally observed that where a community is undisturbed by revolution, a tendency of public opinion in one direction, no matter how singular it might appear to be, was an indication that there was a defect somewhere, which required to be rectified, and that this tendency was one means of rectifying it. There is no necessity for supposing that there is any such thing as a grovelling propensity among the American people, to search among the descending rather than among the ascending ranks of society for candidates for the presidency. The man of commanding talents is not sought after, because he represents too faithfully one part of society; and by so doing, fails to represent all other parts. On the other hand, the man of moderate abilities, the man who has no very strong and salient points of character, by failing to represent any one part exclusively, succeeds more fully in representing the whole.

There is another compensation for the disadvantage of excluding superior men from the first office in the government. A great writer of antiquity has remarked, that the Grecian commonwealths were absolutely compelled to the employment of the ostracism, in consequence of the despotic control which popular favorites exercised. The American government has no need of resorting to any such instrument. But a president who possesses pre-eminent abilities, has a sort of magical control over his party. He may retain the influence he has acquired, notwithstanding he has committed the greatest faults. The man whose fame has never made any noise, the moment he is guilty of any serious blunder, begins to feel the foundation on which he stands tremble. Instead of molding public opinion to his wishes, public opinion controls him, and stops him in the commencement of his career. The selection of men of moderate talents may have been fallen upon as an expedient to subserve the selfish interests of a party. But of all plans, it is the one least calculated to promote that object.

CHAPTER IV.

THE CLASSES OF SOCIETY.

No one man—no one class of men—is able to represent all the attributes of humanity. It is a fine provision, therefore, and not a defect, that society should be composed of a great number of classes, alike distinguished for the variety of their pursuits, and the still greater variety of faculties which they exert for the common benefit. The greater the number of classes the less powerful will any one be, the distance which separates them will be less, and the influence which they exercise upon each other, will be proportionably increased. The ultimate effect of a great number of differences, will be to produce more uniformity, a greater identity of interests and opinions among the whole. It may then be said that society is balanced by the various classes of men.

But what is it which gives a distinct character to this great variety of classes. Evidently, the communication of freedom to all. So that the enjoyment of a privilege, which European statesmen have fancied would open the door to a countless train of disorders, may not only carry with it an antidote to those disorders, but may be productive of the most direct and positive advantages.

Among the various orders of men, we may enumerate as most prominent, the young and the old, the rich and the poor, capitalists and laborers, the rural and the town population, professional men, and lastly, the parties of majority and minority.

No one who has been an attentive observer of public events, can have failed to observe that society is frequently subject to periodical revolutions of public opinion, and that these revolutions, some how or other, correspond with the growth of successive generations. In the United States this important and very interesting fact has been more distinctly manifested than any where else. In 1776, one of these revolutions took place; in 1801, a second; and in 1829, a third. It would seem that they depend to a great extent upon the present generation, which, after the lapse of twenty or thirty years, rises up to take the place of the older, and that the younger men of the community exercise a very sensible influence upon the whole course of public events. This influence may be for good, or for evil, but as a philosophical fact, it is entitled to great attention.

As in every society of even tolerable duration, a fresh generation arrives at manhood every year, and every day, as much as every twenty-five years; it may be supposed, that the influence of these successive populations, one upon the other, is greatly exaggerated. And doubtless such would be the case if the term influence did not import two things: agents capable of acting, and a material upon which they may act. Now the laws and institutions of every country are not only intended to endure much beyond a year, but it is absolutely necessary that they should do so, in order that there may be any experience of their character, and a subject matter for public opinion to exert an influence upon. But this we may say, that the constant succession of one generation to another, breaks the force which would otherwise be exerted after a lapse of years. Something is achieved every year toward the advancement of society, but that there is a marked influence after more distant intervals, is a fact which forces itself upon the attention of every one.

In a well constituted community, this influence will be advantageous. It is in this way, that provision is made for renewing the elements of society, and modifying old institutions by the action of new and more liberal opinions. As this influence in a democratic republic is not stifled by the power residing in the government, it is gradual, and never leads to those violent changes which in other countries threaten the dissolution of society. Instead of a French or an English revolution, the result of the accumulated abuses of centuries, society passes by an easy transition to new tasks, new habits, and an improved social organization.

Very important conclusions may be deduced, in reference to particular countries, from the fact, whether the average duration of life, or mean age of death is high or low. In England it is said to be as high as twenty-five or twenty-seven. In the United States, it is probably as low as sixteen. For it depends principally upon the rate of increase of the population. If this is rapid, and consequently the births numerous, the average duration of life will be comparatively low, since the majority of deaths occur in infancy.

In New England, taken separately, I presume that this average is considerably above sixteen. A society, however, in which the mean age of death is high, will be apt to be led and controlled by those who are past middle age; and where it is low, men under that age will come in for a large share of offices and of public favor. Men who are past middle age constitute a larger proportion of the population in the first instance, than they do in the second. Thus where the population is nearly or quite stationary, society will be most controlled by those whose views are most stationary; and where it increases with most rapidity, it will be apt to be controlled by those whose feelings and opinions are most easily modified. There is a natural foundation then for the existence of a movement and a conservative party. The first may wish to move too fast, the last may be averse to move at all. The mixture of these two classes, so as to insure that each shall have a due degree of influence is the great desideratum. In the western states of America, the population increases faster than in any other part of the world. The movement party, therefore, has a tendency to become the predominant one. This tendency, however, is in a great measure counteracted by another circumstance. The institutions are all taken from the older states. They embody the experience and opinions of an old class of men. They transfer the influence of that class into younger societies. The laws and institutions may be modified, but the fundamentals of government are adhered to tenaciously by all.

But whatever may be the rate of increase of the population, and the proportion between the young and older men of a country, a very great deal will depend upon the nature of the political institutions. The United States and Russia are the two countries in which the population increase most rapidly. But the aspect of society in the two is very different.

Free institutions introduce men at an early period upon the active theater of life. They hasten the period when they shall take part in political affairs, because they hasten the time when they shall engage in the pursuits of civil life. The last constitute a state of preparation for the first. If a greater degree of enthusiasm is imparted to the character of public men, a greater amount of experience is acquired at an early age, and the judgment is sooner matured than in those countries where men are not permitted to meddle with the interests of others, and hardly with their own, until the age of thirty or forty.

But it is not merely the part which the younger men of a country take in the active business of society which is important to be considered. The influence of the feelings and opinions, which are acquired by men in youth, upon their after life, is of great consequence also. Both species of influence are dependent upon the nature of the political institutions. In aristocratical and monarchical government the period of youth is to a great extent one of subjection and rigid discipline, from which the mind does not escape until the feelings and opinions have been completely molded. And the generation which has emerged from it know no other rule than to act the part which their fathers did by them, to maintain their youth in a state of the strictest discipline, and to transfer similar habits and modes of thinking to the walks of public life. But in a democratic republic, although there is no unnecessary relaxation of parental authority, the feelings and opinions which are acquired in youth are permitted to expand freely ; and they, therefore spread their influence upon the whole of the subsequent period of life. In such a community education has a meaning which it has no where else. It then becomes the duty of the government to take care that the elements of instruction shall be imparted to the whole people. In other words, as every new generation after certain intervals gives a fresh impulse to society, it is of great importance that this new movement should be controlled by a corresponding share of intelligence. Without free institutions the mind would be motionless, and society inanimate. With free institutions, but without a widely-diffused intelligence, the impulse which would be communicated would be more likely to be for the worse than for the better.

The most general division of society is into the superior and inferior classes. This is a distinction which we have no reason to believe will ever be effaced. The different degrees of sagacity, energy, and opportunity, which fall to the lot of individuals, will forever create a wide difference in their respective fortunes. The only effect of an agrarian law would be, for the time being, to convert the whole of society into a dead level, where there would be neither knowledge, or industry, or active virtue. Our efforts to elevate all men would only terminate in sensualizing all. Instead of lifting the lower classes higher, we should procure the abasement of all classes. The improvement of our condition, whether intellectual or physical, depends infinitely more upon our own independent exertions, than upon all other circumstances put together. One condition is indispensable: that the laws should not render property inalienable, or in any way obstruct its circulation; that it may be won by those who have industry, activity, and judgment, to win it. In the United States, neither the wealthy nor the merely independent class is composed of those who inherited property, but of those who commenced life with little or nothing.

The existence, then, of two very large classes, is the result of certain laws of our nature, which have a fixed operation, whatever may be the form of government. And the true inquiry is not whether either can be gotten rid of, but whether the influence of the one upon the other, is not part of the machinery by which the welfare of society is designed to be promoted. American institutions have existed a considerable period, under circumstances calculated to give activity to the exertions of every one. And yet even in America we can discern a well-defined line between the higher and lower orders of men. Free institutions do not obliterate the distinctions; on the contrary, they are eminently favorable to the accumulation of wealth in private hands, since they add to the natural gifts of some, the further advantages of opportunity, and the protection of a system of laws which is equal and invariable in its operation. It is like the addition of a new faculty to some men. The resolute, the enterprising, and the industrious, move forward with rapidity; while those who are differently organized, or whose will is subdued by causes which are almost inscrutable to observation, remain in the back ground, less prosperous, less fortunate in every respect, but not the less fitted to perform a very important part in the machinery of society. The most valuable qualities may belong to men in the inferior walks of life: although do what you will, these qualities may never be made to tell in the improvement of their condition. And it is the express design of free institutions, to give to this class a position and weight in the commonwealth which no other form of government has ever accorded.

It will be readily conceded, that the superior class exert a salutary control and influence upon the inferior. But it is not so easily perceived that the influence which the last exercise upon the former is equally important. The two orders of men represent two antagonist forces; the action of one upon the other, prevents either from running away with the power of the community, and establishes a powerfully-regulative principle which, although it is independent of the laws, yet constantly co-operates with the laws.

It may then be inquired, where is the difference between a democratic republic and the artificial forms of government. The last are founded upon a classification of men, and the preceding views suppose that each class plays a very important part in society, and that the influence of both is necessary to give system and regularity to the movements of the government. And this simple statement, which I have purposely adopted, is sufficient to explain the very wide difference between the two cases. In monarchy and aristocracy, the superior class is placed in the government, and the inferior thrust out. In a republic all classes are admitted to the enjoyment of political franchises. The influence therefore which is capable of being exerted by the one class upon the other, and of both upon the government, is totally different in the one instance from what it is in the other.

To talk of the influence of the inferior classes will seem out of place, perhaps even absurd, to those who figure every thing which is low and vulgar as belonging to them. Even if this were the case, their agency might be very important. If they imparted nothing positive to the rest of society, they might at any rate act as a check upon the excesses, the splendid vulgarity, if I may so term it, of the higher orders. If one effect of wealth and refinement is to corrupt and sensualize the rich, and at the same time to make the acquisition of political power more easy of attainment by them, and if we cannot get rid of wealth without destroying all incentives to industry and enterprize, the only alternative is, to raise up a class which will be too numerous to be bought, and which will be constantly interested in watching the movements of the class above them. This control will be negative in its operation at first; but it cannot exist long without compelling this class to the cultivation of more wisdom, moderation, and virtue, than could possibly be the case if they had the whole field to themselves. Providence never intended the inferior classes to be mere instruments for the gratification of the power and ambition of the wealthy, but rather to act as a corrective of the great defects which are incident to the enviable situation of the last, to prevent unbridled licentiousness from taking entire possession of the community, and by putting the refined and the educated on their good behavior, to make them exert in their turn a salutary control upon the ignorant and unenlightened. No control is effectual, if it is all on one side. It must be mutual. It is then more than a control ; it is a positive benefit.

In surveying the walks of private life, one is frequently struck with the numbers of individuals whose tempers are soured, and who seem to be every way uneasy in their condition. An air of pleasantry may be assumed, and is almost universally so when men meet in companies, but a close and practical observer will easily penetrate through this thin disguise. The cause of this discontent is that all have defects and infirmities, and yet the defects and infirmities are not the same in each, or at least manifest themselves in different forms. This causes individuals to run against and to incommode each other. If the infirmities of all were the same, there would be much more placidity of temper : for each would then cordially sympathize with each, and although these infirmities led to much vice and ignorance, they would be tenderly cherished, because there was no one to frown upon them. There would be less discontent perhaps, but this disadvantage would be greatly counterbalanced by the injury done to man as a rational being. An easy good nature would take possession of every one, and this would terminate in a species of mere animal enjoyment, or in a state of absolute vacuity of mind. By coming into contact with and incommoding each other, individuals for the first time hear of, and are made to realize, their defects. Great numbers are put upon all sorts of exertion to cure them, and to raise themselves in the scale of intellectual beings. Now precisely the same process, and with the same good effects, is witnessed in the action of the different classes of society upon each other. If all were alike, all superlatively prosperous and happy, or if the reverse were the case, society would become a barren waste.

If then the agency of the inferior classes is so important as a check upon the superior, the institution of slavery must be attended with some disadvantages. Its tendency would seem to be to lead to what we may term an unbalanced state of society. Slaves have no personal or political influence whatever, and the higher orders are thus freed from a restraint upon their actions, which is beneficial in the highest degree.

Doubtless they who live in a state where the institution is established, suppose that their condition is peculiarly fortunate; they may even persuade themselves that society is better balanced than it would otherwise be, inasmuch as it is exempt from the turbulence and insubordination which frequently take place among the class of free laborers. But as, in private life, there would be no domestic happiness or morality without numberless cares and anxieties, perhaps even adversities, so there would be no public virtue and felicity without very many trials of the same kind. It was the dissolution of the old form of society in Europe, the breaking up the system of servitude, which gave rise to the middle class, and caused the whole frame of society to be better adjusted than it was before. We may go further and say, that this revolution gave birth to the superior ranks, and substituted in the place of a boorish, ignorant, and turbulent aristocracy, a class which is in a high degree distinguished for its urbanity and intelligence. There would be no superior class in Europe at this day, in the proper acceptation of the term, if it had not been for the disfranchisement, and consequent influence, of the classes below them. The European states in which the higher ranks are most polished, most enlightened, and at the same time most numerous, are those in which the greatest amount of civil and political liberty is accorded to the bulk of the population. Much discomfort and annoyance may be experienced in a society so constituted; but that very discomfort and annoyance are the source of nearly all the blessings which have fallen to our modern communities.

In many respects the negro slavery which exists in the southern states of America, is not open to these objections. Slaves there do not fill up as in the commonwealths of antiquity, and the European states of the middle ages, nearly all the departments of industry. There is a very numerous class of freemen occupying the middle and inferior walks of life. But if one only knew how to deal with so difficult and delicate a subject; if one only had the ability requisite to remove the institution without leaving worse consequences behind, there can be no doubt that it would be better that all the occupations of society should be filled by a free population exclusively.

The men of the south cannot reasonably contend that the institution of slavery is a benefit "per se." But they may well insist, that the character which it has assumed among them is totally different from what it is any where else; and that as it is impossible to emancipate in communities where the slaves are very numerous, and of a race entirely distinct from their own, without producing the most disastrous consequences to both masters and slaves, it becomes not so much their right as their duty to maintain the institution. They may also insist, that there are many compensations attending the system, notwithstanding the disadvantages under which it otherwise labors; that slaves are kept under a domestic surveillance like the children of a family, each master superintending the behavior and actions of those who compose his own household; that in this way innumerable infractions of the laws are prevented, which other communities are only able to punish after they have been committed. I observe that the people of the north are sensible of the disadvantage of their situation in this respect. They accordingly make prodigious exertions to educate themselves, and to raise the lower classes to the level of the middle class. They have gone a step further than this. Experience has taught them that the use of ardent liquors is one of the most fruitful causes of crime and of every other species of disorder; they have, therefore, made immense efforts to exterminate the practice. They hear it defended in a great many plausible ways: that it contributes to good cheer and conviviality. The people of New England and New York have turned all these specious arguments in their minds, and have found that after all infinitely more mischief than good is the consequence of the habit; that the indulgence in it, whether by the rich or the poor, whether moderately or in excess, almost invariably disturbs the judgment and clouds the moral faculties. This, as has been remarked in a preceding chapter, argues an uncommon degree of reflection among a class to whom reflection has not been usually ascribed. For it is among the great body of the population, and not among a select few, that these just sentiments prevail; and even if this body do not actually constitute a majority, so as to insure the enactment of corresponding laws, it is at any rate so large as to demonstrate the existence of a sounder and healthier condition of society than has ever existed before. I cannot help thinking that the control of a popular class which is distinguished for such rare intelligence and virtue, cannot but be salutary in a high degree; that it will contribute essentially to a well balanced society; and that it may even be difficult to foresee all the good effects which will ultimately spring from it.

It has been noticed, as a characteristic difference between the northern and southern people of the United States, that among the former, all sorts of novel and startling doctrines in religion, morals, and politics, are constantly propounded; while among the last, opinions on all those subjects have acquired a degree of fixedness and uniformity which it is uncommon to meet with in the oldest settled communities. This difference is supposed to indicate a better social organization in the south, than in the north, and to afford a proof, that if education has been the means of imparting more knowledge to the northern people, it has been at the expense of bewildering them, and of filling society with all sorts of mischievous opinions. This view is very incorrect, however. Inquisitiveness, and a reaching after knowledge of any sort; the desire to form independent opinions upon all subjects, and the ability to discuss them, argues a development of the popular mind which should never be treated too lightly. If there were no crude and half-formed opinions in the world, there would never be any thoroughly matured ones. The speculations which are constantly afloat in a society where information is widely diffused, constitute the philosophy of the people. They not only give an impetus to the popular mind, but they rouse and set in motion the cultivated understandings of the country. The germ of almost all the great truths in philosophy and politics may be traced to the working of the popular mind.

It has been supposed that democratic institutions give too much control to the inferior classes; that they favor inordinately the elevation of persons of indifferent character and low attainments. But in practice, the effect does not take place to anything like the extent which has been predicted. The tendency to it is counteracted by two causes: first, by the consciousness which is ever present to the great majority of uneducated men, and from which they are never able to free themselves, that they are unequal to the higher offices in the state. This feeling, in spite of all the encouragement which is given to popular ambition, may be calculated upon with as much certainty, as any other propensity which influences the actions of men. It is even desirable sometimes to overcome it, to draw men of humble acquirements into the walks of active life, in order that free institutions may answer the end for which they were designed: that is, to make the faculties of men of all conditions as available as possible to the public service. Second: it is counteracted by the jealousy which ignorant men entertain of each other. They are only occasionally brought into contact with the enlightened; but they live in perpetual juxtaposition with one-another. They are accordingly more incommoded by each other, than they are by the superior classes; and feel a greater degree of envy of any remarkable good fortune which may fall to the lot of their own number.

I think, however, that I can at present discern symptoms, in all parts of the United States, of a decided movement in the opposite direction. The dispersion of knowledge in a democratic community, multiplies the numbers of the well-informed to such a degree that the members of this class begin also to incommode and interfere with one another. So many of this class are necessarily disappointed in obtaining office, that they very soon lay schemes for selecting candidates among the class below them, and once the example is set, these new favorites are not backward in availing themselves of such good fortune. The former may not be actuated by any liberal or patriotic views: they probably wish to make a merit of their disappointment; or by forming a close alliance with the masses, to lay the foundation of their own advancement at a future day. Nevertheless, the course they adopt is, without any intention on their part, productive of great advantage to society. The elevation of persons of even ordinary capacity, to places of trust and responsibility, stimulates them to exertion, and frequently awakens dormant qualities which were never suspected to exist. The minds of all are improved by being made conversant with interests which look much beyond the farm or the shop.

Thus the educated and influential set on foot a revolution which gradually undermines their own importance; but it is only accomplished by raising a great number of men in the inferior walks of life to their own condition; in other words, by creating a counterpoise to their own selfishness and ambition. The great works of internal improvement which have been executed in the American states were debated and matured in assemblies composed for the most part of ordinary farmers.

The town and the rural population constitute another division of the classes of a community. These two orders of men no longer live apart from each other, with habits and manners as distinct as if they were separated by different ages. This change is much more remarkable in the United States, than in any other country. Free institutions, which commence by individualizing men, ultimately tend to draw them closer together. The greater the amount of personal independence which each one enjoys, the more numerous are his wants, and the stronger is the desire and the aptitude for society.

Civilization commences in the towns; for it is only by congregating together, that men learn to defer to each other's wants, and are led to co-operate in plans which are calculated to promote their common interests. The city constitutes a nucleus of civilization, around which the country population gathers; and the more frequent the communication between the two the more rapidly will the whole population advance in every species of improvement. In some countries, burdensome and vexatious imposts are levied upon the trade between the towns and the country. I do not know how far the necessities of any particular government may render this mode of taxation desirable, but it is certain that it creates a very serious impediment to a free and liberal intercourse between the two classes; nor is the degree of this impediment measured merely by the amount of the number of duties which are levied, but goes greatly beyond. Any obstruction to a communication between two classes, whose habits and manners were originally different, lays the foundation for still greater differences, and keeps them wide apart for centuries.

Although the people of the United States are eminently an agricultural one, yet in no part of the world is there such a disposition to build towns. The town and the country have constantly advanced, hand in hand. The same causes which give rise to a distribution of the political power of the community, produce also a more exact distribution of the population. The growth of the cities is not determined by the residence of a court and nobility, or by any other causes equally artificial; but takes the course which is most natural, and therefore most favorable to the general prosperity. And although foreign commerce will always rear some very large towns, it may be predicted with certainty, that internal commerce will build up a still greater number nearly as large; and that, in America, there will always be a more equal balance between the town and country population, than in any other state which does not possess the advantage of free institutions. The effect of a thorough intercourse between these two great classes, is to diffuse intelligence, to render the civilization more uniform, and to cause a more exact equilibrium of power among the whole. This operates as a protection against those violent revolutions which take place in other countries, where the cities, having acquired the supremacy, are in a condition to lord it over the whole country.

A city presents an organized force, somewhat resembling that of an army, and unless the country population is raised to a level greatly above that of the European peasantry, it cannot exert the influence which naturally and legitimately belongs to it. The French revolution offers a striking example of this fact: the city of Paris ruled with absolute sway over the provinces, because the provinces were composed of an abject population. In the United States, the people of the country are always willing to obey a summons which calls them to suppress an insurrection in the towns; and their conduct on the very few occasions where their services have been necessary, has been alike distinguished for humanity and bravery.

A prime object of political institutions should be to neutralize the power of great masses, and thus to ward off even the approach of revolution; and the most certain way of effecting this is by dispersing knowledge and property among the whole population. The laws of France restrict the electoral franchise within such narrow limits as to give an undue preponderance to the towns. The qualifications are so high, and the division of the soil so minute, as to place the great majority of the electors in the towns. Bustle, activity and enterprise are characteristics of the towns; while to the rural population, belong greater simplicity of manners, more hardihood of character, and a peculiar aptitude for cool reflection. By establishing a close communication between these two classes, the whole population is bound together by one common interest, and the general standard of character is greatly elevated.

Capital and labor give rise to another division in society, not materially different from the classification into the higher and lower orders, but pointing more directly to the causes which, in a thriving and industrious community, lead to the distribution. The relation of lord and serf at one time swallowed up all other distinctions, and paved the way every where for the establishment of aristocratical or monarchical government. On the other hand, the existence of the two great classes of capitalists and laborers, is an infallible indication of a tendency toward an improved condition of society. In the United States, these two classes not only compose the population of the towns—they compose also the population of the country. Agriculture, in that community, has become a great trade. The division of the soil, while it is unfavorable to the acquisition of political power by a few, procures independence to a very large number. The proportion between laborers and capitalists is, as every where else, determined by the principle of supply and demand; but the condition of the two classes is greatly modified by the influence of free institutions.

The struggle between capital and labor is one of the most striking facts in the history of modern communities. The forces of society seem to have taken an entirely new direction. Instead of efforts to acquire political power, which must necessarily be confined to a few, the great effort of every one now seems to be to acquire property. Two good effects flow from this: 1st, the political institutions enjoy more repose,—the government is not so much endangered by the cabals and conspiracies of the few, as was formerly the case; 2d, by interesting so great a number in the acquisition of property, the value of property is generally felt, and the population are insensibly trained to habits which best fit them for self government.

In the United States, the struggle between capital and labor presents a much more difficult problem than it does any where else. For if the class of laborers outnumbers that of capitalists, and the present system of nearly universal suffrage prevails, may not the public tranquility—nay, the very being of government, be endangered?

The struggle may be harmless, so long as the reward of industry is so liberal as to allow a competent share to both classes. But when the population has doubled and trebled, the condition of the laborer will no longer be so fortunate; for although capital will also have accumulated, yet the objects upon which it can be employed will not have increased in the same proportion, and the double effect of an augmented competition among both capitalists and laborers, will necessarily reduce the amount of the products of industry, and cause a much less quantity to be partitioned among the two classes. The condition of both will be altered for the worse; but that of laborers much more so than of capitalists. The last may be able to live in comfort, while the first may be reduced to a mere subsistence. The struggle will then become infinitely more intense than it has yet been. It may give rise to formidable associations among laborers to raise their wages, and if these efforts are not successful, it may lead to serious riots and insurrection, or the ballot box may be resorted to as a more peaceful and effectual means of curing the supposed evil. Laborers may outnumber all other classes, and by the simple exercise of the right of suffrage, may cause the laws to be shaped to suit their own wishes. This is presenting the dark side of the picture, and it is necessary to view a question of so much interest and magnitude, in every possible aspect, so as to form a valuable opinion of what is to be the future destiny of a country hitherto so fortunate in its career, and to find out if certain evils are necessarily incident to a state in which free institutions are established; whether there may not be some way of alleviating them—whether they are not attended with many compensations—whether, in short, they may not be turned into advantages.

The reason why the struggle between capital and labor, presents so threatening an aspect in the United States, is that laborers are placed in a much more advantageous condition, than in any other country. They stand higher in the scale, both physically and morally. They have on this account, a more resolute and independent character. The very circumstance which renders their condition so enviable, is regarded as ominous of the future tranquillity of the country. We thus look into the future from a wrong point of view. We suppose, that the demand for laborers, will never be counterbalanced by the demand for employment; or that the present independent feeling of laborers, will continue, even after their condition is changed. As society advances, there is a constant tendency to a fall of wages. This is inevitable, whether we ascribe it to the increase of the number of laborers, or to the increased difficulty of procuring the means of subsistence. The vast extent of cultivable land in the United States, will retard the fall; but come it must, whenever the population has attained the density of that of France, or Great Britain. Nature will then impose a powerful check upon passions which would otherwise be ungovernable. For I have constantly observed, that poverty, straitened circumstances, the humility of feeling which these create, have a wonderful effect in subduing the will, and producing a submission to circumstances which are beyond our control. It would be infinitely better, if the present independent condition of laborers could be maintained. But if the fall to lower wages, at a period more or less distant, is unavoidable, the mischiefs which now threaten society, will wear a different aspect; and I do not see, how it can be denied, that the safeguard to the institutions, will be as strong as it is now, and that it will increase in intensity exactly in proportion as it is needed. Discontent will be much more common, but it will not be accompanied with the same degree of power as now. The laborer will have much more cause to complain; but 1st. the change in his condition will be brought about by certain laws of society, which neither he, nor any one else can control. 2d. The same causes will enfeeble his will, and deprive him of the effective power to do mischief. Outbreaks will be much more common; and they will of course take place among a much more numerous body of men; but they will be powerless, compared with what they would be, if laborers possessed the same independent condition as at present. 3d. There is a constant tendency, as society grows older, to an augmentation of capital, and an increase of the number of capitalists. All those institutions which embody wealth, and power, will become stronger, so that not only will the ability to invade property be diminished; but the ability to protect it, will be increased. I predict that the civil aristocracy, which will grow up in the United States, will be more powerful, more intelligent, and more pacific, than any political aristocracy which has ever existed.

The originally equal distribution of the soil in the United States, is a circumstance which has never been sufficiently appreciated. It explains the secret of the private comfort, and well being of the population; and it may be regarded also, as the hinge on which turns the stability of the institutions. The soil of Ireland is distributed among less than one thousand proprietors. Ohio with very nearly the same area, and one third of the population, is divided among two hundred thousand. It is obvious, that this great disproportion, in the one case, between the numbers of the people, and the distribution of the soil, must exert an influence literally immense, upon the condition of the people, upon their manners, character, and powers of exertion; and that it must to the same extent, affect the structure, and the whole machinery of government. Ireland is an extreme case; but the same causes which have produced so striking a disproportion in the division of property there, have acted with more or less force, in every other European state. All have commenced the rudiments of life in the savage state, and all have submitted at one period or another, to the dominion of a foreign enemy, who have camped down among them, and parcelled out the soil among the chiefs of the army. In England and Scotland, in France and Spain, in Italy and Germany, the effect of these revolutions is perceptible at the present day. And if the question were asked, what has rendered possible, the establishment of free institutions in the United States, and what has rendered their existence so precarious in Europe, the decisive, and the satisfactory answer would be the originally different distribution of the soil, has produced these opposite results.

The distinguishing feature then of American society, that which differs it from all others, either ancient or modern, is that the tiers etat, or middle class, is not confined to the towns, but is diffused over the whole country. In Europe, it comprehends the Burgeoise, in the United States, it comprehends in addition, a vastly more numerous class, to wit, the country population. This is a circumstance of infinite moment, in the study of American institutions. It has made a profound impression upon them already, and may exert immense influence upon the future destinies of the country. Until in Europe, the middle class is composed of both the great divisions of the population, the cause of free institutions will be involved in great uncertainty. 1st. Because until then, the population cannot be said to be fairly amalgamated. It is not necessary that the population should all be melted down into one class; but it is necessary that there should be a certain degree of uniformity, in order to prevent an incessant conflict of interests and opinions, and to make the institutions of government something more than the representative of a section of society. 2d. Until then, the middle class will not be sufficiently strong and enlightened, to command that respect which silently and without the employment of force, molds the institutions to its own purpose. The revolution which annihilated the legislature and elevated Napoleon III to the throne, could not possibly have taken place if France had contained a powerful middle class. No individual can have power to take to pieces the government if the population who live under it can agree among themselves; and this is impossible where the inequalities of society are so great and so numerous as to create the greatest diversity of opinions and interests. That merely tacit understanding which takes place among the members of a community in which there prevails great uniformity of condition, imposes an instant check upon all attempts to revolutionize the government. The artificial institutions of monarchy and aristocracy are resorted to for the single purpose of repressing those great disorders which grow out of the inequalities among the different parts of the population. A standing army, then, becomes part of the regular police. It is only a more thorough organization of the constabulary force. If it took from the christian era to the French revolution to create a tiers etat in the towns alone, in continental Europe, how long will it take to create one among the rural population? In private life, an individual entitled to respect, generally commands it. The same is true in political society. Where a strong middle class makes its appearance, it does not stand in need of a standing army to protect it. It may even give control of the army to the executive. No one attempts what is impossible, but at the utmost what is only improbable.

Are there any causes in operation in the United States which are calculated to diminish the numbers and to weaken the influence of the middle class? I have alluded to the difficulty of procuring food, and the consequent fall of wages, which takes place when a country becomes densely peopled, and the greater part of the arable land has been appropriated. There is another circumstance, however, which is beginning to exercise a powerful influence upon European society. Within the last fifty years a great revolution has taken place in the whole system of industrial pursuits, in agriculture, manufactures, and commerce. The tendency every where is to the creation of vast capitals and the extermination of small ones. An infinitely greater net produce can be obtained from the soil where it is cultivated in large farms, than when it is divided into small ones. As the population residing on and supported by it, is much less, the expense of cultivation is much less also. The employment of a large capital, and the application of those improvements which none but the wealthy proprietor can command, enables him to sell cheaper, as a moderate profit upon such a capital produces more riches than the same profit upon a small capital. The effect of this system has been to expel from the soil the former cultivators, and to introduce in its stead the system of day labor. Until within the last fifty years, the English laborer lived on the soil which he cultivated—it was his permanent home. It is very different now. The cultivation is almost entirely performed by day laborers, who are dismissed whenever there is no occasion for their services, and who are consequently without employment during the greater part of the year. In England the agricultural laborers only amount to about 1,061,000. This great revolution has not been unnoticed by writers on political economy, but the comprehensive genius of Sismondi * first pointed out its connection with some of the most important problems in political philosophy. The same revolution, but with still greater effect, has taken place in manufacturing industry. Vast numbers of laborers, driven from the soil, are collected in the towns where manufacturing establishments have grown up. Their wages are very moderate, and they are liable, on every disaster of trade, to be left in a state of destitution. Immense capitals are employed in these manufactures. Formerly fifty thousand dollars was considered an ample capital. At present less than half a million is not considered adequate to the successful prosecution of the business. The larger the capital, the cheaper can the proprietor afford to sell. The same amount of profit which on a small capital would only maintain his family, will yield an immense income on a large one. The constant tendency, then, is to the creation of colossal fortunes in the hands of a few, and the consequent creation of a vast army of proletarians.

The introduction of industrial pursuits first broke up the feudal system, and established the metayer system of cultivation, It has now almost completely broken up this, and introduced the system of day labor. The lower classes have been freed from the direct control and authority of the landed proprietor, but they are placed in a state of greater dependence than ever. Instead of living on the soil, where the means of subsistance was assured to them during the year, or rather for life, they are now employed and dismissed at the

* Economie Politique.

pleasure of the proprietor. It is difficult to predict what will be the result of this system, so entirely unknown either in ancient or modern times. An overwhelming mass of proletarians has been created both in town and country; and although a corresponding increase of the enlightened classes, and the concentration of wealth and power in the hands of landed, manufacturing and commercial capitalists, renders it as easy, or even easier, to govern the masses than formerly; yet it is evident that the system may be pushed so far as to cause its own ruin. The extermination of small capitals on the land, in manufactures and commerce, may cause the middle class to dwindle into insignificance. The class of proletarians may be augmented indefinitely: they may be driven to despair, their overwhelming numbers may enable them to combat successfully against the most solidly established authority.

This is the unfavorable side of the picture; and it is necessary to understand what is possible, in order to comprehend the probable, or even the present. But there are two remarkable circumstances connected with English society, which show that there is a power of resistance somewhere to this extreme state of things. The first is, that the wages of labor have varied very little during the last five hundred years.* A peck of wheat a day has been the average during the whole of that period. The extraordinary improvements which have been made in the science of agriculture, and which have kept pace with the increase of the population, have retarded the fall of wages. It is true that a peck of wheat a day may be a very insufficient reward to the laborer, when he is only employed six months in the year; although in consequence of the fall of price in all manufactured products, he may be able to purchase with it, more of the necessaries of life. The operatives in manufacturing establishments, however, are not subjected to this disadvantage. They are hired during the year. The second circumstance which is entitled to our attention, is presented in the British income tax returns of 1812 and 1848. From these, it appears that there has been an increase of the number of moderate, and a comparative diminution of colossal fortunes.

	1812.	1848.
Between £ 150 and £ 500,	30,723	91,101
500 and 1000,	5,334	13,287
1000 and 2000,	2,116	5,234
2000 and 5000,	1,180	2,586
5000 and upwards,	409	1,181†

*Malthus' Political Economy.

†Nat. Intelligence, March 20, 1851.

M. Sismondi has' not noticed these two circumstances. The mind to which new and striking views are presented, is very apt to run them out to extreme consequences. Nor is this to be regretted. They would not make so strong and distinct an impression if they were not pushed to extremity, nor would those circumstances which contribute to modify them, be so easily found out. The consideration of what is possible, as I before remarked, sheds light upon the probable, and even upon the actual.

The employment of immense capitals in every department of industry, is the secret of the commercial prosperity of England. The complete centralization of capital causes all commodities to be produced, and sold cheaper, and compensates, in some degree, for heavy taxation, and the increasing difficulty of obtaining food. But it is doubtful whether the great mass of the population are placed in more favorable circumstances. The number of the poor, instead of diminishing, is augmented by the increase of riches. Never was industry productive of such brilliant results, and never was the class of proletarians more numerous.

This system is evidently springing up in the United States. There is the same tendency to the employment of great capitals in every department of industry. It will be a very long time before the system attains its maximum; but to the political philosopher, one or two hundred years are but as a single day. There are some circumstances, however, which will contribute to counteract the effects of this system. 1st. The general standard of comfort is higher than it has ever been in any other country; and inveterate habit will render it very difficult to depart from it. 2d. The principle of equal partibility prevails in the descent and devise of estates. Equal partibility, however, may be carried so far as to create an immense army of proletarians, or it may terminate in an opposite result. Great capitalists may purchase a multitude of these small estates, and the system of great landed properties may ultimately be introduced. The principle of equal partibility, however, will be applied to these large properties also, and they will be crumbled in a few generations, into small fragments. The desirable medium may in this way be attained; and the high standard of comfort, together with the alternate creation and destruction of overgrown estates, may place the great mass of the population in more advantageous circumstances, than anywhere else.

M. Sismondi is silent with regard to the condition of the French population. This arises from the adoption of an exclusive theory, the strength of which might seem to be impaired by admitting any important exceptions to it. The theory is entitled to great attention; but it is indispensable to be acquainted with the whole ground on which we travel. France affords a very instructive lesson. There is the same tendency there, as in other countries, to the employment of large capitals in manufactures and commerce; but it is otherwise in agriculture, and agriculture constitutes the occupation of the great majority of the population. The rule of equal partibility has prevailed for more than half a century. The number of proprietors has consequently augmented prodigiously. According to M. Dupin, France, in 1834, contained twenty-four millions of proprietors, in a population of thirty-two millions. Such is the number inscribed on the public registers. A very ingenious writer insists, that as the report made by M. Guion to the chamber of deputies, the same year, shows that the land is incumbered with a debt contracted by proprietors, to the amount of thirteen thousand millions of francs, those who owe this debt are only nominally proprietors.* The mortgagees of the land may ultimately swallow up these innumerable small properties. The fact, at any rate, shows the wretched condition of the agricultural population, and that the division of the soil, and the cultivation of it by those who reside on it, has not been more favorable to the general comfort than the opposite system of large farms and large capitals. More than twenty millions of this people can neither read nor write; twenty-two millions earn only from six to seven scus a day, and of the twenty-four millions of proprietors, twelve or fourteen millions have not always even coarse bread to subsist on. It would seem that neither the English system, which aims to produce the greatest amount of net income, nor the French, which is directed to the production of the greatest amount of gross produce, have succeeded in placing the great bulk of the population in a state of even tolerable independence. Here are two opposite experiments proceeding simultaneously in two countries, separated only by a narrow channel, and the result in each has been to produce a vast army of proletarians.

If we suppose then that all the overgrown estates in Great Britain and Ireland were broken up and sold in small parcels, there

*P. Considerant Dest. Soc., v. 1, p. 152.

is no absolute assurance that the condition of society would be permanently ameliorated. The effect of the division of property is to give a fresh stimulus to the population. The abolition of the laws of primogeniture, and entail, would almost necessarily produce this great change. Properties would be subdivided every generation, and the British peasantry and operatives might be reduced to the same fare of black bread as the French. In applying these views to the United States, we must again revert to the circumstance to which I before alluded. The division of the soil was originally, and continues to be, incomparably more equal than in any European country. This original difference in the structure of society, combined with the high standard of comfort, each acting upon and contributing to fortify the other, may forever ward off the existence of either the French or the English system. And when we add to this the influence of those political institutions, which grew up at the very foundation of their society, habits absolutely indelible may be grafted upon the whole population. As the experiment stands alone, in the history of human nature, the results may be different from what they have been in any other country.

I have now pointed out some of those general causes, which impede the regular march of society, and which raise or depress the condition of the various classes. But there are some circumstances of a more hidden character, which act with more or less force upon multitudes of individuals, whatever may be the structure of society, and however wide the arena of exertion may be. Thus, in the United States, where it is strictly correct to say, that the great bulk of the population belongs to the middle class, there are very great diversities in the condition of individuals. It is because these circumstances are confined to individuals, and do not characterize classes, that it is difficult to unravel them. The history of the individual has never been written. The character and habits which are common to classes, are easily seized and appreciated, those which belong to individuals are indefinitely diversified, and we search in vain for a clue to guide us to some general rules.

It is not necessary to inquire why, in the great majority of countries, one-half, sometimes a much greater proportion of the population, is in straitened or destitute circumstances. But why in the United States, where the field of exertion is almost unbounded, there are the greatest diversities in the condition of individuals, is a problem for the inquisitive mind to ponder upon. The present may be termed the golden age of the republic : there is not the least reason, so far as physical comfort is concerned, that, as a whole, anything better will succeed. It is the first time in the annals of mankind, that the wish of Henry the Great has been realized, "that every man had a piece of meat to put in his kettle." Do the differences I have alluded to arise from difference of capacities ; taking capacities, in its most detailed signification as denoting good understanding, acquired ability, shrewdness, manners, acquaintance with the world, etc. ; or, second, from a difference in the affective faculties, or of constitution, health, temperament ; or, third, from difference of opportunities ; fourth, from difference of organization, disposing some instinctively to exertion, and inclining others to love of pleasure, repose, and inaction ; fifth, from so many having little or nothing to begin life, the families to which they belong being numerous, and leaving little to be divided ; sixth, or from receiving so much, as to corrupt their character, and enfeeble their exertions.

To trace the operation of these causes, not only singly, but in their complication with one another, and with a multitude of others so minute, as almost to elude scrutiny, would be the work of a lifetime. To trace their operation in a society of ten, or fifteen thousand, would be impossible, without a close and minute knowledge of the individuals who compose it. But how shall we obtain this knowledge in a society of millions. The human countenance and manners, even in the commonest individuals, draw over the mind and character such a disguise, that it is difficult to penetrate the interior. Persons, the most dissimilar in understanding, in affective faculties, in organization, constitution, and health, frequently wear pretty much the same face and demeanor ; and yet a difference in any one of these respects, not merely in the broadest signification, but a difference of shade only may give a direction to the whole of life.

Is there any way of legally removing the great inequality of property. Can those who accumulate wealth be considered as appropriating to themselves the just proceeds of the labor of others ; and if they can, would those others appropriate these proceeds to themselves ; or would they, for want of the industry and energy which set labor in motion, cease to be produced at all. These are all inquiries of great nicety, as well as of great moment, in determining what is to be the nature of the struggle between capital and labor, and what the form which the institutions of society will ultimately assume.

I am very far from regarding the struggle between capital and labor as of ill omen to the future prosperity and well being of a country. It is a pretty sure indication that the laborious classes have risen in intelligence and importance, and that they, as well as capitalists, are enabled to exercise some judgment as to the standard of comfort which befits them. It is this very struggle which permits the former to maintain something like a respectable and independent station. The man, distracted by poverty, has no time to look beyond his mere animal wants; the man who obtains due wages, feels his faculties unbound, He can look around him, and gather up some of the information which is scattered about. He feels new motives to a regular and virtuous conduct, and is rendered an active and useful citizen, instead of being a brute machine. If this introduces a new element into every calculation which has for its object the determining the proper amount of wages due to the laborer, so much the better. It cannot be doubted, that capitalists enjoy a great advantage in this respect, in consequence of their superior intelligence: that this intelligence does count for something, and although the relation between the supply and the demand of labor, is the over-ruling principle, yet that like all other general principles, it is capable of being greatly modified in practice. There is every reason, therefore, why, if the class of capitalists are raised in the scale of intelligence, the class of laborers should be also. For when we speak of the struggle between capital and labor, we necessarily intend something more than the mere fortuitous or customary adjustment of the two, by causes independent of any human control; we intend that the judgment is exercised, and that active efforts are made use of by both parties in every contract of service. To denounce the struggle between capital and labor, therefore, would be in effect to lament over the improved intellectual and moral condition of the lower classes. But this we cannot do consistently. If there is any one object which every man, philanthropist, patriot, or statesman, has at heart, it is to diffuse education as widely as possible, and to lift the greatest number of men possible to the rank of intelligent beings. That there must be a limit to our efforts is obvious; but when one compares the condition of the lower classes, even in Europe, at the present day, with what it was two centuries ago, it is evident that infinitely more may be effected iu this respect than any human sagacity would have predicted. That laborers and operatives are able to exercise some judgment as to the amount of wages which are justly their due, that, in other words, the struggle between capital and labor is not a struggle all on one side, is every way favorable both to the prosperity and the tranquillity of the country. It gives to the community a body of more effective laborers, and tempers the misguided feelings which would otherwise take possession of them, whenever a season of distress occurred to interrupt their enjoyment, as well as that of capitalists. The reflection which their improved habits impart to them, draws them back, whenever they are in danger of running into excesses.

It must not be supposed because people are poor that they are therefore rendered insurgent and revolutionary. In order to produce this effect they must, as a general rule, be able to connect their disadvantageous condition with the hand of government as its cause. Poor people, as a class, are fully as much disposed to be orderly as people in a higher condition. Prosperity of any kind administers so many provocatives to the passions, that it requires to be counteracted by powerful motives of self interest. A humble condition and the constant occupation which it renders necessary, are apt to have a subduing influence upon the temper and character. It is when government undertakes to make discriminations prejudicial to the inferior classes, that they are most disposed to acts of insubordination. Doubtless the institutions of America are environed with many difficulties ; and it is in order to lesson the weight of these, that I desire to see the great body of operatives raised as high as practicable in the scale of society. The contest between capital and labor will then not be settled by brute force on the one side, or by superior adroitness on the other ; but will be conducted with some degree of judgment and caution, and will terminate, in the great majority of instances, in a compromise advantageous to both parties. What are termed "strikes" are by no means uncommon in the United States. Sometimes there is no well-founded cause for complaint ; and then workmen recede from their demands and return quietly to their occupations. But the reverse is frequently the case ; and then each party concedes something to the pretensions of the other. A new agreement is made, which, without sensibly impairing the productiveness of capital, adds something to the comforts of laborers, and smoothes all those difficulties which had for a time suspended their accustomed occupations. But capitalists will forever possess one advantage over laborers. They can afford to lie idle for six months, or even longer; while the last, having accumulated little, are obliged to depend upon their regular wages. And this advantage increases just in proportion as combinations among laborers become most dangerous; that is, in proportion as the population becomes more dense. It is fortunate, therefore, that as society advances to the period when the circumstances of so great a number will be very much straitened, there should be some causes in operation calculated to raise the standard of both physical and moral comfort, and to present the only natural corrective which exists to an absolute redundancy of the population.

I observe that it is not unusual in the United States for workmen to specify their grievances in writing, and to cause them to be published. This circumstance is no small indication how much that class are elevated in the social scale. To be able to analyze our thoughts, and to frame reasons for our conduct in any important conjuncture, is precisely that sort of mental ability which it is so desirable to encourage, in order to temper the passions of the multitude by the exercise of calm judgment and reflection.

And the practice of giving publicity to these complaints is particularly worthy of commendation. It affords very strong evidence that those who complain are themselves convinced of the justice of their complaints, and that they are willing to put them to the test of an open and manly avowal. Instead of those secret combinations, which were formerly so common, and with regard to the merit of which no impartial person could form any judgment whatever; workmen who set themselves up in opposition to the exactions of their employers, feel themselves under an obligation to sustain their conduct by a fair and intelligent exposition of their case. The public is, for the most part, an impartial spectator in affairs of this kind; it is not apt to be moved by inflammatory appeals, when these appeals, however common, are made by distinct bodies at different intervals, and never comprehend at any one time any considerable class of the population. I cannot refrain from copying one of those memorials, which expresses the justest sentiments, in language of the greatest terseness and brevity. The journeymen house carpenters in one of our cities made a strike for the ten-hour system, and this is what they say in their statement: "We are flesh and blood; we need hours of recreation. It is estimated by political economists, that five hours labor per day, by each individual, would be sufficient for the support of the human race. Surely, then, we do our share when we labor ten. We have social feelings which must be gratified. We have minds which must be improved. We are lovers of our country, and must have time and opportunity to study its interests. Shall we live and die knowing nothing but the rudiments of our trade? Is knowledge useless to us, that we should be debarred the means of obtaining it? Would we be less adept as workmen? Would the trade, of which we are members, be less respected or useful? Or would the community, of which we are members, suffer less because we were enlightened?"

We need not fear any ill consequences from the influence of the class of working men, when we find them capable of taking such just and liberal views; views which denote that they have a true perception of their own rights, and that they desire so to use them as to make them subservient to the common weal. We should rather hail this influence as the symptom of an exceedingly sound and healthful condition of society. It is fit that the relations which this class bear to the class of capitalists, should be adjusted by these two parties, instead of by appeals to governmental regulation. An European community may be obliged to resort to the last course. But wherever the first is pursued, we may be sure of two things: that the class of working men has risen greatly in the scale; and that there is a high probability the affairs of society will continue to be conducted in a peaceful and orderly manner.

Even admitting, therefore, that the inferior classes should come to predominate in the United States, while the present laws of suffrage continue to exist, it does not therefore follow that the conntry is to be converted into a bedlam. On the contrary, there is every reason to believe, that things will continue pretty much in the same even tenor which they have hitherto held. In progress of time, there will be both a more numerous class of rich, and a more numerous class of poor. But the middle class will forever outnumber both the others. The distribution of the rural population, so different from what it is in any other country, insures this, whatever may be the growth of manufacturing industry. It is to the exertions of this class, that the operatives in England are indebted for the amelioration of their condition. And it is upon the permanent influence of this class, that we are entitled to fasten all our hopes of the future in America.

If we were to suppose the operatives of the manufacturing establishments to constitute a majority of the electors, and even a majority of the legislature, what laws could they pass which would better their condition ? To make a division of incomes between the capitalists and themselves, would instantly annihilate capital, and would render the condition of the last unspeakably wretched. If the income of all the rich was equally divided among all who were not rich, it would not amount to a week's support to each. And admitting that there would be a large number who were incapable of foreseeing these consequences, there would be a still larger number who would clearly discern them.

The ignorance of the ignorant is rarely so great as to blind them to the perception of the few elementary principles on which their own interests hinge. After making every allowance, therefore, for those popular excesses to which society, in whatever form it may be cast, will forever be occasionally liable, I cannot help thinking that the enjoyment of political liberty by the inferior classes, instead of being a hindrance to good government, will assist in promoting it. Nor is there the least probability that these classes will ever compose the majority in the American legislatures. There are certain laws of human nature, the operation of which may be calculated upon with nearly as much certainty as those which preside over the physical world. Every man would gladly be his own lawyer and his own physician, and, whenever occasion required it, show himself master of every other department of knowledge. It would save a great deal of expense, and would administer mightily to human vanity if such could be the case. But the impossibility of the thing is so manifest, and is so universally felt, that, although all professions should be laid open to general competition as are already all other branches of knowledge, the great majority of people will apply to those who have skill and experience, and would consider it the greatest misfortune in the world to be cut off from their advice and assistance. The same is the case with matters of government. The most ignorant men may desire to become legislators; their interest and ambition would seem to be as much gratified in this way as by becoming their own lawyers and physicians. But a desire which, as soon as it is formed, is sure to be smothered by an overwhelming sense of deficiency, can never have any effect.

It is not merely as a political privilege that the electoral franchise is so valuable; the influence which it exerts upon the general manners is inestimable. It causes men to respect and to defer to each other's opinions. It accustoms those who are invested with any species of influence, whether of a political or a merely civil character, to use it equitably and prudently; and it disposes those who are any ways subject to this influence, to regard it, not as an odious privilege, but as a source of peculiar benefit to themselves. Doubtless the very general enjoyment of the electoral franchise in the United States, is one reason why the system pursued in the management of manufacturing establishments is placed upon a so much more advantageous footing than in any other country. By learning to respect others, we are made acquainted with their interests: and this respect then becomes something more than a dead formality. Not merely are the operatives in these establishments better fed and clothed, but they are treated much more as reasonable beings. Their education and religious instruction are considered as having some place in the economy of these institutions.

The enjoyment of political privileges by men in the inferior walks of life, is in reality the only way of effectually conciliating the interests of all classes. It may be said, that as the management of public affairs requires skill and information of a particular kind, it should be devolved upon those who have time and opportunity to acquire them; on the same principle as a division is made of all the other pursuits of society; that inasmuch as the mechanic and the farmer do not undertake to interfere with each other's calling, nor either to dictate to the physician or the lawyer as to the right way of applying their information and experience, there would be the same propriety in confining the whole business of government to a class set apart for that purpose. The two things are in truth very properly compared, and it is because they are similar that the management of political affairs is not conferred upon a particular order of men; although the professions and trades are exercised by those who have skill in them, yet all who have need of legal or medical assistance are free to choose their own physician and lawyer. If this were not the case, if a monopoly were established in favor of a few select practitioners, the same skill would not be exercised by them, and the public would lose all confidence in their ability and integrity. The perfect freedom of choice which every individual enjoys, does not prevent the various professions and trades from being separated from each other. And the same is the case with political affairs. The right of choosing their own rulers does not convert the whole population into lawgivers or judges, nor interfere in any degree with the weight of such public men as are remarkable for their talents and information. The division of labor in America is, in this respect, as strict as it is in any other country, The institutions may fit a greater number for political employments, but the employments themselves are distinct from any other pursuits as they can well be made. If the citizens did not enjoy the right of voting for their public officers; if a monopoly of all public trusts were created in behalf of a few, there would be no effectual check upon the conduct of public men. They would do pretty much as they pleased, and instead of being overawed by public opinion when their actions were reprehensible, they would themselves create public opinion, and compel all others to yield obedience to it.

The dark side of the picture, as I have termed it above, supposes that the operatives and laborers may become so numerous as to control the elections, and ultimately to undermine the most wholesome and the most solidly-established institutions. The error consists in supposing that what is possible is therefore probable, and that whatever is probable may be strictly reduced to practice; whereas, the probable is subject to as determinate laws as the certain. We do not always will to do what we desire, for the motives to human action are derived from without as well as from within; moreover, we find innumerable obstacles in the mere will of other individuals. And although, if we are the majority, there is a physical possibility of bending their actions to suit our purposes, yet, invariably, in practice, a limit is imposed upon our efforts. The moral possibility must be taken into the account, fully as much as the physical; and although the laws which govern the first are more undefined, more dimly seen, than those which govern the last, yet the difficulties which surround any novel and violent enterprise are not on that account lessened, but are, in the greater number of instances, very much increased. So far as the history of human nature is handed down to us, in the history of the various communities which have existed, we find that in no one instance have a majority of men ever accomplished those things which they may be supposed to have desired to do; and this is calculated to suggest the thought—whether moral hinderances do not, in fact, impose as insurmountable obstacles to action as physical ones, although, when we view each in the abstract, we say, of the former, that they are something which can invariably be overcome, and of the latter, that they can never be. What is the reason that whole peoples have lived for centuries under despotic governments, although those who desire a change constitute an immense majority? The change could be easily effected, if there were only the determined and the united will. Moral obstacles, then, it would seem, are absolutely insurmountable sometimes, even when the physical impediments are capable of being removed.

There must be some wise reason for this constitution of our nature. When we deal with the actions of other men, when we meddle with the institutions which preside over them, as well as over ourselves, we require a good deal of knowledge in order to see our way clearly, a good deal in order to carry us successfully through, and still more in order to inspire us with the requisite assurance and self reliance. The want of these presents as real obstacles to human conduct as any physical impediments, and we may, therefore, calculate with as absolute certainty upon part of the actions of whole communities as we do upon the happening of physical events.

We will suppose that a large majority of the members elected to the American legislatures was composed of day laborers and operatives, and that the favorite scheme with these two bodies was the passage of an agrarian law,—not one like the Roman, which confined itself to an equal distribution of the public domain, and exacted an adequate rent for it,—but one which contemplated an equal division of all the property, already in the possession of individuals, and the result of their independent exertions. These bodies would no sooner have met than the spectacle would be one so repugnant to the common sense of mankind (including, in the term mankind, all those who belong to the class elected,) as to frustrate, in the very beginning, all schemes which had been set on foot. For what can be conceived more unnatural than that a considerable part of the population of any civilized community should cut themselves off from all communication with the educated and enlightened, that they should refuse to listen, in any respect, to the counsel and assistance of those whose superior opportunities pointed them out as indispensible guides in every public emergency, and that they should so act for the express purpose of committing an act of gross injustice to all proprietors of land and personal property in the country. I venture to say, that the exceeding awkwardness which those legislative bodies would feel, in finding themselves placed in so unheard of and so startling a position, would strike with impotency every resolution which may have been formed: I go further, and say that this single consideration proves that no such bodies ever will or can be elected in America.

The most plausible supposition that we can make, is not that the day laborers and operatives should elect representatives from their own body, but rather that they should choose from among the other classes persons who had some pretensions to education, and some acquaintance with the general run of public affairs; and who, having little stake in the public weal, should be every way inclined to fan the embers of public discontent, in order to gain a name in the world. In the first instance, we introduce into the legislative halls members who would feel themselves absolutely powerless at the outset, in the discussion or concoction of any measures whatever. In the second we introduce persons there, whose advantages of one kind or other place them in near communication with the enlightened and influential. But these men's actions will be governed by some fixed laws. They only differ from other men, in being very discontented: and discontent and envy, we know, often drive men to do many things which they feel to be wrong. This feeling, the consciousness that they stand in a false position to society, cannot be shaken off; it will introduce an element of discord into all their actions. In order to act with vigor and promptitude, they will be obliged to make efforts to conciliate public opinion. They either fall to the ground on every encounter with members who are superior in moral and intellectual accomplishments, or they seek to win both sides by pursuing a middle course.

The third and the most rational supposition we can make, is, that the class to which I have alluded, although never so numerous as to elect anything like a majority of the members, will always have sufficient influence to cause their interests to be represented, that they will even sometimes send members who will entertain the same ultra view as themselves. If they did not, it would be to be feared that ultra views on the other side would take possession of society. No harm, but on the contrary, very great benefit, will be the consequence. There are many problems in the social organization which remain to be settled, and which can only be settled by the mutual and earnest co-operation of all classes. But a revolutionary movement invariably jeopardizes every thing; it is sure to be followed by a reaction, and after an interval more or less considerable, men are compelled to begin anew, to set out with reflection and a due regard for the rights of all others. If any one should still insist, that these considerations are not sufficient to show that the evils of universal suffrage will not be averted, I have no objection, but rather prefer that this apprehension should constantly press upon the mind of every one. It is, as I have often repeated, a most wholesome provision of our nature, that our apprehension of the mischief which may ensue from our own conduct, should have a perpetual influence upon us. The feeling in great part supplies the place of reflection, where this is deficient. My desire is never to pursue the analysis to the utmost limit, for fear of impairing the strength of that feeling; or to speak more correctly, I am denied the ability to do so, because it would interfere with an essential part of the machinery of society.

Professional men constitute another division of the classes of society. The influence they exert is immense; nor is it easy to conceive of a well-balanced society, unless they were a constituent part of the population. The intellectual men of a country are the hinges upon which society turns; and the members of the three learned professions necessarily compose a very large part of the class of intellectual men.

It is a fortunate circumstance that some degree of knowledge and education is absolutely necessary to even the physical well being of society. If such were not the case, it is doubtful whether men would ever have made any advances in intellectual improvement worth naming. The three professions grow immediately out of wants which are common to all mankind; and as they render study, information, and mental discipline essential to those who practice them reputably and successfully, they serve both to diffuse and to perpetuate knowledge. But these professions are either directly or indirectly connected with all other departments of science; and this lays the foundation for a general system of education, and creates a fourth profession: the teacher whether in schools, academies, or universities. It is a fine provision, therefore, in the constitution of society, that our physicial wants and the passions which grow out of them, render necessary the employment of our higher faculties; and that the more those wants and passions increase in strength and become dangerous to the state, the more certain is the tendency and the encouragement to knowledge. Without knowledge, or at any rate, without the influence which knowledge imparts, men would be condemned to a condition very little above that of the brutes; and with power infinitely greater than that of the brutes, to injure and torment each other. As the individual who exercises all his faculties has the best balanced mind, so a society in which education is widely diffused, and knowledge is permitted to have its rightful authority, is sure to give rise to the best balanced community.

The influence which professional men are capable of exerting upon the rest of the population, will depend in a great degree upon the manner in which they are distributed through the state. There is the greatest difference imaginable in this respect, between the legal profession in the United States and Great Britain. In the former, lawyers are scattered over the whole country, while in England and Scotland, the greater part congregate in London and Edinburgh. I do not now speak of attorneys, but of barristers, the correlative of which in America is the term lawyers. Attorneys in Great Britain, practice a trade, rather than a profession, and a trade so mischievous in many respects, that it is not surprising the abolition of the order should have entered into the plan of the commissioners who were appointed under the act for the reformation of the law. The offices of attorney and barrister, are for the most part performed by the same persons in the United States. Where this is not the case—where the business is of such an amount, as to render necessary a division of labor, a partnership is formed, one member of which devotes himself to the duties of an attorney, and the other to those of barrister and counsellor. The existence of a partnership, however, is no evidence that the duties are separated; for the instances are much more common, where both the members practice equally, in the different walks of the profession. There is at any rate no such class known as the corps of attorneys. The lawyer is responsible for all the business which he transacts, or is connected with; there is no race of jobbers behind his back, whose conduct is withdrawn from his supervision, and almost veiled from the rest of the community.

The very equal distribution of lawyers among the population, is a remarkable feature of the social organization in the United States, and is attended with the most salutary consequences. Something similar to it may be observed in France, where the system of local courts is now established; but the difference between France and the United States, in this respect is as great as between France and Great Britain.

The intellectual influence which professional men exercise is two-fold. They apply much learning and sagacity to the subjects with which they are particularly conversant; and this insures the existence at all times of a certain amount of knowledge in the community. The lawyer assists in protecting our property and personal rights from invasion, the physician preserves our health, and the clergyman teaches and unfolds those truths, without which, all other truths would be impotent and valueless. In order to accomplish these tasks, the best-endowed minds in each profession are obliged to bring a very considerable body of scientific information to bear upon the practical interests of men. This gives to that information a tangible character, and introduces even unprofessional men to a very tolerable acquaintance with it. The clergyman and the lawyer appear before the public in the discharge of their professions. The practice of the physician is necessarily of a private character, being confined to his office, or to the sick chamber, which is doubtless one reason why there is less general acquaintance with the science of medicine, than with either law or divinity: although it is not more abstruse than the two last, and although the great majority of mankind have so great a desire to pry into its secrets. But the acquisition of any one branch of knowledge, is an easy introduction to a fund of general information on other subjects. The intelligent clergyman, lawyer and physician, will not be satisfied with a knowledge of their respective callings; they will each strive to go beyond, in order to render themselves both more useful and more respectable. Hence, professional men are apt, as a general rule, to be the best informed class in the community.

Now it is obvious that the location of lawyers in the United States, the fact that they are distributed through the whole population, instead of being congregated at one spot, gives them a great advantage in spreading not only the benefits of their profession, but in diffusing the information which they have acquired; and it is productive of equal advantage to all other men, by exposing them to an influence which, however imperfect, must necessarily count for something in raising the general standard of improvement.

It is easy to estimate the different degree of influence which is exerted by the members of the legal profession in the United States and Great Britain, when one considers that their location in the former is not a consequence merely of the confederate form of government, which would very naturally assemble a certain number within each of the states. But their dispersion within these as is wide as it can well be conceived to be. Lawyers are established at every county town or seat of justice, frequently in several towns in the same county ; and as the counties are reduced greatly below the size of English counties, they are much more extensively distributed than would be the case in Great Britain, if English barristers were addicted to the same custom. In the United States it is not at all uncommon to meet with lawyers in towns of three or four thousand inhabitants, who are as profoundly conversant with their profession, and whose intellectual endowments are to the full as high in every respect as can be found among the leading men of the same profession in cities of three or four hundred thousand. It needs no argument to show the multiplied advantages which spring from this arrangement of society. A very large proportion of the population are present from time to time at the debates which take place in the halls of justice ; nor are the persons who make a figure in these removed to a great distance during the rest of the year, so as to impress other men with a notion that there is something so mysterious and beyond their faculties to comprehend in the learned profession of the law, that they may not aspire to educate their sons to the same pursuit.

But lawyers exercise a political as well as an intellectual influence upon society. The acquaintance which they have with the laws of their country is necessarily greater than that of any other class ; and this points them out as among the fittest persons to be elected to the legislative body. But this affords an additional reason why they should be distributed as equally as possible among the rest of the population. By mixing much with all other classes, they acquire a knowledge of their habits, an insight into their interests, and a degree of tact in both, which could be gained in no other way. I am not at all insensible to the counter influence which is exerted upon their character. Much of this is undoubtedly mischievous; but, in the aggregate, the influence is of incalculable benefit to society.

Where lawyers are congregated together at the capital city, they soon acquire the "esprit du corps," which either unfits them for political pursuits; or, if they do take part in them, disposes them to be arbitrary in their conduct, and to deal with public opinion as if it were governed by the rigid rules of their profession. British lawyers when elected to parliament have almost always disappointed public estimation. Brougham is the only remarkable exception to the contrary of which I am aware. Even Erskine and Jeffrey appeared to be out of their element in the house of commons, though it is clear that they were equaled by a very few of those who were conspicuous for their talents or influence. The reverse is the case in the United States; eminent lawyers have always been among the most distinguished members of congress. Such men display no lack of ability from their first entrance into the legislature. This only can be accounted for from some difference in their previous training; and I know of no other difference but this: that the position which they occupy in society necessarily forces upon them a very general acquaintance with the political history and interests of their country; and that the discipline which their minds have received from the abstract science of the law acting upon the body of information thus acquired, renders their views both more comprehensive and more practical than those of most other men.

I have mentioned the majority and minority in enumerating the different classes of society. But these two grand divisions of the community not only comprehend all inferior divisions, but serve to regulate their conduct, and to bring the actions of all into some sort of general agreement.

CHAPTER V.

NOTICE OF THE FRENCH CONSTITUTION.

The French "charte" differs from the American constitution, fully as much in the source from which its authority is derived as in the character of the government which it undertakes to establish. It was not the act of a popular convention. An assembly of that kind has never been witnessed, except in America. And yet the popular will in France did manifest itself so far as to obtain some decided advantages on the side of liberty. Magna charta was wrested from the English kings by the barons alone. The chamber of deputies, which assisted in procuring the French "charte," was elected by eighty-seven thousand citizens. The provisions, therefore which are intended to guard the rights of the subject are altogether more comprehensive and systematic in the last. The character of a political constitution will then depend upon the degree of elevation which the popular mind has attained. In the thirteenth and fourteenth centuries, the English commonalty had acquired little or no weight; in France, at the present day, the "tiers état" compose a body whose opinions and interests every French statesman is compelled to consult; and, in America, the middle class has swallowed up all other distinctions in the state. The constitutions of each of these three countries, at these various epochs, partake exactly of the character of society in each. In England, civilization had made feeble advances among any class at the date of the great charter; in France, in 1830, it had made very considerable progress; in the United States, it is more widely diffused than in any other country.

A constitution of government which has been extorted from a

prince is an important event in the history of a nation. It indicates that very considerable changes are taking place, or have already taken place, and it smooths the way for more important alterations in future. If power has a tendency to increase, so also has liberty; and if the last can succeed in advancing to a certain point, it is almost sure of making further conquests. Thus a charter of privileges constitutes a vantage ground upon which to stand in defense of regular government. It may be the work of a week, or a day, but into that short interval an immense mass of experience and wisdom may be crowded. As such an instrument will possess an openly-recognized authority, it will be resolutely appealed to by the oppressed. It has been wrested from the monarch of right, and is, therefore, entitled to greater respect than the power which it has displaced.

Public opinion in England had acquired so much authority in 1688, that the revolution was a bloodless one. In France, in 1830, the popular will had been so much strengthened by the deliberate and repeated concessions made to liberty, that it cost little more effort than in England to effect a revolution. A constitution, therefore, however imperfect it may be as to the source from which it emanates, or the provisions it contains, is a great step in the progress of government. It shows that public opinion has acquired some appreciable weight, and that it is in a fair way of becoming an important element in the constitution of society. The way is prepared for the acquisition of liberty on a still wider scale,—the public mind begins to be trained after a new fashion,—the thoughts of men are occupied quite as much with the interesting subject of their own rights as with the prerogatives of the king and nobility. Thus, although the English nation made a very feeble beginning, yet as they begun early, they have run ahead of every other European state.

An unwritten, or partially written, constitution, like the English, may have this advantage. If the community is not prepared for the thorough introduction of free institutions, and is yet capable by single efforts, at different intervals, to make considerable approaches in that direction, the form of government may be made ultimately to reach a higher standard, and to acquire greater consistency, if for a time a wise and prudent forbearance is observed as to some things. To set forth "in extenso" the maxims of liberty, when popular opinion was weak, would be to endanger the whole undertaking. It is because liberty and power have so seldom been brought into direct conflict in Great Britain, that the former has silently acquired so much influence.

On the other hand, it cannot be doubted, that the establishment of a form of government which is greatly in advance of the manners, may be a powerful instrument in molding society, and lifting the people to a higher condition. A remarkable example of this is afforded in America, where the introduction of the most enlightened institutions and laws into the western states, at the earliest possible stage, keeps the minds of men in one track, and trains the whole population to the same habits and manners as prevail among the oldest members of the confederacy. It is the most striking instance I am aware of, of the immense control which the political institutions may be made to have upon the social organization.

France, like these new states, commenced the fabric of a constitution amid the light of the nineteenth century, and after a struggle the most trying and momentous which any nation has undergone. It was not a time for sudden and irregular leaps. That day had passed by, the period had arrived, when in order to bind together the confused elements of society, an entire system of government must be adopted. The sufferings endured by the whole population during the revolution, were a necessary preparative to this end. Adversity, when it is not pushed to the extent of benumbing the mind, has a wonderful effect in collecting and balancing it, and the griefs and distresses which men of all classes had endured, brought about that degree of reflection which was necessary to the establishment of regular government. As the states general had been abolished nearly two centuries before, there had been no opportunity for public opinion gradually to mold the institutions into a conformity with the altered structure of society, For a legislative body not only performs the office of making laws, it fulfills another office of equal importance : it opens a communication between the government and society at large, maintains an exact equilibrium between the manners and the institutions, and carries both to a higher pitch than could possibly be the case otherwise. The throne and nobility in France had domineered so long, and had acquired such formidable strength, that there was no way of proving that they might be controlled, but by first breaking them in pieces. On the opening of the states general in 1789, powers the most discordant were, for the first time, placed side by side of each other, without any fixed position in the state, and therefore without any distinct recognition of their authority, on the part of society. The "tiers état" had gathered strength and risen into influence, before any one was aware of its existence; so that the whole kingdom was startled from a dream, when the Abbe Sieyes with a single dash of the pen proclaimed that a new power had risen up in the state. This mixture of heterogeneous elements, this encounter of so many hostile interests and pretensions, necessarily led to a bitter conflict: for where all was undefined, what individual, or class, could have influence sufficient to impose just and precise limitations upon the rights of all. No party could do it, for parties neither understood themselves, nor each other. They were placed in collision, by a train of unforeseen and uncontrollable events, and some equally imperious law of necessity must deliver them from their situation. This collision was indispensable in order to inspire a knowledge of their relative rights, and wisdom sufficient to moderate their lofty pretensions. The struggle which took place, disclosed clearly the existence of a great middle class in France, and proved that this class must sooner or later, become a co-ordinate power in the state. The consulate and the empire succeeded an anarchy of many years, as the protectorate of Cromwell, and the arbitrary government of Charles II, succeeded to the English civil wars. The absolute rule which was imposed in both instances, only suspended for a while the spirit of liberty. The military triumphs of Bonaparte, and Cromwell, and even the careless gaiety of Charles's court, relieved the minds of men from the tormenting anxieties which had harrassed them, and gave rise to a species of good feeling, before there was any union of interests. This second stage of the revolution in France, contributed to balance the understandings of men; for it not only showed them the peril of both extremes into which they had run, but it closed a period of considerable duration, and one eminently fraught with matter of reflection for all classes. Certain it is, that the deplorable excesses into which France had fallen, and the opposite calamity of absolute government, prepared the way for the establishment of regulated liberty, whenever the opportunity should present itself.

In 1799, the Abbé Sieyes drew up the plan of a constitution; but it failed, because it was neither accommodated to the old nor to the new order of things. A grand elector as chief magistrate, without any administrative functions; a legislative body without the power of debate; a conservative jury, or censorial body, sovereign and irremovable, but endowed with authority to depose all other officers, were things entirely new in the history of society. The value of the experiment consisted in its proving the worthlessness of mere theory, and in disposing the minds of men to fall back upon some simpler and more practicable scheme of government.

Two apparently opposite conditions are required in a political constitution, that it should give stability to the institutions, and yet render those institutions susceptible of further improvement. No government can be permanently secured against assault from without, unless it is capable of being acted upon by the regular and gentle influence of public opinion. Nor is it difficult to conciliate the two ends I have pointed out, since government after all must rest upon opinion of some sort or other, and the wider its influence, the more enlightened it becomes, the nearer is the approach which it makes to what we denominate public opinion, and the greater the strength which is imparted to the institutions. The tendency to improvement, is as much a principle of our nature as is the attachment to law and order; and the existence of a wise frame of government, like any other enlightened body of ideas, suggests new hints and causes any imperfection to be easily detected and remedied. If most constitutions have failed in giving stability to the government, it is because they have contained so little provision for giving activity to the principle of improvement. That of Great Britain, notwithstanding its imperfectly-constituted house of commons, has permitted very great freedom of opinion, and has consequently contributed mightily to elevate the general standard of intelligence. The extension of the electoral franchise, therefore, in 1832, was effected without occasioning any shock to old ideas, and with infinite advantage to the just authority of government. The wisest plan is always to place the institutions somewhat in advance of society; yet this is a plan from which European statesmen generally recoil, as one fraught with trouble and insecurity to the community. The general population must not only attain a certain degree of intelligence; it must acquire a certain rank, a positive authority in the state, before it is deemed prudent to accord any priviliges to it. Yet there is no truth more important and more obvious at the present day, than that the political institutions are among the chief instruments at our command, for raising the general standard of the manners. To place government upon a liberal foundation, to give to the great majority of adults some stake in the hedge, is one way of impelling men to rise above their mere animal wants, and of connecting them in reality, and not merely in name, with the general weal. And if the cultivation of the popular mind is a thing of so much consequence, what can be better calculated to promote it, than a system of institutions which act as a perpetual discipline, and set every one a thinking, because their knowledge and their interests are then so closely connected? The free institutions of the United States, so far from being based upon a general system of education, preceded it by half a century in the middle and southern states. Those institutions, for a long time, atoned for the want of a system of popular instruction. The plan of education is not now as complete in some of those states, as it is in several of the European monarchies. The idea seems first to have been suggested to the American mind, that youth is not the only season for learning; that the whole of life is a school, and that the information which men acquire, the subjects of thought with which they become conversant after they have attained to manhood, are a more severe exercise to the mind, than all that has been previously learned.

There is no maxim, therefore, more unsound and mischievous, than that which teaches that the institutions of a country can never rise higher than the manners. If this maxim had been acted upon in Great Britain and France, the inhabitants of both would be in the same condition they were in, in the first century. Roman civilization and Roman institutions were planted in both countries, when the people were in a half-savage state, and gave the first start to Britons and Saxons, to Gauls and to Franks.

In every civilized country, a large proportion of the laws is in advance of the condition of the great bulk of the population. This is the case with the body of civil law, the code which regulates private rights; nor can it well be otherwise; for although this species of laws originates with those who take the lead in public affairs, it is difficult, as a general rule to adapt them to that class only. For instance, those rules which determine the title and transference of estates, have an indiscriminate application to men who have small, as well as to those who have large properties. But when we come to the system of political law, the case may be widely different. The reasons for holding to an equality of political rights may be equally strong, but they are not near so apparent as those which lead to an equality of private rights. Government, in most communities, is regarded as something totally distinct and apart from society; it is viewed as the guardian, not as the representative, of the citizens. Hence a rigorous control is exercised over political rights, at the very time that the most just civil regulations are in force.

The accident of birth gives to one man the exclusive right to govern. The same circumstance determines the constitution of one branch of the legislature; and the electoral franchise, and the qualifications for office are then easily disposed of, by a power which is deemed to be beyond the interference or comprehension of the people. Thus those institutions which are capable of exercising the most powerful and durable influence upon society, are frequently found to be the least enlightened. Very much the same code of civil law which was framed under the Roman emperors exists in the democratic republic of Louisiana. Such a code might well be administered under a form of government purely monarchical, for the prince cares little about the equality of men among themselves, provided he is lifted immeasurably above them all. But in Louisiana, as in Ohio and Kentucky, free institutions, as well as an enlightened code of jurisprudence, were introduced at an early day, and the effect is seen in the thorough diffusion of civilization and the high standard of popular intelligence. The political laws, then, act more thoroughly upon the social organization than does a mere body of civil regulations, and the reasons are stronger why they should always be considerably in advance of the population.

The French constitution of 1799 annihilated the regal authority and the privileges of the aristocracy, and yet failed to create a popular branch of the legislature. The electoral franchise was not employed to elect any of the public officers, but simply to create a body from which the government might select; and very soon after this grotesque form of a constitution was proclaimed, even that privilege was taken away.

If public opinion in some of the European states should continue to gain strength, as it has done during the last half century, it is not at all improbable that the office of king will finally give way, and be superseded by systems of government which will be both wiser and stronger, because they will enlist the support of a so much larger portion of the population. I can easily conceive that the day may come, and that it may not be very distant, when the superior classes will feel it to be their interest to co-operate with the rest of the citizens in the most fundamental plans of reform. Every concession, which those classes have hitherto made has been for the sake of securing peace and tranquillity to themselves; and this is a feeling which increases in strength in proportion to the diffusion of popular intelligence. The king gets tired of wearing the crown, when he must either consent to be a mere automaton, or to be stretched upon a bed of thorns. The nobility become wearied with a perpetual struggle for the maintenance of privileges which have no longer any root in the interests or affections of the people. The expression of an eminent English statesman, recently, "we must work up our institutions after a more democratic model," if uttered in the house of commons a century ago, would have been as startling as the invocation of the "tiers état" by the Abbé Sieyes. Nevertheless, the sentiment, like many others which are never uttered above a whisper by Englishmen, is full of meaning at the present day, and speaks, in a way not to be mistaken, to the personal interests as well as to the intelligence of the higher ranks.

France has now a house of commons, as well as Great Britain, and it is chiefly upon the influence which will be exercised by it, that we must rely for any great advance in popular intelligence and liberty. As soon as government makes any even tolerable provision for giving expression to the popular will, all the artificial institutions begin to be in danger. Two forces are then in existence, one of which is constantly tending to the acquisition of more authority, while the other is as constantly declining in both power and influence.

The European governments will undoubtedly experience immense difficulties in reconstructing society, and in consequence of not possessing one advantage which America has. They are mostly consolidated states. The state governments of the United States perform this admirable office; they serve, if I may use the expression, as breakwaters against the authority of the central government, morseling the whole power which is wielded by the community intc smaller fragments, and thus contributing essentially to the maintenance and solidity of free institutions. In one respect, the condition of France is better than most of the European communities, although incomparably inferior to that of the United States. She has a regular system of departmental administration, in which the people participate to a considerable extent, and by which they have been disciplined to some knowledge of self-government. The notion of a confederate government, which was perpetually revolving in the minds of French statesmen during the early part of the revolution, shows the value which was set upon this species of government, as auxiliary to the introduction of free institutions; but how to make the leap, any more than how to make the leap from two hundred thousand to six millions of electors, is the great, the tormenting problem. The people may, in a general sense, be ever so well prepared for representative government, that is, they may be educated and informed, but if the entire authority of the state is wielded by a single government, no matter whether it be republican in form, the institutions will stand upon an insecure foundation.

The territorial division of France created at one period immense obstacles to the formation of regular government. The feudal principalities which existed during the middle ages, were the source of constant disorders, and their extinction and reunion with the crown, were of the utmost importance to the prosperity of the nation. On the other hand, the municipal jurisdictions of departments, arrondissements, and communes, which have superseded them, are of the greatest advantage. They effect a distribution of power, and yet do not disturb the action of the central government. This organization of the power of the state, has then a shade of resemblance to the division of America into states, counties, and townships. Each department has an executive officer, or governor, termed the " prefect," and he is assisted by a council, composed of from three to five members, who transact the details of business. In addition to this, there is a general council of the department, consisting of twenty-five members. But the powers of this mimic legislature are exceedingly limited, when compared with those of the state legislatures of America. It has this advantage over the other council: that it is an elected body, and has the privilege of choosing its president and secretary; whereas, the council of the prefect, as well as the prefect himself, are appointed by the king.

The arrondissements, which are about the size of an American county, are also presided by an administrative officer. Attached to each is a council, with powers resembling those of county commissioners in the American states. And as the general council of the department legislates concerning those interests which are common to the arrondissements comprised within it, the arrondissement, besides disposing of its own local business, superintends the general interests of the cantons and communes.

The government of communes is not confined, as in Great Britain, to city corporations, but is extended over the rural as well as the town population. This is a fine arrangement; each commune is a nucleus of civilization, a school in which, as in the American townships, the people are gradually initiated into the practice of self-government. And this salutary influence, thus extended equally over the whole surface of the state, may become an important means of elevating the country as well as the town population. France has the skeleton of free institutions, and it remains for time to determine whether it is possible to communicate an animating soul to this skeleton. The officers of the communes, the mayor, and council were never, properly speaking, a popular body until recently. During the reign of Louis XVI, government usurped the power of appointing them. Up to 1771 they were elected; but the election was not placed upon the same liberal footing as at present. The number of persons who now exexercise the electoral franchise is not as large as in the incorporated towns of the United States, but it greatly exceeds the number of national electors in France, and is larger than that of any electoral body out of America. For, by a "comte rendu," made by the minister of the interior in 1839, it appears that two millions eight hundred and eighty thousand one hundred and thirty-one persons voted at the communal elections; that is, more than fourteen times as many as the national electors.

Great Britain contains no local jurisdictions at all resembling those of the French departments, arrondissements, and communes. The islands of Jersey, Guernsey, and Man, with their separate parliaments, are too inconsiderable and too much detached from the body of the community to form exceptions to the remark.

A system of lesser governments, as I have had occasion repeatedly to remark, whether the government is a consolidated or confederate one, is indispensable to the thorough and orderly management of the local interests. That no inconvenience is felt for the want of them is no proof of their inutility. Mankind have a wonderful ductility in adapting themselves to circumstances. If a Frenchman had been asked, in the reign of Louis XIV, whether any inconvenience was experienced for want of a national legislature, or of a regular system of courts, he doubtless would have answered, no ; that everything was in the hands of the grand monarch, who was competent to take charge of the most weighty and the most minute interests of society. The French departments are about the size of Rhode Island and Delaware ; they are eighty-six in number, a territorial division which seems to have existed at a very early period. For, in the ninth century, France had eighty-six districts. Similar institutions have existed at one time or another in every state ; but they have not answered the same end in all countries. In some they have been made completely subservient to the centralization of power, while in others they enjoy a sort of independent authority and contribute to distribute power. If the departments were fewer and their privileges more extensive, while at the same time the arrondissements and communes were retained as a part of the system, a plan of local administration would be introduced, which could not fail to be advantageous. The very general taste which prevails in England for a country life, the residence of so large a number of intelligent and influential proprietors upon their estates during a considerable part of the year, compensates in a small degree for the absence of local governments. But the effect is incomplete so long as the institutions contain no provision for training the popular mind to habits of self-government.

The French revolution, which threatened to destroy everything, terminated in reforming everything. No man assuredly would have made such a revolution with the uncertain chance of procuring a better state of things. But the laws which rule over human affairs are frequently placed beyond the reach or even comprehension of individuals, and when lawgivers and statesmen cease to govern wisely and beneficently, a superior power interposes, and overrules all the plans and enterprises of the enlightened as well as the ignorant.

Among the great benefits which the revolution has conferred upon France, we may enumerate the following : It has caused the abolition of feudal services and feudal tribunals, as well as the antiquated system of corporate bodies. It has elevated the condition of the communes, and other municipal bodies. It has given birth to a representative assembly, reorganized the judicial system, abolished the privileges of the clergy and nobility ; diminished the personal authority of the king, separated the regal from the executive authority, diffused education, established the freedom of the press, suppressed entails and primogeniture, introduced trial by jury in criminal cases, and caused such trials to be conducted in public. It has armed the tribunal of public opinion with ten-fold authority, augmented the numbers and power of the middle class, given rise to a better organization of the departmental authorities, compelled the abolition of the conscription, and gradually inclined the minds of men to the quiet pursuits of peace. It has been the means of introducing a system of order and accountability, into the administration of the finances, rendered the debates of the peers and deputies public, abolished the hereditary quality of the peerage, provided a regular and legal mode of punishing all public officers, supplanted the uncouth and heterogeneous laws and customs which existed in the provinces, by an uniform and enlightened code of jurisprudence. It has, consequently, given rise to habits of reflection, and imparted to all classes a more independent tone of thinking and speaking; and for the first time, introduced a written constitution into an European community.

These constitute material and radical changes in the framework of society ; and yet, it seems as if nothing were done, so much remains to be accomplished. A nation in this respect, is like an individual. Every step in advance, which the latter makes, enlarges the circle of his horizon, and the progress which a people have made in reforming its condition, unfolds new wants, and makes all deficiencies more striking and palpable. But the more unsatisfied it is with the position it has already attained, the greater the hope for the future. When M. Guizot, one of the finest minds France has produced, made to the chamber of deputies the following declaration, certainly the most remarkable which has yet fallen from any European statesman, that "it was impossible not to recognize in American society, and by consequence in its influence, principles of justice, of humanity, of regard for the well being of man, which have been wanting in the greater part of the communities which have been great and powerful in the world," he pronounced a sentiment which has relation to America, but which was listened to with profound emotion in France, and over all Europe. That a statesman high in authority in a monarchical government, should give utterance to such an opinion, is a sure indication that the human mind is not standing still in the old world; it reveals to us, that thoughts are perpetually crossing the minds of the most elevated men in that quarter, which look to something not merely as better, but as practicable. The course of events, with its irresistible current, is bearing forward all opinions, and conquering minds which seemed least disposed to submit to its influence. In former times, it was no part of the business of an European statesman to concern himself with schemes for the improvement of society. Their interests seemed to lead in a totally different direction. The ignorance and helplessness of the great mass of the population rendered the influence of public men more conspicuous, and they felt no desire to part with an advantage which was so cheaply and so easily secured. Lord Brougham, when in the English house of commons, was the first European statesman who devoted himself systematically and earnestly to the improvement of the condition of the people. Mr. Burke prided himself chiefly for his exertions on East India affairs; but Lord Brougham, with a mind equally comprehensive, will go down to posterity with "the plan for the education of England" in his hand.

The superior social organization of the British community above that of France has been sometimes ascribed to an inherent difference of character. But what is meant by an original difference of character? It is easy to understand its meaning when the comparison is between two races, between the white and the Ethiopian, or the white and the mongolian. But when the race is the same, there must be some other way of accounting for the difference. The minds of men are formed to so great an extent by outward circumstances, that the greatest diversities of character may very well grow up among the same race. Some nations, like some individuals, are not masters of those circumstances at as early a period as others. But as soon as they are, many hidden qualities begin to develop themselves. Emigrants from among the peasantry and artizans of continental Europe are continually arriving in the United States. They have none of the quickness and ductility of mind which belong to the American character. But their descendants, after a few generations, cannot be distinguished from the original population. They are trained in a new school, and are subjected to the influence of a new set of moral causes. The descendents of the English and Dutch in New York, of the Swedes and Fins in Delaware, of the English and French in South Carolina, are all pretty much the same sort of people, about equally distinguished for sagacity, industry, and intelligence ;—a memorable fact, and which should teach all European statesmen that the only effectual way of elevating the condition of the people, is "to work up their institutions after a more democratic model."

The freedom of the press, the establishment of the representative assembly, the creation of even two hundred thousand electors, and the abolition of a hereditary nobility, are immense achievements for civil liberty in France. The foundation is at any rate laid, upon which to build all sorts of liberal institutions. A very considerable share of the political power is now deposited with the middle class; and it is easy to foresee, that this class, in spite of the subdivision of the soil, will increase and acquire still greater importance. It is the first time in the history of France that any regular scheme of government, any scheme which combines liberty and power in something like due proportion, has been established; thereby affording unequivocal evidence that great changes have been wrought in the structure of society since the revolution.

In all human probability the electoral franchise will be further extended ; for although two hundred thousand electors are a great boon to a country which but the other day was a military despotism, yet this number is grossly disproportioned to the substantial population. No one is entitled to vote unless he pays a tax of three hundred francs. If the qualification were lowered and the electors raised to a million, there is no reason to believe that "France would be blotted out of the map of Europe." On the contrary, there is every reason to believe that she would for the first time find her true position among the nations of the earth. Great Britain and Ireland, with a population of less by six millions, have as many as eight hundred thousand electors. France commenced with fifty thousand. The number was enlarged to one hundred thousand, then to one hundred and fifty thousand, and finally to the present amount. Experience has shown that the surest guarantee of public order is to be found in the co-operation and influence of the substantial population; and that the moment a government divorces itself from all care for the interests of the people, it legalizes within its own bosom a power which will allow it no rest.

The plan of indirect suffrage, or of choosing by a body intermediate between the primary electors and the candidate for office, has been repeatedly tried in France, but was finally abandoned in 1817. The principal objection to it is that it reduces the number of the last electors to so inconsiderable a number as to render them a close body, instead of a popular assemblage. Hence they were denominated "electoral colleges," an appellation which grates harshly upon an American ear. An electoral body chosen directly by the people may be fit enough to make a single appointment,—for public opinion will then be sure to influence the determination of the body; but an electoral college removed by one or more gradations from the people, invariably degenerates into a mere clique, or school of intrigue. The effect is to annul the control of the popular will, and to render the chamber of representatives as irresponsible as the electors.

But the most extraordinary part of the plan was, that the colleges were chosen for life, that the king nominated an officer to preside over them, and that their proceedings were conducted in secret. Vain effort to reconcile the worn-out idea of a by-gone age with the institutions which belong to an improving society. There is but one way, in the nineteenth century of curing the dissensions of a civilized state, and communicating order, regularity and strength to the government, and that is by giving to the people a direct and palpable interest in their institutions.

France with two hundred thousand electors, has made a much nearer approach to constitutional government than when the primary electors amounted to two or three millions, but the actual choice was made by a few close bodies, collected in different parts of the kingdom. All sorts of contrivances have been fallen upon for the purpose of endowing government with a certain amount of strength, and of conciliating, at the same time, the popular will. But statesmen every where will be compelled to have recourse to the very simple plan of founding government plainly and directly upon the interests of the people.

In the Roman commonwealth the plan of arranging men into classes, according to their various professions and trades, was at one time industriously pursued. The comitia of the centuries, the then legislative body, was organized in this manner. But to marshal the various orders of men into distinct classes, and yet to make sure that one or two of these classes should decide the vote, was the very way to prevent a reconciliation of the interests of all. This assembly was, accordingly, superseded by another legislative body, the comitia of the tribes, in which the members voted "per capita." This is the true way of preventing classes from being arrayed against each other, and of giving unity and vigor to the public will. Nothing is more common in America than to find individuals of the same class or occupation enrolled in different parties. Our opinions, when they are free to express themselves, do not depend upon the callings we pursue, but are modified by numberless other causes. But the moment we draw men up in classes, and make this arrangement a fixed political institution in the state, we diminish the chance of uniting the interests of all. The "esprit du corps" starts up, and disposes the members of different classes to look upon each other with a hostile eye. The Roman and the French commonwealths were never so prosperous as after all circumlocution in the mode of voting was abolished.

The constitution of France, in its general outlines, is modeled after the British. The chief points of difference are—that in France (by the law of 1831, now incorporated into the "charte," as provided for by its sixty-eighth section), peers can only be created for life, and no endowment of property can be bestowed upon them. There is also, in the ordinary acceptation of the word, no ecclesiastical establishment. Religion may be said to be established by law, but no one sect has a preference. The clergy of all denominations are equally provided for by the government. The life tenure of the peerage, however, throws that body into a greater dependence upon the king than is compatible with constitutional monarchy. The only remedy short of the abolition of the order, is to cause those members who sit in the house of lords to be elected by the general body of nobility, instead of being placed there by the king. There is much more reason for adopting this plan in France than in Scotland and Ireland. The French nobility are exceedingly numerous, amounting to several thousands, while the nobility of Scotland and

Ireland are a very small body each. Moreover, the institution would more quietly and gradually give way to a different and better organization of the upper house. The tenure for life is one step toward this end. But without the intermediate preparation I have indicated, the transition from a privileged body to a senatorial assembly would be more abrupt and violent than would be desirable.

It has been supposed, that the minute division of the soil in France, was unfavorable to the formation of a middle class. That such a class does exist however, is certain, from the fact that there are two hundred thousand persons, the least wealthy of whom can afford to pay a tax of three hundred francs. These two hundred thousand persons, with their families, will give nearly a million of individuals. There are not many countries in Europe, where so large a proportion of the population is placed in more independent circumstances. Something more, besides primogeniture and entails, is requisite to prevent the creation of small properties. In Italy, where the eldest son succeeds to the estate, the division of the soil is carried further than in France, yet it is surprising how large a number of proprietors in the former, can afford to lease their land even upon the metayer system of cultivation, and at the same time live comfortably upon their proportion of the produce. The number of idle persons is larger in Italy than in France. The younger sons are disinherited, feel little or no incentive to exertion, and live as they can, upon the pittance doled out to them by the eldest brother. Land in Italy, and a great part of France, can bear to be divided into smaller estates, than in northern and central Europe, because the productions of the soil are monopoly ones, and therefore give monopoly prices. Certain it is, however, that the abolition of primogeniture and entails in France, by placing men more on an equality, has driven them to greater self-exertion. Large properties give rise to a larger surplus, but for the same reason, they create a host of laborers, both in the town and country. If there is no class in France so rich as the country gentlemen of England, there is none so poor as the manufacturing population of the latter country. The views with regard to both countries, have been doubtless exaggerated. The subdivision of the soil in France is not so general as is represented, nor are large properties in England so universal as is sometimes supposed. A large proportion of the land which belonged to the French "noblesse," before the revolution, has got back into their hands, and very extensive farms are common, throughout the northern part of the kingdom. The majority of the French population live in the country, the majority of the English inhabit the towns. The employments of the people, and the means of subsistence which they derive from these employments may, after all, be as much divided in the one country as in the other. The location only of the poorer class in each may be different. In France, this class will be found principally in the country; in England, it is congregated in the towns.

Up to the time of the revolution, it was the king and nobility who were set over against each other, for the purpose of maintaining the equilibrium of the government. Now, it is the "tiers état" and the king. The middle class have figured greatly in all the revolutions which have occurred since the reign of blood. It was that class which was chiefly instrumental in closing the period of anarchy. It was the same class which ruled during the memorable three days of 1830, and succeeded in establishing constitutional monarchy. The "charte" of Louis XVIII, was an act of mere grace; that of the present king was fairly extorted by public opinion. Indeed, when one considers that all the revolutions in Europe, in Germany, and Italy, as well as in France, have been accomplished chiefly by that class, it is evident that very important changes have taken place in the structure of society; that there is, in other words, a very general tendency toward depositing some part of the active power of society in an entirely new quarter. When this state of things has lasted long enough to exert a positive influence upon the manners, and to persuade all public men that in order to govern securely, as well as wisely, it is not enough to defer in some small degree to public opinion, but that it is necessary to enlist its active co-operation in the administration of the government, the difficulties which have hitherto obstructed the progress of enlightened institutions, will be in a fair way of being overcome. For admitting, that it should never be possible to carry out the plan of the American government in its full extent, so as to make the public will, in its genuine signification, the moving spring of government, yet unspeakable advantage will be procured to all orders of men, by communicating to the middle class a political weight, corresponding with the rank which it has attained in society. The unbalanced governments stand in need of some such support, of some mediatorial power, which, standing between the two extremes, the highest and the lowest classes, shall control the excesses of the last, and make it the interest of the first to be just to all parts of society.

CHAPTER VI.

IS THE AMERICAN GOVERNMENT A BALANCED ONE?

If by a balanced constitution we intend one in which the principal checks to power reside within the government, the American government is not a balanced one. The materials are happily wanting, with which to construct a political system of that character. There is no order of nobility, no hereditary prince, no ecclesiastical establishment. These are necessary elements in the composition of what is ordinarily understood by a balanced government. There is no commonalty as distinct from the rest of the population. The people are not divided into active and passive citizens: the electoral franchise is enjoyed by all, and the government is thoroughly elective in all its branches. The political institutions, though destined to perform different functions, have one character, and conspire to one common end. As they are not the accidental growth of circumstances, but have been formed with design, the power which created them continues afterward to uphold them, and to regulate their movements. So that the American government, although not a balanced one in the European acceptation of the term, is so in a still higher sense. None of the departments possess a self-existing authority, none exercise an independent will of their own: for they are all controlled by a great outward force which resides in the community.

Political checks are of two kinds; those which exist in the society, but are exterior to the government, and those which are inserted in the government, and which for the most part, compose that organized body which we denominate the political system. The first is of two kinds: it may consist either in that omnipresent control which the public reason, or public opinion exercises, or in the more delicate and complicated control which several governments, united together in a common league, exert upon each other, and upon the central authority. The second class of checks is also two fold; they are either such as exist by virtue of a self-derived and independent authority, possessed by some, or all, the departments of the government, or such as are created by the deliberate act of the community. The two classes may be characterized, the first as perfect, and the second as imperfect checks; the reason of which will readily appear. The first represents the moral force of an entire community, the second represents the isolated strength of the bodies themselves. If the last do more than this, it is because in the societies where they exist the first species of checks acts with more or less force. This is a distinction of the utmost importance: the not making it, is a source of the greatest error and confusion. For instance, if on surveying the structure of the English government, in which two of the departments exist, by a self-derived authority, we were to assert, that the happy balance of the constitution was attributable to that circumstance, we should commit a fatal mistake. The balance of the constitution, the adjustment of the various departments to each other, is in spite of, not in consequence of, the self-existing authority, which those departments possess. The public will, or public opinion, is more potent and more pervading, than in any other government, ancient or modern, except the United States. That this affords the explanation, is obvious, as I have observed in preceding chapters: for until public opinion had grown to be a great power in the state, England was no better, and often not as well governed as many of the continental states at the present day. And the adjustment of the political departments, in other words, the balance of the constitution has kept pace exactly with the growth of that public opinion.

I have considered the second class of checks as of two kinds; those which possess an authority independent of the community, and those which are created by the community. An hereditary monarch and hereditary nobility are examples of the first, and the various departments of political power in a representative government, of the second. I have characterized both as checks of an imperfect kind, but for different reasons. The first act from an impulse within; if they borrow any authority from abroad, it is accidental, and is no part of their original constitution. The second, being created by the community, do, on that very account, possess, and possess designedly, a still larger share of this borrowed authority. It is only because it is borrowed, that is, derived from the power which creates the first class of checks, that it is not of so high a character as these; it is the same in kind, but inferior in degree. The question, which is the best of these subordinate checks, may be viewed in two lights. Each may be best under certain conditions; that is, best relatively. But to the question, which is the best absolutely, that is, of two societies, each of which possesses the system of interior checks, appropriate to it; which will be best governed? the answer must be the last. In other words, the states of continental Europe, from Naples and Portugal to the Baltic, have not been as well governed as the United States. And although we should endeavor to escape from this way of viewing the question, by saying that those states have a very imperfect social organization, and that the social is the parent of the political organization; yet this would be reasoning in a circle, and contributes to fortify the position that I have taken. The checks which exist in those governments are comparatively feeble, because there are inherent causes which prevent them from being otherwise.

Where the check consists in the exercise of a power independent of the society, it may be viewed in two lights. It will represent the body in which it resides; or it may represent the body, and together with it, a portion of society, more or less considerable, which do not belong to it, but whose interests are similar. The last species of representation, however, will be merely virtual. France, with the exception of the interval between 1815 and 1848, Poland and Hungary, all the Italian and German kingdoms, etc., are examples of the first. Great Britain is the only fair example of the second. One, and a very important cause of this difference, is to be traced to the small body of nobility in the last, and its disproportionate size in the former. In Great Britain, the number is about four hundred and fifty; in France, Poland and Hungary, it was from two hundred thousand to half a million. In these three states, the nobility had not only exclusive titles, but they had exclusive privileges also. Their interests, therefore, were set in direct contradiction to the rest of society, In Great Britain, the privileges of the body are few and inconsiderable. The nobility there represent, not only their own order, but they represent virtually the whole body of gentry and landed proprietors. They do not represent the entire landed interest; not the numerous class of farmers, for instance, because the interests of the two are not the same. At the present day, the English nobility may be said also to represent virtually, and to some extent, the manufacturing and mercantile classes. Trade and industry, which for the first time became popular after the establishment of the commonwealth, has now become fashionable; and the fortunes of numbers of the nobility are now embarked, directly or indirectly, in manufactures and commerce.

When two or more bodies with rival interests are placed in opposition to each other, the design is to prevent each from pursuing a separate interest of its own. It is intended that they shall mutually control one another. The course which they will actually pursue under these circumstances, says an eminent writer, (Brougham), will be a mean between the extreme wishes of each. It will be a diagonal, and not in the direction of one side of a paralellogram. The illustration is a happy one, and is a conclusive answer to the theory of Jeremy Bentham, that all checks are ineffectual. But why will this be the result of so disposing different bodies. It must either be from a calculation of the ability of each to resist an encroachment on its rights, or from a calculation of the superior ability ot that power which exists out of the government, but is ever ready to enter into it, when any derangement of the system occurs. The last affords the clue to the efficacy of those checks which are inserted in the government. For it is obvious that it is impossible to construct two or more political departments, whose power shall be so skillfully proportioned, that each shall be a counterpoise to the other, much less to two others combined. But if a powerful check exists outside of the government, although it is habitually of a preventive character, and only occasionally active, the knowledge that it may be roused at any moment will discourage all attempts of one department to invade the rights of the others. The passage of the "reform act," in 1832, and the repeal of the corn laws, about sixteen years later, are memorable examples of this. These are the two most important acts which have been passed by the British parliament within the last hundred years. They both run counter to the opinions and prejudices of the nobility, because they contributed to fortify the power of the middle class. But public opinion run with so mighty a current, the commonalty of England took so decided a stand, that a refusal to concur in their passage would have endangered the existence of the body. Indeed, the reasonings of all those who insist on the efficacy of the system of interior checks, imply the exercise of a check beyond and above these. But not one has noticed it as a distinct fact; all consider the last as merely subservient to the checks within the government, instead of as a distinct and independent counterpoise, differing both in kind and degree from every other species of checks. In a half civilized, or in a civilized, but unsettled state of society, the knowledge which individuals have, that each stands ready to protect himself, does not prevent insults and perpetual combats. But when society has so far advanced that a well-defined public opinion has grown up, such occurrences fall wonderfully into disuse, although the motives and occasions for them are greatly multiplied. It is precisely the same with rival bodies of men. As society advances, public offices become more lucrative and dazzling, the incentives to ambition are hightened, and the desire of encroachment is greater; but this very advancement gives birth to a public opinion, whose circumference is constantly enlarging, and which exerts a more and more searching influence in every part of society. There is no other way in which we can account for the irregular action of the same checks, at different periods in the history of the same government; how it is, that at one time they exert little or no influence, at another have even a pernicious tendency, and at a third, act with precision and efficacy. What we are accustomed to call a healthful operation of these checks, is nothing more or less than the omnipresent control of a power which is external to the political departments, and which, for that very reason, is better able to control their movements.

In order to illustrate the different structure of the American and European governments, we will suppose two associations of individuals, each composed of one thousand persons. In one, the members are for the most part in good circumstances, possess a competent share of intelligence, and elect their own officers. In the other, a large proportion of the members are in an exceedingly dependent condition enjoy none of the advantages of education, and are unable to form to themselves a true notion of the qualities which make up the character of a citizen. In this society, the principal officers perpetuate themselves in office, and have power to appoint such other subordinate ones as they please. The machinery by which the business of these little societies is transacted may be the same: that is, the various functions and duties which the officers of both perform may be nearly alike; yet it is obvious that there will be the greatest difference imaginable in the amount of personal influence and positive authority, which will be exercised in the two cases. In one, the officers will govern the members; in the other, the association will govern itself. This original difference in the constitution of the two societies will give a totally opposite direction to their future destiny. The various officers in each, may occupy the same relative position to each other; but they will stand in very different relations to the members. In one, the introduction of a thorough system of responsibility will prevent encroachments upon the rights of the members; in the other, the officers will continue to check and balance each other's authority; but they will be uncontrolled by any force of sufficient authority to prevent a combination against the interests of the society.

What is true within so limited a sphere, is still more true when we come to consider the large scale on which civil government is constructed. There are then such an infinity of objects to manage, the interests of society become so numerous and complicated, that the machinery by which public affairs are set in motion, may be easily concealed from those who are most deeply concerned in understanding all about them.

Free institutions afford to the mind the very assistance which is desirable: they facilitate the process of analysis which it is so necessary to employ, in order to have any tolerable insight into what are usually termed state matters. The exercise which the mere enjoyment of the electoral franchise gives to the mind, produces that effect. Few are so little inquisitive, or so much absorbed in the cares of life, as not to be led to form their own notions of the character of public men, of the general tenor of public measures, and thence by an easy step, to gain some acquaintance with the practical working of the government.

The great objection to the plan of checking one part of the government by another, is, that it is impossible to give to the various departments sufficient power to produce this effect, without endowing them with so much as to enable them to rule over society, instead of society ruling over them. And although one may figure to himself the greatest licentiousness as the consequence of the opposite plan, yet this licentiousness, I imagine, will generally be found to proceed from some defect in the character and manners of the superior classes, rather than from any natural proneness to insubordination on the part of the people. If we could suppose the numerous body of the French noblesse, in the reign of Louis XVI., to have consented to alter their character so far, as to view with unmingled satisfaction the prospect of establishing a constitutional government; if we could suppose them to have lent themselves sincerely and unreservedly to the plans of the enlightened leaders of the "tiers état," the revolution would have been unnecessary. Now I do not blame men for having modes of thinking, and habits of acting conformable to the system in which they and their ancestors had been nurtured. I only speak of the fact, the ease with which unheard-of calamities may have been warded off, and the blessings of civil liberty secured, if the influential and the high in rank had voluntarily consented to lay aside those hateful privileges which they now do so well without, and which few of them would recall, if they were able. The same may be said of England in the time of Charles I. And we may go further, and say, that if the nobility and gentry of that country, in spite of the habits in which they have been bred, could be supposed to take the same natural view of the office of civil government which is entertained in America; if we could only suppose them to lay aside the antiquated notion that the populace can only be ruled by strong government, and that there can be no strong government without a prince and nobility, the transition from hereditary to elective government might be made without occasioning any shock to society. And if this view be correct, the consequences to which it leads are of the utmost importance to all governments. It shows that the introduction of enlightened liberty is unembarrassed by those extreme difficulties with which it has hitherto been surrounded. The proposition is not an abstract one; that if a thing is willed to be done, it will surely be done; for of all things, nothing is more dangerous than to meddle with abstract propositions, when we have to deal with the actual affairs of men. But the proposition is, that if a thing is willed to be done, and if that thing is nothing more than a scheme of civil polity such as has existed quietly and securely for a great number of years in one community; and if the best faculties and the sincere desires of the influential are made to co-operate with the will to do, that the thing will not only come to pass, but that it will work so far beyond expectation, that all men will wonder why it should have been postponed to so late a period. And if this reasoning is correct, several very important conclusions would seem to flow from it; that there is no community whatever, provided only it be entitled to the appellation of civilized, which will not admit of the infusion of a much larger amount of liberty than was supposed practicable; that there is no necessity why the transition from monarchy or aristocracy to elective government should be violent and abrupt; and that invariably, it is fully as much in consequence of the want of intelligence among the superior classes, as of ignorance among the lower, that the most important reforms of government are ever postponed to a day when there seems to be no other alternative. I have in another place spoken of the great benefit which is procured to the cause of regular government, by delaying the steps by which it is finally achieved; the advantages which are thus gained are unobserved and occasion no alarm, while they add to the ability to obtain still greater. But this is only upon the supposition that to any plan of reform which was at once thorough, comprehensive, and effective, we should be unable to gain the influence and co-operation of the great body of intelligent men in the country. On the same principle, in other words, that if any one had risen up in the reign of Elizabeth, or so late as the time of George I, and proposed the formation of religious, benevolent, and educational institutions, like those now existing in Great Britain, the plan would have been derided as chimerical, and as fraught with little or no value. Yet it is most certain that the spread of these associations at the present day marks one of the most memorable eras in the history of the human race. They may more than any thing else contribute to falsify the notion so generally prevalent, that there is a point to which the civilization and prosperity of a nation may rise, after which it is necessarily doomed to decline. So that in speaking of things which are impracticable, we must distinguish between those which are rendered so in consequence of some imperious law of our nature which cannot be gotten rid of, and those which would be practicable if men would only consent to make an active use of the faculties with which they are actually endowed.

Thus, if the great body of intelligent men in Great Britain, on surveying the manifold abuses which exist in every part of the government (abuses which they never deny, except when challenged to admit them), an ecclesiastical establishment which wrings a princely support to itself from all other sects, a national debt which can never be redeemed, a prince whose vast and unnatural prerogatives conciliate public approbation either in consequence of their antiquity, or of the seductive patronage which enlists a great multitude of the influential in their support, a nobility, a handful of well-educated gentlemen, yet possessing an absolute veto upon the representatives of the people; a chamber of representatives a majority of whose members are elected by less than one half of the electors; the electors themselves with qualifications unnecessarily restricted; a judicial establishment so expensive and so inadequate to the wants of the community, as to shut out men of moderate property, or to beggar them if they enter the halls of justice: I say, if on contemplating these things, and a great multitude of others which indirectly grow out of the system (and to detail which would be to run over innumerable transactions of public and private life), the enlightened men of all England were with one accord to devote themselves to the establishment of free institutions, there would not be as much difficulty as in bringing about the revolution of 1689. The difficulty would be overcome by the simple act of making such a resolution. When we talk of the shock given to society in consequence of any material change of the government, we mean the shock occasioned to the superior classes only. The placing king, lords, and commons in the constitution for the purpose of balancing each other, was never attended with the desired effect until very modern times. But for another circumstance they may have continued to stand side by side of each other as in the reigns of the Henrys and Stuarts, each struggling for the mastery, and filling all England with disorder and misrule. It is the influence of the popular will which now maintains them within their proper spheres.

It may, indeed, be laid down as a maxim of universal application, that the system of interior checks can never be relied upon where there exists no power external to the government, to act upon all the departments, and to maintain each in its proper place. And this necessary condition can only be attained where free institutions are established; not merely because these presuppose the existence of a power without, which has authority to command, but because the parts of which government is then composed have so much simplicity, and such an intimate connection with the community without, that the influence of public opinion is both easy and certain in its operation, As government is then framed with design and deliberation, the share of authority allotted to the various departments will be adapted to the functions which they are intended to perform, and these will have a precise and immediate relation to the interests of the community. Government after it is built up will not be left to the scramble of ambitious men; for the power which created it will be in constant activity, and will continue to preside over each act of the public administration. Encroachments by the executive upon the legislature, or by the legislature upon the executive, will no longer be viewed as an affair in which public officers are concerned; they will be regarded as invasions of the rights of the whole body of society. In the artificial forms of government, the several departments of power represent distinct and contradictory interests in the state, and not the state itself. And the idea of balancing the authority of one by that of the others, is the necessary consequence of a society so organized. Not that in that form of government there are not as strong and even stronger reasons for checking them all by some other influence. But no such influence can grow to maturity where the original constitution of the departments is such as to endow them with a self-existing authority.

If the inquiry is made, in what way the controlling power out of the government is made to operate in America, the answer is, that, in framing the institutions, precautions are in the first instance taken to prevent any of the departments from obtaining an undue ascendency. The powers of all are materially abridged. Instead of a chief magistrate clothed with immense prerogatives, and an order of nobility possessing exclusive privileges, the executive is chosen for a short term, and is intrusted with a very moderate authority. Instead of a chamber composed of hereditary nobles, both branches of the legislature are elected,—although the principle on which the choice is made is not the same in both. All the public agents are thus made directly responsible to the people. Not only is the power which is conferred upon the government less, but the means of controlling it are greatly increased. Instead of one department being accountable to another, they are all rendered accountable to the community; and although this might seem to lead to licentiousness, and to give rise to the most unbalanced government imaginable, yet in practice it is found that the greater the number of persons who are interested in the exercise of political privileges, the greater is the number who prize the advantages of regulated liberty and of public order,—that so far from the laws being weak and inoperative, they command a ready and almost universal obedience.

Nor is it difficult to explain the reason why this should be so. If there were no self-interest, there could be no general interest. But if we would, we could not contrive a society better calculated to augment the number of persons who have some private interest at stake, than one in which free institutions are established,—none in which so great a number of persons are interested in the protection of property. But this protection can no more be obtained for private than for public rights, unless the authority of the law is supreme. This notion is forced upon the observation of every one; it is not left to be worked out as a problem in ethics, by those who have acquired a refined education. The right to property, as well as all other private rights, is from the earliest period of life indissolubly connected with the maintnance of the laws.

Government, then, becomes a personification of the law, and individuals no more think of rising up in rebellion against it, than they do of abjuring any of the other obvious advantages of life. Exceptions there will necessarily be, but it is with general and permanent results that we have to deal; and it would seem to be almost a self-evident proposition that the greater the number of individuals who have interests to be protected, and whose situation and habits enable them to appreciate the connection between those interests and the authority of the government, the greater will that authority be. Foreigners, on arriving in the United States, are frequently surprised to witness the even tenor with which the administration of the law is conducted in the most remote parts of the country. They learn that all the public officers are elected, and yet they see these officers exercising an authority as complete as they had ever witnessed in Europe. Whether they walk the streets of the largest cities, or penetrate into the interior, they find the same system in operation, —the same rigorous and impartial dispensation of justice; and after reflection they come to the natural conclusion, that if the people voluntarily created the government, and passed the laws, they must not only be interested in upholding them, but, more than all other people in the world, they must be disposed to lend an active assistance in their execution.

If then we desire to strengthen the arm of the civil magistrate, and to give to the government the greatest possible authority, what plan more likely to produce the effect than to give force and importance to the popular will ? For even if the class of the disorderly increase, as society grows older, the class of those who are interested in the maintenance of public order will assuredly increase still more. In the large cities of America, the police are invariably more strict, more alert, more resolute in the performance of their duties, than in the small towns or country districts. The officers are elected by the people ; but this only adds to the weight of their authority.

Thus the American government is, in the strictest sense, a balanced one ; but the principle on which this balance is adjusted is different from what it is elsewhere. The political departments are as numerous, and perform duties very similar to those which are performed in other countries, but possessing no inherent and independent authority, the idea of balancing the one against the other would be futile, unless a new motive power had been introduced—a power which, because it resides without and not within the government, both controls and strengthens the exercise of political power.

As public opinion is indispensable in order to give efficacy to this great principle, the extent of that public opinion, the number of people who contribute to form it, and who are in turn themselves affected by it, is a matter of great consequence. In some countries, so limited is the range of intelligence and information, that both opinion of right and opinion of interest help to fortify instead of controlling power. If, in a country of twenty or thirty millions of people, one or two hundred thousand make up all the active citizens of the state, this affords no proof that a much larger number are not entitled to be placed upon that footing ; but it indicates how very small is the force which is brought to bear upon the solid and compact machinery of the government. It also indicates, that the millions who are left out in the formation of public opinion, may be disposed at one time to combat on the side of power, and at another, to run into the opposite extreme of licentiousness.

There is no better way of arriving at a fair estimate of the force and extent of public opinion, in any country, than by ascertaining the number of public journals which are circulated in it. Even though the majority of these should not be conducted with great genius and ability, it would afford no objection to this view, but rather the reverse. It is a proof that what is termed public opinion does not comprehend the highly educated merely; but that it extends to a great number of people in the descending ranks of society, who, although they may not be gifted with learning, or eloquence, yet have a very ready apprehension of those things which most deeply affect their interests, and are capable of forming a very sensible estimate of the manner in which government is administered.

The number of newspapers and other journals published in Great Britain and Ireland, is five hundred and fifty-five. On the whole of continental Europe, it does not exceed twelve hundred; while in the United States, they amount to nearly two thousand. Doubtless they are cheaper in the last than in any other country. Their cheapness brings them within the reach of the great mass of the population: and they are cheap, because it is more profitable to supply a large number of effective demanders, at a low price, than a small number at a high one; and from this circumstance, a very important consequence follows; that a great proportion of those classes, who in other countries are mute and inanimate spectators of public events, are raised to the condition of active and intelligent citizens. The circle of public opinion is wider, the principle of responsibility more stringent and efficacious, and the influence which is brought to bear upon the government is increased tenfold. Government is intended to restrain society, and yet society is intended to restrain the government, and the first species of check is not lessened but is greatly increased by enlarging the basis of popular power.

The establishment of local governments in the United States constitutes another class of checks very different from what exists in any other country. In order that the popular will may exercise an influence both salutary and effective, it is not enough that power should be divided in the first instance between the people and the government; it is necessary that it should be distributed among different jurisdictions. A consolidated government, although republican in its structure, would be an object too large for ordinary apprehension, and would be removed to too great a distance to be watched and controlled by the people. The federal and state governments act as checks upon each other. They exercise distinct powers; and so do the king and parliament; but, in the first case, these powers are inclosed within different spheres, and do not act in conjunction. The force of the check, therefore, does not depend in any degree upon the interests or ambition of those who hold office, but is exerted whether they will or no. The two governments are not only confined to the management of different affairs, but are placed upon different theaters and it may be supposed that on that account this form of government does not very readily afford a notion of what is understood by a system of checks; nor does it indeed in the ordinary acceptation of the term. But it is for that very reason more deserving of attention. Those who wield the political authority of these different communities are not brought into immediate contact, so that the will of one may directly control that of the others. But it will be admitted, that if the original constitution of lords and commons were such that neither could well move out of the position assigned to it, the check would be much more complete than it could otherwise be. It would be so, because so much was made to depend upon the structure of the institutions themselves, and so little upon the personal views and ambition of individuals. A check does not lose that character because it is more comprehensive in its operation, but is the more entitled to the appellation on that account. The constitution of king, lords, and commons, approaches much more nearly the idea of a system of checks and balances since the revolution, and the various ordinances which followed it, than in the reign of Henry VIII, or Charles I. The same is true of France. The king, the legislature, and the judiciary, since the constitutional "charte" of 1830, are infinitely better restrained than in the reign of Louis XIII; for so feeble was the control upon the royal power, at this last period, that a single decree was enough to abolish the legislative body.

The establishment of the local jurisdictions of America, then, gives efficacy to the influence of public opinion. The men of Ohio would have a world of business to attend to, if they were called to watch the management of affairs in every other part of the country. But it is no very difficult matter for them to give an eye to everything which is transacted within their own borders; nor for the men of the twenty-nine other states to do the same. The confining the domestic interests of these communities within a comparatively narrow sphere, not only renders those interests more readily appreciable, but it gives a fairer opportunity to become acquainted with the working of the central government also, since its powers are rendered both fewer and more simple than would otherwise be the case. In other words, the force of public opinion which is brought to bear upon the central government, is increased in the same proportion as that which acts upon the state governments.

Not only is this the case, but the authority which these various governments exercise over the population is more full and extensive also. If the influence of public opinion is brought nearer to the government, and therefore falls upon it with more weight, for the same reason the authority of government is brought nearer to every part of the population, and therefore exerts a more constant and palpable influence upon it. Thus the American government is truly a balanced one; but the system is "sui generis." The checks are not only more numerous, more wide spread than in any other community; the power out of the government is not only as great as it can consistently be made, but it is so distributed as to create a countervailing power on the part of the government which renders the institutions both freer and stronger

CHAPTER VII.

THE INFLUENCE OF AMERICA UPON EUROPE.

A TRAIN of accidental causes no doubt assisted in the establishment of free institutions in America. But now that they have grown to maturity, their influence is in no way dependent upon circumstances. The thinly-peopled country of which the first emigrants took possession, its seclusion from the disturbing influence of foreign politics, presented the golden opportunity. But when this novel experiment had succeeded, its power of reacting upon other communities was, like any other system of conduct, dependent upon the ordinary principles of human nature. The minds of men became more interested in the inquiry, what these institutions gave promise of, than how they came to be put together. It is like the case of an individual in whom a happy train of incidents has awakened great powers ; once these are matured, his influence, whether for good or for evil, is independent of fortuitous circumstances.

The influence of one nation upon the manners and institutions of another, is no new fact in the history of society ; but the way in which this influence operates is different from what it formerly was. Conquest, the incorporation of one people into another, the exercise of authority in some form or other, were the chief instruments in establishing this influence. America is the first instance in which the institutions of one country have been permitted to spread their influence abroad, without the intervention of any force—without even the desire to employ any. It is consequently the first instance in which a deep and general impression has been made upon the manners and habits of thinking of other communities. In order that one people should exert a decided influence of this kind, there must be some point of approach, some easy way of opening a communication between the two. The wide commercial intercourse which subsists between the United States and Europe, affords in part this necessary condition. That species of communication is the most constant and the most general which can well take place. It engages a greater number of persons, and what is of more importance, it brings the American people into a close correspondence with that part of the European population, the middle class, upon whom the strongest and the most lasting impression is likely to be made. It is because the United States is almost exclusively composed of this class, that its commerce has attained such an unexampled growth. The country presents a greater number of effectual demanders for commodities than any other. But commerce cannot well advance the prosperity and social condition of one nation, without communicating some portion of these benefits to others. It will improve the condition and rouse the faculties of all who partake in that commerce. The influence abroad of the Grecian and Roman commonwealths was next to nothing, because their commerce was so exceedingly limited. Commerce multiplies the numbers of the middle class, and creates a community of feelings and opinions, between different people, how widely soever they may be separated from each other. My first proposition then is, that American commerce has assisted, directly or indirectly, in promoting the growth of the middle class in more than one country in Europe.

Here, a question very naturally presents itself: why should American institutions exert a more marked influence upon Europe, than European institutions exert upon America ? The answer has already been hinted at. Under any the most tolerably favorable circumstances, the tendency of most communities is one of progress rather than of retrogradation. Circumstances of one kind or other, foreign conquest, or long-continued civil commotions, may check this tendency for a time, but it is sure to re-appear, and to become the rule not the exception in the history of a nation's life. But if the middle class constitute the great bulk of the population in the United States ; and if this class, in consequence of its favorable position, is enabled to make rapid and substantial advances in everything which concerns individual and social well being, its influence, or the influence of the community it represents, will be proportionally great abroad. It will be so, not merely in consequence of the numbers who go to make up this influence, but because of the number upon whom it is fitted to act.

Now, the form of government established in the United States (one peculiarly adapted to a country in which the middle class predominate), is the most striking event of the age. It excites the inquisitiveness of all classes in other countries; of the common people, because such a scheme promises to lift them higher in the scale; and of the speculative, because having worked so well in practice, the doubts which have troubled them so much are in a great measure resolved. There are symptoms, not to be mistaken, that this new system is exercising the minds of the thoughtful and enlightened in every part of Europe, more than at any preceding period.

Free institutions contribute to produce uniformity in the manners and laws, and this again contributes to produce a more uniform civilization. But the unequal civilization of different parts of the same country is the most fruitful source of all the disorders to which society is liable. A system, therefore, which is calculated to repress licentiousness in one part, and too much power in another, is no longer regarded as a startling theory. Sober and discreet individuals everywhere put to themselves the question, whether the time is not coming when there will be no other alternative than such institutions, or a frightful conflict between liberty and power; and whether it would not be the part of true wisdom to ward off, by forestalling the evil day?

Morality, knowledge, the prevalence of good manners, denote what we term civilization; and as these are all set in motion by freedom of thought, the more widely freedom of thought is diffused, the more powerful will be the impulse given to civilization. A community which exhibits cultivation and refinement only in the higher ranks, can exert no sensible influence upon the mass of the population in another country; but when a people are lifted so high as to be within reach of the superior classes, and yet not so high as to be alienated from the inferior, a door of communication is opened with both. And this explains more precisely the reason why America is destined to exert a more marked influence upon European institutions than it is possible for Europe to exert upon American institutions.

What, then, it may be inquired, is to be the ultimate effect? Are the European states destined to be republicanized? That is not a necessary consequence. The existing governments may be greatly improved, without possessing the perfection or, we may say, without having the precise character which the American constitutions have. It may be admitted, that it will be difficult to arrest the progress of free inquiry, if, after liberty has gained any great advantage, the authority of government is found to be firmer, and yet the people are rendered happier. Wild license may be checked, perhaps totally suppressed; but it is not easy to set bounds to any general movement of the human mind. As soon as in any European state the middle class have become the influential one; and this is, perhaps, already the case in more than one or two, it indicates that the tribunal of public opinion is fairly erected there; and this is very nearly the same as to say that such a state is ripe for free institutions, although these may not in every instance be modeled after the same plan.

Difference of languages, among different nations, has hitherto created great impediments to the exercise of any general influence of one upon another. Governments have acted upon each other, but the people have found no channel of communication. Thus different languages have contributed to form and to perpetuate dissimilar manners and institutions; and these in their turn have caused the people of different countries to look upon each other as belonging to different races. A taste and a capacity for free institutions places all more nearly upon one common ground, creates a sort of universal language intelligible to all, and brushes away those distinctions which had drawn a line of separation between them.

The construction of a system of government like the American, one which is thoroughly representative in all its parts, may not be exactly entitled to the appellation of a discovery, but it approaches so nearly to the character of one, as to render the dispute little more than verbal. The new application of a great principle may be quite as important, and display as much fertility of invention, as the discovery of the principle itself; or rather, the discovery cannot be said to be complete and perfect, as long as any material application of it remains to be found out. Until then, it is the subject of conjecture, but not an item of knowledge, no more than it is one of experience.

We see a plain illustration of this, in all those sciences which have reference to the physical world. Great laws of the human understanding may be discovered, and the discovery necessarily terminate there. But a principle in mechanics, in chemistry, etc., may be almost null, until it is applied. Until then it may be thought over, but cannot be said to be fairly grasped. Newton transferred the principle of gravitation from the terrestrial to the celestial world; and the application is justly regarded in the light of a discovery. Very frequently the problem presented is not, does a certain agent exist? for that may be a matter of general notoriety; but whether an untried and therefore unknown application of it is practicable. The finding out this application is a real discovery, more or less important in proportion to the importance of the application. Almost all the discoveries in physical science present us with the application of some previous knowledge. To deny on that account that they were discoveries, would be to erase from the history of the mind the entire list of discoveries to which it lays claim. Fulton made discovery of the application of steam. It was this application which substituted a principle in the place of a mere fact.

Prior to the existence of the American government, the plan of representation had been applied, however imperfectly, to one political department, but never to all in the same government. The Americans transferred the principle to the entire system of government, as Newton transferred the principle of gravity to the whole material universe. And as in chemistry, the mixture of two substances will often produce a third, differing in all its qualities from either of the others, so a new combination of two political elements, may produce a result different from any before witnessed.

If we admit that the American government is a valuable scheme, then the two great problems which it has solved, are: first, the practicability of conferring the electoral franchise upon the great body of the people; and secondly, of making all the political departments elective. And if this scheme is not entitled to the name of a discovery, it comes so near to one, as I before remarked, that the dispute is little more than one of words. For, what questions are there in political philosophy, which press with so much weight upon the minds of all thinking men in Europe, as the very two to which I have referred? What other questions are there, which by them are still considered as debatable and unsettled? One has no right to quarrel with those who are disposed to view these questions in that light; but once admitted that they are settled, although it should be for America alone, and the system is assuredly raised to the rank of a discovery.

The introduction of written constitutions into some of the European states, is the first instance I shall notice where the influence of American institutions abroad is clearly visible. France, Belgium, Holland, as well as some of the German and Italian states, have resorted to this species of fundamental ordinance, by which to balance and regulate their governments. Prior to the formation of the American constitutions, there was not a single example to be found. A written constitution, however imperfect, will never be a change for the worse, and can hardly fail to be one for the better. But it is very doubtful, whether if some powerful influence from abroad had not occurred to furnish hints to the thoughtful, a single European state would at this day be in possession of such an instrument.

As a happy suggestion, concurring with favorable circumstances, or bending circumstances its own way, has frequently had power to change the fortunes and alter the destiny of an individual, the striking example of a wise and yet novel system of government, in one community, rouses great multitudes of people in others to new views, and may give an entirely new direction to their future career.

It is a fine observation of John Taylor, of Caroline,* that constitutions, or political laws, are intended to restrain governments, as civil laws are intended to restrain individuals. It is because the former are so efficacious in producing the effect intended that the public men of Europe made so much resistance to their introduction. They apprehended, that whatever power was subtracted from the government would constitute an addition to the ill-regulated power of the masses; and that full vent would be given to the worst passions and the most unbridled licentiousness. But this is a great mistake, for a constitution, as I have before remarked, acts as a double restraint; it is a restraint upon the people to fully as great an extent as it is upon the government. And what may appear still more surprising, it is more stringent, more efficacious in its operation, in both respects, when it is ordained by the people than when it is a grant from the ruling authority.

---

*"Tyranny Unmasked," p. 255.

Until the formation of a written constitution, the great majority of mankind make no distinction between the will of the government and the will of the community. The two are considered identical. What the former commands is deemed to be lawful, and what it forbids to be unlawful. Thus, although there is a well defined rule for the observance of the people, there is no law by which we can arraign the government. Hence the maxim, "the king can do no wrong;" a maxim which, although professing to be applied to one person, yet cannot well subsist without rendering all public men less amenable to public opinion than they would otherwise be.

Government, in many communities, bears a close resemblance to the ecclesiastical system of antiquity. A thorough separation was effected between religion and morality. That a dogma was incredible, that it shocked human belief, and ran counter to all the precepts of virtue, only served to recommend it. The highest notions were formed of the priesthood, when it could make things the most incongruous stand together. In the same way, dogmas in government, which contradict the common sense of mankind, acquire a hold upon the mind because there is no rival authority to dispute their rectitude.

America has also exerted an influence upon the structure of the legislative authority in Europe. When the American constitutions were established, Great Britain was the only state in which there was even the semblance of a representative chamber. The plan upon which the legislative body in Europe was originally formed was that of representation of estates, not of persons. This at one period was the case in England; and in Scotland it continued to be so until the union. The same system is still preserved in the Swedish monarchy. This plan invariably denotes a rude and uncultivated society. For independently of the very imperfect manner in which these estates are represented, such a scheme of government exhibits the community as divided into distinct tribes or clans rather than as composing one aggregate community. Hence a legislative body which represents citizens, not classes or orders, is one of the finest expedients for correcting the numberless discrepancies in the manners, customs, and modes of thinking of different sections of society. The creation of the French house of deputies has assisted greatly in bringing about this result in that country, as much as the formation of its celebrated civil code. Both conspire to the same end. The one establishes a uniform rule for the government of men in their civil relations, the other renders them one people as regards their political interests.

The plan of popular representation is still very imperfect in all the European states. But that a great impulse has been communicated to the public mind in that quarter; and that this dates from the establishment of free institutions in America, and has kept pace with them, are undoubted facts, and the very ones I am intent upon showing.

As soon as the antiquated system of a representation of estates in one chamber of the legislative body begins to give way, a very important step is taken toward discarding it altogether. A chamber of nobles may exist for a considerable period afterward; but in several of the European kingdoms a hereditary peerage has been abolished; and this is a second and very decisive step toward a thorough reorganization of the legislative authority. A house of lords is a remnant of the old scheme of dividing men into classes. In order ever to get rid of it, it is important in the first instance to do away with the hereditary principle. This shakes the institution without producing any convulsion. It deprives the nobility of a large share of the prestige which before surrounded them, and by weakening the hold which they had obtained upon the imagination of the people renders it easier to reconstruct the whole institution. By going thus far, say European legislators, we follow the example of Solon, who gave the people not the best laws, but the best which they are at present capable of bearing.

Senate is a term the meaning of which had been almost lost from the political world, until it was revived in the United States. Several of the European states, copying after America, now designate the upper house of the legislative body by the name of senate. There is "power in words," and however short these bodies may fall of the American senate, the change of name is an index of a very material revolution in the state of public opinion. National assembly, the name given to the French legislature in 1789, in the place of that of "general estates," was no further important than as it indicated which way the strong current of public opinion was running, and served as a rallying sign to gather the friends of liberty together. But this was importance enough. It foreshadowed the rise of the present house of deputies.

How long the British community will deem it expedient to retain the house of lords we can form no conjecture. The spread of popular intelligence contributes to weaken its authority; and, yet, this very diminution of authority assists for a time in fortifying the institution. How long the opposite working of one and the same principle will last, we are unable to predict. Popular intelligence, carried to a certain point, acquires the double character of a conservative as well as of an innovating agent. It is where the disorders of society become so frightful as to baffle all efforts to reform, that it assumes the last character exclusively. The immense influence which public opinion has acquired, in the present century, puts both king and nobility very much upon their good behavior. So far from committing outrages upon the popular will, they become more and more disposed to fall in with, nay, even to succumb to it. The abolition of the institution of a hereditary chamber is thus indefinitely postponed, because the practical working of the system is such as to refer nearly all the legislative power to the house of commons.

But so many causes are in operation to elevate the popular mind, and to cause public opinion to be the representative of the middle class, and not, as formerly, of the nobility and gentry, that the same revolution which banished the Gothic system of a representation of estates in one chamber, is silently undermining it in the other. If the house of peers were to stretch its authority so far as the theory of the constitution supposes, it would be in immediate danger. The history of the events which attended the passage of the reform act goes very far to show this. Chartism has been silenced, but it is difficult to conceive how there can have been so decisive a manifestation of opinion as that association indicated, unless there had been some general movement in other parts of society. Chartism, no more than the house of lords, can be triumphant, because the triumph of an extreme opinion would involve the demolition of all others, when the use of opposing opinions is to limit and correct one another. But we may with propriety assert, that the opinions of that body of men were powerfully instrumental in rousing the legislature to enter upon the task of reform; and that these occurrences afford very strong evidence that the notion of free institutions has taken deep hold of the public mind.

Municipal reform is another department of legislation, in which America has exercised an influence upon Europe. Until a recent period, the government of the towns in Great Britain, especially in Scotland, was wielded by a close aristocracy. In the latter, the town councils were self-existing bodies, and supplied all vacancies in their own number. In England and Wales, the government of the towns was not so thoroughly defective; but there were faults enough to call for the most speedy and extensive reform. The commissioners who were appointed, in 1833, to inquire into the state of the municipal corporations of England and Wales, conclude their very able report, by declaring that these bodies "neither possessed nor deserved the confidence of his majesty's subjects, and that a thorough reform must be effected in them before they become what they ought to be, and might become useful and efficient instruments of local government." The act of 1835 carried out the views of this remarkable paper, and the system of municipal government throughout Great Britain for the first time resembles very nearly that which has constantly existed in the United States. Amid the agitation of the human mind in the nineteenth century—amid the bold and independent spirit of inquiry which has seized all classes, and is bent upon sifting every question of political right, the composition of the most inconsiderable local jurisdictions becomes a matter of the gravest importance.

In France, similar alterations have been made in the structure of the communes. Two years prior to the revocation of the edict of Nantes, their privileges were greatly curtailed. But a portion of the inhabitants still participated in the choice of some of the officers. At present, as I have already had occasion to notice, the communal electors in all France amount to nearly three millions. Men are first taught to manage their private affairs, because they are the first which are brought close to their view. The intimate relation which exists between the inhabitants of a commune, resembles the association of a family, and the transition is easy, from the management of their private business to that of the corporation. When they are fairly initiated in this they begin to look beyond, and discover that the prosperity of these local jurisdictions is linked in numberless ways with the prosperity of the whole state. The knowledge which they acquire by exercising their minds upon a new theater, so far from interfering with their private pursuits, renders them more skillful and more prudent in the conduct of their public affairs. The observation of this fact, as forming a striking feature in American institutions and manners, has caused those institutions to exert a wide and extensive influence upon European society.

The spirit of reform has penetrated even the Austrian government. An edict has been proclaimed this year (1846), which abolishes all guilds, corporations, or jurauda of trades and professions, leaving every one to follow whatever business he chooses. Butchers, bakers, and keepers of public houses are alone excepted. These guilds, corporations, and jurauda, are so entirely unknown in America, that the inhabitants of that country have great difficulty in even understanding the import of the terms.

There are some institutions which appear to be of secondary importance, but which on a close examination, and viewed as parts of an extensive system, are found to be of primary value. The plan adopted in the United States for collecting the votes at all popular elections, is an example. The minute division of the electoral districts, which are established for that express purpose, elude our attention in consequence of their extreme familiarity. Yet it is this very circumstance which renders the plan valuable. If we say that a mere regard to convenience was sufficient to have suggested the idea, the question still recurs: whose convenience is consulted? And as the answer is, that it is the convenience of the electors, that is, of the people, which is sought to be promoted, the whole plan is indicative of the elevated position which the popular body in America occupy. Behind a rule, which appears to be one of mere detail, we find concealed a principle of the highest magnitude.

In the United States, the votes for a member of congress are sometimes given at sixty or seventy places in the district. In those states where townships exist, the votes are collected in them; in those where there is no such territorial division, they are collected in parishes; and in those where there are neither townships nor parishes, artificial districts are created under the name of "precincts." This is a great convenience to the country population; and this regard for the convenience of individuals, is attended with immense public benefit. The presence at the polls, of the substantial class of citizens, is insured. The industrious, the orderly, the reflecting, are punctual in their attendance. Little time is consumed in going to and from the polls, and the private business of no one is interrupted. The assembling of a great multitude at one spot, would lead to infinite confusion, to riots, intoxication, and every species of disorder. It is a remarkable trait in the human character, that when people are abroad and collected in considerable numbers, they not only feel themselves licensed, but they even feel under a sort of obligation, to take liberties which they would not dream of at home. Until very recently, some English statesmen were accustomed to congratulate themselves on the advantages of this plan. Writers of the liberal party insisted that the periodical bursts of popular feeling which took place at the hustings, were indispensable to keep alive the spirit of liberty, and to countervail the influence of the king and aristocracy. Popular opinion, it was said, wore an air of more authority, in consequence of these tumultuous assemblages. There is great force in this view ; but it is doubtful whether the plan was not attended with some disadvantages, so great as even to counterbalance all the good which might be expected from it. It is doubtful whether great numbers of well-disposed persons, those who were sincerely desirous of tempering the authority of the government, by an admixture of more of the popular element, were not driven to take refuge in that very authority, from the greater evils which impended in another quarter. The effect was to fortify the influence of the crown and aristocracy, rather than to introduce those staid and orderly habits which fit men for self government. At any rate, I observe that the party which magnified so much the advantage of collecting the whole votes of a county at a single spot, have abandoned it and adopted the American plan. In conformity with a provision contained in the reform act of 1832, the counties are divided into a number of smaller districts or precincts, in which the votes are taken. There is another advantage attending this plan : the polls are not kept open for six or eight weeks as formerly. In analogy to the American laws on the same subject, they are kept open two days in the counties, and but one in the cities. The course of legislation in France has followed the same direction. The elections, instead of being holden at the chief town of the department, are held separately in the arrondissements. Thus the polls are opened at four hundred and fifty-nine, instead of at eighty-six places only. This number, however, is below that which exists in many of the American states, taken singly. In Ohio it is more than double.

For every arrangement of detail in matters of this kind is an indication of something important lying at the bottom. Ohio has three hundred thousand electors, and all France has only two hundred thousand.

In another respect the French legislature have likened the electoral system to that of the United States. There is no distinction, as in Great Britain, between members from counties and from cities. The representation is proportioned to the amount of the population, not its locality. If a city is large enough to send one or more deputies, the elections are held for it exclusively as in the United States; but not because it is a city. The consequence is, that a majority of the deputies cannot, as in Great Britain, be returned by a minority of the electors. The separate representation of boroughs and counties, is another relic of the antiquated system of representation by estates. The members do not compose different bodies as formerly; the veto is transferred from the estates to the electors who choose.

A national bank was established in the United States in the year 1790. It continued to exist, with the exception of a short interval, until 1835. The most striking and original feature in the plan consisted in the organization of branches in all the chief cities. But it is remarkable that at the very time congress were engaged in deliberating upon the law which terminated the existence of the institution, the British parliament were busily employed in modeling the bank of England upon the same plan. The act of 1833, which renewed the charter, authorized the establishment of branches in various parts of the kingdom. And it cannot be doubted, that if it be wise to create an institution of this kind, the advantages of which it is capable should be diffused over the whole country. It is but the application of the great principle of distributing power and privileges. The operation of this principle is witnessed in all the political institutions of the United States. It is equally displayed in all those institutions which are of a mixed character, or which are semipolitical and semicivil. There are two ways of distributing power; one is, by rendering all the associations who exercise it independent of one another; the other, by creating a single institution, and causing its benefits to be spread over as large a population as possible. The first plan guards as well as, humanly speaking, can be done against the condensation of power. But the second may have a totally different effect from the one intended. And where this is the case it is plainly antirepublican. It is true, the more an institution scatters its agents, the more it is exposed to the scrutiny of the public eye. This acts as a check upon it. But the check may be insufficient notwithstanding; the tendency to centralization where all the officers are parts of one and the same corporation, may still be too strong. A national bank was an experiment in America, and the plan of creating branches was a fine idea. It is no wonder, therefore, that it was first seized by France, and afterward by Great Britain. One design of the institution in America, was to act as a check upon the over issues of the local banks. But, in order to compass this end, it would be necessary at the present day that it should wield an enormous capital. And this leads to the inquiry, whether it is ever wise to endow an institution, half civil and half political, with so great an influence; or, as a corporation of this character must necessarily be conducted by beings of similar capacities and passions with those who preside over the local institutions, whether it would be prudent to risk all at one stake, instead of diminishing the chances of a great loss by the multiplication of banks.

The bank of the United States was on the eve of bankruptcy in 1819. In 1835 it became totally bankrupt. The refusal of congress to recharter it may have this good effect. It may compel the state governments to adopt some effectual plan for preventing the disorders of their own currency. So long as a national bank was looked to as the great regulator of state issues, it did not occur to any one that it was possible to place the local institutions upon any other than the precarious foundation on which they had previously stood. But it is plain, that if it is possible to secure the fidelity of the first, it must be equally so to secure that of the last. Thus the disuse of a national bank, may now have the same effect which its establishment was originally intended to have. One design was to make it act as a check upon the issues of other banks; but these have multiplied to such an extent as to render the check totally insufficient; while at the same time, the multiplication of local banks is an indication that these have become institutions of the people and not of a separate moneyed interest, and we have the same security that they will be governed by the same wholesome laws which pervade every other part of society. I do not know that any device will be completely effectual to guard against their misconduct and to prevent the fatal revulsions to which the community is exposed. And yet they are so thoroughly incorporated into the habits of the American people, that it would be a herculean task to abolish them. We cannot do with them, yet we cannot do without them. The bank of England stopped payment from 1797 to 1817. Notwithstanding the control which it exercised over the provincial banks was more complete than that possessed by the bank of the United States over the state banks ; yet in 1825, more than seventy banks out of London, were crushed by the temporary pressure of that year. And 1814, 1815, and 1816, (says a distinguished writer*), "a greater destruction of bank paper took place than had ever previously been known, except perhaps at the breaking up of the Mississippi scheme in France." The notion that banks have contributed materially to further the prosperity of the country, has had great influence in reconciling the American people to them. Every one feels as if they were some how or other connected with that prosperity. And this is undoubtedly the case. But it may be that they stand in the relation of effect, and not of cause. The Americans do not believe that they have explored and mastered every department of political knowledge, but they do believe that the circumstances in which they are placed have permitted them to make more constant and earnest endeavors to do so, than it has fallen to the lot of any other people to be able to make.

The amelioration of the criminal code is one of the most decisive marks that I know of, of the general progress of society. It is an indication of a high state of civilization, in contradistinction to a merely high state of refinement. In no country have so great efforts been made in this department of legislation, as in the United States. And these have had a very perceptible influence upon the European states. It has been said with great force, that the humane treatment of animals can in no sense be regarded as a duty toward them, for duty imports a relation to intelligent and conscientious beings; but it is most clearly a duty toward ourselves and other men. Every species of brutality, toward whomsoever it may be exercised, adds strength to the lower part of our nature, which stands in needs of checks instead of provocatives to its exercise. And when such treatment is exhibited toward criminals, and is

*M'Culloch. "Statistical View of Great Britain," vol. 2, p. 29.

sanctioned by the laws, the fountain of morality is poisoned at its source: the whole community is involved in a species of guilt. The desire of witnessing exhibitions of cruelty and suffering, we should characterize as unnatural, as a deformity in the human character, if it were not so general. But no matter what it proceeds from, whether from an instinctive curiosity to know every thing which affects our common nature, or as is most probably the case, from a desire to hide and to suffocate our own infirmities and vices, it invariably terminates in corrupting the whole of society. On this account, the amelioration of the criminal code of a country has a much more extensive bearing than at first appears. Even if it were attended with no absolute diminution of crime, and had but little influence upon the band of criminals, it contributes mightily to purify the moral atmosphere of society, and to make other men more humane and more virtuous than they would otherwise be.

The system of penitentiary discipline in the American states has almost entirely superseded capital punishments, the pillory, branding, etc., and it has commanded an unusual share of attention from the public men of Europe. Commissioners from England, France, and Prussia, visited the country, in order to become thoroughly acquainted with it, and to make reports to their own governments. The eastern penitentiary at Philadelphia, the most remarkable institution of the kind then existing, attracted their notice in a particular degree. I believe all of these commissioners concurred in the opinion that the plan adopted there answers all the ends of punishment better than any other which has been fallen upon. In England, it was immediately carried into effect. The secretary for the home department, to whom this interest is confided, issued a circular, in 1837, directing all the prisons of the kingdom to be placed upon that footing. I have no exact information as to the course which has been pursued in France and Prussia. It is exceedingly important that the efficacy of the plan of entire seclusion, which is adopted in the Pennsylvania penitentiaries, should be thoroughly tested; it has not been introdued in the other states, and the public mind is in great hesitation as to its propriety. The experience of the English public will, therefore, contribute greatly to settle this difficult and interesting question.

When Dr. Rush, and other eminent men in Pennsylvania ventured the opinion, that cruel punishments increased instead of lessening the number of crimes, people were exceedingly slow in comprehending how this could be the case. And yet no experiment which has been made upon human nature has been more decisive than the substitution of mild in the place of severe punishments. The ferocity which used to be practiced toward criminals roused their ferocity the more; they were converted into a band of soldiers, who believed that they were of right called upon to make war upon the unnatural institutions of society.

In England criminals were executed by thousands where they now are by dozens. Romilly and Mackintosh, as illustrious for their virtues as for their intelligence, commenced the work of reform. No great alterations were made for some time; but a powerful impulse was given to the public mind, and that was enough to insure ultimate success. Sir Robert Peel threw the whole weight of his influence into the scale; he procured the abolition of capital punishment in a great number of instances. For more than a century prior to 1827, every species of forgery had been punished with death. The various statutes on this subject have been one by one repealed. In the first year of the present queen, the last hand was put to the work, by abolishing the punishment in the only two remaining cases. In the three years ending with 1836, no execution for any offense took place in London. But not only has the number of executions diminished greatly, but what is of much more importance, the commitments for offenses which were once punished capitally have also decreased.

It was, I think, in the year 1836, also, that the American custom of permitting counsel to all accused persons was for the first time introduced into England. The reader is familiar with the anecdote told of Shaftsbury. This statesman had a powerful understanding, but as a speaker he was awkward and hesitating. While speaking on this question he became embarrassed and was thrown off his guard by some trifling circumstance; but recovering himself he appealed strongly to the good sense of the house, demanding what must be the condition of the prisoner, forsaken by every one and yet perhaps innocent, when he who stood up as a member of the most illustrious assembly in the world was so easily abashed and confused.

The bill, however, did not pass. The plan seemed to be unworthy of attention, at a time when it was the common sentiment that accused persons did not stand within the pale of humanity. It is only ten years ago, that Lord Lyndhurst succeeded in procuring the passage of a bill which permits counsel to prisoners in felonies as well as in treason. The French government had preceded the English in the work of reform. The emperor Napoleon was so much struck with the reasonableness and humanity of the American law, that he caused a similar provision to be inserted in the criminal code. It had been said in England, that the judge was the prisoner's counsel, a saying which comports little with our knowledge of the human heart. A judge would not be very apt to err in summing up the testimony; and yet I recollect a trial which took place a few years before the late act of parliament, when a prisoner, arraigned for a capital offense, corrected the judge who delivered the charge, upon a matter of fact, on which the whole issue depended.

It is very common in the United States to hear the remark, "all our jurisprudence has been borrowed from England." But I am persuaded, that if any one would be at the pains to examine the codes of the several states, he would find that the diversities between the English and American law, were both striking and numerous. The alterations which have been made at any one time, are perhaps inconsiderable; but when we sum up the whole, the aggregate is very imposing. I am not sure but what the differences are as great as between the common and the civil law. Roman law was the "substratum" of English law. It could not be otherwise; for the Saxons who settled in Britain were among the most barbarous of the European tribes; while on the other hand, the Romans were a highly civilized people, and their institutions of every kind had existed uninterruptedly for four centuries. But the Roman law was modified by the new customs and altered condition of society, which grew up gradually after England became an independent state. A similar revolution has taken place in American jurisprudence. Very great changes have been wrought directly by the operation of the political institutions and a still greater number indirectly, by the manners and by the habits of business consequent on those institutions. The abolition of primogeniture and entails is one example among many of the first; the abolition of fines and recoveries, the disuse of real actions and the simplification of the modes of conveyance, are instances of the second. The speech of Henry Brougham on the reformation of the law, although the most remarkable effort which has been made to remold English law and to give it a more democratic character, contained very few suggestions which had not long before been anticipated in America. The commissioners who were appointed under the resolution offered by that great statesman, made elaborate reports on each department of the law, and so striking are the similarities in some instances, even in detail, between the changes proposed by them, and the actual state of American law, that one might be inclined to suppose that the codes of some of the American states were before them at the time. Mr. Humphreys, an English lawyer, has written an able and instructive work on real property. But its great merit consists, not in an exposition of what the law is, but in pointing out various important changes which should be made, many of which have long since been introduced in America.

The "procedure" of the courts of justice, makes up a very important part of the jurisprudence of a country. I shall notice a few differences between the English and American law. A few are enough to set the intelligent reader athinking. English writers have remarked that the way to an English court was over a bridge of gold. In America, it has been supposed that this is true only of the court of chancery. But I find that in the king's bench, the expense of recovering so small a sum as twenty-five dollars, even where no defense is made and judgment goes by default, was not less than seventy dollars prior to the late reform acts. The constitution of the courts, however unexceptionable it may be in theory, may dwindle into insignificance, if the practical working of the system is attended with such enormous expense as to bar the entrance to them.

The time which is allotted to the hearing of causes is a matter of equal importance. In England, the average number of days set apart for this purpose, in the six circuits is two hundred and eighty-five. In the single state of Ohio, the average number in each of the fifteen circuits, is one hundred and fifty-two, independently of the terms of supreme court. The business transacted in those fifteen circuits corresponds exactly with that which is transacted by English judges on their circuits, with the addition, in the former instance, of complete chancery jurisdiction. The population of England is more than fifteen millions, that of Ohio is two millions. The pressure of business in the English courts is so much beyond the ability of the judges to transact, that great numbers of suitors are necessarily precluded from appealing to them. This defect has to some extent been lately rectified by referring the trial of cases of small amount to tribunals similar to those of American justices of the peace, and by obliging counsel in the higher courts to make a statement in writing of the facts in controversy, and the points relied upon. This frequently cuts short the whole matter, and the case is settled summarily and satisfactorily. This practice is of familiar occurrence in many of the courts of the American states.

The difference between English and American jurisprudence (a difference which is visible both in the civil codes and the codes of procedure of the two countries), arises from this circumstance: that in the latter, the laws are made by the representatives of the people, and are accommodated to the wants and exigencies of the people; in the former, the laws are viewed as parts of an artificial and complex system, and to interfere with them extensively might have the effect, although indirectly at first, of displacing, in some part or other, the authority of the government.

I believe there is but one of the American states in which land is not liable, precisely like personal property, to the satisfaction of all debts. And in that one it is capable of being reached, although the process is a little circuitous. A sweeping reformation of this kind is of more moment than a hundred other enactments which sometimes engage the attention of the curious and learned inquirer. We may pardon the human mind for its obliquities when it is condemned to grope its way in the dark; and when we learn that the reason why, originally, certain creditors could only extend one-half of the debtor's land, was, because the king might want the other half in his wars, we make allowance for the uncouth notions which everywhere prevailed in the middle ages. But the law has continued to exist long after England has been blessed with a succession of wise statesmen and enlightened lawyers. The cause of the difference between the two countries, then, must be sought in the fact, that in America the people are very generally landed proprietors; and that in England the case is otherwise. A law which exempts real property from the payment of debts is not so much a civil as it is a political regulation. It contributes to fortify the authority of a landed aristocracy.

When we learn that in two of the three English courts of common law, the practice of the profession is a strict monopoly, that in the common pleas none but sergeants are permitted to practice, and that in the exchequer the business is confined to four attorneys and sixteen clerks, as the practitioners in that court are denominated, this may not strike all minds alike. Some will view it as a mere arbitrary rule, and as a matter of indifference, one way or the other; others will regard it as an arrangement adapted in some way or other to institutions different from their own, and, therefore, not to be tried by the same standard. But others will take the plain and direct view of the matter, and considering courts of justice as established for the express purpose of adjusting the numerous controversies which arise in every civilized community, will conclude that an institution which confines the transaction of legal business to a few privileged persons, will be fatal to the ambition of others—will render those who do manage it less able and assiduous than they would otherwise be, and render the administration of justice both more dilatory and expensive. The mischiefs which grow out of this curious system, as well as those which result from the exemption of land for the payment of debts, have within a few years arrested the attention of English statesmen and lawyers, and it is not at all improbable that the laws, in both respects, will be so altered as to partake of the very simple character which belongs to them in the United States.

For this is an age different from all others in one particular:—The enlightened of all countries begin to sympathize with one another, in the efforts which each is making to ameliorate the condition of the community to which he belongs. People of different nations are learning to look upon each other as members of one great commonwealth, each of whom is interested in the advancement and prosperity of the others.

All laws which affect private right have an important bearing upon general society; so much so, that from the general character of the civil code we may very nearly determine what is the general state of the manners. But there are some laws which act more directly than others upon the social organization;—such are the laws abolishing primogeniture and entails. If the design of the legislator is to establish an aristocratic form of society, and to strengthen it on all sides by institutions, in private as well as in public life, there is no surer way than by legalizing primogeniture and entails. If, on the other hand, the design is to introduce free institutions, and to make the faculties of the greatest number of men available to the public weal, the first thing he will do, after modeling the political power, will be to establish the rule of equal partibility, and remove the obstacles to the free alienation of property. If the Scotch and English people still cling to primogeniture and entails (the relics of feudal institutions,) the Americans, at any rate, were in the right in believing that the abolition of those laws was indispensable to the working of their own institutions.

Mr. Malthus and Dr. Chalmers have undertaken to vindicate the propriety of these laws. The last has even gone so far as to maintain that government is bound to make provision for younger sons, in order to prevent their becoming idlers and vagabonds. There are some minds which do not permit themselves to look far enough into the future; there are others which, seeing far enough, are yet content to sacrifice the noble ambition of usefulness to mankind to the opinions which they find prevailing in the ruling class of society. There may be difficulty in getting rid of those laws now (perhaps on trial this would be found to much less than is imagined), but if they had been dispensed with two or three centuries ago, in all the European states, a division of property similar to what exists in America would have been the consequence, the general standard of comfort would have been raised, the preventive check to population would have acquired strength, and the people would have been both stronger and happier.

France and Belgium have introduced the rule of equal partibility, and I do not perceive that any ill consequences have ensued, but the reverse is the case. Mr. Malthus supposes that the subdivision of properties will create a race too feeble to make head against the throne and aristocracy. But it does not follow that because an intestate's (or even testator's) property is divided among his children, that any thing like an equality of property will be preserved. The effect of primogeniture and entails is to accummulate property in the hands of those who may or may not render it productive; and the effect of their abolition is to make sure that whenever such an accumulation does take place, from purchase and as the reward of industry and enterprise, it shall redound as much as possible to the general wealth.

There is every reason to believe, that the "tiers état" in France, so far from being weakened as a body, by these laws, have been raised in the scale. Certain it is, that popular opinion was never so strong as it is at present: the abolition of an hereditary peerage, and the formation of a written constitution, are incontestible proofs of this. Many enlightened individuals in Great Britain, still have misgivings. They do not feel enough assured of all the consequences of so great a change, although they believe that in many respects it would be advantageous. We sometimes lament in secret over the ills which pursue us in public and in private life. We perhaps cherish them the more closely on that very account, and even assume an air of indifference or cheerfulness, in order to be revenged upon them. But time and reflection at last drive us to meet them full armed, and then they vanish as the mists of the morning.

It has been my intention to glance at a few only of the differences between European and American institutions, as a clue to the influence which American legislation has exercised, or is likely to exercise upon the old world. A few instances are abundantly sufficient to suggest matter for thought, and to lead the reader to the recollection of a much greater number.

A remarkable instance has just occurred in Scotland: and this revolution consists simply in the introduction of what in America is termed the "voluntary principle" in religion. At the head of this movement stands Chalmers; who, notwithstanding the reasoning he had employed to vindicate the customs of primogeniture and entails, yet takes the lead in weakening, indirectly, the hold which they have obtained upon the public mind. For all the institutions of society which are any ways of a kindred character, are intimately connected; and whatever contributes to strengthen or to lessen the authority of one has a similar effect upon all. To introduce liberal and enlightened notions into some of these, therefore, and to resist vehemently their influence in others, is to run counter to the end we propose, and to neutralize the good we effect, by the ill we leave behind. Doubtless, one reason why American congregations are able to compensate their ministers so handsomely, is because the repeal of all laws which fetter the transmission of property has given an unwonted energy to individual enterprise, and increased the number of those who are in independent circumstances.

At the date of the American revolution, nearly all the states had an ecclesiastical establishment, similar to that of England and Scotland. The introduction of the voluntary system, was one of the fruits of that revolution. The scheme was a new one. In Europe, it was predicted, that religion would fall to decay. So powerless is the mind in forming its conclusions, when it is left without the help of experience. The support afforded to religion, in the United States, is larger than in any European State except Great Britain; the professors of religion are numerous, and public order and morality, to say the least, are as well preserved as in any other part of the world.

In France, the disproportion between catholics and protestants is much greater than in Great Britain; yet the plan of an established church has been dispensed with. All sects are placed upon an equal footing. But, as government makes provision for the clergy, the change can only be regarded as one step, though a very important one, toward the complete dissolution of the connection between church and state.

The catholic church was mainly instrumental in building up our modern civilization. If it became corrupt, it was in consequence of the absolute supremacy which it attained. To prevent the like corruption from visiting the protestant church, there is no way but to accord equality to all sects.

But the revolution in Scotland is in a particular degree fitted to engage the attention of the statesman as well as of the religious man. The opinion has been general in Europe, that the people were no more capable of taking care of their political than of their religious interests. If the experiment in Scotland succeeds (of which no one has any doubt), the notion will very naturally insinuate itself into the minds of all enlightened men, that self government is not impracticable in political any more than it is in religious affairs.

I have heard persons of great good sense insist that the voluntary principle was nugatory in its operation so far as regarded the choice of the clergymen; that there is no congregation in America, in which the nomination is not determined by a very few influential members.

But the knowledge which these members have, that it is in the power of the congregation to overrule them, will forever prevent any abuse of their influence. It cannot happen, as in Scotland, that ministers highly offensive to the congregations should be thrust upon them, and thrust upon them because they were thus offensive.

Popular education is another of those public interests upon which America is likely to exercise an important influence upon Europe. Perhaps no material changes will be made in the plan of instruction. But the true idea of popular education is, that the system should be administered by and through the people, as well as for the people. In other words, the management by the people is itself a chief element in the scheme of popular education.

America affords a practical illustration of the close connection between education and government. But it does so, because the former is throughout of a popular character. Whenever monarchical government draws to itself all authority, and establishes a complete system of centralization, the good which was intended for youth is in great part undone for men. If the system of popular education never can be complete until free institutions are introduced, this is an argument for and not against their introduction.

What we ordinarily term a plan of popular instruction is one adapted to the minds of youth ; but, if this is not followed up by a system which confers independence of thought in after life, the faculties and knowledge which were acquired at schools and academies will become inert and fruitless. The governments of Prussia, Denmark, and Holland, may continue their well-devised schemes of education for an indefinite period ; but if their youth, on entering upon the world, are unable to make application of their knowledge, they can never become as enlightened citizens as the men of New England and New York. It is not improbable, however, that the system of education prevailing in these countries will gradually change the political institutions. One of them is already converted into a constitutional government. And there are very clear symptoms that both the others are on the eve of becoming so.

America is above all others the country of private associations. These societies had existed elsewhere before, but they were never applied to such an infinite diversity of subjects as in the United States ; and they were almost invariably connected with some sort of influence in church or state. In America, they are altogether of a popular character, and are consequently both more numerous and more effective than in any other community. They supply the want which the mind feels for the employment of its faculties after the schools are left; and the discipline which they impart helps to prepare men for the theater cf political life. Associations, religious, benevolent, political, literary, and industrial, abound in every state. They may be regarded as bulwarks for all time to come against the corruption of the manners, the usurpations of the government, and the decay of popular liberty.

If I desired to contrive a plan by which individual freedom, and the general interests of the people, might be easily conciliated with the just authority of the government, I would set about the formation of private associations. Government is never so able to exert and to maintain the influence which of right belongs to it, as when the citizens voluntarily submit themselves to a discipline, the effect of which is to spread knowledge, industry, and benevolence throughout the land. The present has been termed the age of licentiousness. It less deserves the name than any preceding age. Nor would it ever have been so characterized, if the venality and vice which exist were not seen in contrast with so many and such striking monuments of benevolence and morality. These associations, which are fast springing up in every country, are alone sufficient to redeem the age from the imputation. Doubtless, they will never exterminate vice and ignorance, but they will assist mightily in setting bounds to them.

We need not inquire whether the notion of popular associations has been borrowed by other countries from America. At the present day the spread of an institution, the application of it to new and unthought purposes, is much more important than the question where it originated. The diversified forms which these associations have assumed in the United States, and the multiplied advantages which have accrued from them, have rendered them popular abroad, have indeed produced a profound impression upon the European mind. Mr. Pitt succeeded in suppressing a debating society in London, at a time when such societies existed in every town in America.

The example which America has set in endeavoring to make peace the permanent policy of the country, is destined to exert great influence upon the European communities. There is no more unequivocal proof of a sound and healthful condition of society, than a general repugnance to warlike pursuits. This state of feeling indicates many things :

First. The existence of habits of reflection among classes of people who were before supposed to be deficient in that quality.

Second. The prevalence of more exact notions of justice and morality, than have usually been popular.

Third. That the population are so addicted to the pursuits of industry as to render war incompatible with their plainest interests.

The war which has just burst out, may seem to contradict these views, but it affords complete illustration of their truth. For never in the history of any nation has there been so deep and so general a manifestation of public feeling in opposition to military pursuits.

The war was sprung upon the people when they least expected it. It was a false step in politics, soon to be retrieved, and never again to be repeated. Nor would the contest have continued one month, if peace could have been procured. But being commenced, and overtures of peace being refused, it did not strike people generally that there was any other way of prosecuting it than according to the old-fashioned plan, of inflicting heavy blows upon the enemy in order to bring him to terms. The Americans have been so long inured to the arts of peace, so unaccustomed to wearing a military armor, that they not unnaturally prosecuted the war on the same principles which have been followed by other civilized states. But what I wish particularly to notice is, that the conflict has only existed seven months, and already an entirely new system of operations is proposed. This is to abandon all notions of an offensive war, and even for defense ; to occupy the line assumed, as the boundary between the two states, and to concentrate the small military force which will be necessary, in that direction exclusively. This plan is even proposed by a military man, who has displayed the greatest genius for war, and whose ambition and interest would seem to consist in prolonging the contest. It is one of the most signal proofs I am aware of, how completely the character of the soldier in the United States is swallowed up in that of the citizen. The plan is a fair index of the genius and dispositions of the American people. It has made a deep impression upon men of all parties and all classes, and will afford instruction in any future difficulty in which the country may be engaged.

I know no spectacle more sublime, than was witnessed during the pendency of the Oregon controversy: the presentation of addresses from all parts of Great Britain, to the American people, in favor of peace. Mr. Pitt, and his immediate successors, exerted themselves to make war the habitual occupation of the people. At the very same period, the United States were earnestly engaged in maturing a scheme of administration which should render peace the settled and inflexible policy of the country. This system had never before been pursued by any civilized nation. And I cannot help thinking, that when the fruits of this policy were distinctly seen in the unparalleled prosperity of the United States, it exercised very great influence upon the European states. The Pitt policy has lost ground. It is not merely considered vicious, but what is sometimes of more consequence in what concerns the manners, it has fallen out of fashion. Peace societies in England, Scotland, and America, made the noblest exertions during the late difficulty, to maintain peace. It may be said that the masses, the substantial population in both countries, leagued themselves together with a sort of tacit understanding, that their respective governments should be withheld from going to war.

It is not difficult to understand the cause of the great influence which America exercises upon Europe; it is equally easy to understand the way in which it operates. When we learn that more than one hundred thousand Europeans annually arrive in the United States, we know that the unoccupied land is not all that constitutes the attraction; we know that the noise of American institutions has gone abroad, that their influence has spread over millions, who avail themselves of every opportunity to take shelter under the shade of those institutions. I do not perceive that these people ever show a disposition to cling to the habits and prejudices amid which they were reared; but on the contrary, that the feeling is one of congratulation at being delivered from their influence, that the most substantial and intelligent among them fall in with American notions, and lend a ready and cordial support to American institutions. I know, then, that the influence is on one side; that it is America which acts upon Europe, not Europe upon America.

The channels through which this influence finds its way are so numerous, that it would be difficult to count them up. There are probably two millions of persons in the United States, who have relatives, friends, or correspondents in Europe. If we had access to the epistolary communications which constantly pass between them, and could read the vivid and yet simple picture which is frequently drawn of American institutions, we would be able to form a more just and complete idea of the power which they exercise than in any other way. This would be sufficient to solve the mystery, and to let us understand, not only why such crowds are drawn to the American shores, but why so deep an impression is made upon the population which remains behind.

The commercial correspondence is necessarily immense; nor will letters upon business be written without very frequently affording an insight into the curious machinery by which so wide an arena has been opened to man's exertions, and such a mass of unfettered industry has been set in motion. This species of correspondence only serves to confirm the speculations and conclusions contained in letters written professedly to impart information; and Europeans very naturally put the question to one another,—sometimes in a whisper, sometimes out loud,—why, if so great prosperity and so much public order are the fruit of free institutions in America, the same institutions may not be made to work equally well in Europe, since Americans are only Europeans, or of European descent. No other example of self government is to be found, and the obvious inference is, that it is the institutions which have made them what they are. But as soon as the people of the old world begin to interrogate one another, although it should be only in a whisper, as to the causes which have given birth to this new form of society, it is clear that they have placed themselves under an influence from which they cannot afterward escape. That an important change has been produced in the mode of thinking of Europeans, on all those questions which pertain to the social organization, is, I think, certain. The precise amount of influence which will be exerted upon the political institutions it is impossible to calculate.

America is also made known to the European world by books of travels. Within the last twenty-five years, travelers to the United States have been incomparably more numerous than at any preceding period. The greater part have been persons of enlightened understandings, and the most enlightened are precisely those who have done most justice to American institutions. At the head of this class, at the head, indeed, of the European mind, stands De

Tocqueville, who, like Plato, visited a foreign land with the single view of seeking instruction, and who, to the fine genius of Plato, unites the severe analysis and calm observation of Aristotle. With powers of generalization absolutely unrivaled, in the department of political philosophy, he seized the clue to American institutions, and taught Europeans to view them in a totally different spirit from what they had been accustomed to. He taught them that those institutions were neither to be slighted as something gross and familiar to the common apprehension, nor to be viewed as a startling paradox in government. Writing for Europe, not for America, he felt the weight of the task which had fallen upon him. He readily conceived that although ancient institutions were not to be shaken to the ground in a day, yet that by a wise, skillful, and delicate survey of his subject, mingled occasionally with doubts as to the absolutely unexceptionable character of American institutions, truths of which no one could be directly persuaded might be gradually and profitably insinuated into the minds of all. This work has spoken with a weight and authority which belong to none other, treating of the institutions of a foreign country.

American works have contributed to the influence which is exercised upon Europe. Although these works for the most part, are not addressed to the philosophical mind, they are calculated to have a wide circulation among the general run of readers. Works, historical, statistical, and economical, afford a clear insight into the working of American society. They are easiest of apprehension to general readers, and yet open an unlimited field of inquiry to profounder understandings. There are certain pauses in the history of the human mind, when it leaves off philosophizing and speculating for a season in order to recollect itself, and to set in order the vast pile of materials which have accumulated in the interval. The age prior to Bacon's was one of those periods; and this is another. The revolution wrought by that great man in the mode of philosophizing has laid open a vast range of inquiry in physical science; and this enlargement of the bounds of physical science, has communicated an impulse to all other branches of knowledge. It has shaken all, and yet perfected none. An infinity of new views is perpetually crossing the mind, without time being allowed for arranging them and binding them together as a whole. The literature and philosophy of the present age, eminently tentative in their character, and superabounding in materials for thought, make it probable that we are on the eve of an intellectual revolution, similar to that of the seventeenth century. The superficial character of the literature which prevails in America, and to some extent in Europe, sometimes dealing in matter of fact, and sometimes venturing upon speculations the most mysterious and fanciful, may be only the prelude to that revolution. I believe any one who pays close attention to the character of mind of a very numerous class of readers, both in Europe and America, will find that there is something besides ennui, or the mere desire to gain a respectable share of information, which is at work; and that even where the surface of society gives evidence of nothing positive, there never was a period when the human mind was so deeply stirred.

The rank which the United States has now attained, as one of the three great powers of christendom, has invested American institutions with that sort of prestige which gives title to unquestioned influence abroad. A nation, no more than an individual, is proclaimed great until it is able to move the will as well as the understandings, of others. The great danger is, lest the will should run away with the understanding, and that a nation untrue to itself should engage in acts of external violence, inconsistent with its own prosperity and with the welfare of mankind at large. America has hitherto avoided this snare. Peace has made her both powerful and prosperous; nor is it possible for her to continue to uphold free institutions, unless peace is her cardinal policy. Occasional interruptions there may be; her ascendency will soon be such as to place her beyond the reach of these, if she holds a strict guard upon herself. What I most desire to inculcate is, that peace, as the habitual policy of the country, as the policy which it of choice marks out for itself, is indispensable to the enjoyment of genuine freedom, and to the maintenance of that great influence which it exercises upon Europe. An individual does not strengthen his moral and intellectual nature, in order to give full play to the lower appetites. No more will a nation do so, which is mindful of its true interests. The utmost amount of power which a community is able to acquire is never more than enough to set in motion the springs of improvement within, and to dispense the blessings of civilization to its own population. So that the influence of a nation abroad is never so great as when it is least intent upon asserting it, and when its whole efforts are directed to the development of its own resources.

In surveying the changes which have taken place in the laws, manners, and social organization of some of the European states, it is impossible to say how much is due to the separate influence of America. It is very remarkable, however, that they have all been crowded into the space of the last fifty or sixty years. Even in the absence of any definite facts on which to hinge, the presumption would arise, that America has come in for a large share of the influence which has produced these changes. Certainly, the European commonwealths were on the advance, when the American frame of government was established. For the growth of industry had given an impulse to knowledge, and the spread of knowledge was step by step, lifting the bulk of the population to a higher level, and making men somewhat better acquainted with their rights and interests. I will not quarrel with the European reader (if any such there should be) who believes that there is exaggeration in these pages, confident, that after some reflection, he will recur to very nearly the same views, and that what he at first regarded as exaggeration, will only be viewed as an effort to render more distinct, truths which in substance are correctly set forth.

CHAPTER VIII.

ULTIMATE DESTINY OF FREE INSTITUTIONS.

In contemplating the great improvement which society and the art of government have undergone in very modern times, the inquiry instantly presents itself: is there a probability that this improvement will continue, to what extent can it be carried, and have we a reasonable assurance that it will be permanent. These are problems of great importance, and require a distinct and clear examination. There is this great difference between physical and political science. In the first, all we can do is to observe and collect the facts, and to elicit the principles which govern them, and which are constantly the same. In the physiology of society and government, the facts, and therefore the principles, are subject to variation. But this gives rise to a double progress in the last. In physical science. every department has made rapid strides during the last century. This improvement consists in a more thorough and exact acquaintance with the laws of the physical world. If the improvement which took place in the political science, were of the same character, and none other, all the accession which it would have received, would consist in a more thorough and orderly redaction of the principles which had governed society up to that period: for all the improvement in physical science, consists in a more complete knowledge of physical phenomena. These phenomena existed always precisely as they do now, but they were not perceived and thought out; so that we were ignorant whether they existed. But in the political world, the facts, the phenomena, are not always the same; they have varied greatly, although these variations are themselves limited within certain bounds. Beyond these they cannot go, in consequence of the radical sameness of the human organism, at all times and all places. But this variation is something entirely different from anything which occurs in the physical world, and it gives rise to what may be termed a system of secondary laws of political society. The physical world also, has a set of primary and secondary laws ; but the difference consists merely in the character of inferiority of the last, to the first ; for the phenomena on which both depend, existed always precisely as they do now. But the phenomena on which the secondary laws of political society depend, did not exist always, but have been revealed to our observation in very modern times. Hence the double improvement, that is, the improvement additional to that in physical science, which takes place in political science. Not only is an improved method introduced, but an improved state of facts, on which to found an improved method corresponding with it. The astronomy of Newton, and the physiology of Leibig, lay open to our knowledge phenomena which always existed, but which required thought and penetration to bring to light. The political work of De Tocqueville reveals not only new laws, but an entirely new class of phenomena. Indeed, when we speak of the improvement of society and government, we convey this idea. No change, no improvement, which we know of, has taken place in the phenomena and laws which govern the planetary motions ; all was perfect from the beginning. But a visible and marked improvement has taken place in both the social and political organization, within a hundred years.

The chief obstacle to a successful investigation of this subject, is the belief that unless some state of very high perfection is attained, all efforts to re-construct society and government, so as to render them stable and permanent, and to endow the last with both the ability and disposition to rule wisely and justly, must be abortive. In considering the limit to which society may go, we must at the outset, discard all idea of any radical and fundamental change in the character of men, and boldly avow, that this unchangeable character of human nature is the inevitable consequence of the infirmity and defects, physical and moral, of individual man ; for as society is made up of individuals, and all its institutions are administered by them, everything must partake of that infirmity and those defects.

We may figure to ourselves two ends as worthy of attainment in political society. 1st. The elevation of the whole population to a very high standard, in the scale of physical, moral, and intellectual being; or 2d, the elevation of so considerable a number, as to ensure their own good conduct, and as a consequence, the wise and upright government of those whose advancement beyond a certain point is never attained. The first is impracticable; all schemes to bring it about must be abortive, for they would prove in the end inconsistent with the existence of an elevated class in any part of society. The steady and regular augmentation of the middle class, may accomplish the second. The diffusion of property and knowledge will capacitate them for this position; and the conviction which long and painful experience may force upon every other part of society, that that class have the fairest title to govern, will clothe them with that weight and respect which are so necessary in order to exert a legitimate influence over other men. This will take place not in consequence of any optional or arbitrary determination on the part of the population, but in consequence of certain laws of human nature, which operate steadily and invariably. "If universal suffrage, (says an enlightened writer) were introduced this day into England, not a single peasant would be elected to parliament." We may conceive of a society subsisting so long under the influence of these elements, that even the lower classes may have common sense and judgment sufficient to discern, that to break it up would make shipwreck of their interests. For reflection, which is a prominent characteristic of the superior classes in the present age, has increased greatly among the lower. It must also be borne in mind, that although the last are inferior in all the advantages of fortune to the first; they perform a very important part in checking them, and restraining their actions within certain limits. It is doubtful, if in the imperfect condition of our nature, which requires restraints from above and below, we could succeed at all without this instrumentality. If the reformation I have referred to, a reformation falling infinitely short of any utopian plan, is deemed chimerical, we have only to compare the condition of every European country in the first fourteen centuries, with what it is at present. The same proportion of advancement would give us as a state of society, as eligible as I have supposed.

First. The faculties, propensities, and passions of men, are on an average, the same which they always were ; and yet the influence of civilization is such as to produce very perceptible differences in their actions, at different periods. It might be supposed that the offspring of those who have lived in a highly civilized society might after several generations have their physical organization so much changed as to give rise to different propensities, or to propensities so materially modified, as to amount nearly to the same thing. We know nothing of the laws which govern our physical organization ; but observation and experience militate strongly against the supposition, and seem to prove that these propensities can be no further altered, than by giving them different objects on which to expend themselves. Domitian, Nero, and Commodus, as well as Trajan, and the two Antonines, were descended from ancestors born in a highly civilized society. The conflict between our selfish and social propensities, the constant predominance of the former, in consequence of our feeble condition, which causes nearly the whole of life to be spent in devising means of improving even our physical state, are a great obstacle in the way ; for the selfish propensities, the propensities which are personal to us, are as necessary to the advancement of the individual as the social propensities are to that of the race. And although among great numbers, the passions may be gratified otherwise than in acts of cruelty, rapacity, an insurrectionary spirit, and lawless disorders, there will always be a large body, increasing with the advance of civilization, who will be depressed to a very low point in the scale, and whose dispositions will be marked by great ferocity.

In order to test the practicability of elevating the whole population to a high and equal level, for it would be of no importance to place all on a level, unless that level imported a highly eligible condition ; we will suppose that all the land of a country were now to be divided equally among individuals, and that the proportion allotted to each should be two hundred acres ; for less would be insufficient to rear and educate a family. The plan would be encompassed with all sorts of difficulties. 1st. The common sense, sagacity, judgment, and habits of industry of different men, are exceedingly different even in the homely occupation of improving their physical condition. 2d. Even if the country were already cleared, the demand for labor to cultivate it would far exceed the supply. For by the supposition, all the men above twenty-one are proprietors ; nor would it be possible to establish any other rule, as our design is to elevate all, and we cannot effect this, unless all, at the period of manhood, are permitted to enter upon life with an equal facility of bettering their condition. Each individual, then, has a tract of land given to him, and at the outset, he finds himself totally unable to cultivate more than the tenth part of it; for the great majority of laborers, at present, are above twenty-one, and none of them could be hired to perform work for others, when they had more of their own than they could attend to. But we will for a moment suppose that the experiment is successful. The comfortable circumstances in which every one is placed, will give a prodigious stimulus to population. The unmarried, who would have waited until they could, in the ordinary course of things, acquire the means of subsistence, will now marry. Numerous families will be the consequence : the land will be partitioned among a greater number, and in a few generations, the division of the soil will be carried to such an extent, as to mar the whole scheme, and to forbid all idea of elevating the whole mass to the station which was contemplated. Society will retrograde, and will continue to do so, until it reaches the lowest point in the scale. Two circumstances will contribute the hasten this downward progress. The number of children of different families, will be very unequal. This difference will occasion large possessions to be engrossed by some ; while others are confined to a meagre subsistence, or become paupers. The skill, industry, and aptitude of individuals for their calling, will also be very different, and this will contribute still more to hasten the retrograde march. The original division into proprietors and laborers, will be re-established, and we shall neither secure to each an equality of property, nor succeed in lifting all to a high level. When we speak of elevating the whole population, we must mean morally, and intellectually, as well as physically. I have supposed two hundred acres to be least quantity which would be required to attain this end. No one would have the means of educating a family, nor the opportunity of devoting a considerable part of life to the acquisition of knowledge with less. But I have made no mention of the other classes, merchants, manufacturers, artizans, etc., whose agency is so necessary to attain anything like a high state of even physical civilization. I have separated one thing from another, in order to render the analysis more striking and complete. Without the intervention of those classes, every one would be obliged to build his own house, to manufacture and make his own clothing, to construct all the tools and implements of agriculture; which would absorb so much time, if time were possible, as instantly to arrest all progress, and to blast the fruit of what had already been made. Or if we suppose the separate existence of those classes, all idea of a distribution of property is at an end. It is physically possible, for the moment, to make a division of the soil, but we cannot make a division of the qualities which are necessary to the prosecution of other departments of industry. We cannot decree that the skill and dexterity of A and B, acquired by a long apprenticeship to a calling, and sharpened by natural aptitude and sagacity, shall be distributed to C and D. The reader will fill up the outline with the numerous suggestions which will crowd upon him, confirmatory of the view I have taken. Our nature is as it is. The constitution of society is the result of that nature, and we must make up our minds to submit to it, if we would do anything valuable and useful to advance it.

To what extent may we consider the beings who now live in the most civilized societies. Great Britain and the United States, for instance, as radically the same, as endowed with the same appetites and propensities as those who acted a part in the proscriptions and massacres of Marius and Sylla, in the atrocities of the French revolution, and in numberless enormities and cruelties which disfigure the history of England, down to the revolution of 1688? Although nothing of the kind now appears on the surface of society, it does not follow that the same passions do not exist. They may be disguised or diverted into a different channel, and yet be ready to break out, if any unhappy conjuncture should occur to give a violent shock to the institutions. For it is clear, that unless our structure is radically altered, those passions and propensities must be found at bottom the same. In a state of profound tranquillity, there is but one way of ascertaining the fact; and that is by studying and analyzing the characters of men in private life, and as far as we are able, in public life also. To pursue this inquiry vigorously, it would be necessary to draw aside the curtain which conceals the most secret thoughts and transactions; so secret, that if any application were made to individuals, it would be in the power of each, and that with the greatest plausibility, to exclaim against such unjust imputations. But the philosophical inquirer must not be deterred, by such difficulties, from at least stating the fact, and leaving it to individuals who have sufficient acuteness and observation to make the application to all but themselves; and in this way, already so familiar to every one, we shall succeed in comprehending all the individuals of the species; the problem will be solved with the unanimous consent of all, but without any knowledge, on their part, of the result. He is the true friend of mankind who pursues the truth fearlessly; and he may be sure he has attained it when the assent which is given to his deductions is a secret, not an avowed one. Every one who has the skill to unravel these subjects will be convinced that the same heart-burnings and envyings which have ever existed, exist now, and that these malignant passions have been the sole cause of all the cruelties, massacres and judicial murders which pollute the page of history. The annals of other countries and other times wear a foreign and antiquated air. They are regarded as the recital of strange things, and the reader has neither the disposition nor the ability to make a direct and immediate application of what they record to the men and transactions of their own times.

I must now refer again to what I have said of our original structure. Our nature is made up of qualities which are eminently social, and also of qualities which are selfish, that is, personal to ourselves. If the last are not the foundation of the first, they open free scope to them, and render them more pleasurable and agreeable than they otherwise would be. The laws of society, then, are like the laws of the physical world: the same centripetal and centrifugal forces reign over both, and by their united operation, both worlds may be maintained in harmony. But there is this difference: the selfish propensities are much stronger than the social, and unless they can find a sufficient number of objects on which to exhaust themselves, they almost invariably interfere with the other set of qualities. They are stronger than these, because they are necessary to the existence of the race, which the last are not. The procurement of the means of subsistence is felt as a first and imperious want, without which all other wants would be valueless, because they could not be gratified. This is the first occasion on which the order and harmony of society is disturbed. But man, besides partaking of the qualities of the lower animals, is also an intellectual being; and this, although it affords an opportunity for conciliating the two rival qualities of his nature, opens in reality, a greatly extended arena to the operation of his selfish propensities. For the gratification of all those wants, which to subsistence adds comfort, to comfort affluence, to affluence respect, to respect influence, and to influence power, are for the most part selfish, or personal to ourselves. And yet the gratification of all these is necessary to the perfectionment of the individual, and to any considerable progress of society itself. But the exceeding difficulty of maintaining a just equipoise between these two contending principles, will be evident to every one who reflects upon our feeble and imperfect condition. Our selfish wants, both the higher and the lower, are so urgent and so multiplied, that it seems as if they must forever obtain the mastery, and encroach more and more upon our social being. All the efforts to gratify the wants I have enumerated, and many subordinate ones which I have not enumerated, are directed without any immediate regard to the welfare of society. All of them are like instincts, acting without premeditation: or if accompanied with this in some individuals, lending additional force to them.

It is very true, that a state of things may be supposed, in which this constitution of our nature would not be inconsistent with the maintenance, in their utmost vigor, of the dispositions which lead men to society. Society is itself a collection of individuals. If each member succeeded in providing for his well being, both physical and moral, all, that is society, would attain the same end; and the greater the intensity with which each one prosecuted his own interests, the greater the probability that the last end would be accomplished. For, by the supposition, the faculties of all would be directed in channels, the united influence of which would make up the happiness of all.

But this state of things, although there is a constant tendency to approach it, can never be realized. The difficulties in the way are so numerous, that it is impossible to enumerate them all. A few are sufficient. In the first place, life is commenced at a period when the faculties are immature, when there is a total want of experience and observation and when the passions are so strong as to threaten to swallow up the whole being. Mistakes of all kinds are constantly made so common as never to be noticed. And yet these are incurable, in consequence of the inherent defects I have referred to. 2d. Even in the adult, the faculties, both intellectual and affective, are extremely imperfect, while at the same time, there is the greatest imaginable inequality among different individuals. 3d. The constant increase of the population multiplies these difficulties, and renders them more obstinate. The more favorable the condition of the society, the easier the means of subsistence; the stronger is the impetus given to the population. And as this increase is gradual, and the inconveniences it produces, take place silently and unobservedly, men are, by little and little, familiarized to them, and ultimately forget the high standard of comfort which they once presented to themselves. This fails to operate as a check upon a further increase. Reflection has ever exerted a very imperfect influence in this matter, although there are very perceptible differences among different peoples. But these differences are insufficient to prevent the greatest inconveniences and mischiefs among all; and when combined with the other causes to which I have alluded, they present the most formidable obstacles to the realization of that utopian scheme of society, which is so easily imagined precisely because it is so unnatural. All the circumstances I have referred to, spring from certain inherent principles of our nature, which can only be changed by a radical change in our organization.

Can it be matter of surprise, when millions of beings are collected in one community, that there should be an infinite deal of jangling, disorder, and confusion, and that the good order of society and the wholesome control of government should be perpetually threatened. The great majority of these beings, in a country the most happily favored, are struggling for a comfortable subsistence. This sets in motion a host of passions, which, by this straitened condition, are disarmed of the power to do any immediate mischief, but not sufficiently so to prevent society from being infested with a multitude of domestic evils. When we come to the classes above, not so numerous, and yet formidable enough, we perceive the same defects of character, the same inequalities, the same passions, and propensities, but all greatly hightened in consequence of the more complicated struggle in which they are engaged. The constant interference of so many, and such imperious desires, prevents society from assuming that fair aspect which it would be so delightful to look upon; and, at first view, it seems as if it would be better if we were unable to form the conception of such a picture, if our reason did not assure us that it is only by having an ideal standard before us, that we are impelled to make efforts to attain what is really practicable.

In the preceding observations, I have represented human nature as it is. I have supposed our wants, desires, and propensities to be a necessary part of our structure, and as having been implanted for the wisest purposes; to lead us, in the first instance, to even physical exertion, and afterwards, to the employment of our higher faculties. I have spoken of the existence of different classes of society as inconsistent with the scheme of perfection which we may form to ourselves, and yet as indispensable to the maintenance of a condition much raised above that of the lower animals, as indispensable, in fine, to the maintenance of civilization in any part of society. But when to the wants and appetites of the class which is struggling for subsistence, are added the more numerous, and the more complicated wants and desires of the superior classes, all armed with a greater degree of strength and influence than among the inferior ranks, we must not be surprised if society never exhibits a perfectly quiet aspect, nor if it is sometimes torn by the most bitter and cruel dissensions. I have represented every thing as depending upon certain fixed principles, which may assume different forms among different people, as operating unerringly within certain limits, although these limits are not every where the same. This it was necessary to do, in order to answer two inquiries proposed in the commencement of this chapter; to what extent can social improvement be carried, is it possible to effect the elevation of all to a high and uniform level. 2d. Although the advancement of all to a high point in the scale of physical, moral, and intellectual excellence is impracticable, may not the social and political organization, with or without our contrivance, be so ordered, as at least to insure a wise and equitable government of society? This is the only alternative remaining. It is entirely distinct from the other, and must be constantly kept separate from it, otherwise we shall be unable to extricate ourselves from the confusion of ideas which two things compatible in theory, and yet incompatible in practice, will occasion. Up to a certain point, the two are closely connected. The wise, prudent, and upright administration of public affairs depends upon the moral and intellectual elevation of the population; but it cannot depend upon the equal elevation of all. If it did, our destiny would be most stern indeed; for we should be unable to avail ourselves of a contrivance visible in every other part of creation; the making compensation for defects in one part, by the possession of counterbalancing advantages in another. I venture to lay it down as a maxim in political philosophy, that the institutions may be skillfully contrived, and wisely and happily administered, although all classes are not wise and virtuous; nay, although a large proportion are lamentably deficient in these qualities. The principle alone, may so outrun the growth of those principles which are calculated to elevate and improve the race, and to call out its good qualities, as to retain a great number in ignorance, poverty, and bad habits; while there may be a larger number than has hitherto existed in any known country, on whom those incentives will act powerfully and invariably. In this way only, can we gain a glimmering of light in the dark path we are pursuing, and be prevented from tormenting ourselves with the belief, that because all manner of good is not attainable; none is worth pursuing. If we are able to succeed to the extent which I have indicated as practicable, the benefit to the class which is excluded from the advantages of property, intelligence, and education, will not be less than to the more fortunate classes. The former will be governed with more wisdom and prudence than is practicable under any other scheme of society.

The actions of men depend upon two causes; the faculties, of one kind or another, with which they are endowed, and the circumstances which are external to them; including in the last, not only the physical world, but other intellectual beings, together with the institutions, public and private, in the country where they reside, and even those of other countries, wherever they are capable of exerting an influence upon them. On the joint influence of these two causes, depends the whole conduct and behavior of men. Diminish the influence of one, and you alter, or annihilate the influence of the other. This law prevails among societies, governments, and nations, as well as among individuals. It is impossible to conceive that it should be otherwise, since all actions imply something beyond us, affecting our faculties, and, at the same time, affected by them. In the general, the fact is admitted by every one; it is the precise appreciation of facts, and the rigorous application of them which is so difficult to be attained.

Thus a vast deal depends upon the circumstances in which an

infant society, growing up to be a great nation, is placed: its position on the globe, with respect to climate, or its position in relation to other nations; the state of the country in which they are placed, the period when its members began to congregate as a society, the institutions which had previously shaped their conduct, and the causes which originally led to their formation. As an individual, born to-day in Sparta or Athens, will be very different from what he would have been if born two thousand years ago, a society growing up in one country, at one period, may be very different from what it would have been, if planted in another country, and at another period. This will be the case, after making every allowance for the remarkable sameness of organism which prevails among the human species. That organism is not an unit, but is a collection of the most diversified faculties: and hence results the apparent anomaly, that notwithstanding the sameness in the groundwork of the human character, the actions of men are so different. If powerful incentives, or uncontrollable circumstances are applied to some faculties, while others are acted upon feebly, the conduct of the individual will be very different from what it would have been if the state of the case had been exactly reversed; if those faculties and propensities which are powerfully stimulated and developed in one direction, lay dormant, and those which are feebly influenced, were very strongly acted upon. In the same way, the aptitudes, capacities, and habits of some nations may be shaped by outward circumstances, very different from those which surround other nations; and their life and destiny may be very different When the institutions of a country, happily circumstanced, are matured and consolidated, they become a cause external to other nations, and may powerfully influence their conduct.

There is no knowing to what extent this part of the machinery of society may be carried, in modifying the character of individuals and nations. The field within which it may operate, is very large, although we may be assured that the fundamental organization of our nature forbids all idea of making men gods. The general principle is this: if strong incentives are applied to call out the better qualities of human nature, they will be called out among great numbers; and if the incentives to vice, idleness and disorder are also enfeebled, a still greater number will be powerfully acted upon. The whole scheme of punishment proceeds upon the idea that the actions of men may be rendered different from what they would be, by the presentation of motives, which are external to them: not merely that the conduct of those who have already violated the law will be changed, but that a much greater number will be deterred from michievous habits and abandoned courses. And when, in addition to this, the circumstances which surround individuals and societies, are such as to present strong positive motives to the formation of good habits, there is not a probability, but a certainty, that they will be formed among great numbers. All this is true if men are endowed with good as well as bad qualities, of which, I suppose, there will be no question. The beginnings of society in the United States are very remarkable. If we compare them with the early history of every other country, ancient or modern, the contrast is very striking. The first centuries in the annals of Greece, Rome, France, Great Britain, &c., exhibit a scene of eternal warfare, domestic, civil, and national. The circumstances which surrounded the people of the first country, were very different from those which surrounded the people of the four last. The first were born at a period when civil and religious liberty ran high; they planted themselves in an empty country, remote from the theater of European contention, and free from any disturbing causes within. The land was uncultivated, and habits of industry and frugality were imposed upon them; their private institutions were not subjected to the control of any authority without, and for the first time in the history of the world, organised a system of common schools. They were so remote from England that she meddled very little with their political institutions, the members of which they were composed, were so much on an equality that they established a republican government. The effect of all these causes, acting from without, was the formation of certain habits, which became a new cause, and an additional incentive to further improvement. Domestic government was maintained with great strictness and purity. The offspring of people thus trained, were, of course, more susceptible than themselves to external influences; they obeyed the discipline prescribed to them; a character of industry, energy and intelligence, has been handed down from generation to generation; and from these elements, has arisen a nation, in whom the possession of these qualities in a much higher degree, is not only conceivable but practicable, is yet perhaps more remarkable for them than any other.

To the question proposed in the commencement of the chapter: Will the improvement which has taken place among all civilized nations continue to advance? the answer must be, that it will. No nation has ever been known to recede, unless some overwhelming calamity from without has violently arrested it progress. The principle of progression is the rule, that of retrogradation the exception. The reason why this is so, is obvious. Progress implies something higher, and therefore something desirable. It would not be something higher unless it were also desirable. This ensures at any rate a certain tendency at all times to advancement. But the gratification of the appetites and propensities, in all stages of society, is also desirable, and this undoubtedly will disturb the regular operation of the first principle. But it is only where these appetites and propensities are in excess; for the moderate, that is the natural, gratification of them is not only consistent with the development of the higher part of our nature, but contributes to it. On the other hand, the gratification of our higher faculties, to any degree, is not detrimental but serviceable to society. Hence, where the circumstances by which individuals are surrounded, are at all favorable, there is always a disposition to leap forward. If they are alike favorable to all, this tendency will be general; if only to a part of society, it will take place in that part; and it will be correct to term Great Britain, France, Germany, as well as the United States, highly improving societies, although this improvement is not the same in all parts of their populations. Nor can it be doubted that if it were carried, not to some imaginable point, but to a degree perfectly practicable, institutions might be established in those countries, where they are not already, which would provide, not during a few generations, but permanently, for the wise and equitable government of all classes. This is the only reply we can make to another question proposed in the opening of the chapter; To what extent may social and political improvement be carried? It cannot be carried to any thing savoring of perfection; and yet it may be carried indefinitely, because it may take an indefinite time to reach the point which is attainable. It may be carried so far at least, as to ensure a steady, impartial and judicious administration of the government; and this will be an inestimable acquisition, and a reasonable compensation for that radical infirmity of our nature, which forbids all idea of attaining a state of great perfection.

With regard to the great problem, what is to be ultimate destiny of free institutions, we can only offer probable conjectures, not certain opinions. In the body of this work, I have represented these institutions as eminently favorable to the development of the faculties of the greatest number of men, and to the advancement of both civil and political freedom. Apprehensions of their instability will perpetually cross the mind. But these I have described as a wise provision inserted in our nature, and as contributing mightily to ward off the very mischiefs which are apprehended. The stronger they become, and the greater the number who entertain them, the stronger will be the resisting force of society, the greater its ability to arrest disorder of all sorts before it has gone to extremities.

But first, it is remarkable that in proportion to the amount of popular freedom which has been breathed into governments which are not republican in their structure, the more stable they have become, and the more prudent and circumspect has been the conduct of all public functionaries. This is remarkably exemplified in the case of Great Britain, a government which neither commanded the undivided force of its people, nor ruled wisely and judiciously until a large share of popular liberty was engrafted upon it. This change dates from the revolution which placed William III. on the throne, and it has become more and more marked every reign since. There is, indeed, this mischief attending a government whose institutions are partly free and partly not free, it is rendered preternaturally strong, and is able to postpone further reforms, which would be advantageous at an earlier day. I do not intend to pronounce an unqualified opinion against mixed government; but it should be regarded only as a temporary state, and not as political writers have viewed it, as the standing model of government. The may be applied to the French, though their correctness there, will not be readily perceived. There can be no doubt, although the executive remarks which I have made in respect to the English government, is styled emperor, which seems to denote the exercise of monarchical authority in its greatest plenitude, that the government is administered with vastly more prudence and discretion, than under the reigns of Louis XIV. or Louis XV. This is due to the reforms which were executed between 1789 and 1799, which still exercise immense influence upon the opinions of the people, and the conduct of the government. Nor can it be doubted that the empire is only a provisional state, and will sooner or later be succeeded by a constitutional government, in which public and private rights will be more firmly established than they were between 1815 and 1848. The revolution of 1848 is an illustration of all I have said. The difference between it and the revolution of 1789, is entitled to the deepest attention. In the last, the monied men, merchants, and principal tradesmen, and men of letters, were the chief actors. In 1847, it was the reverse: and this can only be ascribed to one or other of two circumstances—either the abuses were not near so hideous and alarming, or the frightful calamities which were brought to every one's door during the first revolution, sunk so deep into the minds of men, and exercised their reflection so powerfully that they recoiled from the commission of any atrocities and cruelties. In either event, it is evident that the general manners have undergone à great regeneration. The middle class in Paris is now the predominant class, and it understands its interests, infinitely better than when, as in 1798, it was just emerging into importance. It is composed of two hundred thousand proprietors, rent holders and tradesmen, and of one hundred thousand clerks, the interests of all of whom are mutually interwoven, and who have so just a sense of these interests as not to dare to jeopardize them, if it is possible to avoid it, and yet exert so decided an influence upon the government as to constrain it to act within the bounds of a constitutional monarchy.

II. Free institutions best fall in with the natural desire of improvement. They afford scope and opportunity to a greater number to lift themselves in the scale ot physical and intellectual improvement. It is not merely because they afford a wider arena to the exertions of all: this is a necessary condition, but it is not the moving spring. Such institutions are fatal to the authority of prejudices and opinions, which spring up in a society, legally divided into classes, and which impose an invincible spell upon the faculties of men. It was not until after the French revolution, that industry became popular in France. There were some symptoms of a tendency in this direction in the time of Louis XV.* These only concurred with innumerable other causes to hasten the revolution. They were too feeble to render industry really popular, until the authority of opinion was completely demolished by the thorough

*Reign of Louis XV, by De Tocqueville.

reform in the ground work of society, which afterwards took place. It was not until then that the gothic system of corporate bodies of tradesmen, endowed with exclusive privileges, was abolished, as well as the regular course of apprenticeship, companionship, etc. These hung like a dead weight upon the industry of France, not only confining it within the smallest possible compass, but imposing, for centuries, an universal belief that the settled order of things could not be departed from. It was not until after the English revolution in the time of Charles 1st, that a like change was effected in the opinions and habits of men. Then, for the first time, it became customary for the gentry to bind their sons as apprentices to the merchants.* This at once rendered industry both popular and fashionable, and from that period, dates the prodigious impetus to popular intelligence and popular power in that country. The complaint now is, that industry has become too fashionable;† that both nobility and gentry have entered into competition with the middle ranks of society; that their fortunes are embarked in commerce, in vast manufacturing establishments, or in enterprises not less costly for the improvement of their estates. In the reign of Louis XV, the only kind of industry which was permitted to the impoverished noblesse, was that of blowing glass. This did not imply the use of their hands; and it was manual labor which was supposed to degrade the man. The objection that industry has become too fashionable, discloses one of its chief merits. Although in very many instances the higher classes in Great Britain, France, Germany, Italy, etc., do superintend the employment of their capitals; in a greater number, they are placed at the command of the classes below them. They thus contribute to fructify and invigorate every branch of industry. But the chief advantage of this consists in its introducing habits of order, economy and industry among an idle and turbulent aristocracy, as well as among an idle and vicious populace. It has aided in melting down differences of opinion which were apparently irreconcilable, and has caused the higher classes to partake of the qualities of the lower, and the lower to partake of those of the higher. If England ever becomes a republic, that is, if the principle of representation is carried into every department of the government, the new form which industry has

---

*Clarendon. †Sismondi.

assumed, foreign as it may seem to the subject, will be principally instrumental in bringing it about.

III. Free institutions cause a greater number of beings to b civilized, than could possibly be the case otherwise. This follows from the preceeding remarks. The rise of a powerful middle class is the most striking fact in the history of modern society. But the whole meaning of the fact is contained in the observation that free institutions extend civilization to a greater number of individuals than any other form of government. The more thorough the civilization of a country, the more completely it pervades every part of society, the more orderly and contented will be the population, the more singleness of purpose will be imparted to the government. This results from the greater harmony among the elements of which society is composed. It is only because the public cannot agree among themselves, that one man, or a few men, are able to seize the supreme power. A close league among a comparatively small body, is sufficient to overpower the efforts of a disunited multitude. This effect of a more or less thorough civilization of all parts of society, is entitled to great attention. It is greatly promoted in the first instance, by the freedom of the institutions; but more than all other things, it contributes ultimately to give them durability and strength. "I found the crown rolling in a gutter, and only put it on my own head," said the first emperor Napoleon; nor could it be otherwise, when the lawlessness of the feudal system first, and the uncontrolled despotism of kingly authority afterwards, crushed every germ of popular improvement. There is at present a strong middle class in France, not strong enough to rule, but strong enough to influence the notions of the government. It is that class which has consented to the elevation of another Napoleon; and by so doing, may be considered as saying to him: *there is a body of anarchists in our midst, small compared with the body of the population, but firmly leagued together. We cannot afford to be ever on the watch, and ever under arms, to resist their machinations. The mere title of emperor will operate as a spell upon the imaginations of these beings. In order to pursue, unmolested, our private occupations under the title of emperor, we make you the chief of police of this troubled country, and thereby design to augment the constabulary force of the kingdom. If you abuse the trust, we will abandon our occupations and expel you. This you know, and your knowledge is, humanly speak-*

ing, a guarantee for the fulfillment of that trust. Such is the unhappy condition to which a nation is subjected when it is partly free and partly not free.

IV. A greater degree of reflection is instilled into men of all classes, and their conduct is consequently more cautious and prudent. It is reflection which enables men to control their appetites and passions, to exercise self-command, to forsee the mistakes they will inevitably commit, if they pursue a certain line of conduct. This office it performs, not from any persuasion on their part that such conduct is abstractly right and proper, but from a perception of the consequences which will ensue, if they follow the impulse of passion and prejudice. The mere diffusion of property diffuses reflection. The possession of property is a something, and that too of no inconsiderable importance, on which the affections, hopes and aspirations of the great majority of men in a republic are fixed. Their interests, and not any imaginary qualities of mind, render them in the first instance reflective, and, by and by, reflection swells these interests to a greater magnitude, and causes them to be guarded with still more judgment and discretion. We are thus delivered from the necessity of supposing that men must possess very elevated qualities in order to be reflective. To be so in a very high degree, they must possess these qualities; but they are not demanded in the ordinary vocations of life; they are not necessary to the bulk of mankind in their conduct, either in private, or public life.

These considerations, together with many others, in the preceding part of this work, to which the reader will recur, afford a reasonable assurance for the perpetuity of free institutions. But we cannot speak with absolute certainty. An excessive growth of the population alone, may disappoint these expectations. I say may, for it need not necessarily have this effect. China is more fully peopled, than any other country on the globe, and yet the institutions, established twenty-five hundred years ago, have subsisted without alteration to the present day, and it has enjoyed profound tranquillity during a vastly longer period than any other country.* It is not because the form of government is regal; for all the European kingdoms, have been torn with dissensions, and involved

* From 1650 to 1850.

in the most cruel wars, during the same period. The high standard of comfort, to which the people of the United States, have been habituated, may repress the excessive growth of the population. We see this exemplified already. The average age of marriage in this country, is twenty-five; in Ireland, it is twenty. The Irish have been familiarized to a very low standard, and they enter recklessly upon marriage, without any prospect of being able to maintain a family. The mere habit of living under free institutions, contributes powerfully to fortify their spirit. The Americans are the only people, who have been able to make a fair beginning; and that is all-important. They have never lived under any other than free institutions* : they have no prepossessions in favor of any others; nor are there any materials for the construction of them. But it may be inquired, whether the rule of universal suffrage, will be always adhered to! Although the numbers, and importance of the middle class should always secure to them the ascendancy, will not a formidable body of proletarians, in the process of time rise up, and constantly disturb the regular movement of the government? I have already suggested, that the American people, have long been familiarized to a limitation of the right of suffrage, not merely in the large cities, but in hundreds of smaller towns, throughout the country. The principle is then already recognized, as one which is both just, and practicable. It is so recognized, because it has been ordained by the majority in those cities, and towns; and the same species of power, the majority of the people in the states, may give it a wider application. The will of tho majority is a wonderful sedative to the disturbances of society. The only reason, why the legislatures of the states do not carry the rule of limitation, beyond their municipal governments, is that the middle class is so numerous, as to render the action of any other, comparatively harmless. But I predict, that if the time ever arrives, when the danger to the institutions becomes imminent, from the banding together of the lowest class, the right of suffrage will be limited. The maxim of equality, is a great regulative, but not a constitutive principle, of society; a distinction of great importance in the political world: when it ceases to perform the first function, it ceases to be a principle in the construction of the government.

* The colonists did pretty much as they pleased, although they were an appendage to a monarchy. ADAMS' DEFENSE.

It is not probable, that the hereditary principle will be ever introduced into a country where free institutions have taken deep root. The materials for founding an order of nobility, will be wanting; the prejudices against it, will be deep, and difficult to eradicate, and the natural aristocracy of the country will be so numerous, and powerful, that they cannot be brought to agree in vesting the supremacy in a close body. An oligarchy only, would be practicable: but this, of all the forms of aristocratic government is the most difficult to establish. It has never succeeded to any extent worth mentioning, except in Venice, where the natural aristocracy, were only as one in a thousand to what it will be in the United States. Take away the overgrown estates of the English nobility, and you annihilate them: destroy the illusion, which has grown up during a long tract of time, and which has persuaded the nation, that it is an order superior to any other, and you undermine its authority: render them as numerous as the great landholders of America, and you introduce the democratic principle into the body, and fritter away its power. It has been said, and with great justice, that the people themselves may be persuaded of the expediency of establishing one or other of the artificial forms of government: that viewing the political institutions as ordained for their advantage alone, they may consider monarchical, or aristocratical government, as on the whole, best adapted to promote their interests. This has been said in countries, which have never known any other form of civil polity, and in which immemorial usage has so long swayed public opinion, that it is very difficult to form any other notions. Opinions are sometimes more difficult to be eradicated, than institutions. All I mean to say is, that where the course of human affairs, has drawn the opinions of men in an opposite direction, where the manners, the laws, the distribution of property, and the form of government, have all partaken of the genius of republican government, it will be exceedingly difficult to lay a foundation for aristocratical, or even mixed government to rest upon. There is great difference between permitting such a government to stand, when it is already existing, and calling it into being, in opposition to inveterate and deep-seated opinions.

The difficulty is as great, with regard to an hereditary chief magistrate, as with regard to an hereditary nobility. Kingly authority, is undoubtedly founded on an illusion of the imagination.

This illusion may be of infinite advantage in some periods of society, when it is necessary to give something like unity, to the discordant materials of which it is composed, and to control the imaginations of men by a supreme imagination. But if in the first rudiments of society, and for centuries after, opposite opinions have prevailed; if more homely faculties have been cultivated, at the expense of the imagination, the illusion vanishes, and the foundation on which we would build is taken from under us. The question is no longer, is regal 'government expedient; it is, is it possible.

The idea of an elective, is still more incongruous, than that of an hereditary monarchy. The condition of society, which imposes a king as a necessary evil, presupposes a state of things, entirely at war with the exercise of popular power. It is for this reason, that the elective principle may in a monarchy, be employed in the choice of representatives, but never of the prince himself, without introducing greater disorders, than those attempted to be cured.

We must then discard all idea of lifting the whole body of the people to a very high standard in the scale of physical, and intellectual improvement: but the social organization, may at least be carried to such a degree of improvement, as to insure wise institutions, and a prudent, and judicious administration of public affairs. And when time, and inveterate habit, have confirmed these institutions, they may acquire a self-existing authority, which will perpetuate them. The problem of government is not at all different from the problem which is presented to every individual in private life. He is born into the world, without any choice on his part: from the commencement of adult age, he finds himself surrounded by inconveniences, physical, moral and social, which he did not create, and which are too wide-spread and obstinate, for him to control. After a few years experience, he is brought to accept this, as something which is inevitable; and as it is inevitable, he does not recoil, but falls upon a plan of life, which will enable him to overcome these obstacles, and to avail himself of the good which is invariably mixed with the evil. The enjoyment of liberty in its highest degree has opened a great volume of experience to the American people; and this experience, not the possession of any natural qualities, superior to those of other people, *may* bring them to see, that the manifold inconveniences, which beset society, are of precisely the same character, with those which they encounter in private life : that they are indestructible, but not unmanageable, and that the plainest maxims of common sense, powerfully urge them to cling to the eminent advantages which they possess, and to venture upon no devious, and untried paths.

www.ingramcontent.com/pod-product-compliance
Lightning Source LLC
LaVergne TN
LVHW021049110826
845150LV00001B/24

* 9 7 8 1 4 2 5 5 6 8 1 9 1 *